WORKING-CLASS EXPERIENCE

WORKING-CLASS EXPERIENCE:
RETHINKING THE HISTORY
OF CANADIAN LABOUR,
1800-1991

Bryan D. Palmer

M&S

Canadian Cataloguing in Publication Data

Palmer, Bryan D., 1951-
　Working-class experience

2nd ed.
Includes bibliographical references and index.
ISBN 0-7710-6945-6

1. Working class – Canada – History – 19th century.
2. Working class – Canada – History – 20th century.
I. Title.

HD8104.P35　1992　　　331′.0971　　　C92 – 093078 – 6

McClelland & Stewart Inc.
The Canadian Publishers
481 University Avenue
Toronto, Ontario
M5G 2E9

Printed and bound in Canada

For my graduate students and for Nicole and Melanie

The serious and critical reader will not want a treacherous impartiality, which offers him a cup of conciliation with a well-settled poison of reactionary hate at the bottom, but a scientific conscientiousness, which for its sympathies and antipathies – open and undisguised – seeks support in an honest study of the facts, a determination of their real connections, an exposure of the causal laws of their movement.

Leon Trotsky, "Preface," *History of the Russian Revolution* (1932)

Contents

OF CLASS AND CULTURE AGAIN; WITH THE STATE AND NATION, GENDER AND IDENTITY, CONSCIOUSNESS AND DIFFERENCE THROWN IN (FOR GOOD AND BAD MEASURE)

This book is obviously a revised and updated edition of my earlier study, *Working-Class Experience: The Rise and Reconstitution of Canadian Labour, 1800-1980*, first published in 1983 and written, for the most part, over the course of a hectic academic year, 1981-82, that saw me move from Montreal to Vancouver. It was received warmly in some circles, but in others the reception was decidedly more cool. Labour historians, like the subjects they study, are a fragmented and fractious lot – anything but the monolithic clique they are often perceived to be from outside of their own ranks. And the sociologists and political economists with an interest in working-class studies are no less likely to take the political and interpretive challenges that emerge, necessarily, out of a history of Canadian workers at face value, without offering their own counterstatements. This is as it should be. Readers of this revised account will therefore want to know how it is changed from its predecessor.

My answer is seemingly a cagey one: this book is quite different from the first edition and yet it is also very much the same. To many this response will strike an evasive note, entirely fitting in these times of scholarly and political fence-sitting and "openness" to any and all interpretive possibility. And yet my understanding that this book is both different and similar to its previous version captures what needs to be said when comparing the first and second editions of this volume.

What is different about this text can be grasped, superficially, by glancing at the title and the chapter subheadings. This book is a "rethinking" inasmuch as it represents my own attempts to grapple with the history of Canadian workers in light of the legitimate and not so legitimate responses to what I wrote almost a decade ago, to address what it was in my first synthetic statement that drew justifiable critique, to temper those instances of analytic exuberance that simply handed those who disagreed with me my own conceptual head on a platter. It is also a "rethinking" in line with the historiographic advances that have been made in a number of specific areas, advances that I have generally accepted but with which I also occasionally take exception. It is apparent from the subsections added to most chapters and the sentences and paragraphs that have been rewritten or appended throughout the entire book that there is now a great deal more on gender, law, and the state in this account of Canadian working-class history. As my own subjective "rethinking," as well as a "rethinking" necessitated by new writings and evidence, this book is also a call for others to "rethink" labour history.

However much all of this "rethinking" suggests a movement away from my past interpretive focus, this should not be taken as some kind of confessionary retreat. This book is different, to be sure, but it is also the same. In its general arguments and orientations it refines and extends what I wrote in the early 1980s, but it follows in the footsteps of that initial effort rather than charting any new, oppositional paths. Where I depart from a past emphasis, develop a new interpretive stance, or reconsider a specific historical process or moment, the substance of the book is not, in my understanding, altered. This remains a text unlike any other in Canadian labour history precisely because it refuses to collapse the history into some cul-de-sac designated "the working-class past." Instead, it insists on an appreciation of the ways in which workers' lives were lived as totalities rather than carved up into particularities. It may well be that any book striving to explore such totality will fail to capture every detail and nuance of the complex wholeness of experience. But there is little to be gained by embracing a cautious and conservative refusal to look past the particular in order to try to comprehend the general. Every synthesis will thus understandably require "rethinking," both as it is conceived and written and after it has appeared. That should be one of its purposes and consequences. And yet, for the most part, that has not been what overviews of working-class experience have either tried to accomplish or succeeded in doing.

When I and others embarked – now more than two decades ago! – on our collective project of reconceiving the Canadian working-class experience it was with the explicit intention of breaking out of certain moulds, in which labour's history was limited to an appreciation of workers' institutions, politics, and episodic confrontations. We wanted to break the back of what we understood to be the routinization of labour history. Many things were involved in this effort to chart new directions of empirical inquiry and to develop different analytic sensitivities. We insisted that the working class was not reducible to its unions and the political parties that ostensibly espoused its cause, and with which so many early historians of Canadian labour identified. Nor was this history of labour born in the twentieth century, as so much of the pre-1970 historical writing assumed implicitly. If we did not understate the importance of trade unions, political mobilizations, and social democratic parties, we had tired of seeing history written as if these important components of working-class life were the only objective experiences worth studying; we wanted to get a little closer to other objective developments and into the subjective lives of labour as well. In our quest to understand and appreciate the meaning of class formation, relations, and identities in the past we looked at the workplace and the contested terrains of civil society, but we also examined, or suggested the need to probe into, fraternal societies, sporting associations, neighbourhood life, ritualistic behaviour, and families.

At this point the term "working-class culture" entered substantively into the discourse of Canadian historiography. What it conveyed was no doubt problematic, but it managed to proclaim that our histories were about more than organizations. However much this reconceptualization of working-class history was and remains labelled with the designation "cultural," it is nevertheless centrally important to understand that the project itself was never one in which culture was either the ultimate object of inquiry or the final determinant of behaviour. We studied this ambiguous and ambivalent realm in order to connect fragmented histories and illuminate in new ways how class mattered in Canadian society. Whereas most of our predecessors had viewed the process of class formation through a telescope focused on discrete phenomena, we insisted on at least the need for more telescopes, if not a new way of seeing. Our project thus tried to address the formal and the informal, the obvious and the obscured, the organizational and, for want of a better word, the cultural, by which we meant the actual activities of men and women as they lived out their lives beyond the exactions of the workplace and the public campaigns of conventional politics. Particular communities and personalities, as well as facets of everyday life previously considered immaterial in the march of historical "progress," often ended up being our direct concerns, but they were in fact always secondary to the primary aim of getting inside specific reciprocities: of work and life; of public and private; of politics and identities. These connective tissues of experience had long been suppressed in the writing of all Canadian history, and their importance in working-class experience had been tacitly denied. Indeed, as our studies began to appear in print, these reciprocities would be rejected explicitly by an empiricist and intellectually conservative assault launched by those conventional labour historians who saw any attempt to broaden the scope of working-class history as theoretically threatening and politically dubious.

Canadian working-class history as it came to be written in the late 1970s and early 1980s, and of which the first edition of *Working-Class Experience* was a specific expression, thus fractured the historical profession. On one side stood those who demanded that history must be narratives built on the accumulation of unproblematic evidence, innocent of theoretical (often "foreign") insights, above the suggestion of the political projects of the contemporary moment, usually anchored in a pragmatic acquiescence to the long-established relations of a respectable, reform-oriented questioning of power and inequality. On the other side were those practitioners who wanted the history rewritten in various, often contentious, ways: feminists, working-class historians, or those interested in race and ethnicity might well disagree vehemently with one another, but such argument actually masked the more basic, if blunt, divide that now obviously ran through the centre of the historical profession. It was not that this divide had never existed before the emergence of new writing on the Canadian working class in the 1970s and 1980s. Regionalists, including Francophone historians, had perhaps precipitated the rupture, but they did so, for the most part, in ways that subdued the theoretical and political process of differentiation. What the working-class historical writing of this period did was accentuate this fundamental break, place the accent firmly on the theoretical and political nature of historical interpretation, and consequently make divisions in the community of historians more visible than they had ever been, a process of separation that would be furthered and deepened by historians of women, aboriginal peoples, and various marginalized social groups.

This basic divide should not be forgotten. It is because this rewrite of *Working-Class Experience* remains committed to a particular kind of interpretive history that it is the same as its predecessor. Whatever the deficiencies, rhetorical excesses (which I have always been prone to and will likely continue to be burdened by), and problematic conceptions of the first edition of this book, there is no denying that it, and the larger collective project of which it was a part, moved working-class history forward rather than backward. That is now being denied in some quarters, but these denials are intellectually vacuous and, at times, rather silly.

And yet there are signs that among those who were a part of this project of pushing working-class history forward there are now differences of considerable import. Some feminists construct histories of major class battles in which the determining influences of the Cold War and the overwhelming authority of corporate power fade as the importance of gender identities is brought into a sharp relief that overshadows and obscures the nature of a history necessarily embedded in a particular political economy. Labour historians and sociologists with a keen eye on the labour process draw the map of class relations in ways that leave no room for a topography of politics, let alone acknowledgement of the subterranean maze of cultural activity. New surveys of labour collapse the history of workers into the very containers many of us tried to crack open decades ago. Historians who have pioneered new and rigorous conceptual understandings of working-class experience adapt to the fashionable, if cavalier and simplistic, contemporary repudiation of Marxism and so-called "essentialism," gravitating to the celebration of discursive identities, proclaiming confidently the end of nation, class, and, seemingly, history itself. All of this is happening among my "friends"; I often ask myself if the old "enemies" and their blunt and crudely ideological campaigns are not preferable to this.

Of course they are not. That is why this book is different: it is a reaction to the debates and discussions and disagreements that have been launched by "friends," and that have been generated directly by the first edition of *Working-Class Experience*. I thought much of the critique of the first version of this book, both as enunciated in reviews and as tossed out in classrooms, study groups, and taverns (where, after a few drinks, academics tend to let their actual views out of their usually partially closed and cautious mouths), was insubstantial and disingenuous, entirely too easy. That is why this book is the same; basically I am pretty much unrepentant. But I am not blameless, and certainly not blind to my own responsibilities: I allowed this critique to unfold in the way it did because I had been insufficiently careful, perhaps to the point of naiveté. Perhaps this was how it had to be. I was young and inexperienced in the ways of the academic game, mostly because I did not see scholarship as a Parker Brothers project of studious moves and predatory accumulations. If I continue to refuse to move my marker with the required professional calculation, throwing dice that I understand are loaded against me, it is not because I remain unaware of how the game is played. But years ago I actually thought that reviewers and historians would try to address books seriously instead of grasping for the quote that proved their own prejudgements.

Much of this relates to what is undoubtedly the single most common disagreement with the first edition of this book: the supposed stress on the 1880s and, in particular, the Knights of Labor. From many quarters came the charge, voiced most cogently by Desmond Morton, that it was "a little eccentric to find the 1880s and the Knights of Labor as the climax of the Canadian labour movement." Aside from the fact that I actually said no such thing, and indeed stated explicitly that a "reversion to the practice of the 1880s would, of course, be inadequate in light of present-day issues," it is nevertheless true that I had been sufficiently impressed with the accomplishments of the Knights of Labor (I had just completed, with my friend Greg Kealey, a study of the Order entitled *Dreaming of What Might Be*) that I opened the door to this kind of dismissal. In this rewrite I hope that the accomplishments of the Noble and Holy Order are conveyed to the reader without placing too much onus on the Knights as an exemplary class organization.

This problem of allowing the critics too much rope with which to hang me also appeared in my overly enthusiastic embrace of culture. On one level this deficiency was more apparent than real, a product of tilting the sails of "culture" against the winds of traditionalist institutional inquiry. If what was said in the original *Working-Class Experience* concerning the cultural realm was hardly as outrageously "culturalist" as many critics charged, there were nevertheless difficulties with my presentation. Chapter titles, for instance, conveyed a simplistic sense of working-class culture, which was also too often depicted one-sidedly as struggle, rather than as both the site of forms of resistance and processes of accommodation. The highly different cultural histories of the nineteenth and twentieth centuries fed into the view that I regarded the post-1886 history of Canadian labour as a descent. My depiction of labour and its culture stressed too much the positive side of the cultural impulses of the late nineteenth century and gravitated too easily to the negative consequence of mass culture's largely twentieth-century impact on workers. On balance, I think this interpretation remains right, although that may be nothing more than prejudice scaffolded on a particular politics. But it is certainly the case that there is a need for more subtlety and a more nuanced appreciation of this history than originally appeared.

There are of course other areas where new literatures are engaged with in ways that produce new interpretive stands. One such topic is that of domestic life, where, confronted by increasing feminist concern with authority and violence in the home, I am more questioning of the discussions of seemingly consensual working-class family "economies." Another is the history of the law of regulation of trade unionism, a subject understudied ten years ago but now the concern of a detailed and sophisticated literature.

These are some of the matters addressed differently in this book. What follows is more than an updated edition; each line has not been rewritten, but each word has been rethought. Some of the nineteenth-century detail has been curbed, but the substance of the argument remains. Those who want the empirical findings of the tables and appendices of the original volume will have to keep their old copies next to the new book, for I have dropped this material. In cutting back on this pre-twentieth-century content I want to stress that I am not succumbing to what I take to be the curiously ahistorical prejudices of Canadian labour historians. Many commentators expressed their disdain for a text that spent slightly less than one-half of its pages on the years 1800-95 and the remainder on the period

1895-1980. I am astounded that such a treatment was considered skewed and wrong-headed. I would have thought balanced would have been a more appropriate designation, especially given the failure of so much commentary in Canadian labour history to address the nineteenth-century world.

The reaction of many historians, sociologists, and political scientists to my supposed overemphasis on the meaning of the 1880s was, in part, I suspect, a consequence of a fundamental disinterest in the nineteenth century. This manifests itself in many ways. Craig Heron's recent *The Canadian Labour Movement: A Short History* (1989) covers the pre-1900 history of workers curtly and inadequately. Laurel Sefton MacDowell reviewed *Working-Class Experience* in the *Canadian Historical Review* and argued that since the Knights of Labor "did not last" there was a need to spend far more time on the modern period of Canada's "permanent" labour institutions. Historical "losers," it seems, should get written out of the record of the past, a practice that those of us engaged in writing the history of the working class have always opposed, for obvious reasons. What we have in the case of Heron and MacDowell are instances of presentism uniting historians who supposedly differ in their political and historiographic allegiances. Presentism masks ideological purpose in the facade of progressive relativism. It has nothing to do with whether one studies the past or the present but, rather, how one relates these two moments in history, simultaneously continuous and discontinuous. Proclaiming that history must be relevant, presentism emphasizes the utility of historical writing, but it does so by assuming and asserting an ideological pragmatism, in which what exists now is elevated to the height of a presence that must be dealt with as a *given*, virtually unquestioned and unchallengeable. So pervasive are presentist assumptions in Canadian history that it is widely and unthinkingly accepted that what we have is somehow separable from some ill-defined but nevertheless discernible distant past, severed irrevocably from more proximate histories that somehow relate to the present.

This has many uses, for various *status quos*, but I see this kind of positioning as ahistorical and politically accommodating. But it now unites many who write about labour and assume that while we have much to learn from the history of 1946, there is little need to look at 1919 and even less reason to excavate the experience of 1886. What presentism does, often in alliance with a narrow parochialism that refuses theory and a broad-ranging concern with international phenomena, is truncate our appreciation of how the past conditions the present and of what kinds of possibilities, lived out in various historical contexts, might exist in the changed contours of the here and now. Against presentism stands the insistence, of which this book is a part, that history matters and that possibility is never simply and only determined by the obviousness of the conjunctures of the current moment. This does not mean that the past can be translated directly to the present. History is not a blueprint. But neither can "useful" histories be premised on amnesia.

For this reason I have tried to redevelop an appreciation of the twentieth-century history of Canadian workers with more attention to the ironies of class struggle, particularly as they relate to the state, industrial legality, and the rise and fall of what some historians now denote the Fordist regime of accumulation. Characterized by workplace technologies dictated by mass production, class relations coloured by high wages, unionization of core industries, and social pacts between capital and labour, sealed by the state and designed to stabilize profit and productivity, Fordism was sustained by an economy of relative and historically unprecedented affluence, expanding consumer potential, and a governing authority that was, for the first time in history, unashamedly interventionist. Regulation of the social order was the state's prime concern, an agenda it buttressed with a plethora of agencies and bureaucracies, an array of social welfare programs, and a general ideological commitment to Keynesian premises that social spending paid social dividends redeemable in class harmony. This Fordist social formation, which had its origins in the early twentieth century, but exercised its most decisive impact in Canada in the 1945-75 years, was always uneven in its hold over the working class. In terms of region, gender, and segmented labour markets, it could be argued that Fordism was always circumscribed. Yet clearly the twentieth-century social formation was coloured by Fordism and within this Fordist period the ways in which state formation, class struggle, and cultural life were scripted are fundamental to appreciating the new historical context. It also highlights the need in any synthetic overview of Canadian labour to develop an understanding of the state, culture, and class.

We know little about state formation in Canada, although our knowledge is expanding constantly with new research and writing. But we do know enough to suggest that the rise of the state in Canada was clearly related to the development of class differentiation, specific class interests, and, at certain points, the critical necessity to contain and regulate, in ways that would be perceived as legitimate, the threatening possibilities of working-class resistance. So fractured and complicated is this history of state formation, with its federal-provincial jurisdictional contests, its local manifestations, its gendered and racial construction, and its friction-ridden relations of legislation and law as written and practised, that I can make no claim to have covered anything approaching the entirety of this long story. But by focusing more on the state in this text, the history of workers as a collectivity is brought into sharper relief. Many of the contemporary analytic trends of our time de-emphasize that history by stressing difference: of how workers have been divided and fragmented by the structures that oppress and exploit them, as well as by their own acts and identifications, which have often privileged locale, race, skill, or gender over and against class.

Yet an understanding of the state and its historical making illuminates how one structured presence within the working-class experience can also override difference by imposing on workers forced apart in so many ways something of a common experience. In this sense the state reproduced what had, loosely, happened before, in terms of the capitalist transformation of life in an admittedly regionally variegated Canada. Labour processes under capitalism differed markedly from St. John's to Victoria, from Windsor to Yellowknife, and no sensible historian would claim that workers in such diverse settings could possibly be homogenized into an undifferentiated proletarian mass. Nevertheless, there is a point at which it is impossible to deny that these peculiar settings and their consequent workplace differences were not subject to *some* common capitalist dictates, which served to shape class in common ways. The state's role was not dissimilar.

We don't so much need to drop the fine theoretical net over Canadian workers, then, discovering that they exist only as *individuals*, for this is what we might well expect in a political economy and a culture in which all that is solid melts into the illusory indulgent air of conditioned self-interest and widely promoted self-identification: this, after all, is what a bourgeois order works quite hard to promote. More important, I would suggest, is grasping how that same bourgeois order works constantly at cross-purposes. What it proclaims and what individuals, workers among them, internalize is sometimes not what it produces. There are collective experiences beyond subjective sensitivities; there is a collective history even as it is suppressed and masked. The history of labour is about the two sides of this street of outcomes and obscurities, about when and why these sides emerge in bolder relief.

Historians who want to insist that differences of region, skill, gender, ethnicity, and race silence class identity in a babble of contending tongues do have a point: on the surface it does appear that Canadian workers, not unlike workers in other nation-states, fail to speak in a single, articulate voice. This book attempts to recognize the diversity that is indeed the voice of Canadian working-class experience, but it does so by refusing to jettison the platform capital and the state erected – a capitalist Canada – and on which all workers talked. Difference and commonality, individualism and collectivity, combined and recombined on this platform, the outcome of this mix taking on new connotations in specific historical contexts. However much historians want to debate the existence of working-class self-identity, they should at least occasionally stop and consider the extent to which capital and the state (themselves, of course, far from unproblematic unities) saw the working class as a dangerously coherent whole.

To rest an understanding of class experience entirely on this view from above would, admittedly, be no answer. Capital and the state often reacted out of panic, and ruling class fears and insecurities ran amuck in outlandish extremism that, as in the case of 1919, unleashed an ugly and unconscionable repression. If the working class was as much of a threat as capital and the state apparently believed in 1919, the outcome of that moment of class war would undoubtedly have been much different and we would be living in another kind of Canada today.

But where a ruling order driven to unreason by the threat of working-class revolt might see an undifferentiated labour challenge, historians need to understand both why this threat appeared when it did and why it failed to sustain itself. This demands appreciation of mobilization, organization, and the political-institutional history of workers, especially in moments of labour upheaval, but it also necessitates looking at periods of quietude, when the working class was in retreat. Within this oscillating history of challenge and complacency there was never an either/or dichotomy of *only* rebellious uprising versus *totalizing* (a term quite different in meaning than my earlier reference to the totality of working-class experience) acquiescence.

Because of this it seems to me that historians do need to address that awkward historical presence that, for want of a better term, some of us have been calling culture. This realm is not some all-encompassing entity, sweeping entire nations, genders, and classes into a common container. The very term "working-class culture" is therefore something of a misnomer, and I have backed away from it somewhat in this edition. But I do continue to use the term, albeit more self-consciously as description: it connotes diverse realms of everyday life that, however much they differ from place to place, time to time, and among sections of a hierarchically ordered working class, are nevertheless coloured and framed by the dependence of workers and their families on the wage. There is no doubt, as well, that at particular times and in specific places this cultural ensemble took on a more overtly political, indeed mobilizing, character. To say this seems to me unchallengeable, and I and others have never meant more than this. No one, to my knowledge, and certainly not me, ever made the argument that there was some kind of "free-standing class culture," a transhistorical culturalist class essence of unambiguous unity. Rather, those of us who attended to culture saw it as the connective tissues of an ambiguous realm of everyday life that bridged the chasm separating class as a silent structure and class as a potential force for revolutionary change. Those connective tissues were never, however, simply one-way threads tying class place to the realization of class consciousness; more often than not they wrapped themselves around class experience in ways that produced web-like mazes in which little was direct and obvious.

We can appreciate the resulting fragmentation and heterogeneity of working-class cultural life in Canada, as elsewhere, without turning our backs on the persistence of cultural distinctiveness, which has historically rested on the hard realities and persistent antagonisms of the wage relation and exploitation common to all workers. No religious affiliation, ethnic identification, political cross-class party, skill distinction, regional context, or gender gulf will override this totally. They may assure, at times, that the cultural will remain only a ground upon which an advanced class consciousness fails to fall. This has certainly happened throughout much of Canadian history. It is out of just such processes of difference, in conjunction with much in the ideological and economic realms, that the ruling order fashions its particular hegemony. But that hegemony, as the persistent character of class conflict in Canada attests, is never just a *given*; it is a ubiquitous contest, in which there are as many instances of arm-twisting as there are handshakes. Moreover, as historians know well, the very same religious, political, ethnic, sectional, regional, or sexual concerns that may reinforce the handshake can also, in altered circumstances, add muscle to the class involvement in direct combat.

Thus I reject the notion that culture is insignificant or non-existent, although, as will be apparent with respect to my earlier comments and how I justify the framing of the chapter on the 1975-91 period, culture is hardly the driving force of the history of class relations. There is no denying that the fragmentation of culture is a central aspect of the historical experience in general in Canada, and cultural life has, on more than one occasion, reinforced accommodation to the established ruling authority. Fragmentation, at certain historical moments, has weakened class resistance, and this process of undermining working-class opposition has definitely had its cultural sides. Yet, for all the divisions that have driven workers apart, weakening class conflict, labour as a collectivity has also been forced to deal with the reality of its separation from its rulers, a separation lived in the workplace but also experienced in the home and domestic world (which often reappeared in the mill, factory, or mine), reinforced in the political arena of parties and elections, and discovered and deepened as well in hours of robust or relaxed leisure. Often the cultural separations that resulted were differences within differences, reflecting little more than common-sense understandings or, worse, baffling confusions. Rarely were they more than an inarticulate way of life that emerged in the seating arrangement of a church or the particular ways that workers and employers spent their Sunday afternoons, the one on the baseball diamond, the other at the country club. This was, for long periods of our history, an inert culture. For all of the cultural inertia of the working class, however, its apparent fragmentation, acquiescence, and accommodation could change with the drop of a hat or, more precisely, the drop of a wage, the demise of a skill, or the restructuring of a job. In confrontations that turned on such developments, cultural experiences might resurface and be moved beyond the passivity of a way of life to articulate a rejection of acquisitive individualism or affirm class identity in demonstrations of mutuality and collective aspiration.

Culture is not, therefore, the last instance of analysis. Rather, it is part of an interpretive framework that builds on recognition of the limitations imposed on experience by economic constraint, places the moment of self-affirmation of the working class within the context of particular stages of development and levels of conflict and struggle, and, finally, attempts to bridge the gulf between culture and the forces that are both a part of it and work upon it. Such forces include those that may fragment as well as unite (family, gender, ethnicity, religion, and politics) in conjunction with those that seek to take culture to a higher level or, in their absence, mire it in the accommodation to the commonplace (class consciousness and leadership).

This attention to the cultural is thus a necessary bridge that connects, across a certain analytic river of fire, the objective presence of class as a relationship to the means of production with the rarely developed subjective realization of a class consciousness that reflects a fully grasped understanding of the necessity of working-class revolution and the creation of a society in which class exploitation is eliminated. I am surprised by how much huffing and puffing in historical and sociological critiques of the first edition of *Working-Class Experience* grew out of a perplexing blurring of these analytic categories. It was as if dealing with culture obscured class as a structured socio-economic presence and diffused class consciousness throughout a social order that had been undeniably insulated from it, except in rare periods. In the interests of avoiding such laboured posturing with respect to comment on this edition, let me make certain things absolutely clear.

Class is conceived in this book in orthodox Marxist terms. It is fundamentally an objective relationship to the means of production. Those who work for wages, lack decisive control over their conditions of labour, produce a surplus for others who own the physical environment of production and its tools as well as working-class time on the job – these people and their familial dependants, who nurture and reproduce on a daily and generational basis the labour power and personnel that do all of this, are the human material of the working class. Being of the working class thus presumes a relationship to those people who are not, as well as a relationship to surroundings and things, from buildings and technologies to paycheques. However well remunerated, it entails specific alienations and many anxieties.

This working class, throughout history, has been constantly changing. It is by no means an undifferentiated mass. This fragmented, constantly shifting reality is registered in the ways working-class people often identify themselves as other than working class. But this does not mean that a working class cannot be located. Even today, as class lines admittedly blur and more and more people earn their livings in ways that create illusory flight from clear-cut working-class self-identification, there is still a basic understanding of who is a worker and who is not. Rarely are identities constructed that entirely and categorically repudiate the material moorings of class place. "Professionals" experience the erosion of their authority

and the routinization of their work; jobs in the old strongholds of traditional blue-collar labour and industrial unionism disappear, but those
created in government bureaucracies and fast-food outlets are no less
alienating. In all of the most basic ways, workers remain workers, whatever
the contemporary process of economic restructuring.

Class in this objective sense, however, is nameless, faceless, a fundamental but inarticulate social entity. *It* produces, by definition, although the
understanding of what production is and how it is valued has undergone
shifts and transformations over the course of the nineteenth and twentieth
centuries. But beyond this production, class as a structured objective socio-
economic relationship does nothing. It takes on its voices through what it
does out of this material situation. It speaks, not so much with words of
surplus produced, profits generated, and labour forces restructured (for
these, after all, are more capital's words than labour's), but with languages
of resistance and accommodation. The translation, if not the grammar, is
often cultural, however much the meaning is one of political economy.

These translations vary greatly and are capable of shifting dramatically.
Over time, through space, in contexts, the tone and content of such translations differ. My sense of the history is that one can appreciate in Canada the
proliferation of many working-class identities. These identities can seldom
be separated decisively from class experience, but they rarely embrace a
fully formed class consciousness in which the clarity of a proletarian program for revolutionary change appears. A study of class consciousness in
Canada for the most part would be an exploration of silences and absences.
For many Canadian historians this relegates class to a category of marginal
significance: other factors matter, but class does not. I see things differently.

This book is an attempt to synthesize working-class history by starting
from the premise that workers are a social grouping rooted in productive
relations. It proceeds to explore the meaning of those relations as they are
lived out both on and beyond the job, expressed in politics and union
organization as well as tavern and family life, church and sporting team. In
the absence of sustained waves of class consciousness, this is what labouring life is all about.

All of this needs to be said because those historians and others who claim
that there is no working-class identity left, if ever there was one, have
confused class and class consciousness. They have done this, in part, I
suspect, because they have no sensitivity to cultural difference. Working-
class identity is being confused with class consciousness, the lack of which
is now routinely marshalled to question the existence of class itself. And in a
classic presentist push, the current moment and its ambivalences are
colouring much of our understanding of the past. The limitations of class in
the present, which are formidable, are determining our view of the past,
when things were different and class possibilities often seemed more open-

ended. Whatever these limitations, however, this all too blanket-like repudiation of class is not only a disservice to the workers of the past. It also distorts our understanding of the contemporary working class.

Ironically, this process of distortion can be furthered by developments of critical analytic insight. If there is a single most influential body of literature and set of concerns addressed in this rewrite, it is undoubtedly those associated loosely with feminism, itself a highly differentiated school(s) of thought and political positioning. Feminist writing and argument have taught us that gender matters in the history of the working class. I have tried to pay attention to this message. Many feminists will not agree with what they read here, but I do not think it possible for any of them to write, as Mariana Valverde did in an earlier, legitimate comment on *Working-Class Experience*: "Bryan Palmer tries to rectify the productive-relations bias of Canadian labour history by using the insights of British studies of cultural aspects of working-class formation. . . . In spite of his refreshing interest in culture and family, however, he tends to treat the family as a black box: sexism and struggles within the family are not mentioned." I have tried to get myself and the history out of this black box in what follows. No doubt there will be many who will see this effort as failure, suggesting that I have paid insufficient attention to gender and denigrated the relationship of gender and class with my explicit focus on workers and their experience.

Certain feminist positions, and even much feminist writing that tends to counter those positions, have argued forcefully or implied less directly that gender identity has, historically, superseded class identity. This book does not argue such a case. This is a book about the working class. This working class cannot be conceived or understood as *un*gendered, but neither can its history be reduced, as some would have us believe, *only* to gender and its oppressions. While the insights of contemporary feminism can certainly not be discounted in forcing reconsiderations of the past – as I believe this book shows – they should not be marshalled to decontextualize history and deprive women and men of earlier generations of their right to a hearing on something approaching their own terms. These terms were not those, for most of our history, of contemporary feminism, just as they were not those of Marxism. I am in fundamental agreement with Elizabeth Fox-Genovese, who writes in *Feminism Without Illusions* (1991):

> Class oppression like racial and ethnic discrimination deprive many women of the "protection" under which many middle-class women have chafed. Forced by economic necessity to work outside the home, frequently deserted or abused by husbands or other male kin, poor women have never been restricted to a domestic haven. And whatever abuse they have suffered at the hands of the men of their own communities, most of them have understood that the greater oppression has come from outside

that community – from a society that has denied their men as well as themselves . . . fundamental respect.

This simple passage calls into question some timeless gender oppression uniting all women and separating them from all men: gender and class demand treatment as connections, not separations; women and men demand treatment, not as biological and social dichotomies, but as possibilities themselves severed by other possibilities, of which class is perhaps the most fundamental. Those feminists discontented with what follows should consider how they have handled class: in Valverde's stimulating and well-received *Sex, Power, and Pleasure*, class is addressed in a few rather idiosyncratic pages.

These positionings on class, identity, culture, and class consciousness produce, I think, the last irony of this text: its concluding chapter. Many will question the tone and content of this final commentary on the history of the contemporary period. They will wonder why so much ink is spilled on politics and leadership and so little on the self-identifications and cultural lives of workers. I find no contradiction here. My highlighting of the current struggles and dilemmas of Canadian workers is posed the way it is because I believe that workers who appreciate the lessons of a past rich in overt class struggle and cultural forms of varying oppositional meaning will understand that the contemporary working class faces obstacles and challenges that demand attention if labour is to recover the strengths of its past to challenge the weaknesses of its present and the bleakness of its future. This is what is required, I would contend, if a host of special oppressions, linked to class but separate from it, are to be overcome. I spend less time on the cultural and more time on the structural and organizational experience of workers because, simply put, in the current assault on labour the objective destruction of the economic, institutional, and political lives of working-class Canadians looms largest in the history of 1975-91. The cultural fragmentations of workers and the inadequacies and possibilities of the cultural experience of working-class Canadians and their institutions are situated in such debilitating developments.

Those who will claim that my critique of the contemporary workers' movement and, especially, its leadership – electoral and economic – is unduly "political," shifting the treatment of class away from that of earlier chapters, quite frankly will have misread the meaning and intention of preceding sections. And, finally, those who see this concluding chapter as unduly politicized should at least appreciate that no Canadian overview of working-class history and/or the labour movement has not ended on a highly political note. What differentiates this history from others is that my note is not appended to the current trade union bureaucracies and social democratic parties as either endorsement or mild-mannered plea to become more progressive. My note is discordant.

As this book goes to press nothing that has happened recently has forced me to reconsider my stand in that final chapter. The federal state continues to bash public-sector workers, who have fought valiant battles of resistance only to be marched back to work by leaders who, days before, promised that they would go to jail rather than succumb. Mulroney's Conservatives do indeed look to be on the way out, but they have a lot more damage they can do before making their exit. Moreover, it is unlikely that a changing of the guard on Parliament Hill will give workers much to cheer about. If the Liberal Party is being groomed for power, it will be no more likely to befriend the workers' movement than were the Tories. And the rise of the Reform Party will only push all federal politics decidedly to the right. Those leftists who like to think globally but act locally are no doubt taking great comfort in the politics of provincialism, but a serious scrutiny of the contemporary context should actually dispel mythological notions that advances are now being registered.

With social democratic governments ruling over 50 per cent of the nation's population, the NDP rise to provincial power in the economic malaise of the early 1990s occurred at precisely the moment that labour's challenge needed to be subdued and other oppositions quieted. Who better to police working-class militants, keep the lid on inflation, deflect aboriginal claims to the land, and patch up the provincial holes in the roof of "national unity" than the party of the "people." The recent revival of the NDP electorally will no doubt be touted as a breakthrough for the left. It is nothing of the sort. Percentages of the popular vote going to New Democrats have not altered much. What has changed is the political demeanour of social democracy, its countenance no longer disfigured by socialist wrinkles or the economic blemish of opposition to the capitalist market. Thus the rather small potatoes of provincial power in the early 1990s have less to do with a reinvigorated left political presence than with the diffusion of right-wing ideas and the organizational and programmatic apostasy of the so-called left. The NDP is winning, in 1990-91, against what remains of its left traditions and past, not because of it. And it is allowed the small ground of provincial-territorial rule precisely because, in the political and economic climate of this period, it can be counted on to do the right thing.

As classic liberals in a hurry, the NDP slowed down to taste the spoils of provincial political office. Ontario showed the way forward, but nothing in the record of Bob Rae's NDP in power, which forms a substantial discussion in this book's concluding chapter, prompts me to revise my rather jaundiced assessment of contemporary social democracy. A party that, throughout its long years in opposition, never yielded in its hostility to legislating striking workers back to their jobs was capable of discussing the possibility of such a coercive law on the first day of a Toronto transit worker walkout. Mike Harcourt's New Democrats swept the British Columbia polls late in 1991 with promises of no socialism, balanced budgets, and a new political civility, while behind-the-scenes Socred power-brokers, sensing that their ship had now sunk, cast a piece of their lot with the Liberals, who finally elected some MPPs to the legislature. When liberals in a hurry put on the brakes, Liberals apparently speed up. Harcourt's first move, after getting a free haircut, was to curry favour with international capital and proclaim the province "open for business." It was all very much a repeat of the Rae performance, with the notable difference that Harcourt saw fit to portray himself as fiscally more conservative than his central Canadian counterpart. Roy Romanow now heads an NDP government in Saskatchewan; it appears to be charting an even more cautious political and economic path. Claiming there is no money to be spent addressing the maldistribution of wealth, Romanow and other Saskatchewan New Democrats are fixated on the provincial deficit. Pre-election press coverage of the Romanow/NDP surge found it difficult to differentiate social democrats, Liberals, and Tories: all seemed governed by Milton Friedman, dean of New Right economics. Western social democratic premiers actually made Ontario's NDP government look almost left with its deficit spending and its posture of fostering a "caring" society. But this comparative viewpoint distorts as much as it reveals. It depends on where you are doing the looking from. In the 1990s, most eyes, including those of established parties that claim to speak for the workers, are focused right. Those that glance left wink at Keynes, not Marx.

Communist Party of Canada leaders, for instance, want to water down what is left of their program, moving into the social democratic void created by an NDP galloping, not drifting, to the right. The aged stalwart supporters of Canada's party of Stalinism disagree, and actually stormed the CPC's national headquarters, forcing the Communist leadership to flee the scene in limousines. At issue was no doubt politics of substance, with advocates of "democratic socialism" standing against those who called for a renewed communism, but the central issue was also supremely ironic: the CPC leadership wanted to sell off party property that had historically been regarded as belonging to the membership.

As social democracy abandons even the pretence of socialist programs and politics, as the Communist Party squabbles over who owns what and looks to appropriate political ground to its right vacated by the electoral reformist left, and as trade unionists take a beating their own bureaucratic leaders urge them to resist up to the point that those leaders themselves will actually have to feel some blows, it is apparent that Canadian workers lack anything approximating an adequate leadership. In this context of what we might call voicelessness, working-class needs get short shrift.

This, in good part, explains why so many are so ready to see any identities beyond class as real, and class itself as little more than the figment of what remains of a leftist imagination. However different this version of *Working-Class Experience* is from its predecessor, it is the same inasmuch as it refuses to refuse class. For those who read it and continue to think that workers in this country are incapable of thinking of themselves as workers, I suggest a simple exercise: go talk to some. And listen with both ears. They will tell you of their personal problems and gripes. Talk will zero in on the cost of groceries and the eagerly anticipated consumer purchase, as well as on their resentments toward the GST and the mounting state recourse to wage "freezes" and "capping." Women will complain of their companions, and regional grievance will surface; among the religiously devout or the so-called "deviant" there will be particular concerns. Yet there will be, throughout these conversations, an unmistakable divide separating "them" and "us." In one ear you will hear about individual identities and needs, about acquisitions, accommodations, and fragmented selves seemingly unconnected to wider worlds; in the other ear will echo an appreciation of the past, the necessity of struggle, and the experience of collectivity. These are, and for years have been, the voices of class. They may not be all that some of us would want them to be, but they exist today as they did yesterday.

PREFACE TO THE FIRST EDITION

> The chief defect of all hitherto existing materialism . . . is that the thing, . . . reality, sensuousness, is conceived only in the form of the *object* . . . or of contemplation . . . , but not as *human sensuous activity, practice*, not subjectively.
>
> Karl Marx, "Theses on Feuerbach," (1845)

As I was preparing to pack this manuscript off to the publisher, Eugene Forsey's monumental compilation of data on the workers' movement of nineteenth-century Canada arrived in one morning's mail delivery. *Trade Unions in Canada* presents, for the first time, a wealth of factual information necessary to interpret important realms of labour's formative experiences. Unlike so many of his contemporaries and successors, whose perspectives on the Canadian working class were influenced directly or indirectly by the social democratic milieu of the 1930s and 1940s, Forsey broke decisively from an explicitly political and implicitly presentist concern with labour in its twentieth-century guise. Much of recent working-class history has dealt with the more visible development of the labour movement in this century, and concentrates on a specific set of questions: leadership, the emergence of collective bargaining, the role of the state in "industrial relations," the development of unionism as an economic and political force, and the contest between social democracy and communism for the allegiance of Canadian workers in the 1930s and 1940s. However important such issues may be, they inevitably focus our attention on labour's more contemporary history, to the exclusion of an understanding of the formative years of class formation and class conflict. Forsey, however, has begun at the beginning, and his study provides a tacit critique of those who have, for three decades, been implying that labour history starts in 1919 with the Winnipeg General Strike. But this critique is, understandably, a muffled one. Concentrating on unionism, he has explored limited realms of working-class experience and has presented, by his own admission, "few opinions or arguments" and "few analyses."

This book necessarily aims to be both something less and something more than Forsey's exhaustive history of trade unionism from 1812 to 1902. It is less, for it can of course make no pretence to fill the gaps in our factual knowledge in even one small corner of the vast field that encompasses working-class experience from 1800 to 1980. About unions, labour politics, family life, leisure activities, patterns of conflict, relations with the state, material circumstances, or a host of other facets of working-class life much more will have to be written than I have presented here. But this study is more, in that it is not simply a presentation of facts, a project always destined – given the nature of the sources – to be limited and inhibited. Unlike Forsey's *Trade Unions in Canada*, it is an attempt to generalize, to interpret, to locate periods of similarity in which working-class experience shared certain characteristics, and to separate them out from other epochs, in which the history appears to take other directions. This book, then, is conceived as an argument about working-class experience, rather than a definitive chronicle of labour's history.

It is only by portraying the collective experience and by probing areas outside the realm of labour unions and politics that a sophisticated under-standing of workers' experience can even be approached. Although politi-cal and union activities have both measured and influenced the tenor of the working-class experience, they are far from being its sole aspects. Likewise, the factual presentation of specific events and particular developments provides a good starting point for study but cannot stand as a full charac-terization of Canada's working class. This book attempts to create a unified portrait by bringing together diverse regional experiences and by drawing on many levels of working-class life. Two issues arise from such a treatment, and they have long been points of debate among historians of Canadian labour: the significance of regional disparity and the validity of examining the sparsely documented areas of working-class experience that lie outside labour organization and electoral activity.

First, as to *region* (and, by implication, *chronology*, for Canadian regions developed at an uneven pace and at different times): this book does not neglect regional peculiarities. But it does offer generalized arguments that may be developed out of attention to specific regional entities, as with, for instance, the focus on central Canada in the portrait of labour's early years. But throughout the book, the argument is developed as a "national" argument only where there is evidence that regional experiences shared certain similarities. Ironically enough, I would argue, this took place most prominently in the nineteenth century, prior to the erection of a Canadian state and the full impact of policies that might be construed as serving the interests of central Canadian "imperialism." Such policies and the class forces behind them – which always presented themselves as the embodiment and voice of "national" interest – slowed development in the Maritimes and structured the West along particular paths. In the twentieth century, the consequences of such processes would be felt in the world of the working class, manifesting themselves in regional identification, different forms of organization or political practice, and divergent experiences, both materially and culturally. But in British North America or the early Canada of the immediate post-National Policy (1879) years, such divisions were less pronounced, and shared experiences were, to some extent, more prevalent.

Second, and perhaps more contentious, is the way in which this book addresses working-class experience. Obviously the approach here breaks from previous attempts to survey the history of Canadian workers in its insistence that *working-class life extends beyond labour organizations and labour politics*. There is a need to study the place of workers in their communities and families, as well as in their unions and political parties, and this need has been insufficiently recognized by many labour historians. Church and tavern, printers' chapel (the name of the printing trade's organization), and election-night "treating" are all spheres of working-class life, interconnected and linked to the material realities of the workplace and the larger political economy. They are complex parts of a process of class formation that need to be analysed in order to comprehend how workers came to see their interests as antagonistic to those of employers, and how workers whose experiences were constantly atomized through social institutions and ideologies came to embrace a collective response to the industrial-capitalist transformation of the late nineteenth century.

This book therefore differs from other labour history surveys in that it lays stress upon the totality of working-class experience. It is *class*, as embedded in the structural, primarily economic context of specific social formations, that is at the conceptual root of this study, not labour as an interest group fighting its way into a pluralist society by way of its unions and its political platform. The development of distinct working and non-working classes was a protracted and contradictory process. It grew out of the economic relations of production, but was also clarified and reproduced over time in other formal and informal ways: through ritual and revelry, culture and conflict, family and funeral and, of course, through the strengths, weaknesses, and character of the workers' movement itself. At times new initiatives – from capital and/or the state – drove it into retreat, but its potential was never relinquished entirely.

None of this is to argue that workers' experiences inside and outside their unions and their political activities bore the distinct marks of class consciousness. Social and cultural life, like day-to-day developments at the workplace or in the political arena, were ambiguous, and class as an idealized, conscious expression of worker antagonism to capital and the state has been a rare phenomenon in Canada. But there are indications in the history that at specific moments there was an unprecedented merging of class institutions and perspectives, which produced organizational, political, and cultural ferment. To explore such activity, and to discover why it has been more intense in some moments than at others, is one of the most difficult tasks before labour historians.

Part of the difficulty lies in the interpretive and historical divide that runs through our historiography, separating the history of the nineteenth century from that of the twentieth. These two periods have, for the most part, been studied by different kinds of historians. Nineteenth-century experience has been probed by those concerned with class, community, and, to a lesser extent, culture, while the twentieth century has been examined in terms of labour and the left (in its "syndicalist" face of the World War One years and its social democratic stance during the period of the Great Depression and the 1940s). So little is known of the explicitly cultural in the post-1900 years that it is impossible to make more than tentative statements in the discussion of such experience. Although historiographical developments have accentuated this rift, a part of its cause can be found in the history itself.

In earlier periods, workers lived far more localized and less commercialized lives than their more recent counterparts. Their politics, their unions, and their social and cultural experiences turned on community concerns and possibilities, and unfolded within specific settings. Later, by the 1920s, national markets, the presence of powerful North American states, monopoly capital, the potential expansion of consumer credit, and the rise of conspicuous consumption shifted workers' perspectives and moved labour in two complementary, if apparently divergent, directions. The class no longer lived in local communities, but in a larger, less personalized national or international community. At the same time, there was a retreat from the immediate community into the narrower unit of consumption represented by the family. In nineteenth-century workers' experience, family life was far more likely to have been integrated into neighbourhood activities and collective forms of working-class leisure than in the twentieth century, when the nuclear family probably became a haven, both psychological and consumer-oriented, in an increasingly alienating world.

But in the absence of any convincing discussion of this question and of countless others, it is necessary to proceed cautiously. There are, moreover, important discussions of organization and labour politics that can be used to address this twentieth-century experience. These facets of workers' lives may well have become more significant as the localized experiences of the nineteenth century gave way to the nationwide labour movements of the twentieth century. This is not to imply, of course, that labour's struggles to unionize and develop a political presence consumed, in its entirety, the experience of twentieth-century workers. Rather, they remained, as they had been in the nineteenth century (where they were undoubtedly weaker), but parts of a larger whole, and it is the understanding of this totality that is central. If it cannot yet be fully created because of immense gaps in our knowledge and conceptualization, we must nevertheless still try to gesture toward it, exploring the economic, institutional, political, and cultural experience of workers. This book attempts to suggest how this experience was forged, how the Canadian working class has been made and remade over the course of two centuries. In this rise and reconstitution of Canadian labour lies an interpretation of a part of our past and a suggestion of what must be attempted if the working class is again to reach toward its potential.

ACKNOWLEDGEMENTS TO THE FIRST EDITION

In a book such as this, covering a wide and interpretively problematic span of Canadian history, I have been sustained by a number of individuals who willingly shared sources and perspectives with me. Among the most generous have been Donald Akenson, Dale Chisamore, Michael Cross, Russell Hann, Peter DeLottinville, Robert Malcolmson, Ian McKay, Richard Rice, Wayne Roberts, Terry Ruddel, John Herd Thompson, and Brian Young. Debi Wells gave me access to her own research and took the time and trouble to read the manuscript in its entirety, as did Gregory S. Kealey and Allen Seager. George Rawlyk suggested that I do this book originally, forced me to rethink specific sections, and helped me to cut the manuscript down to a size that publishers deemed appropriate. My students in various seminars at Queen's and McGill produced papers and remarkable criticisms of my own way of looking at working-class experience that have enabled me to write differently than I once would have. A Department of Labour grant provided research assistance, while the offices of the Dean of Arts and the History Department at Simon Fraser University facilitated the final typing of the manuscript. I am grateful to Bernice Ferrier, Jenny Alexander, and Wilma Whiffin, who typed with skill, patience, and good humour as we all struggled to meet deadlines.

Finally, my deepest thanks go to two historians at Queen's University. Their support will never be forgotten.

ACKNOWLEDGEMENTS TO THE SECOND EDITION

I am especially indebted to all of those academics and workers who wrote to me upon publication of *Working-Class Experience*, letting me know what they liked and what they did not, informing me of lapses of judgement and errors of fact. I have tried, in this revised edition, to correct the wrongs. My thanks go out to Allan Greer, who pointed out problems in the first chapter, and to George Samas, my friend, neighbour, and unrepentant pragmatic social democrat, who disagreed with all I wrote in the final chapter, but nevertheless read it with an eye to keeping me from making embarrassing errors of fact. Graduate students at Queen's University have provided me with substantial, ongoing critiques, as well as much new material, upon which I draw liberally in the text. I thank them all. Indeed, I would like to dedicate this book, with much appreciation, to the graduate students I have learned from over the course of the last ten years and, as well, to Nicole, who listened when she did not have to. And for Melanie, off to social democracy's last best frontier, good luck.

Chapter 1

PRODUCING CLASSES, PATERNALIST AUTHORITY
1800-1850

THE SOCIAL FORMATION

The early history of the Canadian producing classes begins with the harvesters of fish and fur. Portuguese, Spanish, French, Irish, and English fishermen laboured to secure the cod that fed much of Catholic Europe and helped to keep the absolutist states of the seventeenth and eighteenth centuries financially afloat. Native peoples hunted and bartered in the trade in furs that made the fortunes of European companies and American entrepreneurs. Finally, there were the voyageurs and engagés upon whose backs the Montreal and Quebec merchants relied. Out of these experiences would be written the first paragraphs of resistance to authority and labour discipline, as well as introductory chapters in evolving relations of expropriation, exploitation, and subordination.

Some historians and sociologists consider these early producers workers, structured into relations of dependency through their accumulated debts to mercantile capitalists and increasingly reliant for their sustenance on wages. It was not quite this simple. The transatlantic fisherfolk had no sustained presence in Canada, the aboriginal peoples central to the fur trade were never totally reduced to employable hands, and the more proletarianized voyageurs and engagés always maintained a persistent, seasonal connection to the land, from which they drew a part of their material support and an ideology of independence. Allan Greer's conclusion that "there was little place in the fur trade for a genuine proletariat" might well stand as a comment on the entire overlapping set of economies that made up the pre-1800 Canadian social formation.

Such complex social relations of production extended into the nineteenth century, as did much of the history of craftsmen's associations and apprenticeship training in New France and shipyard labour in the port cities. However, the demise of the fish and fur empires occurred quite abruptly, and by the beginning of the nineteenth century, lumber and wheat had become the main staples of British North America. In New Brunswick, as Graeme Wynn has shown, a "timber colony" emerged, while wheat dominated central Canadian development. To be sure, in parts of the Maritimes, sea staples remained critical: as late as 1857, 90 per cent of the classifiable employed males of Newfoundland were engaged in sealing and fishing. Over the course of the 1800-50 years, however, the old staples gave way to the new exports of square timber and wheat. Both of these items linked up more easily with other diversified economic production than had the staples of fish and fur. They were connected with more stable populations of resident producers and conditioned new forms of production related to those populations and to the harvesting needs of the staple. Square timber and wheat production thrived under the protection of British mercantilist practice for much of the first half of the nineteenth century, although periodic economic downturns made lives dependent on these staples precarious. As Britain's powerful Industrial Revolution unleashed demands for free trade and a general questioning of the "protections" afforded colonial hewers of wood and drawers of water such as the outposts of the Canadas, the assured markets of the Empire were gradually undermined. When Britain chose in 1846 to repeal the Corn Laws, a symbolic and material expression of colonialism that allowed Canadian staples a preferential access to Britain's teeming urban markets, the staple producers of the Canadas were clearly entering a new age of difficult adjustment.

Similar problems faced French Canada. Recent historical writing suggests that an older interpretation of a "crisis on the land" in Lower Canada has been greatly exaggerated. Wheat yields may not have dropped as precipitously as Fernand Ouellet once suggested, and soil depletion and *habitant* impoverishment were not likely the universal features of a generalized agricultural crisis. Still, there can be no doubt that the seigneurial system stifled some initiative and contributed toward increasing population pressure on the land. When crop disease exacerbated matters in the 1830s there was genuine distress in many *habitant* communities, where impoverishment, landlessness, and the semi-proletarianization of sectors of the population indicated changes in the social structure.

Imperial concerns were many and varied, and they hardly worked uniformly to aid development in colonial Canada. Often, as in the mercantilist barriers against actual production, they curtailed economic activity directly. But the course of development followed strange and often unanticipated paths. The British desire to defend its North American colonies in the aftermath of the War of 1812, coupled with the transportation needs of the new staples, stimulated improvement of the St. Lawrence rivers and lakes system, and between 1821 and 1848 a series of new and improved canals were completed.

Immense sums were pumped into the Canadas in these years to finance this canal system. Completed by the 1840s, when railways began to rival water transportation, this water-based network of natural and man-made navigable arteries facilitated the export of timber from Quebec City and Saint John and the massive Upper Canadian shipments of wheat to Britain, the United States, Quebec, and the Maritimes. Such activities were paralleled on the east coast by the Halifax merchants' involvement in the trade in staples, their commercial connections to the West Indies and the United States, and their role in the construction of the Shubenacadie Canal.

These economic endeavours and public improvements turned on the demands of commercial capital as well as changing colonial imperatives, both of which were transatlantic in origin. Yet, their impact would be greatest in the Canadas, where commerce and colonialism would sow the seeds of their own demise. For as these forces adapted policies and practices to their self-conceived interests they created factors that would usher in a new age of industrial-capitalist expansion. Prior to 1850, three distinct but related phenomena characterize the epoch as the culmination of a centuries-long prelude to Canada's Industrial Revolution: merchant capital, independent commodity production, and the orientation to land and its ownership all prepared the way for industrial capital's post-1850 surge.

The mercantile fortunes accumulated in the staples trade sought speculative and investment outlets, looking for monopolistic advantage but fostering the growth of productive capital and creating the domestic development that would give rise to the basic structures of an internal, home market. Hat manufacturing in Quebec City, of course, grew directly out of the fur trade and was an implicit and early blow against mercantilist doctrine, which saw direct colonial production as harmful to the interests of the metropolitan centre of Empire. Even more dramatic was the case of shipbuilding, a logical extension of the timber trade and a mammoth enterprise that employed over 3,350 workers in Quebec City alone in the peak production year of 1825. As Richard Rice has shown, shipbuilding in the years

1809 to 1854 may have employed anywhere from one-quarter to one-half of the male work force in Quebec City. Shipyards there employed upwards of 200 hands and turned out one of every five tons of ships built in British North America. Eastern Canadian yards – in Saint John, along the Miramichi River, or in the rude schooner and sloop-producing outports and rural river locations of the entire region – employed far smaller numbers of workers. Naval dockyards in Halifax and Kingston also produced ships, especially in moments of military crisis. During the War of 1812 over a thousand "artificers" were recruited from Quebec and Great Britain to be transported to the Kingston site between 1813 and 1815.

Often the mercantile pursuit of development extended beyond a simple link to the traditional staples. In Halifax, commercial waterfront capital sought productive opportunity through the creation of the Stanyan Rope Works in 1826-27. Montreal businessmen exemplified this process: Peter McGill, George Moffatt, Joseph Mason, James Ferrier, and the Molson family all embraced wide-reaching economic interests during the first half of the century. Upper Canadian merchants such as William H. Merritt in St. Catharines pumped their profits into the expansion of the St. Lawrence canal system, an economic endeavour that resulted in spin-off industries producing shovels, wheelbarrows, and other utensils. Such generalized activity, undertaken by merchants primarily interested in moving goods rather than creating them, nevertheless stimulated production and partially overcame some of the impediments blocking the creation of a diversified economic home market in which manufactories existed. Merchant capital, then, in varied ways and uncertainly, to be sure, provided one path to industrial development.

The second path was a more modest one. Independent commodity producers – saw and grist millers, carpenters, shoemakers, tailors, iron forgers, and others – captured local markets and expanded productive concerns. Many artisan producers, such as the Upper Canadian blacksmiths studied in great detail by William Wylie, were hemmed in by commercial capital and its capacity to dominate specific, especially rural, locales. But other small producers battled the odds to launch the beginnings of capitalist enterprises. Especially pronounced in those urban centres where the home market was most advanced, this activity ran headlong into mercantilist restrictions, American competition, and chronic shortages of skilled labour. A 1799 petition to establish a Chippewa, Upper Canada, ironworks commenced: "Your honours are knowing how difficult it will be to get labourers." By the 1840s, however, capitalist handicraft production was established in cities such as Toronto and Montreal, and it was making inroads elsewhere. Belleville and Cobourg boasted paper and woollen mills that employed more than 100 workers.

Such firms were exceptions that pointed to the possibilities of an industrial future. Manufacturing establishments in the pre-1850 years were normally small: the average Upper Canadian manufactory employed less than five workers. Still, there were 3,300 such establishments in Upper Canada at mid-century, employing almost 12,000 hands. The largest work forces were found in the shingle, carriage, cabinet, and boot-and-shoe sectors. Technology had yet to transform such spheres and when it did, after 1850, especially in the rise of steam engines and the transformation of the metal trades, the consequences would be monumental. Out of the once handicraft-dominated manufactories of the 1830s and 1840s would emerge the fully mechanized, larger factories of the industrial age. Like merchant capital, independent commodity production provided a varied and uncertain path to capitalist development. Both paths converged most often and most dramatically on the towns, where the producing classes were concentrated.

Yet, developments in rural areas were not without a role to play. Upper and Lower Canada were approximately 85 per cent rural at mid-century, but various developments ensured that many in the countryside had no access to landownership. Farm families found it more and more difficult to provide land for their children and many newly arrived immigrants necessarily turned to wage labour to provide for themselves.

The work force thus obtained helped to overcome impediments to the creation of a capitalistic labour market and was therefore essential to the economic development of the Canadas. This work force was not only a vital prerequisite to the large public works projects of the canal era, it was also a central component in the emerging social relations of urban life (where servants were much in demand), in early manufacturing and construction, on the docks of a commercially oriented society, and in the fields and forests of a wheat-and-timber economy.

Land was alienated, or access to it blocked in various ways. Moving from east to west, we see that agriculture and permanent settlement were never easily accomplished in Newfoundland, where it was early felt that ownership of the land would undermine allegiance to the fishery, threatening monopolistic profit and striking a blow at the training ground for the Empire's seamen. Settlement proceeded, but slowly and unevenly. Absentee landowners were granted huge tracts of Prince Edward Island, Nova Scotia, and New Brunswick before 1800. Township granting and the long-standing practice of seigneurial tenure (not abolished until 1854) in Lower Canada contributed to landlessness and population migration to the cities, the United States, and the barren lands of the northern shield. On the Upper Canadian frontier, early speculators held much of the best land, church and state took their appropriate share, and free land grants were curbed in 1826 and forbidden by the Land Act of 1837 (the provision being overturned in 1841).

The rationale behind such acts and the motivation of those elite figures who crafted them are difficult to ascertain with certainty. Lord Goderich, the Colonial Secretary in 1831, provided one assessment when he stated: "Without some division of labour, without a class of persons willing to work for wages, how can society be prevented from falling into a state of almost primitive rudeness, and how are the comforts and refinements of civilized life to be procured?" Goderich insisted that in every society there should be "a class of Laborers as well as a class of Capitalists or Land-owners."

This appeared to be happening across the diverse expanse of the developing Canadas. An irate Kingston mechanic complained in the midst of tough times in the 1830s that "country mechanics, like birds of passage, this summer are pouring into undertakers, working late and early for *twelve dollars a month* subject to be hired out again like slaves, to others at advanced wages – a degradation that the meanest bushwacker swaying an axe, who neither spent years nor months in practice or study of his calling seldom submits to." By 1851, in the rural areas of the Home District to the east of Toronto, some 10,172 out of 14,994 labouring-age males (67.8 per cent) were landless. Rates of pay for some occupations, according to Peter Russell, actually declined over time: female servants saw their labour command less in 1840 than it had in 1818; many skilled tradesmen experienced marginal wage declines between 1815 and 1840.

J. K. Johnson has recently argued bluntly that "There was no conspiracy on the part of the 'ruling class' to create a landless wage earning proletariat in Upper Canada." Perhaps not, but the evidence of concentrated owner-ship of land, alienated in huge parcels, is unmistakable. Those who owned that land, and who also often played pivotal roles in drafting land policy, were amenable to using whatever schemes they could to enhance the value of their plots so that their immense holdings would command higher and higher prices. Johnson charts the history of one short-lived such scheme, the Canadian Emigration Association of 1840-41, by which prominent Upper Canadian landowners were willing to provide settler immigrants with free fifty-acre tracts in order to increase the possibility of selling off companion lots of 150 acres. Forced to such a policy of enticement because of declining immigration in the aftermath of the political turmoil and economic difficulties of the late 1830s, elite landowners folded up their colonization scheme when it became apparent that somebody had to pay the bills and when the number of immigrants soared in the early 1840s. Conspiracies, of whatever sort, were far less significant in the history of class formation than broader social and economic processes and trends.

The early nineteenth-century social formation of the Canadas proper was therefore based on the authority of commercial capital and rooted in a social structure unquestioningly agricultural. At the same time, however, a manufacturing sector was coming into being and the process of class differ-entiation was under way. Such a perspective underscores the close link between town and country, and reveals the importance of the home market and of the early producing classes – precisely those forces often obscured by the traditional historiographic stress on the mercantile and rural essence of Canadian society before 1850. Moreover, in approaching the social formation in this manner, we are led toward an understanding of the economic dislocations and political instability characterizing these years. Given these disruptive realities, what were the elements that helped to stabilize early Canadian society?

PATERNALISM

Few attempts have been made to come to grips with the character of social and productive relations in early Canada. An original and significant statement is that of economic historian H.C. Pentland in his 1950s study *Labour and Capital in Canada*, published in 1981. Pentland has come under sustained assault from various critics, among them Donald Akenson, who, in one of the great polemical overstatements of our historiographic time, reduces Pentland's contribution to infusing the so-called new Canadian social history with a vile racism and defensive ethnocentric nationalism, and Allan Greer, who challenges Pentland on the grounds that he misunderstood the central importance of Marxist analytic categories. These critiques have undermined Pentland's credibility as an authority in many quarters, but they have failed to offer any substantive interpretation of how, in a period predating unambiguously capitalist productive relations, the producing classes and their various masters related to one another. Where Pentland's argument remains insightful, and where it demands refinements and extensions, is in the assertion that social relations in the pre-1850 years developed within a system of "status, hierarchies, symbols, privileges, and loyalties" where a particular style of leadership and economic organization evolved in ways that reached beyond the simple force of material superiority.

Those who ruled did so, of course, because of their economic might and control over resources and jobs, but in the 1800-50 years they were forced, because of material circumstances such as localized shortages of skilled labour, to justify such power in ways that reached beyond the economic. And they lived their lives as rulers partly out of such justifications. A social order unfolding within such boundaries can be described as paternalism. This does not mean, as one labour historian has implied, that we should be wary "of conjuring up images of kindly father-figures patting the heads of respectful workers." No historian who has studied paternalism – from the slave South to the mills of Victorian England, to the Japanese factories of the twentieth century – has ever conceived specific forms of paternalism in simple-minded dichotomies such as these.

As a widespread ethos that often defined the social relations of production in early Canada, paternalism grew out of the necessity to justify exploitation and mediate inherently irreconcilable interests that had not yet hardened into class antagonism. It rationalized inequality and provided for a hierarchical order, but it did so in diverse ways. In its historical manifestations, it included kindness and affection of superiors toward subordinates, but it rested on power and its capacity to abuse the powerless in acts of cruelty, harshness, and gross insensitivity. Paternalism's ultimate significance, regardless of its character, lay in undermining the collectivity of the oppressed by linking them to their social superiors. This did not necessarily imply an absence of social, even overtly class, conflict, for not a little of the sustaining power of paternalism was its forced recognition of the humanity of those it both relied on for labour and supposedly guarded from the impersonal assault of economic downturns, unpredictable misfortune, or natural calamity. The paternal master was responsible for those who provided him with labour. If this was believed by those who laboured, it could result in resistance and demand, as well as accommodation.

The history of paternalism in British North America from 1800 to 1850 is thus a varied and complex one, understandable only in terms of the different political economies within which it grew. Although it began to recede as bourgeois forms of authority and capitalist structures encroached on social and economic life more and more toward mid-century, paternalism cast its varied shadows across the diversity of early Canadian life. Regionally, it offered many faces, from the disgruntled seigneur displeased with his *censitaire's* disregard for authority, to the oldest ship fisherman in a Newfoundland outport, who appropriated the title of "King" as a measure of his authority.

At the St. Maurice forges, the aristocratic paternalism of a Scots "monarch," Matthew Bell, was directed at what one commentator referred to as the desultory habits of French ironworkers originally imported from Burgundy. The workers were supposedly superstitious traditionalists given to bad manners, cursing, and quarrelling. They often grieved about conditions and the cost of provisions in the iron-producing community. Such views of the working classes in early Canada were quite common, and it is difficult to separate the chaff of class prejudice from the wheat of actual historical relations. Bell's "labour relations," however, seemed to grow out of a need to stabilize productive life through an active intervention in the non-economic world of St. Maurice. He continued long-standing practices, guiding his workers like the concerned paternalist, providing them with "certain and uniform labour" and encouraging them to intermarry with local women. The end result was an insular, supposedly contented industrial village. This was paternalism's benign face. But it always had an uglier countenance. The hatter Matthew Hall, for instance, secured the imprisonment of a disobedient female apprentice who was seven months pregnant. After nine years of service, Isabel Webster had violated her apprenticeship agreement by committing fornication, one of the many pleasures denied workers under various forms of indenture. Hall reacted with the barbaric repression of the defied paternalist.

Danny Samson's recent researches into communal resources and the transition to capitalism in Minudie, Nova Scotia, in the first half of the nineteenth century detail the consolidation of Amos Seaman's paternalism in the 1840s. Seaman's Cumberland Basin estate was composed of landed holdings and the lucrative, if legally imprecise, seashore ledges, which extended well offshore and from which grindstones had been quarried since the 1730s. For generations transient stonecutters known as "the Fraternity" governed the quarries and regarded them as a communal resource. Only by legally appropriating these ledges as his property, monopolizing the marketing of the grindstones throughout the northeastern United States, and evicting pauper tenants and squatters was Seaman able to secure his hegemony at Minudie. This proved a bitter struggle, marked by pronounced popular resistance. Aided by the Colonial Secretary and backed by powerful Boston allies, Seaman eventually found himself in control. Then, to placate his disgruntled work force, he quickly assumed the postures of paternal authority. He christened himself King and called his house Grindstone Palace. His motto was, "I feed the poor I scold the Nave & working hard the Ship to Save." Work, lodging, steam mills, churches, and a school were built for the people, now obviously dependent on Seaman. But he was never, in his own eyes, just an employer. He was "their leader." As Samson points out, class struggle could force the hand of capital to open out in paternalist gesture.

Such examples of paternalist practices could be reproduced extensively. Their meaning is not so much that isolated instances of rebellion and resistance took place within the paternalist order; rather, they cultivated a notion that authority was constituted in the hands of people who were born to rule or who had earned the right to rule. These rights of rule were reinforced in ongoing acts of negotiation, many of which recognized smaller spheres of restricted rights for the producing masses at the same time as they buttressed the ultimate authority of powerful individuals and groups.

As work commenced on the Lachine Canal in July, 1821, a celebration was held in which French and Irish labourers were treated to a dressed ox and plenty of beer, allowed to brawl harmlessly, and sent on their way so that the contractors and local gentlemen could retire to a nearby inn for an ample dinner. Such a ceremonial beginning or ending to a construction project was commonplace and left no doubt as to the particular responsibilities of masters and men. Almost three decades later, 150 carpenters met in Saint John in 1849 to give "three hearty cheers . . . to the British Ship Owners" and to establish the ten-hour day. The hours of labour were a more substantial claim than a piece of meat and a barrel of beer, and the ship carpenters, craftsmen with the bargaining power provided by a commercial boom, were in a better position to extract concessions than a heterogeneous group of unskilled labourers. But their cheers for their employers hinted that they, too, lived within the paternalist confines of connection and separation.

In Upper Canada, a society hierarchically ordered since the first settlement of the 1780s, the paternalist structures were of three discrete sorts: economic, political, and socio-cultural (ethnic and religious). They consolidated within the three critical sectors of the social formation: merchant capital, petty production, and landed property.

Paternalism was, of course, strongest when all these sectors were interconnected, as in the case of the Garden Island timbering community at the junction of Lake Ontario and the St. Lawrence River. There, the merchant-manufacturer "Governor" Dileno Dexter Calvin built an empire that encompassed timbering, shipbuilding, merchandising, lake and river towing, freighting, and salvaging, employing approximately 300 settled and highly skilled workmen and an equal number of transient (often native or French-Canadian) raftsmen. Calvin's enterprises commenced in 1836, founded on monopolistic control of the St. Lawrence and the trade in hardwood, and came to a close in the late nineteenth century with his death in 1884. Fervently opposed to unions, drink, and ostentatious living, Calvin concerned himself with all aspects of life on "his" island, where he was patron, employer, and neighbour, the spiritual leader and first citizen of a self-enclosed community. Cash was seldom needed, accounts being settled "on the books." With wages authoritatively established by Calvin's all-powerful hand (and in times of depression he might actually keep workers on the payroll to his own short-term economic detriment), and goods and services (food, lodging, banking, education, and health care) dispensed according to his judgement of need, Calvin was lord of a sixty-five-acre timbering manor. Workers remained under him for their entire lives, as did their children and grandchildren, who, like their fathers and mothers, shared in the company profits on a small scale. Three generations of sail-makers worked for the Governor. Calvin's arbitrary dislikes (which extended to dogs and short men) and unquestioned authority (manifesting itself in charges for lost or broken tools and acquiescence at election time to the political choice of the Governor), as well as the gruelling pace of work dictated by the seasonal arrival of ships, meant that Garden Island was no haven for the small of stature, the independent-minded, or those shy of hard work. But Calvin's paternalism succeeded, and an American visitor to the island in the 1870s noted that life seemed "saturated in traditions and memories." This visitor idealized the community as one where employer and workmen lived in co-operative harmony. No doubt there was an underside to Calvin's rule, but Garden Island was obviously a milieu in which paternalism elicited certain loyalties.

One reason for this was Calvin's visible involvement in all work operations and social events. He could be seen captaining river tugboats, shaping morality in the local Baptist church, or advocating temperance in the island's Mechanics' Hall. In artisan workshops across the country, this same kind of bond may well have existed. The intimacy of handicraft production and the promise of mobility up the craft ladder – from apprentice to journeyman to master – often strengthened ties between employers and workers. Houses built to accommodate working families and the staging of festivals, dinners, and parades championing the virtues of producers reinforced such tendencies.

Paternalism was also nourished on the land, where an uncompromising grip on property could be its economic foundation. Colonel Thomas Talbot, settler of the St. Thomas-London area, was a landed paternalist notorious for his practices. Known as the "Baron," Talbot used his land as a final bargaining tool, granting it freely to incoming settlers but retaining ultimate control, merely pencilling in settlers' names on a survey so that they could later be erased at his whim. Gruff and unconcerned with commercial activities or administrative functions at York (later Toronto), he projected the style of the eighteenth-century gentry. Like Bishop John Strachan at York, who toured with a ponderous state coach, valet, and elegant cassette with a dozen glasses, out of which the finest wines were ceremoniously drunk, Talbot was capable of using an impersonal commodity like drink to reflect the paternalist ethos and its firm understanding of class place. Those who bought their liquor by the barrel, rather than the jar, and those who took their spirits with style and couth, rather than debauched indiscipline, lived their superiority. This kind of ritualized display of authority was coupled with occasional and well-placed acts of kindness as well as hard-nosed squashing of dissent to produce awe and respect, not to mention fear. Talbot ruled his "principality" for over thirty years. Scattered across the colony were variations on the Talbot theme: near Napanee, Joseph Pringle and his wife were paid homage by the district's settlers as "King and Queen" of the Salmon River, while in the town itself "the King of Napanee," Allan Macpherson, resided in splendour on the bank of the Napanee River; in the backwoods of Victoria County, Newcastle District, Admiral Van Sittart carved a wilderness estate out of a 1,000-acre grant, dressing for formal dinner each evening and never being without champagne.

In an age characterized by the political influence of mercantile wealth, paternalism also reached beyond petty production and the estate to embrace wider constituencies. On large public works projects, such as the construction of the Niagara dockyards, the passing of Sir John Colborne in a steamboat might draw a salute from the works, followed "by the cheers of about 200 workmen, mechanics, and others employed thereon." One group of mechanics ended a meeting with a toast:

May commerce flourish, troubles cease,
And tradesmen smoke their pipes in peace.

Kingston mechanics closed an 1841 address with the hope that the government would retain the backing of "all classes" and enjoy the unshaken "affections of the People."

Economic forms of paternal authority were thus inseparable from the whole context of political rule. While even dissident political figures might be advised to follow the paternalist "guidelines," it was in Tory circles that paternalism worked its forms, language, and consequences most obviously. It is true that no uniform Toryism existed before 1850. This was a period of faction, rather than party, and the nature of paternalism varied according to the different socio-economic contexts from which various elites and compacts emerged. Talbot and Calvin, for instance, used all of their paternalist influence to stifle any dissent from their political views. In an 1836 election one pensioner near St. Thomas was asked who he voted for. "How the devil do I know . . . when the Colonel is not here to tell me," he replied. As Tory factions competed for the support of plebeian constituencies or opposed Reformers, they handed out material and political favours, rolled rum and whisky barrels into the streets, and put the wheels of the Orange Order in motion to ride roughshod over all comers that challenged their grip on political office. In constituencies such as Leeds-Grenville, every electoral contest in the years 1833 to 1836 saw riotous Orangemen clash with those standing in opposition to the local compact.

Much of this was no doubt the everyday rough and tumble of politics in the pre-1850 period. But it often was embellished by the paternalist touch and its various negotiations. In the midst of widespread opposition to the Kingston Penitentiary's practice of teaching inmates craft skills and marketing their wares, one Tory leader wrote to another to assure him that Christopher Hagerman had "made all right here with the Mechanics and is sure of election." When Cornwall canallers, known for their riotous behaviour, settled into "a very orderly and quiet mannered" posture, a special Act of the House of Assembly provided for their winter relief and 632 of their number were employed throughout the off-season, rather than being dismissed in the usual peremptory fashion. Paternalism responded to the tug at its arm or the poke in its face as much as it noted the bowed head and the doffed cap.

A final aspect of the paternalist presence in early Canada was even more amorphous than the diverse manifestations of economic and political forms and substance. Turning on an ethnocultural axis, this paternalism could work within the parameters of order and hierarchy as defined by the official culture, or it could march defiantly against it. It could be successful, or it could fail. Thus priests were often a stabilizing force among the Scots Catholics of Glengarry or the Irish Catholic canallers. They could usually impose their own authority in the face of the obvious weaknesses of a removed and Anglican Toryism. But the head of the McNab clan near Arnprior, described as unique in his reliance on "feudal grandeur," never quite knit his settlement together. His public appearances, headed by a piper, were apparently not enough to stifle the contentious lawsuits, bitterness, and bad feeling among his "subjects." *The* McNab, as he was called, tried hard to sustain an ethnocultural paternalism on the basis of tartans, Gaelic speeches, and silver buttons first worn by his ancestor in the uprising of 1745; it was never enough.

More successful was Peter Aylen, "King" of the Ottawa Valley Shiners in the late 1830s. Orchestrating the every move of these raftsmen, who battled French Canadians for control over jobs on the river, Aylen was the great defender of the oppressed Irish "race" at the same time that he was lining his pockets with the surplus he extracted from their overworked hides. He would eventually move the Shiners beyond brawls on the riverbanks and into the very arenas of symbolic authority, defying the staid and outraged Bytown gentry. Led by Aylen, the Shiners terrorized local residents, disrupted the annual meeting of the Bytown Horticultural Society, and forced a split in the ranks of local magistrates. Ultimately driven back, and abandoned by the opportunistic Aylen, the Shiners raised the spectre of a paternalism run amuck in social disorder. These and other developments indicate that where Tory compacts could not sustain paternal authority through economic and political means, others might well step into the breach, playing on ethnic and religious loyalties to weave together their own small organic communities.

In all of this, paternalism was one part self-conscious creation by the merchants, independent producers, and landed gentry, and one part negotiated acceptance by the various plebeian subjects of the producing classes. But these two parts did not constitute the whole. Paternalism was reinforced by the material constraints of the social formation that had spawned it. For much of paternalism's staying power lay in the unique and localized economic, social, political, and cultural make-up of a wide range of early Canadian settings. Paternal authority gained strength from physical separation, diverse sub-economies, and the realities of wielding power in an age that predated the establishment of a powerful state, welfare services, and an impersonal labour market. Equally significant was the social fragmentation that ensured that this very same authority would not be challenged decisively, either through sustained class conflict or through coherent political opposition. It must not be forgotten, however, that the paternalism sketched briefly above was in constant evolution, adapting to social and economic change. And although localism and social fragmentation dominated life in the early nineteenth century, trends toward greater unity did exist. Paternalism was an ethos marking time, and the men who practised it were a passing breed. In bringing about the demise of paternalism, the emergence of the beginnings of class division in society and the resulting tensions and conflicts would not be an unimportant factor.

MATERIAL EXPERIENCES: DIVERGENT/CONVERGENT

Producers during the pre-1850 years were hardly a unified class. They lacked self-definition and clarity of purpose; their organizations, when they did exist, were immature and locally based, although they could, on occasion, appeal to trade groups widely separated by geography. Attached to their craft, their religion, their ethnic experience, perhaps even to their city, town, or region, producers in this period remained part of a broad amalgam cut off from the paternalist elite but nevertheless connected to it through shared circumstances. The producers were isolated within various social classifications that ranged from age, gender, and status (apprentices, female servants, journeymen) to style of life (rough and respectable). Difference, rather than collectivity and solidarity, was at the centre of daily labouring life in the early Canadas. Canallers from the farms of French Canada or the villages and fields of Cork, Connaught, and Munster huddled in temporary shanties along the Lachine and Welland canals, they and their families numbering in the hundreds or thousands, wondering where they would be next year. At the same time, the shipwrights of countless small yards exhibited a settled continuity that embraced generations. Out of such divergent contexts no clear and categorical class presence could emerge, and it is therefore impossible to compile a history of the working class in this period. Instead, we will look at the varied histories of components of the producing classes.

These histories, with their particularities of region and status, were rooted in material circumstances. Often, the producing classes were stratified according to the level of their earning power. In one sample of approximately 430 Montreal workers, 20 per cent earned less than £2 monthly, 61 per cent between £2 and £5, 14 per cent between £5 and £10, and 5 per cent over £10. Those at the low end of the spectrum obviously lived in a situation of advanced poverty, expending 60 per cent of their income on food and the remaining 40 per cent on lodging, clothing, and health, but the few at the pinnacle of the wage chart faced little of this financial pressure and insecurity. The social structure of mid-nineteenth-century Hamilton reveals a comparable social ordering. Of the 342 labourers in the city, three-quarters were among the poorest residents. If you were a printer or a baker, however, your chances of getting into the ranks of the affluent were much better, and approximately 30 per cent of such tradesmen accumulated sufficient property to place them among the richest 20 per cent of Hamilton's population. As a rule, Upper Canadian skilled mechanics and artisans earned at least twice as much for their day's labour as their unskilled counterparts. But even being a craftsman did not assure one a place in the economic elite: 44 per cent of Hamilton's bakers were among the city's poor, as were 40 per cent of the machinists, masons, and moulders.

Wage differentials were thus a fundamental feature of early Canadian class experience, drawing lines of separation between labourers and craft workers. Those lines often signified the difference between dire poverty and making do. Field hands reportedly earned three shillings/nine pence daily in the Toronto area in 1840; masons in Quebec City almost doubled that figure in their established 1845 daily rate of seven shillings; miners in Pictou County, Nova Scotia, could supposedly count on ten shillings a day during the 1840s. Canallers would have thought such wages extraordinary: their normal rate was two shillings/six pence, and it was being constantly reduced by contractors. Such variations were reinforced by many factors, including the regional peculiarities of inherently unstable political economies. An 1849 Newfoundland report, for instance, suggested that the unquestioned oscillations of the fishing economy, in which summer work gave way to winter distress, undermined the morale of the producing classes and predisposed them to "lean altogether on public charity for support."

Even within the same region, such as Upper Canada, considerable disparity existed across the sub-economies of a highly differentiated material context. This is revealed most dramatically in an average wage-ratio compilation for selected occupations in the various districts of Upper Canada in 1840. Constructed by Leo Johnson, these data indicate that if the colonial average was set at 100, wage rates would have fluctuated from a low of 87 in Ottawa to a high of 111 in Niagara. Such a static picture, of course, does not take into account important variations over time, both in terms of years and seasons. In the absence of precise data on the cost of living – from year to year and throughout the various regions and sub-regions – differences in wage rates cannot be easily interpreted. They do, however, point to marked separations among various strata of the labouring people.

Those separations reached beyond the basic mechanic-versus-labourer division and past the usual peculiarities of regions and sub-regions. Pushing difference further were gender and age, the worst paid labour being that provided by women and children. Robert Gourlay, agitator and early critic of the Upper Canadian elite, reported that female servants could expect only twenty to thirty shillings a month, plus board and lodging, in 1818. Things actually worsened over time, with the rate dropping to fifteen to twenty shillings by the 1830s. Dairy women were among the worst remunerated: in Ottawa they commanded little more than a shilling a day, while in Toronto they might, if lucky, get double that meagre amount. Semi-skilled female labour fared a little better, but it never drew much more of a wage than that of the canal navvy. In Portsmouth, near Kingston, women toiling in the shirt and stay-making industries were said to be subjected to "female slavery . . . to the manifest detriment of the poor rates and the morals of [those] employed." Of the young "advantageously hired out" but not formally apprenticed, we know little. In the mines of Pictou County, boys might make as much as three shillings a day if they were over fourteen years of age but a mere one shilling/six pence if between twelve and fourteen. In Lower and Upper Canada, and in the port cities of the Maritimes, they undoubtedly worked for much less, when and if they could find paid employment. More often than not they likely scrounged and scraped to help out families in dire need.

If there were divergent material realities within the producing classes sufficient to warrant recognition of a variety of circumstances, there were also commonalities of experience that appear to be important. Many early workers, isolated in their own trades or callings and locales, faced similar threats and trends, but geographical separation prevented them from recognizing the fact. Most producers and workers, as Judith Fingard has shown, were subjected to the seasonal work stoppages and harsh winter climate that led to hardship, poverty, and dependency for so many British North American workers. The growing incursions of the market and the beginnings of an impersonal and exploitative division of labour took a toll on canaller and petty producer, marginalized *habitant* and youthful apprentice. In Montreal, manufacturing nailers, hatters, and founders brought employees together by creating specialized divisions of labour as early as the second decade of the nineteenth century, and even in highly traditional work spheres such as the Gaspé fisheries, villagers from St. Thomas (near Quebec City) were orchestrated into discrete work routines of cutting, salting, and packing. Paternalism may have played off old divisions and entrenched allegiances for a time in settings like these, but the gathering of large numbers of workers on the impersonalized canal sites of the 1830s and 1840s was a precursor to the collectivization of labour that marked future productive relations.

Out of converging experiences would come the first recognitions of class structure and of common discontents. Even respectable mechanics found that, in the eyes of the elite, they were little better than the unskilled whom they regarded as far beneath them in the social scale. Mercantile pillars of society made it clear that tradesmen were not the stuff of polite society and political power. Alongside such sneers, the desertions, turn-outs, riots, worker organizations, and other collective efforts of the producers indicated that grievance existed at the bottom of the social order as well. The voice of the labouring poor emerged in a petition circulated in Merrickville, Upper Canada, in June, 1837: "The Monopoly being Enjoyed by the owners of Mills in this place is such as to cause General Dissatisfaction and in the present state of the country, the poor destitute inhabitants have greatly suffered through want of bread, when at the same time, there was plenty at the above mills . . . and the owners would not sell in small quantities for the accommodation of the poor, even for money." In the early history of Canada's producing classes, the shocked indignation of these workers would be reproduced in diverse and diverging contexts. As the paternalist order deteriorated to the point that bread itself was hoarded for profit, a conception of class distinctions slowly began to be formed among those various groups that provided the human material fashioning the country's first generations of workers.

THE IRISH AND OTHERS: SOME QUANTITIES

Canadian workers, like all workers, had to be recruited, a process that entailed an unusual amount of disruption and displacement. It was premised on an original expropriation, aboriginal peoples having been subjected to a three-centuries-long contact with Europeans that culminated in the forced disruption of their relationship to the land and the near-obliteration of their way of life. Ravaged by disease, liquor, superior technologies, and religious imports, native peoples suffered severe dislocations and depopulation. One does not have to embrace a mythologized and romanticized notion of the innate environmental nobility of native people to recognize that their contact with an imperialistic intrusion of white colonizers left them, for the most part, marginalized. Over the course of the nineteenth century, especially in central Canada, aboriginal peoples found themselves increasingly shunted into the restrictions of the reserve system. To be sure, as Rolf Knight has shown, native people on the west coast were incorporated into the working class and laboured in canneries and other sectors of a late nineteenth-century industrial-capitalist political economy. Pockets of such aboriginal proletarianization existed across the diversity of Canada's regions, but the dominant experience of native people was not one of full integration into the exploitations of wage labour.

Canada's first producers were therefore aboriginal, but its first working class was not. Workers were instead drawn from the ranks of English-Canadian farmers, Francophone *menu peuple*, and Yankee immigrants. Even more important were those pulled to the emerging labour market from European fields and factory towns.

English and Scots immigrants provided one early source of labour, especially the Highland Scots, the most important group prior to 1816. By that date perhaps 10,000 Highlanders had come to the Canadas. Of these, only half remained, the rest departing for the United States. After 1816 the English became more numerous, with up to 10,000 arriving yearly at the port of Quebec between 1823 and 1850, although many would, once more, find their way to the cities and farms of the United States. In Nova Scotia the Scots remained the predominant immigrant stream; 22,000 landed there between 1815 and 1838, and many of these went to Cape Breton. Such figures do not allow for much precision, and even basic occupational information is lacking. But many of the newcomers were farmers, while significant numbers were drawn from the ranks of labourers and mechanics. By mid-century, such English and Scots immigrants comprised approximately 36 per cent of the more than 400,000 British-born in Upper and Lower Canada.

If we are to believe the reports of chagrined landowners and other paternalist figures, such English and Scots migrants easily adapted to the ways of the other significant immigrant group, the Americans. The Reform leader William Lyon Mackenzie considered Yankee workmen "as stiff, as self important and as calmly insolent in their behaviour, as if they had, each, in his own proper person, achieved their national independence." Ironically enough, Tory opponents considered Americans the very kindling that ignited Mackenzie's radical fires. One anonymous observer wrote to the Lieutenant-Governor that "The very chips of democracy are those Mechanicks from the United States. . . . And no sooner do they arrive here than they list the Corps of rebellious miscreants and sow the seeds of discord and disaffection and were it not for them, the faction of which Mackenzie, Ryerson, and Bidwell are the heads would have died away long since." When a brief flurry of activity for shorter working hours broke out in Kingston, Cobourg, and Belleville in the late 1830s the sarcastic rebuke of the press left no doubt that the "graceless proceedings" had been the work of "certain calculating Yankees" bent on promoting "the pernicious, treasonable, and democratical doctrines of Atheism, Republicanism, and Revolution." American workmen were obviously regarded as a troublesome lot. They also seemed to be everywhere. In the late eighteenth century United Empire Loyalists settled in Nova Scotia, Prince Edward Island, New Brunswick, the Eastern Townships of Old Quebec, and the western frontier of Upper Canada. Before the War of 1812, thousands of so-called "late loyalists" crashed the Canadian land market, taking advantage of available plots. By 1815 they may have numbered around 100,000, as much as 80 per cent of the English-speaking population. This early Americanization of town and country lent a particular coloration to the process of class formation.

Another source of labour recruitment was the natural increase of the *canadien* population, descendants of the indentured labourers, soldiers, salt smugglers, and marriageable women from France who had emigrated to the Canadas before 1760. These provided the demographic basis of the *habitant* class, which began to experience limited proletarianization in the pre-1850 years. As early as 1800 Kingston-area farmers were hiring French-Canadian harvest help, and many raftsmen were drawn from Lower Canadian farms no longer able to support their expanding populations. The massive exodus of *habitants* to the New England milltowns had its origins in this period, but it was mainly a post-1860 phenomenon, with as many as 500,000 French Canadians migrating to the United States in the period

1860-90. Far less momentous were migrations to the Eastern Townships and the northern shield, which throughout the 1840s could not have exceeded 4,000 annually.

There was *habitant* movement to the cities, but Fernand Ouellet has suggested that in this period it was overtaken by immigrant arrivals. Coloured by his intellectual investment in the notion of a severe agricultural crisis, Ouellet's argument is that while the Montreal and Quebec districts contained large percentages of landless rural labourers in 1842 (38 and 28 per cent, respectively), the French-speaking percentage of the producing classes was actually declining over time. Having once constituted the majority of the producing classes (51 per cent in 1831), Montreal's Francophone workers, according to Ouellet, had been reduced to a minority (42 per cent) eleven years later. With the influx of English-speaking labour, Ouellet suggests, pressure was exerted on distressed *habitants* to stay on the land and eke out a living as best they could, thus deepening the agricultural crisis. Joanne Burgess, in a study of Montreal leather workers, challenges Ouellet's depiction of French-Canadian craft communities under siege, arguing that the trades did indeed recruit from the countryside. She shows that over 30 per cent of the French Canadians who became shoemakers in Montreal between 1825 and 1831 came from the surrounding rural villages, suggesting the importance of the countryside as a source of labour recruitment.

But, across the regions, the Irish provided the most awesome numbers to the newly developing class of producers. Comprising anywhere from 47 to 85 per cent of the total number of immigrants landing at Quebec City and Montreal between 1817 and 1847, the Irish stocked the labour pool of early Canadian society. As Terrence Punch has shown in an unpublished study of the Irish in Halifax, they made up approximately 40 per cent of the city's producing classes in 1838, *before* the famine migrations of the late 1840s. Fully 55 per cent of Halifax labourers, 77 per cent of its servants, and 85 per cent of its truckmen were Irish in 1838, and among the skilled the number of Irish, although less, was also substantial, hovering between 20 and 25 per cent. Michael Katz found a similar situation in Hamilton, where at mid-century almost one-quarter of the city's mechanics were Irish, as were 57 per cent of its labourers. In Montreal the Irish numbered 9,500 in 1844, congregated in working-class neighbourhoods such as "Little Dublin" and "Griffintown." They had established themselves in such key work sectors as canal labouring and carting.

As Donald Akenson has shown, most Irish migrants to areas like Upper Canada ended up settling on the land: as late as 1861 three-quarters of all of the Irish in Ontario lived in villages or on the land. But this does not mean they were unimportant to the cities. Their sheer numbers meant that, quantitatively, the Irish were a central demographic component of the urban labour market. As more than 100,000 Irish landed in Canada during the famine migration of 1846 they swamped the cities. Regardless of how many went to rural areas (where they might also feed into labour recruitment by becoming landless labourers), thousands found themselves in towns, mired in poverty, especially if they were Catholic. Between 1851 and 1861 the percentage of Irish Catholics among the poorest one-fifth of the population of Hamilton more than doubled to almost 45 per cent. While Irish Catholics comprised barely 19 per cent of the total Upper Canadian population in 1851, they made up almost 35 per cent of urban dwellers.

Although the cities may not have been the main destination of Upper Canadian Irish immigrants, the Irish, especially the Roman Catholics, were thus vital to the cities. In Halifax, where access to Nova Scotia farms had long since been closed, baptismal registers from 1827 to 1847 suggest that a mere 5 per cent of the Irish headed for the land. Almost 50 per cent remained in the city, where the Irish comprised 35 per cent of the population in 1851; the remainder made their way to the "Boston states." Had they been able to find their way to New Brunswick they might have fared better, but a study of Charlotte County reveals that while Irish Protestants represented 54 per cent of all farmers in 1861, the Irish Catholic percentage was about half of this figure. Moreover, while Irish Protestants comprised only 15 per cent of the landless labourers, Irish Catholics made up a far greater proportion, at 43 per cent. In Lower Canada, where the seigneurial system and loyalist settlement imposed more rigid barriers to Irish settlement on the land, the urban labour market of Montreal exercised considerable magnetic pull.

From these peoples, then, the early working class would be fashioned. Migrants and dispossessed farmers, Irish, English, and Scots, Yankee mechanics and *habitants* moving to the city – these were but some of the streams that flowed into the labour pool. And these differentiations were reproduced in experiences that separated components of the early producing classes.

APPRENTICESHIP

Urban newspapers in the pre-1850 years often carried advertisements offering rewards for the apprehension of apprentices who had deserted their masters. Apprenticeship was a binding relation, in which both master and apprenticed youth had established rights and responsibilities. These desertion advertisements, announced under a woodcut caricature of a runaway slave, indicated two things: the extent to which the apprentice's rights were obviously in a state of deterioration that prompted young workers to bolt their masters' workshops and homes; and the chattel-like status of the apprentice. This process of debasement was accentuated by the reward "price" runaway apprentices commanded: *one penny*.

The nineteenth-century legal agreement of apprenticeship, in spite of this obviously deteriorating context of master-apprentice relations, nevertheless remained substantially unaltered in form from its eighteenth-century antecedents. A typical turn-of-the-century agreement would have seen a widowed mother or a father bind son or daughter to be taught a said "Trade, Science, Or Occupation," "to dwell continue and serve" a particular master for a set period of time (anywhere from three to ten years) or until the age of twenty-one. The apprentice was to keep the craftsman's "secrets and trade commands" and not to "imbezil or waste" the master's goods or suffer him to be wronged. In addition to these work-related responsibilities, the apprentice could not commit fornication, contract matrimony, haunt taverns or playhouses, frequent dice tables, play cards, secure unlawful gains, or absent him/herself without the master's leave.

These duties fulfilled, the apprentice was to be "well and sufficiently taught and instructed," provided with meat, drink, washing, lodging, apparel, and all other necessities, in sickness and health. An additional suit of clothes, "as is fit and usual for such an Apprentice," was to be provided, and masters might be legally responsible for fines levied against mischievous apprentices. At the completion of his or her time (when all days lost to absence, misconduct, or negligence had to be made good), the apprentice might expect a parting gift of clothing, tools, or money. This was a legal relation, but it was also a highly paternalistic form of labour organization.

Studies of apprenticeship by Jean-Pierre Hardy and David Terence Ruddell (Quebec City) and Pierre H. Audet (Montreal) indicate that changes in work relations were under way as early as the period 1790-1815. A once highly personalized form of craft training and work organization was turning into little more than a source of cheap labour, giving rise to discontent among apprentices. More than 200 young apprentices deserted their Quebec City masters in these years, while in Montreal the number of runaways rose appreciably after 1805. Despite the formalities of apprenticeship, paternal authority clearly was not unchallenged.

This opposition proceeded from the escalating economic rationality of these years, as apprenticeship became less craft training supplemented by moral and educational supervision and more a form of bound labour. As masters accumulated capital, stepped up production demands because of market considerations, and hired increasing numbers of apprentices to do the heavy and often unskilled work needed in the shop, apprentices began to see only the tyranny of their obligations. They grew resentful of the master's failure or refusal to fulfil his responsibilities. And they took to their heels in protest.

New forms of apprenticeship would emerge in the post-1860 years as new skills came into being and international craft unions formed around them. Printing, for instance, would point to the way of the future as early as the 1830s. But the essentially eighteenth-century form of apprenticeship, although surviving into the nineteenth century, was a traditional practice about to be superseded by the new social formation of the 1800-50 years. At Halifax, in 1845, a record of indenture marked this transformation of the apprenticeship agreement:

> I agree with the consent of my father Robert Cose to serve Messrs. Temple & Lewis Piers from the first day of June 1845 till the first day of June 1851 and to be obedient to their commands, conducting myself in a sober honest and respectful manner, and to be obedient to the Foreman of their Rope Works, or to any person under him who may have authority to direct me. It being understood that I am to have the privilege of learning to spin before the expiration of the above term, and that I am to be paid for my services at the following rates, viz: 5/a week till the 1st day of June 1846 ... 18/a week to 1 June 1851. Said Piers being bound by this Agreement, while they continue the manufacturing of Corrdage, provided I conduct myself to their satisfaction.

Masters thus began to exempt themselves from responsibilities and traditional apprenticeship was replaced with a more market-oriented variant. The protections once offered by masters disappeared, but some of their paternalistic interest was preserved in the retention of the proprietary and authoritative aspects of apprenticeship.

THE RESPECTABLE

Young apprentices reacted to this deteriorating paternalist order and its waning sense of responsibility with acts of individualistic rebellion, such as flight and dissolute behaviour. But as apprentices grew to journeymen and as some attained the status of craftsmen, individualism was increasingly replaced by collectivity and the rebelliousness of debauchery was overtaken by a sense of the rights of an eminently respectable social group. And the hallmark of respectability in the years prior to 1850 was the journeyman's capacity to initiate, even to sustain, trade unionism in an age that looked askance at "Meetings and Combinations endeavouring to regulate the rate of wages, and to effectuate illegal purposes." Unions and trade associations were established early in the century, Halifax building tradesmen and shipwrights leading the way with the formation of their trade body in 1798. Under the auspices of benevolent and charitable societies, early Canadian mechanics forged craft unions that espoused principles of mutual aid, respectability, and autonomy. The numbers of such organizations increased in the 1830s and 1840s; by mid-century roughly forty-five trade bodies had been founded, although many of these had lapsed.

Skilled craftsmen were an important component of the urban scene in these years, making up anywhere from 7 to 12 per cent of the population of Canadian cities and encompassing roughly 30 per cent of all heads of households in centres like Halifax. In different regional economies specific trades dominated. Upper Canadian printers and carpenters were among the most active in building unionism and consolidating a craft presence, while in ports such as Quebec City, Montreal, Halifax, and Saint John trades linked to shipbuilding complemented the usual urban mechanics within developing strongholds of skilled labour. Many of the craft bodies formed failed to survive the depressed economic years and troubled political climate of 1837-39, but a collective sense of pride was being cultivated. By the 1840s the phrase "Once a printer, always a printer" had appeared, a reminder that respectability was built on a foundation of self-worth that entailed shared, rather than individualized, experience.

Nowhere was this more apparent than in Saint John, New Brunswick, where building tradesmen and waterfront workers led the way in the creation of a local labour movement that, by the 1840s, was unrivalled in Canada. As Richard Rice has shown, mechanics' meetings and parades in the city drew from 1,200 to 2,000 workers, including blacksmiths, founders, hammermen, carpenters, tailors, painters, bakers, riggers, coopers, shipwrights, coachmen, cartmen, and draymen. One local newspaper described the first of these "trade union" processions (something of a misnomer since not all of the trades marching were unionized): "We have travelled . . . seen some splendid 'turn outs', in New York and other places, but never saw anything that surpassed what we witnessed on Wednesday . . . whether we refer to the respectability of appearance, the appropriate devices on the banners, the badges which were worn. . . ." A second workingmen's parade in 1840 once more elicited laudatory comment.

Mechanics like those who marched in Saint John also participated in a wide range of self-help activities, joining temperance societies and fraternal lodges or patronizing festivals where "habits of steadiness and perseverance" were praised. While leading citizens played prominent roles in all of this, often acting as key officers in fraternal orders and temperance societies or as patrons of early attempts at adult education such as the mechanics' institutes, craftsmen and even the odd labourer had their part to play. In Kingston a large majority of the 350 members of the local Mechanics' Institute were "mechanics and apprentices" who enjoyed attending the lectures and having access to the technical and popular literature in the reading room. Such endeavours cultivated a sense of respectability, which some have interpreted as a repudiation of working-class interests and an attachment to the aristocratic cultural norms established in the interests of stable social relations and the status quo.

There is something to this view, although it is altogether too one-sided. A sense of respectability did link the skilled worker to non-working-class elements, establishing a cross-class cultural alliance in many of these insti-

tutions, cultivating a world view that accommodated the producing classes
to the paternalist order, encouraging a set of chauvinisms that could manifest themselves in craft exclusiveness or in a narrow attachment to national,
local, or individualistic acquisitive priorities. But this was only one side of
the process. Respectability was a two-edged sword. The very attachment to
self-help and self-advancement that led workers to denounce drink and
illiteracy or proclaim their loyalties to the Empire could also motivate them
to take collective action and to unionize in order to preserve and protect
what they saw as the *rights* of respectability. Many saw the need to associate
and unite with their fellows for "mutual support and protection [of] their
trade."

The result was often class conflict, for employers who paid lip service to
the respectability of "their" hands were seldom content when those who
laboured for them demanded better treatment or higher wages. Skilled
workers led approximately half of the almost sixty strikes known to have
occurred prior to 1850. Particularly active were carpenters, tailors, and the
miners of the east and west coasts. Hatters in Quebec City revolted against
attempts to introduce specialized divisions of labour into their trade, while
Toronto shoemakers struck early against "scanty wages . . . beds of straw
. . . tyrannical oppression." Montreal carpenters and joiners attempted to
secure the ten-hour day in an 1833-34 strike.

One of the most publicized class battles of this period was a Toronto
printers' strike that erupted in 1836. The York Typographical Society
formed in 1832 "to maintain that honourable station and respectability that
belongs to the profession." Its first anniversary banquet was addressed by
William Lyon Mackenzie, who praised the union's efforts to "secure
respectability to journeymen without interfering with the prerogative of the
employers." Three years later, class interference was most on Mackenzie's
mind. "If all the journeymen were editors," he railed, "and each had a press
of his own, a more resolute, determined, and *obstinate* body, would not be
found on this continent." Mackenzie clearly saw property as paramount,
and he resented deeply his printers' demands for higher wages, parity with
New York piece rates, and limitations on the number of apprentices hired
per shop. Respectability, once praised by the reform-minded editor, had
given way to "divisions and animosities in society," arraying "classes
against each other who could otherwise be united by a common interest."
The printers' strike of 1836, in Mackenzie's words, was an ungrateful, ill-
informed attempt to "split up the community into so many selfish and
mischievious monopolies."

Perhaps one of the most illuminating testimonies of the skilled worker's
self-image emerged from a meeting of mechanics employed on the Cornwall canal in April, 1835. "Though not gifted with patrician hauteur, nor
Hereditary greatness . . . a very numerous and respectable assembly of
Masons and Stonecutters" convened at Carnerous's Inn to condemn "the

mean chicanery, the unhallowed traffick, and the deep-laid and combined plans for the reduction of prices [wages]" characteristic of "a few designing, speculating contractors." After paying their respects to distinguished forerunners from Archimedes to Benjamin Franklin, the mechanics condemned the peonage that kept men "destitute of capital" and silent in the face of injustice. Resolving "not to sit tranquil while their dearest rights [were] invaded," the masons and stonecutters noted that only two of their number were absent. Their unanimity and their talent, they felt, entitled them "to a voice in the body political of this our adopted Country."

This sense of labour's worth, and of the necessity of preserving it from debasement, extended beyond productive relations. In a July, 1830, action that suggests a level of organization previously unexplored by historians, journeymen tailors rioted in opposition to a circus play, *Billy Button*, convinced that it undermined their respectable status. The play met with two nights of rioting in Montreal in spite of appeals from the master tailors for quiet. When it moved to Quebec City it encountered similar violence, necessitating the calling out of the magistrates and constables, as well as the termination of the satirical performance. This collective act coincided with the first unionization of Montreal tailors, a body organized from 1830 to 1834. Its members were said to be bound by a masonic-like oath reinforced by threats that all defectors who failed to support efforts to raise wages would have their thumbs cut off.

Attempts to extend this craft consciousness and the conception of skilled labour's respectability to all ranks of labour were rare. They do begin to appear, however, in the 1830s and 1840s. The erection of the Kingston Penitentiary in 1833-36 united local labour in a movement to oppose training convicts in craft skills. Fearful that the products of such a system would be "dumped" on the market and wary that prisoners "apprenticing" in a state institution would undercut craft respectability, Kingston's mechanics were able to win support from craft workers and reformers in a number of Canadian cities. With the establishment of newspapers explicitly devoted to the producing classes, the skilled/unskilled dichotomy was being slowly, if incompletely, broken down. Edmund Bailey O'Callaghan's *The Vindicator* (Montreal) championed throughout the 1830s "the classes whose labor is the real source of wealth," pillorying Canada as "the Ireland of America." An obscure Quebec journal, *The People's Magazine and Workingmen's Friend*, appeared in 1842, condemning the political and social inequalities separating rich and poor.

It was even possible for those well beneath the status of craftsmen to begin to push the cause of the lowly labourers. In Saint John, Patrick "Paddy" Bennett led the crusade for respectability and rights from his experience as an Irish immigrant. Bennett played a pivotal role in the organization of waterfront unions and perhaps contributed to the disproportionate role played by unskilled labourers in militant actions and organizational efforts in Saint John. He imparted to his brethren on the docks a hatred of injustice and petty, arbitrary tyranny, leading the ship labourers to a condemnation of incompetent foremen in 1849. In the pages of his *True Liberator* he exposed the suffering of the quarantined famine Irish. But Bennett himself eventually fell victim to destitution. His last days were spent in the Alms House. Bennett's fall was a sharp reminder that respectability, as a way of life embraced by a segment of the producing classes, was perched on a thin edge. When wage rates were cut, jobs lost, injuries sustained, or the economy depressed, the respectable found the gulf separating them from the rough narrowed considerably.

THE ROUGH

Within every trade, of course, there were those who defied the social conventions of respectability. Respectable and rough are thus not meant to be categorical designations and oppositions carved in interpretive stone. Rather, they are a means of locating particular historical identities associated with relatively separate components of the producing classes. Some skilled trades – coopering, shoemaking, and tailoring – were thought to harbour a disproportionate number of dissolute workers, and in the Kingston dockyards (1813-15) or the Marmora iron works (1823) skilled workmen drove their masters to persistent complaint because of their "vile and disorderly conducts," a euphemism for drunkenness and absenteeism. But most craftsmen of this epoch would defend their good names against the vilifications of those who would cite particular cases of dishonourable behaviour to besmirch an entire calling. When one newspaper editor charged that compositors were generally a drunken lot, a Montreal printer was quick to condemn the editor's "insult [to] a whole class for the sake of venting . . . malignity against one or two of its members." This self-proclaimed "sober-setter of type" linked the editor's discontent not to his intemperate hands but to the employer's anger at "the better class of compositors [who] will not work for him on the conditions . . . his hands are forced to submit." In the printing trades, as in all respectable crafts, "certain little necessary forms or customs [were] regularly observed," and editors who arbitrarily neglected them faced the workingman's hostility. But there were those among the producing classes who toiled without such necessary forms and customs. Devoid of the ability to promote themselves as skilled, lacking in apprenticeship training and the knowledge of a craft, earning marginal wages on casual and seasonal work that allowed only bare subsistence, these workmen were the roughs upon whom the respectable stratum of workers often looked with condescension, pity, or contempt.

At the centre of the rough subculture were the Irish labourers who had thronged to Halifax, Quebec City, and Montreal after 1817. They found employment on the docks, at construction sites, and in the homes of the rich: one-half of the adult Irish males in Halifax in 1838 were labourers, servants, or truckmen. But outside of the cities the rough made their presence felt most dramatically. With pick, shovel, and axe they combined and competed with unskilled French-Canadian labour to construct canals or fell trees and get timber to export ports. Canal sites saw masses of these workers congregate, many of them part of a North American/transatlantic migratory work force. Of the 1,200 Irish attracted to the Welland Canal in 1842, for instance, two-thirds were from Ohio, Illinois, and Indiana, while one-third were recently arrived immigrants.

This was the first truly mass employment of labour in the Canadas, prefacing in its impersonality and sheer size the factory experience of later years. But canal labour lacked the permanence and seeming stability of factory production. It took on a more anarchic, chaotic character, a climate in which rough treatment resulted in rough behaviour. Hundreds, often thousands, of canallers gathered near work sites, living out of makeshift shantytowns. Single men and migrant families faced intolerable conditions: gruelling work and long hours; inflated charges for what passed for lodging and supplies; the ravages of diseases (cholera and "fevers" being the most common); the violent animosity of the resident "country folk"; depressed wages paid monthly and often in scrip redeemable only at the contractor-controlled "pluck-me" store; and bosses who absconded without paying their impoverished workers.

Like the skilled, whose treatment at the worst of times was infinitely better, the Irish canallers rebelled at this harsh treatment. Occasionally they even articulated a sense of their own respectability, however much it was trampled on. In the midst of an 1843 Montreal strike one Irish canaller complained to the press that he and his fellow labourers "did not anticipate ... cruelty ... and disrespect from foremen ... connived at and sanctioned by the Contractors ... ignorant of a man's labour in canalling as they were of astronomy or navigation." Indignant at attempts to depict Irish canallers as a charge on the community, drawn *en masse* to charity, the canaller assured readers that "our earning and industry for the last few years, together with the moral precepts of the Very Rev. T. Matthew, has rendered us independent of charity." Finally, he stated that, "notwithstanding the hopes entertained by our enemies, we are fully determined to steer clear of any infraction of the law." No doubt he wrote in all sincerity. But the history of the canallers' response to the oppression and exploitation of the 1821-46 years is hardly one in which "steering clear of the law" was a dominant tendency.

To begin with, the Irish canallers struck work sites with some regularity, and in these work stoppages the spirit if not the letter of the law as it was conceived in colonial Canada was as likely as not to be breached. A partial listing of Canadian strikes in this period indicates that on *at least* twenty separate occasions, Irish canal navvies conducted formal and easily recognizable strikes, which means that this stratum of the producing classes was involved in approximately one-third of the strikes of the pre-1850 years. But riots, more than strikes, provided Irish canallers with a special form of collective bargaining and political negotiation, albeit one, again, that was no more successful than it was lawful.

One historian has identified 400 separate riots in the Canadas in the years prior to 1855. My own researches have uncovered over 200 in the pre-1850 period, and more than one-third of these involved Irish canal labourers. Most common were work-related protests, often relating to wages and intolerable conditions, and clashes with judicial or political authorities with whom the canallers had various bones to pick. But the canallers also rioted among themselves, feuding bands of Munster and Connaught men competing for scarce jobs or reviving an old grievance. When other labouring groups or machines threatened their jobs, the Irish reacted with dispatch. They rioted against French Canadians in 1843, and in the five years that followed they expressed their riotous hostility to an excavating machine, set fire to a steam dredge, and dumped fifty-two wheelbarrows into the St. Lawrence. A state of virtual civil war was said to exist along the Welland Canal in the summer and fall of 1842, as canallers, known as Midnight Legislators, gathered under the cover of darkness to organize bodies of 400-500 that marched brazenly through nearby towns to demand "Work or Bread." Armed and dangerous, this "audacious" and "illegal combination" put up a formidable opposition.

If this was clear on the canals, it was perhaps even more explicit along the Ottawa River, where Irish Catholic raftsmen defied respectable society in a reign of terror that stretched from the late 1820s into the early 1840s. This was the Shiners' War, which had its origins in French-Irish competition for jobs on the river, and ended with the ethnic paternalist Peter Aylen using the brutality and violence of the rough raftsmen to secure his own power and opportunistic ends. Never as socially significant as the canallers (they numbered, at most, a few hundred), the Shiners were the roughest of the rough. They raped women, beat up their opponents, broke out of jail, and were capable of murder. On the frontier of eastern Ontario's timbering community a body of such roughs could terrorize an entire region into partial submission. But the success of the Shiners was never complete. They were often victorious in their crusade to define rafting as an Irish preserve, but they ended up winning little in their attempts to challenge the authority of the Bytown gentry. Their weak position was reflected in their dependence on Aylen; not of the rough, he used them and their ugly capacity to intimidate those around them. But when the elite fought back with vigour to defend their interests, authority, and property, Aylen departed from the Ottawa Valley, leaving the Shiners leaderless and directionless. The Shiners' strength had lain in a weakly developed collectivity, superimposed and

directed by Aylen for ends that had little to do with the long-term empower-
ment of the Irish raftsmen. With Aylen gone, the Shiners as a presence
faded from view.

Both canaller and raftsman, then, raised the threat of disorder in the
early history of the Canadas. They took on the threatening posture of the
dangerous classes. Dissolute, defiant, and undisciplined, the rough challenged the paternalist order by refusing, at specific moments of conflict, to
recognize much of its august authority.

CRIME, ANTI-CRIME, AND CLASS: THE LAW AND THE PRODUCERS

The paternal order rested on many foundations. One was the law, a force of
majesty, justice, and mercy that drew its ultimate power from the fear it
could inspire. Tory judges advocated "terrible examples" to prove that
"justice *dares* array herself in terrors when it is deemed necessary." Hang-
ings were public events; thousands attended executions, where cakes, gin-
gerbreads, and confessional tracts were hawked beneath the gallows. Mercy
was occasionally shown, the condemned being pardoned, the rule of law
reinforced, paternalism showing to good effect its benevolent cheek to the
criminal and the crowd.

Chief Justice John Beverley Robinson and Justice of the Court of King's
Bench James Buchanan Macaulay believed that crime was a consequence
of individualized failings, "uncongenial qualities," and "brutal passions."
The paternal use of the law, in which men of substance dispensed forgive-
ness and punishment in a spectacle of justice that draped itself in ritual and
theatre all the better to serve notice that society was divided into those who
ruled and those who followed, might well curb crime if it was indeed
isolated in this kind of psychological "deviance."

In the Far West of the fur trade, Rupert's Land was presided over by
Adam Thom, the Hudson's Bay Company appointment to the post of
recorder of the Red River settlement. Thom's tenure, stretching from 1839
to 1854, was one of paternalistic condescension for the Métis people of the
region, in which his self-importance and sense of superiority were cloaked
in legal pedantry and disdain for the "primitive" people around him. Yet
even on the historical margins of Canadian society, Thom's high paternalist
posture could not withstand the increasing social pressures of a Métis
community demanding a justice that broke out of the confinements of
Hudson's Bay Company autocracy and relied less on "dissertations on
General Principles" and more on honesty and common sense. By 1851 the
law of Rupert's Land had to be revised, and Thom was left to regret that he
no longer ruled the roost and that the English-speaking segment of the
community, which, according to him, comprised "one half of the popula-

tion, nine tenths of the wealth and ninety nine hundredths of the intelligence," was left in a state of precariousness.

For Thom the passing of the old regime was linked directly to the demise of a particular form of rule, in which the economic dominance of the merchant was maintained by the political authority of paternalism: "It hitherto has been, and still is," he wrote to George Simpson, senior Governor of Rupert's Land, "in its mercantile character alone, that the Hudson's Bay Company governs this country . . . and, as soon as the people shall have advanced beyond the capabilities of this paternal tutelage, The Hudson's Bay Company political power is sure to be either abridged or abolished."

It was apparent, however, that in the more developing Canadian economies the major issue was not the kind of direct political challenge raised by the Métis of the West but rather the rise of a disturbing and problematic criminal underclass. Crime in the country escalated as pressures on the land exacerbated social tensions. In 1846, the *British Colonist* complained of organized gangs of bandits that committed a wide range of crimes that showed "what a remarkable change has taken place, as the settlement of the country has progressively advanced." The Markham Gang was active in this period, and according to one report used travelling tailors to ascertain the wealth and susceptibility of prospective victims. William Townsend, "the Dick Turpin of the Niagara Peninsula," left a marginal coopering shop in Dunnville to become a highwayman. When some of the dispossessed of country and town took to crime as a way of life the limitations of a paternalistic use of law were exposed. As early as the 1820s there were those in authority who recognized the need for a more institutionalized legality; they campaigned for change.

The new Kingston Penitentiary was a symbol of such change: its bleak physical structure was an expression of law's hardening response to criminality, in which the majesty, terror, and mercy of the older and personal eighteenth-century spectacle gave way to a legal order more codified and comprehensive, with recourse to an imposing institution of incarceration. Built in the 1830s, it stood as a reminder of the world the Tories had lost. Crime could no longer be regarded as individualistic malevolence. It was symptomatic of deeper social evils, including the emergence of class cleavages.

To counteract this, new laws addressed new tensions associated directly with problems posed by acts of class resistance. Many such acts remained highly individualistic, but they were also recognized as contained within experiences that were collective. The Master and Servant Act, passed in 1847, was an attempt to "regulate the duties between Masters and Servants or Labourers in that part of the Province formerly called Upper Canada." As Paul Craven has argued, the new legislation was a complex if calculating blend of paternalist persistence, as the very name of the Act makes clear, and concession to the impersonality of the wage nexus. For apprentices, craftsmen, labourers, and servants, the law now institutionalized punishment for "abandoning" the employer. Other legislation aimed to stop sailors' desertions, thousands of which took place annually in Canadian port cities by mid-century. Law was shedding some of its ritualistic paternalism, much of its mercy, and not a little of its majesty. But its range, especially pertaining to class, had been extended. The beginnings of this important process were discernible in the complex history of trade union regulation.

To explore the impact of law on early Canadian unionism is a difficult task, complicated by a long and tangled history of common and criminal law in England that was transferred incompletely and in ways that were complicated to a British North American colonial context. Recent research by Eric Tucker of the Osgoode Hall Law School clarifies much of this history. Tucker begins by pointing out that, in the case of Upper Canada, English criminal statutes passed after September 17, 1792, were not in force in Old Ontario, meaning that the famous English Combination Acts of the 1790s, which prohibited workers from uniting to raise wages or improve conditions, were not technically part of the law; nor were the repealing acts of the 1820s, which provided limited immunity for trade unions from criminal prosecution at the same time as they regulated the activity of organized workers. This may well explain why Nova Scotia adopted its own legislation in 1816, which Eugene Forsey characterized as "a ferociously anti-union act." Condemning the "unlawful Meetings and Combinations" of journeymen and workmen in the town of Halifax and other parts of the province, this repressive legislative assault annulled all contracts and agreements through which workers had attempted to advance their wages, lessen their hours, or control any aspect of their trades. Those who defied this order could face jail sentences of up to three months. Moreover, they could also be indicted, prosecuted, or punished under the common law for combination or conspiracy. This threat hung over labour in Nova Scotia until the Act's repeal in 1851. Indeed, if no such criminal legislation existed in Upper Canada, Tucker suggests that some law relating to wage-fixing, in force in England throughout the eighteenth century and before, might well have been embraced by specific Upper Canadian jurists.

The common law on worker combination was equally ambiguous, but again Tucker shows that certain magistrates were of the opinion that combinations of workers to raise wages and secure improved conditions were illegal. In the end Tucker suggests a distinction between the complexities and ambiguities of the "legal zone of toleration," in which trade unions were subject to diverse and often contradictory interpretations of formal laws, and the "social zone of toleration," the pragmatic constellation of practice and belief within the social formation and, most importantly in terms of law, among lawyers, judges, and magistrates. Tucker concludes that "Even in its unclear state, the law cast shadows on the legitimacy of trade unions and reminded everyone involved that legal and social toleration was contingent on trade unions behaving 'responsibly' both in regards to the ends they pursued and the means they used." Such an assessment of the law's role in regulating trade unions in the pre-1850 period fits well with an analysis, such as that presented above, that stresses the two-sided nature of craft respectability.

It also explains why early Canadian trade unionism was both threatened abstractly by the potential use of law and seldom prosecuted successfully by that law. As early as 1809 an overseer at the Upper Canadian naval dockyards found his carpenters a stubborn and troublesome group. Obviously unsure of his legal position, he requested "authority to employ a Lawyer to bind them down to their agreement as they are a set of men who require it very much." As Marmora's iron works thirty miles north of Belleville were being built in 1822, completion of the facilities was delayed. According to the boss, the problem was "wicked combinations among my work people – whom I have had no power to control." Fifteen years later employing masters had an idea that the law might be used to good advantage. Criminal conspiracy charges arising out of trade disputes were initiated against bakers in Kingston in 1837, but the workers were acquitted. Shortly thereafter, however, in the same city, two officers of a tailors' society were found guilty of conspiracy and fined five pounds. As the tensions of an emerging class order nibbled away at the stability and entrenchment of paternalist authority, a precise and coherent law of trade union regulation was an uncertain vehicle. That it was mobilized at all suggests that the social formation was changing; that it did not drive forcefully over labour was an indication that it did not need to.

ROUGH JUSTICE

The law thus circumscribed plebeian experience; it did not define it. Indeed, there were moments when the producing classes stepped outside the law to defy constituted authority by imposing their own alternatives to legalistic norms, measuring out a moral authority of their own. The strike, in the productive sphere, might be an expression of this conscious attempt to recreate conceptions of appropriate social relations. Beyond work, as well, within the community and in everyday life, the producing classes used ritualistic forms of behaviour to lend force to their views of right and wrong. In a period when law itself was being transformed from a highly ritualized to an increasingly impersonal and distant authority, the producing classes, especially their rougher elements, often resorted to custom and ritualized behaviour to sanction what law could or would not sanction. Enough of paternalism remained in this period that certain elements of the elite might, as well, play off of this popular attachment to tradition to keep the masses under their sway.

Many customary and ritualized practices could be discussed here: when marriages broke down and recourse to divorce was unavailable to the poor a husband might arrange the "sale" of his wife to her new companion, a procedure which, if properly conducted, would unite "illicit" lovers in a matrimonial ceremony regarded as legal and binding and allow the "wronged" husband to resecure his pride in a magnanimous gesture, such as using the proceeds of the transaction to treat the "wedding" party at the tavern or pay for ringing of church bells; convicted prostitutes might be paraded in a cart by the hangman, the taunts and jeers of the crowd expressive of plebeian hostility; journeymen whose wages had been cut could react by "daubing" their employer's entire house with excrement. These and other practices were part of a wide-ranging rough justice that flew in the face of the movement toward a more distanced and institutionalized practice of law. One ritualistic form that illuminates the unfolding contest between law as it was coming to be imposed and law as it was conceived in terms of custom was the charivari.

Persons who violated certain standards and accepted modes of behaviour were often subjected to the charivari. A crowd would gather at the house of the offender, usually masked or in disguise or under the cover of darkness, treating the object of their displeasure to all manner of discordant sounds. The screeching din let the neighbours know that an individual was being ostracized. Money was sometimes demanded for the poor or for drink. Physical beatings, tarrings and featherings, even killings were not unheard of, and charivaris across British North America resulted in a series of local bylaws outlawing such potentially riotous gatherings.

Three types of charivaris emerged. The first was directed against what were judged to be domestic infelicities. Those who married people much younger than themselves or those who abused their spouses or children might be paid a visit by the charivari party. In an epoch when the family was a means through which craft training and property were passed to the next generation, these charivaris were more than expressions of irrational intolerance, although they could, of course, be that: they also stood in firm opposition to the deterioration of the interests of the children of the first marriage bed and chastised those who defiled a cherished and mythologized institution. A second type of charivari singled out those who violated the racial, ethnic, or religious values dominant within a particular region. Finally, charivaris could also be enacted as a form of economic or political protest. Allan Greer has argued that in the midst of the Lower Canadian Rebellion in 1837 charivaris were "a central element in a campaign to destroy government power in the countryside and to assert a practical sort of popular sovereignty." Months later, after the suppression of the revolt, the politics of the charivari experienced an about-face as Tories used the ritual to register their displeasure with the reform sympathies of the Colonial Office.

While by no means the exclusive terrain of the producing classes, then, the charivari nevertheless reveals much about the class relations of the paternal order. Occasionally led by the patrician elite, and therefore indicative of the organic connection linking the top and bottom of the social order, the charivari also exposed social cleavages separating the plebeian masses from their social superiors. Along the Welland Canal, Irish navvies often prefaced their riots with charivari-like activity, one contractor claiming that "the firing of Guns and blowing of horns throughout the night . . . is the sure presage of trouble." In the village of St. Pie in Canada East, a series of charivaris in 1843 was employed by Catholics against a group of French Protestants described as "cobblers and journeymen . . . of the lowest and most ignorant class," themselves well known as practitioners of rough music, debased artisans who made "a trade and merchandize of religion." These charivaris ended in the torching of the house of the leader of the sect.

This was not likely the terrain of the rich and the powerful, and the charivari was most often an expression of how the world of pre-1850 Canada might be turned upside down. An 1804 Quebec City instance, arising out of an act of domestic "impropriety," was described by an English gentleman:

> The other night . . . I observed hundreds of dim and glimmering lights dancing, as it were, towards me full speed. Presently I began to distinguish a multitude of glittering and gaudy figures. . . . They were all in disguise, even to one another; and enjoyed liberty and equality to a very great extent. . . . One of the figures, that was in the character of a female, approached a young girl of genteel appearance who, like myself, was looking on, and in a *rampant* humour began stroking her – cheeks; by degrees lowering his caressing motions to her – petticoats, *bupe*, off he flees like a vision, screaming out loud, *Charivari! Charivari!* A young gentleman who seemed to be the young lady's friend stepped forward. . . . Thousands of hideous figures instantly crowded around him. . . . One in particular, who was dressed in a buffalo hide and brandished a *huge* pair of horns on his head, came balancing along all giving way before him and with a twirl of his *panache* gave [the gentleman] a hoist and left him sprawling, head over heels in the mud. . . . Horns! Charivari! resounded from all quarters. The place seemed in a riotous uproar; and women in *certain* situations were greatly alarmed.

Without glorifying in the assault on the young bourgeois woman, it is important to see past this act to recognize the "liberty and equality" of the crowd, which proceeds outside of any usual constraints. Costumes, masks, the man dressed as a woman: all gave the charivari party a certain licence to defy convention. Deference is rejected, and a young gentleman's attempt to intervene is physically rebuffed; sexual liberties are seized and acted out, "covered" by the female appearance of the man engaged in the outrageously and scandalously public stroking of the young woman. Finally, there is no possibility of turning the crowd back. It does what it wants, within certain understood territory. Charivari here was a carnival atmosphere of ribald ribbing of the paternalist order whereby men, masked and unknown, were freed somewhat from the normal restrictions of the social sphere: you could touch a woman if you were dressed as a woman; you could knock a gentleman down, but you could not finish him off the way you might in a "real" brawl.

The charivari was thus part of a pre-1850 society in which the lives of the labouring classes grew out of a context in which the powerful and the propertied established certain rules and allegiance, but the ruling classes could not ensure that this ordered understanding was always conceived and lived *only* in their interests. Rough justice exposed this set of reciprocal limits, buttressing the paternal order in many ways at the same time as it exacerbated tensions and contradictions. Thus, in 1822 Kingston's master and journeymen shoemakers came together to protest the conviction of one of their number for "assault, battery and Riot." He was sentenced to be imprisoned two months and publicly whipped twenty-five lashes for his part in "riding upon a rail a certain man for having abused his wife." The petitioning shoemakers – substantial masters and propertyless journeymen – knew the man as a shopmate and appealed to the mercy of the magistrates to temper their impatience with such frolic. Custom and law were coming to be counterposed to one another.

As the paternal order grew less secure, it began to appreciate the dangers of such disorders. The charivari was one of the more obvious examples of rough justice that contained within its informal licence the seeds of a larger threat. "That the assembling of a crowd for a Charivari may also be used as a pretence by evil disposed persons, to effect purposes of a very different nature, or more dangerous to the public security," commented one judge in a shrewd assessment in the 1820s, was grounds enough "to be hoped that by the vigilance and exertion of those charged with the administration and execution of the laws, such disturbances will be suppressed, and never permitted to recur in any shape, nor under any pretence." When popular initiatives stepped out of their proper sphere, it was feared, they flirted with the insurrectionary moment.

THE INSURRECTIONARY MOMENT

If the paternalist order was marked by ongoing erosion that was nevertheless not quite capable of toppling it, it should come as no surprise that the pre-1850 years were ones of political turmoil. Entrenched oligarchies found their authority questioned and everywhere the cause of "the people" was championed. In Newfoundland there was a call throughout the 1820s for a local legislature that would "represent the wants and interests of the people," and a newspaper declared in 1828 that "there is not one man within this town who would not affirm that the present order of things in this country ought to no longer exist." When Joseph Howe began to publish letters signed "The People" in his Halifax paper, the *Novascotian*, he found himself on the wrong side of the entrenched powers, charged with "wickedly, maliciously, and seditiously contriving, devising and intending to stir up and excite discontent and sedition among His Majesty's subjects." Howe replied in court that this was small potatoes compared to the way the poor were plundered. In Upper and Lower Canada the political rule of the paternalist elite was also challenged, culminating in open, if decidedly unsuccessful, rebellion.

In this battle to secure a way of life, class was by no means the central issue, and the producing classes did not play the most important role. But neither were they totally inconsequential. At the insurrectionary moment they would be seen and heard, although other shouts and the din of much-studied voices have tended to drown them out in our historiography. To hear them we must listen attentively to voices often ignored; to see them we must look, not necessarily at the main actors of the age, but at a set of moments of defiance enshrined in symbolism and a counter-theatre of resistance and politics promoted as egalitarian.

Indications of discontent and disaffection within the producing classes of Upper Canada were plentiful, predating by a decade and more the famous Gourlay agitation of 1817-19. Early petitions bemoaned the autocratic character of officers of the Crown, protesting that the populace could not live under "such tyranny and oppression." There were statements that "monarchal government" was despised, reports of revolts in the making. Robert Thorpe, Joseph Willcocks, and William Weekes, a patrician trio moved toward dissidence and the people by their own frustrated ambitions, orchestrated this early opposition in the years 1805-12. Led by Thorpe, a Wilkes-like figure who drew upon his Irish heritage and position of authority as a judge to pillory the "servile reptiles" and "Scotch peddlers" surrounding the official compact at York, this group posed the first challenge to a segment of the colonial state.

Thorpe's appeal, which Lieutenant-Governor Gore saw as "sowing the seeds of Ingratitude and Disloyalty," was summed up in the phrase "*I The People.*" It rested, as J.B. Walton has noted, on the imagery and symbolism of the United Irishmen, and when Thorpe decided to contest an election in 1807 he took to the hustings under the "seditious emblem" of a harp without a crown, formerly displayed by the Irish Republicans in 1792. Sporting badges inscribed "Thorpe and the Constitution" and communicating with English Jacobins in self-exile in the United States, Thorpe and colleagues promoted "abuse and disaffection," which angered paternal power. The paternalist power-holders had no use for someone who tarnished "the solemnity of the judicature," disgracing such majestic office with "the rant of theatre." Thorpe was driven from the colony for "preaching and pratting upon harmony and union, . . . fill[ing] one class of subjects with enmities towards another . . . foul suspicions of every man in office but yourself, and . . . destroy[ing] the original confidence so necessary to the existence of civil society."

Hardly a coherent class mobilization, the Thorpe agitation nevertheless hinted at the role that American republicanism and Irish nationalism would play in future reform contests in Upper Canada. By the 1820s "Yankee Radicals" were present in considerable numbers and there were rumours of an Irish conspiracy led by supporters of the radical nationalist, Daniel O'Connell. Mackenzie's reform movement was coming into being. A populist appeal to "the people" gathered momentum, espoused by political figures who were not members of the producing classes (and who might act out their politics of opposition in eminently paternalistic ways), but who realized that political change could only come about under conditions in which the procedures of early government were democratized.

These developments opened up spaces for elements of the producing classes. Reform supporters by the early 1830s were being described as "runaway negroes and people who have neither habitation nor property in the country," and as "Methodists and social levellers." In Brockville, Matthew Howard stood for the Reform Party, and his 1830 electoral effort was pilloried by Jonas Jones's Tory newspaper in a bitter condemnation of the intrusion of class considerations into the polite workings of a politics long orchestrated by gentlemen:

> a great noise was heard at the doors of the Committee, when lo in walked *Mathew Mushroom Howard*, Esq., carrying "*a millstone round his neck*" and supported on the right and the left by the Most Reverend Fathers William Hallock and James Cameron his tail and other habillments upheld by an innumerable host of "Saddle Boys." . . . Gentlemen slaves! Mr. (M.M.) Mulberry Mushroom Howard is a Miller, a grist Miller, A Farmer, a Trader, a straw hat maker, a pumpkin pie dresser, an onion sauce stewer and . . . a mighty, mighty clever man and what more do you want for the good of the country.

Beyond the satirical dig of the elite it is possible to glimpse a counter-theatre of democratic forms that reformers placed in opposition to the theatre of the official Tory culture, with its pomp, ceremony, and elitism. Politics, in the process, was no longer quite the restricted domain of a chosen few.

This counter-theatre escalates in the popular discontent of the 1830s, a shift to the symbolism of republicanism attesting to the drift to insurrection. At a Stouffville rally Mackenzie was introduced, a rifle tied to a pole was placed over his head, and a speaker said "he wished the Governor and the damned Tories were there to see it; and they would know by looking there at what they had to depend on before the lapse of many months." The need for physical force was addressed directly: "There must be an ARMY as well as a CONGRESS. There must be PIKES and RIFLES as well as men and tongues."

Meetings in August, 1837, attested to the use of symbol, rhetoric, and theatre in widening the appeal of this call to arms. At the "Second Great Northern Meeting" at Lloydtown there was the usual talk of erecting a Liberty pole, and flags flew in the breeze, their bearers "conscious of the principle they indicated." The American eagle was prominent, as was support for the central figures of Upper and Lower Canadian reform. One banner depicted "a large star, surrounded with six minor lustres – in the centre, a Death's Head, with the inscription, 'Liberty or Death'." Other flags bore, in huge letters, "Daniel O'Connell" and "Liberty," and the colours of the Irish were prominent. "Of Monarchs tender, Monarchs tough/We thank our stars we've had enough," declared one placard. Lines of verse were supplemented with pikes, swords, trumpets, cannons, and muskets, "by way of relief to the eye." Target practice was directed toward a loaf covered with butter, perhaps a symbolic representation of the appropriated affluence of the oligarchy.

Resolutions were passed in profusion, and the crowds were in agreement that "much could be done without blood." But there was an unmistakable hardening of positions, evident in the aftermath of the repression of the Bond Head-orchestrated Tory election victory of 1836. As "Reform" urged in the pages of the *Cobourg Star*:

> Take this piece of advice from an *ignorant elf*:
> *Let each ipso facto Reform one himself*
> And then my dear Roger, you'll see in conclusion,
> A glorious – a grand – and a great REVOLUTION.

Small wonder that Mackenzie, clandestinely referred to in communications passed among the rebels as "the editor," drew sharp and bitter attack from defenders of the status quo:

> Wha do ye think on a mission was sent,
> The breedin' o' Johnny's bull-dogs to prevent,
> Because they made havoc on Jonathon's hens see?
> Wha but the white-liver't mawkin McKenzie;
> Painche-awimet, sheep shanket, cow-rin' McKenzie;
> Midden-bred, filthy-jakes-scourin' McKenzie.

There was more than a little theatre here, on both sides of the political fence. In a paternalist order that consciously used symbolism and ritual to display its authority, it is no wonder that opponents saw one part of the political struggle as the creation of a counter-imagery.

Awareness of class difference helped to push the resulting symbolic discontent and counter-theatre toward the insurrectionary moment. Of the 855 radical democrats arrested in the aftermath of the Upper Canadian revolt, 375 were yeomen, 345 labourers, eighty carpenters, foundrymen, and other tradesmen, the remaining eighty-five professionals, merchants, and innkeepers. These figures gesture toward the social forces behind the efforts that consumed much of the year 1837. In a recent evaluation of the Toronto poll book from the 1836 election, which recorded how everyone voted, Paul Romney offers some insights into urban artisan producers and politics. His evidence suggests that those involved in luxury trades highly dependent on elite patronage were more likely to vote Tory than those whose product was more plebeian. Impressionistic evidence from other quarters and locales confirms this judgement. Dutcher's foundrymen and Armstrong's axemakers were the men Mackenzie figured could be counted on in Toronto. An anonymous letter to the tavernkeeper Montgomery, seized by the authorities, made cryptic reference to plans to send arms to "the carpenter beyond Thornhill." In Merrickville, the leading radical reformer was one John Graff, a tailor in "low circumstances and not very respectable." From Ingersoll came the report that "A Yankee rascal" threatened that buildings would be burned and property destroyed. "This fellow is a wagon maker," concluded the informant, "has no stake in the country, but is a perfect firebrand."

Certainly Francis Bond Head, architect of the 1836 election victory, which relied on hustings violence that contributed to the frustrations and political impasse that moved some reformers into the camp of revolution, recognized class as a factor in the political contest of these years. He revelled in the 1836 win because, "In the place of blacksmiths and carpenters reeling from daily labour with no farther knowledge than that which appertained to their calling, and with obstinacy and perverseness proportionate to their ignorance and vulgarity; we have for the most part GENTLE-MEN of intelligence, information, and talent, capable of discussing the measures which they are called upon to deliberate and decide." As Graeme Patterson notes in a study of Middlesex (London) politics in this period, "Considerations of 'class' seemed to be outweighing those of 'nation'."

One of the deposed and despised mechanics referred to by Bond Head was Samuel Lount, a blacksmith who arrived in Upper Canada from Pennsylvania in 1811. Elected in Simcoe County in 1834, he was defeated in 1836 by the usual combination of bribery, intimidation, and land grants. A confirmed revolutionary by the fall of 1837, Lount was active in the insurrectionary meetings of that period, proclaiming that "It is the voice of the people, which is power." Bent over his forge, engaged in the wholesale manufacture of pikes aimed at the Family Compact's collective throat, Lount was the expression of what Bond Head could not fathom. On April 12, 1838, along with another rebel, Peter Matthews, he was hanged for high treason. Thousands had petitioned for mercy. But Lount would not be the recipient of paternal benevolence. He was to be an example, a statement of the terror that could be unleashed to subdue insurrection. Most rebels would simply be carted off to the other end of the world or exiled to the United States.

This Tory victory – secured by recourse to superior force, helped along by rebel confusion and an inept leadership, and consolidated in a restrained but well-placed public use of the gallows and of transportation – imposed a measure of calm on what had been a decade of political turmoil. There were plenty of indications that resentments continued, but the producing classes for the most part expressed their resentments obliquely. In 1839, three carpenters, described as possessing "no property, principles or influence" (an appropriate paternalist trilogy of denigration), erected mock gallows on the banks of the Humber River and there hung effigies of three prominent Tories, John Beverley Robinson, Francis Bond Head, and Christopher Hagerman. From the likenesses they suspended signs reading: "I will condemn right or wrong; we must have a rebellion; and I will prosecute unto death."

In Lower Canada, the insurrectionary moment was more protracted, encompassing two distinct rebellions that galvanized not hundreds willing to risk their lives in armed confrontation, as in Upper Canada, but as many as 10,000. Complicated by the question of national oppression and led by a more entrenched and mature petty bourgeoisie, with its economic roots embedded in the commerce of the cities, and by the landed relations of the seigneurial system, the *patriote* agitations drew on a similar counter-theatre of protest, but here the banners and rhetoric of rebellion were cast in terms of *indépendance*.

After the 1834 adoption of the "92 Resolutions," an extensive listing of the grievances of *les canadiens* endorsed by 80,000 signatures (over one-quarter of the adult population), Lord Russell drafted a set of imperial counter-resolutions in 1837 that attempted to suppress French reform initiative. These "coercive" resolutions were condemned by the London Workingmen's Association and in Lower Canada were greeted with the Phrygian cap of republicanism and a Canadian flag of green, red, and white, replete with beaver and maple leaf. The American eagle was Canadianized, a maple branch in its beak. Nor were the Tories without their theatrical thrust, advertising a "Canadian" shooting match, "a plaster figure representing a certain great agitator, to serve as bull's-eye," members of the "British Legion or the Doric Club" being requested to "hold themselves in readiness."

Active before the Upper Canadian rebels, the *patriotes* early declared, "Better a bloody but just and honourable fight than cowardly submission to a corrupt power." Louis-Joseph Papineau, the Daniel O'Connell of the French Canadians, was their leader, a man who could unite a lot that was wrong with nationalism and populist radicalism. The shock troops were the distressed *habitants* and day labourers of Montreal. There the Fils de Liberté, an organization set up by students and young professionals, soon gathered hundreds of journeymen, apprentices, and unskilled and unemployed workmen, not a few of whom were Irish, following the resolute Edmund Bailey O'Callaghan. A military camp at St. Eustache attracted the discontented with its ribald irreverence: "Come with us; we're all armed, we have fun; it's like a wedding; we drink, eat, play fiddles, dance, we're free, we do what we want. . . . It's our right, we poke fun at the King, the Queen, and the Clergy." Here was one grand charivari of revolt.

Perhaps 700 to 800 tradesmen and labourers were drawn to insurrection by the Fils de Liberté, and north and south of Montreal the rural districts provided between 4,000 and 7,000 recruits. Numbers of landless labourers and country artisans gravitated to the movement; they were apparently not critical in the leadership. The 108 court-martialled after the first rebellion were dominated by poor farmers and the petty bourgeois. Only fifteen could be easily identified as coming from the trade or labouring classes. There were apparently no counterparts to the Upper Canadian Samuel Lount, although the second uprising at the end of 1838 carried a more radical tinge, as noted by Fernand Ouellet: "Nelson's declarations of independence in February and November of 1838 proclaimed abolition of the old social regime and also universal suffrage, appealing directly to the urban and rural proletariat." In the aftermath of defeat, this orientation brought the radical minority of workingmen to the cause of Francophone nationalism.

At Quebec City, for instance, in October, 1839, a company of journeymen printers staged a Voltaire play, a tragedy depicting a struggle between father and son in which the offspring kills his parent "for the love of liberty." In the words of the English Tory press, the theatrical staging was "replete with the most extravagant republican declamations and expressions of hatred of Kings," and the disaffected printers were determined to "get up an excitement among the people connected with the fatal source of the misfortunes of the Province, national origin, which they will endeavour to turn to *any* advantage that may offer." This play, and its advocates and opponents, serves as a metaphor for the politics of the 1830s, when paternalistic power was challenged overtly. As the metaphor suggests, that challenge was most visibly acted out by fathers and sons, repulsed by those who stood for King, country, and family. This was a male metaphor. How had the script of the theatres of power and protest come to be gendered in this way?

GENDER, CLASS, AND THE PATERNAL ORDER

Masculine and feminine identities were central to the paternalist order, which drew some of its capacity to command the allegiance of the producing classes through its conscious generalizing of the power of the father into all realms of civil society. This was a period in which domestic authority and the institutions and symbolic authority of the political arena were undeniably linked. Not for nothing did Mackenzie dub the Upper Canadian oligarchy the *Family* Compact, and the situation in other locales, such as Halifax, was not all that different. As we have seen with respect to the Talbots, Calvins, and their like, paternalist power was connected to an elaborate process whereby individuals buttressed their right to rule by socially and economically constructing themselves as *fathers* of their respective communities. Within the developing arena of the primitive state, ruling authority congealed within individuals who aptly dubbed themselves "fathers of the people." As Annalee Golz has suggested in an unpublished paper, the law addressed this unity of family and state and the *Upper Canada Jurist* warned in the mid-1840s of the dire consequences of tampering with the "natural" connection of domestic tranquility and political order: "Domestic duties are invaded, and parental authority disregarded. Children feel themselves no longer dependent, but are ready to indulge in any display of contempt of parental authority, and the fearful consequences that must ensure may ultimately destroy all rule and governance in the state."

Male heads of household thus owned not only the property of the family but the time and productive activity of their wives and children. This was widely regarded, in law and in belief, as one of the many claims of "natural affection." Men were also, of course, responsible for wives and children, both economically and morally, and had rights to seek redress and compensation in the courts for physical and sexual crimes against their family members. Like apprentices, wives and children would be advertised if they absconded from the bed and board of their husbands and fathers, with ritual reward offered for their return and warnings given to all who would harbour or employ them. Cobourg's Samuel Crawford insisted in 1833 that "Any Person or Persons employing my son John Crawford, as Carpenter, I will hold him or them responsible for his time, and further not to pay him any earnings, as he is a minor, and has eloped from me, and can make no arrangement for himself." When wives were similarly noticed, husbands uniformly explained that they had departed "without any just cause or provocation."

The context of pre-1850 society, then, is obviously one in which the unquestioned dominance of males – over property and person – within the family consolidated a domestic patriarchy that was legally enforceable but, more importantly, was clearly understood to be the social norm. Civil society and economic relations were commonly regarded as tied directly to this organization of the household; "patriarch" was a word used to designate figures of social and political authority. Patriarchy was thus male power, virtually uncontestable within the small confines of individual families. Paternalism was the ideology and practice of taking this power in a social formation in which class was emerging as a line of socio-economic demarcation and generalizing it through a purposeful elaboration of commonly understood status and a deliberate, if often disingenuous, recognition of the rights *and* responsibilities of the civil *father*.

This social and explicitly gendered construction of the "natural" connection of family and state infused entire realms of the economy and culture of the pre-1850 years. On one level it was most emphatically about the relegation of women and children to positions of subordination. But it also seeped into the process of class formation and, consequently, was forced into an increasingly pressured process of negotiation, in which paternal oligarchs tried to assert their authority over all subjects, including male workers. In contrast, male members of the producing classes, especially if they possessed any type of skill, sought to establish the "manhood" of their craft, measured in part by their capacity to provide for their entire families on the wage, or "price," it commanded. At issue for such tradesmen was the reinforcement not of subordination to social superiors but of their own rights as fathers and workers with dependants reliant on them and their competence. When William Lyon Mackenzie wanted to cater to his printers he praised their "free, manly independent spirit, . . . always on the side of justice and fair play." But another workshop employer, Toronto brewer and newspaper publisher Thomas Dalton, saw mechanics as the "productive children of every nation," limited by the "incessant toil demanded from them for the support of their families." Resolving the diverging trajectories of these two assessments of the skilled was what a good deal of the class conflict of the 1830s and 1840s was about. And that conflict exposed how varying "interests" were counterposed. Mackenzie the reformer was early attacked by Tory opponents for his failure to live up to the paternalist promise. He was charged with beating his son, ridiculing his mother, and tyrannizing his workmen. "What thinkest though of thy paternal character?" he was asked bluntly by the Brockville *Gazette*, which expressed disgust at "these glances of thy domestic character, as a parent, a son, and a master."

Domestic patriarchy and the wider paternalist ethos thus became contested terrain as economic differentiation, political opposition, and class formation unfolded. But such contests primarily involved men. Most women and children were structured into the confines of domestic units. If a woman married, the husband's authority was primary; if she stayed single, her father maintained his hold into adulthood. Widows might find a space to carry on an artisan business or orchestrate the earnings of unmarried children, but this was highly precarious. Domestic servants and apprentices might escape one parental household, but they lived within the equally rigid employment relationship of servitude. Even women of the elite, whose privileges were considerable, had their station: theirs was the responsibility of nurturing the young and providing the domestic tranquility that would replenish their husbands; if they had a role outside of their own homes it was to reinforce the paternalist ethos and family-centred nature of the social order by doing good works of charity among the domestically deserving poor. As Kathryn McKenna shows in her study of the women of the Powell family, there was no escaping these designated boundaries of patriarchy without suffering complete ostracism.

Ironically enough, domestic patriarchy for the producing classes may well have been much looser. Of course, the lives of workers and their families were materially more precarious and necessitated endless rounds of labour that were always provided by servants in the households of the rich. But on the land and in small-scale production, it is entirely possible that women's work was not only of the narrowly defined domestic sort. Because all members of the family had to work to sustain the entire reproductive unit, male control over women might well have been somewhat weakened. More work, more autonomy was a problematic trade-off, however, given the continual spinning, weaving, sewing, cooking, preserving, hauling, tending, washing, caring, and other tasks of farm women and artisans' wives. And whatever lessening of patriarchal restriction took place, it never elevated women to the status of men: their lives were subordinate and dependent; their work was far less likely to be public and remunerated.

As class was emerging in early Canada, then, and as political opposition was crystallizing against paternal, oligarchic rule, workers and their forms of opposition were simultaneously being contained within boundaries of gender. Thus, as the producing classes struggled to overcome their subordination, their own domestic sphere reproduced inequality and consolidated hierarchy.

PRODUCING CLASSES AND PATERNALIST AUTHORITY – ACCOMMODATION AND RESISTANCE

On balance, the paternalist order was able to withstand the challenges it faced in the pre-1850 years. The producing classes were accommodated to the rule of the oligarchs. Much of this process of accommodation had little to do with the choices and actions of either the producing classes or paternalist authority. Because the dominant economic activity was trade, production and concentrations of workers were curtailed. Merchants as the pre-eminent social class orchestrated a social formation that, by its own definition of economic endeavour, kept concentrations of workers limited

and highly transient. Regional political economies never overcame fundamental separations from one another that grew out of their physical relationship to particular staples and the mercantile cultivation of specific
markets. No uniform working-class presence within or across regions could
possibly develop in this context.

In spite of such formidable barriers to class formation and unity, however, there were signs of collectivity within the producing classes. First,
specific trades and unskilled callings, from tailors and shoemakers to raftsmen and navvies, began to act in concert under the pressures of exploitation
that, however different, contained features in common. Second, there were
signs that various producers could come together in common, essentially
political, battles that pitted them against paternal authority. Third, some
of the separations of location and region were breaking down, albeit very
slowly and quite incompletely, in activity that reached past the narrow
confinements of place, whether geographic or related to social station. The
mechanics' associations in Kingston, Toronto, and Montreal in the early to
mid-1830s were limited expressions of these kinds of mutuality among
producers, just as the labour parades in Saint John, New Brunswick,
established links among different kinds of workers. Occasionally the local
impact of these emerging working-class strengths was quite formidable. A
twelve-week 1841-42 strike of Pictou County, Nova Scotia, miners, which
turned back a wage cut and deterred those who broke ranks with effigy
burnings and other intimidations, convinced one investigator that "There
is no business with which I am acquainted that could sustain itself against
the influence of such a monopoly as this."

Even if the producing classes were a divided set of groups when examined
within the confines of their own experience, the paternal elite was not
always able to draw fine lines of distinction. Too often, authority saw only
the threatening potential of an all too undifferentiated mass of the dangerous classes. The ruling order offered many innovations to counteract this
and in the process unwittingly contributed to the pressured collectivization
of producers. Educational reform, as Alison Prentice and Bruce Curtis
have shown, was in part aimed at reducing class antagonisms. It sought to
inculcate discipline. One chief superintendent's report described the educational system of Upper Canada as "a branch of the national police," aiming
to "restrain many of the grown up population." But like so much of the
cultural experience, education was two-edged. More than a simple imposi-
tion of authority, it produced awareness that certain disciplines and learned
behaviours could be used to resist at the same time that they were meant to
be marshalled in the interests of submission and accommodation.
Working-class leaders such as Étienne Parent, editor of *Le Canadien*, the
paper of the working class of Quebec City's St. Roch district, balanced this
duality of accommodation/resistance in his understanding of the popular
attitude toward the state: "The government may keep us in a state of

political inferiority, it may rob us, it may oppress us. It has the support of an army and of the whole power of the empire to enable it to do so. But never will we ourselves give it our support in its attempt to enslave and degrade us."

Throughout the 1840s producers acted out their limited forms of class power at the same time as they proved, understandably, incapable of mounting a frontal challenge to the status quo. Typical in their blend of accommodation and resistance were the carpenters of Montreal, who in an 1845 strike described themselves as "sound constitutionalists," thus proclaiming their political loyalty to the established order; but they threatened to desert the city if they were not offered protection "from oppression." After many craft walkouts and insulting exchanges between masters and men, the 1840s could nevertheless end with a Toronto Typographical Society anniversary dinner in which the "one and indivisible" nature of capital and labour was proclaimed with enthusiasm. Toasts were drunk to "the better understanding between two parties, who are sometimes carried away with the erroneous idea that their interests are antagonistical instead of being, as they in reality are, mutual and reciprocal." A decade of contradiction and ambiguity, the 1840s provided a reprieve for the old paternal order of the Canadas.

But it was no more than a reprieve. Charley Corncobb, "poet laureate" of reform, set the paternal order's decline to lines of verse:

Toryism's sun is set
'Tis down, 'tis gone forever
Some say that it will start up yet,
But will it? Nonsense, never.

John Macaulay, a member of the old elite, observed as if in mourning, "The most alarming symptom . . . in the country is the decay of old-fashioned loyalty, and a general want of respect for authority and station which once prevailed among us . . . when, whatever the failings of the much abused 'Family Compact', we had a Government of Gentlemen." Even moderate patrician reformers seemed to agree. Robert Baldwin, who had done so much to bury Tory rule, worried in 1851 that "If the sober mind of the Country is not prepared to protect our Institutions it can't be helped." For Baldwin "reckless disregard of first principles" was leading to "widespread social disorganization with all its fearful consequences." In the years from 1850 to 1880 these prophecies and complaints would, in large measure, be borne out as the Canadas entered into an unmistakable age of industrial capitalism and consequent class cleavage.

Chapter 2

CLASS DIFFERENTIATION AND ANTAGONISM
1850-1880

THE SOCIAL FORMATION

The 1840s, more than the 1830s, were years of profound change in British North America. Replacing the bluster of an insurrectionary moment aborted almost before it was conceived were the vast transformations in economic and political life. In 1846 the colonial mercantilist tariffs were dismantled, and a little later the colonies were granted a form of "Home Rule" with the attainment of so-called responsible government, through which the elected representatives of the people finally had their say in the legislative process. A whole way of life, and the patrician paternalists who had stood as guardians of its official Tory culture, was replaced with a more materialist orientation. The state, once little more than a style of rule, was created to address substantive questions of national development and political consolidation. Mercantile capital and unmistakable agrarian dominance gave way to a more pervasive industrial capitalism; urban centres grew; and an impersonal labour market, stocked by the famine Irish, broke down some of the barriers to productive capital.

Economic growth was facilitated by reciprocity with the United States (1854-66) and by the external demand for manufactured goods and the old staples that resulted from the growth of the home market, the Crimean War, and the American Civil War. Technological advances (the introduction of machines in key sectors such as tailoring and shoemaking) and the innovations in banking throughout the 1850s and 1860s, culminating in the first Bank Act of 1870, added to economic growth. New men of power rose out of this context – railway promoters like Allan Napier MacNab and Francis Hincks and lawyer-businessman-politicians such as George-Étienne Cartier and John A. Macdonald – while the Talbots and the Baldwins receded from view. In the years from 1850 to 1880, the foundations of a modern industrial-capitalist order were laid. While these years did not totally overcome the entire range of contradictions and ambiguities so deeply embedded in the pre-1850 social formation, especially in terms of regional disparities and uneven development, they nevertheless stand as the point of entry into an industrial revolution paced by central Canada's expansive economy.

Railways symbolized the new age. From a mere seventy-two miles of railway track in Canada in 1850, mileage expanded to over 2,000 in 1865. Early railways radiated from Montreal and, secondarily, from Toronto. The resulting concentration of industry in these two centres reflected the regional character of future economic growth. As the age of wood, wind, and sail wound down, the arrival of a new epoch of iron and fire left much of British North America to plot its own indigenous path to industrialization, a process sure to leave the Maritimes, parts of rural Quebec, and the Far West locked into a subordinate place of economic subserviency. The construction of a transcontinental railway (the Canadian Pacific) in the 1870s and 1880s and the completion, in 1876, of the Intercolonial Railway linking the east coast and central Canada were ironic mechanisms by which these relations of inequality were perpetuated. A colony but recently removed from the clutches of imperial economic needs was, as Pentland noted long ago, able to absorb its own empire after 1867, when Confederation consolidated an "unequal union" that replicated, in politics, the economically privileged position of central Canada.

As Gustavus Myers noted early in this century, great fortunes were made in this railway construction, and they were accumulated through crass wheeling and dealing that resulted in unprecedented political scandal. The result was not so much a humiliated set of politicians as it was a social formation in which capitalist development and state-building were joined at the vulgar point where cash changed hands. Overzealous, and always able to entice one more grant or guarantee from their allies in the government, the railway hucksters who fuelled the drive of this political capitalism plunged Canada into an orgy of railway overproduction. This process was wasteful in the extreme, and many small investors lost their shirts as schemes soured and unnecessary rail lines proved less than the economic bonanza promised by those who had already lined their pockets. But the railway mania of these years nonetheless generated economic diversification and capital accumulation. Casimir Gzowski, associated with the Grand Trunk Railway, helped to establish the Toronto Rolling Mills in the 1850s, and by 1866 this imposing edifice employed over 300 men in rerolling old rails or puddling iron for new ones. A proliferation of metal-producing shops and foundries emerged in the 1850s to cater to the needs of the railway age, while huge shops like those of the Grand Trunk in Montreal (with a work force of 3,000) and the Great Western in Hamilton (employing 500 to 600) provided additional stimulus to economic development. Small wonder that one early newspaper described the 1860s as a decade that "set agoing an industrial revolution."

This revolution was most pronounced in the central Canadian urban centres. A view of Hamilton, Toronto, and Montreal in the years from 1850 to 1870 reveals the overwhelming changes. The industrial work force of such cities comprised approximately 16-20 per cent of city populations. More and more laboured in larger settings and entire new communities of industrially employed workers emerged out of the economic transformation of the period. Barely one in four Hamilton workers was employed in a shop of ten or more in 1851, but this figure had soared to 83 per cent by 1871. Between 1850 and 1870 the number of machinists in Hamilton climbed 800 per cent. Toronto, which produced about double the industrial output of Hamilton and which employed twice as many workers, saw similar trends. Of considerable importance in the new factories were women workers. Three-quarters of the work force in Toronto's rising clothing industry were female and the *Globe* estimated in 1868 that almost 4,000 women laboured in the city factories or in their homes on outwork. Larger work sites, expanding industrial work forces, and technological innovations did not, however, eliminate smaller, more traditional shops, which survived and remained a significant economic presence.

But the trend was unmistakable, as evidenced in Montreal's mid-century rise to manufacturing prominence. Out of forty-four firms listed in an 1856 booster publication, more than half had been established between 1850 and 1855. Geared toward the export market, Montreal firms were in the enviable and ironic position of benefiting from the city's low wage structure in spheres where technological innovation was of secondary importance and at the same time they capitalized on machinery, steam power, and advanced productive methods in industries where these forces were coming into economic play. The result was that Montreal firms outstripped their rivals in productivity, one estimate being that in the city's leading economic sectors of boots and shoes, furs and hats, and tobacco, value added per worker in

Montreal was greater than elsewhere by anywhere from 19 to 87 per cent. Montreal's diversified and advanced manufacturing sector was said to account for 75 per cent of the total production of Canada in 1875. And it was in Montreal that monopolistic control over the domestic market first emerged. Redpath, established in 1855 with 100 workers, was soon supplying seven-eighths of the domestic demand for white sugar.

On the periphery manufacturing might was more subdued, but industrial capital was capable of making significant inroads on the hegemony of the old staples-oriented mercantile elite. Manufacturing was widely regarded as critical to the economic future of Maritime Canada. In Halifax, this was borne out in the rise of boot and shoe production and the clothing industry, which together employed over 600 adult and child labourers, and in the creation of a mechanized and monopolistic firm, Moirs, that would later totally dominate the baking and confectionary industry. Nova Scotia's "fathers of Confederation" sold the idea of integration with central Canada in part on the basis of attracting capital. Their plan involved using the coal mines, which by 1872 provided 7 per cent of all provincial revenues, as an enticement that would establish the area as "the great emporium for manufactures in British America." This was not to be, largely because of decisions made by the powerful economic and political interests of central Canada.

Pockets of successful industrial-capitalist development were nevertheless visible across the Maritime provinces. Moncton and Halifax sustained industrial structures linked to the Intercolonial Railway and their own domestic markets, while the coal fields of Nova Scotia were industrial communities built around the more than 3,000 men and boys who worked the mines by 1879. These areas were able to support population growth, while many Maritime locales in the 1860s and 1870s were losing people. People went where the industry was: to the burgeoning urban centres of the American eastern seaboard; to the few Maritime cities where jobs were available; and, lastly and in far lesser numbers in these years, to central Canada. While Halifax's population rose almost 20 per cent over the course of the 1870s, many rural and outport Nova Scotia communities stagnated. The rise of manufacturing in the Maritimes was thus a highly uneven process, discernible, to be sure, in expanding industrial-capitalist output but scarred by the difficult dislocations that left parts of the region in a downward spiral of social and economic deterioration.

Things to the west were different, but no less complicated. There the importance of the fur trade still hung over much of the region and the extinguishment of aboriginal title to the land of the western interior was only resolved by a series of 1870s treaties, just as the defeat of rebellions in 1870 and 1885 determined who would rule the territory. The millions of acres of western real estate thus freed for settlement were always meant, as Gerald Friesen has pointed out, to serve the interests of "old Canada," to be an investment frontier that would enrich central Canada. But this dream or nightmare, depending on your regional vantage point, was, in the pre-1880 years, more of a future-oriented vision, at least in terms of its most decisive concrete consequences. Prairie residents in the 1870s worried about the buffalo, not wage labour. The explosive rise of Winnipeg, from a village of 100 in 1870 to a town of almost 4,000 by 1874, signalled the extent to which change would be rapid on the western industrial frontier. But Winnipeg's manufacturing muscle was still rather undeveloped: of 900 buildings in 1873, only twenty-seven were classified as manufactories, and they were overshadowed by the mercantile houses and offices of real estate speculation. Not until the 1880s would Winnipeg consolidate as an industrial centre linked to railways and orchestrated around production. This frontier-like social formation necessarily resulted in a subdued industrial capitalism, evident in British Columbia as well. There, the 1850-80 years were ones of stunted colonization; the social structure was skewed by the economics of fur and the adventure of the gold rush. Whites numbered only slightly more than 9,000 in 1867, and an 1870-71 census recorded only 400 employed in manufacturing, concentrated almost entirely in Victoria, New Westminster, and Nanaimo. Mining accounted for fully 2,300 of the identifiable employed and an overwhelming 75 per cent of all exports.

The economy of British North America had thus advanced considerably since the days of colonial commercial dominance, staple trade, and agricultural production of the pre-1850 years, but it had done so unevenly. Regional imbalance would be the very economic core of "national" development. Domestic production increasingly supplied the needs of Canada's growing demand for agricultural implements, boots and shoes, furniture, machines, woollens, paper, and foundry products. Native Canadian industry was of greater and greater political importance and tariff protection was formally implemented with the 1858-59 Galt-Cayley legislation and expanded in the 1860s. Rising numbers of patent applications indicated that Canadians were no longer willing to let innovation be the prerogative of others. But production and protection and patents were all, for the most part, concentrated in and secured for central Canada. There, too, the home market expanded most dramatically, as urban centres such as Toronto, Hamilton, and Montreal grew markedly in these years. Ontario's urban population had been 133,500 in 1851. Thirty years later it stood at 376,000.

This was not steady, uninterrupted "progress." Two major economic depressions cut into the economic buoyancy of these years, curtailing population growth and severely disrupting life in the years 1857-60 and 1873-79. Both depressions would take their toll on the petty producers and merchant princes, thereby furthering the relative interests of industrial capital. They would also weed out the marginal masters and concentrate economic power in the hands of the larger, more sophisticated employers. Out of these developments would come the highwater mark of nineteenth-century competitive capitalism in the 1880s. Under the impact of the 1873 depression the number of agricultural implements works in Ontario decreased by thirty-two while workers employed increased by over 1,000. One hundred fewer sawmills were manned by 3,000 more hands, and the number of tanneries decreased by 110 at the same time as those employed remained stable. In factories producing railway cars and locomotives a modest rise in the number of firms was paralleled by a thirtyfold expansion of the work force. Depression, in the 1850-80 period, spurred the concentration and centralization of capital and also produced destitution and misery.

By the 1870s, then, Canada had gone through a period of state-building, expansion of the manufacturing sector, and urbanization. The economy was still dominantly agricultural, but not overwhelmingly so. As O.J. Firestone has pointed out, value added by manufacturing in 1870 was 19 per cent of gross national product, compared with 34 per cent for agriculture; manufacturing provided 13 per cent of the total jobs, while agriculture remained the key work sector, with 50 per cent of total employment. Manufacturing activity was heavily concentrated in the Toronto-Hamilton and Montreal regions, which, according to Chambers and Bertram, accounted for a hefty percentage of all value added in manufacturing in central Canada. There were significant signs of manufacturing growth in the Maritimes, and a hint of possibility in the Far West. Although the large shop was beginning to overshadow the smaller concern, traditional work settings remained. As late as 1871 the average firm in Hamilton employed only seventeen workers, but this compared to five in 1851. In Toronto 88 per cent of industrial establishments still employed fewer than thirty workers in 1871, although this large majority of establishments hired only 33 per cent of the work force. An industrial revolution, while in the making, was not yet consummated.

Class differences in these years definitely widened, but consciousness of such differentiation remained somewhat inhibited and constrained. Particularly in the 1870s, with the onslaught of a general price deflation that would continue through to the end of the century, competitive capitalists attempted to widen their share of the market by reducing costs. When directed at labour, this took the form of the wage cut and, taken in conjunction with the severe dislocations of depression, put labour on the defensive. Depression concentrated capital in both body and mind: as it weeded out marginal employers it alerted all who hired labour of the necessity of keeping the wage bill low. Throughout the years 1850-80, labour took advantage of prosperity and capital's productive needs to attempt to gain tangible wage increases, improve job conditions, and combat expanding capitalist authority in the workplace. But as workers reared their collective heads in moments of upsurge, both the strengths and weaknesses of labour would be revealed. Like the economy itself, workers were constrained by the business cycle, subject to the greater power of employers and politicians whose fortunes fluctuated with it. The first stirrings of a labour movement were visible in these years, especially in central Canada, but so, too, were they stilled in the economic crises of the 1850s and 1870s.

AN INSURRECTION OF LABOUR

After a difficult period of adjustment to the economic and political changes of the late 1840s, British North America experienced a pronounced commercial boom. Prices rose approximately 2 per cent annually between 1850 and 1870, with the 1850-54 years marked by a sharp increase in commodity prices that plateaued in 1854-57, dipped in the depression of the late 1850s, and, only in the mid-1860s, settled back to 1852 levels. To counteract the adverse effects of this pre-1855 inflationary surge, workers early resorted to the strike.

Railway labourers on a number of lines in New Brunswick, Quebec, and Old Ontario launched their demands in a series of riotous strikes between 1850 and 1853. Largely Irish, workers on these construction sites re-enacted the scenes of violence and disorder produced in the 1830s and 1840s by canallers. Skilled craftsmen were another group suffering from the escalating prices of prosperity. But a more serious issue to these mechanics was the introduction of machines, which undermined the very basis of their respectable status and diluted their much-vaunted skill.

In Montreal, shoemakers first encountered "Labor-Saving machinery" in 1849, when they formed a Journeymen Shoemakers' Society and declared a strike against the leading manufacturer, Brown & Childs. Toronto's tailors led the struggle against mechanization, reviving in 1852 the moribund society that had been established in the 1840s and dictating a new price list to their employers. One of the merchant tailor firms, Hutchinson & Walker, then introduced the first sewing machine into a Canada West manufactory, bringing a woman operative with the device from New York City. The "knights of the needle" responded with a strike, and upon Hutchinson's capitulation celebrated their victory on King Street. Parading about the town, they ridiculed the detested machine and symbolically buried it, hoisting it high in the air, carrying it on their shoulders after "the fashion of a corpse on its way to the burial grounds." The woman seamstress returned to the United States. Hutchinson & Walker sought to mollify their tailors and provided a dinner for them; the men replied in kind, presenting their masters with "a silver crouching lion, the emblem of the establishment." Two years later "labour problems" plagued the firm again, and Hutchinson & Walker, fed up with what was referred to as the terrorism of organized journeymen, filed legal charges that resulted in one of the best-publicized conspiracy trials of the decade. When Hamilton's Lawson's tailoring establishment, largest of its kind in the Canadas, introduced machines there were the same kinds of protests. The tailors walked out, separating themselves from what they referred to as "the fiend . . . the evil . . . monster." In less than a decade the number of male craftsmen employed at Lawson's fell from 100 to twenty-nine, sixty-nine females had been hired on, and there were ten sewing machines in place. For the male tradesmen, the machine had taken its toll.

These conflicts seem similar to earlier confrontations. The presence of symbolism and the nature of the rhetoric, the localized nature of the struggles, the trade consciousness, and obvious concern with preservation of craft status recall the struggles of the 1830s, while the rough methods of the railway Irish navvies reproduced the history of canallers. Strikes among early British Columbia miners in Fort Rupert (1849-50) and Nanaimo (1855) seem reminiscent of actions taken in previous decades by other isolated and "obnoxious" workmen. But in fact the strikes of the early 1850s represented a preface to a shift in class relations rather than a throwback to the past.

As conflict between master and man continued, polarization occurred. Especially pronounced among the skilled mechanics, this emerging class cleavage widened a breach that had seemed minor and easily contained in the pre-1850 years. The result was an 1853-54 strike wave that was "looked upon by the press and the public as the beginning of an insurrection of labour." Commencing in the spring and summer of 1853, when craft workers took advantage of apparent labour shortages and expanding productive activity to initiate six struggles in Toronto, Hamilton, and Kingston, the insurrection of labour escalated, as Paul Appleton's unpublished Master's thesis demonstrates, to an unprecedented level of confrontation in May-June, 1854. At least twenty-two strikes were fought in south-central Canada. In two months skilled craftsmen waged almost as many struggles as they had in the fifty years prior to mid-century. If employers reacted with surprise and a grudging acceptance of craft-worker assertiveness in 1853, by the next year they were showing signs of impatience with this newly forged stance of working-class aggression.

Accompanying many of these struggles were tactics of intimidation, practised by worker and employer alike. Assaults and implicit threats and warnings were used by some organized workmen; support from the courts was sought by a few employers. A sense of grievance and class distinction was emerging, evident in a statement by stonecutters: "Are rational and intelligent beings, under the banner of freedom to be trampled under the feet of despotic, dollar hunting railway contractors? Are canals . . . instead of stone, to be built on the skulls and marrow of men? Freedom says no! Common sense and public opinion echo no!" Given that this 1853-54 upheaval took place in a context of economic boom, when "every shop and store is thronged; manufacturers and mechanics are working double time, and labourers cannot be had for love or money," workers may have won more than their share of demands and employer recourse to legalistic repression could have been curbed by the need to placate somewhat the skilled mechanics.

Unskilled labourers were noticeably absent from this insurrection that was described somewhat effusively as "all but universal." This was an indication of the gulf still separating skilled and unskilled. Labour shortages in 1853-54 no doubt played a role in securing the unskilled relatively satisfactory wages, especially on the railway projects. Strikes may not have been necessary. Some labourers were actually able to double their wages between 1853 and 1854 without recourse to work stoppages. Of the twenty-eight strikes known to have taken place in 1854, for instance, only six involved the unskilled, and the bulk of these were urban workers with ties to craft labour, many of whom were employed on municipal projects. But a strike of railway navvies working on a Welland Canal bridge near Port Colborne at the end of October, 1854, introduced the unskilled, once more, into the fray. Walking off the job for payment of back wages, these navvies, unlike the skilled, adopted the strike in a stance of defence rather than in an offensive effort to establish mechanisms of shop control, thwart machines, or reappropriate a slice of labour value extracted from their skill.

By the autumn of 1854, and certainly by 1855, the economy was dipping toward the crash of 1857. In this context of economic recession the skilled backed away from confrontation while the unskilled were increasingly forced into it. When Montreal stonecutters struck in November, 1857, the newspaper response was a curt "Are these men mad?" Between 1855 and 1859 only fourteen strikes and riotous worker confrontations are known to have occurred, more than half being mass strikes of relatively unskilled workers. Quebec ship labourers, Grand Trunk workers at Point St. Charles, navvies on the railways of western Ontario and Nova Scotia were all involved in such battles. Often spontaneous eruptions, these conflicts were violent affairs. One, the Ridgeway Riot, led to an American contractor invading Canada to quiet his workmen, while another saw a church sacked, overseers beaten, and attempts made physically to drive imported workmen off the job. In April and May of 1855, Grand Trunk workers in Point St. Charles, near Montreal, struck for better wages and shorter hours. They destroyed eleven labour-saving derricks and managed to spread their protest to other Griffintown workshops, especially the foundries and Redpath's sugar refinery. One senses neighbourhood and kinship ties at work here, emboldening the strikers to proceed to a number of industrial establishments "with a perfect sense of impunity," thus securing a limited victory.

Among the skilled, struggles of this magnitude were rare. Strikes of printers, woodworkers, and shoemakers in the later 1850s tended to be small affairs, and they often ended in defeat. An exception was a large strike of workmen in the Great Western Railway shops in London and Hamilton in November-December, 1856. These large workshops were plagued by shortages of skilled workmen and to overcome this problem and retain its work force the employer cultivated a paternalistic solidarity within the railway community. Managerial rhetoric emphasized "the existence between all classes of the Company's servants, of that spirit of unanimity and cordiality which is so indispensable to railway working." High rates of pay, sick funds, mutual benefit societies, and housing, schools, and churches erected by the company for the workers all served as the materialist cement holding this paternal order together. Testimonial dinners bid farewell to retiring foremen or upwardly mobile superintendents moving on to greener pastures. Gifts of silver tea services and purses of $200 told of the workmen's integration into the relatively harmonious world the Great Western Railway worked so hard to create. Yet this paternalism could become unstuck as class tensions intruded. This was what happened in 1856. When a new superintendent dismissed a popular foreman with the apparent intention of replacing him with a personal favourite, the honour of respectable workmen seemed at stake. Things worsened when the superintendent claimed that the foreman was a drunkard, a charge the men denounced as a "monstrous fabrication." The resulting strike secured the reinstatement of the foreman, squashed a rumoured wage cut, restored the workmen's right to be paid for three-quarters of a day's work (rather than half) if they arrived a bit late on Saturday, and established a system whereby workers rode the railways for half fare.

More noteworthy, perhaps, than this strike to make a paternalistic company live up to its self-image was a massive demonstration of the unemployed in Quebec City in late 1857. Led by the ship carpenters, over 3,000 workingmen congregated at City Hall; they petitioned the Mayor and demanded "work at any price." Speakers mounted the roof of the municipal building to address the throng in French and English, urging "the maintenance of law and order." After proceeding through the principal streets of Lowertown to the St. Roch district, the assembled drafted a public statement demanding action: "Winter is fast approaching and will find us in the midst of a severe pressure. What is to become of our labouring population? The hopes held out of a resumption of the ship building trade, which employs so many industrious hands at this season of the year may be fallacious. No time is to be lost, some arrangement should be made to aid the poorer classes in their struggle with poverty and distress."

This meeting provides a fitting statement on the close of the decade, a reflection of the devastating impact of the 1857 crash on the beginnings of central Canada's first labour movement. Silenced by the close of the 1850s, workers had nevertheless waged at least seventy-three strikes between 1850 and 1859. In the flush of solidarity of 1853-54, they mounted a labour campaign that aimed beyond the sectional interests of craft workers and hinted at a broad-ranging collectivity that might have included some of the unskilled. Retreating into whatever security they could find in the post-1857 collapse and not yet freed of the fetters of paternalism, the skilled dropped their aggressive stance of the early 1850s and sought "work at any price." Nativism seemed on the rise within the society as a whole and this may well have served to divide many workers. Both the strengths and weaknesses of labour at this turning point lay in working-class organization, in a local and international unionism that was forged in the 1850s and carried through to the next period of boom and bust – the 1870s.

UNIONISM: LOCAL AND INTERNATIONAL

The strikes of the 1850s, particularly the insurrection of labour, had been sustained by worker societies, associations, and unions, almost all of them composed of skilled workers rooted in particular local settings. Centred in Saint John, Montreal, Quebec City, Toronto, Hamilton, and London, dozens of isolated trade societies flourished after mid-century, and organization even spread to the Far West, a bakers' body forming in Victoria in January, 1859. Eugene Forsey's exhaustive researches on the early Canadian labour movement suggest that two-thirds as many local unions existed in the 1850s (about thirty) as there had been in the entire first half of the nineteenth century. Seal skinners in Newfoundland were organized in 1855 and in Saint John, New Brunswick, an early centre of labour activism, Richard Rice's study of worker organization reveals the existence of seven societies. Led by carpenters, tailors, printers, and shoemakers, these early unions were as interested in social and benevolent activities as they were in defending labour's economic or workplace interests. Particularly notable, inasmuch as it grew out of the distressed context of 1857, was the Quebec Ship Labourers' Benevolent Society, led by a small contingent of Irishmen known as authentic "'Little' Champlain Street harps." Organized on street corners on summer nights, the body eventually formalized its meetings (gathering regularly at the Temperance Hall) and its dealings with shipmasters and the stevedore middlemen, becoming one of the most formidable associations in Quebec City.

In its heyday in the years 1860-73, which corresponded with the last prosperous phase of the trade in square timber, the Ship Labourers embraced five locals and 2,000 members, 95 per cent of whom were Irish. Brought to public attention by its involvement in a mass strike in 1866, the Society outraged Quebec's leading merchants, increasingly resentful of the "decidedly and undeniably illegal" actions of the labourers, who refused to countenance either "scabs" (and actually invaded the sacred precincts of the naval dockyard to do battle with strikebreakers) or steam-driven machinery on the docks. By the late 1870s the Ship Labourers' Society was in decline. The collapse of shipbuilding in Quebec, traditionally a preserve of French-Canadian labour, pushed Québécois workers into longshoring, and they formed their own body, L'Union Canadienne. Riotous clashes between French and Irish took place in 1878-79, signalling the termination of the Irish reign in the ship-labouring trade. Eventually this rift was healed, French and Irish uniting in the 1880s under the auspices of the Knights of Labor, but it marked the end of an epoch of local unionism in Quebec City.

Over the course of the 1860s and 1870s local unionism thrived, especially in Ontario, where as many as seventy societies existed. In the Maritimes between 1860 and 1875 there were at least thirteen local labour bodies in Halifax, one in Pictou, nine in Saint John, one in Chatham, and one in Charlottetown. Montreal was also a centre of activity, while in British Columbia the shipwrights, typographers, and miners boasted organizations. Much more research and study are required before we can grasp with any certainty the character and structural dimensions of working-class experience in this period.

As with the institutional context, there is a lack of precise figures on the extent of conflict. But the trend toward increasing numbers of strikes is clear. Ontario led the way with 134 strikes, or almost half of all conflicts, followed by Quebec with eighty-four, the Maritimes with fifty-two, and the western reaches of the country with six. Such battles may well have involved workers who had no organized unions, but many conflicts grew directly out of employer hostility to trade unionism.

Some general patterns of conflict, which distinguish the experiences of the skilled crafts from those of day labourers, can be discerned. The latter, for the most part, struck to secure wages and to gain an immediate and tangible end. Victory or defeat tended to depend on local conditions and the availability of surplus labourers willing to fill the positions vacated. Most such struggles were short affairs of one or two days. Workers with a skill to bargain with, however, were more likely to use the strike to achieve a variety of ends: to gain wage increases, to resist wage cuts, and to secure a measure of autonomy or mundane workers' control at their work sites. In the last case, workers often struck to limit the hiring of apprentices, thereby preserving the character of skill and limiting the supply of labour, or to restrict output or maintain the standard wage rate, both of which stood as badges of respectability and craft pride. For the skilled, an appropriate demeanour toward the boss was essential in maintaining craft dignity.

As early as 1861, the *Montreal Gazette* reported that "strikes were becoming epidemic among skilled mechanics." In 1867 Montreal's Médéric Lanctôt, a local journalist drawn to the workers' cause, claimed that strikes had occurred yearly over the course of the previous three decades. Local unions were certainly involved in such work stoppages. By the 1860s, however, while still important, they were less significant than the growth of internationally connected organizations of labour, bodies that sought to create wider solidarities within trade sectors and that linked workers of one locale to those of another. To combat the emergence of expanding national and international labour markets and combinations of capital in these years, workers gravitated to similarly conceived bodies of labour.

At the beginning of 1859, British North America contained only one internationally connected union, the British-based Amalgamated Society of Engineers, which had small branches in Hamilton (fourteen members) and Toronto (eleven members). Twenty years later there were two British internationals (the Engineers were joined by the Amalgamated Society of Carpenters and Joiners) with eleven branches, as well as eleven American craft unions with forty-three locals. Moreover, many international unions, such as that of the coopers, which thrived in the 1860s and early 1870s, had passed away by 1880, victims of bad times, mechanization, and employer hostility.

Entirely restricted to the skilled, international craft unionism was led by moulders, printers, carpenters, cigarmakers, and coopers, buttressed by associations of workers connected to the railway age, shopcraft engineers and the running trades. The short-lived Knights of St. Crispin galvanized Canadian shoemakers in the 1860s and 1870s, and there were possibly as many as twenty-six Crispin lodges from Saint John in the east to Petrolia in the west. They had all but disappeared by the end of the depression of the 1870s.

Like local unions, internationally affiliated bodies were drawn into conflict situations. Craft unionists found themselves up against employers who had no time for their demands and who were increasingly banded together in their own international associations. Over the course of the 1860s and 1870s skilled workers were involved in at least 204 strikes, the unskilled in seventy-two. These figures more than doubled the strikes fought between 1815 and 1859. Unions like the Iron Molders International Union, the Cigarmakers International Union, and the Knights of St. Crispin were not unimportant in this escalating pattern of strike activity.

International union strikes often turned on the question of who would control aspects of the workplace. Thirty-three per cent of all strikes in the 1860s and 1870s related to attempts to secure shorter hours or control some aspect of work life. The Coopers International Union pledged that all barrelmakers should "allow no one to teach a new hand" in order "to control the supply of help." In strikes fought to gain this and other similar ends, however, financial support from international headquarters was crucial. One unsuccessful cigarmakers' battle in Toronto in 1873 was sustained by $1,675 in aid, while the Canadian moulders, whose eighteen locals averaged approximately twenty-five members in the late 1860s and early 1870s, received over $5,000 in support form the United States in 1874-75. This represented nearly one-third of the union's total expenditure on strikes and lockouts, and Hamilton's local benefited from an immense donation of

$3,480, which made it the best-funded moulders' union in North America in its moment of adversity. Aid of this sort lent material meaning to the IMIU seal, which bore impressions of both the American coat of arms and the royal crown, across which stretched the clasped hands emblematic of the international solidarity of labour.

Over the entire period 1850-79, ninety-four international union locals were established in Canada, with almost 76 per cent being in the industrial heartland of Ontario. Taken in conjunction with the local unions, this means that some 165 labour bodies had been formed in Canada by 1880. Far more than mere organizations of economic protection, these unions, associations, and societies were social institutions as well. They had their own rituals and often publicly paraded in ceremonial procession. As centres of benevolence and fraternity, they encouraged workers to come together at the workplace, in conflict situations, and within the community. Leisure, politics, and education became points of collective concern, and at union meetings workers debated temperance and Confederation as well as the standard wage rate.

The social and cultural place of early workers' organizations can be determined partly by examining attendance at public parades. One of the earliest of these took place in Saint John, as an 1853 procession honoured the European and North American Railway. Five thousand marched, with carpenters and joiners, shoemakers, founders, millmen, tailors, shoemakers, stonecutters, and others sporting banners, uniforms, and emblems. A horse-drawn printing press was emblazoned with the message, "Knowledge is Power," while blacksmiths walked under an elaborate banner depicting a woman hanging from an anchor, inscribed, "By hammer in hand, all arts do stand." Artisan pride and the dignity of labour reverberated from such symbols and representations.

By the late 1860s these parades occupied an important place in the world of the Canadian worker. When Montreal's Médéric Lanctôt formed the Grand Association of Canadian Workingmen, he inaugurated the founding of this body with a torchlight procession. From the coopers' blunt statement, "We work well when well paid," to the cabinetmakers' reminder that "Equal justice only will insure permanent peace," the mottoes reflected labour's emerging pragmatism as well as its humanistic concerns. Early support for Canadian national feeling, especially the economic nationalism of a protective tariff, was also demonstrated by workingmen in some central Canadian parades. Hamilton's workers, for instance, marched in a grand "Celebration Day" procession on July 1, 1867, accompanied by the usual craft displays, regalia, and banners.

These public displays of pride and patriotism hardly obliterated rougher methods of airing class grievance. Dry goods clerks in Ottawa who engaged in an early closing agitation in April, 1865, outraged respectable society by "daubing over with filth" the front of one mercantile store holding out against the attempt to have all retail outlets close by 7:00 p.m. In the Red River Valley, Thomas Scott, later to be executed by Riel, led an 1869 strike to secure payment of travelling expenses for a road-construction crew. Upon winning their demand, Scott and others seized the contractor, threatened to duck him in the Seine River, and extorted the wages they would have received had they not been out on their two-day work stoppage. The contractor gave in, but later filed a civil suit for aggravated assault.

However much unions shunned such rough behaviour and cultivated an image of respectable and dignified labour, there were those who saw these efforts as the thin edge of a dangerous wedge. The Halifax *Evening Express* proclaimed in 1874:

> No burning questions of capital and labour divide our people and distress our rulers. Strikes are infrequent, there is not much enforced idleness, there is no tyranny over the workman that he should rise against, there are no laws which oppress him, there is no tariff that he objects to being unfair. . . . We protest against . . . the beginnings of that dangerous species of combination among workmen which gives so much distress to authorities and inflicts so much ultimate evil on the workingman himself.

This depiction of Canadian society may well have been marked by more wishful thinking than acute social analysis, but the anger, indeed fear, evident in such an excerpt was real enough. It had, in part, grown out of increasing class antagonisms and working-class organization that surfaced in the 1850-80 years. For the first time in Canadian history there was a sufficiently industrialized capitalist sector to generate working-class institutions. While escalating local and international unionization and the growing number of strikes were perhaps the most visible reminders of this, they were by no means the only expression of the working-class presence.

ASSOCIATIONAL LIFE

A significant feature of the Victorian cultural landscape was the proliferation of associations, clubs, societies, and lodges during this period. While many of these fraternal, sporting, and benevolent bodies had their origins in earlier years, they now began to supplement seriously the institutions of self-help (mechanics' institutes) and community protection (fire companies) that had their roots in the pre-1850 period. The magnitude of this associational network was quite striking, and in the years predating mass culture and highly commercialized forms of recreation it formed a vital part of everyday life for many males. This gendered structure needs to be kept in mind, for most associational life in these years excluded women. Mary Ann Clawson, studying fraternal orders in the United States, has suggested that this all-male brotherhood was a symbolic rite of passage, especially critical for young working-class men whose identities necessarily suffered through onslaughts in an age of capital's dominance.

Certainly many men joined; and the 1850-80 period of emerging industrial-capitalist strength was when they were most likely to sign up. More than one-third of the Orange lodges that existed in the nineteenth century were established during the 1850s, when approximately 550 were formed. By 1864 this single fraternal order claimed a membership of 200,000. And this was just one example: there were societies associated with people's national origin, like the Sons of England, as well as benevolent bodies such as the Masons, Oddfellows, Foresters, and others. The Ancient Order of United Workmen enrolled over 3,000 members in its Ontario lodges by 1880. There were also large numbers of sporting clubs in urban centres, drawing baseball, lacrosse, snowshoeing, rowing, or fishing enthusiasts to their ranks. Almost every city had a series of volunteer fire companies, which gradually gave way to professional brigades by the close of the century. While by no means the sole territory of the working class, this matrix of lodges, associations, and volunteer groups was not without its plebeian component.

Did working-class involvement in these societies enhance an appreciation of class place and the inequalities of the social formation or undermine class awareness? It is not an easy question to answer. To be sure, fraternal life accentuated bonds of masculinity, nationality, and respectability that often brought journeyman, master, manufacturer, merchant prince, and lowly labourer together in a classless, pluralistic order that was itself a denial of class divisions. Darryl Newbury's unpublished research into the fraternal milieu in Ottawa-Hull exposes this side of associational life nicely: E.B. Eddy, proprietor of one of the region's major enterprises, a large match factory, managed not only to secure the position of Worshipful Master of the Masonic Lodge but also to have the fraternal body named after him. This was not the stuff of which working-class independence would be made.

Still, the workingman could take selectively from the fraternal experience, in ways that reinforced the class awareness and differentiation proceeding apace in the economic arena. The fraternal values of mutuality, co-operation, and equality were not without their place in a society that seemed to be drifting in directions that repudiated all of this. As profit and individualism appeared to be overtaking craft worth and the dignity of labour, the fraternal order offered a language that reasserted values and conceptions in seeming decline. With the insecurities and impersonalities of the new age, friendly societies established death benefits and the promise of a proper burial. The appeal to nationality must have had a similar calming effect in a period of mass migration and fractured ties to homeland, however mythologized such attachments. Moreover, the elaborate ritual and solemnity of the secret societies undoubtedly cultivated a sense of fraternity cherished by skilled workers who themselves had gone through the apprenticeship rites that immersed them in the "arts and mysteries of a trade." As a means of transcending economic constraints and combatting ideological challenges to their implicitly held world view, many workers found their way to the friendly society. Often such bodies had memberships that were overwhelmingly working class, and even in the less plebeian orders it was uncommon for a solid one-third of the advocates not to be drawn from the ranks of labour. By the 1880s one working-class figure would pronounce with confidence that nine-tenths of the fraternal orders' membership was working class. This was an overstatement, but it did emphasize the importance of these societies in the cultural experience of workers.

The friendly society was thus an important locale in a two-sided cultural context in which workers could be pulled in contradictory directions. It was but one site of many. Workingmen also met in mechanics' institutes, fire companies, and sporting clubs. Small towns like Napanee, Goderich, Woodstock, and Paris, as well as larger centres such as Halifax, Montreal, and Toronto, all supported mechanics' institutes in these years. According to Foster Vernon, there were sixty-seven institutes in Ontario by 1858, with a membership of about 7,600; by 1879 there were even more halls and more workers patronizing them. Public lectures at these institutes often promoted a vision of a classless, progressive social order, and the mechanics' institute as a vehicle of self-help contained many of the same contradictory currents as the fraternal society. Usually controlled by upper-class elements, these institutes nevertheless provided a place where workers could sift the pros and cons of the new industrial-capitalist order through a filter that necessarily took some account of emerging class differentiation. This was precisely what happened when Great Western Railway mechanics, aided by their paternalistic better, managing director Brydges, turned the Hamilton and Gore Mechanics' Institute away from its orientation to the middle class and instead secured a change in the bylaws, a fee reduction, the election of Brydges to the board, and classes in the mechanical arts taught by actual railway shop workers.

The fire companies and sporting clubs had similarly constructed histories, in which contradiction and ambiguity were present along with indications of the presence of class. Morgan O'Connell, captain of the Montreal Shamrocks, a prominent lacrosse club, reacted to some adverse criticism of his club in 1874 with the words, "I hope this is not because we are only mechanics, and Irish Catholics at that." There were abundant signs, then, that associational life could override class barriers at some times as well as cultivating notions of class difference.

One area definitely romanticized in this associational life was the home, sustained materially by the benefits of the friendly societies and the ideological shoring up of a mythical domesticity that was in the air in many quarters, including the mechanics' institutes. Thus a Bytown Mechanics' Institute lecture of 1853 focused on "Domestic Affections" and saw the family as the source of political stability. "If the domestic influences have been corrupted at their foundations of life," argued Reverend Johnston, "this deep undercurrent of evil will, in time sweep away every barrier, and engulf society in the polluted waters of licentiousness and anarchy." It was no accident that this gendered message and the gendered nature of associational life in this period came at precisely the time that working-class families were under siege, their incomes eroded by skill dilution, seasonal work stoppages, and economic depression, their idealized mythology of hearth and home disrupted by the entry of women and children into the paid work force.

FAMILIES

The importance of the family in nineteenth-century working-class life emerges out of many developments. Ritualistic practices such as the charivari, which was used to punish violators of domestic norms, proclaimed an attachment to the family itself and pointed to popular attempts to sustain it. In the outports of Newfoundland, as Gerald Sider suggests, work was organized along family lines, and yearly ritualized gatherings such as Christmas mumming may have provided a structured but relatively informal way of reforming work relationships, recognizing the link between domestic and labouring life. Families appear out of the historical record as an essential foundation defended by working people. In spite of a series of hardships and forces working to disrupt the domestic sphere, the family was an institution around which many workers developed strategies of survival. In this process class differentiation was again accentuated, as workers and non-workers lived lives in which class-based variations on the meaning of "childhood" and "domesticity" were constructed and diverging structures of fertility evolved.

Economic threats to the family, of course, were often at the root of working-class grievances and precipitated many social conflicts, especially between skilled mechanics and their employers. "There can be no doubt that the dollar would go farther in a family twenty years ago than double that sum can be made to supply at the present day," explained a discontented workingman in the midst of an 1864 Halifax house joiners' strike. "Under the circumstances, therefore," he continued, "the workmen are justified in looking out for themselves and the dear ones dependent on them for their daily bread." This kind of thinking was at the core of the popular notion that skilled workers deserved remuneration sufficient to allow them to provide for their families in ways that reinforced and displayed the economic and cultural respectability of the father and his dependants: wives were not to be forced into wage labour outside the home; children were to be educated and provided with the skills that would allow them entry into a proper marriage or an honourable trade. Historians have come to call this mindset the family wage, a notion that implied far more than so many dollars a week.

Often associated in the historical literature with the late nineteenth-century rise of industrial capitalism and the economic separation of waged work and the home, this working-class understanding of the family wage defies precise chronological pigeon-holing. As indicated in an earlier chapter, something related to this family wage, however nebulous, existed in the earlier history of gender and class relations, which prior to 1850 were structured around an unmistakable domestic patriarchy. By the 1860s, nevertheless, it is possible to discern a more formidable appreciation of the beginnings of attachment to the idea of the family wage, especially among skilled and organized workers. But this did not mean that the actual history of the family wage was a simple and clear-cut phenomenon.

The family wage was in fact always more of an idealized conception than a historical reality. So many factors worked to undermine it, including many that heightened distinctions between working-class and non-working-class families. Central here was the expanding employment of women and children, ushered into the workplace by increases in plant size, mechanization of trades, and skill dilution. While these years were dominated by uneven development in which routinized factory production coexisted with small handicraft manufactories and artisanal work, the influx of unskilled labour, much of which was under the age of sixteen or female, was considerable. Moulds invented in the early 1860s transformed the cigar-making trade and stimulated an influx of women and children; textile production expanded employment opportunities for women and the young; and the introduction of sewing machines in the clothing industry and the McKay stitcher in shoemaking in the 1860s undermined the position of many male workers.

The proportion of women and children in Montreal's shoemaking and clothing industries increased 50 and 80 per cent, respectively, between 1861 and 1871. One in three workers in Ontario's leading boot and shoe production centres in 1871 was a woman; one in seven was under sixteen years of age. As bakeries expanded from manufactories to factories, the employment of women and children increased. In Halifax this process was especially notable in the 1870s, as the percentage of children increased from roughly 9 to 22 per cent in the labour force in baking; comparable figures for women jumped from 11 to 16 per cent. Tobacco works in Ontario employed 371 male hands, ninety-one women, and 245 children in 1871. One in four boys aged eleven-fifteen living in Montreal worked for wages, where 42 per cent of the industrial work force in 1871 was composed of women and children. Such figures reveal that the family wage – as a level of payment and a way of life – was attainable by only the few. They also provide the starting point for an understanding of working-class family life in the years from 1850 to 1880.

Families of labouring people subsisted, not on an individual wage, but on the combined earnings and unpaid contributions of men, women, and children. As employment opportunities for children expanded with industrial-capitalist consolidation, different sections of the population rewrote their own demographic histories. Katz notes, for instance, that in Hamilton between 1851 and 1871, fertility rates among the business class (composed of professionals, agents, clerks, merchants, manufacturers, and employing master craftsmen) decreased strikingly. Desiring more consumption for their families and more education for their children, the bourgeois and petty bourgeois limited the number of children they conceived in order to appropriate rationally the optimum in material goods and social benefits. In contrast, the fertility rates among skilled workers increased over the same period, while the numbers of children born to poorer labourers increased even more dramatically, at twice the rate of the skilled. This cresting fertility was thus one expression of class need: those social classes most constrained by economic necessity responded positively to the opportunities of an expanding teenage labour market, which could be exploited to help provide sustenance for the family. By the 1880s there is evidence of entire families being recruited to particular work settings, especially the cotton mills. There, family discipline functioned in the interests of capital, but it could also mount a challenge to attempts to fragment family earning power. "Why did you dismiss my daughters?" asked one irate mother, "I have need of their assistance to live."

Indeed, those families whose children had not reached the age of eleven were at an economic disadvantage, for married women were not likely to work for wages in the traditional sense. Employed in their younger years as servants, seamstresses, or milliners, women usually left the work force upon marriage. By the 1870s, with increasing employment chances in factory work, some married women drifted into this type of wage labour, but their numbers were not large. Bettina Bradbury's study of two Montreal wards in 1871 notes only 2.5 per cent of wives resident with their husbands reporting an occupation. If a woman was widowed, of course, the likelihood of her engaging in wage labour would be much higher, but even here it was more common for women to have recourse to the "putting out" system, whereby they did consignment work in their homes at reduced rates of pay. And it was here that most women found employment, structured into the confines of an age-old rationalization that saw "secondary" earners as deserving of only the most meagre payment. A Montreal clothier explained that he hired a number of women who worked in their own homes "for very cheap . . . to buy finery . . . which they would not be able to buy but for this industry."

In fact, however, such women worked out of sheer necessity and were part of a process of family survival. Sometimes survival meant sharing a house-hold with another family, sending children to stay with relatives in the country, or even placing children in orphanages or under the care of some other "charitable institution" until they could be reclaimed at an age when they might be put to work. These were all ways in which the debilitating consequences of unemployment, recession, seasonal curtailment of work, sickness, or the death of a mother or father might be offset.

Because working-class families necessarily had to adapt and survive as units, historians have perhaps been too quick to interpret this experience as one of collectivity and co-operation. The very language of historical analy-sis, in which Canadian historians now routinely refer to the family economy of the late nineteenth century, is evidence of this. Yet families did not so much construct a family economy in this period as they were moved into specific corners by the imperatives of an economy directed by forces very much outside of their control. To be sure, many family experiences were co-operative and consensual, but the structural impossibility of surviving on the earning power of the head of the household should not, in and of itself, be taken as an indication of universal agreement and harmony within the domestic realm.

The family, after all, was not just the site of working-class adaptation and survival, not only a locale where resistance to capital could arise. It was these things, but it was also potentially a fundamentally repressive institu-tion in which the autonomy and interests of women and children were subordinate to those of men. The underside of the adaptive families of Victorian Canada is a history of husbands deserting wives, of brutality in which women and children suffered the presence and power of abusive men, and of males (and, occasionally, females) appropriating the paid and unpaid labour of their spouses and offspring as well as availing themselves of sexual access to those who, emotionally and physically, had few resources to resist. The husband's property rights over "his" woman knew few legal limitations in this period, especially in terms of sexuality. An 1869 judicial statement made it clear that nothing justified a married woman engaging in the unpardonable sin of adultery: "His compelling her to leave by his violence, or her leaving in consequence thereof, or his abandoning her without provision, alike fail to warrant or excuse her subsequent volun-tary living in adultery." Judges often ruled, even in the face of physical assault, that "a man has the right to resort to the moderate correction of his wife . . . [and it] is not . . . for magistrates or courts to step in and interfere with the rights of a husband in ruling his own household." As Kathryn Harvey's study of wife-battering in working-class Montreal in the 1870s shows, male violence against wives was far from uncommon. In the course of a decade some 350 cases of wife-battering were brought before the courts.

Thus, in families both fragile and resilient, repressive and adaptive, the working class reproduced itself and struggled with and against the vicissitudes of the new social formation. As the family became the site where cultural attachments and visions, ideals, and a measure of autonomy were circumscribed by material realities, entrenched powers, and the pervasive influence of work, it was a force shaped by the related currents of conscious human agency *and* structured social necessity. Partly created by working people, the family was also, in part, moulded by the largely impersonal and historically determined developments of an age of nascent industrial capitalism. Men and women walked to the altar, conceived children within intimate bonds, and shared much, but behind their backs unfolding events limited choice and structured behaviour along specific paths. Co-operation was always potentially countered with coercion, and a male authority debased outside of the home often ran amuck within its walls, striking out in sometimes purposeful, sometimes blind, unconscious rage at this ordering of life. The family had its victims as well as its beneficiaries. For some adult males, drink was an avenue out of all of this, at least for the moment, the tavern an alternative to or escape from the confinements of the family, however temporary; other men, without family ties, found the tavern a home away from the homes they never had.

TAVERN LIFE: THE WORLD OF JOE BEEF'S CANTEEN

Taverns had long been of significance in the plebeian world. Innkeepers in Upper Canada were known for their "independence" and republican sentiments, which, ironically, gave them "no zeal to oblige"; their premises were often centres of political discussion and agitation. By the 1840s the proliferation of drinking establishments in urban areas was regarded as a serious social problem, and in towns like Kingston one house in seven sold spirits to the public. Both Reform and Tory politicians cultivated votes through licensing these establishments. As social polarization increased in the years after 1850, the tavern, like many institutions, reflected class distinctions. Fine hotels catered to those with aristocratic pedigree or pretension, while other houses attracted moderate artisans or city swells and dandies. Then, too, there were "the Great Houses of the Vulgar People," and there were hundreds of these "low rum holes" among the over 1,200 licensed establishments of Victorian Montreal. Historians have long known the importance of this tavern underworld, haunted by the "undeserving poor." But it has remained an obscure realm, dimly lit by the rare pieces of evidence that have survived the passage of time. An exceptional study by Peter DeLottinville describes the Montreal waterfront tavern of Joe Beef's Canteen, a meeting place for canallers, longshoremen, sailors, and ex-soldiers. This was a clientele, in one commentator's words, of "unkempt, unshaven, fierce-looking specimens of humanity."

Joe Beef's was established by Charles McKiernan, an Irish Protestant ex-soldier of republican attachments. Patronized by day labourers, his canteen was an environment for the crude and the rude: it was furnished with rough tables and chairs, had a sawdust-covered floor, was adorned with skeletons and bottles of preserving fluid containing mementos of interest, and housed a fantastic menagerie of monkeys, parrots, wild cats, and bears. Beer was sold for five cents, and some of the bears were known to consume twenty pints daily. Their lack of sobriety, as well as the clients' rowdiness, made Joe Beef's Canteen an object of attack by crusading reformers, newspaper editors, and temperance advocates. As part of a criminal subculture that existed on the margins of working-class life, it was a well-known rendezvous for the "sun fish and wharf rats" of the harbour and was much frequented by youth gangs. In his *Autobiography of a Super Tramp*, W.H. Davies claimed that "not a tramp throughout the length and breadth of the North American continent . . . had not heard of [Joe Beef's Canteen] and a goodly number had at one time or another patronized the establishment."

McKiernan's tavern attracted casual labourers, the unemployed, and the transient for three reasons. First, it offered them sustenance along with drink – at one end of the bar huge piles of bread, cheese, and beef were there for the taking by those indulging in a brew. Dollar bills and notes of credit were deposited with McKiernan, tucked into an engraving above the beer taps, drawn upon as regular customers found themselves out of work or behind bars. The tavern even functioned as an informal hiring hall, and McKiernan was known to lend out shovels and picks to the unskilled. Joe Beef's also served as a cheap boarding house, and for ten cents "guests" were provided with a blanket, access to a tub and barber, "medical" advice and "cures," as well as accommodation for the evening. As many as 200 men could be crowded into the sleeping quarters on any given night; newspaper boys aged twelve to fourteen comprised three-quarters of McKiernan's boarders, and for twenty cents a day they received food and lodging. Second, Joe Beef's provided an escape from the cares and troubles of the world in an atmosphere of reckless abandon and hilarity. Any given evening might see McKiernan engaged in a game of billiards with one of his bears, or the dogs set upon this same animal. Musicians were commonly employed, in spite of legal prohibitions, and McKiernan was prone to harangue the crowd in rhyming couplets, drawing from local newspapers and Irish journals from the United States ammunition fired out in an endless stream of debate.

Out of this came the final attraction of Joe Beef's Canteen, its unmistakable role as defender of the poor, an institution with a direct message of the equality of men and the worth of the supposed worthless. McKiernan promoted Joe Beef's Canteen through newspaper advertisements as a house in which social outcasts could find a niche uncrowded by the condescension and deference that "Beaver Hall Bogus Aristocrats" practised and demanded:

> Citizens, we eat and drink in moderation;
> Our head, our toes, and our nose are our own,
> All we want is to be left alone!
> We eat and drink what we like,
> and let alone what we dislike.

Joe Beef's lent this rhetorical flourish substance by offering food and lodging to the poor free of charge if they were destitute and, although supported mainly by the Protestant and English-speaking, by refusing to cater to the prejudices of the age:

> JOE BEEF OF MONTREAL
> Who will feed a Poorman, if [he] is hungry
> Cure him if he is sick – He does not give a damn
> Whether he is an Indian, a Nigger, a Cripple, a
> Billy or a Mick – He never let a poorman die on
> The floor and never went back on the Poor.

Adept at bridging the contradiction, McKiernan could challenge the arbitrary and class-bound nature of the law at the same time that he provided information to local police, vilify the British Empire while ruling his own "den of robbers and wild beasts" with "infernal majesty in loyal style," or satirize the crass commercialism of the age and the tyranny of the "lousy dollar" at the same time proclaiming that "all Joe Beef wants is the Coin." "Son of the people," Joe Beef cared not for "Pope, Priest, Parson, or King William of the boyne." Thoroughly materialist, he provided the transient poor with what they needed to survive – food, lodging, and pride – and denigrated the empty promises and salvations offered by "Churches, Chapels, Ranters, Preachers, Beechers and [other] such stuff [of which] Montreal has already got enough."

Although a notorious partisan of the Conservative cause, who would enlist his ranks in the time-honoured practice of electioneering by riot, McKiernan could also turn his activities toward the unfolding class struggles of his time. The most explicit demonstration of this came in the midst of an 1877-78 strike of labourers on the Lachine Canal. Over 1,000 French and Irish workers on the canal enlargement project dropped pick and shovel to resist a wage cut and protest "truck" payment. Joe Beef's provided the strikers with wagon-delivered daily rations of 300 loaves of bread, thirty-six gallons of tea, and a like quantity of soup. The Canteen housed the out-of-work labourers, 300 finding shelter under its roof. As the private charities closed their doors to the striking workmen and their families, Montreal's working class was provided with a stark reminder of the essential difference between the undependable charity of the upper class and the mutual assistance generated in the name of their own ranks.

McKiernan also offered the canallers an elementary lesson in political economy, complementing the bread and soup donated to the cause:

> My friends, I have come here tonight to address you on "the Almighty Dollar." The very door bells of Montreal seem to ring with "the Almighty Dollar." The wooden-headed bobbies nail you, and you have to sleep on the hard floor provided by the City Fathers, and the next morning the fat Recorder tells you: "Give me the Almighty Dollar, or down you go for eight days." The big-bugs all have their eyes on the "Almighty Dollar," from the Bishop down, and if you die in the hospital, they want the almighty dollar to shave you and keep you from the students. No one can blame you for demanding the "Almighty Dollar" a day. The man who promises 90 cents a day and pays only 80 cents is no man at all. The labourer has his rights. . . . Now I won't ask you to cheer for prince, bishop, or any one, but for the canal laborers.

The "Loud Cheering" that followed this speech helped to prompt one contractor to overstate McKiernan's role in the dispute: "All of the trouble which we have had on the canal this winter has been caused mostly by men that have never worked a day on the canal," he claimed, adding that the conflict was "started in a low Brothel kept by one Joe Beef who seems to be at the head of it all." In the end Joe Beef's role was not an insignificant one, and in popularizing the grievances of the men and helping them to carry out their work stoppage, he contributed to the canallers' eventual victory.

McKiernan's strike support was but a part of a more wide-ranging commitment to that "liberty tree" with which he adorned his wife's grave in 1871. His libertarian stand often vented itself in satirical rage, directed especially at zealous pietists and temperance advocates. He was known to set his bears on those foolish or naive enough to enter his rooms. By the late 1870s, such forces of morality and social order were on the ascent, and Joe Beef's Canteen began to face competition from the YMCA recently established in the waterfront area. When a regular customer died of overconsumption of drink in 1879, the public attack on McKiernan was stepped up and the next years saw the erosion of Joe Beef's reputation as a patron of the poor. As workers gravitated toward more explicit forms of class action, centred in the rising Knights of Labor or the challenge of workingmen's politics, tavern life at Joe Beef's became less and less associated with the class positions, defences, and stands taken in the 1870s. The atmosphere of the Canteen, according to one 1887 report, was no longer one of jocular conviviality but of sombre, dull, and vacant silence, expressive not of the old combativity but rather of resignation.

Charles McKiernan must have found this changed context of the 1880s difficult to adjust to, and his displacement from the centre of the rough waterfront world no doubt proved a hard and bitter pill to swallow. He died on January 15, 1889. "Always the poor man's friend," McKiernan's body was accompanied to its grave by representatives of fifty Montreal labour societies. Not all mourned his passing, however, and one virtuous bour-geois editor scoffed at the accomplishments of Joe Beef's "talented proprie-tor," who had operated a "resort of the most degraded of men . . . actively at work . . . for the brutalization of youth." An advocate of Christian phi-lanthropy, this editor's uncharitable caricature revealed the limitations of a reformism that could not comprehend the labouring poor any more than it could appease them. Joe Beef's, the product of an age of transition in which class perspectives were coalescing, attempted to provide something else for the unemployed, the casual labourer, the tramp. While perhaps an atypical tavern, Joe Beef's Canteen bridged the gulf separating rough and respect-able, all the while refusing concession to the hypocrisies of the consolidat-ing bourgeois ethos. A pioneer who linked the physical, social, and cultural needs of the poor with a system of social welfare that could be perceived as self-generated, McKiernan's place in working-class experience was about to be taken over by other pioneers.

THE NINE-HOUR PIONEERS

In the 1860s the industrial-capitalist Anglo-American world was rocked by struggles to shorten the length of the working day. Originating with the London building trades in 1859, the demand for the nine-hour day captured the sympathies of engineers in Newcastle, England, and led to agitation in the United States from 1866 into the early 1870s for the eight-hour day. George McNeill, a prominent American labour reformer, recalled this movement in the 1890s and explained: "Men who are compelled to sell their labour, very naturally desire to sell the smallest portion of their time for the largest possible price. They are merchants of their time. It is their only available capital."

In Canada the working-class effort to secure shorter hours occurred during the first six months of 1872, coming in the wake of the commercial prosperity and post-Confederation exuberance of the early 1870s. Treat-ment of the Canadian nine-hour movement has generally focused on the struggle of the Toronto printers, an episodic clash involving mass mobiliza-tion of working-class elements, fierce employer resistance led by George Brown of the *Globe*, and the attempt to legally prosecute the twenty-four-member Typographical Union's Vigilance Committee. But as John Battye has noted, the Toronto printers' strike of March 25, 1872, was, in essence, a breach of a much more significant labour effort, a movement that stretched across central Canada in an effort to secure fundamental social reform and a shift in the nature of productive relations. As a defiant refusal to subordinate particularistic craft interests to a co-ordinated orchestration of the struggle, the printers of Toronto, lacking an organized nine-hour league, fought valiantly but in isolation. Their unwillingness to make common cause with Canadian labour as a whole prefaced the future disintegration of the movement. But this is to anticipate, for in the spring months of 1872 the nine-hour day became the major issue in a series of labour-capital conflicts that erupted across central Canada.

As an organized movement, the nine-hour agitation of 1872, like the labour insurrection almost two decades before, originated in Hamilton. Dan Black's Tavern and the Mechanics' Institute were the sites of early meetings of blacksmiths, machinists, and carpenters, and by late January, 1872, the Iron Molders International Union local had lent its support to the attempt to secure shorter hours. James Ryan, a Great Western Railway machinist described as "a Communist missionaree,/An immigrant, late from the Old Counteree,/Sent out by the great International band/To enlighten the darkness of this savage land," quickly emerged as the movement's spokesman, a man dedicated to establishing the nine-hour day throughout "the Dominion." Bringing together union and non-union men, Ryan helped to stimulate the formation of nine-hour leagues in central Canada, especially in Hamilton and Montreal, where large railway shops provided an organizational centre. In Toronto, the *Ontario Workman* emerged as the voice of labour's upheaval, a paper founded on the co-operative principles that many nine-hour advocates must have endorsed.

Throughout February, March, and April the movement initiated a series of meetings and minor confrontations in which newly arrived British craftsmen, likely affiliated with the Amalgamated Society of Engineers and the Amalgamated Society of Carpenters and Joiners, figured prominently. Ryan travelled to Montreal to address delegates from the 2,000-strong English-speaking league, led by James Black, and he proposed strike dates of May 15 in Hamilton and June 1 in Toronto. In return for financial support from the Montreal league, he argued that Montreal workingmen would undoubtedly secure the sought-after shorter work day, claiming that Montreal employers would succumb to their workers' demands "without driving you to resistance." Ryan had thus devised a workable plan, with the highly organized and militant workers of Hamilton materially supported by the larger industrial centres of Montreal and Toronto. He contended that a first strike would provide a show of strength and educate employers in the folly of opposition. But as Ryan told the Montreal delegates, the success of the venture rested on solidarity and support. "Resistance without funds," he said, "is useless." Thus, when Toronto printers refused to support Ryan's plan, launching a premature attack on George Brown and the other leading employers in the trade, they won their strike but abandoned the nine-hour pioneers in Hamilton.

The scheduled strike, billed as a celebration of labour's victory, nevertheless took place in Hamilton on May 15. A giant procession wound its way through city streets as 1,500 men marched four abreast. Wagons exhibited the mechanics' wares while banners proclaimed their beliefs, purposes, and sense of worth: "Wisdom is Better than Wealth"; "United we Stand, Divided we Fall"; "Art is Long, Life is Short"; "Nine Hours and No Surrender." As 3,000 onlookers cheered them on, the workers circled the city, one of their wagons bearing a monument inscribed, "Died 15th of May, 1872, the ten hour system." At a mass meeting and dance at the Palace Grounds, Ryan told the assembled throng that the eyes of the Dominion were upon them and promised that "it was beyond the power of any capitalist to put the movement down." However, the exhilaration of the moment was not enough to win these workers the reduction in hours of labour that they sought. Ryan's assessment of the inevitability of victory gave way to impassioned pleas to "hold on, all depends on Hamilton." The following days were ones of agonizing defeat.

By June, the striking Hamilton workers were back at their employment. Most returned without gaining the reduction in hours, and in those cases where the nine-hour day was won it represented only a minor concession to the highly skilled. Craftsmen in Toronto, Hamilton, and Galt were forced to flee the cities of their work to take up jobs in the United States. In Montreal, the movement was finally crushed in August, 1872. How had the pioneers of labour come to this end? An explanation of the failure of 1872 lies partly in the fact that the 1870s represented a transition in labour organization, one in which a certain ambivalence on the part of workers had not yet been overcome. While the nine-hour pioneers looked forward in their vision of solidarity, the localized, fragmented experience of working life remained a powerful barrier to success, as did the inhibitions of political paternalism. Out of a social formation promising capitalist development evolved a labour movement that could only promise collectivity. If it did not fulfil this promise, it nevertheless presaged labour's upsurge in the 1880s. So, too, however, did the state emerge from this moment of confrontation with its eyes on the future of class relations. Within the law, these years buried archaic and crudely coercive understandings of law as it related to trade unions, charting the faint beginnings of a regime of industrial legality within which working-class organization could be regulated and contained.

LAW AND LABOUR: ESTABLISHING LIMITS

John Hewitt, a leader of the Coopers' Union in Toronto and an activist in the nine-hour agitation, penned an editorial on trade unionism in the *Mail* in April, 1872. "Trade unions are a product of the age," he wrote. In "trying to trample Trades' Unionism out of existence here . . . they might as well try to stem Niagara." As Eric Tucker has argued, Hewitt was right. For various reasons trade unionism was beginning to be accepted as a consequence of industrial-capitalist development, albeit one that was irksome and more than a bit of a nuisance. It was apparent, however, that outlawing unions as illegal conspiracies and combinations was no longer an adequate response. It was still possible, as Gregory S. Kealey has shown in the case of Toronto, for employers to use the Master and Servant Act, and in years of heightened trade union militancy (1870-73) local employers resorted to this piece of legislation to charge many striking workers with disobedience and desertion. But this was an anachronistic Act, and the class relations it tried to keep alive were a thing of the past. So, too, were attempts to use conspiracy laws to stifle trade unionism. As Paul Craven has shown, again in the case of Toronto, they were invoked infrequently and commitments for trial in the absence of other charges were virtually non-existent.

What this suggests is that, in Tucker's terms, a legal zone of toleration with respect to trade unions was emerging out of recognition that they were a permanent and irreversible phenomenon associated directly with the new capitalist order. The task was therefore not to rely directly on eighteenth-century legal forms that turned on paternalistic pique, on the master's legal right to command unquestioning loyalty from each and every one of his workmen. Rather, the aim of the emerging legal regime was to recognize trade unions as the prerogative of labour, yet to ensure that, as legally recognized institutions, unions functioned within specific lawful boundaries.

This process unfolded first and most explicitly in the mines of Nova Scotia. Strikes in the Nova Scotia coal industry were hardly a novelty: the Albion mines in Pictou County were the site of a number of conflicts in the 1840s, and between 1864 and 1876 there were likely at least seven work stoppages in the Pictou and Cape Breton mines. The initial conflict in this later period took place at Sydney Mines. During a bitter 1864 battle the manager asked for state assistance in his efforts to evict striking miners from their company houses. With no statutory powers to act in such circumstances, the government displayed a remarkable capacity to get down to business; within a morning a bill was written and passed through all three required readings. Troops stood by in readiness for use against the miners before the legislation was actually brought into force. The new law, called the Combination of Workmen Act, set a tone for late nineteenth-century regulatory legislation. It did not prohibit worker combinations or associations nor did it strike blows against collective attempts to negotiate wages and other matters. But it did stipulate that the use of force, violence, or obstruction in these ends, against persons or property, was a criminal offence. The new Act justified the provincial militia's intervention in the strike and, according to commentators, "slammed the door against effective action on the part of workmen to achieve their goals or settle their disputes." As "force" was never defined, the law tended to be invoked whenever employers were concerned that striking workers might harm their business interests.

Other regulatory law was put into place throughout the 1870s, most of it aimed at stabilizing production by altering as little as possible an employer's relations with his workmen. Thus the 1873 Coal Mines Regulation Act set limits within which the inspector of mines and the owners/managers operated, but it did nothing to empower workers. Curbs were placed on the hiring of young boys and wages were not to be paid in public houses where alcohol was sold. The new regime of nascent industrial legality trod lightly on employers' toes. All things considered, the legal system created by politicians seemed content to contain class relations in ways that moved decisively against a rather nebulous, open-ended notion of worker "violence," while limiting employers in matters as much moral as economic. Power, consequently, was rather unevenly addressed.

The Nova Scotia Combination of Workmen Act may have provided Parliament with something of a model, for in 1869 it revised the criminal law to include a provision declaring it a misdemeanour to use violence or threat in conjunction with attempts to raise the rate of wages through unlawful conspiracy or combination. This still left the legality of unions somewhat unclear, but by this late date it was apparent that working-class organization was going to be difficult to stop. Judges and politicians were inclining to the view that unionism was an acceptable working-class response to the changing socio-economic terrain of Victorian Canada. Capital had its combinations and it was strong; labour should be allowed to have its own organizations, all the more so since it was publicly perceived to be weak. But there must be limits, beyond which workers could not go.

This was the way matters stood when George Brown, drawing on the legal opinion of Robert Harrison, decided to draw on the full ambiguity of the law to charge his printers with conspiracy to reduce the hours of labour in 1872. The typographers were also faced with nine additional charges relating to threats, intimidations, and other sorts of pressures. But the judge apparently saw little evidence of these criminal acts and committed the printers to trial only on the charge of conspiracy to reduce the hours of labour; it remained to be seen if this was, under law, an offence.

The case was not to be decided in the courts but in the legislature. Regulating trade unions, in 1872, was too important a task to leave to the contradictory and potentially ambiguous judgements of legal authority alone. With the master printers and George Brown demanding that their case against the union typographers be heard, John A. Macdonald chose to act, to secure some political capital and to resolve the issue of the law of unions once and for all. The day following the commitment of the strikers to trial, Macdonald announced that he would introduce bills in the House of Commons that would bring Canadian law in line with British law, thereby offering no discouragement to the immigration of much-needed skilled labour and winning Macdonald and the Tories a great deal of working-class support. With the passage of the Trade Unions Act, the Attorney-General understandably dropped the prosecution that had been proceeding against the Toronto printers.

The new law made it clear that no worker could be criminally prosecuted for conspiracy solely on the basis of attempting to influence the rate of wages, hours of labour, or other aspects of the work relation. For unions to be covered by the Act, they had to register, something that few did. The Macdonald bill did nothing to legalize the means by which trade unionists could achieve their ends, now clearly within the law. Indeed, an accompanying piece of legislation, the Criminal Law Amendment Act, spelled out clearly that a wide array of behaviour associated with trade disputes was now criminal. "Molesting," for instance, was defined as persistent following, hiding tools, and watching and besetting. The CLAA actually created new statutory crimes and reintroduced the matter of conspiracy inasmuch as two or more people acting in combination in ways that violated the Act could be prosecuted for criminal conspiracy. Workers wasted no time in calling for total repeal of "that obnoxious appendage to a measure in itself good, the Trade Unions Act." They were successful in securing some amendments but failed to have the CLAA repealed. In the end, the 1870s would see relatively few prosecutions of trade unionists under the CLAA. Symbolically, however, it was apparent that the law was a limited venue for trade union advance.

What is the meaning of all of this? On the one hand, the Trade Unions Act and accompanying legislation hardly justify regarding 1872 as a great victory for Canadian workers. Macdonald's rhetoric promoted such a view at the time, but his legislation was by no means a categorical defence of trade unionism. On the other hand, recent historical writing has tended in the direction of scholasticism, interpreting the letter of the law rather than how it connected with the realities of class relations. Desmond Morton thus describes the Trade Unions Act as a "dead letter," and Paul Craven concludes that "the legal position of trade unions was more or less the same after its passage as before."

There is a fair bit of class struggle in the spaces between more or less, and events of the magnitude of 1872 seldom get that easily reduced to dead letters. Tucker provides a more sensible assessment. The 1872 legislation legalized trade unionism, but it did so within limits and by defining them as potentially dangerous threats to community stability. There were many drawbacks to the hastily passed legislation, not the least of which was the class-specific language of the law, which would later be modified. But the point is a simple one. Trade unions were now held to be legal, if limited, bodies. Workers could, in the future, struggle to revise and overcome those limits, and they would. The law would not be on their side, but part of its guillotine-like edge, which had been hanging over them for decades, was now vanquished. Like the social formation within which it developed, law in the 1870s represented simultaneously a beginning for labour and an end to a part of its history.

THE 1870s: BEGINNINGS AND AN END

By the 1870s, it appeared that Canadian labour had left behind much of the narrow, trade-oriented provincialism of its past. Unionism was advancing and workers in specific crafts were enlisting in the common cause, not only in the nine-hour leagues of 1872 but also in trade associations and assemblies formed in Hamilton, Toronto, Montreal, Ottawa, and St. Catharines. Out of James Ryan's Canadian Labor and Mutual Improvement Protection Association (CLMIPA), formed May 3, 1872, in the midst of the shorter-hour campaign, would emerge a political voice for labour. It was created by workers from Hamilton, Toronto, Brantford, and Dundas (Montreal would affiliate later), received endorsement from Sarnia, London, Oshawa, Guelph, St. Catharines, and Ingersoll, and there was reason to believe that labour in Stratford, Brockville, Kingston, and Sherbrooke was also sympathetic. The CLMIPA proved the forerunner of the first so-called national central labour body, the Canadian Labor Union (CLU), organized in 1873.

Around this labour centre gravitated the emerging working-class leadership of the 1870s, a contingent of reform-minded skilled mechanics concerned with political representation, immigration, prison labour, the legal position of unions, apprenticeship, child labour, a mechanics' lien law, the hours of labour, the tariff, co-operation, and extension of the franchise. Exhilarated by the prospects of intervention in the political process, workingmen elected their first candidates to federal and provincial office in these years, sending Henry Buckingham Witton of Hamilton to the Dominion Parliament in 1872 and Ottawa's Daniel J. O'Donoghue to the Ontario legislature in 1874. With the *Ontario Workman* and Montreal's *Northern Journal* championing the cause of labour, workers now had access to a press of their own, an important advance over previous years, when labour newspapers had been established but never sustained for any length of time. Militancy, too, seemed to peak. Kealey notes that in the 1870-74 period Toronto workers fought twenty-seven strikes, more than had been recorded for that city in the entire period from 1800 to 1860.

These changes seem to indicate the beginning of labour's public presence as a class, with concerns, institutions, and politics reflective of the unique social position and economic needs of the working class. But while beginnings were made in the 1870s, the period was as much the end of the old order as it was the launching of a new one. The nine-hour movement had failed, and the early organization of the 1870s had foundered on some old inhibitions. Regionalism remained a potent limitation, especially evident in the central Canadian content of much of labour's unfolding dramas; Maritime and Francophone workers were tied loosely to the major events of the 1870s, while western labour's voice was barely audible. The worlds of skilled and unskilled remained distinct, and solidarity, even among craft workers, proved a fragile entity. In spite of the increasing importance of women workers, female labour was not even yet on the margins of working-class activism. Within politics, the sway of labour's paternalistic superiors won the first battle in the war between capital and labour. The working class entered the 1870s riding the crest of a wave of workplace militancy and political agitation, but by the end of the decade it was in a trough of economic recession, stifled militancy, and Tory hegemony.

In the aftermath of the nine-hour struggle there was a revival of the paternalistic mediation of workplace antagonisms. A part of this was imposed, none too benevolently, from above, with employers forcing workers to agree to "pledges" and "documents," eliciting promises to desist from agitation, or establishing shop rules that curtailed efforts to reduce the hours of labour. This was but one part of a collective response on the part of capital, a relentless opposition to the nine-hour leagues that must not be underestimated in the demise of the movement.

But labour itself seemed to slip rather easily back into the "cordiality" of respectable relations between master and man. J.N. Tarbox, manager of the Wanzer Sewing Machine Works in Hamilton, which was bitterly contested ground in the short history of the 1872 battle, was presented with a gift from the establishment's workers upon his retirement in September. Brief months after he had helped to quell the nine-hour rebellion, Tarbox was the recipient of a gracious tribute: "We also regret that near to the close of your stewardship there should have anything happened to mar the good feeling that always existed between master and man. That little incident is now passed, and we desire to remember your former kindness and the gentlemanly manner in which you have invariably treated your men." Wanzer's mechanics may well have regretted these words in the months to follow, as a new price list cut back wages 35-50 per cent on piece work, and militants were driven from the shop. As one dissident argued, "This was very like a new years gift for those men who in the largeness of their hearts went back upon the short time movement and accepted the gilded bait held out to them last summer." A "social revolution," imminent in April and May of 1872, had been reduced to a "little incident" by January, 1873. At root here was a willingness to abandon militancy and organization and rely on other forms of activity and non-working-class "support."

This process was perhaps most apparent in the political sphere, where Macdonald and the Tories successfully manipulated working-class voters.

Outrage at George Brown's efforts to silence Toronto's printers with conspiracy charges was easily translated into working-class opposition to Brown's party, the Grits, and the Tories were the obvious beneficiaries. They assured themselves of the workers' allegiance with passage of the Trade Unions Act in April, 1872. Tory H.B. Witton, riding this support to electoral victory in Hamilton, proved a sorry representative for Hamilton's nine-hour pioneers. Lady Dufferin captured his transformation in a terse line: "We had met him soon after his election, when he dined in a rough coat, but now he wears evening clothes." Witton failed in his effort to secure re-election in 1874, the Tories suffering through the Pacific Scandal; in the 1880s he would be remembered with contempt. "The first situation that was offered him he took," recalled one labour reformer with venom, "and went to Vienna on some government exhibition business."

In Toronto the post-1872 election months saw an even more unambiguous drift toward Tory hegemony, as the *Ontario Workman* was purchased by a triumvirate of Conservative workingmen secretly financed by John A. Macdonald. While the *Workman* remained a working-class organ, advocating a range of reforms and promoting the interests of labour, it avoided direct assault on Tory political rule, narrowing the nature of its social critique. Around this organ, the Toronto Trades Assembly (TTA) and the Canadian Labor Union (formed in 1873) consolidated what Gregory S. Kealey has appropriately dubbed a Toronto "junta" led by J.S. Williams and prominent nine-hour agitator John Hewitt. Committed Tories, the "junta" members dominated the developing central Canadian labour movement in the 1870s, lending it a thoroughly Conservative cast. When the CLU met in Toronto in September, 1873, twenty-six of the forty-five delegates were from Toronto, and the new labour centre became little more than an extension of the Toronto clique. Championing labour's cause in the political arena, this inner ring spoke from the rostrums of the TTA and the CLU and did much to consolidate labour's emerging electoral power, but it did so in a voice muffled by its acquiescence to the party of Macdonald.

Even among labourers far removed from the Tory influence in Hamilton and Toronto, the 1870s proved to be a decade during which potential labour power was restricted by the workers' inability to express themselves unambiguously as a class. Thus, the election of the supposedly "independent" worker candidate Daniel J. O'Donoghue in the Ontario election of 1874 was something less than a victory for autonomous working-class politics. The surprising election of O'Donoghue owed as much to religious and ethnic controversies in the deeply divided Ottawa constituency as to any clearly defined working-class agitation. Supported by Conservatives who saw the need to elect a Catholic in the dominantly Irish and French seat, O'Donoghue would champion independence but was nevertheless loosely allied with Mowat's Reform Grit government. Like Witton, he was a fairly subdued advocate of the working class. By 1875, seeking re-election, he declared himself "a Reformer . . . [and] repudiated the idea that he represented a class of citizens, but [promised to do] his utmost in the interests of all classes." Toronto's Alf Jury noted in 1877 that labour had only one man in the Ontario legislature, "and they had only half of him."

Workingmen might well have moved beyond these limitations to embrace a more definitive independence and class stance in the late 1870s, but just as they entered partisan politics an economic depression occurred. Unemployment, short time, and the voracious demands of deflationary capital for wage cuts put workers in a position where they had to fight for basic survival; other battles were postponed. Few were the unions that weathered this storm; fewer still the individual workers who emerged from it unscathed. Central Canadian workers looked to political representation as a means of remedying the problems of class conflict in a period of prosperity. However, politics held little in the way of solutions for labour in the context of depression. Essential institutions – labour centrals and unions – and rudimentary class perspectives had not yet been consolidated to the point that they could provide a foundation for greater militancy. The price exacted by the depression of the 1870s cannot yet be fully understood, for basic data (such as the extent of unemployment) are lacking. But it is known that labour suffered greatly and that employers used this economic downturn to attempt to destroy unionized adversaries.

Over 500 heads of families were supposedly unemployed in the nation's capital in 1879-80, in spite of indications of a business revival. Deputations of the jobless waited on the Prime Minister but obtained little in the way of relief. Admissions to the Toronto House of Industry soared in the years 1879-82, as over 2,000 applicants sought charity. In Montreal, the changing character of working-class protest followed a logic of escalating demand. December of 1875 saw a series of demonstrations in which labourers pleaded for work or bread. Originally peaceful, these actions drew more than 1,000 workmen and culminated in a confrontation with police and an attack on bakers' sleighs. The municipality eventually hired hundreds of destitute labourers to work on public roads for sixty cents a day, "just enough to keep a man and family from starving." One year later the Montreal unemployed were still seeking work, but no longer were their grievances couched in the language of polite request: they demanded "bread or blood."

In this period of catastrophic downturn, however, three developments guided labour out of the confusion of the 1870s. First, working-class political involvement toward the end of the decade remained dominated by Tory attachments, but the formation of Tory front groups such as the Workingmen's Liberal-Conservative Associations of Ottawa and Toronto unwittingly contributed to limited forms of independence for workers in politics. In the capital, a Workingmen's Association championed working-class aspirations regardless of party affiliation. Second, even among the trades most sympathetic to the non-working classes, the severity of the 1870s depression precipitated a stance of defiance, expressed in the assault of the Brotherhood of Locomotive Engineers on the Grand Trunk Railway in 1876-77. At Stratford, Belleville, and Brockville, labour's supporters attacked strikebreakers and helped the engineers to win a major victory. Third, and finally, as all labouring people confronted the spectre of unemployment, workers across trade and skill lines began to come together to protest. The growth of independence within labour politics, the involvement of the previously non-participating engineers, and the common confrontation with distress all mark the end of an epoch in which labour was subordinate. As well, these factors suggest the beginnings of a period in which working-class opposition could consolidate.

Chapter 3

THE CONSOLIDATION OF WORKING-CLASS OPPOSITION 1880-1895

THE SOCIAL FORMATION

During the 1880s competitive capitalism consolidated in much of Canada, building on past accomplishments and going beyond them. The rate of manufacturing output attained annual growth rates surpassing those of the 1870s, and these rates would not be exceeded until the boom years of monopoly capitalism in 1900-10 and 1926-29. Indeed, the growth of manufacturing facilities in many industries during the cresting fortunes of the National Policy (1880-84) is most striking. Between 1880 and 1890, for instance, the value of cotton cloth output rose by 125 per cent, but even this dramatic increase understated the gains of the decade's first five years: the number of mills, spindles, looms, and capital invested tripled in that half decade. Urban markets for the rising production of the late nineteenth century expanded considerably in the 1880s, with the percentage of the population living in cities growing significantly in the years 1870-1900.

Quebec's urban population swelled from 20 to 36 per cent in this period, while Ontario's actually doubled, rising from 20 to 40 per cent. Across Canada the figures climbed from 18 to 35 per cent. Much of this urban growth was concentrated in expansion of the industrial sector, as in Ontario where the number of employees in manufacturing rose from 87,000 to 166,000 between 1871 and 1891.

Railway mileage expanded as well, shooting up from 3,000 in 1873 to over 16,000 in 1896, but it was the construction of the transcontinental railway that epitomized the attainments of the new age. Facilitating the movement of goods and people, the Canadian Pacific Railway stimulated economic growth and expansion and contributed to a political consolidation that, for the first time in the country's history, tempered regional diversities with at least the promise of a common industrial-capitalist future. But that common "national" future was always skewed by central Canadian dominance and regional subordination to the interests of powerful forces in the Toronto-Ottawa-Montreal axis.

The history of the Canadian West in these years exposes this dualism of development and dependency. On the one hand, the National Policy hardly integrated the West in ways that contributed to a vibrant diversified economy and autonomous development. The state's much-publicized immigration policy managed to bring only 1.5 million people to the country during the more than thirty years separating Confederation and the end of the century, hardly enough to populate the expanse of the Prairies. By contrast, almost 5.5 million emigrated to the United States in the 1880s alone. Railways, praised loudly as a boon to western development, managed to practise what was called "fair discrimination" in ways that, ironically, benefited the rich and populous industrial-capitalist heartland at the expense of western producers. It cost twice as much to ship wheat 200 miles on the Prairies as it did in Ontario. And staples such as wheat were what the region was to be producing. This, which could be multiplied by countless other examples of western grievance, was the downside: a limited economy held back by its relationship to a central Canadian political economy.

There was, however, another aspect of western development in these years. Winnipeg was indicative of this. As railway mania swept through this entry point to the West the city imploded in speculative frenzy. The bubble lasted only a few years and was bound to burst, as it did in the early to mid-1880s. Nevertheless, a metropolitan centre had emerged: growing rapidly to 20,000, Winnipeg developed in the 1880s as a city of discernible class differentiation, its industrial character accentuated by the influential presence of the CPR railway yards and shops that would figure prominently in the future growth of the labour movement. Even further to the west, the CPR secured access to a mineral empire, establishing the Consolidated Mining and Smelting Company as one of its many subsidiaries. Hundreds of thousands of acres changed hands, Vancouver sprung up as a mercantile centre of 5,000, and mining ventures proliferated. Government was little more than the guardian of all of this, its aim being described by one newspaper as to provide the kind of stability that would stifle the "forces of disorder." One such force was to be the rise of radical labour.

Economic expansion was most pervasive in the metropolitan centres of the industrial-capitalist heartland. In Toronto the protective tariff of the National Policy helped to stimulate the local economy, and between 1878 and 1884 thirty-six new major factories came into being. The number of hands employed in large work settings more than doubled, while capital invested and the value of the annual product soared accordingly. Between 1881 and 1891 the total number of productive establishments in Toronto more than tripled, the number of workers doubled, the capital invested increased roughly 265 per cent, the annual product, 220 per cent, and the value added, 215 per cent. This diversified expansion was accompanied by increasing concentration and specialization of particular productive sectors, and Toronto established itself as a leading centre of printing and publishing, chemical and secondary wood production, and the clothing industry. Canada's other leading industrial centre, Montreal-Hochelaga, also experienced considerable expansion in the 1880s, climbing into a position of dominance in the food and beverage industry (almost 40 per cent of the total production in this sector was located in Montreal-Hochelaga) and in the production of transportation equipment (again, almost 40 per cent of the national output, with thousands of workers).

In the Maritimes, industrial expansion was also quite dramatic. Nova Scotia's output increased 66 per cent over the course of the 1880s, outstripping Ontario and Quebec, which had 51 per cent increases. Wholesale shippers, lumber and ship manufacturers, and petty producers attempted to adapt the old staple economy to the new imperatives of the National Policy, basing their optimistic vision of the future on iron and steel, fuelled by the region's coal reserves, and on textiles. While regional interests would be thwarted by the 1890s, Maritime capital experienced its years of boom in the 1880s: coal production, centred in Pictou and Cape Breton, doubled between 1880 and 1890, with over 2 million tons mined. The relative increase in industrial capital, average wages, and output in Saint John surpassed that of Hamilton; ventures like the St. Croix Cotton Manufacturing Company drew on American and Canadian capital to turn once-peaceful villages into "hives of industry." Out of the foundries of Amherst, the rolling mills of New Glasgow, and the sugar refineries of Halifax flowed the products of competitive capital's brief decade of expansion.

As T.W. Acheson has shown, this expanding manufacturing sector was led by a few hundred entrepreneurs, predominantly manufacturers of immigrant origin (first- or second-generation Canadians). Concentrated in the central Canada of the lower Great Lakes and the St. Lawrence Valley, the members of this rising class of capitalists were, in Acheson's words, "the proletarians of the business community," men of small means who had captured a large share of local markets and moved into wider prominence. Competitive, grasping at each opportunity to secure an advantageous market position, these new men of industrial might were often rooted in the small community (over 50 per cent of the manufacturing of Ontario in the 1880s took place in communities where populations never exceeded 10,000). They rose to power and authority out of the depression of the 1870s and the buoyancy of the early years of tariff protection; their collective histories intersect with times of deflation, which, according to one economist, saw the ratio of commodity prices plummet by roughly 25 per cent from 1873 to 1886.

We know little about the social impact of this secular decline of prices in Canada, but if the experience of the United States is at all representative, it might well be speculated that although real wages no doubt rose, employers responded to deflation with increased application of technology, intensification of labour, and, most importantly, wage cuts. The latter would have been most prominent in the troughs that a number of economic historians have located around the years 1879-80, 1885, and 1888, for the wage cut was the most useful mechanism by which competitive capitalists could recapture some of the losses resulting from deflation. Engaged in an anarchic, individualistic, and ruthless quest for the spoils of production, the first true generation of Canadian capitalists soon learned that the way to secure advantage over business rivals was to heighten the extraction of surplus from labour by cutting wages, thus allowing larger amounts of capital to be sunk back into production.

This brief sketch of the economic situation in the 1880s gives a partial indication of why, for the first time in Canadian history, a mass movement of working-class resistance developed. It was present not only in the urban centres of central Canada but also in the small towns. As well, labour resistance sank some roots in the Far West and on the east coast. This organizational upsurge of labour did, of course, develop differently in different contexts, but it also shared many common features. It had critically important social, cultural, and political consequences and to some extent checked consolidated capitalism's unrestrained attempts to bring production under its own control.

The 1880s were a decade of unprecedented working-class militancy, centred in the emergence of an organization called the Noble and Holy Order of the Knights of Labor, a body different from the trade unions inasmuch as it sought to bring all workers into one grand organization. The strength of the Knights of Labor may have helped to create a situation in which the working class kept wage rates at least partially intact – inhibiting capital's assault, resisting employer efforts to implement reductions, or lessening the severity of such wage cuts. If this was the case, then the Knights would have played an important role in depressing the rate of profit and curbing the process of capital accumulation; the social cost of labour would have been relatively high, compared to the Laurier boom years of the twentieth century, and the process of appropriation curtailed. Finally, breaking the back of this intransigent labour movement would have been a political, social, and economic imperative for an industrial capitalism moving away from the stage of anarchic competition toward monopoly. The Knights of Labor, in conjunction with the craft unions and other labour bodies, may thus have helped to rally the individualistic and once-divided capitalists that Michael Bliss has depicted as in quest of "a living profit" to employer combines that led out of the nineteenth-century context of competitive entrepreneurship and into the age of monopoly. And, in Canada, where the state always had a hand in economic endeavours, labour resistance may have helped to consolidate a particularly political form of capitalism, in which intervention in "labour relations" was to be especially acute in the years 1900-20. In this sense, the moment of oppositional self-affirmation of the working class and the structural development of the political economy were part of a complex relationship that will be examined in more detail in the closing section of this chapter. Now let us turn to the working-class experience itself, looking at the varied dimensions of labour activism.

KNIGHTS AND WORKMEN

The most vibrant institutional development in the history of nineteenth-century North American workers began in Philadelphia in 1869 when a small group of garment workers came together under the leadership of Uriah Stephens. They created a secret society, bound by oaths, elaborate ritual, and a commitment to the unity of all workers. More than a trade union, the resulting body, which they dubbed the Noble and Holy Order of the Knights of Labor, combined aspects of a religious brotherhood, a political reform society, a fraternal order, and a pure and simple unionism. Expanding into Pennsylvania coal mines, Pittsburgh shops, and New York factories, the Noble and Holy Order grew slowly in the 1870s, and Stephens was succeeded by Terence V. Powderly, uncharitably described by one historian as a vain and disingenuous rabble-rouser. But under Powderly the Order threw off the cloak of secrecy and, in the 1880s, captured the support of the American working man and woman as had no other labour reform organization.

The Knights drew workers into their ranks through a relatively simple procedure and institutional apparatus. Individual members joined local assemblies, either in mixed assemblies (according to diverse occupational affiliations) or trade assemblies (adhering more rigidly to specific craft categories). For a local assembly to be formally organized, a minimum of ten members was required. Once established, LAs were known to swell in membership to over 1,000. Initiation fees were set by the local, but the minimum fee was one dollar for men and fifty cents for women. Local dues, again, were controlled by individual assemblies, but they were to be not less than ten cents per month. Members were also expected to contribute to the co-operative fund, men paying ten cents monthly, women less. If a specific geographical region or trade contained five or more assemblies, a district assembly could be formed. The Order, then, was a highly centralized body, with a well-defined hierarchy and structure; yet it was also relatively egalitarian, and the local assemblies had a large measure of autonomy, with their own courts to prosecute those who transgressed the disciplines and regulations of knighthood.

Although strongest in the rapidly expanding industrial cities of Ontario such as Toronto and Hamilton, the Knights also penetrated the province's towns, villages, and tiny hamlets. Throughout the 1880s and into its declining years that stretched out to 1907, Ontario's Knights of Labor organized locals in eighty-three towns from Amherstburg in the west to Cornwall in the east, from Port Colborne in the south to Sudbury in the north. A total of 252 locals formed ten district assemblies. The province's five largest cities contained almost half of all local assemblies, but if a town had a minimum population of 3,000 or was anything of a railway centre it was almost certain to have Knights organized within it. Trade assemblies dominated in the large industrial cities where all occupations had sufficient strength to organize LAs; mixed assemblies were much more popular in smaller towns and villages where few crafts and diverse labouring sectors had the sheer numbers to stand on their own.

How many workers were drawn into the Order? This is difficult to determine. Membership peaked at different moments in different regions, and the bookkeeping of the Knights was never all that precise. Across south-central Ontario, membership in the Knights of Labor climbed to its highest point in 1886 and then declined, rapidly in some areas, more slowly in others. Towns near the American border (Brockville and Hamilton, for instance) seemed to experience the Order's impact earliest. But in north-western Ontario and in the timber country of the Muskoka region the prominence of the Knights came later, as it did in some eastern Ontario towns such as Kingston, where the Knights were said to have 1,500 supporters in 1887. In Ottawa, the Order's successes came, not in the 1880s, but in 1891. This conflicting pattern of growth is further complicated by the fact that even *within* industrial cities like Toronto and Hamilton, which followed the classic pattern of cresting in 1886, there were some working-class groups – letter carriers, longshoremen, and unskilled labourers – that joined the Knights even after the organization was in obvious retreat.

A count of peak membership at any static point in time is thus a poor measure of the Order's capacity to draw workers into its halls. Adding up peak memberships across Ontario, for specific points in time, reveals that the Knights organized a minimum of 21,800 workers. A figure double, perhaps triple, this tally is likely a more accurate reflection of the number of workers that passed through the Order. Considering the expansion of the trade unions at the same time, it is apparent that organized labour as a percentage of the Ontario work force was reaching significant levels for the first time in the nineteenth century. In large industrial cities, manufacturing towns, and railway centres, it is entirely possible that the Knights drew 20-40 per cent of all employed workers, and in some locales the figure may well have been much higher.

In Quebec the organizational centre of the movement was in Montreal, where sixty-four local assemblies were formed between 1882 and 1902. Unlike the case in Ontario's metropolitan centres, Montreal's upsurge of the Knights continued throughout the 1890s, with a period of significant expansion in 1893-94. Approximately 2,500 workers were enrolled in Montreal's Order in 1887, and local assemblies in 1886 averaged almost 200 members. A secondary district was that of Quebec City, where at least a dozen LAs were formed. Across the province of Quebec a total of 100 or more assemblies existed, bringing French- and English-speaking workers into the same body and providing the first working-class organization for many *canadiens* in smaller towns.

To the west, the Knights of Labor quickly established themselves in the expanding railway towns and industrial enclaves of the prairie provinces. Telegraph operatives, railway workers, tailors, and carpenters led the way in Winnipeg, where as many as six local assemblies were probably established by 1887. Organization drifted west with migrant workers, and in Calgary an assembly was set up by itinerants from Owen Sound and Winnipeg. But in British Columbia, where the industrial frontier was starkest in the railway camps and mining towns, the Knights of Labor found their most receptive western Canadian audience.

Vancouver Island-based miners battled Robert Dunsmuir's coal empire throughout the 1870s, facing a stern Scot who tolerated no unionist assault on his arrogant and uncompromising rule. Politically and economically omnipotent, Dunsmuir drove his workers to clandestine organization, and they created a Miners' Mutual Protective Association that surfaced in periodic clashes between capital and labour in the years 1877-83. Class conflict in the Vancouver Island mines was always confused by the issue of race and the consciously constructed notions of "white work" versus "Oriental labour." Chinese workers had, since the 1860s, been employed in the mines, where they were relegated to the lowliest labouring job, hauling coal, often on the surface. White workers, in contrast, worked the seams underground and cultivated a sense of themselves as skilled and privileged miners. When the Chinese tried to better their lot through collective action and even early strike activity, they received little support from their white co-workers. As mine managers concentrated on increasing production, some white miners were convinced to allow the Chinese underground with them, where they could be used to do the rough work required if white miners were to up their output. The result was something of a class bargain between white labour and white capital, in which the Chinese were virtually used as beasts of burden while the miners increased their pay packets, being paid by the ton mined, and the owners saw productivity soar.

"White" and "yellow" work was thus rigidly separated, the working class irrevocably divided. As class conflict erupted in the mines in the later 1870s, the Chinese, now underground and having for years observed their white counterparts, were a ready force of strikebreakers. Popular white working-class mythology held that they had been brought into the mines as blacklegs. The truth was somewhat different, but no less destructive of working-class solidarity: white capital and white labour had, in alliance, forced the Chinese workers into a context in which their only recourse was to scab on those who had scabbed on them.

This was the unfortunate background to the labour struggles of the 1880s in British Columbia, in which the Knights of Labor would figure centrally. As Dunsmuir exploited white racism and Chinese need, bringing in more and more Orientals in the face of work stoppages, miners and other white workers formed the Workmen's Protective Association in 1878 to combat "the great influx of Chinese." Building on such precedents, the Knights of Labor entered British Columbia in 1883, establishing six local assemblies in Vancouver, two in Wellington, and one each in Nanaimo, New Westminster, Victoria, Yale, Kamloops, and Rossland. These LAs gained prominence in the mid-1880s and rallied the west coast's white working class in opposition to the Chinese, recently thrust even more prominently into the labour market with the termination of their exploitation on the construction gangs of the Canadian Pacific Railway. In Victoria, the Knights of Labor upheaval coincided with the emergence of John Duval's *Industrial News* and the rise of the Anti-Chinese Union.

The Knights of Labor history on the west coast is thus interwoven with a racist working-class attack on Oriental workers. This attack was sustained as the Knights of Labor constructed an image of the Chinese worker as "the Other," that which was the very opposition of the "manly" mechanic. In a Knights of Labor statement to an 1885 Royal Commission, Oriental labour was denounced as "low, degraded, and servile." Being "without family ties," this sub-species of workers was not only able to work for wages far below those demanded by white labour but to "grow rich" on this inferior pay. Products of "humble submission to a most oppressive system of government," the Chinese were, in the eyes of the Knights of Labor, "willing tools whereby grasping and tyrannical employers grind down all labor to the lowest living point."

The conjuncture of working-class upheaval and organization associated with west coast Knights of Labor and the explosion of an intense anti-Oriental working-class agitation skewed the content of class conflict in British Columbia (and elsewhere) in the 1880s. But the exclusion of the Chinese, however nefarious as a plank in labour's program, was far from the only cause promoted by the Order. Shorter hours, antagonism to monopoly, condemnation of political corruption, organization of workers, and resistance at the workplace were also all critically important, if understudied, aspects of the Knights of Labor presence on the west coast.

On the east coast, the Knights of Labor also secured a foothold, albeit a weak one. Local assemblies existed in Moncton, Saint John, Halifax, Amherst, North Sydney, New Glasgow, Campbellton, and Truro, although they never extended into the working class in any significant way, being almost entirely restricted to the telegraph operatives whose defeat in a momentous 1883 international conflict seemed to seal the fate of the Order in the Maritime provinces. A number of LAs arrived in the late 1890s among the coal miners of Cape Breton, organized in District Assembly 35 at Glace Bay, but this minor organizational growth was but a pale reflection of the east coast's more entrenched and previously established regional labour movement, based on a body that opposed the Knights of Labor at the same time as it seemed strikingly similar.

As workers in central Canada flocked to the Knights of Labor in the 1880s, east coast labourers in the mines, on the docks, and in the shops cast their lot with Robert Drummond's Provincial Workmen's Association (PWA). Originally formed in the woods adjacent to the Springhill Mining Company, the PWA established its pioneer lodge in late August, 1879, and first bore the name of the Provincial Miners' Association (PMA). But like the Noble and Holy Order of the Knights of Labor (also formed by workers of a particular occupation), it soon tried to extend its organizational focus as well as its name, and took as its slogan the words, "Strength lies in unity."

Never as successful as the Knights in broadening its appeal beyond a specific group of workers, the PMA was led by the miners of Springhill, Stellarton, Westville, and Thorburn. It organized loaders, check weightmen, trappers, labourers, and miners in the mainland coal fields of Nova Scotia, and by October, 1879, enrolled almost 650 in its ranks. Wharfmen at Granton, engaged in loading coal on the ships, formed a lodge soon afterward, and following the October, 1880, meeting of the organization in Truro the five-lodge body changed its name to the Provincial Workmen's Association. Drummond was encouraged to bring the Cape Breton miners, previously unorganized, into the cause. Nine lodges were soon established, and the PWA claimed a membership of 1,200 in Cape Breton (probably an exaggeration since there were only 1,725 miners on the island, and they did not attain closed-shop status during this period). Glass and foundry workers in New Glasgow and Pictou County also joined, and throughout the 1880s the PWA expanded; in 1884 it had 1,860 members in good standing. In

Amherst, boot and shoe workers once associated with the Knights of Labor
LA 2209) founded Concord Lodge of the PWA in 1891 after their employer
fired a number of the Order's activists.

By 1897 the PWA claimed to be "the strongest single labour organization
in Canada," but it was already on the verge of an internal crisis as Robert
Drummond followed an increasingly conciliatory policy of refusing to
oppose the "pluck-me" stores of the Dominion Coal Company in return for
the company's willingness to collect union dues regularly. This collaboration angered Drummond's members, who gravitated to the more militant
tactics of the Knights of Labor in the years after 1898. By 1899, the number
of PWA lodges had declined from sixteen to three, and membership dropped
to 1,000. Surviving into the twentieth century (and outlasting the Knights),
the PWA, abandoned by Drummond, would continue to follow a moderate
stance in its dealings with employers and would be used later as a force to
keep the United Mine Workers of America (UMWA) out of the region's coal
fields. Its powerlessness apparent by 1904, the Provincial Workmen's Association eventually succumbed to the larger international union; the body
dissolved in 1917.

Where the Knights of Labor failed, the UMWA would succeed, and in
1918, 98 per cent of the PWA's former membership voted to affiliate with
District 26 of the international union. Ultimately liquidated by its own rank
and file, the early PWA was nevertheless, as Sharon Reilly has argued, and as
an 1886 statement claimed, "a response to the wishes of men who had been
subjected to indignities, who had suffered loss, who were well trodden
down, and yet who had in them a sturdy spirit of independence." Like the
Knights of Labor (which it resembled in its attachment to ritual and fraternity, as well as its message of solidarity), the PWA was an initial announcement of the consolidation of working-class opposition in the 1880s.

The form of that opposition was obviously different in the Maritimes
than it was in central Canada, as Ian McKay has recently suggested. The
PWA shared a good deal with the Knights of Labor, but it also evolved in
ways that reflected the contrasting material experiences of workers in Canada's regions. In Ontario the Knights of Labor reached into virtually every
community and drew on a continental labour-reform vision; the Provincial
Workmen's Association was a more limited body. Yet in its limitations lay a
good part of its potency: militant lodges, few in number but powerful in
their influence and impact, had a greater longevity than the more volatile
local assemblies of the Knights; ethnic and occupational homogeneity
secured the PWA in the world of the Scottish collier in ways that were
unlikely if not impossible in the more economically diversified and culturally heterogeneous industrial heartland of Ontario's Noble and Holy Order;
and Drummond's orchestration of a political alliance with the Nova Scotia
Liberal Party, rooted in the vital importance of coal mining to the region's
political economy, allowed labour a legislative impact that may well have

been greater than anywhere else in Canada. All of this rested on the PWA's commitment to working-class independence. This was never an easy end to achieve, but it was at the heart of the coal miner's conception of himself, was negotiated with employers in complex ways that played on the coal community's paternalist ethos, and was regularly fought out in strikes. As McKay notes, the Provincial Workmen's Association was "the critical force of dissent in the Maritimes," its seventy-two strikes in the 1879-1900 years being the "major nineteenth-century response in the region to the coming of industrial capitalism."

Knights and Workmen, then, dramatically expanded the institutions of the workers' movement in the 1880s, providing the organizational focus of a labour upsurge. Different but similar, these oppositional movements mark a new stage in the development of workers within Canada's regions. The preceding discussion has provided a cursory introduction to this process, a brief listing of some achievements. Workers in the 1880s attained their greatest accomplishments as the ambiguous, fractured, and unfocused raw material of working-class life was moulded into a movement culture of opposition and alternative, a process of working-class self-activity that took the collectivist impulses of labouring experience and shaped them into a reform mobilization.

A MOVEMENT CULTURE

This movement culture was most visible in the Ontario experience of the Knights of Labor, where ritual and procession, symbolism and soirée, combined to proclaim the unity of all labour, an undertaking of opposition and challenge that distinguished the 1880s from previous decades of labouring people's experience. The Order's effectiveness stemmed from its ability to build on the mundane class distinctions of daily life and to construct out of this a movement that attempted to unite all workers to oppose the oppression and exploitation that they lived through both on and off the job. On the one hand, the Knights of Labor developed out of a social, cultural, political, and economic context in which class differentiation had been developing over decades; on the other, they pushed all of this forward, posing alternatives, striking a posture of opposition. Much of this also happened in other regions and among workers unaffiliated with the Noble and Holy Order, particularly among the militant and large colliers' lodges of the Provincial Workmen's Association. But the Knights of Labor present perhaps the clearest expression of this process, providing insight into how the closing decades of the nineteenth century elevated the "labour question" to a previously unanticipated importance.

The men and women of the new movement entered their local assembly halls with deeply held convictions. In the symbolism and richly suggestive ritual of the Order, both the strengths of the past and the purposes of the present were revealed, introducing us, as well, to the class values upon which the Knights constructed their alternative vision and the movement culture that sought to transform the very nature of Victorian Canada.

Indeed, each Knight of Labor entered the Order through a ritualistic procedure that cemented him or her in specific traditions, pledging eternal secrecy, strict obedience, and scrupulous charity toward new brothers and sisters. Every initiate vowed to defend the interest and reputation of all true members of the Knights of Labor – employed or unemployed, fortunate or distressed – and was instructed that "to rescue the toiler from the grasp of the selfish is a work worthy of the noblest and best of our race." The Order endeavoured to "secure the just rewards" of honest work and to prevent the trampling of "poor humanity in the dust." Secret signs, oaths, passwords, and grips further consolidated the attachment to collective principles and protected labouring people from the hostility of anti-Knights of Labor employers. Reverberating throughout this ritualistic and symbolic content of the Knights of Labor was the centrality of class pride, the awareness of the worth of the working man and woman. This, above all else, drew adherents to the cause.

Festivals, dinners, and workers' balls gave cultural force to this developing opposition, "cementing together the bonds of unity," as one early labour newspaper reported in 1873. Picnics and dinners came to assume an importance beyond mere recreation, uniting workers and making them more "competent to fight the Monster (Capital)." Across central Canada in the 1880s – in Hamilton, Toronto, London, Montreal, Oshawa, Gananoque, Belleville, and Ingersoll – workers affiliated with the Knights of Labor mounted huge labour parades and demonstrations drawing thousands to the public proclamation of labour reform. French and English came together in a series of labour demonstrations, picnics, and excursions in Montreal that took place during the 1880s and culminated in a grand Labour Day parade held in September, 1891. Such events, like the earlier trade processions in Saint John, were visible reminders of labour's strength. But unlike the community-based events of 1840 and 1853 in Saint John, the parades of the 1880s linked towns and cities. If the district assemblies of Toronto and Montreal drew 10,000 or more to their gala events, no less impressive were the thousands the Order could attract to manufacturing hamlets like Ingersoll and Gananoque.

Challenged by such public displays of worker unity, segments of the dominant culture were driven to adapt to the new realities of industrial-capitalist society and its class polarization. There is evidence that in some communities established religion suffered setbacks and that the Knights of Labor usurped the traditional role of the church. Montreal labour activist William Darlington claimed: "The Knights preach more Christianity than the churches." Church sources bemoaned "the gradual falling away of those whom the respectability of the middle classes does not see and the dignity of the rich . . . ignores," and were distressed by the "lapsed masses." Historians have long recognized the class tensions inherent in church-labour movement relations, and from the pulpit came many hostile commentaries on strikes and working-class activism. The labour leadership gave as good as it got. A Hamilton leader, using the pen name "Vox Populi," expressed what must have been a widespread critique in labour circles of city pastors and their houses of worship: "You love Jesus Christ, you love to preach about him and do his will, I too with my Br. Knights love his doctrine, and strive to carry out his will, also to obey his command, love one another . . . it is not Christ I find fault with, but the inconsistent doctrines taught in or favored by the church."

Among some sectors of established religion – Methodists and Presbyterians, especially – these words found a hearing, and there were condemnations of "selfish capitalists" and admissions that "upon our land lies a dark reproach. By those in high places the poor are repressed." One Kingston minister proclaimed that "Labor was squeezed and enslaved by monopolies . . . because of this enslavement production was slackened just as land was schackled also, the same effect was produced." Religion, then, was often confronted by labour's upsurge. If it could bare its teeth in class hostility and condemnation of worker activism, it was also on occasion forced to adopt a stance and a language of recognition if not appeasement. Few workers lost totally their conceptions of Christian behaviour, but many reconstructed their religious views in ways that attended more directly to class grievance and need. The movement culture had not so much defeated religious institutions, but Christian practice – both in its organizational sense and in terms of its working-class constituency – might be modified in the face of it.

As Doris O'Dell shows in a unique study of the class character of church participation in Belleville, there were all kinds of ways in which class distinctions, supposedly absent in religious life, were reinforced within congregations. Seating arrangements, uneven financial contributions, styles of worship, differences between evening and morning services, and contrasts between neighbourhood churches of the same denomination all reflected the presence of class within religious life. O'Dell establishes that workers involved themselves in this life at the same time as they filtered its messages and forms through their own class-informed conceptions of the world.

The extent to which enthusiastic religious movements alternative to the established churches, such as the Salvation Army, might attract working-class men and women also reinforces the point that class was, by the 1880s, an unmistakable factor within the spiritual milieu of Victorian Canada. The raucous services of the Sally Ann, its rowdy parades, all-night meetings, and circus-like performers appealed to the unskilled and working-class women who, for a time in the 1880s, flocked to the Hallelujah Army. Lynne Marks has provided an invaluable look at the class content of Salvation Army experience in small-town Ontario of the 1880s, tantalizingly suggesting that the experiences of the Knights of Labor and the Sally Ann overlapped. There is little proof of this since comparable membership lists are simply not available, but a sensitive and sympathetic reading of Marks's excellent research suggests the potency of class identifications in the 1880s as well as the extent to which the Knights of Labor employed religious rhetoric and evangelical language to convey its message and draw workers to its ranks. The Salvation Army was often strong in precisely those communities where the Knights of Labor set up local assemblies, and Marks hints at connections between the working-class soldiers of the Army and the workplace presence of the Knights, noting that Kingston labourers held noon-day prayer meetings in the midst of an 1883 Salvation Army campaign and then, four years later, joined the Knights of Labor and went out on strike. In the same year, there is evidence that Belleville's iron worker Knights attended Salvation Army meetings.

So much was clearly in turmoil in the 1880s and class identification was central to what must have been a turbulent period in the formation of working-class identities. One reading of Marks's exploration of the Salvation Army is that it galvanized class-based religiosity at the very point that mainstream churches were occasionally failing to address adequately working-class realities. This process may have actually pre-dated the mass upsurge of the Knights of Labor, helping to condition a climate in which workers would be drawn to the Order in later years. Many interpretive questions remain, but Marks's detailed examination of the working-class content of the Salvation Army in the 1880s reminds us of the importance of religion within class formation. Like O'Dell, she is suggesting strongly that attempts to see religious experience as only a denial or suppression of working-class needs and aspirations are misplaced. Obviously, the conjuncture of class and religion in the 1880s had many sides, and the experience is not easily collapsed into specific interpretive containers, one receptive to class, the other antagonistic.

Even in Catholic-dominated Quebec, where Church opposition to the Knights of Labor in particular and labour militancy in general probably exceeded that found elsewhere, circular letters from Archbishop Taschereau (February 2, 1885) and all bishops (June 20, 1886) prohibiting membership in this "cosmopolitant" "occult-led" secret society failed to drive the Order from the province. Although the membership did indeed decline after this antagonistic intervention, the Vatican overrode Taschereau, and Richard J. Kerrigan, a Montreal workers' advocate, recalled the "dynamic year of 1886" as one in which the Knights defended themselves against the Archbishop's attack:

The Knights of Labor grew to alarming proportions in the country, and the Province of Quebec, always the political storm centre of Canada, had to get drastic treatment if it were to be kept safe and sane for law and order. Bishop Taschereau of Quebec launched his famous excommunication decree against the Knights of Labor.... This did not hurt the Knights much.... This high-handed action of this over-officious servant of God had the effect of driving the bulk of the intelligent French-speaking proletariat away from the "faith of their fathers" and when the edict was spoken of among the French militant Knights of Labor it was agreed that ... "Of this we will not die."

Across Canada, the bishops' opposition produced only minor problems, and even in Montreal, where one would expect the edicts to have their most far-reaching consequences, twenty-three new local assemblies were organized in 1886. While the ecclesiastical furore may have led to the disappearance of some Montreal assemblies and of a few others at Richmond and Upper Bedford, those throughout the rest of the province survived, and by 1887 the Order in Quebec was approaching its peak strength.

Other aspects of the dominant culture also seem to have undergone change in response to the rise of the Knights of Labor. Temperance, an early plank in industrial-capitalist work discipline, became a mark of working-class independence, a cause for all Knights of Labor to champion vocally and practically. Instead of relying totally on dime novels and popular religious tracts, which were always capable of being produced and read with a content of class differentiation in mind, workers turned as well to works of social criticism and tracts of labour reform. The cumulative effect of these and other developments altered the nature of social relationships in hundreds of Canadian communities.

The most vital contribution of this movement culture was the message of labour solidarity. Long-standing points of division within working-class life – skilled versus unskilled; male versus female; Protestant versus Catholic – were opposed by the Order's conscious and persistent attempt to construct an alternative vision of the possibility of solidarity. In their call for all workers to unite, the Knights of Labor struggled to create a national working class committed to the internationalism of the labour movement. One Hamilton Knight wrote of this in 1887:

When we entered the Order we were taught that in the home of labor there would be no distinctions of Country, Creed & Color because all were of the Earth and with equal rights to Earth, when we understood this great truth that all men are brothers we rejoiced, and we solemnly resolved that we would do all in our power to strengthen the bonds of unity between the workers of the world and we are still steadfast to our principles.

This promise of working-class unity was nowhere more apparent than in the attempts to integrate Irish workers into the labour movement, for in the process of overcoming ethnic and religious prejudice the traditional gulf separating skilled and unskilled was also bridged because many Irish lacked craft skills. The Knights of Labor hailed efforts to unite Orange and Green, declaring that "Sectarian bigotry is now the only weapon that capital has to wield, and . . . [the Order] is rendering it more and more harmless every day." A good part of the Noble and Holy Order's force lay in a radical alliance composed of one part support for Irish nationalism and another part endorsement of labour reform. Thus, Gordon Bishop, a Gananoque steel worker, recalled in the 1940s that the Knights were led "by members of the Irish race who fled the slavery of peonage in their own lands and who hated as fiercely the economic slavery of the New World."

Symbolic and ritualistic practice, coupled with public display and assaults on previously divisive forces therefore stood at the centre of the movement culture's experience throughout the 1880s. As the Knights of Labor swept across Canada, they forged a unity among labourers previously unattained and unanticipated. They found some of their strongest backers and promoters among working-class intellectuals and activists, and achieved new organizational strength by including women, uniting the particular oppression of sex with the cause of the exploited working class.

BRAINWORKERS

In April of 1886, J.L. Blain of Galt wrote to Knights of Labor leader T.V. Powderly, describing himself as a well-educated "rat from the sinking ship of aristocracy." He told of his efforts in the cause of labour reform, of the lectures he had given on "Capital and Labor," where he proposed remedies for the "present unjust state of society in which 50 percent of the products are absorbed by nonproducers." Blain was one of literally hundreds of intellectuals (called "brainworkers"), activists, editors, lecturers, people's poets, and organizers who "spread the light" during the 1880s and 1890s. As both products and producers of labour's upsurge, these working-class advocates emerged from the local assemblies of the Knights of Labor, lodges of the Provincial Workmen's Association, and the trade unions, mounted platforms in labour demonstrations where their talents as speakers were exploited to the full, and penned social criticism that attacked the inequities of the age.

The labour-reform newspaper was their most obvious vehicle for activism. In the pages of well-known Toronto-Hamilton journals, such as the *Labor Union, Palladium of Labor, Wage Worker, Trade Union Advocate, Canadian Labor Reformer, Labor Record*, and *Labor Advocate*, the movement culture of the 1880s and 1890s was at its most vibrant and visible. The existence of other similar organs, from the Victoria-based *Industrial News* to the PWA's *Trades Journal*, demonstrated the scope of the working-class reform presence in these years. Always balanced delicately on the brink of financial ruin, such newspapers kept afloat during these years only by dint of extraordinary effort, personal perseverance, and occasional support from a long-established trade union. They had many differences, but all strove to "take a broader and more comprehensive view of the entire subject of Labor Reform than is embodied in mere unionism, and to grasp and apply those great underlying principles of equity and justice between men which alone can permanently and satisfactorily solve the issues between Labor and Capital." This was an important component of what Frank Watt has referred to as the "freely germinating radicalism" of the 1880s.

In this environment Canada's most significant late nineteenth-century labour reformer eventually came of age as a radical social critic. In the early 1860s, while working for the *St. Catharines Post*, Phillips Thompson started the intellectual odyssey that would take him from the humour columns of the daily press through the Knights of Labor to the post-1900 socialist movement. By the 1880s his writings consistently sought to elevate people's conception of their own sense of self, striking at deeply rooted feelings of inadequacy. For Thompson, as for so many other "brain-workers" in labour's cause, the industrial struggle was waged not just in the factories, mines, and shops but also in the realm of ideas. In his major work, *The Politics of Labor*, Thompson alerted Canadian workers to new ways of viewing history, political economy, and literature, launching a trenchant critique of bourgeois culture. Always suitable for mass consumption, his message represented something of the "high" side of the movement culture's agitational prose: its sophisticated and radical scrutiny focused with rigour on monopoly in the economic sphere and the privileged snobbery of the "uppertendom" in areas of social relations and the arts. Quietly assimilated if not loudly endorsed by local reformers, Thompson's arguments found an echo in the "low" realms of the movement culture, appearing in anonymous lines of verse that chronicled class grievances:

> Oh! ye toilers have ye felt cold and hunger,
> And been warned with poverty's breath?
> Have your hearts been soaked with your sorrow?
> Have you slept in the shadow of death?

or offered words of encouragement:

> 'Tis the foremost thing to do –
> Spread the Light!
> Till the world is made anew –
> Spread the Light!

It is darkness that enslaves,
Those who dwell in dens and caves,
Knowledge strengthens – knowledge saves –
Spread the Light!

This kind of exhortation to activism was at the centre of the recruiting drive that brought the Knights of Labor to prominence and pushed and promoted the ideas and activities of other labour bodies across Canada.

Those cities in which Thompson figured centrally – Toronto and Hamilton – produced labour spokesmen whose impact would be felt across the province: A.W. Wright, Alfred Jury, Charles March, William H. Rowe, George Collis, William Vale, Thomas Towers, Edward Williams, and D.J. O'Donoghue (who had moved from Ottawa to Toronto). In Montreal, activists such as A.T. Lépine and future socialists William Darlington and Richard Kerrigan were prominent, while in the Maritimes the PWA's Robert Drummond and Martin Butler, editor of his own Fredericton-based *Journal*, championed the workers' cause in the 1880s and 1890s. The latter was an exemplar of nineteenth-century radicalism, proclaiming his religion as "universal brotherhood" and determining, in 1893-94, to "abolish the false economic system that makes one man rich out of the blood and sweat of a thousand of his fellow men."

Butler, who lost an arm to a machine while working in an American tannery at the age of eighteen, eked out a living as a pedlar, poet, and journalist, all the while sowing the seeds of labour reform. By the turn of the century his radicalism was tempered by the unpopularity of his anti-Boer War views. In 1900 he noted, "The democratic tree has been pulled up by the roots and the ground seeded down with the seeds of imperialism and aristocracy." Like Thompson, he left behind the nineteenth century to enter the twentieth, where, he told his readers, "One star only shines on the horizon, and that is Socialism, the doctrine that all men are brothers, have the same rights of opportunity, education and enjoyment and the product of their hands, wrung from the bountiful mother earth, created by the Father of all for the equal use of his children." This was a language that indicated how much the developing "progressive" ideas of the epoch were cast in older, familiar vocabularies of religion and masculinist power, but it was also, in its embrace of socialism, an expression of political movement.

What was in part unique about the 1880s, then, was that the decade produced a stratum of bona fide working-class leaders, some drawn from the ranks of labour, others attracted from the outside. These "brain-workers" served, as G.H. Allaby has argued in a study of New Brunswick reformers around 1900, as "prophets of radicalism." In the 1860s there had been only a handful of such types, and they had little continuous, stable presence in the ranks of the working class. Moreover, they often embraced activities and rhetoric that were thoroughly compromised. This had changed by the 1880s. Working-class intellectuals and activists were a significant social force, a dispersed collection of dissidents with a movement at their back and institutions and vehicles at hand to help propagate their ideas. They helped to cultivate, in Phillips Thompson's words, a vision of an alternative society in which universal democracy and co-operation could triumph over war and monopoly. The "beautiful ideal" of the brainworkers was born in the 1880s, when the possibilities of labour reform seemed boundless. This ability to "dream of what might be" if "the world's workers were only educated and organized" was deepened and complemented by significant achievements in drawing an important and previously excluded segment of the working class into the movement culture.

WOMEN

Women had become a vital component of the labour force across North America by the 1880s, representing approximately 15 per cent of the gainfully employed and numbering almost 3 million. Shunned by most labour associations, women were even excluded by the Knights of Labor until, in 1881, Mary Stirling and her co-workers in Philadelphia's Mundell & Company's shoe works defied their employer in a strike and spontaneously organized the Garfield Assembly, named in honour of the recently assassinated president. With the aid of some male Knights, Stirling and her sisters persuaded delegates at the 1881 General Assembly to open the Order's doors officially to women. From that point on, women became a force in the Knights of Labor, and by 1886 almost 200 women's local assemblies had been organized in the United States.

In Canada, especially in the Ontario stronghold of the Order, women became an important presence in the Knights of Labor. By 1891, one wage labourer in eight was a woman, and female workers comprised a low-paid group that the Royal Commission on the Relations of Labor and Capital in Canada (1889) reported could be "counted on to work for small wages, to submit to exasperating exactions, and to work uncomplainingly for long hours." Concentrated in cotton textiles, shoe factories, and domestic service (by far the largest category), women also worked in the sweated trades of garment production and the tobacco industry, and were scattered across a wide array of other employments. Their wages, on average, were approximately one-third those of their male counterparts.

This material divergence had long formed the basis of a profound separation between male and female workers, and the introduction of women into the mass struggles and organizational upsurge of the 1880s began to overcome decades of complacency. While the Order as a whole failed to address decisively the particular oppression of sex, often being inhibited by a confining adherence to the consensual norms of Victorian morality and conventional gender relations, it nevertheless raised the question of the role of women within working-class circles with a seriousness that was unprecedented. In examining the fragmentary historical evidence of the relationship of the Knights of Labor to female workers, it becomes obvious once again that the Order contributed to an alternative vision of social relations, edging the consolidating working-class opposition on to entirely new ground. For if the Knights of Labor remained inhibited by the cultural norms of a society that circumscribed woman's role and established the usual "proper sphere," it did defy those norms in its attempts to build a movement encompassing all workers – male and female. And in this it appears to have gone beyond much of the practice of other working-class organizations, such as the PWA and many of the trade unions, an advance not unrelated to the ways in which gender, skill, and occupation came together in the coal fields or the trades as compared to the more heterogeneous manufacturing milieu the Knights entered into in Ontario in the 1880s.

Hamilton's *Palladium of Labor* reflected the Order's refusal to ignore the plight of the woman worker at the same time that it echoed the confinements of the age. It argued, on the one hand, that women came into the Knights of Labor as the peers of men, equal to them and deserving of the same pay in the workplace and the same recognition in the political and social spheres. There was apparently no position within the movement that a woman could not hold, and women such as Leonora M. Barry became organizers, while others, such as Amherstburg's Rose Le May, became district master workmen. This practice of equality, however, was occasionally undermined by conventionality, and some women's LAs petitioned Powderly to allow them to invite men to chair their proceedings, so reluctant were many women to occupy public posts of authority. Moreover, a commitment to women's advance was often tarnished within the Order by a retreat into the domestic ideology of the times and a chivalrous deference to femininity: "Upon motherhood we base brotherhood, and in our family circle we pledge ourselves to defend the fair name and reputation of an innocent sister even with our lives," declared the *Palladium*. "If there is any preeminence given either sex in our Order," continued the paper, "it is given to women."

The flip side of this "elevation" of woman was, of course, the rights of male protectors, which could run amuck in familial authoritarianism and traditional assertions of patriarchal power. The Knights of Labor thus defied convention by opening assembly halls to women workers at the same time that they extended this invitation to organize with a hand gloved in the traditionalism of gender difference. When Canadian women were won to the cause of labour reform, it was seldom through the strike, the mass campaign, the boycott, or the demonstration. Rather, for the "fair sex," the ticket into the Order was often stamped at the soirée, the hop, or the social, and it was possible for editors like Hamilton's William H. Rowe to contrast the "pining and wasp-waisted, doll-dressed, consumption-mortgaged, music murdering, novel-devouring, daughters of fashion and idleness" to "the real lady" who could "darn a stocking and mend her own dress . . . a girl that young men are in quest of for a wife." Passages like this spoke simultaneously of the Knights of Labor attempt to address class and gender *and* the limitations of that effort.

Rowe's crude moralizing and constricted view of women's place did not deter workers like Katie McVicar, Hamilton's pioneer woman organizer, from posing the issue of central concern to working women in a more realistic manner: "Our employers are organized for the purpose of keeping the selling prices up and the manufacturing prices down, and we ought certainly to accept the assistance and invitation of our gentlemen Knights and organize; remain no longer strangers to each other, but combine and protect ourselves to some purpose." In the years after 1884, McVicar's line of argument would be pursued by others, albeit often anonymously. But women also came out openly for reform, and a few, like Belleville poet Marie Joussaye and Picton social critic and writer Elizabeth Johnson, joined the ranks of central Canadian "brainworkers." These developments helped to instill a sense of sisterhood among working women, but one that was class bound. An open letter to the "working girls" of Canada in 1885 closed on the note that female workers must not look to the law, the church, or "the high-born sister women for help." "Sisters," concluded this address, "by our dignity, co-operation, and organization, we must protect ourselves." As the movement grew and more women became attached to the cause of labour, gains were made, and in the consequent expansion of understanding the restrictions of women's place were cut back and eroded.

Out of this emerged demands for women's suffrage, a recognition of the vitally important place of unpaid domestic labour, attempts to organize previously unorganized women workers, and calls for equal pay for equal work. The act of drawing women into the labour movement – women who had before been isolated on the margins of trade union, workplace, or political struggles – was critical in many Canadian communities, an initial step in the process of overcoming gender subordination within the working class. Over the course of the 1880s approximately 10 per cent, or twenty-five out of 250, of the Ontario local assemblies contained women. Most of these female members of the Order were employed in cotton mills, shoe factories, and the garment industry; isolated domestics and clerks were less responsive, understandably, to the lure of the Knights of Labor. Throughout this recruitment, the Order's defence of "the right of women to be regarded in all matters of citizenship and all relations between the government and the people as the equal of men" was paramount. This, according to Phillips Thompson, could "hardly be denied by any clear-sighted and consistent Labor Reformer." American land reform and single tax advocate Henry

George put the matter in a similar light when he argued before a Hamilton audience that "The women have a right to come into your organizations. . . . The women are the best men we have."

In late nineteenth-century Knights of Labor strongholds like Belleville, Brantford, Hamilton, Montreal, Stratford, Thorold, and Toronto, then, women joined the Order in assemblies named "Hope" and "Advance" with the intention of realizing parts of the possibility of women's emancipation. From today's standpoint, attendance at musical and literary entertainments as "Goddesses of Liberty" or membership in a local assembly named "Excelsior" (which expressed elevated status) might point less to liberation than to an innately sexist idolization of femininity. Yet in the challenge of the 1880s, such honorifics were an articulation of dignity and worth felt to be the birthright of all individuals, including labouring women. To acknowledge the place of working women within the general human condition represented a great advance over past practice and played a not inconsiderable role in changing male workers' views of women and female workers' views of themselves. The possibility, in the end, was far from realized; but it nevertheless existed. The Knights of Labour, and the movement culture of the 1880s, had begun the process whereby the questions of class and gender could be considered as one.

POLITICS

The movement culture of the 1880s shifted parts of the existing terms of class relations, drawing unskilled workers, women, and the Irish from the periphery into the very centre of late nineteenth-century labour-reform agitation. In this attempt to construct a wider-ranging solidarity, workers glimpsed the potential of working-class unity that could change the world in which they lived.

Labour leaders knew that party attachments were strong among workingmen (women, too, had their loyalties, but they could not vote) and many who espoused reform were actually committed to one of the established political bodies, Grit or Tory. But politics of this sort was often regarded as a dirty corner, crowded with manipulators, "wire-pullers," and con artists. There was money to be had from the conventional parties, and many in the labour-reform milieu saw the need to overcome the consequent compromising character of traditional political involvement and influence-peddling. Some opted for simply pressuring the established parties to behave more honestly and operate in the interests of workers, but the more unique and lasting accomplishment of the decade was the initiation of independent political action. Sir John A. Macdonald, leader of the federally entrenched Tories and long adept at turning working-class discontent to his own party's good fortune, worried in the 1880s that he was

losing his grip on the political workingman. In his view there were dangerous "rocks ahead," threatening the Conservative ship. Among them were
the Knights of Labor.

From the moment of its entrance into Canada, the Order engaged in
politics actively. As early as 1882 pro-labour aldermen were elected in
Hamilton, and in the 1883 Ontario provincial election labour reformers
launched independent campaigns to seat working-class candidates. In
some cities Labor Political Associations were formed. Much of this political work was engineered by leading Knights of Labor, who were also
involved heavily in the influential Toronto Trades and Labor Council and
the recently founded Trades and Labor Congress of Canada, which first
met in 1883. They played a key role in the election of W.H. Howland, an
unambiguous reformer, as mayor in Toronto in 1885. Such gains drew
concessions from the Ottawa-ensconced Tories and spurred labour reformers on to new political efforts.

Both the December, 1886, Ontario election and the February, 1887,
federal election saw strong working-class efforts to vote labour spokesmen
into the respective legislative bodies. In the provincial contest, seven
working-class candidates took the field. One ran for the Grits (Reform/
Liberal) and two ran for the Tories (Conservatives), but their labour affiliations were made more important than those of previous working-class
candidates in that they billed themselves as "Liberal-Labour" and
"Labour-Conservative." Four candidates ran as independents, shunning
the established political parties. They would all lose, but often such independents took a major share of the vote. London Knight of Labor Samuel
Peddle, for instance, gave Tory opposition leader W.R. Meredith a run for
his money in the provincial election. Meredith had won his seat by easy
acclamation in the previous contest. Two of the labour candidates who
campaigned on traditional tickets actually won provincial seats: St. Thomas Tory brakeman and Knight of Labor Andy Ingram in West Elgin, and
Lib-Lab candidate William Garson in Lincoln-St. Catharines. The February federal election, however, saw working-class candidates shut out. In
this context of minor victories the Knights of Labor stepped up their
lobbying efforts, establishing a legislative committee in the late 1880s. But
the most accessible political lever was still that of the municipal council,
and combined Knights of Labor-trade union forces won a number of
impressive political battles in this area: Brantford, Chatham, Brockville,
and Ottawa were all sites of municipal victories.

In Quebec, labour's political voice was heard most clearly in the Knights
of Labor stronghold of Montreal. Described in detail by Fernand Harvey
and in unpublished studies by Victor Chan and Robert Cox, labour became
especially active in politics in 1886, when the Order supported three candidates in the provincial election. Another workers' candidate, Charles
Champagne, ran in the industrial district of Hochelaga. All were backed by

the working-class community, all were affiliated with the Knights of Labor, and all would refuse to compromise their independence by running for the established Grit and Tory parties. However, none of these labour candidates won. As in the case of Scots saddler William W. Robertson, defeat was partly attributable to principled political stands against national chauvinism. Robertson refused to placate English-speaking prejudices against French Canadians and no doubt paid the price in Anglophone votes. "Make the labour candidates custodians of the country's morality and integrity," he shouted from one podium, raising the movement culture's banner of an alternative to partyism and corruption. When one French-speaking candidate was wooed by the Liberals, led by nationalist Francophone Honoré Mercier, he declined the bait of easy identification with a party headed by a Québécois. "I will not put the labour question in second place," he replied. Although defeated, the labour trio gained 6,000 of the 18,000 votes cast in the three Montreal districts. William Keys, an Irish machinist employed in various Griffintown shops, took his failure at the polls in stride, assessing his campaign positively: "I consider my candidature to be a triumph as it has shown the wealthier classes what workingmen can do."

This entry into the political fray necessarily moved the established powers in the direction of concession. Defeats conditioned a more tolerant view within labour-reform ranks of those who would combine class interests with traditional party politics, and in an 1888 federal election a Tory workingman and Knights of Labor organizer, A.T. Lépine, won a seat in Montreal East. As in Ontario, however, the most influential victories may well have taken place at the municipal level. The Order elected an alderman and a councillor in Quebec City in 1892, and the mayor and nine of twelve aldermen in Hull in 1894.

Miners on the east and west coasts also took their first strides into the political field in these years. The *Trades Journal*, voice of the Provincial Workmen's Association, declared in 1885 that the "ballot must be the means to secure our just desires, maintain our rights, put good men in power, and hurl tyrants out." PWA candidates ran in the Nova Scotia provincial election of 1886, Robert Drummond as an independent Liberal in Pictou County and James Wilson as a straight workers' candidate in Cumberland. Both lost, but in the process the PWA, Drummond, and Liberal Premier W.S. Fielding began to negotiate a complex alliance that would result, according to Ian McKay, in the PWA securing "the most impressive series of reforms wrung by a Canadian trade union from a nineteenth-century government." Over the course of the late 1880s regulatory legislation did much to establish a regime of industrial legality in the coal fields, key features of which were the introduction of compulsory arbitration as an alternative to strikes and certification procedures for colliery officials. When Fielding, in 1889, extended the franchise to miners living in company housing it appeared that Drummond had indeed secured for the coal miners "the badge of citizenship." This had not so much been won at the polls as it had been accomplished through a mutually beneficial set of parallel understandings on the part of Drummond and Fielding. The personalized icing on this political cake was Drummond's appointment to the Legislative Council in 1891, a posting that would gradually degenerate from one of misguided good intentions to overt enjoyment of the pleasures of office.

There would be other problems with this statist panacea, but the PWA had shown how much of a political presence labour could be in a province in the midst of economic transformation. Tensions between Drummond and Fielding, as well as between Drummond and militants within his ranks, were never easily resolved. When employers consolidated and expanded their operations in the 1890s and increasingly demanded labour acquiescence, Drummond was less and less capable of either directing the PWA response or containing it. In the midst of an 1895-96 strike fought against a wage reduction, one PWA lodge disregarded Drummond's instructions, armed its militants, barricaded 200 miners inside its hall, and used considerable physical force to discourage scabs. The political turn was stopped dead in its tracks; its regime of early industrial legality in the coal fields was over.

In the West, workers raised their objections to the importation of Chinese labour and protested the land-grant system that gave concentrated economic authority to coal baron Robert Dunsmuir. Although not solely the creation of the Knights of Labor, west coast political action was greatly influenced by the Order. Occupationally, the political agenda often seemed set by the influential miners. As Paul Phillips notes, the four worker candidates nominated in 1886 were unmistakably linked with the cause of the Knights of Labor. In Victoria, one candidate, John Duval, was a reform editor whose newspaper, the *Industrial News*, was endorsed by British Columbia's Knights of Labor. S.H. Myers, candidate in Nanaimo, was a coal-miner member of the Order who would later die in a mine disaster. The platform of the Workingmen's Party called for mine safety laws, land reform, and exclusion of the Chinese. It signalled the first political expression in British Columbia of "a basic divergence of interest between the 'toiling masses' and the 'wealthier part of the community'." Municipal politics also became a focus of activity in Vancouver, while in Winnipeg political action seemed restricted to the provincial election of 1886.

These diverse and unco-ordinated labour efforts stand as evidence of an underlying similarity in working-class experience that, in spite of many variations and diversities, fed into the rise of a movement culture of working-class opposition and resistance. Advanced most emphatically by Knights and Workmen, the ideals of this culture were tested in the politics of the 1880s and 1890s, when the first concerted attempts to decrease worker dependence on old-line political parties were made. This often led to a sense of independence within sectors of the working class. Few independent labour candidates won seats, but the gains registered in consciousness and political recognition of class needs extended beyond the failures of the polls. And at the local level tangible victories were being secured: early closing, union wages and jobs in corporation work, just assessment rates, opposition to bonusing capital's consolidation, and responsible public transit were just a few of the issues that were, on occasion, resolved in favour of labour.

In the national sphere, significant concessions were won as both Liberals and Conservatives courted a growing working-class political constituency increasingly aware of its own potential as a "spoiler" in electoral battles. Oliver Mowat, Premier of Ontario, and, to a lesser degree, Macdonald in Ottawa responded to this new development of the 1880s with factory acts, bureaus of labour statistics, arbitration measures, suffrage extension, employers' liability acts, improved mechanics' lien laws, and royal commissions, just as Fielding in Nova Scotia reacted to the miners' tug at his political arm. Hence, the political struggles of this period cannot be cavalierly dismissed as failures. But independent labour politics was still far from a realization in the 1880s and 1890s. The established parties proved sophisticated opponents of this emerging working-class autonomy, and through patronage and concession, power and force, they managed to contain much of the working-class opposition. But in the workplace, where class relations often unfolded in their sharpest, least mediated manner, a growing divergence of labour and capital was becoming apparent.

STRIKES

One expression of the rift between labour and capital that emerged in the 1880s was the rising number of strikes. This willingness to resort to the strike pointed to an increase in working-class grievances that grew out of the movement culture, indicating that labour was beginning to see alternatives to accommodation. To be sure, many of the conflicts of the 1880s were mundane confrontations over wages, but workers also made attempts to retain control over work processes that seemed to be drifting into others' hands as capital consolidated its authority.

The increase in strike activity in this period is indisputable, and this alone accounts for a good deal of the public recognition of a working-class presence in politics, in the pages of the daily newspapers, and between the covers of late nineteenth-century popular novels such as Albert Carman's *The Preparation of Ryerson Embury* and Agnes Maule Machar's *Roland Graeme: Knight*. In Hamelin, Larocque, and Rouillard's *Répertoire des Grèves dans la Province de Québec* (a useful source that nevertheless understates significantly the number of strikes) there are references to 102 strikes between 1880 and 1895, compared to a mere sixty-one conflicts in the entire period from 1843 to 1879. Kealey's *Toronto Workers Respond to Industrial Capitalism, 1867-1892* indicates that 112, or over 70 per cent, of the 156 strikes fought in Ontario's largest city in the post-Confederation period occurred in the years after 1880. As we have already noted, the PWA fought more than seventy strikes between 1879 and 1900. More than 430 labour-capital conflicts erupted across Canada over the course of the 1880s. Compared to the 1870s this represented a rough doubling of the number of strikes and lockouts; if the 1880s are set against earlier decades – the 1850s or 1860s – such figures signal a sixfold increase in conflict. Individual craft unions led the majority of these struggles, but relations between Knights and unionists were so close prior to 1886 that it is often difficult to distinguish the role of trade unions from that of the local assemblies.

Even where craft unions and Knights of Labor were relatively weak or virtually non-existent, as in Halifax, there are indications that the 1880s marked a new period of class conflict. An unpublished study by Ian McKay contends that there were as many strikes conducted in Halifax in the 1880s (fifteen) as there were in the preceding two decades. Communities previously uninterrupted by the upheavals of class conflict, like Milltown, New Brunswick, first witnessed strikes and labour organization in 1886. The 1880s were thus a time of heightened workplace militancy, symbolized by the Halifax Carpenters' Union, which marched on Labour Day in 1888. It displayed the Stars and Stripes, indicative of the internationalism of labour, and for the first time brought before the public a handsome silk craft banner, made in London in 1864 at a cost of $250. Bearing a Latin inscription, "By diligence and perseverance we overcome all things," the carpenters' 1888 unveiling of their union's motto did indeed indicate that finally, after a quarter of a century, their craft pride and organization had moved beyond fear of hostile reception. But lest others miss this message, the carpenters of the 1880s introduced yet another symbolic piece, expressive of the new social climate: an enormous mallet they claimed would be employed to level scabs. As McKay notes, in the conjuncture of the symbols of old and new, workmanship and militancy, lay a part of labour's new perception of itself.

The Knights of Labor epitomized this new self-perception: it grew because it was willing to organize class forces larger than itself, marshalling numerous trade sectors or industrial groupings for particular struggles. Thus, in Toronto the Knights of Labor contributed to the formation of a coalition of forces knit together by experienced labour reformers and trade union militants who all found common cause in the need to support striking women boot and shoe operatives in the spring of 1882. This was apparent again in the summer of 1883 when District Assembly 45 (Brotherhood of Telegraphers) engaged in a continent-wide strike against the monopolistic telegraph companies that united operatives in Canada from Sydney in the East to Winnipeg in the West.

The ultimate failure of the telegraphers' strike and its bitter aftermath, which saw DA 45 withdraw from the Knights of Labor, appeared less important, in 1883, than the solidarity expressed in its course. Workers struggled to obtain abolition of Sunday work, the eight-hour day and the seven-hour night, equal pay for members of both sexes, and a universal wage increase of 15 per cent. They posed the moral authority of what the Knights liked to call "modern chivalry" against the "tyranny and unjust treatment of a soulless corporation." And when they lost this battle it was not defeat they remembered but the importance of labour unity and the necessity of continuing the struggle. "The telegraphers' strike is over," declared Hamilton's *Palladium of Labor*. "The People's Strike is now in Order."

The "People's Strike" took many forms in the years to come. At its most dramatic it involved mass strikes that crippled whole industries or polarized entire communities. Examples of struggles of this magnitude included the two Toronto street railway strikes of the spring and summer of 1886, cotton mill strikes in Merritton in 1886 and 1889, in Cornwall (1887, 1888, and 1889), and in Milltown in 1886. The great lumber workers' strikes in Gravenhurst in 1888 and in Ottawa-Hull in 1891 were also part of this wave. Each of these strikes unified working communities, increased the level of class struggle to previously unmatched heights, and involved workers long excluded from labour action in a wide-reaching solidarity that linked men and women, skilled and unskilled, French and English, in a bond of unity. For the most part these labour upheavals, waged to secure organizational recognition, humane conditions, and better wages, had few parallels in the history of labour before 1880. The only previous strikes comparable in sheer numbers were the canallers' battles, which lacked the level of solidarity achieved in the strikes after 1880, and the ship labourers' conflicts in Saint John and Quebec City, which failed to draw other workers to the cause with the same force.

Beyond these epic battles, Knights of Labor often formed alliances with long-established craft unions to mount smaller struggles aimed at the preservation of particular forms of worker autonomy or limited job control. The Order provided an institutional backing for literally thousands of workers who sought to maintain wage standards in the face of prosperity's inflation and the wage cuts of more depressed years. One of the most massive confrontations occurred in January, 1887, when more than 1,000 primary metal workers led by the Knights of Labor walked out of the Montreal Rolling Mills and two other companies in opposition to a 10 per cent wage reduction.

Among Canadian moulders, perhaps the most conflict-ridden trade in the 1880s and early 1890s, Knights and unionists fought classic battles that turned on the issue of work autonomy and managerial prerogatives. Organized throughout Ontario and Quebec, and to some extent in the Maritimes, moulders were concentrated in agricultural implements shops and stove foundries. Employer opposition to unions, workers' rejections of wage cuts, moulder demands for limited numbers of apprentices, union attacks on employer use of helpers, known as "berkshires" or "bucks," revisions to the standard wage rate or shop book "prices," and antagonism to arbitrary authority all led to a series of worker-employer clashes in the 1880s.

But to discuss only strikes is undoubtedly to distort much of the character of productive relations, however much such conflicts contribute to our understanding of work relations in these years. The labour-capital relationship was a symbiotic one, based on give and take, in which workers appropriated some of the power of decision-making at the workplace, establishing procedures and controlling limited aspects of the production process. This is revealed dramatically in an exciting study of workers' control among the Springhill miners by Ian McKay.

Basing his study on rare papers and minutes of the Pioneer Lodge of the Provincial Workmen's Association, McKay argues that between 1882 and 1886 miners and proprietors existed within a structure of "organic control" in which pit democracy, worker autonomy, and a culture and ideology of independence thrived within the mining community. Workers enjoyed extensive powers over production, although long-term decisions regarding entrepreneurial strategy rested in the hands of the company. The PWA lodge minutes record almost 140 attempts to resolve working-class grievances through labour action in the mid-1880s. Almost 20 per cent of the cases involved discussion of a strike, but only four actual work stoppages occurred. Wages were the likeliest cause of discontent, but the miners discussed and debated matters of hiring and firing, management, and customary working-class rights. Collective bargaining obviously evolved within this particular structure of organic control and resembled a situation in which proprietors (one the owner of capital, the other, of labour) struck a bargain within well-defined relations of reciprocity. But that reciprocity was walled in, as all understood, by the ultimate power and threat of workers withdrawing their labour. Springhill's PWA launched perhaps the first 100 per cent strike in the history of Nova Scotia's collieries in 1890; as the mine began to flood and as politicians rushed to the scene, the company, fearful of the prospects of the destruction of its property, capitulated totally to the workers' demands.

Throughout the 1880s and early 1890s, then, a sense of working-class autonomy, often resulting in conflict, was never far from the surface of class relations. Whether it emerged visibly in a walkout of more than 2,000 lumber workers in Ottawa-Hull, in a riot against Toronto street railway magnate Frank Smith, in a defeated struggle to control the nature of production in a Brockville foundry, or in deliberate debate in the lodge room of Springhill's PWA, the strike was a forceful feature of social relations and everyday life. An elementary lesson was learned in these years, as a movement culture heightened worker awareness, challenged capital, and promoted the cause of labour militancy and unity.

ON THE MARGINS OF THE MOVEMENT

The movement culture of the 1880s touched many workers and, in its various expressions and promotions of collectivity, shifted the nature and meaning of working-class experience. To underestimate all of this would distort the past and be a disservice to those many workers who struggled to create a more just, humane world. But it is also nevertheless true that, however great its impact, the movement culture exercised its influence strongly in some areas, less decisively in others. It could not be expected to transform all of working-class life at one fell swoop, and it did not. In smaller towns and in realms of private life the movement culture may well have registered its presence more weakly than in the larger industrial-capitalist cities and in the more obvious class context of the workplace. A look at the underside of family life and the practice of male violence toward women exposes how resistant some sectors of the working class were to the message of the movement culture, a message that was itself not unproblematic.

As we have seen the Knights of Labor conceived of themselves as chivalrous protectors of women's virtue: they deplored the capitalist degradation of honest womanhood that resulted from exploiting women at the workplace; many took great offence at the coarse language, shared water closets (toilets), and intimate physical proximities that came with virtually all factory labour in Victorian Canada. Nor did the Order turn a blind eye to domestic violence and the ways in which men could take advantage of women sexually. Local assembly courts could try and convict members of the Knights of Labor for wife-beating, and the Ontario Order was a strong backer of the eventually successful campaign to enact seduction legislation.

Three points need making about the movement culture's conception of how best to address the conjuncture of class and sex. First, its very willingness to enter into this realm is a reflection of the undeniable advances the workers' movement was making in these years, reaching past the conventional concerns with wages and workplaces to try to reconstruct the meanings of life in a class society. That the Knights of Labor considered the question of sexuality primarily as a matter of libertine aristocratic philanderers and tyrannical, licentious bosses despoiling working-class womanhood was itself an expression of how much "the labour question" had expanded in the 1880s, of how much class had become a central reality in people's lives. Second, however, as Karen Dubinsky and others have argued, the construction of the relation of sex and class in this way was, as we have seen earlier in this chapter, premised on highly traditional notions of gender in which a hierarchical opposition – man/woman – conveyed distinctions that were themselves antithetical to the project of equality and repressive in their undertones of male protectors, womanly virtues, female chastity, and the sanctities of the home. Third, because of this, the Knights of Labor could only campaign for the kind of seduction law and state intervention into the realm of sexuality that would prove less of a liberation for woman and more of a new, institutionalized regime of regulation. Within this concept of regulation women secured few victories, the working class little in the way of wins.

Research into the extent and nature of male violence against women in late nineteenth-century Canada is just beginning, but it is already apparent that it was considerable and that the law offered women little in the way of security. Judith Fingard's exploration of the dark side of life in Victorian Halifax reveals extensive family violence, with particular wife-beaters charged repeatedly over the course of a decade. Wife battery was often related to drinking and desertion, but in both cases the law was reluctant to challenge the husband's implicit proprietary rights over his wife's person and sexuality. The passage of the Ontario Deserted Wives Maintenance Act in the late 1880s notwithstanding, working-class women got little from the courts. As court cases studied by Annalee Golz suggest, male authoritarianism and brutality were features of family life some women endured for years. Worsened by alcohol abuse, occasionally triggered by unemployment and destitution, usually reflective of an ugly masculinist pride that refused any and all acts that would undermine, however gingerly, a husband's "rule" over his household, male violence was the underside of the mythologized male protector image cultivated by the labour movement, the courts, and the wife-beater himself. If this male violence led to litigation, women had an uphill battle in winning any substantial redress. Judges commonly asserted that wives must bear some indignities, and acts of violence perceived as "isolated" were never grounds for any kind of settlement. If a woman had committed adultery, that, in and of itself, usually nullified any case she might have. Women's characters were constantly assaulted and questioned. The state, clearly, was no better a protector than some husbands.

This was also evident in another expression of male violence, sexual assault. Dubinsky's examination of rape and other sexual crimes explores a number of cases from the 1880s to the 1920s. Her analysis underscores the extent to which the labour movement's early focus on the evils of the industrial-capitalist workplace and the construction of sexual assault/ seduction as the activity of designing employers and aristocratic dandies shielded sexual crime's perpetrators when they were themselves from the working class and, in the case of voluntary sexual activity, denied young women any active agency in the making of their own erotic lives, regulating their sexuality in ways that protected the "rights" of their working-class fathers and families. Most sexual assault actually took place within those families, and when it was work-related the home, not the factory, was the most likely site of attack: domestic servants comprised the most common occupation to come up in the courts. Over half of all the seduction prosecutions involved ongoing and mutual relations between two lovers, not the Knights of Labor image of deceitful aristocrats luring young working-class maidens into the recesses of sexual depravity, promising them marriage, tempting them with sweets and carriage rides, and abandoning them "virtueless" after sating their lust.

This history of physical and sexual abuse, centred in the family, is a revealing reminder that however much the movement culture changed working-class life in the late nineteenth century there were some areas and many workers immune to its impact. The Knights of Labor, the trade unions, and the Provincial Workmen's Association, all of which saw themselves as fighting for working-class respectability and battling to secure the family, regarded male violence against women as distinctly unrespectable. Yet, for all of this, there were locales and personalities they could not influence; most of the cases we have of overt abuse seem to involve labourers on the margins of the movement, unaffiliated to labour organizations of any kind, likely to be living their lives in "cultures" other than that of the movement. Still, there must have been those within the labour movement who were guilty of abuse and assault. The movement culture, for all that it affected them, had not broken through all of the ugliness of particular extremes of male power. And even where, rhetorically, it challenged this ugliness, it did so in ways that sentimentalized gender relations rather than equalizing them. As a result, the movement culture at its best was caught in a web of limitation, a process evident in other spheres as well.

THE CLOSE OF A CENTURY

The modern Canadian labour movement – strongest in industrial-capitalist Ontario and Quebec, prefaced by the short-lived, Tory-linked Canadian Labour Union of the 1870s (which succumbed to the strains of the 1873-79 depression) – emerged in the 1880s. More than a dozen cities and towns managed to establish Trades and Labor councils by the end of the decade, with strong city centrals thriving in Toronto by 1881, Montreal by 1886, and Vancouver by 1889. Often led by Knights of Labor activists, these bodies provided a forum for interaction between Knights and unionists as well as a focus for the labour movement's economic and political work. They also provided local foundations for the creation of the Trades and Labor Congress of Canada, which first met in Toronto in 1883. Forty-eight delegates attended this original gathering (only eleven from outside Toronto), but in the years to come the TLC would grow to embrace a wider constituency. In 1886, 109 delegates were in attendance, and the TLC's conventions would continue into the 1950s. By the 1890s, however, it was clear that labour's ship was battling stormy seas, and in 1893 only seventy delegates appeared at the Trades and Labor Congress meeting; two years later the number had dropped to thirty-nine. The movement culture was in trouble.

Part of that weakening was caused by the breakdown of solidarity in the years after 1886, as Knights and craft unionists began to disagree on more and more. Major rifts erupted across North America between the Knights of Labor, who advocated united concern for all workers, and the international trade unions, which were, by definition, oriented toward more exclusive interests. This division was most acute in the cigarmakers' trade, with the international union endorsing the blue union label and the Knights of Labor local assembly members advocating their own white label. This intra-class rivalry played a part in the collapse of a unified labour movement and affected major centres such as Toronto, Hamilton, and London. Historians have traditionally viewed this parting of the ways in the late 1880s as an inevitable separation in which the utopian and "backward-looking" Knights of Labor lost out to the more pragmatic, less reform-oriented, strictly "bread-and-butter" unionism of the international associations of craft workers. Such an analysis, generally proposed by scholars with little attachment to the Order's humanistic commitment to alternatives to capitalist authority, has only recently come into question in Canada and the United States. But this reigning interpretive orthodoxy has contributed to misunderstandings about the nature of working-class organization at the close of the century.

To stress the craft unions' "victory" over the Knights of Labor and to argue that a committed and intellectually aware stratum of North American labour leaders consciously chose the narrow path of trade unionism over the politically oriented, reformist purpose of unifying all workers is to mistake historical outcome for strategic direction. And surely this also misreads the histories of trade union pioneers, who, in Canada, as in the United States, were often simultaneously Knights and unionists. D.J. O'Donoghue, often depicted as the aristocratic father of the Canadian labour movement, was a labour activist dedicated to the Knights of Labor well into its years of decline in the 1890s and eclipse in the early twentieth century. There were many others like him, and in 1893, four out of every seven delegates attending the Trades and Labor Congress were still affiliated with the Noble and Holy Order of the Knights of Labor.

It will therefore be difficult to understand fully the decline of the movement culture of the 1880s if it is attributed to the inevitable rise of a "superior" trade unionism. Although this culture undeniably was strongest in the industrial-capitalist heartland of Ontario and urban Quebec, and no one can doubt that regional peculiarities remained important and fostered distinctive working-class responses and organizations, it is also the case that the various labour movements of the particular socio-economic and geographic components of Canada dovetailed in the content of their programs and the forms of organization. There were differences, of course, but similarities and commonalities existed as well. Those who would hold to a regionalist explanation of the failure of the movement culture, positing an inevitable insularity, miss a great deal in their inability to see a kind of forest for the specificity of many trees.

A full comprehension of the decline of the movement culture of the 1880s necessitates an examination of the social and political structures within which the culture came to prominence. This analysis will reveal the character of productive relations, the nature of the state, and the limitations these forces imposed on the workers' movement, leading toward the failure of the organizational efforts of the Knights of Labor and the Provincial Workmen's Association to sustain themselves effectively into the twentieth century.

The 1880s represented the culmination of an age of competitive capitalism and political localism, and the movement culture developed as a working-class challenge to those structures. Consolidating a working-class opposition that had long been internally divided against itself, proponents of this movement struggled to unite French and English in Quebec, miner and shopworker in the Maritimes, and Irish and English, man and woman, skilled and unskilled in Ontario's industrial heartland. As Norman Ware argued almost fifty years ago, "The fact is that the Knights of Labor more fully represented the wage earners as a whole than any general labour organization either before or after its peak year, 1886." The bonds of unity did not grow out of economic need alone but were rooted in ritual, a sense of brotherhood and sisterhood, and an activism informed by working-class intellectuals who saw reform as the only hope in an age of degradation. For the first time, Canadian workers struggled for similar political, economic, and social improvements in spite of great differences in region, culture, and working conditions. Both Knights of Labor and Provincial Workmen seemed engaged in a "crusade" to impose "economic order" on an individualistic and acquisitive capitalism. In the process, they became voices of a prophetic, if eclectic, radical dissidence, a "moral universality" pitted against capital's perceived sins.

But in all of this, the movement culture was, ironically, raising grievances that were even more prophetic than they were real. While the movement of the 1880s saw the writing on the wall, it had no conception of just how large the letters would eventually come to be written. At precisely the moment that the labour upheaval of the late nineteenth century erupted, the context that ushered it into being was on the brink of transformation. Opposing

monopoly, labour reformers battled a capitalism that was actually dominated by entrepreneurial competition. Attacking the misuse of political
power, they themselves endorsed the politics of independent working-class
activity in an age that understood little of the eventual authority of the
interventionist state. Staking out progressive ground on the question of
gender, labour reformers nevertheless embraced age-old notions of hearth
and home.

This was not, most emphatically not, a simple question of backward-
looking ideology. The problem was less the movement culture's backward-
ness than its understandable limitations: aware of the awesome change
being effected throughout North American society, working-class leaders
and their followers in the 1880s had only their past experiences to draw on in
forging their collective response. Their experiences inhibited the extent to
which they could reply to changes taking place, yet those changes would
not, in fact, leave their full imprint on the social order until well into the
twentieth century. The movement culture was thus forward-looking in its
realization of capital's potential destructiveness and in its strategic call for
labour unity at the same time that its tactics, learned in the school of the
actual experiences of the nineteenth-century past, were limited and understandably could not meet all the needs of the new hour.

This ambiguity, of a prophetic and visionary stance inhibited by the
limitations of historical context and the awkwardness of being the first to
grapple with new sets of problems, lies at the heart of labour's failures in the
1880s. An eclectic radical critique, capable of uniting the working class
around the perceived threats of a rising economic and political oligarchy,
would eventually see its worst fears confirmed in the late 1880s and 1890s.
As monopoly began to develop and as political power in a nation-state born
only twenty years earlier grew more centralized and more sophisticated, the
tactics of the past proved ineffective. Change was proceeding at such a
quickening pace and the older social relations were being superseded so
dramatically that working-class bodies like the Knights of Labor and the
Provincial Workmen's Association were thrown into conditions that altered
rapidly. What they needed most was time to adapt; this is what they never
had. The whole process of forging a collective response had to be begun
anew. What had appeared as adequate in the movement culture's euphoric
rise in the early 1880s came to be seen as inadequate in the troubled years of
post-1886 breakdown. The "moral universality" fostered by the movement
culture started to disintegrate. In the 1890s the search for solutions to
labour's dilemmas would be renewed in the rise of socialism and the drift
toward a more dominant pragmatic unionism. But by then the damage had
been done, and the movement culture of the 1880s was in a shambles.

All of this explains the supposed failures of the movement culture. Economically, the Knights of Labor have often been criticized for their ambivalent practice at the workplace, and their hesitancy in strike situations is well

known. The enthusiastic reception accorded arbitration and co-operation is often read as a naive and uninformed attempt to create social relations of production in an age of industrial capital similar to those that prevailed during some "golden age" of the artisan producer. Yet, in essence, such orientations and commitments were by no means irrelevant to all that the Knights of Labor and Provincial Workmen's Association leaders and rank and file experienced in an age of competitive capital, when small-scale production and community formed the background of much of economic and social life. That this was in the process of changing just as the movement culture raised these solutions is both understandable and tragic, for it meant that labour reformers lacked an economic strategy at precisely the moment it was most needed.

Capital seized the needs of the hour more decisively, consolidating its own power, moving out of local relations and into wider worlds of accumulation and exchange. Employers grew more and more hostile to any attempt to slow down or thwart this process, seeing in labour organization a brake on their accelerating quest for control over work environments. Workers thrown into conflict with such bosses found themselves increasingly the losers in class battles that now had wider and wider ramifications. Trade unionists began to see that their interests might be better served in a more disciplined and restricted body, such as the union devoted to their particular craft. Employer hostility, as much as any clear-cut philosophical disagreement over the direction of the labour movement, caused the division between Knights and unionists in the last years of the century. It was a separation that broke the back of labour unity, with skilled workers retreating in the face of capital's power, which by the 1890s seemed to grow more awesome day by day. Women and the unskilled, perhaps the major beneficiaries of the movement culture of the 1880s, slipped back into a state of unorganized dependence on capital's mercy and the politician's benevolence, a far from enviable situation.

It should not be possible to regard this as only a product of the reactionary exclusivism of skilled workers, given much of the craft community's support for socialism or syndicalism in the years before World War One, and the Knights of Labor's longevity in certain Canadian circles, especially in French Canada, discredits this view. Rather, we can see the trade union retreat, not as the agency of an aristocratic abandonment but as part of a determined outcome imposed by capital's late nineteenth-century surge toward monopoly. That capital itself understood the necessity of breaking the back of the movement culture and knew well that bodies like the Knights of Labor lent to trade unionism a perniciousness that could not be tolerated is evident from an 1891 statement in the *Journal of Commerce*: "The spirit of trades unionism," declared this pious organ, "is strangling honest endeavour, and the hard-working, fearless, thorough artisan of ten years ago is degenerating into the shiftless, lazy, half-hearted fellow who, with unconscious irony, styles himself a Knight of Labor."

Labour's political failures in the 1880s and early 1890s may also be understood within this context of transformation. In the 1880s the state could not be seen as we know it to exist today: born only in 1867, the Canadian state was actually obscured throughout the 1880s by its essential unfamiliarity, and the workers' movement struggled to devise strategic directions to take toward politics. Given the history of common purpose among labour and owners that preceded the 1880s, the record of achievement and the strides taken by workers in achieving independence should not be underestimated. As early as the 1850s and 1860s, workers entered into an economic-political alliance with manufacturers and far-seeing mercantile elements, forming a common front based on a vision of the Canadian nation as one dominated by producers. This "producer commonwealth," from Confederation on, came to be associated with the pragmatic economic nationalism of Macdonald's Conservative Party. Committed to high tariffs, railroad-building, industrial growth, and westward expansion, Tory policy promised employment for workers caught in an age of insecurity and abated the nine-hour opposition by introducing a Trades Union Bill. A Tory-worker alliance was thus at the centre of working-class politics in the 1870s, visible not only in the industrial-capitalist cities but in the coal fields of Nova Scotia. But in the 1880s, under the impact of the movement culture, working-class independence became an actual rallying cry among significant numbers of labour reformers.

Sceptics will of course point to the failure of the movement culture to elect independent candidates to Parliament, just as they will emphasize the compromises made by labour reformers such as the PWA's Robert Drummond. And partyism continued to exercise its sway. But to focus on these issues is to direct attention away from spheres of vital importance in our understanding of the late nineteenth-century context. The dominant experience within which labour reformers emerged in the 1880s was not national politics, or even provincial campaigns, although these are the most visible and studied realms of past political experience. Even when successful in incorporating labour in an early national policy that promised to speak for a wide amalgam of class interests, the Canadian state was often perceived through working-class eyes that focused on local individuals who concretized a distant, mystical state in particular community settings and neighbourhoods, championing state policies as their own and promising specific benefits to their constituencies. In this personalized, highly localized context, the movement culture of the 1880s understandably saw reform being forged out of the immediate, rather than distant, context: local politics were the neutral ground upon which contending forces battled for political direction.

A pessimistic appraisal of the failures of the political campaigns of 1886-87, therefore, misses much of the point of labour-reform politics in the 1880s. The real failure was that just as the Knights of Labor and Provincial Workmen's Association mounted their seemingly spontaneous and localized political campaigns of the 1880s and 1890s – running candidates for mayor, alderman, and councillor far more often than they contested federal and provincial elections – a new political age was in the process of formation, an age in which the presence of national political concerns gained prominence over local ones. Like its critique of monopoly, the movement culture's political efforts fell short of a mark that demanded a new strategic direction, one in which the state was conceived as a powerful, autonomous force supporting the status quo. Lacking such an orientation, the workers' movement concentrated on the locale, flirted with a larger political reality in 1886-87, and, unaware of the potency of processes of incorporation into the mainstream, slipped back into the traditional party fold as the defeats mounted in the post-1886 years. The cause of labour reform went into its tailspin. Eclectic radicalism had not been enough.

These economic and political changes understandably altered the ideological direction of countless brainworkers, and the eclectic radicalism of the 1880s, once something of a broad and fraternal coming together of dissident minds and thoughts, splintered. Working-class activists who had been loosely associated in the cause of reform now gravitated to diverse camps: socialism, syndicalism, the Independent Labor Party. Divisions previously unknown became paramount as those who had once thought the single tax, theosophy, Irish nationalism, and currency reform compatible became more uncompromisingly convinced that such panaceas were but facades obscuring more precise and programmatic conceptions of change.

And on this note the century ended. With the Knights of Labor in a shambles, with the Provincial Workmen's Association barely hanging on to its members, with the craft unions drawn inwards, with brainworkers now moving in more forceful but occasionally opposed directions, the working class was far from unified. The consolidation of working-class opposition that was both promised and, in part, realized in the year of upheaval, 1886, was now clearly in the throes of dissolution. In the post-1895 social formation there would be much to cause further disruption. But the strength and legacy of the movement culture of the 1880s were considerable, the continuity of personnel, ideals, and forms of resistance sufficient to ensure that in the changed context of 1895-1919 a new kind of labour movement would emerge. Forged in class conflicts as bitter and protracted as anything seen in nineteenth-century Canada, the early twentieth-century workers' movement mounted acute challenges and sustained episodic confrontations before the forces of repression and fragmentation undermined it and forced working-class experience into specific corners in the 1920s.

Chapter 4

THE REMAKING OF THE WORKING CLASS AND ITS OPPOSITIONS
1895-1920

THE SOCIAL FORMATION

As the economy became noticeably depressed in 1893, ushering in a period of hard times that would last until 1896, the political scene also began to change. One casualty of the depression was Tory hegemony, as the political hold of the Macdonald Conservatives weakened with a series of crises in the late 1880s and early 1890s. The Jesuits Estates Act, the Manitoba schools question, and the death of Macdonald himself all contributed to the Tory loss of favour, and when the failure of the economy was attributed openly to the shortcomings of the National Policy, the party was ousted from government. Thus ended the Tories' right to embrace economic nationalism as their particular political property.

Wilfrid Laurier and the Liberals, the lessons of their 1891 defeat fresh in their minds, avoided the temptation to raise, once again, the banner of free trade with the United States. They quietly condoned tariff policies made more suitable to business magnates and won an 1896 electoral victory settled in the industrial heartland of Ontario and Quebec. The new Prime Minister's claim that the twentieth century would "belong to Canada" was based on a conception of the classless society. Such a view may have appeared tenable at the turn of the century, as labour was far from a forceful presence on the political scene, and in the 1890s, at least, there was more political dissidence among farmers than among workers. But in the aftermath of the economic retreat of the 1890s, the presence of labour as a class, felt so strongly in the 1880s, would be evident once more, if only for a brief period. However, the working class existed in a changed context, for the century promised to all Canadians belonged, more correctly, to monopoly capital.

This had tremendous ramifications, and caused a radical restructuring of the working class and subsequent changes in its perception of itself and the place to which it was assigned by non-workers. In the workplace, managerial innovations, technological changes, and newly developing industrial sectors diluted many skills, created a new hierarchy of job classifications, and increased the need for unskilled workers. This last development, a result of the increasing concentration and expansion of productive forces, provided the "pull" required to attract a multitude of immigrants from the fields and factories of eastern, western, and southern Europe. The consequence was a labour market and a labour force fragmented ethnoculturally and structurally. Gains made in the 1880s, as skilled and unskilled workers came together, were outstripped by the complexities of new labour markets that made such primitive distinctions obsolete. The relative cultural cohesion of that decade, moreover, disintegrated as the working class was no longer overwhelmingly Anglo-American in origin.

In spite of these changes, however, the working class remained a distinct entity, with a series of cultures marked off from that of its rulers. This was especially true in new settings like the recently developed industrial-capitalist West. The labour "problem," for all of capital's conquests, still existed. This led to an acute crisis for the industrial-capitalist order, necessitating the intervention of the progressive state in the social relations of production. In fact, the development of Liberal hegemony largely resulted from the recognition of class as a political issue of vital and continuing importance. It was obvious that workers had to be considered as a class with a unified voice and that the *ad hoc* manner in which they had been treated in the late nineteenth century was no longer applicable. William Lyon Mackenzie King, a youthful twenty-two in 1896, was in some respects a product of the interpenetration of politics and class relations, as demonstrated by the positions he held in the years 1895-1920: labour "expert" and journalist, editor of the *Labour Gazette*, deputy minister of labour, member of Parliament, Minister of Labour, architect of labour legislation, freelance labour conciliator, "humanitarian" author, and federal leader of the Liberal Party. In 1921, "Willie" King, the industrial relations authority, occupied the Prime Minister's office, a position he would hold for most of his remaining years. This period, then, consolidated the Liberal Party as well as the contemporary Canadian state, a structure that drew a good part of its early sustenance from the need to respond to class antagonism.

To see the social formation of the early twentieth century in this way is thus to focus on three discrete areas, separable for the purposes of analysis. Economic concentration and the transformation of the workplace were the key factors that led to changes in the social composition of the work force and necessitated the rise of the interventionist state.

The period was marked by great economic change, establishing the years 1900-14 as those of the most rapid growth in the history of post-Confederation Canada. At the root of the accelerating pace of economic life was the increasing concentration of productive power: while enclaves of entrepreneurial capitalism survived in many sectors – Alberta's coal mines, Ontario's garment industry, the realms of resource-processing and manufacturing dispersed throughout the country – the drift was toward highly concentrated forms of corporate production, a far from accidental development orchestrated by finance capital in the metropolitan centres of Toronto and Montreal. Combines and concentration had developed, as the Knights of Labor perceived, even during the 1880s, and that decade witnessed the first movements toward oligopoly in textiles (culminating in the formation of the Canadian Coloured Cotton Company in 1892) and agricultural implements (epitomized by the creation of Massey-Harris in 1891). This process reached new heights in the years after 1900. As Tom Naylor has argued recently, the Great War ushered in a new age characterized by increasing government involvement in economic life, refinements in fiscal policy conducive to capital accumulation, and shifts in income streams available to the propertied.

This was the age of business writ very large indeed. Corporate mergers became a hallmark of the new age, with joint-stock companies emerging as a typical industrial form, displacing the family dynasty and allocating to boards of directors the power that was once wielded through patriarchy and individual autonomy. Fifty-six major industrial consolidations occurred in the years 1900-12, leading to the formation of a number of overcapitalized corporate giants.

Behind such consolidations stood a new breed of industrial financier, professional promoters like Max Aitken and Rodolphe Forget. Aitken, the future Lord Beaverbrook, engineered the takeover of Nova Scotia's regional banks and no doubt applauded the gentleman's agreement establishing close ties between the Royal Bank, whose sphere of influence extended from the Maritimes to the Caribbean, and the Bank of Montreal, which dominated the central Canadian financial scene. More regionally based, Forget, along with his brother Louis, Sir Hugh Allan, Senator Robert Mackay, and

Sir Herbert Holt, created the Montreal Light, Heat, and Power Company, an infamous gas monopoly known as "the Octopus." Managing such overblown affairs became big business and gave rise to specialist managerial magnates like Frank Jones and Joseph Flavelle of the Davies Packing Company.

The merger movement, then, linked finance and industrial capital, concentrated production, and gave rise to new strata within the capitalist class. It changed the very nature of production: 63 per cent of value added in manufacturing in 1890 was produced by almost 2,900 plants, but three decades later a similar percentage of value added was generated by fewer than 950 concerns. Between 1900 and 1920, almost 200 consolidations absorbed approximately 440 firms. Such a trend had a dramatic effect on the quantitative dimensions of industrial output. Production soared. In traditional spheres such as boot and shoemaking and textile, tobacco, and iron production, the net value of goods increased threefold to fivefold, allowing manufacturing to outpace agriculture as the leading economic sector (44 per cent of the value of production in 1919).

The patterns of growth were, of course, coloured by regional economic differences. British Columbia depended on extracted resources of coal, fish, lumber, and non-ferrous metals. On the Prairies, wheat was the prime resource, stimulating new demands for central Canadian manufactured goods, agricultural implements, and processed products, although Winnipeg was itself a manufacturing centre of importance, ranking fourth in the nation. Regional economies, like those of the Crow's Nest Pass and Cape Breton, turned on coal. Production in Alberta climbed to a pre-1945 high of almost 7 million tons in 1920. Quebec's economic well-being was centred in Montreal's financial district and in the explosive development of the pulp and paper industry in the hinterland. Indeed, pulp and paper, along with the automobile sector (as well as related production in rubber, parts, and machinery) and the production of hydroelectric power and electrical apparatus, were among the most dynamic spheres, helping to lend credence to Ontario's vision of its central role in the new industrialism. Automobile production was negligible at the turn of the century but grew markedly in the years 1910-23, the value of production increasing eighteen times. Chemicals, chemical products, and electric light and power saw even more dramatic increases in the value of products from 1900 to 1923: chemical-related goods rose in value by a factor of fourteen, while electric light and power produced in 1923 was thirty-four times more valuable than that generated in 1900. Between 1910 and 1920 these newly established industries displaced older manufactures, laying the groundwork for an industrial structure that survived for decades. The business of Canada was central Canadian business, and social and political practice would turn on this essential recognition.

Illustrative of all of these trends was the history of Canada's steel industry, conceived in the 1880s but actually born in these years. Four groups of

Canadian capitalists were in on the ground floor of this symbolic centre of the new economic age. Growing out of the industrial developments in the Maritimes of the late nineteenth century, the Nova Scotia Steel and Coal Company consolidated in Pictou County. Stimulated by World War One demand, expanding with infusions of Halifax capital, it was eventually taken over by American interests in 1917. With a work force of over 2,000 and many diversified manufacturing facilities, "Scotia" was a regional producer with a national profile. In central Canada its counterpart was the Hamilton Steel and Iron Company. Reorganized by the indefatigable Max Aitken in the immediate pre-World War One years, the Hamilton-based corporation merged with a number of Ontario and Montreal-based producers to form the Steel Company of Canada, which, by the end of the war, was the industry's unqualified success story. Two other steel corporations fared less well. New England entrepreneur Henry Melville Whitney sought to capitalize on the ownership of huge portions of the Nova Scotia coal fields, launching the Dominion Iron and Steel Company at the turn of the century. Its history was more mercurial than those of "Scotia" and "Stelco," however, and while it profited from world war its post-1920 history would be one of disappointment and instability. Even more checkered was the story of Francis Henry Clergue's operations in Sault Ste. Marie. Algoma Steel promised much but ended up delivering far less: by the 1920s it was operating at less than half its capacity.

This mixed message of the steel industry nevertheless contains some essential and unambiguous indications of what was happening economically in the years 1895-1920. A new corporate presence had emerged. Virtually non-existent in the late nineteenth century, the steel industry began in the 1880s and by 1918 it had arrived with a vengeance. In this period four huge corporate enterprises, sustained by mergers and financed by powerful American and Canadian interests, controlled the entire domestic market. Production of pig iron in two short decades soared almost thirty times, and well over ninety times for steel ingots and castings. With a work force of 20,000 this was an industry of monumental importance to the capitalist social formation. But it was not without its problems. American capital was quick to milk profits from existing facilities rather than engage in long-term planning and diversification, and this did much to sink the Algoma operation in the aftermath of World War One. With markets for the new diversified steel products so concentrated in industrial-capitalist Ontario, and with railway orders no longer a reliable source of profit, the industry's concentrated centre became Hamilton's Stelco plant. The margins – Maritime Canada and the new industrial frontier of northern Ontario – were at a serious disadvantage. Corporate concentration and regional advantage thus became the hallmarks of one of Canada's leading industries, an indication of the way the economy was being structured in specific directions in the early twentieth century.

Many areas of the Canadian economy other than steel found themselves inundated by American capital. The increasing concentration of industry, the expansion of output, and the pressure of tariff protection all moved American interests north, and the dependent status of Canadian capital was established during this period. As Marshall, Southard, and Taylor noted in 1936, the years 1900-05 saw the most rapid rate of growth of American-owned firms in Canada, when the number of these enterprises more than doubled. Between 1900 and 1914, American investment in Canada increased five times, and doubled again, to approximately $1.63 billion, in the World War One years. The number of American firms entering Canada rose from an average of twelve a year in the 1900-05 period to over thirty-three yearly from 1915 to 1920. Concentrated in the Toronto-Hamilton-Niagara region and in Montreal, the branch-plant economy was embedded in the centre of industrial-capitalist Canada, although similar dependent economic structures also reached into British Columbia railways and smelters, Alberta coal fields, and eastern Canadian steel production. International Harvester, General Electric, Westinghouse, American Locomotive, Swift's, Singer, American Asbestos, Standard Oil, National Cash Register, Sherwin-Williams, Du Pont, Ford, and Goodyear were among the scores of Canadian branch plants set up in the opening decades of the twentieth century. They brought advanced technology and helped to introduce new methods of managing labour that were eagerly received by indigenous Canadian capital.

In these years, for instance, efficiency experts came on to the shopfloor armed with stop watches and slide rules with the intention of standardizing tasks, minimizing worker autonomy, and, thus, increasing output. This was an age of "scientific management," ceremoniously announced by the "principles" of an idiosyncratic but determined American engineer, Frederick Winslow Taylor. It was also a period of the professionalization of management, of stricter cost accountancy in business, industrial betterment (which often translated into profit-sharing, improvements in working conditions and company facilities, or factory beautification schemes), and closer attention to the hiring procedure and maintenance of stable personnel relations. "System" was the buzzword of the new century; order, the ultimate aim.

While far from universal in its impact, the managerial revolution had its most pronounced successes in the highly concentrated and advanced sectors of textiles, high-technology manufacturing (especially precision-production and railway supplies), and the new industrial staples, notably smelting and pulp-and-paper production. It was notoriously difficult, if not impossible, to manage scientifically a mine, the docks, or the lumber camp, nor was it likely that agricultural labour, the building trades, or relatively small, specialty shops, where social relations retained much of their handicraft character, would fall to the reorganization of the expert. The transformation of the workplace was thus concentrated in central Canadian corporate enterprises where mass production, technological innovation, and expanding markets were all increasingly important. Advocates of the new science of production, however, undoubtedly had an ideological impact extending well beyond the actual implementation of various schemes and plans, making efficient use of labour a prime concern of most employers.

Case studies of the implementation of managerial innovations detail the diversity of particular forms, as well as the underlying motivations of reducing labour costs and increasing productivity. Taylor's hand-picked disciple, Henry Gantt, reorganized the CPR's locomotive repair facilities in Montreal's Angus Shops, while in the Grand Trunk freight yards in Toronto a newly developed system of "intensive" management prevented "Chaos." Management journals such as *Industrial Canada* popularized new supervisory methods, and employers used royal commissions to lobby the government to encourage awareness of systems developed in pace-setting American firms like General Electric and Baldwin Locomotive Works. H.L.C. Hall of the International Accountants' Society restructured working life at Hamilton's B. Greening Wire Company, transferring authority from skilled workmen to foremen, standardizing tasks, eliminating all lost time and motion, tabulating the minutes required to perform each job and the materials and tools employed, and adopting piece rates and premium plans. At the Lumen Bearing Company of Toronto a similar regime increased production from twenty-eight castings a day to sixty-five. "It is the story of economy of time and energy," boasted one advocate, "of making . . . more efficient workmen." Like most such efforts the intention was, "First, to induce economy by the elimination of waste, and second to induce economy by intensifying production."

Such developments – the increasing concentration and expansion of economic power and the reorganization of work – were not received passively by the working class. Those workers who retained a measure of skill and saw their workplace authority whittled down during this period reacted most vigorously. But one part of capital's capacity to effect such growth and change was the structural alteration in the working class itself. During this period, mass immigration changed the composition of the Canadian working class.

Because many of the new immigrants lacked industrial skills, they provided suitable material upon which the productive and managerial imperatives of capital could work. They had the raw muscle and sheer numbers to work the mines, railway construction projects, and mass production industries of post-1900 Canada. Other immigrants found themselves in the semi-skilled positions of entirely new economic sectors, which lacked traditions of labour organization and resistance. Many thousands spoke no English, their workplace communication restricted to acceptance of the wage, which came to them in pay envelopes catalogued with an impersonal number rather than a name. One immigrant worker in Hamilton had been dead for hours before anyone could ascertain who he actually was. Off the job, they relied on their own ethnic community rather than class allegiances, retreating into their own cultures, a move often conditioned by English-speaking workers' open contempt for the immigrant way of life and the ethnic worker's role as a wage-depressing member of an increasingly large reserve army of labour.

Over 2.2 million immigrants came to Canada between 1903 and 1912. World War One of course restricted this inflow, but well over one million immigrants arrived in Canada between 1913 and 1922. The bulk of these were British, although hundreds of thousands came from various corners of continental Europe. Many were at first sojourners attached to their homelands, but the new immigrants quickly became permanent settlers, establishing communities across Canada. By 1921 the Italian population of Montreal had grown to almost 14,000. One in ten workers in Hamilton was European-born by the 1920s, and in 1918 it was reported that "foreigners" did "practically the whole of the heavy and laborious work" in the iron, steel, and metalworking shops and factories. Almost every major industrial centre had similar ethnic enclaves, and in the West most members of the working class had just arrived in Canada. In the coal fields of Alberta in 1911, nine out of ten miners were said to be immigrants, who represented fifteen to twenty separate ethnic groups, including Bohemians, Finns, Poles, Ukrainians, Slovaks, and Swedes. It is not surprising that real growth in population leapt forward by 65 per cent in the first two decades of the twentieth century.

This quantitative transformation could not but affect the nature and position of class forces in Canadian society. With the city replacing the country as the centre of social and economic life, the voice of the working class should have acquired authority. As the percentage of workers gainfully employed in non-agricultural pursuits expanded from 54 in 1891 to 67 in 1921, class discontent should have moved more unambiguously into the social and political arena. In fact, it did. But because class unity was impeded by language barriers and because grievances varied so markedly from sector to sector and region to region, the potential for class solidarity was undercut. Nevertheless, there were instances of episodic class confrontation and efforts to build new movements of class resistance. When this occurred, however, the working class faced yet another hurdle: the increasing authority and power of the state.

The evolution of William Lyon Mackenzie King's particular form of industrial relations paralleled the rise of the Liberal state in the years 1900-11. In his astute recognition of the need to draw "community," capital, and labour together, King attempted to mediate class antagonism by bringing both labour and capital under the jurisdiction of established political authority, creating state bodies that were to act as supposedly disinterested voices of "the community." The conflicting interests of workers and employers were to be subjected to the scrutiny of the "impartial umpire" of the state. The creation of a Labour Department and the passage of the Industrial Disputes Investigation Act of 1907 were part of the new strategy.

Although the progressive, interventionist state claimed impartiality, it more often worked to ends that fulfilled capital's needs and aspirations. The IDIA, for instance, cultivated a measure of industrial peace through its advocacy of compulsory conciliation and endorsement of a "cooling off" period necessary to "reasonable" bargaining between capital and labour. Tripartite boards of arbitration were established, and the need for special treatment of "public interest" disputes was recognized. Designed only for utilities, railroads, and coal mines, the Act nevertheless set the tone for labour-relations policy in the early twentieth century. Between 1907 and 1911, over 100 disputes were handled under the IDIA, and in nine cases out of ten, strikes were averted.

This procedural commitment to "conciliation" was but the velvet glove over the mailed fist. Capital and the state did not hesitate to take repressive action against workers. Refusal to comply with an investigation or to postpone a strike in accordance with the Act could be penalized by fines, the legislation drawing the line between legal and illegal work stoppages. If working people entered somewhat willingly into King's theatre of reconciliation, then, they were also coerced into compliance: during the opening decades of the twentieth century, military intervention in class struggles was on the rise. Of the thirty-three strike-related instances of "aid to the civil" power known to historians in the years 1867-1914, the rate of intervention increased appreciably in the post-1895 years. Well over two-thirds of the total number of militia involvements in strike situations after Confederation took place in the 1895-1914 period. Among the most bloody battles were those that pitched Cape Breton, Springhill, and Vancouver Island miners against their employers and the armed forces of the state. When one considers that monopoly capital began to arm itself ever more effectively in this epoch, drawing on detective agencies, employer associations, spies, blacklists, and open-shop campaigns, it is clear that the working class was indeed a "community under siege." "Whatever King's impenetrable doctrines of conciliation amounted to," observes Ian McKay, "they barely concealed the crucial new fact that, in defence of capitalism, the state was prepared to kill."

Worker organization, of course, was often the stimulus to such violence, threatened and actual, just as it was one obvious response to concentration of industry and managerial attempts to impose a more rigorous discipline at the workplace. In an age of big business backed by interventionist government, it was hardly surprising that large unions found a receptive audience among Canadian workers, who discovered in the years 1895-1919 how little of the century was actually theirs.

MATERIAL LIFE

Studies of real incomes, job security, working-class housing, and health standards in the urban centres of Montreal, Toronto, and Vancouver in the years 1900-21 establish the existence of a labour force struggling unsuccessfully to keep pace with rampant inflation. R.H. Coats's 1915 observation that wage levels did not rise comparably with increases in productivity in the first fifteen years of the century has been substantiated by the arguments of Terry Copp, Michael Piva, and Eleanor Bartlett. Prices soared, with the wholesale commodity index skyrocketing from a 1900 base level of 100 to a 1920 high of over 280. Wage rates, on the other hand, rose and fell between 1900 and 1915, then inched imperceptibly upward. Major wage increases were recorded during World War One, when labour shortages allowed unskilled labour and a variety of skilled trades to extract concessions from employers; hourly earnings increased 20 per cent and more. But the cost of living between 1915 and 1918 wiped out most gains at the workplace by forcing real incomes down.

Working-class incomes were also highly differentiated. Segmented labour markets emerged and consolidated; various "grades" of labour were marked off by a hierarchical wage scale expressive not only of skill, age, and gender, but also of status and ethnicity. Highest paid were the skilled males who, in the opening decades of the century, might draw $2.75 to $3 daily. Labourers would earn less than $1.75, especially if they were Italian, Ukrainian, or members of other non-Anglo-Saxon immigrant groups. Messenger boys might count on eighty cents to a dollar per day, while other male child workers, aged ten to fourteen, might fare slightly better. Women, working at piece rates in the garment industry or as waitresses or domestics (where food and lodging might be incorporated into the wage), experienced diverse scales of payments. But $4 to $5 per week was not uncommon. While a minority of skilled female workers, such as stenographers and nurses, might command as much as $20 weekly, there were instances in sweated or outwork situations of women earning fifty-three cents a week (in 1895) or the equivalent of two cents an hour (in 1901). In general, women's wages were roughly 40 to 60 per cent of men's, although for the rare women who broke into the crafts, wages were almost equal. Such meagre economic prospects for working women made prostitution an attractive alternative to wage labour.

However, the most important effect of low wages was to discourage women from entering the labour market at all. With the man as the primary wage earner, family incomes varied between $550 per year for unskilled labour in Montreal in 1914 and $1,135 for skilled workers in Toronto in 1921. To support the family, the wage earner had to work six days a week, fifty-two weeks a year, without sickness, unemployment, or vacations, spend nothing on drink, furniture, education, or savings, and, with luck, have an employable wife, teenage son, or daughter to "put out" into domestic service or industrial employment. In spite of a series of legislative enactments aimed at keeping children under the age of fourteen in school, many working-class youth spent a good deal of their time earning modest wages to keep precarious families afloat economically.

Working-class well-being was thus quite circumscribed. This was an epoch that predated basic welfare measures, and periodic recessions coupled with seasonal fluctuations disrupting many trades and unskilled callings affected many workers. Even in good times, if the work force expanded faster than the number of jobs available (through a combination of natural increase and immigration), the existence of a labour surplus would keep many workers unemployed. Houses of industry, piecemeal public works projects, and the meagre sums expended on relief (roughly $35,000 yearly in Toronto from 1901 to 1921) achieved little in alleviating the plight of the jobless, while religious societies, the cornerstone of Catholic Montreal's welfare structure, were no more successful. In Ontario in 1914, 14 per cent of all factory workers had been unemployed over the course of the year; in steelmaking, the figure stood at 27 per cent. "The fear of unemployment," declared Toronto District Labour Council secretary William J. Hevey in 1919, "is one of the most dreadful things in the life of the workman."

If workers were fortunate enough to have work, there were still major problems. Hours at the workplace were long, up to sixty a week, and ventilation was poor, safety measures were minimal, and the production process was likely to be accelerated because of the reorganization of work. Factory acts protecting workers were vague and ineffectual, and not until 1909 in Quebec and 1914 in Ontario did workers' compensation reform overcome some of the deficiencies of the old employer-liability legislation of the 1880s, which workers found increasingly unsatisfactory as an effective guard against disabilities incurred through rising numbers of industrial accidents. In the dangerous extractive industries of the West, as in railway construction work, high accident rates actually imposed structural impediments for capital to overcome, creating labour shortages. While improvements were made, they were generally in the interests of capital and had little to do with recognition of the socio-political grievances of workers. "Benevolent" employers were convinced that reform would increase productivity, curtail absenteeism, and forestall unionism. In 1920, it was still possible for one labour spokesman to claim with justification that workers were "left to the mercies of their employers who . . . have in many industries required them to work under conditions that are constantly jeopardizing their lives and their health."

If the shopfloor was a far from ideal environment, neither was the working-class home. In Montreal, 80 per cent of the population rented accommodations, and housing shortages created the opportunity for landlords to gouge tenants, charging $10 to $12 monthly for basement rooms.

This might represent 25 per cent of an unskilled worker's wage. Rents climbed 50 per cent in the pre-World War One years, making it necessary for families to share accommodations. When the Board of Health examined Montreal's housing in 1918, it found almost 2,000 dwellings damp, overcrowded, or dirty. A similar survey in Toronto claimed that in one sample of 235 houses, half were occupied by more than one family, and one-fifth to one-third were without basic sanitary facilities. A larger Toronto investigation, also undertaken in 1918, established that of 13,000 domiciles inspected, 8,000 were overcrowded, a product once more of landlords attempting to secure whatever the market would bear. One zealous entrepreneur took two $11-a-month cottages, divided them into four units, and almost doubled his intake, charging rent totalling $42. Ameliorative efforts, such as the Toronto Housing Company's proposal to build low-cost housing for rent rather than for sale and Quebec legislative reforms, made only a modest impact in the pre-1920 years. If the Canadian-born working class experienced privation in this realm, the immigrant worker fared even worse. Ethnic slums drew the early ire of J.S. Woodsworth, who quoted a mission worker's report to convey the character of one immigrant household: "John Klenbyel and wife and six children, and from fifteen to twenty boarders live in four rented rooms. The place is 'beastly' dirty. The boarders bring home kegs of beer nearly every day. Two of the older girls are 'working out'. One of them told our visitor the other day that she cannot stay at home; she is happier away." "Comment is hardly necessary," snorted Woodsworth.

Working-class wives and families could do much to overcome such conditions, and domestic lives were often structured around coping with these less than adequate conditions. Victories were won. But such living arrangements, exacerbated by inadequate sewage systems, a primitive notion of how to combat disease, low nutritional intake, and food and milk that were often contaminated or adulterated, bred poor standards of public health. One in three Montreal infants died before reaching the age of twelve months in the years 1897-1911, with gastro-intestinal diseases taking a particularly heavy toll. In Toronto, infants fared better, but in the first two decades of the twentieth century more than one in ten died young. Those who survived might face the ravages of tuberculosis or typhoid, illnesses contributing to high death rates in industrial cities. At the root of persistent health problems was nothing less than inadequate working-class incomes, one doctor reducing the issue to its lowest common denominator: "The destruction of the poor is their poverty."

To be sure, it would not be appropriate to depict all workers in all regions as economically downtrodden, poverty-stricken, and diseased. Some historians, such as Ian Drummond, have scrutinized the industrial-capitalist experience of these years in Ontario and concluded that the period 1900-13 was a Great Boom. Real wages crept upward, according to the rather generalized and imprecise figures marshalled by Drummond, but even he acknowledges the problems in the data and concedes that the war and immediate post-war years introduced turmoil and uncertainty in the economic realm that adversely affected working-class lives. No doubt assessment of the standard of living of Canadian workers in this period will continue to pit optimists against pessimists. The data are fragmentary, of course, and much depends on the proclivity of historians of opposed political positions to interpret this sketchy evidence in ways that often seem to bear little relationship to one another. An appreciation of the differentiation of the working class and of how specific layers of labouring people reacted to the changing conditions of the time is central to understanding the complexity of this debate.

The period afforded the privileged pinnacle of labour – skilled, unionized, English-speaking, often regionally embedded in central Canada's capitalist heartland – some small chances of material advance. Yet in regions where such workers were not the norm, or among the growing underclass of those urban slums mired in the marginalization of capital's burgeoning metropolitan centres, the Great Boom and its denouement were hardly a time of abundance. Even so-called protective legislation, supposedly aimed at insulating workers and the poor from the excesses of the market, might be experienced differently. Thus restrictions on child labour, strengthened (though hardly effective) during these years, could benefit the generational possibility of mobility for privileged workers by allowing their children access to education and the appreciation of new possibilities. But for other segments of the labouring poor the enforced loss of child income might prove a severe and immediate deprivation. Nor was this process without its gender implications, as women found their lot confined increasingly to economies either domestic or marginal.

No hard and fast conclusions can be drawn from this, but it would seem that for the majority of the working class, perhaps, life was simply not getting all that much better, certainly not unambiguously so. Among the minority who did manage to register gains, the rising expectations of the moment might well be deflated by the alienating restrictions of the workplace, where the relatively high wage was no guarantee of contentment. In addition was the perception that whatever small advantages some workers could secure, capital was accumulating more, both in power and in dollars. Out of this complex swirl of material circumstances and understandings some workers responded with resignation, others with resistance.

INTERNATIONALISM

Material difficulties constrained most workers, albeit differently; if craft workers and their unskilled brothers and sisters remained distinctive status groupings, many were reminded of the harsh commonalities of class experience. In the face of what were perceived as deteriorating conditions, significant numbers of workers, especially those with a remnant of skill to be undercut, turned to the most powerful proponent of labour's interests. The Canadian history of international craft unionism, as we have seen, commenced in the 1850s. Although they played a secondary role to that of the Knights of Labor in the 1880s, the craft unions, not the Noble and Holy Order, survived into the twentieth century.

The eclectic radicalism embraced by many craft unionists and the consequent willingness to make common cause with the unskilled were, however, somewhat tamed by events of the 1890s. All unions avoided confrontation in these depression-ridden years, and some internationals, like the Molders', suffered serious setbacks in the face of a virulent capitalist offensive in 1890-92. But even in defeat, organized workers were still poised for limited, yet significant, action; the cause of international unionism was given a boost by the aristocratic railway conductors and trainmen, whose orders and brotherhoods won a critical victory against the CPR and William Van Horne in 1892. But this was a victory narrowed into craft union needs rather than reaching out to larger class interests. The lesson of the 1890s was clear: to fight and win one had to define the struggle quite precisely and rely on the strengths of specific groups of workers who had skills that were needed in the marketplace and traditions of collectivity that could be counterposed to managerial authority. In the words of the Toronto *Globe*, no union could expect recognition "until it [was] strong enough to force it."

That strength flowed not only from the internal state of the crafts, but also from the external conditions of economic life. As the clouds of hard times lifted in the late 1890s, craft unions reasserted themselves, and their collective fortunes over the course of the next two decades, like the pattern of strike activity, followed the crests and troughs in the business cycle. Organization boomed in the 1897-1904 upswing, settled into a holding pattern until 1915, when the war brought the country out of a major recession, and exploded thereafter, union membership expanding from 166,000 in 1914 to 378,000 in 1919.

In the post-1896 upsurge, the craft unions established their supremacy within the Canadian labour movement, capturing the one-time stronghold of the Knights of Labor, the Trades and Labor Congress of Canada. As late as 1893 the Knights dominated this institutional centre of organized labour, but at the historic Berlin (Ontario) Congress in 1902 all who opposed supremacy of the powerful international craft unions were banished. Driven from the ranks of officially organized labour, the Knights and other "dual" unionists formed their own "national" labour centre, the National Trades and Labor Congress, which gave way to the Canadian Federation of Labor in 1908. But these were only a minor threat to the TLC. Internationalism was the central tendency within the Canadian labour movement in these years, a trend that Robert Babcock once dubbed American labour

continentalism. Samuel Gompers, craft union boss of the American Federation of Labor, one-time socialist cigarmaker in the 1880s but by the turn of
the century a committed pragmatist given to demanding nothing but
"more, more, more" for his membership, cast his shadow into Canada.

His influence spread across the country with efforts of men such as
Hamilton's John A. Flett, a carpenter and former Knight appointed as the
AFL's first full-time general organizer in Canada at the turn of the century.
As the AFL established itself, volunteer advocates from all parts of the
country finally became officially recognized and commissioned agents of
Gompers and the Federation. These men, and many others, bore much of
the credit for the 250 per cent increase in the number of chartered interna-
tional unions in Canada in the years 1897-1902. By 1902, well over 1,000
AFL-affiliated union locals existed across the country. Fifty-nine per cent of
these were in Ontario, 13 per cent in British Columbia, 11 per cent in
Quebec, 9 per cent in the Maritimes, and 7 per cent on the Prairies. Urban
centres like Toronto, Montreal, Hamilton, Winnipeg, and Vancouver had
the highest concentrations, with from thirty-five to 105 union locals each.
By 1914 the number of Canadian locals had risen to 1,775, with an average
membership of seventy-five.

Some scholars claim that international craft unionism had the effect of
quelling the resistance of Canadian labour, acting as an agent of incorporation and quiescence. The Canadian labour movement in this period has
been viewed as ideologically confined by American bureaucratic unionism,
a pragmatic Gompersism that kept labour politically subdued and economically contained. There is some truth in this, and no doubt the exclusivist
"bread-and-butter" unionism of Gompers left less room for the unskilled,
the woman, and the class-conscious than had previous organizations, such
as the Knights of Labor, or more militant rivals, such as the Industrial
Workers of the World. But craft unionism was never some monolithic
structural process of incarceration, in which workers were only stifled and
moved in the directions that business unionism allowed. Members of these
skilled bodies of workingmen played a fundamental role in socialist reform
politics and battled at the workplace, where they confronted a determined
resistance to any notion of unionism.

The lessons of the 1880s were still remembered by some in this craft union
milieu. Gompers's assertions that Canadian and American workers were
"one and the same in spirit, in fact, in union, with one common polity and
policy; with identical principles, hopes, and aspirations," was purposeful
rhetoric when it came from the head of the AFL, which had neither the
capacity nor the intention of dealing with the many differences between the
Canadian and United States political and economic contexts. Nevertheless,
it rang true in many workers' ears. "There is no 49th parallel of latitude in
Unionism," declared one British Columbia miner. "The Canadian and
American workingmen have joined hands across the Boundary line for a

common cause against a common enemy." Internationalism still meant something noble and necessary to workers, in spite of the fact that the exclusivist Gompers was always guided by a tacit premise of "unionism in one country." If the international unions failed to provide all the answers for all workers, they still offered tangible solutions to some immediate problems. It was the first step toward organizational revitalization. Only time and twenty years of change and conflict at the workplace and in the realm of politics would reveal the fatal flaw in craft unionism's Pyrrhic victories during the years 1897-1902.

WORKPLACE CONFRONTATION

Strikes, as we have seen, were not unusual in the nineteenth century; between 1901 and 1914, however, they became something of the norm in the social relations of production. In an exhaustive survey of Canadian strikes between 1891 and 1950, Douglas Cruikshank and Gregory S. Kealey point to the importance of this period as the site of two major national strike waves. The first, stretching from 1899 to 1903, involved 726 strikes and was concentrated in Ontario, where skilled workers seized the opportunities presented in the aftermath of the depression of the 1890s. Aggressive, and often victorious, these strikes tended to take place in the manufacturing and construction sectors; in transportation and mining there were fewer strikes, but the size and militancy of the conflicts were greater. The second wave, in 1912-13, was more geographically dispersed, with western workers more of a presence. In this shorter two-year period 308 strikes were fought, but the industrial range of conflict was extended; garment workers were particularly active and the strike could occasionally take on the character of a military campaign, as in the coal fields of Vancouver Island, where a two-year strike was ended only by the outbreak of world hostilities in August, 1914.

Strike activity in the three Maritime provinces and in the structural core of capitalist Canada, south-central Ontario, points to the pervasiveness of conflict, the important place of regional peculiarities, and the influence of the character of the workplace in conditioning the nature of class struggle. Finally, studies of these confrontations look beyond the obvious battle over the wage, envisioning the strike as an essential confrontation over power.

Across the Maritimes 324 strikes were fought in the years 1901-14, with the tempo of class conflict following closely the fluctuations in the business cycle. Strikes tended to be fought in the "good times" of 1904-05 and 1909-11, rather than in the years of recession associated with 1908 or the pre-World War One downturn, commencing in 1913. But the particular character of specific Maritime groups, as Ian McKay points out, loomed large in strike activity. Unskilled labour fought a large percentage of these battles (37 per cent), the skilled crafts were involved in 28 per cent of the confrontations, and miners led 18.5 per cent of all strikes. Less skilled workers responded almost immediately to changes in the economic climate, and the pre-depression year of 1907 represented the highwater mark in the number of labourers' strikes. Craft workers had more diverse reasons for striking, but the building boom associated with the construction of the steel works at Sydney in the first years of the century created a tight labour market and rising prices that provided the structural inducement to strike. Miners, something of a community apart, tended to follow a unique pattern, and the years 1909-11 overshadow all others in the history of class conflict in this period.

Labour's discontents extended well beyond the coal fields of Nova Scotia, with 56 per cent of the strikes in these years taking place in the port cities of Saint John and Halifax, but the miners accounted for 76 per cent of the days lost to strikes. Most dramatic were the massive confrontations in the coal communities of Glace Bay and Springhill, where battles were fought and lost over recognition of the United Mine Workers of America. Involving over 1.3 million striker-days, the coal conflicts of these three years were among the most protracted and vehement battles in the country. In the region itself, they were of unquestionable significance in the twentieth-century pre-war years, making up over 80 per cent of days lost to strikes in the coal fields and over 60 per cent of all days lost in the Maritime provinces.

Such strikes often turned on the wage, which workers perceived to be losing ground to inflation. Sixty-five per cent of Maritime strikes in these years, by one method of classifying issues involved in industrial conflicts, were related to wage-increase demands or opposition to reductions. But there were other issues as well, including union recognition, control of apprenticeship, objections to forms of payment or new work systems, and opposition to supervisory personnel. Broadly conceived, these and other discontents relate to workers' attempts to secure or retain some hold on a measure of autonomy at the workplace.

The strike was thus a privileged moment in which, to employ English socialist R.H. Tawney's phrase, "autocracy [was] checked by insurgence." There was a sense in which workers grasped intuitively that monopoly capital was about more than the appropriation of their labour power; it was also about the taking of their dignity. Indeed, a voracious capital seemed to want to devour both with equal dispatch. As a consequence, the history of workplace relations turns not only on the reappropriation of the wage but also on various attempts to seize the pride that workers sensed they were losing. In the mines, this related quite directly to matters of life and death, for the workers themselves saw that their own standards and ethics could ensure safety, whereas management's flirted with disaster.

If Maritime workers did not use the strike to oppose mechanization (no strikes were fought on this issue alone) and the "scientific" reorganization of work (only seven conflicts might have related to this problem), this "quiescence" relates more to the economic context than it does to worker passivity. Both grievances were of only minor significance in the pre-war history of port workers and coal miners, the dominant regional occupations. Labour, however, was quick to react to tyranny on the job. In 1909 one miner declared, "[A] time comes in the life of nations, it comes in the life of communities, and in the life of organizations when THEY CANNOT ENDURE ANY LONGER THE IMPOSITIONS FORCED ON THEM BY AN AUTO-CRATIC AND OVERBEARING SPIRIT."

Strikes in the Maritimes thus follow complex patterns resulting from national developments, regional peculiarities, and diverse experiences within the working class. From the dramatic challenge to capital expressed in the coal confrontations of 1909-11 to the frustrated defeats of women, immigrants, and the unskilled, through the ambiguous job actions of craftsmen, who might strike to retain the exclusive status of their trade (a losing battle, in the long run), industrial conflict ran the gamut from the heroic to the tragic, from the limited victory to the defeat that nevertheless signalled the beginnings of a class stance. Employers imported strike-breakers by the thousands, stood fast against unionism, drew on the state and the law, and, in the end, constructed an elaborate hegemony that would carry them through the war years and into the period of the regional economy's ultimate collapse. They had won the battle, but they would lose a war in which there were no winners.

At a superficial glance, the history of Maritime strikes in the years 1901-14 is weighted down with defeat. But in the midst of labour's crushing losses in these years emerged solidarities and organizational forms, strategies, and understandings that would resurface in the class conflicts of the 1920s. In 1903 a Springhill miner articulated the class resolve associated with that period of the miners' revolt, declaring in the midst of a strike: "We are prepared to stay out fifteen years. . . . No, we will not tolerate the interference of politicians or any one else this time. We are running the affair and will settle it to suit ourselves." Words like these would be rare in central Canada at this time, but if they were spoken they would come, not from a miner, but from skilled craftsmen, concentrated in the metal trades, where managerial revolution and technological change provided the incentive for workplace protest.

Craig Heron and I have argued that strikes in ten south-central Ontario cities were also numerous in these years, and at least 421 struggles were waged. As in the Maritimes, strikes were commonly resorted to in times of prosperity. Locale also played a large role, with the urban centres of Toronto and Hamilton accounting for 47 and 22 per cent of all strikes in these ten cities, involving over 50,000 workers or an overwhelming 89 per cent of all strikers. But unlike on the east coast, here the strike was the particular weapon of the skilled and was less likely to precipitate a mass upheaval. More common were smaller, shorter confrontations – an ongoing theatre of conflict. Workers in the building and metal trades led fully half of all of these strikes, and the unskilled a bare minimum of 6 per cent. The diversity of the economy of south-central Ontario and the range of manufacturing pursuits explain some of this, as does the rise of the branch plant and the implementation of various efficiency schemes and managerial innovations. Whereas labour in the mines and on the docks dominated the Maritime work force, south-central Ontario moulders, machinists, carpenters, painters, and bricklayers made up a greater part of those employed.

They struck, of course, against the wage cut and for supplements to the wage payment. But they also engaged in battles for control: over apprenticeship, against arbitrary foremen, in opposition to new systems of payment and management. As efficiency-conscious employers restructured the nature of work, subdividing tasks, accelerating the pace of work, and intensifying operations, workers fought back. In 1907, female operators at Toronto's Bell Telephone struck unsuccessfully against a particularly unreasonable managerial dictate that they would have to cut hourly wage rates at the same time that the work day was to be extended from a rigidly monitored five hours to eight. Electricians, female knitting-mill workers, carpet weavers, and garment workers waged similar struggles against the modernization of the labour process, but often to similarly unsuccessful ends. More often victorious were the skilled trades, which might extract concessions before recourse to the strike or adopt workplace strategies of resistance that flowed from their unique knowledge of the technical and human components of production.

But regardless of their situation within the work force, all workers came to resent the incursions of zealous innovators, whose purpose was to engineer men and women as they did the symbols of the new age, machines. "The 'one man two machines', the 'Taylor', 'Scientific', 'Premium', 'piece work', and other systems introduced into the metal shops are making of men what men are supposed to make of metals," declared one labour journal. An anonymous poet expressed a generalized class sentiment when he addressed his lines of verse to an "Efficiency Expert in Hell." Strikes were one expression of the class resentments bred of the changed conditions of these early twentieth-century years; anti-labour initiatives on the part of capital were yet another.

In central Canada these management initiatives included employers' associations (more than sixty in Ontario alone) such as the National Founders' Association and the National Metal Trades Association, which joined their American counterparts in a crusade against unionism. Capital also looked to the courts, where it secured legal victories prohibiting picketing and boycotting (the systematic use of the injunction against the workers' movement dates from a Toronto metal trades dispute in 1902), blocking legalization of the union label, deflecting legislation establishing the eight-hour day, and amending the Alien Labour Bill to allow employers a free hand in importing workers. Flooding the labour market with British workers and European immigrants, of course, undercut the viability of any working-class resistance. Supplemented by increased supervisory rigour, paternalistic policies, and welfare-capitalist measures, as well as the armed intervention of the state and the conciliation of the IDIA, these tactics helped employers carry out their strategy of subordinating labour by driving unionism from the country.

Opposition of this order stimulated class conflict across Canada. In Quebec, according to Stuart Jamieson's review of the strikes enumerated in the *Labour Gazette*, the centre of the storm was in the labour-intensive sector of the "light" industries – especially textiles and clothing – that figured prominently in the provincial economy. A 1908 royal commission investigating conditions in the cotton textile industry cited wage cuts, long hours, and evasion of laws regulating child labour as critical areas of working-class grievance in Quebec. A classic confrontation erupted in October, 1900, at the Montreal Cotton Company's Valleyfield plant, a centre of conflict throughout this period (strikes took place in 1901, 1907, and again in 1908). Precipitated by unskilled labourers doing excavations for the company, the strike expanded to include many of the 3,000 textile workers, who were outraged when the company summoned the militia from Montreal. Federal mediation was required to bring the workers back to their jobs.

To the west, the years from 1900 to 1914 saw an unprecedented escalation of conflict. In burgeoning cities such as Winnipeg and Calgary a wide range of urban workers embraced the strike: railway shop workers, street railwaymen, saddlers, machinists, and carpenters. "The great lesson which organized labour learned here in 1903," declared Calgary's *Bond of Brotherhood*, "was the fact of the class war existing here as naked and unashamed as in the older cities most of us have recently left." The dominant forces within the western class struggle, however, were the coal miner and the railway worker. These years represented the heroic years of international unionism in the coal fields of western Canada, the United Mine Workers of America battling for the rights of a membership that employers were dedicated to blocking. Organizational strikes, like that of the massive two-year confrontation between 7,000 Vancouver Island miners associated with the UMWA and Canadian Collieries Limited, led to the importation of Chinese and occidental strikebreakers, riots, and military intervention. After outlays of $16,000 weekly, totalling $1.5 million, the international was forced to concede defeat, and after 1914 the union was driven decisively from the island, just as organization had been after earlier confrontations. The power of the Dunsmuir coal interests and their successors, the Canadian Collieries, proved more than the union could bear.

Equally powerful was the Canadian Pacific Railway, symbol of monopoly and its intimate connection with the state. As an industrial crisis deepened in 1903, the United Brotherhood of Railway Employees challenged the CPR, opposing the "secret warfare" of capital's attempt to break the union through intimidation, dismissal of activists, and use of labour spies. Wedded to the organization of all railway workers rather than subdivided craft bodies, the UBRE battled from Revelstoke to Winnipeg "to perpetuate their union, nothing else." Initiated in February, 1903, the strike continued into March, when sailors from Victoria, longshoremen in Vancouver, and Calgary teamsters stopped work in sympathetic job refusals to handle "scab" freight. Winnipeg's Trades and Labor Council declared the CPR "unfair" across the West, and other city centrals took up the same stance of opposition. Public outcry developed as strikers were jailed and one militant socialist, Frank Rogers, was shot dead by company thugs while picketing the CPR tracks in Vancouver. But the craft brotherhoods, condemned for their "scabherding" policies and "reprehensible and traitorous conduct," refused their support, and with their aid and the availability of strikebreakers, the CPR was able to crush working-class resistance. The UBRE suffered defeat, its major accomplishment being the creation of a royal commission whose findings simply heightened class tensions and elicited yet more indignation from British Columbia workers.

In the southeastern British Columbia and Alberta coal fields of the Crow's Nest Pass, the workers and their union, the UMWA, fared better. Unlike the immensely powerful CPR and the Vancouver Island mining communities, the Pass was characterized by small employers, all scrambling to make ends meet. Over 300 mines were in operation by 1918. Pitted against weaker employers than had been confronted either in the East or on the west coast, unionists gained a foothold here early in the twentieth century. From the outset, radicalism was associated with organization, the Western Federation of Miners (later to associate with the Industrial Workers of the World) pioneering unionism in the mines. In British Columbia, Fernie, Coal Creek, Michel, and Morrissey were early centres of strength, and strikes were fought. But effective unionism dated from the UMWA breakthroughs in 1905-06 and the first major instance of class war, the Lethbridge, Alberta, strike of 1906.

Although far from a union victory, the Lethbridge confrontation won wage increases, other concessions, and the company's promise of non-discrimination against union members. It thus secured the UMWA a foothold in the region, known as District 18, and was a landmark in the history of western miners. As Allen Seager and William Baker have shown, the Lethbridge strike was won as much by Mackenzie King as it was by the miners and their families. They fought for almost nine months. Scabs were escorted home with charivaris by strikers, and strike leaders condemned both Liberal and Conservative parties as "merely committees of the capitalist class," refusing the intervention of state agents at "any price." This strike, and the resulting "coal famine" in large parts of Alberta and Saskatchewan, simply heightened the need for the presence of the state, and King eventually proved successful. As in most cases, King's involvement managed to produce a settlement that, in the words of the local Frank, Alberta, paper, the *Frank Paper*, had "the look of being a decided victory for the men." But compared to other union agreements in District 18 it was a setback, and the majority of the miners' original demands were quietly forgotten or fundamentally altered in the final compromise.

The Lethbridge strike was therefore a fitting introduction to the contradictory developments of this period. Proving the mettle of miners' unionism in the pre-World War One years, it and another strike in 1911, of the ten major Alberta work stoppages waged between 1905 and 1945, remained the only conflicts to be supported by significant financing from international union headquarters. At the same time, however, it introduced into the coal fields an undependable third party in the form of the state. Indeed, the 1906 confrontation laid the foundations for the Industrial Disputes Investigation Act. In the years when the Act was in force, miners in the Crow's Nest Pass would be forced to take up the strike again, three times between 1907 and 1911. While some workers' interests were incorporated in the Act, the IDIA permitted the establishment of the open shop, "limited" recognition of the union being all that the miners could now legally wrestle from the employers. In the coal fields of Alberta and southeastern British Columbia, the "impartial" umpire of the state assumed the same series of roles fulfilled in south-central Ontario by scientific management, employer associations, and the selected use of injunctions.

The history of workplace confrontation in the years 1900-14 hints at the vast changes that swept over working-class experience in these years and indicates the resilience of class forms of resistance, attachments to respectability and autonomy, and the potency of new organizational efforts. While the period was often one of harsh defeats, it also saw significant victories; working-class initiative and solidarity were all the more impressive because of the range and diversity of monopoly capital's opposition. Economic change, the transformation of the labour process in specific sectors, the rise of the interventionist state (in both its military and conciliatory dress), and the flooding of the labour market with new workers all forced Canadian labour to fight back in ways that broke from old forms of resistance. In the process, workers reminded capital that they were not resigned to the lot cast for them, a position of challenge also evident in the political sphere.

THE POLITICS OF DISSENT

The tendency within the craft unions was to support electoral candidates who endorsed specific reforms associated with working-class demands or those who, in addition to their commitment to the movement's aims, also came from the ranks of the toilers. Centred in the Trades and Labor Congress of Canada, this political orientation was never more than a trend, and the period actually opened with the Socialist Labor Party's admission to the TLC. One year later the SLP was removed from the Congress because it was not judged to be a trade union, the conventions of 1895 and 1896 serving notice of socialism's presence within trade union circles as well as its controversial status. Over the course of the 1895-1920 period, working-class politics were pushed beyond a Gompersite policy of rewarding labour's friends and punishing its enemies by the emergence of two strands of dissent: labourism and socialism.

Labourism's platform was codified as early as 1898, although its impact in the political realm would not be felt until a few years later. Always severely compromised by its affinity with the Laurier Liberals, labourism nevertheless played a vital role in moving the working class beyond accommodation and toward the stand of political independence. Its origins lay in the first political stirrings of labour in the 1870s and 1880s and in British experience; its most explicit statement was that of the sixteen points and preoccupations laid out at the 1898 meeting of the Trades and Labor Congress. A compilation of progressive demands that could be endorsed by most Anglo-Saxon organized workers, labour's program included free compulsory education, the eight-hour day, a minimum wage, public ownership of railways and telegraphs, tax reform, abolition of the Senate, extension of the franchise, prohibition of prison and contract labour, and legislative elimination of child labour. Supplemented by the demand for equal suffrage for men and women, appended in 1917, these and other demands formed the backbone of labourism's attempt to inject democracy and humanitarianism into the body politic. However, also included among labourist political planks was an assault on Chinese immigration. Anti-Orientalism continued to highlight the exclusivism of labour's parliamentary program.

Originally stimulated by western labour reformers, labourism experienced some setbacks before it spread throughout the land. Two Liberal-backed labour candidates, Arthur W. Puttee, editor of the Winnipeg worker reform paper *The Voice*, and Nanaimo miners' leader and head of the TLC, Ralph Smith, won federal seats in 1900. Such victories stimulated discussion of an independent labour party, although the practice of Smith and Puttee was, as A.R. McCormack and others have pointed out, always subordinate to the interests of the Liberal Party. Concessions were won, to be sure, but they were not so much demanded and extracted from authority as they were begged and bargained for in yearly meetings between labour representatives and Laurier and his cabinet.

Although working-class candidates secured victories in provincial elections in British Columbia, by 1904-05 labourism appeared to be on the wane. Puttee was defeated in 1904, Smith defected to the Grits, and the president-elect of the TLC, Alphonse Verville, suffered a loss in his attempt to gain election in Quebec City. Puttee had been abandoned by the Liberals, who were attempting to capture the growing East European immigrant vote in Winnipeg. The Liberals healed a number of party rifts that had kept them divided and hence were no longer as dependent on labour for votes as they had been in the earlier 1900 contest. Puttee's campaign was forced in certain directions and ended up being fought along class lines. Unlike the case in 1900, when he had presented himself as the reform candidate of all people, in 1904 he ran as the advocate of "Mr. Workingman."

Labourism defeated nevertheless represented the beginnings of labourism as a legitimate expression of class interest. In Quebec, Verville's defeat induced a Montreal delegate to the 1905 convention of the TLC to urge labour bodies in Quebec to unite in the formation of an independent labour party. Such calls for action received increased support from organized workers in the TLC, who by 1906 had elected Verville to the House of Commons in a sweeping Montreal victory, passed a resolution endorsing "independent political action," and made moves to establish the Canadian (Independent) Labor Party. Much of this political ferment was of course related to workplace confrontation, which conditioned a climate of class antagonism. As Ralph Smith noted in a letter to Wilfrid Laurier, society appeared on the verge of breaking into two armed camps, "just as Marx had predicted." Some would view such a development with fear and loathing; others could applaud it. Eugene Debs, central figure in American socialism and symbol of working-class repudiation of Gompersism, visited Toronto in 1906 and found the Canadian labour movement in "a more healthy condition" than that of the trade unions to the south.

The CLP/ILP proposed in 1906 was slow to emerge, and when it did develop it took many forms. Blocked by socialist strength in British Columbia, the creation of a labourite party proceeded in Manitoba where a similar body had existed as early as 1895. Puttee and other "old country" reformers founded the Winnipeg Independent Labor Party in 1906, a year of confrontation on the street railway and public appearances by British labour advocate Ramsay Macdonald. Active in municipal politics, the Winnipeg ILP was to be hampered by divisions created out of a debate over collective ownership of the means of production, a stand advocated by the popular British leader Keir Hardie. Middle-class single-tax proponent Fred Dixon captured some of the ILP supporters in the post-1910 years and, through alliances with Liberals, sustained victories on the "Independent" ticket. Labourism, increasingly moderate, won political stature but lost its role as the sole exponent of the working class.

In Ontario, the CLP/ILP seemed more vibrant. Six hundred delegates, representing the major industrial and manufacturing centres of the province, convened to establish the party in 1907. Heartened by the provincial election of labourite Allan Studholme in Hamilton in 1906, the Ontario CLP/ILP seemed the centre of labourism by 1907. Studholme himself would carry the banner through the war years until his death in 1919, securing his seat in the Ontario legislature at repeated elections. Hamilton East's "little Labor Man" rode to victory in the midst of the class solidarities cultivated in the 1880s and consolidated around the struggles of street railway employees in an epic 1906 clash with their employer, city authorities, and the militia.

Other ILP supporters from Hamilton – Samuel Landers and Walter Rollo – also stood at the centre of Ontario labourism and, along with Toronto's James (Jimmy) Simpson, helped to orchestrate the movement's revitalization in the war years after a post-1908 decline in fortunes. By 1917, numerous local labour parties were united under the auspices of the newly created Hamilton-based Ontario Labor Party. Farmer-labour co-operation swept the Conservatives from office in the October, 1919, provincial election, the United Farmers of Ontario electing forty-five candidates and the ILP winning an unprecedented eleven seats, with particularly impressive showings in Hamilton and London. Two labourites served as cabinet ministers in the UFO-ILP government.

Nowhere else did labourism gain such victories. In Quebec, the Labor Party exerted its limited strength in Montreal, where Gustav Francq and Verville promoted the cause of independent labour representation, the latter winning at the polls in 1908 and 1911. These years also witnessed the rise of the labour town in the coal fields of Vancouver Island, the Crow's Nest Pass, and the East. Two socialist aldermen were elected in Nanaimo in 1914; in Fernie, B.C., Tom Uphill of the United Mine Workers of America was first elected mayor in 1915 – he would hold this civic post for most of the next forty years. Among Alberta's miners, socialism, rather than labourism, prevailed, but the ILP drew some support, especially among those of British descent. As ongoing research into the nature of the Socialist Party of Canada uncovers more and more indication of a *practice* of co-operation among different components of the labour left, an historiographically entrenched view of the *ideological* division separating various radical tendencies may well be displaced.

In industrial Cape Breton, labourite candidates ran for federal office as early as 1904. By 1918, the ILP was well established, tending to dominate town politics in coal centres like Glace Bay. A coal miner was elected mayor in 1918, and the ILP ran candidates for town councillor in five of the six wards. Campaigning under the slogan "Corporations vs The Masses," all five labourite candidates were victorious. After another election in 1919, Glace Bay's town council took on the appearance of a working-class body. Joining a manager, an engineer, and a contractor were two machinists and seven coal miners. Besides Glace Bay, workers won control in New Waterford and Dominion, as well as securing minority representation in Sydney,

Sydney Mines, and on the county council. David Frank has argued that these early labour victories reflected a shifting balance of power in the Cape Breton coal towns, and they were not without their material ramifications: the coal companies were challenged, the use of the police in strike situations curtailed, and the assessment of taxes revised. In Halifax, as Suzanne Morton has shown, labourism peaked in a 1919-20 effort to establish a local labour party, an undertaking coinciding with a massive shipyards strike.

It is thus in the understudied realm of local politics and class action that labourism's history is to be found. As Craig Heron has argued, labourism as the main political voice of Canadian workers prior to 1920 was intimately connected to industrial struggles and a generalized set of class grievances that grew out of the tensions associated with the many changes of the 1900-20 years. Highly decentralized, labourism, like the trade union movement and the class struggle, ebbed and flowed with a distinct calendar: its presence was most noticeable in the first years of the century, in the period leading up to the outbreak of war, and, finally and most acutely, in the context of heightened class struggle of 1916-20. As a turn toward the political arena, labourism was never an attempt to deflect workers from the industrial battleground but to turn that struggle in the direction of broader, more unified class initiatives.

The rise of labourism was therefore the political expression of the various forms of limited, semi-autonomous, working-class organization and activism that had been developing across Canada since the 1880s. As the annual report on labour organization in Canada pointed out in 1921, fully 271 working-class candidates ran for office in forty-four municipalities in 1920: 111 were elected, including mayors in Westville, Moncton, Sault Ste. Marie, Port Arthur, and Fort William. These political campaigns had their origins in the rise of labourism in the 1900-20 period, as well as in the emergence of one of its left opponents. For within the politics of labour the orientation of independent representation was challenged, not only by partyism and the employers but by socialism.

Socialism was always something more than mere votes cast. *Cotton's Weekly* estimated the socialist vote across the country at a mere 3,500 in 1903 and an improved, but still disappointing, 17,000 in 1913. Yet socialist influence in the workers' movement reached well beyond such limited numbers.

With the vast changes wrought by the full-scale impact of industrial capital and the emergence of concentrated economic power, the moral universality of the labour-reform critique of the 1880s faded, its eclecticism lacking substance and strategic direction. The essential solidarity and working-class character of this pre-socialist radicalism of the 1880s was a moment of great achievement, as we have seen, yet its disintegration in the 1880s was simultaneously a loss and an advance. The emerging socialist movement, while always divided – not only from moderate labourist elements but also against its own, factionalized self – and never capable of drawing masses of workers to its ranks, did indeed encourage the spread of a socialist body of thought and, in some cases, contributed to organizational and political breakthroughs. Major socialist organizations appeared for the first time in the 1890s: followers of the American Marxist Daniel DeLeon, later the recipient of a rare commendation from Lenin, formed the first Ontario branch of the Socialist Labor Party (SLP) in 1894, while the more mass-oriented Canadian Socialist League (CSL) was initiated by George Wrigley, former Knights of Labor and farmers' advocate, editor Phillips Thompson, and others in 1899. If the Socialist Labor Party was supposedly doctrinaire and opposed to moderation and reformism, the Canadian Socialist League presented a mild Christian socialism premised on the need for democracy and public ownership.

An Ontario Provincial Socialist League was formed in 1901 and, after contesting the 1902 election, changed its name to the Ontario Socialist Party. Organizers spread the socialist word to the West, cultivating support in Winnipeg, and the Socialist League gained adherents in the East, with Fredericton a centre of activity from 1902. But the real foundation of Canadian socialism lay in British Columbia, where allies of the Canadian Socialist League led the way. Miners associated with the Western Federation of Miners, workers affiliated with the Vancouver Trades and Labor Council, and Christian co-operators were especially active in the new politics.

On the west coast, in fact, DeLeonite and reformist wings of Canadian socialism joined. Prior to 1904 these two factions battled for labour's allegiance, and both often lost to the labourites. The Socialist Labor Party's insistence on a critical stance toward the unions, which it often considered a barrier to the attainment of true class consciousness, won it few friends among the Ontario and Nova Scotia communities where it was active in the opening years of the twentieth century. But in British Columbia, by 1903, a combination of factors merged ideological and ethical differences within the socialist camp, forging a unified grouping of radicals that would result in a rejuvenated socialist movement.

DeLeonite socialism on the west coast had a stormy history that encompassed the formation of an SLP local in Vancouver in 1898 and the creation in 1899 of the party's trade union arm, the Socialist Trades and Labor Alliance, which was dedicated to waging relentless war on the collaborationist AFL and craft unions. Subsequently, part of the organization split from the mainstream to form a socialist club that became the United Socialist Party in 1900. More conciliatory toward the unions, the new party soon became the leading socialist body in the region, enrolling 250 members and running a respectable electoral campaign. As class struggle escalated in these years, especially in the coal mines and on the railways, and as American socialist literature and organizers filtered across the border, the validity of the socialist attack on capital appeared to be confirmed and recruits to the revolutionary movement increased. By 1901, attempts to unify the restructured DeLeonites and Christian socialists led to the drafting of a socialist platform and the creation of a provincial organization, the Socialist Party of British Columbia (SPBC).

The more revolutionary wing of the movement, Nanaimo's miners, feared for the loss of socialist principle and imported a propagandist from California, E.T. Kingsley. He was a former state organizer for the SLP, a man converted to socialism on his hospital bed, where he had read Marx while recovering from an industrial accident that took both of his legs. Not one to soften socialist doctrine with faith in capitalism's capacity to effect reform, Kingsley would leave his mark on British Columbia's movement and, in the process, stamp the pre-war socialism of Canada with a particularly vehement advocacy of class struggle in the political arena.

Kingsley's successes mounted in 1902-03, as employer hostility to unionism and a series of defeats in the mines left workers "ripe for socialism." Organizers claimed the province was reaching "the beginnings of the final stage of capitalism," and socialist candidates were occasionally polling an unprecedented 40 per cent of the vote. New converts to the socialist cause were being made every day; one authority estimated that half of the new SPBC's membership had been drawn to socialism in the years 1902-03. A Cumberland miner testified to the transformation in workers' consciousness before a 1903 royal commission when he spoke of the inevitability of workers controlling production and capturing the reins of government. "If you want to obtain the scientific analysis of the situation," he boldly told the commissioners, "you could procure a copy of Karl Marx's *Capital*," adding for good measure, "that is the groundwork of modern socialism . . . the scientific analysis of capitalist production." Confronted with words like these, the royal commission was quick to condemn unions as political bodies, claiming the existence of "a class of so-called union men developing rapidly in Western America, which is really not a trade union at all, but a secret political organization whose members are bound by an oath. . . . The primary object and common end of this class of organization is to seize the political power of the state for the purpose of confiscating all franchises and natural resources without compensation."

In April of 1902, sixty representatives of socialist and labour organizations met in Kamloops to establish the Provincial Progressive Party (PPP). Had the socialists been victorious, this body would have fulfilled the worst fears of the commissioners. As it was, reformers carried the day, signalling the beginnings of a contest between labourism and socialism in British Columbia. The gradualist labourites won the first battle, but the ultimate victory would go to Kingsley and the revolutionaries. While the socialist movement would never descend to the pre-1900 DeLeonite assault on trade unions, a series of developments reinforced the socialist rejection of reformism and also eased the labourites from power in British Columbia. Crucial successes came in the 1903 provincial election, when the uncompromising platform of the SPBC shattered the reformers' arguments that mass support would never go to such supposedly doctrinaire radicals. Socialist candidates won election in Nanaimo, Newcastle, and Slocan, while in Vancouver socialists averaged over 1,100 votes each. This gave Kingsley and company all the evidence they needed. Orthodoxy became the key issue, and prominent printer-agitator R. Parmeter Pettipiece articulated the new self-conception prominent in B.C. socialist circles: "fate has decreed this position in the world's history to us and we should prove to the workers of the world that we can rise to the occasion; let us stand firm; keep our organization iron-clad, aye 'narrow' and see that we shy clear of the rocks of danger that have wrecked so many well-meaning movements." By the end of 1903, the labourite-dominated PPP was disbanded, revolutionary socialists controlled the provincial executive of the SPBC, and Kingsley sat in the editorial chair of the *Western Clarion*, regional voice of socialism. Revolution, rather than reform, was now on the agenda.

These advances served to encourage eastern socialists, who gained a new respect for the effectiveness of the "uncompromising principles of revolutionary socialism." Kingsley and his allies were seen as the new vanguard, pacing developments not only in Canada but in the socialist world. Negotiations with socialists in Winnipeg and Ontario led to the founding of the Socialist Party of Canada (SPC) late in 1904. The SPC proclaimed that capitalism could not be reformed, that trade unions could not benefit workers in the long run, and that class-conscious political action designed to seize the state in the interests of the proletariat was the only way to destroy the wage system, the necessary beginning of a new working-class order.

All of this earned the SPC the rather condescending label "impossiblist." Those in the party saw things differently, regarding themselves as the most steadfastly revolutionary socialist body in the world and rejecting, with pride, affiliation with the reformist Second International. In practice, such high-blown rhetoric was often tempered by reality, and the SPC was always less dogmatic in its day-to-day dealings with the working class than it was on the pages of its leaflets and newspapers, a divergence that has often misled historians into taking the organization at its literalist word. Perhaps as much as 75 per cent of SPC membership belonged to trade unions, and they functioned well within these bodies, often working jointly with the leaderships of unions such as the UMWA. The much cited hostility to trade unions, recalled Wallis Lefeaux in 1960, was little more than an issue promoted in the pages of the *Western Clarion* for a few years.

Between 1905 and 1910 the new party spread across the country. There were fifteen locals in the Maritimes and a number in Ontario and Quebec. But the real strength of the SPC lay in the West, where Keir Hardie's admonition, "none but socialists need apply," seemed to hold true. In the Crow's Nest Pass, miners' leader Frank Sherman was active in SPC work in District 18. Between 1909 and 1913 the Rocky Mountain coal communities elected socialist candidates with regularity; often they polled 65 per cent of the vote. Allen Seager notes that one such socialist, Charles M. O'Brien, combined the rhetoric of the Wobblies, the imagery of Jack London, and the prestige of Eugene Debs. He was described in 1911 as "broad enough to be friends with everybody and everything except the capitalist system . . . a ripened and mature revolutionist, a sturdy rebel." The fact that he was regarded as the UMWA's representative in the legislature gives further evidence that the SPC's anti-union stand was far from uniformly carried out in practice. Among Vancouver Island coal miners the party was equally popular. They regularly sent socialist candidates to the B.C. legislature, where they made a mockery of parliamentary decorum.

With a total membership of only 3,000, the SPC managed to exert an influence within the working class far out of proportion to its small membership. In British Columbia, for instance, it increased its share of the provincial vote in contested constituencies from 10 per cent in 1907 to 22 per cent in 1909, winning 11,000 votes and returning two candidates. Narrowly defeated in other ridings, the socialists claimed to have wiped out "the Liberal Party [and] cleared the field for a struggle to the death between the two extremes of capitalist society; capital on the one hand, dominant, aggressive, and brutal; on the other, labour, awakening from the lethargy of ages and determined to conquer its freedom from class rule and exploitation."

Among immigrant workers, the SPC also made early gains, breaking down the Anglo-American stranglehold on Canadian socialism. By 1908, Ukrainian branches of the party existed in Winnipeg, Portage La Prairie, and Nanaimo; Ukrainians were active in at least four other locales, the newspaper *Chervony Prapor* declaring itself the voice of the SPC, "serving that section of the proletariat that spoke the Ukrainian language." Other ethnic groups, such as the Finns, Italians, Germans, and Slavs, also made common cause with the SPC. Such alliances tended to disintegrate over time and the party's ultimate inability to transform itself into something more than an exclusive contingent of English-speaking migrants and militants manifested itself in the exodus of many of its ethnic supporters. But it would be wrong to underestimate the importance of this brief moment of class possibility, which secured tangible victories and symbolized the internationalism the party proclaimed.

In spite of this early success, the SPC began to fade, losing support from 1910 to 1917. During these years it was wracked by internal dissension, state-directed repression and harassment, revolts among its Ontario and foreign-language sections, and the pressure of the rising tide of a resuscitated labourism, which it failed to stem. Moderate British socialists and

East European immigrants led the exodus from the party and gravitated to the newly established Social Democratic Party (SDP), founded in 1910. Confronted with this new opposition and facing the difficult context of war-induced patriotism, the SPC failed to revitalize itself. By 1912, Kingsley admitted that locals were "either semi-defunct or in a state of philosophical dry rot."

Recent unpublished research by Peter Campbell suggests that while Kingsley may have been correct in his assessment of the SPC's institutional and electoral health, he underestimated his party's capacity to retain those workers committed to Marxism. After 1912 a "second-generation" of Socialist Party of Canada activists – Jack Kavanagh, Bob Russell, Bill Pritchard, and others – emerged. More likely to embrace the possibilities of trade unionism as fertile ground to spread the educational message of socialism, these Marxist workers also had a less sectarian relationship to bodies like the Industrial Workers of the World. As intuitively drawn to the Rosa Luxemburg of *The Mass Strike* as they were to Marx's *Capital*, this was a breed of revolutionary connected to Kingsley but different from the old "theoretical war horse." When this new layer of SPCers assumed leadership of the "impossiblist" forces, their organization was finished in terms of its capacity to win parliamentary representation, but it remained capable of forwarding class action, particularly in terms of new forms of industrial organization. The vanguard had lost its power to lead in its own name, perhaps, but its "second-generation" leadership would influence working-class events in the momentous upheavals of the post-war period. It would provide the advanced cadre of One Big Unionism.

Labourism and socialism, of various kinds, thus contended for the labour movement's support and votes in the pre-war years. James Simpson and R.P. Pettipiece of the International Typographical Union and Frank Sherman of the UMWA failed to convince the Trades and Labor Congress that the SPC should be recognized as the legitimate political voice of labour in British Columbia and Alberta. From this point on, the labourites and socialists would clash repeatedly. To be sure, both political tendencies were capable of working together and the two constituencies were never completely divorced from one another. Schisms and differences did exist within the House of Labour, but there was also overlap.

On one side, seemingly, were the pure socialists, readers of Marx, Engels, and Bebel; on the other, the more moderate reformers were apparently influenced by Fabian tracts, social gospel texts, and copies of *Merrie England* or *Progress and Poverty*. But it was actually more complicated and intellectual influences were more interrelated. At first, the beleaguered miners of British Columbia and Alberta, labour intellectuals, and European radical immigrants affiliated themselves with the first group, while the second was more likely to attract urban craftsmen of British descent. Had these been the only two political streams within the working class, the politics of dissent may have developed and flourished. But the loyal ties of many workers still lay elsewhere. The casually employed, the unskilled, and the tradesmen who refused the independence offered by labourites and socialists tended to resign themselves to voting Liberal and Conservative, as their fathers had. If denied the franchise, they might eschew political action altogether. In Winnipeg, in 1906, for instance, less than 8,000 people out of a population of over 100,000 were listed as municipal voters. Many immigrants, by definition, were outside of the political process. Canada's regions experienced this process of labour politics differently. In the rapidly developing West, with its immigrant masses and stark industrial conditions, radicalism often seemed an option. Elsewhere, other factors structured the possibilities for the working class.

REGIONALISM: RADICALISM/RELIGION

Capitalism stamped its imprint on the developing Canadian nation-state during the 1900-20 period and structured the regions of Canada into a national market composed of specific subsets, each with its own role to play in a differentiated division of labour. Generalized trends developed alongside particularities and peculiarities. Thus capitalist transformations and escalating class struggles were apparent everywhere in Canada at the same time that they took specific forms in what were increasingly different contexts.

For many historians only one side of this process is visible, and they ignore commonalities and general trends in order to accentuate the extent to which radicalism was regionally based and bound. But ironies abound, and complexities undercut any simple equation of regionalism and radicalism. The labourist impulse, for instance, was perhaps felt earliest and strongest in the so-called radical West, while the first stirrings of socialism occurred in the supposedly accommodated central Canadian metropolitan centres where Gompers's AFL unions were long entrenched.

Radicalism was never an entirely western phenomenon. Workers, intellectuals, and petty proprietors rubbed shoulders in Hamilton's Marx Club; small Ontario towns, such as Brockville, boasted militantly leftist locals of the Socialist Party of Canada. Critically important revolutionary leaders, such as industrial Cape Breton's J.B. McLachlan, gained widespread popularity in this period. Enclaves of radicals could be found in many trades. In Toronto, metal polishers wrote to their craft journals under the pen names "K. Marx" and "Sansculotte." Patternmakers in the same city declared themselves unhesitatingly for the abolition of the wage system. A May Day parade in Montreal in 1906 was headed by the red flag and drew 5,000. Newfoundlanders elected Fisherman's Protective Union Party candidate George Grimes, a lay preacher and self-proclaimed socialist, to the legislature in 1912.

These instances of radicalism could be reproduced indefinitely, and as we will see shortly, the upheavals associated with 1919 were national in scope. Still, there is no denying the extent to which radicalism was most widespread in the West. One expression of this was the rise of the Industrial Workers of the World, an organization that appealed to those migratory, often immigrant, labourers who found themselves caught in the very exploitative centre of capital's frenzied pace of accumulation.

The Industrial Workers of the World, as A.R. McCormack and David Bercuson have argued or implied, made few inroads into eastern Canadian industrial communities. To be sure, the IWW could be found among the unemployed of Hamilton in 1914 and in the coal fields of Cape Breton, where the famous Wobbly "Big Bill" Haywood lectured in 1909. But these were sporadic appearances, and the favoured terrain of the Wobblies was definitely the West. In the mines of the Kootenays, where the IWW had five functioning locals by 1907, and among the western blanket stiffs who migrated from the head of Lake Superior to Vancouver Island to find work in the logging camps and harvest fields or on railway construction sites and docks, the Wobbly message fell on receptive ears. It was a simple but effective statement of self-worth, directed at workers who toiled incessantly for low wages, under intolerable conditions, without the hope of security.

Western workers, told that they were the basis of the economy and that they had it within their means to stop the wheels of production if only they were organized into one united contingent, began to see the potential power they wielded. By 1912, according to McCormack, approximately 5,000 had become associated with the IWW, joining a dozen large locals stretching from Victoria to Winnipeg. One IWW source claims a membership of double this by 1911. Among workers who built western railways, the industrial unionism of the Wobblies was particularly attractive: 40 per cent of railway construction workers in the region carried the red card of the IWW. Ethnically heterogeneous, the IWW advocated the organization of all workers, even the Orientals so long opposed by the labour movement. "Wops" and "Bohunks" comprised a large component of its constituency, just as they provided the bulk of unskilled labour at many job sites. Foreign-language locals thrived, and the Vancouver longshoremen and lumberers who fought the first IWW strike on the west coast were drawn from eighteen different nationalities.

Founded in Chicago in 1905 as an expression of hostility to what militants in the workers' movement chastised as the American *Separation* of Labor, the Industrial Workers of the World owed their name, in part, to the intervention of a B.C. delegate, who argued that the proposed designation – the Industrial Union of America – was inadequately internationalist. Present in Canada from its inception, the IWW's impact was greatest in the years that bridged the 1908 recession and the immediate pre-war collapse of 1913-14.

Egalitarian to a fault (any Wobbly could act as a full-time organizer as he travelled from job to job), the IWW charged low fees and transferred membership cards without inhibition. Camaraderie was cultivated, and Wobbly halls served as dormitories, mail drops, and employment agencies. For the alien worker without a vote or the unskilled and illiterate, the Wobbly brand of radicalism was perhaps the only one that offered adequate solutions. The only training required of members was that of working-class life itself; the only classics demanding attention were those that came from the oppression and exploitation of labouring experience. "Everything is founded upon the job," explained one B.C. Wobbly, "everything comes from conditions on the job which is the environment and life of the toiling slaves. The job is the source of civilization." And the job would also be the basis of change. The IWW considered every strike a "miniature revolution," and saw social transformation being attained through a general strike that would leave the workers in control of production.

With the economic recession of 1913-14, the collapse of the railway boom, and the scattering of its Wobbly labour force, the IWW was weakened. Canada's entry into World War One provided a context in which employer hostility to the Wobblies would be supplemented by increased state repression: IWW organizer Dick Higgins was tried under the War Measures Act in Vancouver, and late in 1918 Diamond City mine union leader Tom Shannon was imprisoned for possessing "IWW literature." Always closely tied to the larger American-based movement, Canada's Wobblies also suffered organizational disarray when over 100 IWW leaders were arrested on conspiracy charges in Chicago in 1917. By 1918 the organization was nearly non-existent. But its vision, its hope, and, in many ways, a good part of its strategic orientation to the working masses would be taken up with renewed vigour in another movement of western radicalism, the more distinctively Canadian challenge of the One Big Union.

If the IWW was no longer a force to reckon with as the war neared its conclusion, conditions in the mines and shops of the West and the agitations of SPCers and pre-World War One social democrats in the SDP nevertheless conditioned a particular stance of defiance within the western working class. Rampant wartime inflation forced large numbers of western workers into strike actions and set off sympathetic strikes among other trade groups. The railway machinists' bulletin noted that the "ability of individual trade unions to enforce their economic demands is becoming less as the master class unite." Militancy crested in this period, pushing aside many moderate labour leaders. Among western workers, opposition to capital grew. But these alienated and increasingly radical elements saw little that encouraged them among their eastern labour counterparts. Resentments against employers would soon be translated partially into antagonism toward a cautious, eastern-dominated craft union leadership. A split within the Canadian labour movement was in the making.

At the Quebec City convention of the Trades and Labor Congress in September, 1918, the implosion occurred. Westerners, with the support of some eastern radicals, launched a direct attack on the Congress leadership. Since the West had been able to send only forty-five delegates to the convention, or less than one-tenth of the total, its voice of opposition was easily ignored. Convinced that TLC conventions discriminated against western labour because they were often held in the East and therefore had more delegates from Ontario, urban Quebec, and the Maritimes, the radicals from the West decided to hold their own conference before the TLC reconvened in Calgary in 1919. Prior to this there was much debate, an escalation of state repression against wartime radicals, and considerable international development, including the rise of the One Big Union movement in Australia and the armistice of November 11, 1918.

In the midst of such developments the Western Labor Conference met in Calgary in March, 1919. Orchestrated by radicals committed to socialism and industrial unionism, much influenced by an SPC in which the events of the Russian Revolution stimulated a minor revival of the sense of what was possible in the workers' movement, the gathering, originally conceived as an attempt to plan a radical comeback within the TLC, quickly took on a secessionist hue. Before the opening speech was made, the *Western Labor News* proclaimed, "The more effete East is burdensome to the West and the slavish subservience of parliament to the interests of vested wealth has filled the cup of the West to overflowing." The radicals were finally getting their say. A Vancouver trades council secretary and SPC member, Victor Midgley, astutely arranged for the radical-dominated B.C. Federation of Labor to hold its annual convention in Calgary just prior to the Western Labor Conference, thereby assuring the presence of a distinguished core of committed radicals. In the words of Desmond Morton, they "completely managed" the convention and "railroaded" moderate delegates. What Morton ignores is the extent to which such "management" and "railroading" had been long-standing practice at TLC meetings. The difference, in 1919, was that it was being orchestrated from the left rather than from the right.

The Western Labor Conference, a forum called into being by western radicals and composed of delegates not unsympathetic to radical claims and aims, required less railroading than radical rhetoric. Resolutions passed quickly. They denounced censorship, made common cause with the Bolshevik Revolution, eschewed traditional political action, raised high the banner of the general strike, and advocated the foundation of a new labour movement unencumbered by the exclusivist trappings of the American Federation of Labor. As Peter Campbell has recently shown, the "second generation" of SPC leaders, drawn less to theoretical refinement and the educational platform of the political campaign than its Kingsleyite predecessors, had been working the trade union side of the agitational street since

1913, promoting the idea of one big unionism. In 1919 this battle of ideas was finally translated into practical accomplishment as "Midgley & Company" (historian David Bercuson's characterization) led the way in founding the One Big Union.

Historians like Bercuson and Morton consider the OBU little more than the expression of "chialistic faith," "designed by the maneuverings and machinations of a small handful of millenarians while the tens of thousands of western workers ready to revolt against capitalism and craft unionism had no chance to determine what the vehicle of their discontent would be like." But the events of March-June, 1919, and the background of the previous two years call into question this kind of interpretation. Miners in District 18 had adhered to revolutionary demands for workers' control since 1918, and the 5,100 members of the UMWA were staunch industrial unionists. Trades councils in Victoria, Vancouver, and Winnipeg (where 75 per cent of the city's organized workers embraced the new militancy) were overwhelming in their support for the OBU, while 5,500 organized loggers lined up behind the old SPC agitator W.A. Pritchard and the OBU by a ratio of nine to one. To be sure, there were centres of opposition, especially among British urban craftsmen in Alberta, where Calgary was a TLC stronghold, and in Saskatchewan. But as Glen Makahonuk points out in the case of Saskatoon, a labourist centre, significant support for the OBU existed along with great hostility to the TLC and its eastern leadership. As A.R. McCormack argued long ago, the anti-OBU forces were far from effective, and in the turmoil of the spring of 1919, militant industrial unionism won a short-lived but significant mass base in the West.

Radicalism was, then, something more than a matter of faith. If it lacked precise programmatic direction, it was nevertheless rooted in working-class experience and discontent. The manoeuvrings and machinations, the conspiratorial intrigues of "sterile" and "fuzzy" socialist thinkers, were in fact less important in its creation than other conspiracies and machinations. Miners who had tasted the autocratic authority of the Dunsmuir interests for decades and railway workers who knew the anti-labour practice of the CPR were not about to oppose those who held out the hand of solidarity as the salvation of the class. Those who had heard the story of Vic Midgley being forced into the street by vigilantes, made to kneel so that the Union Jack could be rubbed across his lips, the press there ready to report that the revolutionary socialist kissed the flag, had other conspiracies and manoeuvres on their minds.

Almost 90,000 "enemy aliens" were "registered" in Canada during World War One and over 2,200 were interned. Many others were deported; some went back to European deaths at the hands of right-wing regimes. The 64,000 Russian subjects present in Canada at the time of the Bolshevik Revolution bore the brunt of a particularly hostile nativism. Violence directed at these immigrants, many of whom were socialists and workers, as well as attacks on ethnic clubs, called into question moderate reform thought and action, just as the perceived complacency of labour statesmen in the East provoked western workers to split with the mainstream trade union movement. In eastern industrial cities, too, in immigrant quarters as well as among some of the skilled, there were signs of radicalism. A Montreal organizer expressed his astonishment that "the Soviet idea was so rampant . . . among the foreign-speaking iron and steel workers" of Hamilton.

Faith, then, was less an explanation of western radicalism than were conditions and contexts, all with histories. But in another region, its political economy less structured by resources and the accumulative pace of the industrial frontier, faith would intersect with the trajectory of class organization and activism. In French Canada, where regionalism was less a matter of landscape and its exploitation and more a function of demographic difference, the labour movement shifted gears in the years 1900-20, but by no means in ways that were easily linked to developments in the West.

In Quebec, the long-standing struggle between national and international unions has been mediated by the French fact, by the particular and unique culture and perspective of Quebec workers. The Knights of Labor, for instance, existed far longer in Quebec than in any other Canadian province, and when the Berlin decision of 1902 forced the Knights from the Trades and Labor Congress of Canada, many French-Canadian workers in the Order were driven to form their own "national" unions. Those attracted to the local assembly of a particular locality, and hence attached to a set of common experiences, found it far easier to transfer their loyalties to the local Catholic confessional *syndicats* than to join the larger English-dominated organizations of international craft unionism. The result was the formation of the curiously named National Trades and Labor Congress on September 18, 1903. This maverick TLC, composed of so-called national unions (Quebec's Knights of Labor, despite their formal affiliation to the Philadelphia-based body, considered themselves national unions), represented a conservative, largely French-Canadian alternative to the internationalism and materialism of Sam Gompers, but it soon lost support and by 1907 had been severely weakened by internal splits and factionalism.

Out of the ashes of the National TLC rose the Catholic *syndicats*. These confessional bodies had their origins, as Fraser Isbester has argued, in the confluence of three streams of intellectual and social endeavour. First, they were themselves carried along in the general labour upheaval that swept North America immediately after the turn of the century. Second, the separate structures of French-Canadian unionism were manifestations of the popularity of nationalism in Quebec, strong since the execution of Riel and given new impetus under advocates such as Henri Bourassa and Lionel Groulx. Third, the Catholic unions could also trace a part of their origins to the shift toward social action noticeable in the pontifical reign of Leo XIII, dating from 1891. Conscious of its waning influence among the working masses, evident from the point that threats of excommunication associated with membership in the Knights of Labor fell on all-too-deaf ears, the Church sought to re-establish its influence among the labouring poor. "The scandal of the nineteenth century," noted one concerned Catholic authority, "was the loss of the working man to the Church." If labour organization could turn that setback into advance, the Church would sanction trade unionism, albeit worker organization of a specific kind.

The first Roman Catholic *syndicat*, headed by a priest, was formed among paper workers in Chicoutimi in 1907. Over the course of the next fourteen years Catholic unionism grew in Quebec. In 1921 some ninety-six confessional unions banded together in the Confederation of Catholic Workers of Canada (Confédération des Travailleurs Catholiques du Canada, CTCC), a body that claimed 26,000 members. Endorsed by Church and state, it was a far cry from the OBU, which was vociferously denounced and attacked by such pillars of established authority. The pairing of regionalism and radicalism in the West in the same period was counterposed to the linked fortunes of regionalism and religion in Quebec, where Catholic unionism formed an early conservative and otherworldly counterpart to both international unionism and socialism. It would be too easy to take these Catholic unions strictly at their word, emphasizing the pro-employer, anti-strike rhetoric and the conscious construction of an image of French-Canadian labour as passive and deferential. Within this *ideological* limitation it was quite possible for workers to negotiate with employers and use their priestly leadership and Church favour to good advantage. But there were also limits beyond which the Catholic unions could not go, and the boundaries within which *syndicats* existed were, compared with developments in the West, substantial if not stultifying.

The workers' movement thus faced common threats in the years 1900-20, just as it dealt with generalized developments such as the hegemonic rise of the Trades and Labor Congress of Canada. But regional political economies and socio-cultural contexts ensured that no common ground was found on which a unified *national* labour movement could walk. Nor were the experiences of men and women easily assimilated to some essential class response.

GENDERED RADICALISM

Radicalism obviously did not sweep all Canadian workers into its enthusiastic embrace of the project of social and economic transformation. To be sure, it could be found anywhere, but it was bounded by region and occupation. It was more likely to be discernible among western resource and transportation workers and bindle stiffs or among a militant minority within the crafts, contexts characterized not only by their peculiar political economies but also by the dominance of men. Radicalism took on the trappings of a masculine project as its advocates assailed the boss and challenged the state, calling forth an opposition of proletarian manhood.

The emergence of this gendered radicalism was a consequence of a dual process. One part was structured by the sexual division of labour that developed out of the increasingly concentrated and regionally differentiated forms of production in the 1900-20 years. Another part was made by labour radicalism itself, which approached the woman question in a particular way.

Undoubtedly the most significant factor in the making of this gendered radicalism was the fundamental and varied divide that separated men's work and women's labour in these years. Complicated by the consolidating regional division of labour, this meant that where women worked for wages in the industrial-capitalist centre of the economy or in the urban settings of the West, they were isolated from the major constituencies of radicalism, the militant minority among skilled workers in the craft unions. Certain types of jobs, including laundry work and the sweated, subcontracted, and subdivided sectors of the garment trades, became female job ghettoes; technological and marketing innovations led to the proletarianization and, in some cases, feminization of accounting, general office work, clerical tasks, and sales. One Toronto bank increased its female staff from 200 to 8,000 in two years. In this instant proletarianization there was not all that much room for a radical response to develop. The predominance of women in teaching, which was a nineteenth-century phenomenon, continued apace in these years and, as in other female work sectors, poor conditions and low wages prevailed. Such female labour was isolated, and while efforts to organize were made, they were far from effective. Attempts to unionize, as Wayne Roberts and Star Rosenthal have shown in studies of Toronto and Vancouver, were frustrated by workplace ecologies that defied collectivity, by employer hostility, by demographic realities (most female workers were young and single and, after a period within the work force, left to marry and engage in unpaid domestic labour), and by the absence of any traditions of organized resistance.

When women workers actually found themselves employed in factory settings that promised some possibility of transcending these forceful limitations, as in the boot and shoe sector of industrialized Quebec studied by Jacques Ferland, gender's influence could still be forceful. Ferland's insightful depiction of the material culture of the workplace illustrates how separate were the spheres of men and women, who did different work. Women, for the most part, bound the upper part of the footwear; men worked in the bottoming, lasting, and heeling departments. The large factories of this period isolated "women's departments" by reserving a whole floor for the upper-stitching room. Technology, too, was gender-bound, with women working small machines, confined to chairs; men worked larger machines in standing positions. (Ferland, with some justification, refers to the men's machines as phallus-like, alluding to their elongated, linear, erect structure, in contrast to the oval complexities of women's machines.) Skill and strength had little to do with such assignments; more important was a technological design that perpetuated and deepened long-standing conventional wisdoms about the physical incapacities and abilities of women. And because the division of labour in the industry dictated a certain chain of interdependent and minutely structured processes, work stations were compact and contained. All of this ensured an explicit gendered division of labour, with male and female work separated by material barriers that translated into pay differentials and a work force organized into a fragmented set of male craft "brotherhoods" that often ignored women and usually excluded them from participation in the union.

Other sectors, such as the cotton industry, could be contrasted to the boot and shoe experience, to draw out the possibility of women's activism. Cotton mills were not gendered to the same extent as the boot and shoe industry, and men and women interacted more within the labour process, facilitating resistance to the boss that united men and women over time. Indeed, as Ferland points out, women often led the way in class conflicts in the industry, rejuvenating organizational efforts in the cotton mills and forming the first Quebec-wide male and female Federation of Textile Workers of Canada in 1907. But when these women struck in 1908 against an obnoxious and vindictive foreman known for his outrageous conduct on the shopfloor, their male union leadership talked tough in the beginning only to collapse in the end, unwilling to use union authority and power to address a grievance that related directly to gendered discontent.

The union leaders who eventually backed away from this Quebec class struggle flowing out of gender demands were by no means radicals. Indeed, had they been members of a radical organization such as the Socialist Party of Canada, it is doubtful that they would have walked away from the conflict so complacently. Nevertheless, as Linda Kealey has shown, the radicalism of the pre-war years was indeed gendered. While organizations of Christian socialists, "impossiblists," and social democrats differed on how they understood and related to the "woman question," there was an identifiable tendency. Most radicals, including women in the socialist movement, saw the class struggle as central and the overthrow of the bourgeoisie as the primary goal. Women were acknowledged to suffer special oppressions and certainly socialists demanded that their rights – as citizens capable of exercising the franchise, for instance – be extended. But women's main task was often conceived quite conventionally. Maintaining the home, nurturing and training the young, supporting the political struggles of their husbands – these were essential contributions that women could make to the socialist movement. As in the craft unions, where women were often active in auxiliaries, label committees, and boycott campaigns, the familial, consumer-focused activities of women were stressed. It would be wrong to assume that such women's working-class activities were marginal or unimportant, for they often tipped the scales in contests between workers and employers. But there is no denying the gendered nature of working-class life in this period, the extent to which production was a man's world, reproduction a woman's.

In the radical coal towns of Cape Breton, J.B. McLachlan described the miner's wife as "the greatest financier in the world," while a miner's wife herself wrote in 1921, "A house is a woman's work-shop and she is there night and day the whole year through." McLachlan appealed to women of the coal towns in 1917 under the heading "Wives, Mothers, Sisters, and Sweethearts of Men, Attention," asking them to respond to the union's call for a minimum daily wage of $8.50 by detailing their family budgets. The result was letters that both indicated how difficult it was for a family to survive on such meagre earnings and how meticulous miners' wives were in stretching limited resources to sustain the working-class household. Where the division of labour dictated that men work for wages and women labour in unpaid domestic duties, this construction of women's role had substantial material moorings: this was certainly the case in the coal towns of the East and West, as it was in the more radical centres like Vancouver, where less than 10 per cent of the manufacturing work force was female. In the lumber camps and on railway construction projects, where the IWW might gain converts, women were not so much structured into the family as they were simply not present. This is not to say that women could not march on picket lines and contribute to the class struggle, which they did, time and time again. But gender roles were conceived differently.

All of this occasionally lent the radical relation to gender a particular otherworldliness. As the debate over women's involvement in the socialist movement hardened in the Socialist Party of Canada, for instance, spokeswoman Ruth Lestor dug in her heels and consistently espoused the view that a woman's class position, not her gender, was paramount. In a party whose membership was only 10 per cent female, led by male radicals steeled in opposition to reformist politics that left the exploitation of one class by another unaltered, this was no doubt a majority position that many socialists rightly embraced. But Lestor's succinct insistence that "A woman is a man – that's all," was unnecessarily blunt and angular, a reflection of how blinkered the gendered radicalism of the pre-war years could be.

The powerful ideology of "woman's sphere" and the structural gendered determinations of divisions of labour, regional political economies, and processes of production all combined to ensure that radicalism spoke in a masculine voice in this period. To be sure, there were those, such as Christian socialist May Darwin and Helena Gutteridge, a British immigrant who joined the SPC after World War One, who challenged this gendered radical-ism with an insistent demand that the special oppression of sex be addressed alongside the exploitation of class. But as Linda Kealey suggests, "by and large, men and women socialists subscribed to prevailing notions of wom-an's role in the home and stressed the social and educational roles of women socialists in supporting their husbands and bringing up the next generation of socialists." That project was to be shaken to its very foundations by the war. The catastrophic events of 1914-18 transformed both the ideological and the structural context in which workers and their oppositional move-ments – not only in Canada but around the world – operated. After 1914 radicalism and unionism, employer authority and state power, would never quite look the same.

THE WAR FOR DEMOCRACY

World War One proved to be a watershed in the history of Canadian workers. It brought the country decisively out of the 1913-14 recession: in those years trade union membership fell 20 per cent and the number of strikes declined to a twentieth-century low. But with the new demands for production, especially in wartime industries such as coal mining and muni-tions, the post-1915 years revitalized labour's bargaining position. By 1917, the country's employers faced a shortage of 100,000 workers, and this tight labour market increased the chance of success in a strike, enhanced the likelihood of *de facto* union recognition, and created a new structure of demands that radicals were able to exploit.

With unemployment no longer a great threat and with wages sometimes increasing at rates higher than inflation, the labour movement appeared to be regaining lost ground. By 1917 the number of strikes climbed to levels approaching those of the 1912-13 strike wave. More strikes, over 300, were initiated in 1918 than in any previous year in Canadian history. Equally important, as Douglas Cruikshank and Gregory Kealey point out, were the successes workers were scoring: by 1917 outright working-class victories reached their highest level in the entire 1890-1950 period. New workers were drawn into these struggles, most notably federal employees, the Associa-tion of Letter Carriers waging a national walkout that commenced in Toronto, spread to twenty cities, and gave rise to numerous sympathetic work stoppages. Many such struggles were waged as rank-and-file revolts, against the urging of reluctant union leaderships and, on occasion, in opposition to the advice of stalwart radicals, some of whom remained affiliated with the Socialist Party of Canada.

Coal mining was perhaps the leading sector within this new militancy. For the first time in the new century, Alberta's miners' wages increased more quickly than soaring prices and were on a par with those of their

American counterparts. During the years 1914-20, 12 per cent of all strikes, 20.5 per cent of all workers involved in conflict, and 23 per cent of time lost to strikes and lockouts were accounted for by miners. The West, in this wartime strike wave, replaced Ontario as the dominant region of conflict. Alongside the battling miners, loggers and civic workers in Victoria, Vancouver, and Winnipeg challenged employers and took job actions, many of which culminated in threatened general strikes.

The war years were also the years of the "Red Scare," as the Bolshevik Revolution of 1917 raised the spectre of communism for the first time in North America. When the Western Labor Conference declared its full acceptance of "the principle of proletarian dictatorship as being absolute and efficient for the transformation of capitalistic private property to communal wealth," it sent fraternal greetings to the Russian Soviet government and the German "Spartacans," recognizing that they had "won first place in the history of the class struggle." Prime Minister Robert Borden's fears of western labour's "absurd conceptions of what had been accomplished in Russia" were another part of this same development.

Out of these years, as the Royal Canadian Mounted Police's official historian, S.W. Horral, has reminded us, the RCMP was born. The counter-revolutionary panic of the Canadian ruling class cultivated a sense of need, and the regionally limited Royal North-West Mounted Police was merged with the Dominion Police, hurriedly converted to a national police force. The RNWMP thus entered the national arena, experienced in the art of counter-subversion. By April of 1919 it had managed to infiltrate every important revolutionary organization in the West, and two of its agents had been delegates at the Calgary Western Labor Conference in March. The enhanced powers of the state in wartime, secured by the War Measures Act of 1914 and expanded in subsequent orders-in-council and initiatives of the Secretary of State, established mechanisms to "register" and restrain supposed "enemy aliens," impose censorship, and disrupt socialist organizations. All these powers were exercised in the wartime climate of statism and anti-Bolshevism.

The repression of the war years continued into the post-war reconstruction period. Alien registration, prohibitions on movements and the freedom to possess firearms and to publish newspapers in "foreign" languages, forced labour, deportations, the banning of certain organizations, and private vigilante actions unpunished by the state all confirmed the radical beliefs of many ethnic workers. At the same time, these state actions drove less resolute immigrants into passivity. Almost 200 immigrant "anarchists and revolutionaries" were rounded up in summer raids that followed the outbreak of the Winnipeg General Strike. While Canadian workers fought for democracy abroad and, in the aftermath of the war, mutinied, rioted, and struck for better conditions for themselves and returned soldiers, those focused on the home front were engaged in their own war for the rights of citizenship. The war for democracy at home was waged most forcefully in the Alberta coal fields and in the munitions industry, where a 1916 strike in Hamilton challenged state, employer, and the powerful appeal of "patriotism."

Explored by Allen Seager, "the great fight for democracy" in the coal communities of Alberta commenced in 1916-17 with a series of limited victories that won war bonuses, wage increases, and the repeal of some harsh clauses imposed on the men under the adverse conditions of 1915. Another strike in 1918 secured further concessions, and the miners returned to work. As their union, the United Mine Workers of America, was recognized by the bulk of the operators, and conditions and wages were better than those previously known by the foreign-born and native English-speaking miners, the coal fields should have been models of stability and contentment.

Pinkertons, government spies, and employers interpreted the situation differently, however, and saw the ideological and social components of an alternative culture of resistance. One miner militant was a firm believer that "as soon as this war is over . . . things will be alot better for the working men and women . . . this will be what the Aristocrats and Plutocrats will call Anarchy . . . then the men that are living off the earnings of us poor devils will either have to work or else not eat." A workers' mock parliament in Blairmore defined the community's war aims as "the establishment forever of government for, by and of the people." In Drumheller, colliers built a new Miners' Institute where they held union meetings. Here were signs of an emerging autonomy, the creation of an institutional foundation for the "new culture," the "working-class culture," that the *One Big Union Bulletin* saw at work in the coal fields in 1919. Something of the strength of that culture was felt when nearly 7,000 workers walked off their jobs in District 18 in May of 1919, enforcing the first 100 per cent strike in the mines, pulling out the unionized maintenance men, and thereby threatening not only capital's profits and production but its property.

Even within the confines of more conventional forms of social interaction between labour and capital, the war years were ones of class polarization and unprecedented militancy. The International Association of Machinists, for instance, was a union struggling to establish itself in the early twentieth century. It fought major strikes on the Grand Trunk Railway in 1905-07, against the CPR in 1908, in Kingston (1902-05), and in Toronto (1907-09). But the most dramatic confrontation unfolded in Hamilton in 1916.

On Monday, June 12, 1916, approximately 2,000 workers struck over thirty Hamilton plants engaged in the production of munitions. Among the plants affected were the Steel Company of Canada, Canadian Westinghouse, the National Steel Car Company, and Dominion Steel Foundry, a representative sample of monopoly capital's leading firms. Myer

Siemiatycki's discussion of the conflict stresses the range of workers drawn to the strike and the hostility of the bosses and the state. Nine hundred unionized machinists affiliated with the IAM, 338 associated with a rival craft body, the Amalgamated Society of Engineers, and 800 unskilled and unorganized shellmakers came together in a struggle for improved conditions that escalated quickly into a challenge to capital and the state. Employers formed an association and attempted to fan the flames of public opposition with patriotic hysteria. After a month-long battle the machinists were forced to return to their jobs. Less radical than actions in the West waged by supporters of the OBU, such struggles pushed workers toward new awareness. "If the machinists of the world were to strike today," said Hamilton's oldest member of the IAM local, "this war, large as it is, would immediately cease, the world would stand still, because this is a war of machines and an age of the same."

As statements such as these were being made workers were also fighting their own particular war for democracy in resisting the state's attempts to conscript workers directly into the ranks needed overseas. The Borden-led governments of the war years never considered that the trade unions should be consulted on domestic or foreign policy. Trades and Labor Congress resolutions in 1912 and 1913 had confirmed even the cautious, mainstream labour movement's opposition to war, and this held doubly so for radicals in the trade unions. With the declaration of war in 1914, the Congress softened its stand, but enough anti-war sentiment existed within labour's ranks that even TLC president James Watters was restrained in his statement that, "If there is any right in this war, we hope that right will prevail," and condemnatory in his charge that "profits have been a motive prompting manufacture of essentials." Still, Watters and his allies in the upper echelons of the TLC contented themselves with attempts to secure "fair wage" clauses in war industry contracts and to lobby the government not to conscript labour. Little was gained by such moderation.

In June, 1917, the Conscription Bill was introduced into the House of Commons. Radicals were immediately galvanized to outraged opposition and there were calls for a general strike. Western radicals were the most vehement in their denunciation, but in Quebec the anti-conscription mood, rooted in a national sense of grievance, was more widespread. Huge demonstrations in Quebec City and Montreal drew tens of thousands into a protest movement that seemed to coalesce with the strike movement then gaining ground and the radicalism of western labour. Alphonse Verville, past-president of the TLC and sitting member of Parliament for Montreal Hochelaga, thundered, "There were two major views on the War, that of the exploiter and that of the exploited." But the federal election of December, 1917, saw the conscription forces victorious and the TLC leadership accommodated to Gompers's AFL position that labour should aid the war effort.

Many radicals continued to oppose conscription, but they faced the repressive capacities of the Borden Unionist government and its Dominion police. As the shooting of Ginger Goodwin, an SPCer, union organizer, vice-president of the radical B.C. Federation of Labor, and draft dodger, near Cumberland on Vancouver Island indicated, the state was willing to take extreme measures in its fight against radical anti-conscriptionist workers. Labour countered with a one-day general strike in Vancouver. That working-class opposition, as well as such state extremism, would carry over into the post-war upheavals associated with 1919.

GENERAL STRIKE

Nineteen-nineteen was a year of strikes. More than 420 were fought, far exceeding the number of conflicts in any previous year. The number of workers involved in strikes (almost 150,000) and worker days lost to conflict (over 3.4 million) also peaked, as did the number of workers organized in unions (approximately 400,000): these figures doubled or tripled those of earlier years. In 1919, the Labour Department began calculating time lost to strikes as a percentage of time worked annually. That percentage was 0.6 in 1919, a figure yet to be surpassed. Employer victories, however, began to increase, relative to the more favourable ratio of worker wins to losses of 1917-18. Clearly, the class struggle was heating up to the point that it was mandatory for ruling authority to put a stop to what appeared to be a threat to the very foundations of civil society. Twenty years after the event, the Prime Minister of the day, Sir Robert Borden, noted that "In some cities there was a deliberate attempt to overthrow the existing organization of the Government and to supersede it by crude, fantastic methods founded upon absurd conceptions of what had been accomplished in Russia. It became necessary in some communities to repress revolutionary methods with a stern hand and from this I did not shrink."

As Gregory S. Kealey has argued, 1919 was a moment of international working-class revolt: it erupted in Canada not only in the radical West but in the metal trades of industrial centres, among railway workers in the North, and within the militant minority of urban craft workers in eastern cities. Fuelled by the radical rhetoric of an activist contingent of soapboxers, socialists, and agitators/organizers, the 1919 revolt was driven by belief that capitalism could not be reformed but had to be overthrown. A single slogan recurred time and time again in worker discontent of the period: "Production for use, not for profit." Shaping the contours of the thoughts and struggles of a diverse set of working men and women, rooted in different conditions and contexts, was a powerful mythology of the potential of One Big Union. Although embodied in the organization of the same name, the mobilizing *idea* of the One Big Union was in fact more powerful than its smaller, more localized institutional expression. Where the OBU itself failed to consolidate, the *myth* of One Big Union could nevertheless spread, often like wildfire. This unique conjuncture of class activism and ideological ferment pushed metal tradesmen, machinists, miners, and transportation workers into the generalized revolt of 1919, drawing into the fray new contingents of strikers. Women and civic employees figured prominently in the latter process, the former establishing Women's Labour Leagues and Women's Labour Councils in such cities as Toronto, Winnipeg, Calgary, and Vancouver.

In all of this, remnants of the Socialist Party of Canada were evident. No longer a potent organizational force in its own right, the SPC had withered as a party but had become a steeled cadre of working-class leaders committed to the OBU, as organization and idea, and these leaders were well placed to figure actively in the events of 1919. No longer capable of playing a vanguard role, the SPC nevertheless provided the men and women who would personalize the OBU myth in the heady days of 1919. Many of them, after years of experience in the pressure cooker of class struggle and ultraleft politics, were moving away from the failures of the SPC toward a committed Bolshevism that would later find its institutional expression in the founding of the Communist Party of Canada. Indeed, the early 1920s establishment of communism in the Canadian workers' movement was a product of the class upheavals of the war and post-war years, the ideological debate associated with the Russian Revolution and the fractured SPC, and the lessons learned from the advances of 1919 that nevertheless could not be translated into workers' power.

Most visible among the countless struggles of 1919 was, of course, the Winnipeg General Strike, which spurred Canadian labour to action across the land. Originally viewed by historians drawn to the statist pronouncements of leading politicians like Borden as a conspiratorial attempt to establish a Soviet-style government, contemporary scholarship has revised this view of the confrontation, casting the struggle not as a Bolshevik plot but as a simple battle to improve wages and working conditions and to implement the essential structures of collective bargaining. This revisionist stance has been drawn from a reasoned assessment of evidence, although it has also often been based on assumptions that workers are never interested in anything other than the size of their paycheques. The new analysis has clarified the strike's aims, but it does not offer any explanation as to how non-revolutionary demands can, in specific circumstances, form the foundation of a challenge to authority that proves radical, even potentially revolutionary, in its implications. And that, in a few words, was what the Winnipeg General Strike was all about.

David Bercuson's *Confrontation at Winnipeg* provides the essential chronology and narrative of the conflict. Class relations in the city had undergone a certain polarization as early as 1906, when strikes by street railway workers, blacksmiths, and moulders exacerbated class tensions. Pre-war depression, wartime inflation, and workplace militancy further set the stage for the reconstruction period. With labour leaders warning of the necessity to "adopt stringent measures to force a recognition of [worker] rights," and radicals and socialists firmly implanted in the institutions of the workers' movement, the city was a centre of early discussion of the efficacy of the general strike. The return of soldiers, many of whom were still unemployed, the radical commitments of the ethnic community, and the general attachment to the mythology of One Big Union all created an explosive climate.

May Day, 1919, provided the spark. Building trades workers demanded wage increases to offset what they claimed was a 57 per cent decline in purchasing power of their earnings over the years 1913-19. However, the Building Trades Council employers complained of a recession in construction, an impasse was quickly reached, and May opened with the traditional spring strike. Similarly, among metal trades workers, the last week of April was a time of working-class demand for higher wages and a forty-four-hour week. Although the metal tradesmen did not demand union recognition, the employers were resolute in their opposition; only three of twenty-eight employers bothered to reply to the worker demands. The larger employers, in particular, were adamant in their refusal to bargain. As a result, the workers unanimously agreed to strike, closing down the shops on May 2 for the third time in as many years. The issues were far from revolutionary: wage parity with the better paid railway shop workers; the eight-hour day; and, to up the ante a bit, union recognition.

Other workers were embroiled in similar controversies. Telephone operators had come to a confrontation and nearly gone on strike, while street railway workers and even the policemen's union were locked into negotiation with employers. The weekly Trades Council meeting convened in this atmosphere of discontent. Workers became irate when they heard testimonies of the arrest of a German metalworker, of labour spies and government-hired *agents-provocateurs*, and of increasing employer hostility to unionism. Winnipeg seemed to be emerging as a test case. Across Canada, the eyes of labour were focused on their struggles, claimed the radical R.B. Russell. He exhorted workers to take "no more defeats" as the working-class standard. Amidst "tumultuous applause and scenes of the greatest enthusiasm," the Council voted to take up this rallying cry with a general strike. On May 13, the Council met again to report the overwhelming support the proposed general strike received from the city's organized workers: they endorsed the action by a vote of 11,000 to 500, and the general strike was called for May 15, 1919. Over 22,000 (eventually as many as 35,000) workers would stop work, the bulk of them unorganized, in a city populated by 175,000 people.

By the early evening of May 15, Winnipeg was paralysed. The strikers controlled the press, putting out the *Special Strike Edition* and the *Western*

Labor News, the police were sympathetic to the labour cause, and the Central Strike Committee functioned as something of a labour government. The Labor Temple saw a steady stream of employers marching to its door, begging permission to carry on essential services such as milk delivery, a reversal of roles of subordination that pleased the radicals among the leaders of the strike. By early June, as Donald Avery has stressed, ethnic workers such as Oscar Schopperlie (later to be arrested and deported) were growing more and more successful in their efforts to bring immigrant organizations and the ranks of the strikers closer together, while radical leaders were increasingly influential in segments of the returned war veterans. Thus, the strike became something more than a struggle for mundane workplace and bargaining rights, and its constituency expanded beyond the ranks of the skilled Anglo-Saxon craftsmen among whom it originated. In this movement of working-class initiative and innovation, capital and the state saw dissidence and challenge that had to be eradicated.

A Citizens' Committee of 1,000 moved quickly to suppress the Winnipeg strikers, sweeping aside the issues of collective bargaining in paranoid condemnation of the "deliberate, criminal and fantastic attempt to make a revolution." Closely in touch with the municipal, provincial, and especially federal levels of government, the Citizens' Committee served as capital's watchdog in its moment of crisis. Expenses incurred were, on several occasions, paid by the government in Ottawa, which kept close watch on the proceedings to determine if any of the strike leaders' actions were "seditious or treasonable."

Many of these so-called Bolsheviks were actually labourites, Liberals, or Conservatives; on the fifteen-member Central Strike Committee only R.B. Russell was a known advocate of the organizational OBU, which had yet to be formally constituted. The Strike Committee kept workers off the streets and confined to mundane tasks of keeping the city going, a stance of moderation that served only to further enrage the political and entrepreneurial "leaders" of Winnipeg. "Permitted by authority of strike committee," a placard that allowed the movement of goods and persons through the strike-stopped city, was a symbolic but tangible reminder that business was functioning in a manner far from usual. As pressure mounted, nativist attacks on aliens and "foreign Bolsheviks" increased, and the federal government intervened, Minister of Labour Gideon Robertson dismissing all the postal workers who refused to report for their duties. Arthur Meighen, Minister of the Interior and future Prime Minister, condemned the "revolutionists of various types, from crazy idealists down to ordinary thieves," who threatened those Winnipeg economic interests with which he was closely allied.

Pro- and anti-strike forces clashed across the city, many war veterans casting their lot with the workers but other soldiers proclaiming their opposition to labour radicalism. Parading supporters of both sides merely exacerbated tensions, which reached a new high in the second week of June, when 240 policemen were dismissed for their suspected sympathies with the workers. When 1,800 "special police" were recruited by the Citizens' Committee responsible for public order, the crisis was nearing its violent resolution. Between June 16 and June 21 the RNWMP raided labour halls and strike leaders' homes, arresting and imprisoning key spokesmen, as labour mounted a countrywide protest culminating in a silent Winnipeg parade that was attacked by the "specials" and the Mounted Police, injuring more than thirty and killing one. Aldermen John Queen and A.A. Heaps, as well as R.B. Russell, the Rev. W. Ivens (editor of the *Western Labor News*), and six others, four of whom were described as "foreign Bolsheviks," were jailed, and when some of their duties were taken over by a new corps of strike leaders such as J.S. Woodsworth and Fred Dixon, another wave of incarcerations followed. On June 26, 1919, after six weeks of constant battle, the strike was finally declared over, the Central Strike Committee urging labour to "speak in no uncertain terms at the next municipal election."

Given what was at stake in the international class struggle, this was to collapse the cause into a rather small container. Defeated but not demoralized, the Committee insisted that "Labor must fight on until she wins the long war for freedom." Just how that was to be done, however, was never spelled out with much force. Meanwhile, the state focused its repressive attention on the leaders of the Winnipeg General Strike and the OBU, pushing the cause of law and order into 1920 with a series of state trials that lasted from December, 1919, through April, 1920. The results were a bankrupted workers' movement and a number of jail terms, as well as some eloquent defence statements and influential propaganda.

Labour radicalism thus failed the test of 1919. For all the revolutionary rhetoric, working-class initiatives emerged out of the course of events rather than guiding those events in a strategic assertion of programmatic change. To be sure, this would have been a monumental achievement, attained against all odds and in the face of the most concerted anti-labour offensive ever waged in Canadian history. But it is nevertheless the case that the more aggressive, disciplined, and effective actions came from employers and the state. Winnipeg's General Strike revealed, as had no other single development in the 1895-1920 period, the power marshalled by the state and capital in the age of monopoly. It told, as well, of the price to be paid if that power was not recognized and combatted with workers' organizations of equal power, with class directives, with preparations for all eventualities, especially those of repression, and with extensions of workers' autonomy and authority. David Simpson, founding member of the policemen's union, recalled in 1979 the impact of the state assault on Winnipeg labour: "After the arrests the strike was bust, blown away." Blacklisted, forced to flee the city and then to return to work as a bailiff, Simpson felt something of the long-term consequences of the working-class defeat, a victory secured for capital by a consolidated state power.

STATE AND CLASS: LAW AND THE INDUSTRIAL ORDER

The most significant developments in the early twentieth-century history of the Canadian working class were thus twinned. Increasing class struggle, manifested in a spreading and subversive radicalism as well as in rampant conflict at the point of production, was countered by the developing presence of the state in class relations. To be sure, there was no monolithic, coherent state; its role and importance over time changed and at any given historical moment it always existed as a multifaceted, layered structure of various bodies and regionally constructed forces – parliaments, municipal councils, conciliation boards, and the judiciary. For all of this complexity, however, the rise of the interventionist state in this period, complementing in the sphere of politics the consolidations in the purely economic realm, is of central significance in the unfolding dramas of class relations.

From the very moment of the turn of the century, the state groped toward a solution to the "labour problem." For a time, this took the form of what the sociologist Bob Russell has recently dubbed voluntary conciliation by the patron state. A Conciliation Act was passed in 1900, establishing a federal Department of Labour that, under its own initiative or the invitation of one of the parties involved in an industrial dispute, could appoint a conciliator or launch an investigation into any strike or lockout it judged warranted inquiry. In force until the passage of the Industrial Disputes Investigation Act in 1907, this legislation coincided with the first wave of twentieth-century strike activity and was associated with the national wanderings of chief conciliator William Lyon Mackenzie King, who managed to involve himself in some twenty-eight of the thirty-one instances in which the provisions of the Conciliation Act were invoked. Most of the settlements benefited capital, and this early exercise in patron-state voluntarism was constructed largely as an exploratory and preparatory entry into class relations. Hesitant and uncertain of how to proceed, the state allowed its presence in the class struggle to be personalized around King, whose job was to impress on workers the possibilities of state intervention and to pressure capital to offer at least some minor concessions. This was a beginning that could only be left behind in the face of escalating class conflict.

The modest impact of the Conciliation Act paled before the upwardly racing spiral of class conflict. Between 1900 and 1907 over 1,300 strikes and lockouts took place, some 733 of them registered with the Department of Labour. Some of these conflicts, in the eyes of the state, posed a grave threat to public welfare and industrial order. Moreover, specific struggles exposed the Achilles' heel of the Conciliation Act: given voluntarism's recognizable tilt toward the interests of employers, labour was loath to co-operate in procedures it could readily see worked to its disadvantage.

This set the stage for the passage of the Industrial Disputes Investigation Act in 1907. Covering an important array of industrial undertakings in the mining, transportation, and public utilities sectors, the IDIA provisions were unilaterally extended in 1916 through the emergency powers of the War Measures Act. Under the IDIA, workers and employers were to provide thirty days' notice of any changes in employment conditions and, in the event of a likelihood of conflict, labour or capital could petition the state for a board of inquiry that had the power to investigate and make non-binding recommendations. During the period that this tripartite board (composed of representatives of capital and labour, as well as a chair acceptable to both disputants or appointed by the state) met, strikes were illegal. The IDIA thus represented a formal departure from the *ad hoc* interventions of the state in class relations, institutionalizing a new regime of industrial order through the regulation of class struggle. Russell has found that 90 per cent of the boards convened in the 1907-14 period were at the request of employers. He also suggests that where labour was organized and strong, it could do far better through direct negotiations or, even, illegal strikes than through recourse to the IDIA. But where employers were powerful and obstinate, and workers weak and divided, it was possible to secure, especially in times of prosperity, some positive results from an IDIA intervention.

What a legislative act could not accomplish, moreover, the state tried to secure with a staunch commitment to the theatre of conciliation and discussion, institutionalized in the increasingly common recourse to royal commissions exploring aspects of class relations. Pioneered in the late 1880s, this exercise in reconciliation through public inquiry proliferated in the 1900-20 years, with the state striking a number of royal commissions that addressed, among other matters, Japanese and Chinese immigration, technical education, and industrial conflicts. This public theatre intended to harmonize class antagonisms reached its zenith, predictably, in 1919 with the appointment of commissioners instructed to "enquire into Industrial Relations in Canada."

It is critical, however, not to mistake the new tripartist trajectory of compulsory state intervention coupled with the promotional possibilities of the royal commission as the sum of state involvement in class relations. Rather, even acknowledging its tilt toward employer interests, this was the carrot meant to entice workers; the stick was always in readiness to beat them back. Military intervention in strike situations was by no means an everyday occurrence, but it did increase after the turn of the century, the use of direct coercive power of the state more than doubling in the post-1900 years. Given the rising number of strikes this increase may not be particularly noteworthy, but when troops did move to secure industrial order they provided a clear object lesson in the brute power of the state. In specific circumstances, mostly related to coal-mining struggles in the East and West, the state used its military might to occupy entire communities: its poised bodies of armed men and its strategic parade of Gatling guns and other firepower let all know that the price for industrial disorder was potentially a fight to the death, a battle, moreover, that would necessarily be fought on quite unequal terms.

During wartime, with the country engaged militarily elsewhere, this kind of armed resolution of class conflict was understandably rare, but the state measures of repression were, as we have seen, extended: censorship, deportation, conscription, and counter-subversive activity on the part of police, who spied on and infiltrated radical groups and unions, were all part of the arsenal of repression. The IDIA, its reach extended considerably, continued in place until it was declared non-constitutional in 1925, but it was supplemented by a plethora of wartime orders-in-council that limited workers in their rights to strike and resist employers.

Russell has studied 663 cases of capital-labour conflict in the years 1915-24, all of which were covered under the IDIA. He finds that strike activity that actually pushed beyond the legally defined boundaries of the IDIA was the only strategy that offered labour any chance of success, with roughly 80 per cent of all labour victories secured by such means. State intervention in this period, when labour activism was on the rise, was thus a direct attempt to restructure class relations to allow capital to regroup and offset the trend toward working-class victory evident in the 1916-18 years. In the changed context of wartime militancy and radicalism and increasing workplace conflict, state intervention ran even more strongly to the advantage of capital than it had in the earlier 1907-14 period. With the crushing of the Winnipeg General Strike and the all-out state assault on the One Big Union the state signalled, decisively and unambiguously, that tripartist "compulsory voluntarism" was limited to those times when labour actively embraced industrial order and offered no fundamental challenge to state authority.

What emerges from this brief overview of state initiatives is the extent to which labour lagged behind, handicapped by its inability to grasp the extent to which the state, as a powerful national force, was engaged in a constant project of regulation and containment. To suggest that this was a coherent and strategic formulation on the part of an omniscient state would be to strain the historical reality considerably. But it is nevertheless the case that in its gropings from voluntarism to tripartism, and in its willingness to use coercion and repression, the state was redefining the very nature of class struggle. One price of labour's defeat in 1919 was that this consolidation of state power overrode the working-class revolt, channelling the workers' movement into a new period of dissolution.

UNDERSTANDING WORKING-CLASS OPPOSITIONS AND 1919

At a superficial glance, the General Strike in Winnipeg and the emergence of western labour radicalism seem to represent an unprecedented consolidation of class consciousness. General or sympathetic strikes erupted in Brandon, Regina, Saskatoon, Calgary, Edmonton, Medicine Hat, Prince Albert, Prince Rupert, New Westminster, Vancouver, Victoria, Amherst, Toronto, Lethbridge, Fort William, and Port Arthur. Within French Canada and southern Ontario, workers reacted more cautiously, but Montreal and Toronto were nevertheless centres of sympathetic activity. At a May 22, 1919, strike rally of Canadian Vickers plant employees in Montreal, approximately half of the 4,000 later involved in the strike passed resolutions promising material and moral support to the Winnipeg strikers. Although Montreal workers failed to mount a general strike in support of the western workers, they were far from acquiescent. By mid-June, nearly 13,000 workers were on strike in the city; rallies in favour of the Winnipeg General Strike and OBU propaganda produced a volatile atmosphere in which workers' militancy and radicalism were apparent.

A similar situation existed in Toronto, where, from the time of the Russian October Revolution well into 1919, revolutionary socialists had been leading a campaign against capital. By May, 1919, demonstrations of 5,000 would be headed by banners declaring, "We Fought for Democracy – Not for Capitalists." A future Communist leader, patternmaker Jack MacDonald, placed the new demands of labour squarely before the workers' movement: "We want the world for the workers," he yelled, "and we are going to have it." On May 30, a general strike was called; 12,000 responded, although four days later they were back at work. MacDonald insisted that the struggle was far from over. Labour, he claimed, was fighting "for control of the means of production."

These and many other similar developments show 1919 to be a unique moment in the history of Canadian workers. Attempts to suggest that time lost to labour conflict continued at extremely high levels into the 1920s miss the point that in 1919 labour's revolt was generalized across regional and sectoral boundaries, but in years like 1922 and 1924-25 the high recorded levels of strike activity were isolated in pockets of radicalism and militancy associated with groups such as the eastern Canadian coal miners. Elsewhere, class relations were far more subdued.

In Winnipeg the events of 1919 left their mark on the local political scene, as J.E. Rea has shown, well into the 1940s, if not to the present day, with a noticeable pattern of confrontation between labour and Citizens' Committee candidates continuing to characterize debate on the city council. The symbolic power of the general strike, moreover, would retain a privileged place within the Canadian trade union movement and would be drawn on once more in the difficult years of the 1970s. Among historians, too, Winnipeg 1919 is considered to be significant, and synthetic accounts of Canadian labour generally treat the confrontation not as an event in the history of workers but as the very starting point in labour history. "Labour's trauma started at Winnipeg in 1919," writes Irving Abella. "Until then its horizons seemed unclouded and propitious." Kenneth McNaught places his analysis of the General Strike in somewhat different, if complementary, terms: "the Winnipeg strike was a most significant occurrence in Canadian history, if for no other reason than that it was the first and only time in Canadian history that a majority was split clearly into two opposing camps." Such views, however correctly they point to the importance and novelty of 1919, obscure the extent to which class relations and antagonisms in Canada have a history that predates the 1919 labour revolt.

To compare the upheavals of the 1880s with those of 1919 is to emphasize the extent to which the later revolt was a reflection of both the continuity of class struggle *and* the changes that had taken place as a consequence of the twentieth-century conditions of monopoly capital, state intervention, and labour market segmentation. In the 1880s, when an eclectic radicalism bred of entrepreneurial capital's undisputed conquests captured the sympathies of a significant element within the working class, the Knights of Labor constructed a workers' opposition premised on the need to organize all workers and activated by a moral universality that challenged capital and the early state in ways that were unprecedented in nineteenth-century Canada. Much of this happened in the Canadian West in the years from 1899 to 1919, albeit in ways that sharpened the challenge and upped what was at stake. Capitalist development in the West lagged notably behind that of central Canada in the late nineteenth century, but in the Laurier years of the wheat boom and the integration of the West into the newly consolidating empire of Montreal-Toronto financial interests and Ottawa's proclaimed nation-state, the material foundations of class distinction emerged sharply and quickly.

This was a classic case of the shifting locale of the industrial frontier: that frontier gravitated from East to West over the course of the nineteenth and twentieth centuries. In the years before 1850 the "industrial frontier" was stunted by the hegemony of commercial capital, but it nevertheless thrived in the shipbuilding centres of Saint John and Quebec City. By the 1850s, manufacturing and entrepreneurial capital became established, and the industrial frontier passed into central Canada, encompassing a region bordering the Great Lakes and the St. Lawrence, stretching from London to Montreal. That frontier spawned monopoly and the integration of finance and industrial capital. In the epoch dominated by these forces, wheat, on the one hand, and other staples like coal, lumber, and non-ferrous metals, on the other, emerged as the foundation of resource-based capitalism in the East and, more particularly, in the new frontiers of the West and northern Ontario. Each of these industrial frontiers produced distinctive working-class structures, in terms of both organization and social and cultural life. Uneven economic development conditioned a specific unevenness in class formation.

Western labour radicalism from 1899 to 1919 was thus in some senses the counterpart of central Canada's labour upsurge of the 1880s. The links here are quite direct, from the Western Federation of Miners, a body tracing its origins to the Knights of Labor, to the attachment to the idea and myth of the One Big Union shared by the Knights, the IWW, the socialists, and the OBU. Early socialists such as George Wrigley, Phillips Thompson, and Richard J. Kerrigan found their way from the Noble and Holy Order to the radical socialist and industrial-union formations of the early twentieth century. It is true that the economic, sociological, and ideological climate of the West, indeed of all regions in the country, was quite different from that of the 1880s, and this resulted in a radical movement that differed from the more eclectic movement culture of the earlier period. By the time industrial capitalism transformed the West, it had already entered its powerful monopoly phase and the state had begun to chart a formal path of regulation and legal intervention in class relations. At the same time, the workers' movement underwent an ideological evolution that was a product of peculiarly North American dealings with corporate capital and of international developments led by European revolutionaries. This new advancing class consciousness, admittedly cultivated and embraced by a minority within the workers' movement, clarified many, though not all, of the deficiencies and ambiguities inherent in the eclectic radicalism of the 1880s.

Such developments were impressive; but they did not give rise to an unambiguous class consciousness and solidarity. Indeed, at the pinnacle of labour's revolt in 1918-19, working-class radicalism assimilated a rhetoric of class consciousness that was unfortunately unmatched in the realms of class organization and programmatic conception of how society would be transformed. In the new ideological and material conditions of the twentieth century, diverse strategies that covered the spectrum of "pure and simple unionism" of the craft/business sort, labourism, Christian socialism, syndicalism, and revolutionary Marxism all competed for worker allegiance. Region and gender remained divisive realities. Where the ideological eclecticism of the 1880s resulted in a movement that was sometimes hesitant and unusually unfocused, the radicalism of the turn of the century (especially in the West) consisted of a contentious, if more advanced and sophisticated, body of competing ideologies and organizational directions. If these ideologies and strategic directions appeared to come together in the upheaval of 1919, however, it was through the suppression of difference rather than explicit debate and a formally established united front. But many questions went unasked, as well as unanswered.

A newer, more proletarian radicalism, admittedly infused with socialist principle and rhetoric, emerged in the exuberance of wartime militancy, international working-class advance, and a climate in which workers' power seemed realizable. Labourite and socialist, syndicalist and revolutionary, Christian moralist and pragmatic unionist were all drawn into labour's struggles. However different all of this was from the 1880s, there was a similarity: eclecticism remained and the alliance was sustained through times of upheaval and victory, but when the powerful forces of capital and the state clamped down on this labour revolt defeat would fracture the loose ideological and organizational foundations of the workers' movement. Across Canada the lesson of 1919 was brought home to the working class in blunt and unequivocal language: to fail to take into account the combined power of capital and the state was to court decisive defeat. The class stand of 1919 thus proved unsuccessful, as had eclectic radicalism before it. Many lessons of the class struggle had been learned; many more remained to be taken up. Much of the history of the 1920s and 1930s would emerge out of just this conjuncture of what was understood and what was not: communism, social democracy, labourism, continued partyism, and the contest between craft and industrial unionism can all be interpreted as part of this process.

This ideological and organizational fragmentation was reinforced by demographic change. In the 1880s the Knights of Labor succeeded in minimizing (not, of course, eliminating) ethnocultural divisions within the working class. However, this vitally important achievement extended only to the English-speaking and French-speaking workers who formed the absolute bulk of the Canadian working class. Irish and non-Irish, Catholic and Protestant, were brought together to some extent and even in French Canada, where language and culture posed acute problems of unity, the 1880s saw a number of common responses to a range of similar problems among members of the working class. In the opening decades of the twentieth century, with immigrants flooding the labour market, ethnic divisions became more pervasive and more distinct. While significant and historically creative efforts to bridge the gaps of ethnic heterogeneity were made, especially in the West and in the radical enclaves of urban industrial-capitalist Canada, no fundamental, lasting unity between indigenous and immigrant workers was achieved. Immigrant workers formed the backbone of a reserve army of labour, structured into cul-de-sacs of casualism. Almost universally blocked access to routes of attaining recognized skills, they were isolated in specific job ghettoes, often lived in urban slums, and suffered ethnic prejudice that was institutionalized by corporate and state power and personalized by countless individuals. Whether considered as "dangerous ʁ reigners" given to radicalism, primitive peasant communalists prone to the violent and chaotic resolution of specific grievances, or slovenly and docile workers incapable of sustaining working-class organizations of self-defence, the immigrants were generally far removed from their English-speaking counterparts in the newly restructured Canadian working class.

To pose the matter in these highly abstract terms is to capture the large picture but to risk missing some of its complex details. For even within the immigrant working class, there were divisions of significance. At the most basic level, politics fractured working-class ethnic groups. The Finnish community was split between its Red and White components. The tactics adopted by some of these subcommunities were as different as night and day, the disciplined socialism of the Red Finns contrasting with the violent strikes undertaken by Italian and Greek workers at the Canadian Lakehead, described in detail by Jean Morrison. The socialist activism of segments of the Ukrainian, Russian, and Jewish communities was much different than the generally ineffective and often apolitical protests of immigrant workers in centres of heavy industry such as Hamilton. At the same time that the radical Ukrainians editing the newspaper *Robotchy Narod* (*Working People*) challenged English chauvinism, defended radical anti-militarism, and insisted on a class stand of resistance, the early sociologist Edmund Bradwin was describing Slavs in the northern bush as "just plodders in the day's work – withal, that pliant type that provides the human material for a camp boss to drive." Even acknowledging Bradwin's ethnocentrism and racism, it is impossible to deny that these extremes – radical activists versus the raw, apolitical apathetic human material of exploitation – did not constitute real poles of opposition within the immigrant community.

The demographic remaking of the working class in the post-1900 years was thus a factor of considerable importance in the remaking of working-class oppositions, evident in the many schisms that rocked the Socialist Party of Canada and the Social Democratic Party. Immigrant socialists left the SPC in 1910 to form the radical base of the SDP. No sooner were these ethnic radicals allied with moderate, labourite-leaning Anglo-Saxons like Jimmy Simpson, however, and other splits were in the making. After 1917 a plethora of revolutionary foreign-language federations were established, many of which would feed directly into the developing Communist movement.

Much of this was a necessary process of political realignment. But it was also a reflection of the structural impositions of capital, which rigidly segmented labour markets that divided workers in myriad ways. Region, skill, and gender, as we have seen, were all part of this process of segmentation, simultaneously structured by capital and assimilated and internalized by labour. But race and ethnicity, in relation to class, were perhaps most obviously and purposively constructed in oppositional terms. In the words of one contractor: "We distinguish white men. Austrians and Italians we don't call them white men. I don't know that it's hardly fair but it's customary." Allen Seager has insightfully suggested that even the census category "labourer" in British Columbia was in part "a racial category into which low-status Asian immigrants were habitually structured, literally as well as figuratively," a point reinforced by the researches of Gillian Creese, which document the undeniable duality of a west coast labour market separated into spheres of "white" and "yellow" work.

Race and ethnicity thus stand as something of a symbol of how materially embedded structures of difference, imposed by capital and often assimilated by labour, undercut the possibilities of working-class oppositions in the years 1895-1919. This process was never, of course, total and unchallenged, and much in the history of working-class oppositions and the upheavals of 1919 struggled, often successfully, to overcome the many barriers monopoly capital was able to erect in the path of class solidarity. Still, these barriers were formidable, and they were lent more substance by the repressive thrust of the newly consolidated interventionist state. Against the invigorated initiatives of capital and the state the impressive mobilization of working-class oppositions associated with 1919 did not prevail. And once defeat came, as it did in 1919, it ensured that the conflicts between fragmentation and solidarity within the working class, between capital and labour in the larger social relations of production, and between accommodation and resistance within the political realm would all be resolved in favour of the former tendencies and forces at the expense of the latter. The causes of solidarity, labour, and resistance would live on, throughout the 1920s and 1930s. But as new assaults on the surviving remnants of working-class oppositions and organizations were being mounted, labour faced an increasingly uphill battle.

Chapter 5

DISSOLUTION AND RECONSTITUTION
1920-1940

THE SOCIAL FORMATION

The 1920s and 1930s were monopoly capital's years of boom and bust, its moment of consolidation followed by deep crisis. World War One proved to be monopoly's "adolescence," separating its years of maturity from those of its infancy. Before 1914, business life had come to be dominated by the close connections between finance and industrial capital, while the economy tended increasingly toward concentrated holdings and mass production. These methods were developed further in the late 1920s as Canada emerged from a post-war recession to take its place in the world capitalist order, a place that would be shown, in the collapse of 1929, to rest on a precariously unstable material foundation. The country and its working class were plunged into a depression both unexpected and unprecedented in its severity. The Liberal and Conservative parties retained their hold on the electorate, although new challenges arose in the form of third parties of dissent. But the forceful initiatives were taken by the Liberals, and Laurier was succeeded by the architect of class conciliation, William Lyon Mackenzie King. His term as Prime Minister – broken only briefly in the 1920s and again in the early 1930s – provided labour with a promise of participation in decision-making that would prove as hollow as it was appealing.

In the 1920s, new patterns of investment and corporate organization were pioneered, facilitating concentration not only of industry but also of chartered banking. Much of this activity centred on resource-based industrial development, the new staples of hydroelectricity and pulp and paper being of particular significance. The bases of many of Canada's contemporary corporate giants were laid in this decade: especially noteworthy was the creation of a series of investment companies. Among the most powerful were the Brazilian Traction, Heat & Light Company (1912), Power Corporation (1925), and Alcan Aluminum Limited (1928). Such holding companies, as Jorge Niosi argues, provided one way of centralizing and concentrating economic power. Mergers presented another complementary path. Beginning with the formation of the British Empire Steel Corporation in 1920, which amalgamated the coal and steel interests of Nova Scotia, the decade was dominated by a wave of industrial conglomerations. In the merger movement of 1924-30, 315 such mergers took place, involving firms with assets of nearly $1 billion. Such concentration of economic power established monopoly as the dominant force within the economy, and in the next merger wave the dimensions of concentration were substantially reduced. From 1931 to 1935 only 232 mergers, involving less than $400 million in assets, took place.

Much of the actual joining of corporate interests was orchestrated by financial intermediaries, investment houses such as Wood Gundy and Company or the chartered banks with which they were closely associated in *de facto* partnerships. Wood Gundy, for instance, "created" Canada Cement in 1927, and Canada Power and Paper, Simpson's Limited, and the reorganized BESCO, or Dominion Steel Corporation, in 1928. Allied with the Royal Bank, Wood Gundy was represented on the boards of fifty of the largest Canadian corporations by J.H. Gundy and was at the centre of some of the most spectacular bankruptcies in the history of Canada when economic collapse took some of its offspring in the early 1930s. The banks, for their part, also concentrated their power, and from a high of fifty-one banks in 1874 the number declined to thirty-six by 1900 and to a mere eleven in 1925. Three of the largest – the Royal Bank, the Bank of Montreal, and the Commerce – accounted for about 70 per cent of banking resources in 1927, and in alliance with a range of investment houses, trust companies, life insurance outfits, and industrial corporations, these banks attained a previously unmatched consolidation of economic power and authority.

Concentrated forms of production stimulated real manufacturing output, which grew at a compound rate of 4 per cent between 1919 and 1925 and at the exceptionally high level of 9.8 per cent between 1926 and 1929. American capital flowed into Canada to exploit this economic potential until, in 1934, there were 1,350 U.S. firms operating in the country. Thirty-six per cent of these corporations had been established between 1920 and 1929, and a further 26 per cent came to Canada in the years 1930-34. As a percentage of foreign investment in Canada, American capital more than doubled between 1913 and 1926, rising from just under 22 per cent to 53 per cent. Direct U.S. investment was clearly overtaking British portfolio investment, seizing upon a set of new economic opportunities.

American capital was particularly active in resource-based production and in the new mass-production consumer goods industries. In mining, American-dominated giants like the Sudbury-based International Nickel Company of Canada were products of the 1920s, and forest resources crossed the border at increasing rates to fulfil expanding American needs. As the 1924 royal commission on pulpwood revealed, as much as 30 per cent of particular regional timber lands were leased or owned by foreign capitalists, the bulk of them from the United States. Within the automobile industry – a symbol of the expanding production of the 1920s – Ford and General Motors were drawn to Canada to exploit domestic sales and to operate within the tariff walls of the British Empire, selling to overseas markets. By 1929, 250,000 cars were produced annually in Canada, of which 100,000 were exported. So pronounced was the American impact on the Canadian economy that by the 1930s U.S. capital controlled almost one-quarter of the nation's manufacturing, and in automobiles (82 per cent), electrical apparatus (68 per cent), rubber goods (64 per cent), machinery (42 per cent), and chemicals (41 per cent) the dominance was even more pronounced.

The combined processes of consolidation and Americanization of Canadian capitalism stimulated technological change and automation. In the 1930s, 30 per cent of new mining equipment was imported, largely from the United States. Because American investment was concentrated in large industrial firms capitalized at over $200,000, economies of scale were implemented freely, sustained by branch-plant profits between 1926 and 1933 of nearly $550 million. To compete with such giants, indigenous Canadian capital was also forced to modernize. Drawing on new energy sources, especially hydroelectricity, the manufacturing sector expanded greatly. Between 1911 and 1931, the installation of electric motors in Canadian manufacturing establishments increased sixfold in Ontario and forty-fivefold in New Brunswick. Other innovations and developments – refrigeration, steel ships, rail and road penetration of the North, and the discovery of new mineral deposits – contributed to growth, pushing capital formation and gross national product (GNP) to near-record highs in these years.

As profits consequently soared, work forces expanded, technological innovations proliferated, and managerial perspectives shifted. Many of the economic sectors in which growth was so pronounced throughout much of the 1920s were bastions of the open shop. The craftsman's regime of limited worker control and powerful unionism, which had appeared as such a brake on capitalist expansion in the first phase of monopoly's consolidation at the turn of the century, was curbed and undermined, if not obliterated. This meant that the brute restructuring force of pure-and-simple Taylorism, although still a presence, was supplemented by what has come to be known as welfare capitalism schemes.

Factory beautification programs, profit-sharing plans, industrial councils that smothered unionism in a suffocating rhetoric of worker-employer co-operation, personnel departments, and company-sponsored leisure activities were all hallmarks of the new age. Such initiatives had their origins in earlier times, but they became more systematic and common in the aftermath of the upheavals of the 1916-20 years. In the steel industry studied by Craig Heron, companies introduced pension plans, self-promotional monthly magazines, recreation programs, and highly publicized safety campaigns. Women workers in the Penmans mills of Paris, Ontario, remembered the labour relations of the 1920s as dominated by the company's Pleasure Club, which organized dances and card parties in a hall on a floor of the underwear mill. These monthly gatherings were supplemented by picnics, sporting tournaments, and annual train and boat excursions, where the paternalism of the corporation was reinforced by a familial ideology that feted the "best baby" and largest family in attendance with prizes. One worker described life in the Penmans empire as a "family affair." Along with more traditional corporate tactics of union-busting, blacklisting, and well-placed firings of militants, these welfare measures and paternalist practices combined to dampen, if not entirely drive out, working-class impulses to organize and resist. Strongest in the 1920s, the welfare plans so consciously crafted by capital likely faded somewhat with the economic collapse of 1929: as unemployment and joblessness drove workers to accept what little employers could provide there was hardly as much need to sweeten the pot of corporate offerings. At least in the early stages of depression, unionism and militancy were so thoroughly stopped in their tracks that welfarism would have been little more than redundant.

For all of this expansion and change, then, there nevertheless existed a fundamental divide in the history of the 1920s and 1930s. The Great Depression separated out histories of capital, labour, management, and the state, with 1929 marking an historical moment that fractured trends and forced recognition of new and changed realities. Of course, there were locales where such trends were not evident, the lines of demarcation softened by powerful continuities. But the blunt economics of difference separated out the possibilities for many workers with the crash of 1929. What happened?

Put simply, the expansion, profit-taking, and much-proclaimed prosperity of the mid- to later 1920s were sustained by serious imbalances within the Canadian economy, which was, as ever, regionally structured. In addition, this "national" economy was highly dependent on a world capitalist order, which provided much-needed markets for exports but which was also quite unstable. Domestically, the prairie wheat sector never recovered from the depressed prices of the post-war years and was overextended beyond levels sustainable by peacetime prices for foodstuffs. Cultivated acreage actually declined. In certain key sectors, central Canada so dominated output – as much as 90 per cent in some realms of production – that it structured the country around the existence of "have" and "have-not" regions. Within Atlantic Canada the dislocations bred of shipbuilding's unambiguous collapse, plus the weakness of a coal and steel industry looted by absentee capital and abandoned by powerful central Canadian financial interests, were patently obvious by the 1920s. Ottawa, as the site of political decision-making, and Montreal and Toronto, as locales of finance capital's power, cultivated Atlantic Canada's dependency on central Canada. After 1928, Cape Breton was called on to stock the countrywide labour market and provide a reserve capacity for "national" energy and steel needs; in the Maritimes as a whole, 42 per cent of the region's manufacturing "disappeared" in the years 1920-25.

Built on consumption and its seemingly endless elasticity, the economy of the 1920s was nearing its breaking point: overproduction seemed endemic, the overextension of credit an unhealthy indicator of the lack of stability in the "boom" of the twenties. The automobile companies of Windsor and Oshawa, for instance, were willing to drive 400,000 cars off the assembly lines in 1930, although Canadians already owned one million autos and never, in any year, had more than a quarter of this number been sold. The beginnings of economic crisis appeared visible to some, even in the midst of a bloated prosperity. A reversal of twentieth-century population trends resulted. Prior to 1920, 1.2 million Americans entered Canada from the United States, as opposed to 900,000 Canadians emigrating south. But in the 1920s there was a turnabout, with a drain of some 700,000 to the United States.

International markets, too, reached their limits and could no longer absorb Canadian goods: agricultural exports dropped in value from $780 million in 1928 to just $253 million by 1932. The world capitalist order, perched precariously on the edge of war debts and excessive supplies of primary products, took a turn downward in 1928-29. In Canada, where economic boom relied heavily on such primary products, the effects of worldwide depression were felt immediately. Excess production was the norm before 1930. In newsprint, for instance, the years 1913-20 and 1920-29 saw production triple, with Canada producing 65 per cent of the world's total, 90 per cent of which went to the United States. After the downturn, such overproduction was curtailed, regional economies dependent on resource output were abandoned, and workers were thrown out of employment. The bubble of the 1920s burst; the stock market crash of "Black Thursday," October 24, 1929, was simply the decisive signal that something, economically, had been quite wrong for some time.

Within a few short years, real GNP declined by almost 30 per cent, the value of exports was reduced by 25 per cent, new investment dropped to only slightly more than 10 per cent of its 1929 level, and unemployment hovered around the 25 per cent mark. More than one-tenth of the Canadian population depended on relief. Diverse regional experiences led to a range of responses to crisis, but the Conservative and Liberal leadership of the country offered little in the way of alleviation. R.B. Bennett presented his "Iron Heel" and then his "New Deal," while King preferred to retire behind constitutional questions or draw inspiration from criticizing Conservative failures. "King or Chaos," neither a disciplined response to crisis nor much of an actual choice, nevertheless carried the Liberals to electoral victory in 1935.

It was left to others – Communists, social democrats, community groups, industrial unionists, relief advocates, the unemployed – to articulate new needs in the deteriorating context of the 1930s. That they did so only with modest success was in part a consequence of monopoly capital's unique capacity to undercut the foundations of solidarity. The 1920s had been a decade of anti-union violence, strikebreaking, wage reductions, and industrial paternalism and welfare capitalism. When depression struck with all its force in 1930, labour was stripped, in large measure, of its institutions and part of its political traditions. It had to begin anew.

LABOUR DEFEATED

Capital's relentless quest for hegemony quickened its pace in the early 1920s. Labour, at the centre of social and political life in 1919, seemed to take two steps backward for every forward leap of its adversary. A wide array of forces and developments combined and seemed to leave workers at the mercy of ever more powerful employers. Not all working-class efforts ended in defeat, of course, but there is no question that more and more struggles were ending in outcomes favourable to capital. Strikes resulting in unambiguous employer victory were a markedly higher percentage of all conflicts in the years 1921-24 than in any other twentieth-century period, save for the exceptional annual figure for the recession-ravaged 1908. While this percentage figure dropped in the more economically favourable climate of 1926-29, it still remained relatively high compared to earlier years.

Union membership was also trailing off, dropping from roughly 380,000 in 1919 to 240,000 half a decade later. Workers affiliated with the Trades and Labor Congress of Canada fell from about 175,000 in 1920 to a low of just over 100,000 in 1926. Established craft unions suffered severe setbacks, while in specific sectors – agricultural implements, meat packing, construction, and oil refining – industrial councils brought worker and employer representatives together in a Mackenzie King-inspired attempt to bypass traditional forms of worker organization and collectivity. Estimates from various sources indicate that between 145,000 and 200,000 workers were represented by such councils in the 1920s. Closely associated with Canadian subsidiaries of such American corporate giants as Imperial Oil, International Harvester, Bell Telephone, Swift's, and Consolidated Rubber, this works council movement also thrived among indigenous Canadian firms, especially Massey-Harris in Toronto. These businesses epitomized the open-shop tendencies of the times, blocked organized workers whenever they could, and only encouraged labour's fortunes to decline.

Radicalism was also on the wane, although its collapse was not quite as precipitous as most historians have assumed. Peter Campbell's recent unpublished research into the lives of Socialist Party of Canada and One Big Union activists R.B. Russell, W.A. Pritchard, and Ernest Winch illuminates how these radical bodies and individuals hung on through difficult and often desperate years. This revises past assessment (including my own) that the SPC was virtually defunct in this period, and it broadens our understanding of the staying power of the OBU, as an attachment and principled commitment, if not a permanent class organization. Having drawn over 50,000 to its ranks in 1919, there is no denying the extent to which the OBU was debilitated by factionalism, employer hostility, state repression, and economic recession in the early 1920s. Still, the conventional wisdom that the OBU could only muster the support of 1,600 dues-paying members in 1927 understates, as Campbell indicates, the potential and possibility that the OBU stood for in many working-class circles. Among Nova Scotia and New Brunswick miners, Montreal packinghouse workers and railway labourers, eastern building tradesmen, and northern Ontario miners, the OBU was still organizing and eliciting a positive, if not permanent, response. As the 1930s presented workers with the threat of layoffs and unemployment, the OBU and its stalwart advocate, R.B. Russell, continued the radical fight; even the SPC threatened a bit of a revival. To acknowledge all of this is to grasp the extent to which radicalism had, however, fallen on tough times. Leftists in the workers' movement knew well that they were living through a difficult period in the 1920s.

The decade began with high strike levels, more struggles being waged in 1920, 445, than ever before. But this figure obscures the extent to which the tide had turned to employers: compared to 1917-19, when workers won outright an average of almost 35 per cent of such strikes, in 1920 they managed to secure clear-cut victories in only 18 per cent. This percentage of worker wins would continue to decline in 1921, 1922, and 1924 before picking up again in the later, more prosperous years of the decade. Militancy thus tapered off noticeably in the post-1920 climate of hard times and antagonism to job actions. In 1921, the Department of Labour reported more than eighty-five defensive strikes against wage cuts, the bulk of them ending in defeat for workers. This set the stage for a good part of the history of the 1920s.

Outside of the coal fields, where the 1920s witnessed a series of violent confrontations, Canadian labour seemed submissive. It had been forced into a temporary quiescence. The vast majority of class conflicts were fought in the 1920s simply to preserve what was increasingly coming under attack from capital: the wage, the union, the customary conditions of work. Clearly, the 1920s were, in general, a period of marked deterioration of labour's power.

Much of labour's defeat can be attributed to the particular social formation of the early 1920s, when monopoly capital sat atop Canadian workers with a new sense of itself and its powers. Defeat was a structural consequence of the increasing power of employers, a power that was, for the most part, unmatched in working-class circles. One group particularly subjected to the power of capital, but which fought vigorously to resist its campaigns, was the coal miners.

BLOOD, GUTS, AND CULTURE ON THE COAL

"Blood on the coal" was a gruesome reality for Canadian miners. It shaped attitudes toward the operators and conditioned a particular defiance in union workers, who fought to win "compensation fully compatible with the dangers of our occupation." Between 1871 and 1939, more than 1,600 men were killed in Nova Scotia mines; in Alberta, over 1,000 miners died on the job in the years 1905-45. Miner militancy was never simply a reflection of the danger of the job, but along with the impossibility of rigid supervision and the negligible impact of machines in the early mines, it contributed to the process whereby coal miners cultivated a pride in their work and a code of ethics that followed class lines. "We built up a certain pride. This is mine. This is my section of the mine," recalled one Cape Breton miner. In Alberta and Cape Breton coal fields in the opening decades of the twentieth century, this pride was centred in the rise of effective unionism.

By 1919 in Nova Scotia and by 1920 in Alberta, the United Mine Workers of America represented coal miners. The history of this ascendancy was not always an honourable one, and in Alberta it had been generated in a conspiratorial drubbing of the One Big Union that involved the federal government, the coal barons, and the international officers of the UMWA. In the East, nothing this sordid took place (the international union's moment of disgrace would come later, in 1923-24), although the rise of the UMWA involved a contentious jurisdictional battle between the militant international union and the more collaborationist remnants of the old and thoroughly discredited Provincial Workmen's Association.

Recent histories of mine workers in the 1920s provide insight into the complex interaction of economic factors, cultural traditions, and ideological currents in the battles of the 1920s. For if the rest of Canadian labour was in retreat, the coal miners refused to capitulate in the face of employer hostility and the weakening of the industry. Coal mining accounted, by one count, for almost 17 per cent of all strikes in the 1920s, approximately one in every two strikers, and more than half of the striker days lost across the country.

The miners could not have chosen a more inopportune time, in terms of traditional collective bargaining moments, to wage their fight. Just as a rejuvenated miners' movement peaked the coal market became saturated, and by the end of the 1920s the coal miners' movement was in disarray. Oil and electricity were replacing coal, and marginal mines, thrust into production during World War One, were closing. Prices for coal dropped 50 per cent over the course of the 1920s.

Overproduction in American fields resulted in the flooding of central Canadian markets in the immediate aftermath of World War One. Cape Breton's traditional markets were virtually captured by competitors, and inadequate tariff protection and high transportation costs ensured that throughout the 1920s Nova Scotia sales would be undercut by an unstable market. Production and miner days worked in Nova Scotia fields dipped 33 per cent between 1917 and 1921. The newly created, financially unstable BESCO and its Montreal-based magnate, Roy (the Wolf) Wolvin, sought to break out of this impasse by making wage cuts, workers' pay comprising 60 per cent of production costs at the time. When BESCO negotiated a contract with 12,000 employees in 1921-22, it proposed a wage reduction of 33 per cent, setting the stage for four major strikes that would total well over two million miner days of strike activity.

As David Frank notes, these were years of constant confrontation, and between 1917 and 1926 at least sixty-four strikes were fought by the miners over wages, political concerns, the status of the union, the length of the work day, and a range of other issues that included the right to celebrate May Day or take one-day holidays to "discuss" questions of vital importance to the mining community. Out of this context of conflict surfaced workplace militancy that embraced mundane slowdowns in the form of restriction of output, as well as more spectacular actions such as the 100 per cent strike. Motivated by radical ideas extending from moderate labourism to Bolshevism, the miners demanded worker control, fought battles against the international union bureaucracy, and assaulted the "pluck-me" stores. Community solidarity was pitted strongly against corporate arrogance and economic might.

Antagonism grew, not only at the coal face, but on a foundation of traditional cultural attachments enriched by more recently established institutions, ideologies, and practices. While the Cape Breton fields were not ethnically homogeneous, they were dominantly Scots Catholic, and miners drawn from other national/ethnic backgrounds had been assimilated into the local milieu by the 1920s. The Scottish moral and clan tradition translated into the miners' collective condemnation of the "tyranny" and "slavery" to which they were subjected. Although a devout people, these Scots Catholics were disappointed in the churches' ties to the corporations and, while they remained members of the flock, they distanced themselves from those clergymen who appeared too willing to subordinate miners' needs and aspirations to company profits and policies. Drawing on religious commitments, the *Maritime Labor Herald* proclaimed its 1922 "Christmas Message": "The social revolution is the economic fulfillment of the gospel message."

Oral traditions reinforced this essential process of cultural adaption and, like the forms of struggle at the point of production, embraced subtle and ironic methods of rebellion as well as more unambiguous and open revolt. In a society comprised of Scots with similar or identical surnames, nicknames, for instance, might reflect grievances with the wage and its injustice, as well as a means of identification. Sandy MacDonald found one payday that, after a series of company deductions, he had collected a mere two pennies. "Did you have a good pay?" he was asked. "Well, yes," came his sardonic reply, "I had a very big pay." When the miners told this story, Sandy was popularly christened "Big Pay" and his sons the "Big Pay" MacDonalds. More direct means of political expression also emerged out of the oral tradition, as militant poets and storytellers like Dawn Fraser championed the people's interests in epics that might arouse the class passions of thousands of discontented miners. Bitter in his denunciation of that "monster," BESCO, Fraser wrote lines of condemnation in the near-starvation conditions of the winter of 1924-25. His "The Case of Jim McLachlan" chronicled the "dark and dismal days of old" (it was supposedly recounted to children in 1994) when "the world and all was ruled by Gold."

Fraser's memorializing of McLachlan was a tribute to a mainstay of the "Red" culture of the Cape Breton coal fields (something Fraser would later abandon and attack), McLachlan being the centre of a Bolshevik presence that reached beyond politics into the very way of life of the mining community. J.B. McLachlan joined the Communist Party of Canada in 1922. He had already established himself as the leading trade union figure in the Nova Scotia coal fields and was linked with the region's major labour newspaper, the *Maritime Labor Herald*. As class conflict peaked in 1923-25 McLachlan and other Communists constructed a "Red" culture in Cape Breton, a literal island of Bolshevism surrounded by the Canadian seas of reaction. Miners congregated behind the Glace Bay post office, a place known as "Red Square." The largest UMWA local was dubbed "the Kremlin." Communist members numbered no more than 250, but they reached into many quarters, cultivating supporters and sympathizers through their involvement in May Day organizational efforts, Women's Labour Clubs, and celebrations of the revolutionary calendar. Miners and Communists promoted the anniversary of the Russian Revolution and Lenin Memorial Day at a jammed Savoy Theatre, where rousing renditions of "The Red Flag" and the "Internationale" competed with filmed accounts of the Second Comintern Congress, featuring Lenin, Trotsky, Zinoviev, and the Red Army and Navy. Revolutionary orators such as Malcolm Bruce kept audiences on the edge of their seats for hours, while meetings ended with a performance of the Young Communist League "Junior Red" choir. Couples were married under the red flag. In newspaper articles and regular educational talks, McLachlan and others hammered home the messages of class struggle, proletarian internationalism, and the evils of capitalism.

The "Red" culture of these years was never a majority tradition, but in conjunction with the more traditional solidarities of the mining community, it helped to sustain the Cape Breton miners over the course of mass struggles that ended in defeat. It also helped to pressure an attack from within the labour movement as John L. Lewis led a devastatingly destructive move against McLachlan and the Cape Breton miners. As Lewis and the hierarchy of the UMWA dug in their heels in opposition to the Nova Scotia miners' public affiliation with "Reds," union headquarters challenged the district's right to strike, suspended its autonomy, and removed its radical and popular leadership. In conjunction with the repression unleashed by the state and the hostile actions of Wolvin and the BESCO empire, this represented a formidable foe, and McLachlan and the miners went down to a hard defeat. From 1923 on, when a sympathetic strike called in support of striking Sydney steel workers culminated in violent clashes among police, scabs, and strikers, Cape Breton was a war zone. McLachlan and another UMWA leader, Dan Livingstone, were arrested, with the former charged and convicted for seditious libel.

McLachlan's jailing and the Lewis-led crushing of the union reinforced corporate arrogance, epitomized in one boss's contemptuous challenge that the miners could not "stand the gaff." But stand it they did, even to defeat, and Wolvin and BESCO, after riding the union into the ground in 1925, succumbed to bankruptcy in 1928. At this point, the coal industry in Cape Breton was able to survive only on government subsidies. McLachlan retained his reputation and stature among the miners, but the "Red" culture was eroded, and with it much of Communist influence in the coal fields.

Unlike the Cape Breton mining community, the Crow's Nest Pass was not dominated by any single ethnic group. The coal towns of Alberta and southeastern British Columbia had taken in a great part of the mass immigration of 1895-1919. Coal communities like those at Blairmore, Drumheller, and Hillcrest were populated mostly by European peasants, many of whom, before coming to Canada, "had never [seen] a mine in their life." This ethnic diversity, in which Anglo-Saxon workers rarely comprised more than 25 per cent of the mining work force, created some of the fragmentation that led to the dissolution of working-class unity. Immigrants were commonly employed as strikebreakers. However, the widespread impact of the OBU in the western coal fields and the solidarities associated with 1919 helped to establish the social force of the slogan, "No Alien but the Capitalist." Out of the immigrant cultures, the coal miners fashioned class purpose and forms of resistance that would help fuel the battles of 1922-26.

United Mine Workers' District 18, like Nova Scotia's District 26, was the centre of a series of bitter disputes in the mid-1920s, as class war erupted in the mining West. In a district-wide strike in 1922, western coal miners joined forces with their brothers in the United States, taking half a million North American miners out of the pits. Two years later, a seven-month strike followed, lasting from April to October, 1924. Led by the UMWA, these struggles, like those to the east, were mounted to oppose proposed wage cuts (of 50 per cent) designed to buttress a declining industry. Involving up to 10,000 miners, the constant confrontation in the West came to a head in the 1924 strike, which saw the usual opposition to the companies complicated by worker resentment of the international union leadership's conciliatory tactics and refusal to endorse the 100 per cent strike that would include the withdrawal of maintenance men and thus threaten the property holdings of the owners. With militant strikers parading under banners adorned with the hammer and sickle, proclaiming, "NO SURRENDER, NATIONALIZATION OF THE MINES," the UMWA literally abandoned the district. One year later the international union, where it survived, was little more than a "company union," and the name of its leader, John L. Lewis, a dirty word in "wild rose country."

Defeated or not, the radicalism and solidarity of the coal fields served as an impressive demonstration that there was still some fight left in the working class. Western and eastern miners forged a movement of alternative that proceeded from work-related experience and grievance but became consolidated within the community. Exploring the fabric of this experience has led Allen Seager to conclude that "a real flowering of genuine proletarian culture" took place in Alberta's coal towns in the 1920s. The Women's Labour League in Drumheller established child-care facilities "free from bourgeois influence," while meetings, boxing matches, and poetry recitals in the district brought together English, Irish, French, Scots, Italians, and Ukrainians.

Miners, however, differed from most Canadian workers at this time in that they embraced the fragile, minority "Red" culture of the 1920s far more readily than most occupational groups. They were also a community apart in that they comprised a front that battled capital at the point of production when most other workers were far more subdued. The coal miners often believed and acted as if "the capitalist system as they knew it was coming to an end."

This was a product of exploitation in the mines, of course, but it was also a consequence of a highly politicized effort to offer new answers to age-old problems of inequality and alienation. A part of such opposition was generated spontaneously, out of the conditions of existence. But that part could not carry groups like the miners into the struggles they waged (and the accomplishments they secured) against the odds and in the face of a more general working-class quietude. What differentiated the miners from other workers was their leadership, in which a new breed of radical, the Communist, figured prominently. A Finnish-Canadian miner's wife recalled her "moving" introduction to the Finnish Socialist Organization, when she first sang the "Internationale." May Day paraders in Glace Bay marched under "the biggest red flag in Canada," measuring some twenty feet by twelve feet. Miners' slogans were blunt statements of this politics: "Workers of the World, Unite" and "Long Live Communism." Communism entered the politics of Canadian workers in these difficult years of the 1920s, when, in the context of labour's defeat, the left wing of the workers' movement consolidated, challenging capital at the very height of its power.

COMMUNISM

Communism developed surreptitiously in Canada, forced underground by the repressive and nativist assault on radicalism and the "Red Scare" of 1919. Born of industrial crisis in Canada, the convergence of various radical streams previously allied with other organizational constituencies, and the example of the Russian Revolution, Canada's first Communists put forward a seven-point program on April 30, 1919. Calling for "the forcible seizure of the governmental power and the establishment of the dictatorship of the proletariat," they advocated the confiscation of private property, the destruction of capitalist institutions, and worker control of society. "Your only hope lies in revolution – the sweeping away of this rotten system of exploitation," their clandestinely distributed leaflet proclaimed. "You must achieve a victory over the capitalist class so that you can celebrate May Day along with your fellow-workers in Russia." This message was delivered to working-class neighbourhoods, not in the radical West or the militant coal towns, but in Montreal and in southern Ontario industrial centres.

After overcoming some initial factionalism and organizational divisions, a secret convention of Communists met near Guelph, Ontario, in 1921 to formally constitute the Communist Party of Canada (CPC). Among the early figures of Canadian communism were Matthew Popowich and John

Navisisky of the Ukrainian Labor Temple Association in Winnipeg; the patternmaker and archetypal proletarian, "Moscow Jack" MacDonald of Toronto; an Irish-born lithographer, Tom Bell, once affiliated with Ontario's Socialist Party of North America; Bill Moriarty, an English immigrant and one of the first SPC members to join the new Communist movement; former SPNA founder and school teacher, Florence Custance; and the leading intellectual, Maurice Spector.

Spector was only twenty-three at the time of the Guelph meeting, but he was already a theoretician of stature who had been a member of the Young Socialist League (the SDP's youth section), a contributor to socialist newspapers, a student activist and editor of the *Toronto Varsity*, and an early advocate of the United Communist Party of America. Joined by a committed core of early Communists, among them the machinist and future party head, Tim Buck, this body of working-class advocates took the message of communism "to the masses" in the early to mid-1920s. To better reach a large constituency they created a legal party, the Workers Party of Canada, and established a newspaper, *The Worker*. The underground apparatus ceased to exist on orders from the Communist International. While the membership of the new legal party consisted of 4,800, the bulk being affiliated with foreign-language federations, the Workers Party exerted an influence far out of proportion to its small numbers.

Communists were active in the Canadian Labor Party, contributing to municipal campaigns in Toronto, Vancouver, and elsewhere, and by early 1923 had won the Workers Party provincial affiliation in Quebec, Ontario, and Alberta. For three years they offered a vocal and substantial opposition to Conservative craft union leadership within the Trades and Labor Congress of Canada, opposing the presidency of Tom Moore. In 1923-24, Workers Party presidential candidates at the annual TLC conventions polled almost 25 per cent of the vote. They drew on the old OBU constituency, the artisan-immigrant quarters of the city, and the coal towns of Districts 18 and 26, which, as we have seen, were strongholds of the new, Russian-inspired communism. As McLachlan was railroaded to prison and District 26's UMWA charter revoked by the international office, a Cape Breton Communist and former prize fighter, Lewis MacDonald, led Drumheller's miners in a sympathetic work stoppage. Known as "Kid Burns," MacDonald was both a Communist and a nativist, epitomizing the strength and weakness of the working class in these years. His radicalism and his atheism, however, in conjunction with assault charges stemming from a 1925 strike confrontation, earned him incarceration in 1926. Further to the west, the Workers Party gained access to the important voice of British Columbia workers, the *B.C. Federationist*, and although control of this paper produced serious divisions and unhappy political consequences, it did speak of the Communist impact in trade union circles.

As labour across Canada was driven into retreat, as the coal miners suffered defeat, and as cautious practice and conservative ideas gained widespread credence in restricted groups within the trade union movement, the ethnic Communists turned inward. In the early period of the CPC, as Ian Angus shows, the autonomy allowed the foreign-language sections permitted such sheltered development. The Canadian movement was also distant from Communist struggles in other parts of the world as it moved to devise tactics and a strategy that would implant communism within the consciousness and activities of Canadian workers. But in the years 1923-29 the Communist International experienced a profound Stalinization, and Communist parties around the world were subordinated to the needs of "socialism in one country," policies being dictated by the changing imperatives of Stalin's consolidating Soviet regime. The potential of the early 1920s, fading in the face of domestic circumstances that were anything but propitious, was further undermined by Moscow-conceived directives that stripped the CPC of its independence, casting a competent leadership aside, and submerging the movement in a sectarianism that alienated it from the ranks of labour and much of its membership.

The beneficiary and eventual Canadian perpetrator of this development was Tim Buck, whose ascent to the leadership of the party was accompanied by the creation of a "cult of the personality." Buck's rise was others' fall: Spector was slandered and expelled, along with MacDonald, and Custance made her exit. But the most emphatic loss of this period, concentrated in the years 1928-31, was that of many ethnic members and their loyalties to communism. Under attack by the Comintern since 1925, the foreign federations were supposedly enclaves of "opportunism, federalism, and nationalism," and the word came to the Canadian party that Communist work must be based on class rather than language. As the central proponent of this new line, Buck earned little respect among the party's Ukrainians, Finns, and Jews, and demands were made that he be removed from the leadership. The tension within party circles mounted in 1928, as Stalin predicted the imminent collapse of the capitalist world order and called for immediate working-class mobilization, thereby implicitly challenging the very right of ethnic language sections within the Canadian movement to exist. Such "Bolshevization" drew its blood in 1929, as numbers of Finns were suspended and others left the party in disgust. By 1930, the Comintern's position on "Bolshevization" had stiffened, Ukrainian and Jewish comrades were hostile to the Buck circle, and the ethnic associations were saved only by their leadership's recantations. These hollow confessions of "guilt" acted only as a coverup of the internal crisis of the party and left a residue of suspicion and hostility among the remaining ethnic Communists.

The crisis was a product of the so-called "Third Period" of the international Communist movement, although it originated in the mid-1920s. Prior to 1928, the party had been engaged in "mass propaganda, maintaining and broadening the party contact with the masses, preparing and training the reserves of the working class and educating party cadres." But between 1928 and 1935, the Communist leadership stressed that the radicalization of the masses was now a fact of social and political life and that the task before workers was to foment revolution. "Little do [people] realize," said Stewart Smith, an early Buck ally and graduate of Moscow's Lenin School, "that in a very short time the streets in Toronto will be running with blood." Communist strategy thus centred on the creation of dual revolutionary unions (affiliated with the Workers' Unity League), the conquest of the streets, and a divisive assault on social democracy and reformism within the workers' movement.

In this period of revolutionary posturing, much was lost on the political and cultural fronts, as well as in the industrial realm. These were years that set the stage for the irrational, for the blind faith in the "party line," however far removed from Canadian reality it may have been. The late twenties and early thirties served as an introduction to the drastic shifts in Communist policy resulting from the wartime needs of the Soviet Union in 1939-41. As such, these years have presented historians with ample ammunition to disparage and discredit the entire Communist experience, to denigrate the accomplishments of rank-and-file Communists, and to erase the achievements of militancy, struggle, and resistance – often paced by Communist effort – from the pages of Canadian history. But when we consider the odds against the workers' movement in the 1920s, which Communists and coal miners defied, there is much to appreciate in the activity of those who inherited the legacy of 1917, especially in the early years of the 1920s, when prospects for the Canadian working class looked so bleak.

THE THEATRE OF MASS CULTURE: THE FIRST ACT

Much of the difficulty faced by workers in the post-1920 years related directly to the relative increase in the powers of capital and the state, a shifting in the balance of class forces that flowed directly out of structural change in the political economy. There were, however, other factors that pushed class relations in specific directions inimical to the workers' movement. Ironically, one such force in this period was the first act of mass culture's theatre, a commodification of leisure time that provided some workers in some locales with the possibility of escape from a part of the bleak features of life in capitalist Canada. Because the new business of entertainment was controlled by capital, it differed from past working-class experience beyond the job, which was often generated spontaneously out of class and community settings and might well highlight class differences. But in the beginnings of mass culture in the 1920s this kind of process was blunted as the new leisure structured workers into a relatively passive relation with their non-work time and promoted a subtle, but nevertheless important, message of pluralistic classlessness. In the context of labour's defeat and the absolute decline in militancy and unionism, this cultural development could not help but complement capital's project.

As Suzanne Morton has suggested in a sensitive study of men and women in a Halifax working-class neighbourhood in the 1920s, the impact of mass culture was necessarily filtered through a complex sieve in which occupation, age, ethnicity, and gender all ordered class experience. For many males active in the trade union movement prior to the 1920s, their involvement in labour causes was central to their leisure time. One Halifax machinist noted that "He liked the labor movement [and] it was a hobby to him. He had spent time and money on it, he had not been interested in much else." But five years later an American Federation of Labor organizer suggested that committed labourites like this were being displaced by younger men disinterested in trade unionism as a cause. Another workers' advocate claimed that, "In these days of flivvers, flappers, and road houses, horse races and prohibition, I find it a difficult matter to secure volunteer workers for the interests of the Union." According to this trade unionist, by 1929 most union members wanted "increased wages and better conditions" but did "not want to make any personal effort."

For young women the temptations to forsake their class backgrounds were also great. Parents who had tightened their belts to provide their daughters with a good education and a decent start in life found that they were rewarded with contempt. One daughter elicited this comment in 1928: "she despises us, her home, our poverty and our ignorance. We have scraped and saved to get her lots of the good things in life, but now she has become a 'cut above us'." No doubt generational tensions had been part of working-class family life for decades, but mass culture accentuated them just as it exacerbated the individualist/collectivist divide within trade unionism. It was a problem recognized by W.A. Pritchard and others once affiliated with the Socialist Party of Canada and the One Big Union. Radicals in the 1920s, forced to grapple with this dilemma, began to address the unnerving impact of new cultural and leisure forms.

The character of mass culture and its impact on class relations remain understudied, and much of what follows is inferential and speculative. Some interpretive caveats are therefore necessarily in order. First, much of the work done in cultural studies suggests ways in which class audiences negotiate mass culture and, in turn, how the leisure barons marketing the products of this realm appeal to class instincts. This results in a process in which contemporary mass culture cannot simply be seen as imposing itself on class audiences; rather, production and consumption within mass culture are not one-sided but complex and multifaceted, and always capable of producing, in the sphere of class relations, awarenesses and tensions associated directly with struggle and resistance: mass culture, many authorities tell us, is not just accommodation. No doubt this is true, and studies of the dime novel and working-class audiences in late nineteenth-century America point in this direction.

But here the *historical* context is primary. Mass culture in the 1960s, after generations have grappled with it as a persistent presence in their lives, may well be an arena of contest, as the cultural theorists of our time tell us. Historically, however, the first stirrings of mass culture must have been experienced by workers differently: the possibility of resistance growing out of this initial cultural "revolution" and the chances of renegotiating its many and contradictory meanings were rather limited. More important in this arrival of mass culture was the economic *appropriation* of the cultural realm and its incorporation into capital's expanding and acquisitive hold over all aspects of life. This relates directly to what some theorists identify as a new regime of accumulation associated with the high wage, mass production, increased leisure time, and the conscious structuring by capital of labour into the republic of consumption. Fordism, as this regime of accumulation has come to be known, with deference to Henry Ford's pioneering introduction of both the assembly line and the five-dollar day in his Michigan automobile plants, restructured life on and off the shopfloor. It revitalized capitalism in the age of monopoly and aggressively colonized previously insulated areas of working-class life.

The second interpretive point that needs bearing in mind is that this Fordism, while undoubtedly present in Canada in the 1920s, was in its initial stages of development. As such, it and the mass culture associated with it were uneven in their impact. Not all workers, of course, were subjected to the Fordist arrival in these years, nor did all workers experience mass culture. Coal miners, as we have seen, were restructured in ways that made Fordism seem absolutely benign, and the casually employed, unskilled, and immigrant workers saw little of the high wages, job security, and consumerist potential of mass culture that the new age was promoting. Whole regions remained locked into poverty and underdevelopment, their class relations a stark reminder that capitalism's ugliest side still prevailed in parts of the country. Yet, for all of the limitations of Fordism and mass culture, some workers were affected by these developments. That this segment of labour was the predominantly English-speaking, skilled, respectable, central Canadian, urban contingent predominating in the organizational centre of the country's Trades and Labor Congress-affiliated unions only reinforces the necessity of looking at forces that must have registered an influence within the workers' movement.

For all of these reasons I characterize this as a theatre of mass culture, and I set discussion within acknowledgement of this as only a first act. This was theatre because it was not generalized to the point that it could be construed as centrally influential in the historical experience of the time; but it did illuminate what was happening. As a first act, this period was mass culture's beginning, but not its final and forceful realization. The curtain of depression would lower on this first act in 1929, postponing mass culture's full impact until the post-World War Two years.

To look at the 1920s is to see a hint of how old cultural modes could be displaced by a range of activities that redefined the nature and meaning of time away from work. The material foundations of the localized and often class-based cultures of an earlier epoch were being undermined by new products, concentrated control, the expansion of urban markets, and monopoly capital's campaign to profit from any and all saleable commodities. Culture, once at least partially based in social or group experience, was in the throes of transformation: spectator sports, the rise of the mass media, and the power to overcome distance transformed culture into a potentially purchaseable item. The collective endeavours that had formed the foundation of nineteenth-century working-class culture, however limited and ambiguous, were by the 1920s being gradually eroded by privatized forms of leisure, which increasingly turned on the purchase rather than participation. In spite of its capacity to reach and exploit huge markets, mass culture was an individualized activity that moved workers who could afford to buy into it away from social interaction and into the confines of the unit of consumption, the nuclear family.

To integrate a stratum of Canadian workers into the margins of consumer capitalism, it was necessary to increase the disposable income of the family and to provide sufficient leisure time to allow numbers of workers to divert earnings previously earmarked for basic necessities into new realms of consumption. Specific state reforms to establish old age pensions and allowances to the blind, widowed mothers, and orphans undoubtedly secured, for some working-class families, a portion of income once diverted to needy relatives. Minimum wage legislation for women and children may have buttressed family incomes. Shorter hours – the eight-hour day became the norm in many sectors in these years – allowed at least some of the more privileged industrial workers time to consume. To be sure, the 1920s were hardly a decade of unambiguous advance, as Leonard Marsh pointed out in a pioneering 1931 survey and Terry Copp has reiterated in his study of Montreal. Real wages did not rise dramatically. But if a series of studies pose contradictory assessments of the material well-being of the working class, a trend does seem clear.

Average wage rates across the industrial spectrum peaked in 1920 and, according to statistics compiled by Urquhart and Buckley, reached a point not surpassed until 1940. Purchasing power, low in the spiralling inflation of 1919-20, began an ascent in the recession of 1921 and continued to climb in the prosperous mid-1920s, plateauing during the latter part of the decade. By 1928 it was possible, for the first time, for the average male manufacturing worker to raise a family on his wages alone, while it was only in the 1920s that the average woman worker rose above a starvation wage and status of dependency. As figures from the *Labour Gazette* indicate, the weekly family budget, computed on the basis of average prices in sixty Canadian cities, dropped from over $26 in November, 1920, to just over $21 in November, 1927. These averages, of course, distort a great deal. Working-class material well-being may have advanced in the 1920s, but considerable numbers of people hardly lived the good life. In 1929 a family of four needed an estimated $1,200 to $1,500 to survive in minimum comfort, but 60 per cent of Canadian working men and 82 per cent of labouring women earned less than $1,000 yearly. The combined earnings of family members still kept many demographic units domestically afloat. Too much stock should not be placed in these average figures, but on balance a segment of the Canadian working class likely found its disposable income increasing over the 1920s, especially in the flush years of mid-decade. This was reflected in escalating productivity of both labour and capital and in rising real GNP.

Moreover, even if the economic collapse and unemployment of the 1930s made a mockery of working-class purchasing power for tens of thousands, those fortunate enough to have work might still retain a small piece of the consumer society. Drastic cuts in wages were outpaced by price declines that resulted from decreased demand for goods. As a consequence, real wages may well have risen; from 1929 to 1933 money wages declined by 14 per cent, but the cost-of-living index fell by almost 22 per cent. Goods that had cost $10 in 1926 could be had for $7.50 six years later. Some employees, such as full-time civil servants, actually saw their standard of living increase by as much as 25 per cent during these years.

These generalized averages and trends on the side of income are paralleled by similar figures with respect to consumption. The 1920s witnessed increasing expenditure on a wide range of consumer goods: automobiles and radios, household appliances and furnishings, and less durable commodities in the entertainment field. Per-capita consumption of cars in Canada was second only to that of the United States, and Canadian production surpassed that of the United Kingdom and of major western European countries such as Germany and France. Almost one in seven Canadians over the age of fourteen owned a car by 1930, and although the bulk of such automobile purchasers were not workers, some of them must have been.

The automobile craze, accelerated by easier terms of credit, declining costs of products and fuel, and suburban expansion, helped to transform the nature of some workers' lives. It separated labour and leisure decisively and structured new possibilities for working-class families. No longer did all workers necessarily have to congregate in neighbourhoods near their jobs, ride to work on the same streetcars, or travel to outings, sporting affairs, or holiday excursions in large groups on rented railway cars or teamster-driven waggons. Courting, superficially a most private affair, had once been done in the almost collective context of the promenade, where young lovers were visible to one another. But in the age of the automobile, the ride was a more solitary undertaking. The car thus symbolized the transformations in leisure activity in the 1920s: by no means a possibility for all working-class consumers, some workers could attain it. Automobiles meant that travel to and from work and cultural events could be done as a family rather than as a class.

The radio, with broader purchasing potential, served a similar function, also contributing to the breakdown of localized participation sports like baseball, which had long thrived on specific neighbourhood rivalries, work-related subcultures, and class allegiances. Union leagues, common at the turn of the century, survived, and in some centres baseball teams even preserved a class character rooted in earlier times but transformed by new ideological currents and economic developments. On Hamilton's "Mountain," the all-star team was an independent group called the "Marxian Youth." But this was a rare occurrence and company leagues, part of capital's welfare-oriented conquest of working-class initiative, were more common. As Suzanne Morton shows for the Halifax working-class neighbourhood of Richmond Heights, local baseball leagues in the 1920s were often a contradictory blend of class and commerce, participation and spectatorship. As radio began broadcasting professional events, however, sports like baseball and boxing may have become less related to class and locale and more mass directed. Radio drew large numbers of listeners around the family table or living-room mantel to hear of the victories of Gene Tunney and Jack Dempsey or the home runs of Babe Ruth.

Mass culture was thus developing from the same concentration and Americanization that dominated the economy as a whole. Radio emerged immediately after World War One, and particularly in border cities, on the Prairies, and along the St. Lawrence-Great Lakes system, American broadcasting was heard. Most of the stations were owned by powerful newspaper companies such as the *Toronto Star* and *La Presse*, and like the papers, these stations took a good deal of their news reporting from such international services as Reuters and Associated Press, even as early as 1923. As a result, radio stations resisted attempts in the late 1920s and 1930s to initiate public regulation. A nascent Canadian film industry was quickly eclipsed in the 1920s by American production, and with the rise of Hollywood in the 1930s the collapse of any existing Canadian cinema was assured.

As early as 1919 similar trends within the sphere of mass-circulation magazines roused the ire of Canadian nationalists. Over 300 such American journals inundated Canada in the 1920s, led by the immensely popular *Ladies' Home Journal*, *Saturday Evening Post*, and *McCall's*. "The mentality and morale of impressionable young Canadians is being merged in the reeking cloud of lower Americanism," complained the *Vancouver Sun*. "Something should be done to dam this trash flowing over the border."

Government tariffs, the "high" culture nationalism of painters associated with the Group of Seven, and efforts of the Canadian Authors' Association did little to stem the tide of mass culture sweeping into Canada. American publishers and film producers simply jumped the tariff wall and found a ready audience among Canadians.

This commercialization and diversification of culture necessarily affected the character of working-class life and consciousness. Workers in the 1920s were a diverse lot; many were too poor to partake of the mass culture, while others were excluded because they spoke little English or lived on the margins of the country where the new leisure had a negligible impact. Still, for some, the radio, automobile, and increased levels of disposable income undercut the experience of collectivity, replacing it with individualized or family-centred behaviour. Consumer goods could never totally undercut class antagonisms and differences, but they could enhance the ideological message of a pluralistic, classless society. Even among the immigrant poor, mass culture may have reinforced patterns of class segmentation evident in the labour market. Largely excluded from the products of mass culture, immigrant workers could, nevertheless, by ruthless underconsumption and communal pooling of resources and skills, acquire their own homes, symbol of "making it" in modern Canada. Tightly knit, ethnically homogeneous communities thus evolved, further separating the English-speaking and the "foreign" sections of the working class, widening rifts that first appeared in the post-1900 years and nativist upsurge of World War One.

Leisure and its growing commercialization also had a gendered content. The superficial signs of the loosening of women's subordination commonly associated with the flapper of the 1920s, in conjunction with the growing opportunities for female employment in monopoly capital's clerical and service sectors, no doubt threatened some men whose masculine identity was bound up with "breadwinner" status. Halifax's labour newspaper, the *Citizen*, asked with some worry in 1922, "What will be Man's Place in Society of the Future?" Its answer must have troubled many: "Every sort of clerkship and factory job is done nowadays by a woman or a child where a man used to earn double the pay and support a family. Where are the men to go if this keeps on? What is to become of family life? Many towns in the United States are already known as 'She-towns'."

Many working-class men no doubt resolved the gender identity ambivalences that must have been common in these years by reinforcing their "manliness" in the pursuit of recreations such as hunting and fishing. Like work itself, these pastimes could feed the family, sustain a sense of self-worth, and demonstrate the skilful conquest of nature. Suzanne Morton notes that in a Halifax working-class neighbourhood, stores commonly promoted fishing and hunting gear, while Halifax County residents purchased thousands of big-game licences over the course of the 1920s. As hunting and fishing captured the imaginations of working-class men and addressed certain gender-related perceived needs, this realm of mass culture served to divide men from women at the same time that it understated class identification.

To look at workers off the job in the 1920s is therefore to glimpse a part of what weakened the workers' movement. We can imagine scenes, not so much of conflicts and solidarities but of ethnic workers gathered on their porches, men escaping their homes to fish or hunt, Canadians huddled around the first automobile purchased on their block, older workers listening to the radio in their dens or kitchens, and working-class youngsters reading mass-circulation magazines at their lunchbreaks or dancing the night away to the sounds of American bands. With working-class institutions like the union, the labour church, and the radical club no longer as central in social and cultural life, and with employers and much of the media and educational system lauding the accomplishments of individuality and personal advance rather than collectivity and struggle, mass culture and capitalist need combined to stress acquisition. The real fruits of this would not be tasted until well into the 1940s and 1950s, but its seeds were planted in the 1920s. And as much of the above might indicate, the theatre of mass culture was one in which women were particularly active, structured as they were into roles associated with consumption, nurturing, and socialization.

WOMEN OF THE NEW DAY

The 1920s have often been viewed as bringing in a new day for women in general and for women workers in particular. Suffrage agitation, largely a middle-class activity but drawing working-class advocates such as Flora MacDonald Denison and Helena Gutteridge to the cause of votes for women, developed from the 1880s and peaked in the World War One years, winning women the franchise. Women workers entered new jobs during the war years, helping to fight the battle for production and widening women's access to employment for a brief period. The great increase in the number of women employed during the first decade of the century dipped over the years 1910-20 but increased again in the 1920s, when the percentage of females over the age of ten in the total labour force rose from 15.5 to 17 per cent. Old trends continued, however, and most of the women engaged in wage labour were single. Nevertheless, married and divorced women gradually entered the labour market, comprising roughly 17 to 20 per cent of female workers. As Mary Vipond has shown, mass-circulation magazines depicted great transformation in the role of women, and in the legislative sphere, provincial minimum wage laws affecting women were passed in seven provinces between 1917 and 1920. But appearances proved deceiving.

Women's working lives may have been "modernized," with processes of innovation, concentration of capital, and expanding work forces in new areas of economic life leading to more opportunities for women in clerical, service, and sales spheres. More "middle-class" women, as well, entered professions. Nevertheless, women still suffered from lower pay, marginal status, and subordination to patriarchal authority; men were defined by their lives beyond the home, women by existences bounded by family and its responsibilities. Women also remained outside the mainstream of unionism, with one superficial assessment of their organizational potential claiming that they did not "seem to possess that spirit of solidarity characteristic of men in industry." As Veronica Strong-Boag concludes, women's relationship to waged work in the interwar years was a highly ambivalent one. More and more women experienced the extra-familial socio-economic relations associated with working for wages outside the home, but home remained a pervasively limited structure within which female lives were grounded.

One reason for this was that while wage work opened up for women in the 1920s, it was labour of a particular sort. Female employment was often ghettoized – poorly paid and confined by its isolations and rigid supervisions. Domestic labour, almost the sole service employment for women in the nineteenth century, was now supplemented by waitressing, as restaurants proliferated in the 1920s. Between 1919 and 1929 the number of telephones in the country doubled, creating new work for female operatives, who were often judged to be suitably malleable material for efficiency-conscious, bureaucratically run corporations like Bell Telephone and Maritime Telephone and Telegraph. At these companies, employee "team spirit" was cultivated in the interest of profit. Marketing innovations, especially the growth of chain drug and grocery stores such as Loblaw's and Tamblyn's and the continued expansion of mail-order department stores, also attracted women to work outside the home, but it locked them into menial sales positions. Among typists, stenographers, and female clerks in the federal government, this structured inequality was also an unwritten rule of the workplace. In many of these occupational settings, the social relations of production were privatized, subject to an authoritative male supervision, and conventionally defined as temporary, due to the single "girl's" tendency to flee the workplace upon marriage, assuming woman's proper station of wife and mother. Such was not the stuff of which unions or persistent resistance was built.

In manufacturing there was a greater trend toward collectivity, as women reacted sporadically to the conditions prevailing in the low-wage competitive sectors of clothing, textiles, and food-processing, among others. But a multitude of forces served to undercut solidarity. Caught between innovating employers and craftsmen who were especially protective of their jobs because of threats of dilution and displacement, women were often barred from skilled, well-paid employment.

This did not, of course, mean that resistance on the part of women was impossible, simply that it was less visible than even the modest challenge raised by male workers. Strikes, though far from common, were an indication of resentment and resistance. Textile workers in Stratford (1921), waitresses in Calgary (1923), match workers in Hull (1924), cotton mill workers near Welland (1924), and knitters in Hamilton (1928) were but some of the female strikers of the decade. As women workers faced scabs, hostile foremen, police, and hired thugs, they were not reluctant to use physical force, and in a 1926 Montreal Amalgamated Clothing Workers strike, four teen-aged girls were charged with assaulting a constable. At E.B. Eddy's match company in Hull, striking women employees were dismissed as the corporation shifted its operations to a Deseronto, Ontario, plant, a tactic available to mobile and diversified monopolies. The women's response was to seize, push, jostle, and hit a manager and, after some time, they resecured their positions, although demands that forewomen be hired and union activity allowed were eventually denied. Other struggles turned on women's attempts to resist managerial authority. In 1929 female employees struck Hamilton Canadian Cottons Limited, so that "things [would] be like they were before the efficiency experts came along and changed them." Such collective challenges to capital may well have been buttressed by individual acts of sabotage, absenteeism, and worker turnover, but in the end they more often than not came to little.

The working women of the new day thus found themselves generally facing limited horizons. Conditions at a wide range of work settings were either hygienically deplorable, as in the case of many industrial factories, or routinized, as in the example of clerical/communications work. Regardless of whether women worked in service, manufacturing, or commerce and finance, they often found themselves assigned to the lower rungs of particular job hierarchies; advance to positions of authority and recognized, remunerated skill were uncommon. Wage discrimination was notorious to the point of being institutionalized, the much-proclaimed breakthroughs of the new day failing to crack the wall of gendered pay differentials separating men's and women's work: between 1921 and 1931, women sold their labour power for 54 to 60 per cent of the male "price," revealing a structured continuity in inequality that reached back into the nineteenth century. Even with legislative reforms on the issue of minimum wages, few gains were recorded, so obdurate were the companies and so poorly informed and protected the woman worker.

In addition, state institutions, such as the Ontario Minimum Wage Board established in 1920, actually functioned to keep women workers poorly paid by perpetuating the gendered understanding of class. Margaret McCallum notes that the Board assumed women could look to men for economic support if they had children to support or became too ill, old, or feeble to work. Ignoring statistics that established that many married women had to support entire families and were forced into the labour market by necessity, the Board proceeded to construct women's minimum wages on the basis of a narrow conception of working women as "single girls" attached to an established household. It never consulted with organized labour. As Strong-Boag concludes, in the 1920s "sexist discrimination remained an integral feature of economic organization, however modern." Things were not all that different in those left-wing political circles where one would have expected the women's question to be addressed with more sensitivity. As Joan Sangster has shown, both the Communist Party and the Co-operative Commonwealth Federation grappled with the nature and meaning of women's oppression, but both political formations came up rather short in their theoretical and practical contributions to gender equality.

Although this did not cause female workers to become passive and acquiescent, it may well have conditioned a measure of escapism for some, a process facilitated by aspects of the new mass culture of the time. Dances like the "Blackbottom" and the "Charleston" were a way of relieving the drudgery of alienated labour, while in a dress factory conversations might turn, not on the union or radical politics, but on "dress and boys and movies all day long." After work, "the girls all fix[ed] themselves up, the paint and powder [was] put on thick, and they pretend[ed] not to be working girls." Feminine identity might be formed, in some quarters, on a repudiation of class. A Parisian commentator was surprised to see the parade of working-class women making their way to jobs in Halifax in 1930. They flooded the downtown, decked out in heels, stockings, smart coats, and chic hats. In Paris only the wealthy were well dressed, "But in Halifax all women look well and all are most charmingly dressed."

Dominant gender relations within the working-class thus consolidated on the basis of fundamental continuities of difference. That difference was generally expressed in separations that reached well back into the nineteenth century: men did certain kinds of work, women others; men received fatter paycheques and realized much of their self-conception on the job; women worked for lesser wages and often conceived of themselves in relation to non-waged social activity. Historians have begun to probe this making of twentieth-century gender identities and while much confirms older, entrenched understandings of how men and women co-existed within the working class, new insights into the complexities of labouring lives have emerged.

Joy Parr's impressive reconstruction of the gender of breadwinners in two Ontario industrial towns indicates that as capital consolidated it might carve new spaces for women as well as burying them deeply in old ones. One of the towns studied by Parr, the furniture-making community of Hanover, was dominated by male workers who "provided" for their wives and children in classic "breadwinner" fashion. In the paternalist-ordered milltown of Paris, however, class formation took a turn away from the structuring of work along masculine lines. There, the Penmans firm relied on relatively high Canadian wages to attract skilled female emigrants from the British Isles into the expanding knit-goods industry. Paris became by the 1920s "a woman's town," in which assisted female immigrants found lifelong work. Wage labour, not marriage, was the continuous thread along which the female life cycle progressed. Unionism was virtually non-existent in this consolidating women's community, power residing undeniably with the corporation, whose profits flowed from the production of its largely female work force.

In this context, even state policies might take on a gendered content, the tariff protection afforded the "light" clothing industries of Paris where women worked being invoked as the perfect complement to male-dominated "heavy" industry in nearby towns such as Hanover. Fathers could labour in one setting; daughters in another. "Expensive" labour, through the availability of work for "cheap" labour, could be spared some of the costs of reproducing the work force. All of this, of course, implied that the woman's town or the woman's workplace might well be a site where accommodations could be allowed to women subjectively creating the conditions of everyday life, but little could be granted to class mobilizations that threatened to unite men and women in active organization. Strong bonds between women, weakened links with male kin, tolerance of female-headed households – all might well figure in the life of a community peopled in economic part by skilled, strong-willed emigrant females.

Mock wedding ceremonies provide a window of insight into this process. In Paris mills these were practised by the emigrants. Set in the workplace, they surrounded the supposed solemnity of marital union with the inversion of normal roles and ribald joking. With women and men dressed as each other, power based on gender alone was deflated. These ritualistic celebrations thus ridiculed conventionality in raucous parodies of domestic life, setting limits to the normal patriarchal powers of the household: cross-dressing apparently sanctioned role reversals, and the hierarchies of the workplace, as well as the home, were exposed as fragile and subject to the normal constraints of "fair treatment." This was a context in which women secured something for themselves, but it cannot be stressed too strongly how much this security and gain were won at the cost of a great deal – and with capital's purposeful acquiescence.

Penmans power over its work force was never more evident than in the Great Depression. It doled out work, one and two days at a time, to its grateful dependants, and in the process rode out the tough years while consolidating a hegemonic hold over both its workers and the entire community. Many Canadian towns could not weather the storm of economic collapse in this way, and with the rise of joblessness in the 1930s the struggle against unemployment became a central narrative in the history of workers.

WORKING AGAINST NOT WORKING

The economic collapse that was under way in 1929 reached its lowest point in 1932-33, and among Canadians the wheat farmers of the drought-stricken prairie West, the marginal small business people, the young with no employment possibilities, and the working class, especially those without skills, suffered the most. Statistics reveal much, but they convey only a sense of the dimensions of the problem and are subject to great variation because of the lack of uniformity in their essential foundations and definitions.

From any point of view, however, the assessment is the same: more Canadians were out of work during the 1930s than at any previous time. Over the course of the entire decade conservative estimates placed the unemployed at 10 per cent of all wage earners. The winter months of 1933 were the worst, and figures compiled for Prime Minister Bennett stated that over 32 per cent of all wage earners were without work. By 1937, such compilations revealed a drop in these unprecedented rates of unemployment to 12.5 per cent; but in 1938-39 the figures rose once more. Not until the war machinery was in high gear in the early 1940s did unemployment cease to be a problem. The capitalist order overcame one moment of crisis only when another was substituted.

These measures of unemployment were reflected in similar statistics revealing dimensions of workers' economic dependency. The most important data focus on the massive numbers of people who could not survive from one year to the next without public aid. Between 1933 and 1936, about 12 per cent of all Canadians received emergency relief, while another 5 per cent relied on charitable aid, mothers' allowances, or old age pensions. More than 1.5 million, in a total population of 10 million, were reduced to the humiliation of state dependency. Charlotte Whitton, of the Canadian Welfare Council, estimated that in 1935 1.9 million were public dependants, roughly 20 per cent of the entire population. As one authority, Leonard Marsh, commented at the end of the decade, the fine distinction between unemployed and unemployable had become increasingly obscure.

Yet little was actually done to confront the vast problem of unemployment and deteriorating standards of living. In the cities, single men were often not entitled to relief (in Kingston, for instance, the unmarried were eligible for only one day of assistance, enough, presumably, to let them leave town). Moreover, in many municipalities, such as Montreal, married and unmarried relief applicants were required to establish proof of consecutive residence in the city of six months to three years. Other barriers were also erected, in what appears to have been almost a deliberate attempt to keep the indigent away from relief offices and off the public assistance rolls. Montreal restructured its relief apparatus three times between 1931 and 1937. In Kingston, a public clamour initiated by the *Whig-Standard* secured the dismissal of a relief officer who was a former labourer. A concerned public replaced him with an army major, whose military background, it was claimed, suited him well to the role of dispenser of relief.

Strict controls were developed within which relief "benefits" could be "consumed." Cash was never simply handed out. Instead, ration cheques were issued, and rents and light and gas bills were paid directly to landlords and utility companies by the relief office or the city. Everyone dealing with a relief recipient would know that he or she was "on the dole." Grocers, dealers, and vendors were often sent special "menus" or food lists and were told to censor relief purchases. In Ontario, as elsewhere, liquor could not be bought by relief applicants, and those sustained by assistance were forced to disconnect their telephones, if they had any, surrender their driver's licences, and deduct all casual earnings from their relief payments. Across the country municipalities responded to the depression unevenly within a set of individually defined rules and regulations. For some, the burdens of providing relief were particularly taxing. In British Columbia, five municipalities were eventually forced into virtual bankruptcy and placed under the scrutiny of a provincially appointed commissioner. Not until August, 1941, did national unemployment insurance legislation come into effect, a measure that historians generally agree was "too little too late."

Reading between the lines of this history of unemployment, it is not difficult to comprehend how pervasively gendered the phenomenon of joblessness was throughout the 1930s. As Ruth Roach Pierson has recently suggested, notions of "the family wage" obviously lay behind the relief provisions that spelled out the difference between single and married men and assumed all women to be properly located in the private sphere of the home, rather than the larger public arena of political economy. Single working mothers, young women entering the labour market, and married women with jobs could not be accommodated in the prevailing conventional wisdoms of gender relations in a period of escalating unemployment and its attendant social and political pressures. When the state began, slowly and tentatively, to reach toward policy initiatives that might address the crisis of worklessness, early unemployment insurance discussions presumed men's breadwinner status and women's dependency, further constructing class in gendered ways. Where legislation itself might be blind to gender difference, conveniently ignoring women's low wages and insecurities, it almost always accepted implicitly a dichotomy that ordered men and women along paths of inequality. The realities of a gendered division of labour were thus never addressed by the state initiatives, however tardy, and the history of unemployment itself and reform efforts to alleviate its distress only served to confirm and perhaps even deepen long-standing differences among the varied class experiences of men and women.

This summarizes the official response to the debilitating and catastrophic impact of these years. Within such confines, the experience of the working class turned, in good part, on the response to joblessness and destitution. Some workers became resigned to their lot and appealed to authority for some tangible dispensation that would carry them through these difficult years. They wrote, in prose that spoke only of the immediate needs of survival, to the millionaire Prime Minister, R.B. Bennett.

Between 1930 and 1935 thousands appealed to Bennett, and Linda Grayson and Michael Bliss have assembled 168 such letters in the collection called *The Wretched of Canada*. Western farmers, urban dwellers, the elderly, students, and industrial workers begged Bennett for aid: five dollars, a suit of clothes, a chance in life. But others were demanding, and far more critical. A Toronto carpenter attacked the Prime Minister in 1934: "Us fellows down here are getting fed up with all your paper talk, what we want is action and pretty quick, we have been bluffed along by your big talk. Why don't you cut off about 2 or 3 thousands dollars from these big men and put men to work out of it what you are doing this taking all you can get your hands on taxing us poor people so as you can make enough money to go to Florida for a vacation." From British Columbia came this terse close to a letter of condemnation: "this will take my last 3 cents, but we hope it goes to the bottom of *you*, and that you will hand us out *both work* and *living wages*. You have caused lots of people to kill their families. . . . Now you are trying to get war going to make yourself richer. Well, R.B. Bennett, I hope you get your share of bullets." Leo Gadali of Toronto simply enclosed a newspaper clipping announcing the suicide death of an unemployed bookkeeper, commenting, "I would say the Dominion Government was the murderer of this young Canadian, in that it is in their power to do something for the unemployed, but have not done so." Letters like these demonstrated to political authority the social forces that could potentially lead to a movement of opposition.

In the separate Dominion of Newfoundland, however, the Canadian federal government obviously could not play a role. Government revenues declined sharply during the 1930s as fish prices plummeted; costs of relief soared, even when individual monthly allowances were set at the staggeringly low level of $1.80 per adult. With its credit no longer extendable, the government was unable to pay debt charges out of incoming revenue, and after a 1933 royal commission investigated the situation, Newfoundland suspended operations and placed itself under British rule. But this was merely the official response to popular forms of resentment that had already swept much of political authority aside. A riotous crowd of 10,000 attacked the legislature in St. John's while the House was in session in April, 1932, looting government offices and destroying files and records. Parliamentary government was suspended as state liquor stores were pillaged and streets were barricaded and littered with debris and smashed office equipment. Not until a militia of ex-servicemen was sworn in and a British cruiser summoned to the port was some form of order restored in St. John's. Three years later, the city's unemployed formed a more disciplined contingent, headed by a committee of five that demanded specific reforms and acceptance of their list of those suffering from want of work. "We want work, not dole – which is poison to an independent industrious people as ours is," they declared. Ignored by the ruling British commissioners, the unemployed mounted protests and another riot ensued. Although four of the five leaders were arrested and tried, none was convicted by the sympathetic jury.

In the more isolated outports of Newfoundland and Labrador, merchants had long kept fisher families locked in a perpetual cycle of debt and exchange of their product, salt fish, through the truck system. Supplied with necessities throughout the winter and difficult times, fisher folk were then forced to "market" their treated catch to their mercantile creditors. As the ravages of the early depression struck these already economically precarious outports, families responded by acts of intimidation that sometimes forced merchants to undermine their own truck system, appealing instead to the state to provide relief that could then be channelled through the firm allowing the distribution of much-needed supplies.

More formal bodies were often successful in wringing other kinds of concessions from local and regional authorities in industrial-capitalist central Canada. The Ontario Federation of the Unemployed, the Quebec "Front Populaire," the Verdun Workingmen's Association, and the East York Workers' Association are among the better known. Most locales of any industrial significance likely gave rise to a movement of the unemployed. Where Communists were not present or were weak, socialists might take the lead; Conservative and Liberal working people were also commonly involved in numerous initiatives.

In the East York Workers' Association (EYWA), studied by Patricia V. Schulz, militancy, radicalism, and conservatism coalesced, as Communists, socialists, and Tories shared grievances against the relief system. By 1934, the EYWA had enrolled over 1,600 members, and meetings drew more than 800 to nights of entertainment, song, and discussion of Marxism and political economy. A train of visiting speakers drew up to their door: Salem Bland, J.S. Woodsworth, Angus McInnis, Frank Underhill, Jack MacDonald, and J.L. Cohen. Women's groups were formed, mass meetings called, a strike launched, and political affiliation to the recently established Co-operative Commonwealth Federation (CCF) endorsed. This occurred in the face of Communist opposition and earlier attempts to set up a rival organization of the unemployed. Radical and conservative were able to co-exist because, in the words of one ex-member, "at the time most everybody felt just a little bit revolutionary and I think that it got to the point of desperation that something radical had to be done to better living conditions."

As a thoroughly typical instance of the activism of the unemployed, the EYWA was a product of troubled times and constituted authority's inability to provide for people thrown out of work. It and its counterparts drew on cultural forces and economic grievances to fashion a social and political challenge. When organizations of unemployed workers from eastern and southern Ontario met in June of 1933, they had common complaints but were drawn into dispute over whether to sing "God Save the King" or the "Internationale." No symbol was more potent than the Union Jack, which might be draped over a tenant's door as a protest against eviction. The struggle against unemployment thus brought many workers together in a common fight, but it left unanswered many questions about the ultimate political loyalties of this newly mobilized army of the jobless.

Nowhere is this more evident than in the work camp agitations of the single unemployed. Cut off from relief, stigmatized when they were reluctantly given aid, and directed to isolated work camps where they could be forgotten, these unmarried, unemployed men occupied a particularly tragic place during the depression years. Abandoned by most, they were courted by Communists, who formed an organization, the Single Unemployed Workers' Association (connected to the Workers' Unity League), to appeal directly to their needs. In the work camps themselves – Saskatchewan alone had twenty-three – they organized Relief Camp Workers' Unions and conducted propaganda campaigns designed to heighten the already tense atmosphere of the camps.

Labour efficiency on some relief sites was less than 50 per cent of that of ordinary labour and declined further as time passed. Resentments quickly surfaced and were merely exacerbated by the incompetence of some of the senior supervisory staff, military discipline, poor medical care, and irregularities in the payment of wages or the allocation of rations, some of which were pilfered by supervisors.

As Lorne Brown has noted, unrest spread from camp to camp in the spring of 1933, continuing well into 1934. Camps large enough to report to the Department of National Defence experienced fifty-seven disturbances between June, 1933, and March, 1934. At an Ontario camp in Long Branch, 700 inmates refused to work, shutting down the operation. Thousands of men were expelled from camps for disciplinary reasons, and more than a score received prison sentences resulting from their role in demonstrations and violent disturbances. Wasted lives and seemingly calculated indignities by an arrogant and authoritarian supervisory personnel bred discontent that erupted in 1935.

The major protest occurred in April of that year, when 1,500 relief camp workers in British Columbia "struck" and descended on Vancouver, demanding "work and wages." After two months, in which they failed to elicit a response from the national government, they began a trek to Ottawa. Buoyed by a straw vote of almost 27,000 endorsing the abolition of the camps and immediate relief for the strikers, generous donations to the reliefers on "tag days," and a May Day march of more than 15,000, a core of unemployed "rode the rails," destined for Ottawa. Communist-inspired and led, headed by Slim Evans, the On-to-Ottawa Trek (which had a lesser-known counterpart in Ontario, as marchers moved from Windsor to the capital, often accompanied by a friendly police escort) picked up supporters along the way. It drew men from the camps of the West and generated enthusiasm and warm welcomes in the towns of the interior and the Prairies. As a travelling display of grievance the single unemployed were held up in Regina for several days, and then, on Dominion Day, RCMP forces and the trekkers clashed in a battle designed to stop the protesters before they gained too much momentum and before they had a chance to reach that centre of western Canadian radicalism, Winnipeg. When the Regina Riot was over, one policeman was dead, many trekkers were injured, and a hundred protesters found themselves in jail: Bennett's 1931 declaration not to "put a premium on idleness" had been translated, through the coercive might of the state, into a reality.

Other protests would be launched: a strike prevented work in one Saskatchewan camp in December, 1935, to January, 1936, and in 1938 a veteran of the On-to-Ottawa Trek, Steve Brodie, led 1,000 jobless men to occupy Vancouver's post office, art gallery, and a major hotel. Like the trek, however, it ended in a violent confrontation on June 19, 1938. By this date – known as Bloody Sunday – the camps had long since been disbanded, and the unemployed were once more a part of the more general process of resistance in the cities. With war literally around the corner, the need to work against not working was coming to an end.

One historian, Desmond Morton, has dismissed much of the unemployment agitation led by Communists and others with a cynical turn of phrase. "A union of the unemployed," he states, "is composed of members who want to get out." This, of course, is true, but it is no less true that a union of wage workers is about something other than wages, forged by people who know, pragmatically, that they labour for a living but have aspirations that make them something more than automatons who draw their weekly paycheques. Organization is also about dignity and collectivity, which are political and cultural as well as economic matters. In creating one of the first truly mass movements of the unemployed – there had been other stirrings among the workless in the depressions of the late nineteenth century – workers of the 1930s raised the demand of "work and wages" at a critical point in history when such a claim to essential human rights necessarily extended beyond the economistic. The resulting agitation certainly produced little in the way of lasting organization, and even less in terms of combatting the cause of depression. But these are not the sole criteria by which one must judge the movement of the unemployed.

There were other accomplishments not easily charted along the Whiggish and linear "progress" of modern unionism, as it is conceived by so many Whiggish and linear historians: of standing up to the state, of fighting for human rights rather than succumbing to resignation and defeat or collapsing the meaning of struggle into the immediately attainable or the institutionally recognizable, of taking up the cause of those for whom no one battled. In all of this, the unemployed drew on the spontaneous energies of class experience, as well as the disciplined leadership of Communists, socialists, and other non-aligned militants. They charted paths that would be followed by others on the industrial union front, and that would find expression in agitational propaganda and proletarian literature. And in doing so, they intersected with non-working-class elements that saw in capitalism's crisis of the 1930s the need, not for a Communist revolution, but for progressive, if moderate, socialist reform.

REFORMISM

Although the Communists made considerable achievements in the struggles of the unemployed, the party and its cadre charted a nearly suicidal course in these early depression years. The Workers' Unity League (WUL), certainly, pioneered new strategies of class action and was intimately involved in the beginnings of industrial unionism in the mass production sector. But it was also isolated from the masses of workers affiliated with unions, Canadian and international, that had little concern with revolutionary politics. One part of this process of isolation was internal and stemmed from factionalism, an exodus of members in the 1929-31 years, and the entrenchment of slavish adherence to the now thoroughly Stalinized Communist International. But another part was imposed from outside the party. The Trades and Labor Congress expelled Communist unions in the late 1920s, and the state initiated a "Red Scare" by outlawing the CPC in 1931 and jailing eight of its leaders. Employers, too, opposed all radical initiatives. These factors set the party in the direction of a sectarian and irrational adventurism, which made a parody of Communist calls for the "United Front." Once an integral part of the workers' movement in the early to mid-1920s, communism became an embattled periphery, eschewing close relations with mass labour parties and a wide range of reformers.

By 1929, progressive socialists like J.S. Woodsworth were regarded by the CPC as the "most dangerous elements in the working class," and Jack MacDonald summed up the Communist view when he characterized Woodsworth as "the main representative of the bourgeoisie in the ranks of the working class." It was not uncommon for Communists in this period to condemn all those outside their ranks as "social fascists," an ugly, uncomradely designation that created divisions throughout popular mobilizations, unions, and unemployed agitations. Such a sectarian stand did much to marginalize the party. It seemed that the achievements of the Communists among the jobless and the unorganized were made in spite of the sectarianism of "official Marxism."

Because so many rank-and-file Communists were such dedicated and able organizers, and because they willingly defended the weak and members of the new industrial work force, a great deal of historic importance must be attached to their activities in the 1930s. But the policy and practice of the party dictated that it would not lead a generally leftist upsurge. At the very moment that labour needed a political leadership of the left, the Communist Party was embroiled in confrontation with which only one segment of the Canadian working class could identify. In abdicating its larger responsibility and substituting for it ritual exhortations of revolution, the CPC helped create the conditions in which social democracy would experience its rebirth. But in the process of being born again, social democracy would necessarily change. Mostly dormant in the 1920s, save for significant pockets of non-Communist socialists/Marxists concentrated in British Columbia, the proletarian social democrats of the early twentieth century had come largely from the urban immigrant masses. As progressive farmers and moderate, religious Anglophones kept social democracy alive in the 1920s, its character was altered. In the 1930s, social democracy would be a political movement of intellectuals, farmers, and a few assimilated but more often Anglo-Canadian workers and Marxists.

The social democracy of the 1930s had its roots in the social gospel – an early twentieth-century crusade to put Christian social principles into practice, to transform religious concerns into demands for the reform of society – the farmers' agitations of the war and immediate post-war period, and the class conflict associated with 1919. Its early leaders were J.S. Woodsworth and William Irvine, both alienated clergymen who abandoned their churches to lead a small but influential parliamentary group of dissidents known as the "Ginger Group" in the 1920s. By 1930 Woodsworth and his allies in Parliament were searching for new means to combat the increasing unemployment and acute poverty of the depression. In William Irvine's parliamentary office, on May 26, 1932, "co-operating independent" MPs agreed to form a "Commonwealth Party." Two months later, representatives of western labour groups, farmer organizations, and socialists affiliated with declining parties met in Calgary and the new movement christened itself the "Co-operative Commonwealth Federation (Farmer Labour Socialist)," proclaiming its intention to establish a political program that would regulate production and exchange according to principles of human need rather than profit.

Over the course of the next year, the early CCF aligned itself with the League for Social Reconstruction. Formed in 1931 and headed by University of Toronto historian Frank H. Underhill, McGill law professor Frank Scott, U of T social scientist Harry M. Cassidy, and economist Eugene Forsey, the LSR was the Canadian counterpart of the Fabian Society. Concerned to distinguish itself from the Communists and the fascistic "national socialists," it prefaced every statement with a note regarding its "democratic" allegiances. Among the LSR's demands were public ownership and operation of transportation, communication, electric power, and other monopolistic industries; nationalization of the banks; the establishment of co-operative institutions to produce and market agricultural goods; social legislation to secure worker rights, including freedom of association and insurance against accident and unemployment; publicly organized medical services; graduated income and inheritance taxes; and a foreign policy securing international co-operation, disarmament, and world peace. Explored fully in a study by Michiel Horn, the League for Social Reconstruction represented the social democratic intellectual response to the Great Depression and world crisis. The democratic reformers affiliated with the League, however, had little connection with labour or farmer groups, and conceived of their roles as educational. They directed their efforts at the intelligentsia and used their position to gain platforms from which they posed a running critique of the lack of public policy aimed at overcoming the distress of the early years of the depression. They also fought for essential civil liberties, defending Communists like Tim Buck, for whom they had no great love, from the repressive assault of the state. By 1933 there were seventeen branches of the LSR in Canada, with a membership of 500.

Originally founded as a non-partisan body, the League, led by Underhill, was drawn to the CCF. It played no role in the Calgary conference that created the CCF, but late in 1932 Woodsworth was urging Underhill and Scott to help draft the new party's manifesto. To accommodate non-working-class/farmer supporters of the new movement, CCF clubs, in which LSR members could function easily and comfortably, were established. These progressive intellectuals were not above an elitism that made them uncomfortable in the "coarse" ranks of the people for whom they advocated change, and many were unsure of whether they could embrace an organization considered "socialist." When the CCF's Regina Manifesto was drafted on July 19, 1933, Underhill, Scott, and other League members could congratulate themselves on their efforts: whole segments were written by them, and the academics had an important hand in redrafting those sections they proposed but that were rejected by the CCF's 1933 convention.

As Norman Penner has argued, the Regina Manifesto was a parting of the ways in the history of Canadian socialism. Unlike all previous socialist bodies, the CCF was a "federation of farmers, labor and socialist organizations," rather than a working-class body. Not only did the Manifesto reject revolutionary upheaval as a means of change, but it spelled out clearly that it would seek "its ends solely by constitutional methods." Oriented toward immediate reforms, fourteen of which were spelled out in the Regina statement, the CCF was dedicated to "the eradication of capitalism" through ameliorative reform and parliamentary debate rather than revolutionary action. After years of left-leaning ideological debate, the Regina Manifesto represented a return to the eclectic radicalism of the 1880s.

But within the context of extreme crisis, with the uncompromising CPC pursuing revolution and denigration of reform, the CCF's program offered much to alienated intellectuals and socially aware small property owners, as well as to devastated farmers and some embattled workers. It became for many the embodiment of Canadian socialism, identified with public ownership and nationalization. Even a small group of committed Marxists, unable to join hands with the CPC, tried to keep the idea of revolution alive within social democratic circles. They might champion the cause of industrial unionism or join a committee to aid the Spanish Civil War effort. For these radicals it was the CCF's anti-capitalism that mattered, as well as a conviction that the CPC would never become the party of the revolutionary masses.

This, of course, did not necessarily make the CCF a working-class body. When labour gravitated to the Co-operative Commonwealth, it was through already established, usually organizational channels: remnants of the ILP, the Canadian Labor Party, and the Socialist Party of Canada found their way into the new movement. Local unions could affiliate, but few did, and there was no constitutional means by which national unions could cast their lot with the CCF. While social democratic leaders like Woodsworth spoke for labour in the House of Commons, they did so unofficially. Contacts between the CCF and the labour movement, then, while present, were only barely formalized and structured into political alliance. The CCF would not officially associate with the labour movement until the 1940s, well after the emergence of an industrial unionism that rocked class relations in Canada in the post-1936 years.

INDUSTRIAL UNIONISM

Industrial unionism predated the 1930s. In certain sectors, most notably mining, it existed before the turn of the century, and both the Western Federation of Miners and the AFL-affiliated United Mine Workers of America were *de facto* industrial unions. Other ostensibly craft associations, including early union efforts in some realms of the garment trades and even in the steel industry, either approximated industrial organization or flirted with it. The Knights of Labor upheavals of the 1880s and those of the One Big Union in 1919-20 constituted attempts to introduce industrial, rather than craft, organization, inasmuch as they aimed to organize all workers into labour bodies that cared less for sectional interest than they did for class solidarity and workplace unity.

But it was not until the establishment of mass production, marked as it was by increasing plant size, technological change, and managerial innovation, that industrial unionism became a forceful presence in the Canadian workers' movement. The industrial form of organization, potentially one path to take in the making of unionism, was thus associated directly with the age of monopoly. Although industrial unionism could adapt itself to virtually any political climate, its legacy as Canada entered the 1930s was two-sided. On the one hand, bureaucratized industrial unionism of the sort practised by the Amalgamated Clothing Workers concentrated on institutionalizing complex bargaining procedures in the industry, following a course promoted early in the century by John Mitchell and the American-headquartered leadership of the United Mine Workers of America. On the other hand, a more socially venturesome industrial unionism, linked to the eclectic radicalism of the 1880s and the militant upheavals of the OBU era, still beckoned to some in the workers' movement. Events and actions in the 1930s would straddle both traditions: there was enough of the latter tendency present to hold out hope that union breakthroughs promised to alter socially the map of class relations; but the weight of the bureaucratic form of industrial unionism bore sufficiently heavily on the developments of the later 1930s that, by the time industrial unionism actually broke through to large successes in the 1940s, its meaning had been confirmed as far from revolutionary.

Communists set some important precedents in the early to mid-1920s. As members of the Trade Union Educational League, activists like Buck supported the amalgamation of the craft unions in 1923, but as this was before the Third Period of Stalinist-declared revolutionary upsurge and dual unionism, they worked within existing trade union structures. Only when established unions collapsed, as with the UMWA debacles of 1923-25, did Communists endorse the creation of new unions. Along with social democrats and unaffiliated militants, Communists led a minority of western miners in the creation of the Mine Workers' Union of Canada, a body that opposed both the bosses and the UMWA, which, by 1926-27, was clearly identified as a company union. While it claimed a national membership, the MWUC attracted few eastern coal miners. Communists played pivotal roles in District 26, cultivating antagonism to John L. Lewis, a task that was not all that difficult. Eastern miners, however, remained associated with the international union for a time. Only in Westville, Pictou County, did the MWUC attract a following. But the miners withdrew from the Canadian union in 1928 as the Canadian Legion red-baited its radical, Comintern ties. When the Legion, a community centre, took the harsh step of barring the MWUC miners from its premises, cutting them off from leisure activity and entertainment, the workers surrendered their charter.

Western miners were therefore the strength of Communist trade union work, just as the immigrant quarter was the CPC's most productive recruiting ground throughout most of the 1920s. One opponent in the 1940s argued that the Communist presence in the mass organizations of the ethnic community allowed them to conceal their seditious actions "under the guise of cultural, educational, and athletic activities, in order to lure more flies into the web." Whether this was true or not, their community involvement did give them a base from which to champion the cause of industrial unionism. By 1929, Communists had led the way in a number of industrial union drives. They controlled the MWUC and the Lumber Workers Industrial Union, which drew its main sustenance from 1,000 to 2,000 Finnish workers in northern Ontario.

In the doldrums of the 1920s, these unions launched a number of strikes, and Alberta miners participated in at least seven confrontations with the operators between 1926 and 1929. The lumberworkers of the Algoma District gained a reputation for radicalism through their participation in May Day celebrations, support for cultural-agitational propaganda, commitment to publishing their own ethnic newspaper, and militant job actions in the strikes of 1928-29 in the Port Arthur, Cochrane, and Thunder Bay region. Communists were also prominent in the Auto Workers Industrial Union, claiming a 1928 membership of almost 700 in three locals, and in the Industrial Union of Needle Trades Workers. This last body was supported by militant garment trades workers expelled from the International Ladies' Garment Workers Union and the Amalgamated Clothing Workers. The ILGWU briefly organized in Windsor, a difficult city in which to gain early support, while the ACW consolidated its membership in Winnipeg, Toronto, and Montreal.

These unions, and a number of Communists active in them, made common cause with the All-Canadian Congress of Labour, formed in 1927 by A.R. Mosher of the Canadian Brotherhood of Railway Employees, a body expelled from the TLC in 1921. An unlikely alliance of nationalists, radicals, and conservatives, joined by a superficial commitment to industrial unionism, the ACCL was by no means a centre of Canadian trade union unity. Built on implicit and explicit hostilities to the centralization of international unionism and to the craft-dominated Trades and Labor Congress of Canada, the ACCL was a temporary meeting ground for Communists and reactionaries. The former were in the initial states of subservience to the shifting "lines" of a Stalinized Communist International; the latter were an opportunistic trade union grouping, top-heavy, which eventually opted for "co-operation between capital and labour" in order to oppose American unions in Canada. By 1929, the ACCL's policy of "Canadianization of labour organizations" looked more to the state and the employer than it did to worker initiatives and militancy. It never succeeded in capturing the sympathies of Canadian workers and likely won no more than 50,000 adherents, approximately one-third of the membership of the TLC.

Communists were drawn to the ACCL through a combination of indigenous developments and changes originating with the Communist International. The conservatism of the AFL-TLC pushed some toward alliance with secessionists like Mosher, and within the party some saw the need to address the influence of American imperialism. But the deciding factor was far removed from the peculiarities of Canadian conditions and related more to the broad searching out of new orientations to trade union work that proceeded, often, from Stalin's rigidly formed and poorly conceived theoretical "laws of motion," some of which made abrupt turns in this period.

From 1928 on, there was a movement away from the Leninist practice of the early to mid-1920s, when Communists were instructed to "bore from within" established trade union centres to win the masses to proletarian internationalism. Instead, greater emphasis was placed on the treacherous role of the reformist leadership of the trade unions and the need to build autonomous revolutionary organizations. This was the trade union component of the Third Period, and had been prefaced by Stalinist directives to Canadian Communists to concentrate less on TLC unions than on the "progressive" ranks of the nationalistic ACCL. However, the most substantial new development came in October-November, 1929, when both the TLC and the ACCL were attacked as "the bulwark of the Canadian and Anglo-American bourgeoisie." Early in 1930, the Communist Party followed the logic of this denunciation and formed the Workers' Unity League (WUL), dedicated to creating new unions under Communist leadership and displacing the established trade union centres. The WUL served, in effect, as a complement to other bodies, including the TLC. By no means a majoritarian tendency within the labour movement, it nevertheless attracted more than 40,000 to its ranks by 1932.

Dramatic confrontations involving the WUL included the bloody Estevan-Bienfait, Saskatchewan, strike-riot in 1931, which left three miners dead at the hands of the police, firemen, and the RCMP, and the Stratford furniture workers' battle of 1933, where the intervention of the state again secured victory for the employers. But the lessons of such defeats were not lost on workers across the country, whose resentments of the military arm of political authority increased considerably in these years. Across the country, other strikes unfolded and similar results ensued: Manitoba Premier John Bracken used the RCMP to crush Communist-led workers in Flin Flon, while British Columbia miners' picket lines were dispersed by bulldozer-driving police. On Vancouver Island, Cumberland workers lost their struggle to attain collective bargaining rights, a conciliation board condemning the "communist agitation" that opposed a company that had managed to stifle organization in its mines for sixty-six years. Eastern miners, unaffiliated with the WUL, were more successful, and McLachlan launched a series of job actions in 1931-32, many of them ending in victory, securing the workers a rotation system that divided available work among union members in the face of mine closures and mass layoffs. In 1932 they formed the independent but Communist-led Amalgamated Mine Workers of Nova Scotia, a union that failed to last the decade.

Aside from defensive struggles led by the two internationally affiliated garment trades unions, the WUL provided much of the strike leadership of the early 1930s, substantiating Communist claims that they led 75 to 90 per cent of the strikes in the years 1932-34. Among the Canadian workers encouraged to strike under the banners of the WUL unions in the years 1931-35 were Montreal garment workers, sawmill workers in New Westminster, lumberworkers in northern Ontario, loggers on Vancouver Island, fishermen on the Skeena and Nass rivers of British Columbia, longshoremen in Vancouver, textile and furniture workers in Toronto, Kitchener, and Waterloo, chicken pluckers in Stratford, and miners in Noranda-Rouyn. Quebec furniture workers, teamsters and shoeworkers across western Ontario, and, most importantly, automobile, steel, and rubber workers in central Canada were also organized by the WUL, which was active in Windsor, London, Hamilton, Toronto, Montreal, and Sydney.

At the very moment that the WUL appeared to be on the threshold of an organizational breakthrough in the mass production sector, however, new imperatives came from Moscow. In conjunction with indigenous North American developments discussed below, these altered Canadian Communist practices in the labour movement. The rise of fascism, according to Stalin's spokesman, Georgi Dimitroff, necessitated a United Front and demanded the disbanding of all dual unions and an end to labour's divisions. The WUL was to liquidate itself, transferring its members back to the appropriate unions associated with the TLC. J.B. McLachlan, among others, refused to chart such a course and resigned from the Communist Party; he died later in the decade.

The call to return to the fold coincided with developments of immense significance in the United States, where John L. Lewis was putting aside his collaborationist, red-baiting clothes of the 1920s to don the late 1930s cloak of working-class spokesman, championing the cause of industrial unionism and promoting the organization of the unorganized. Always aware of the impact of symbolic gestures, Lewis crossed the floor of the 1935 AFL convention to land a punch on William L. (Big Bill) Hutcheson, president of the craft-conscious and exclusivist Brotherhood of Carpenters and Joiners. That act announced publicly the birth of the Committee of Industrial Organization, later renamed the Congress of Industrial Organizations (CIO). The ties between Lewis and the AFL were severed. Along with what was perceived to be President Franklin Roosevelt's encouragement of unionization under various disputed sectors of his New Deal, this led to an unprecedented organizational boom in the United States.

The CIO had no official presence in Canada, but as its historian, Irving Abella, notes, Communist activists and rank-and-file workers were captivated by the great breakthroughs being made by a revived labour movement to the south. By 1936, with some signs of industrial recovery present, Canadian labour also appeared to be on the move once again: union membership climbed approximately 15 per cent over the course of the previous year and stood at almost 325,000, which represented a greater expansion of union ranks than had occurred at any time since 1919-20. In steel, textiles, and mining, the CIO attracted Canadian workers, although the lack of funds and support from Lewis retarded growth. Sit-down strikes broke out in Chatham, Windsor, Oshawa, and Point Edward, an industrial periphery of Sarnia, in 1936-37, demands ranging from the establishment of union shops to increases in wage scales. Once more the state intervened, this time with Ontario Premier Mitchell Hepburn struggling to keep the CIO from organizing the province, proclaiming that law and order would be preserved and invading unions turned back at the border. At Oshawa, auto workers won the key strike in a series of labour-capital clashes through subterfuge. Denying affiliation with the CIO, union negotiators Charles Millard and J.L. Cohen (the former, a war veteran associated with the CCF and president of the local union, the latter, a radical Toronto lawyer) achieved almost all of the workers' substantive demands. The process of denying acknowledgement of the role of the CIO, pointed out a defiant Millard, was "just child's play." The Oshawa strikes of February-April, 1937, were, like an earlier confrontation in 1928, "a demonstration that the spell of industrial slavery [could] be broken down even in the automobile industry." Despite his posturing and reliance on tactics of repression, Hepburn proved, in Abella's words, "the most successful organizer north of the border."

Thus, Oshawa created a CIO presence in Canada in the absence of actual CIO organizers. Lewis appointed only one recognized CIO leader, Silby Barrett, who was directed to use his base as leader of the eastern UMWA to organize Nova Scotia steel workers at the Sydney DOSCO plant into the Steel Workers Organizing Committee, or SWOC. A Lewis loyalist, Barrett had demonstrated his worth in the international union's red-bashing exploits of the 1920s. Ironically enough, given Barrett's high CIO profile and history as an ardent opponent of McLachlan and the Communist miners, the push toward industrial unionism was driven, in good part, by able young Communists under the guidance of J.B. Salsberg.

Even in the case of Barrett and the Sydney SWOC, as David Frank and Donald MacGillivray argue, basing their claims on the oral biography of Cape Breton radical George MacEachern, union agitation at DOSCO commenced well before Lewis's Canadian lieutenant appeared on the Nova Scotia scene. Having cast his lot with the Communist Party in the early 1930s, MacEachern worked in the Sydney steel plant and used the workplace council, established in the aftermath of a 1923 strike, to promote the need for unionism. By 1935 MacEachern and others managed to win 600 workers to an independent local union, which supported a newspaper and initiated a push for a Canadian Federation of Steelworkers. Not until all of this had been accomplished did MacEachern and other industrial union pioneers turn to the CIO, setting the stage for Barrett's appearance in late 1936. Within months the Sydney steel workers, aided by the miners and bankrolled by the treasury of the initial local union, enrolled thousands in SWOC and Barrett was taking the bows for the breakthrough that others had in fact created.

The MacEachern story could perhaps be repeated, with numerous variations, across the landscape of industrial Canada in the mid- to late 1930s. The history of the early CIO was thus one of initial, often startling successes, almost universally orchestrated by local radicals, Communists, and rank-and-file militants. To consolidate and continue their gains, these working-class organizers turned to Lewis and the CIO, but lacking strong organizational backing they tended to fade. In Quebec, Hepburn's anti-labour policies were surpassed by those of Maurice Duplessis, whose repressive Padlock Law was used to confiscate SWOC records and to disband the 1,000-member lodge in Montreal. Employers followed the lead of such state actions and refused to bargain with the struggling CIO unions. In March, 1938, only 16 per cent of the SWOC recruits who had signed in 1937 were still paying dues.

State and employer opposition to the CIO was exacerbated by political wrangling and factionalism as Communists and social democrats literally came to blows in union circles. Even "Mr. CIO," Charlie Millard, was driven out of the United Automobile Workers, where his anti-communism won him little support from a leadership that was often more than a little sympathetic to known "reds." He was immediately hired as the CIO regional representative in Ontario. However, he encountered serious difficulties, for by the time of his appointment in May, 1939, the CIO and the cause of industrial unionism were in decline: membership, which had stood at 65,000 in 1937, dropped precipitously. Unions in auto and steel lost thousands, while the wood and rubber workers experienced drops of one-half to one-third of their membership. And in January, 1939, in a move that spoke more to the concerns of American craft union leaders than to the needs of the Canadian workers' movement, the Trades and Labor Congress of Canada suspended all the CIO unions affiliated with it. Repudiated by his own union, yet expected to orchestrate activities among other trade bodies also led by Communists, Millard faced months of turmoil. The situation continued to deteriorate when, later in the year, the CIO unions were officially barred from the TLC. By mid-1939, the CIO reported that of the nearly 1.3 million workers in its Canadian jurisdiction fewer than 5 per cent were organized and affiliated with the Congress. Most workers were living below the level of minimum subsistence, and Canadian workers, unlike their counterparts to the south, lacked legislation protecting their rights to organize. The workers' movement, after such impressive progress in its attempts to revitalize labour organization, was dealt a series of blows by state forces, obstinate employers, internal ideological disagreement, and an accentuation of depressed business conditions that would not lift until war resuscitated the world economy. Not until the 1940s would the euphoria and promise of the early CIO years, when a mobilizing unionism took on some of the trappings of a social movement, again spread among Canadian workers, leading to militant action and dramatic advance for labour.

AGITPROP/PROLIT

The crisis of capitalism, the rebirth of social democracy, the rise of industrial unionism, and Communist agitation among the jobless combined to bring the working class to the forefront of public consciousness. This awareness was deepened through unprecedented activity on the literary front as the written word became a potent weapon in the class struggle. As Frank Watt has stressed, a literature of protest paralleled the rise of capitalism in Canada, and was especially pronounced in the labour upsurge of the 1880s, producing a range of critical writing that was reflected in the social gospel-type novels of the 1890s. With the escalating class conflict of 1919, new journals of social criticism were founded, led by *Canadian Forum*, which aimed to "secure a freer and more informed discussion of public questions." In the 1930s this organ would be used regularly by CCF and LSR writers: *Forum* exemplified the restrained radicalism of an intellectualized social democratic milieu, although it did have room for Communist commentary, especially with J.F. White as its editor. During the depression years it was joined and challenged by a major anti-capitalist literary movement. For the first time, plays and short stories, literary magazines and cultural journals, intersected with the class struggle, producing agitational propaganda and a proletarian literature.

Communist journals such as *Masses* (1932-34) and *New Frontier* (which began publication in 1936) provided a public outlet for left-wing writers and intellectuals affiliated with the Progressive Arts Club. Evolving out of a Saturday afternoon discussion group set up by poet Abraham Nisnevitz, the Toronto-based Progressive Arts Club was active in the late 1920s, and by 1932 it included sections for writers, artists, and theatre workers. Among the more active were Dorothy Livesay and future historian Stanley Ryerson. Theatre troupes developed around the Workers' Experimental Theatre in Vancouver, Winnipeg, Montreal, and Toronto. Plays such as Ryerson's *War in the East*, an anti-imperialist piece depicting Japanese soldiers who refused to fight the Chinese, and Dorothy Livesay's *Joe Derry*, a children's pantomime about the arrest of a Communist cadre, were performed throughout Ontario in the summer of 1933. The direct appeal of agitprop theatre, on the picket line or in the street, was an innovation of considerable importance. There was tangible impact in the unemployed themselves staging a play about their situation, as in Trevor Maguire's *Unemployment*.

Short stories and poems published in literary journals also attracted attention. The new mass production industries were subjected to blunt artistic condemnation in creative writings entitled "Juggernaut" and "Production." Poets addressed their verse "To a Generation of Unemployed," their products appearing under titles such as "Depression Chants" and "Hunger." As Watt notes, it was not so much the artistic merit of such work that was at issue as it was the attempt to create an entirely new aesthetic in the literary realm. Agitprop, proletarian literature, and a people's poetry helped to stimulate a movement toward contemporaneity, political purpose, and realism in the arts that had been woefully lacking in what had come to be an established Canadian tradition.

In art, too, the depression exerted an influence. Leonard Hutchinson switched from painting to printmaking in the 1920s so that ordinary people could afford his artistic creations. By the time of the Great Depression, however, his work was considered political commentary, and he strove to "make a record of the terrible injustice that was thrust upon these people." His slogan was, "Wherever people worked, I'd be there," and he claimed to have glimpsed "the bravery of them – they had the spirit in them that you couldn't kill." A small November, 1981, exhibit of Hutchinson's work depicted farm labourers, logging camps, main streets in small-town Ontario, and Port Dover's fishing boats. As John Bentley Mays, art critic for the *Globe and Mail*, suggested, these artistic endeavours were and are "documents of real working life ... a resolute, important, and little-researched experiment in Canadian socialist realism." Convinced that there was a need to fight back and to oppose the authorities, Hutchinson was called "an agitator, bolshevik, Communist, Marxist – everything under the sun." As curator of the Hamilton art gallery, during the 1930s he taught classes on art to young children and bought classical works, but he also opened up the basement to vagrants and used his woodcuts and prints to address obvious social issues that were identifiable in their titles: "Bread-lines" and "Protest." An accomplished artist, elected associate of the Royal Canadian Academy, Hutchinson was part of a struggle to bring "high" and "low" culture together in an understanding of the 1930s that would lend itself to solutions and activist intervention.

A literature of protest was thus united, on the left, with a popular art of dissent that challenged complacency, encouraged resistance, and resisted the lure of mass culture. To be sure, mass culture's public appeal was severely circumscribed by the economic collapse of the period, but explicitly politicized stories and pictures or agitational street theatre brought culture into the process of protest. That this agitprop/prolit consolidated in the 1930s was itself an expression of the extent to which debilitating economic times opened people up to new ways of looking at the world. But as they glimpsed something of hard times in the woodcuts of Leonard Hutchinson or the plays and poems of others sensitive to the ravages of unemployment or the relentless alienation of factory production, Canadian workers also looked directly into the glare of the coercive power of the state.

STATE POWER IN THE SERVICE OF CLASS INTEREST

Frank Scott, prominent in the League for Social Reconstruction and a literary figure of importance, penned some "Social Notes" in the 1930s:

After the strike began
Troops were rushed
To defend property.
But before the trouble started
Nobody seems to have bothered
To defend living standards.

These lines of verse introduce us to the duality of state power in the 1920s and 1930s: repressive in its defence of property, profit, and political order, it was essentially abstentionist in attending to the needs and rights of those outside of these social relations. It is difficult not to see the interwar years as the last stand of a particular type of state, given to enforce its and capital's will through brute might at the same time that it avoided a more subtle regulatory role. Out of the dilemmas and contradictions posed for this coercive/abstentionist state in this period, however, would emerge a new kind of state power, one that sealed a future "compromise" between labour and capital based in industrial legality, welfare provisions, and a social Keynesianism judged affordable in the new prosperity of the post-World War Two world.

As we have seen, efforts were made, from the nineteenth century on, to construct a regime of industrial legality. The early twentieth-century chapters in this historical narrative culminated in the passage of the 1907 Industrial Disputes Investigation Act. But that federally scripted story came to a close in 1925 as the British Privy Council found the IDIA *ultra vires* of Section 91 of the British North America Act. In fact, the declared unconstitutionality of the Mackenzie King-inspired legislation was little more than a denouement. With the unprecedented class conflict of 1919, both King's public commitment to harmonizing class relations and his project of constructing the state as representative of *the* "community" of Canadians faded, being either overtaken by more explicit needs or proven untenable. In the aftermath of the post-World War One labour upheavals and their repression, it was no longer possible to cultivate the illusion of state impartiality with respect to class struggle. The out-and-out victory of capital by the early 1920s, moreover, simply ended the need for the facade of the IDIA. With employers no longer requiring the cover of state intervention and workers unlikely to see it as producing anything positive for them, the two-sidedness of state policy evident in the pre-war years – coercion and concili-ation – collapsed inward, exposing the remaining repressive powers of the state.

For the most part, then, the interwar years are noteworthy as ones in which the state failed to integrate itself into the emerging Fordist regime of accumulation that arose from the restructured mass production of this period. Employers could chart new paths of productive relations, in which shorter hours, welfare measures at the workplace, and higher pay opened out into the new consumer potential of a capitalism increasingly attuned to extending the definition of commodities and rethinking the meaning of the market. But as long as the state was not prepared to secure this social formation with an equally expansive notion of its regulatory role, interven-ing in new ways and developing extensive safety nets to secure a political and economic order of a new kind, Fordism in Canada would remain inhibited. That, in contrast to the United States, was precisely what hap-pened in the interwar years.

With the judicial dismissal of the IDIA, the making of industrial legality – the state-orchestrated construction of a codified system of collective bar-gaining and industrial relations – was put somewhat on hold. To be sure, a number of provinces passed legislation that effectively recognized the IDIA provisions within their jurisdictions. Federally sanctioned boards of concil-iation and inquiry still existed, then, but their role was far more limited than it had been when Mackenzie King's IDIA was unambiguously in force. Whereas third parties intervened to resolve fairly high percentages of strikes in the World War One years (almost one in four strikes in 1918), throughout the 1920s the role of the third party lessened markedly; not until the later 1930s did such intervention, so characteristic of industrial legality, again reach high levels.

Specific crafts in some regions might well move into something approx-imating industrial legality, cultivating a pragmatic business unionism that relied on contracts, fair wages legislation, and a rejection of the politics of labour radicalism associated with 1919. This, according to Ian McKay, was exactly the route followed by Halifax building tradesmen in the 1926-31 years. They could secure a toehold on this precarious system of industrial relations in the prosperity of the late 1920s, but with the economic collapse of the 1930s there were increasing demands for explicit state intervention. Nova Scotia's building trades workers and contractors were actually united in their call for government action, and this pushed the provincial govern-ment to produce an Industrial Standards Act in 1936. This had the effect of standardizing wage rates and hours of work in the Halifax-Dartmouth construction industry, giving legal status to collective bargaining. For lab-our this was judged a great victory, to be preserved and defended at all costs; to contractors it meant the stabilization of their business milieu, lessening the economic impact of fly-by-night interlopers and curbing the potential threat of rural craftsmen.

One year later, Nova Scotia reached beyond the limitations of a piece of legislation aimed at one industry to pioneer the first contemporary Canadian Trade Union Act. The legislation legally recognized trade unions, provided for employer recognition of unions that were the majority choice of employees, and established that where companies checked off any deductions they were also to check off union dues if workers expressed their desire for this in a Minister of Labour-monitored vote. Massive working-class effort went into securing such provisions. Trade unionists saw this legislation as a monumental step forward, but they no doubt blanched at the Act's insistence that all union financial reports and constitutions be filed with the Provincial Secretary. Nor were they likely to feel kindly toward the legislation's recognition of an employer's right to suspend, transfer, lay off, or discharge workers for cause, or to accept gladly its age-old condemnation of intimidation.

Such legislation showed the way forward to a wider and more sustained industrial legality and the labour organization that prefaced its passage indicated the ways in which workers could mobilize to secure change. But its effect in the late 1930s was limited. First, employers were given rather wide latitude in their interpretation of what it meant to follow the provisions of the Act, especially, for instance, if union drives seemed to carry the odour of Communist influence. Second, these guidelines meant little in the face of the state's more widespread and overt policies of brute repression of labour activism, just as their impact was weakened in the face of the pressing problems posed not so much by conditions on the job but by the desolation and destitution of unemployment itself. In both of these areas – repression of activism and response to joblessness – the interwar state followed highly traditional courses of action and inaction.

Overt military intervention in strikes in the 1920s and 1930s was far from commonplace, and in fact seemed to be declining from higher levels in the pre-World War One years. When order appeared threatened by class struggle, however, the federal and provincial states were willing to act decisively, as the 1922 Cape Breton coal strike indicated. Almost 1,000 troops were called into Cape Breton, another 1,000 special police were deputized by the provincial government, and the coal fields were declared a police zone. A UMWA official later recalled that 1922 amounted to something like negotiating "under the muzzle of rifles, machine guns, and gleaming bayonets with the further threatened invasion of troops." Later strikes were no different.

But more important in the 1920s and 1930s than overt military intervention was increased picket line violence, an indication of the escalation of hostilities between strikers and local police. However one measures such strike-related collective violence, the incidence of violence in the 1930s soared above previous decades, doubling, at least, the figures for earlier twentieth-century decades. Kealey and Cruikshank identify ninety-eight instances of violent strikes in the 1930s, compared with a total of only 118 in the entire preceding thirty years. And as local authorities winked at anti-labour vigilante activity, class conflict often ended in bloodied heads or worse. In December, 1929, one year after a series of strikes in the northern Ontario lumber camps, Viljo Rosvall and John Voutilainen, two Finnish organizers for the Lumber Workers Industrial Union, disappeared. Their badly mutilated corpses were found the next year. Five thousand workers marched in the funeral parade, engulfed in the darkness of a rare solar eclipse. "God himself . . . is ashamed of this heinous crime, ashamed that the murderers remain free," noted one of the eulogists. After the Estevan shootout, workers carved "Murdered by the RCMP" on the common tomb-stone of the three dead Ukrainian strikers.

Those workers killed in the class conflicts of the 1930s were often immi-grants. The state's repression of "alien" workers was indeed quite unmis-takable, with massive deportations taking place in the interwar years. Amendments to the Immigration Act and the Criminal Code were reissued, allowing the state literally to expel any immigrant dissidents whose alle-giance to capitalist order was questioned by their political or economic activities. An eightfold increase in deportations of "unproductive" immi-grants occurred between 1931 and 1933, and Barbara Roberts has detailed how the state bureaucracy matured over the course of the 1920s and early 1930s, shovelling out the redundant, the red, and the restless. Municipali-ties and provinces aided and abetted Ottawa's national program of removal, which coincided, in its beginnings, with a concerted "Red Scare" that used the legacy of 1919, Section 98 of the Criminal Code, to jail eight leaders of the Communist Party of Canada.

This state repression was the complement of state inaction on the funda-mental issue of unemployment. Indeed, it might be argued that in the place of an effective program of relief and a forthright policy on unemployment, the state directed its energies to *managing* unemployment and *containing* the threat posed by the unemployed: deporting "unproductive" immi-grants, jailing reds who agitated in the streets against the human costs of capitalism's collapse, and providing passage through picket lines of those unemployed willing to "scab" were all actions consistent with the purposes of various levels of state power in the 1930s.

A survey of this history of state power in the service of class interest shows that Scott's brief lines of verse captured a good deal of the history of state/class relations in the interwar years. These were years when the state secured property and did little to defend living standards. Perhaps at no other time in the history of Canada, save for the very event that set the tone for the state's program of class relations – the repressive onslaught of 1919-20 – was the facade of state impartiality stripped away to expose such naked self-interested class purpose.

THE PRE-WORLD WAR TWO CONTEXT: LABOUR ON THE DEFENSIVE

The 1920s and 1930s had seen labour's dissolution in the period of capitalist hegemony and its attempted reconstitution in the crisis-ridden decade of the Great Depression. Gains were registered and advances made, but on the eve of World War Two the Canadian labour movement was fragmented, its militant sectors in retreat and a conservative wing drawing inward. Regionally, the radical miners' enclave in the East was in disarray, while the western-based Mine Workers' Union of Canada, which waged over forty strikes in the early 1930s, involving most of its 3,000 members, had been liquidated within the UMWA's District 18.

In Quebec, the advances of the workers' movement also showed signs of being stopped in their tracks. The CIO's major triumph, after a WUL defeat in 1934, was the 1937 recognition strike of the International Ladies' Garment Workers Union. Five thousand workers struck and succeeded in cutting women's hours of work from eighty to forty-four weekly, securing a wage increase of more than 30 per cent, and winning approval of the closed shop. Yet, even in the midst of victory, solidarity was undercut, the Catholic *syndicat* opposing the ILGWU, which in turn accused the rival confessional union of "selling out" the workers through personal deals between the priests and the employers.

The Confédération des Travailleurs Catholiques du Canada (CTCC) was formally constituted in 1921, organized in 120 locals with a declared membership of 45,000. (Effective membership may have been much lower, possibly 17,600.) Based on the Church's role in developing study groups among autonomous Canadian trade unions during World War One, the CTCC emerged out of a close and working relationship established between the priests and Francophone trade unionists. In the ensuing dialogue, workers' leaders explained tactics and the realities of class distinctions separating labour and capital, while the Catholic priests interpreted the papal encyclicals. The confessional unions that were amalgamated in the CTCC, led by priests or *aumôniers* (chaplains), were thus rooted in a two-sided interaction, which has been explored by Jacques Rouillard. On the one hand, Catholic confessional unionism grew out of the Church's bitter antagonism to socialism and the godless materialism associated with international unionism. One the other hand, *les syndicats nationaux au Québec* were a product of the resistance to Gompers's insistence that Canada be treated as "a state federation of labour."

At first, Quebec workers in the *syndicats* appeared overly quiescent, as the priests' prohibitions of sympathy strikes, justifications of private property, and rationales for hierarchical social relations all created barriers blocking class struggle. Resisting the internationalism of the American Federation of Labor craft unions in the interests of Quebec's national survival, Catholic unionism was originally more concerned with preserving the status quo than with militant defence of workers' rights and material interests. But in the harsh climate of anti-unionism in the 1920s, employer hostility forced the hand of Catholic unionism: workers ceased to adhere strictly to Church doctrine, priests adopted more militant postures, and opposition to the international unions receded.

Both the internationals and the *syndicats* suffered losses during the 1920s and their common plight encouraged them to combine forces. Rouillard shows that by the end of the decade the two rivals were linked in joint legislative and strike activity. As AFL leaders softened their attacks on the CTCC and avoided comment on the Church, the confessional unions endorsed the closed shop, the eight-hour day, and collective bargaining procedures. As early as 1925, the CTCC repudiated its own origins, taking its stand with the workers' movement. Father Maxime Fortin declared that the days of exhorting workers to "practise renunciation" were over, that no longer would Catholic labour devote itself to "fighting the International." Instead, like all unions, the *syndicats* would "take care of the interests of the working class."

Still, there were differences between the confessional bodies and other labour unions. Separate union centres existed, and sometimes they opposed each other. The trade unions also continued to be more militant than the confessional bodies. One estimate claims that between 1915 and 1936 more than 500 strikes were waged in Quebec, involving over 150,000 workers. The confessional unions apparently led a mere nine of these struggles (4,300 workers), and they were still regarded by many outside of their ranks as thoroughly compromised in the arena of class struggle. Forced into joint action at times, the internationals and the confessionals harboured deep distrust of one another. A Canadian trade union leader, writing to an AFL spokesperson in 1927, claimed that the best policy to pursue was to "pay little or no attention to these rival dual national Catholic . . . movements, thereby allowing them to peter out over time."

But as the CIO cause captivated Canadian workers in the 1930s, it stimulated expansion among all unionized workers and the CTCC grew to its pre-1940 peak of 52,000 workers associated with 285 locals in 1937. In this climate of union growth, CTCC and AFL-TLC unions again found themselves fighting similar battles. CTCC condemnation of trade union violence and calls for the arrest of foreign Communists and rival unionists (all of which divided confessional and international unions in the early years of the depression) no longer appeared relevant as hitherto unorganized industries such as asbestos mining and shipbuilding became the sites of bitterly contested strikes.

The most dramatic struggle turned on efforts to secure recognition of the National Textile Federation of the Canadian and Catholic Federation at the Dominion Textile works in 1937. Strikes erupted across the industry, and much of the malingering conservatism of the confessional unions was broken down as an American manager was kidnapped, driven to the United States, and told to stay there, and as an inkpot was thrown in the face of the president of Dominion Textile. But the union was nevertheless defeated, ushering in a new period of traumatic decline for the confessional unions. As the CIO achieved some significant breakthroughs in Quebec in the late 1930s, the Catholic unions lost prestige. After almost two decades of attempts to bring together the rival sections of the trade union movement in Quebec, they remained apart. Labour's divided ranks were no doubt weaker for this disunity, and whatever temporary gains were registered by the CIO before 1940 were more than offset by Catholic union losses.

Regional and religious peculiarities also coloured the Maritime response to the fluctuating fortunes of these years. In the late 1920s and 1930s, the Antigonish Movement flourished in eastern Nova Scotia and gained a foothold in New Brunswick and Prince Edward Island as well. As an attempt to organize adult education to stimulate self-help, co-operation, and associations of social action, the Antigonish Movement was led by clergymen, professionals, and government employees centred in the Extension Department of St. Francis Xavier University, bringing together farmers, fishermen, and coal miners. By 1938 it had organized 1,100 study-for-action clubs, thirty-nine co-operative stores, and almost forty other co-op plants, factories, or purchasing associations. Courses in the "Antigonish Way" were offered, enrolling people in discussion groups where co-operation was extolled. Part of a long history of regional griev-ance, the Antigonish Movement emerged out of the dissolution of the 1920s, which saw the farmers' political challenge discredited, the Maritime Rights Movement collapsed, and the coal unions assaulted by capital and divided by rifts between moderates and militants, bureaucrats and indige-nous reds.

Conflicts also existed between craft and industrial unionists. In spite of efforts to preserve some form of unity, the emergence of the CIO unions and the hostile reception afforded them by the TLC separated the labour move-ment into opposing camps. After being expelled from the TLC in 1939, the CIO unions formed an alliance with Aaron Mosher's All-Canadian Con-gress of Labour, a body ostensibly antagonistic to international unionism. After the Oshawa auto workers' strike of 1937, Mosher congratulated Ontario Premier Hepburn's attempt "to curb domination by foreign agita-tors and Communists." But the ACCL, as it had been when it was connected with the Communist-led Canadian unions of the late 1920s, was as oppor-tunistic as it was nationalistic and reactionary. It needed the buoyant CIO to keep its sagging fortunes from receding from view. And within the CIO an emerging social democratic leadership sector saw in the ACCL a force that could be directed against the Communists, who could control policy in the SWOC, the United Electrical, Radio and Machine Workers, the Leather and

Fur Workers, and Mine-Mill, as well as holding considerable power in the UAW and the United Shoe Workers.

The 1930s ended, then, with Canadian organized workers aligned with the newly established Canadian Congress of Labour (CIO-ACCL), the TLC, or the Quebec Canadian and Catholic Confederation of Labour. Many more workers, however, remained unorganized; fully 83 per cent of the non-agricultural work force did not belong to unions. Divisions of ethnicity and gender remained of considerable importance, and sectional and regional barriers remained. As late as 1939, for instance, the 638,000 employed women formed a mere 6 per cent of the total labour force and but a minuscule portion of unionized workers. In certain provinces, such as Quebec, where women still did not have the vote, there was direct opposition to their working in industrial situations, and across the country they were concentrated in poorly paid industrial and unskilled economic sectors. They presented a visible reminder of the persistent divisions of class experience.

So, too, did the extreme case of the racially divided work force in British Columbia, where militancy and class consciousness were diminished by white antagonism to Oriental (Chinese, Japanese, and East Indian) members of the population. These disparate groups comprised 8 to 12 per cent of the province's people in the years 1920-40 and, like women, were structured into the lowest-paid categories of a highly segmented labour market. While historians such as W. Peter Ward have overestimated the extent to which such divisions undermined class, these social cleavages did present a significant barrier to unity. The Chinese, of course, worked in Canada since the nineteenth century, and the labour opposition they faced was quite pronounced during the 1880s. But in that earlier context, the Chinese had been the only exception to the rule of class solidarity, at least at the rhetorical level.

By the 1920s, however, a multitude of eastern and southern European immigrants entered the labour market. To be sure, these ethnic minorities sometimes encouraged radicalism and often joined with their English-speaking counterparts to resist the encroachments of capital. But they were also potential strikebreakers, and employers and the state did much to see that they were used to segment the labour market. In conjunction with the antagonisms of the native-born workers and the immigrant cultural distinctiveness and ethnic loyalty, these factors ensured that ethnicity was as much a force that undermined class unity as it was an agent that contributed to collectivity.

Anti-communism also began to influence numbers of trade union leaders, social democrats as well as conventional Liberals and Conservatives. Among rank-and-file workers, the Communist Party's many "turns" introduced them to a history of oscillations and questionable practices that tarnished the image of many of the more militant fighters within the workers' movement. Nothing would serve to discredit the Communists more than the flip-flops over their relations with social democrats – at first shunned as "social fascists" and then solicited as popular front allies – or the shifts in policy that emanated from the Hitler-Stalin Pact of 1939 and the German invasion of the Soviet Union in 1941. Subservient to the needs of "socialism in one country," international Communist movements were expected to reorient themselves immediately to Stalin's directives.

Canadian Communists were among the most pliant. From being staunch advocates of class unity against fascism in the 1935-39 period, they turned to attack Canadian capital and the state in 1939-41, arguing that these warmongers must not be supported. With German tanks rolling toward Moscow in June of 1941, however, the Communist Party changed course and became the advocate of the national government and the employers, at times going so far in some unions as to lend its support to no-strike pledges and to whip the membership into patriotic fervour for the progressive cause of Mackenzie King's liberalism. Honoured more in words than deeds, such "pledges" were broken regularly in a 1941-42 strike wave, but they did provide anti-Communist forces with a forceful critique of the CPC's claim to be *the* voice of the working class. Many workers considered that the war and the defeat of Hitler had become the sole concern of Communists in the labour movement, and it was difficult, once the war ended in 1945, for the party to re-establish credibility as militant voice for the workers.

With labour thus divided and subjected to conflict and shifting ideologies, Canadian workers entered the 1940s unsure of their status and politically ambivalent. Social democracy had consolidated some support among labour in British Columbia, Winnipeg, Cape Breton, and Ontario, but it was pre-eminently a farmers' movement, with its most tangible electoral strength in Saskatchewan. Unable to win more than 8 or 9 per cent of the federal vote in the years 1935-40 and running poorly in the industrial heartland of Ontario, where it secured only 6 per cent of the provincial vote in 1937, the CCF was a party in search of a labour constituency. Liberalism remained the political choice of the majority of the Canadian population, workers and non-workers alike. Since King had absorbed the protests and challenges from the farmers' movement in the 1920s he may have felt confident in his abilities to accommodate labour's emerging political voice of dissidence. But in the late 1930s the Liberal regime of Mackenzie King actually did little to encourage unionist support. In the 1940s and 1950s, war and the resurgence of mass culture and consumer capitalism set the stage for a new chapter in the unfolding drama of the social relations of labour and capital. Workers began to search out a new legitimacy and raise the challenge of a unified political voice that would speak for the working class.

Chapter 6

CLASS, CULTURE, AND MOVEMENT
1940-1975

THE SOCIAL FORMATION

In the post-1940 years Canadian workers, along with employers and the state, restructured class relations. The period from the late 1940s into the early to mid-1970s is fondly regarded by contemporary labour leaders as something of a golden age for trade unionists, a time when collective bargaining rights were won, wages were pushed to new heights of consuming power, and job conditions were improved substantially. There was, of course, a price to be paid for such gains, and employers and the state gave no more than they had to, and certainly no more than they could justify on the grounds that it stabilized class relations and put profit on a more certain, predictable ground.

The basis for this trade-off involving labour, capital, and the state was an unprecedented post-World War Two prosperity, which fundamentally altered the material context in which workers lived their lives, both at the workplace and off the job. This prosperity, a result of the realization of Fordism's promise of productivity and expansive consumption, placed North American workers in increasingly privileged positions compared to the economic realities of labour in European capitalist nations or, more starkly, the Third World. The high wages and rising living standards of workers in the United States and Canada were but one aspect of the United States takeover of the economic world and the penetration of the goods and standards of the U.S. into all corners of the globe. Canada, America's richest colony, an ally that had enough corporate strength actually to mount its own imperialist agendas in lucrative parts of the underdeveloped world, such as the Caribbean, was uniquely situated to reap the benefits of the American Century at the same time that its relation to the United States was always capable of unleashing contradictory impulses.

The very fact that the Canadian state pursued a different, more welfare-oriented path into the age of high Fordism than its U.S. counterpart indicated that there were and would be national differences that separated out the histories of these two countries in the post-World War Two period. Some of those differences would be experienced within the workers' movement. But there were also marked similarities, the most fundamental being the joined fortunes of the Canadian and American socio-economic systems in the age of high Fordism stretching from the late 1940s to the mid-1970s. This would be a period of social Keynesianism, in which the state orchestrated the antagonisms of capital and labour into a placatory regime of industrial legality that it judged well worth the costs of bankrolling the bureaucracies of the emerging collective bargaining system. Complementing this expensive and cumbersome infrastructure of class conciliation was a correspondingly expansive welfare state that set up safety nets to catch those falling away from the protections of industrial legality or prohibited from entering into them. Underlying all of this largesse was the astute assessment that the expense and effort were worth it: employers and the state, as well as the emerging labour hierarchy, agreed that class harmony was perhaps the most valued commodity of the post-World War Two period.

Supplementing the fundamentally economic trajectory of class relations in these years was the ambivalence of the economics of culture. Mass culture's origins, as tentatively suggested earlier, may well have undercut class solidarities and institutions in the context of labour's retreats and defeats in the 1920s. Its first act of appropriating whole realms of class experience and restructuring them as commodities quite possibly forced class allegiances and identities into the background as it promoted pluralistic consumption. But doing this, not only in a period of setbacks for labour but in a decade in which material want and basic economic insecurity still plagued many sectors of the working class, necessarily limited the impact of mass culture. In the post-World War Two years the context of mass culture's influence within the working class was dramatically different. First, labour was aggressively consolidating its presence, not reeling from the repressive onslaught of capital and the state. Second, many workers had tasted at least some of the fruits of mass culture, allowing a palate of discrimination to develop. Third, in the economically expansive times of the post-World War Two period, mass culture became truly mass in its possibilities. Unlike the 1920s, mass culture might be enjoyed by a wide spectrum of workers; the consequence was that it was less and less of a divisive badge, worn conspicuously by the privileged few but denied to the many. For all of these reasons, the mass culture of the post-World War Two years was far more likely to be two-sided in its consequences – on the one hand integrating workers into the capitalist order; on the other, conditioning sets of demands and cultivating aspirations that pitted labour and capital against one another – than the earlier, and far more limited, experience of mass culture's first act in the 1920s.

In the post-1940 years the Americanization of mass culture proceeded apace, going well beyond the beginnings established in the 1920s. Especially in the late 1950s, when the western Tory populist John Diefenbaker was in power, the invasion of things American created a hostile questioning of the American takeover of Canada. This culminated in the O'Leary Commission's 1961 report recommending that restrictions be placed on such American-controlled magazines as *Time* and *Reader's Digest*; because of their massive circulations, these journals were felt to play an influential role in the Canadian marketplace, especially in terms of their capacity to mould public opinion. But as Frank Underhill stressed early in this period, the mass culture of these years was not characterized only by increasing American content. It was also, at root, a democratizing force, and in the 1940s and 1950s the extension of consumer power, a promise of the 1920s, was achieved and widened considerably.

As material acquisition became a common feature of working-class life, mass culture in the 1960s and 1970s became more complex and diverse. By this time, all spheres of mass culture proceeded from market considerations and profitability. Commodities ruled much, but in an oddly contradictory way. Dependence on acquisition conditioned accommodation to capitalist structures at the same time that it could convey a message of resistance and questioning of the social order. This was evident in the explosion of mass culture in the 1950s. Pizza was a craze that may well have been classless. The rich might not have eaten much of it, but certainly workers, small property owners, independent businessmen, and professionals all had a go at this new "cuisine," just as they shopped in the malls that began to undercut and outsell the small stores of downtown central business districts.

Mass culture did more than anything to create the generation gap later pseudopsychologists and pop journalists would spill much ink on in the 1960s. Elvis Presley arrived, to the dismay of many staid parents, his hips gyrating in an unmistakable celebration of a sexuality that was as uninhibited as it was public. Tame compared to the black jookin' of American ghettoes, Elvis's mass market appeal, an undeniable consequence of his colour, announced a frightening opposition between young and old that could widen out into a resistance that set the powerless against the powerful. With the young lining up to watch Marlon Brando in *On the Waterfront* and James Dean in *Rebel Without a Cause*, singing "Shake, Rattle, and Roll" and "Jailhouse Rock," it was apparent that the emerging mass culture was something of a Pandora's box. After all, a year or so before pop culture's big hit had been "How Much is that Doggie in the Window?" Innocuous banality seemed to be taking a back seat to potentially subversive cultural forms. Where would it all lead, some were asking? Mass culture thus expanded consumer demand in the 1940s and 1950s – a process that certainly had the potential to incorporate workers into the status quo – at the same time that it did this in ways that might raise questions about the social order and encourage limited forms of resistance. Only in 1948 did consumption actually decline, and by the 1960s and early 1970s new products and cultural developments were proliferating in ways that often related directly to radical interrogation of the social and political order.

The new mass culture expanded because of demographic and economic developments. Until at least the late 1960s, the Canadian economy grew impressively, and output increased yearly with the exception of 1945-46 and 1954. Immigration, inconsequential during depression and war, was revived, and 1.5 million new Canadians arrived between 1948 and 1957. Population rose substantially in the years from 1945 to 1980, almost doubling to approximately 24 million, while the average family head's real income between 1944 and 1978 also increased, from about $2,500 to $5,400. Such figures, of course, make no allowance for those many losses – in the environment, in personal satisfaction, in the quality of life – but they do speak to particular gains. As an absolute magnitude as well as a percentage of the labour force, unemployment fell throughout much of the pre-1960 period. In the early 1950s it generally hovered between 2.5 and 5 per cent, but in the downturn that followed the Korean War it rose to 6 per cent and in the recession of 1956-59 it climbed to roughly 10 per cent, dangerously close to 1939 levels. Between 500,000 and 750,000 people were jobless. "It's a crying shame that in a country with all the natural resources we have, we have to see people on the street," declared an auto worker in 1958. By 1960, however, the situation was improving, although between 1951 and 1971 for every 100 jobs created, 117 men and women entered the labour force. The Maritimes and Quebec fared particularly poorly, with the comparable regional ratios standing at 128 and 120 to 100, respectively. Still, unemployment dropped yearly until 1966, when it was approximately 3.75 per cent, but then it rose to almost 8 per cent by 1976, an indication of the rough times that were ahead in the 1980s for workers.

For the earlier years of the fifties and sixties, there is no denying that many workers had greater capacity as consumers, and this prosperity was enhanced by demographic trends. Because fertility rates decreased in the depression-ridden 1930s and during the World War Two years, Canadian society was relatively aged throughout the 1950s and into the early 1960s, and the adult-to-youth ratio was skewed. This meant that family incomes were undoubtedly larger and, perhaps, accounted for youth being indulged more than at earlier times in history. All of this also culminated in the post-war "baby boom," which peaked in 1959. "Today," wrote A.R.M. Lower in 1958, ". . . the five-room bungalow [is] the object of life and every woman in sight [is] pregnant." The children of this epoch would become the young workers of the years after 1965, men and women who had known little of the immediate post-war economic expansion but whose expectations arose from their parents' lifestyles and the economic buoyancy of the early 1960s. However, this prosperity did not continue, and from 1965 on there were indications of many new constraints: inflation, unemployment, industrial crisis, and political turmoil all affected workers. All the consumer "attractions" of the 1950s, when durable goods, cars, gasoline, housing, and land were relatively inexpensive and earnings seemed high, were, if not disappearing, becoming less easily attainable. The norm of two cars, a home in the suburbs, and four children, which many workers had come to see as their realizable dream, now seemed harder to secure. Yet, the urbanization that helped to establish this norm still continued. The percentage of the labour force employed in the agricultural sector declined from 24 per cent to less than 6 per cent between 1940 and 1970. By 1956, two out of three Canadians depended on urban sources of employment.

In this context, workers began to conceive of alternatives and to develop new strategies of resistance. No longer circumscribed by the need to fight for survival wages, workers with unions at their back came forward with a new set of demands. With essential rights of association and collective bargaining established during the 1940s, when organized labour finally attained legitimacy, the workers' movement of the 1950s consolidated wage and condition agreements in many industries and often attained compulsory check off of union dues through a formula devised by Mr. Justice Ivan Rand. Labour's institutions, hived off in competitive quests for affiliates, were even partially brought together to some extent in the 1955-56 merger of the Trades and Labor Congress of Canada and the Canadian Congress of Labour.

Such accomplishments provided the foundation upon which a youthful and demanding working class launched a new series of initiatives after 1964. The sixties began with the smallest amount of time loss from strikes and lockouts since World War Two and fewer numbers of strike participants than in any year in the 1950s. But from this modest beginning, strikes increased throughout the early 1960s and reached an unprecedented peak in

1966, when over 617 strikes involving more than 410,000 workers cost corporations over 5 million worker days and 0.33 per cent of working time. Especially noteworthy were the "wildcat" strikes, "illegal" walkouts not sanctioned by unions and usually undertaken to resist the ratification of contracts negotiated by union officers but rejected by the membership. Such strikes were often violent, and defied convention and attempts to impose legal restraints. They numbered in the hundreds in 1965-66, when they comprised 20 to 30 per cent of all conflicts. As industrial relations "experts" were quick to observe, these struggles represented a departure from the traditional confines of class relations: "Much of this unrest is characterized by militancy that is less the product of labour leadership than the spontaneous outbreak of rank-and-file restlessness. . . . In some cases the rank-and-file have been rebelling as much against the 'union establishment' as against the 'business establishment'."

In this oppositional stance, breakaway unions emerged, the nationalistic antagonism to the American-based internationals that had been dormant since the founding of the All-Canadian Congress of Labour in the late 1920s resurfaced, and raiding (one union's attempt to draw another union's members into its ranks) became a critical problem for the labour movement, causing strains and tensions within the newly forged merger of 1956. Quebec's rejuvenated Catholic *syndicats* challenged international unions and drew new strength from a socially conscious unionism that blended ascendant Québécois nationalism, militant syndicalism, and political action in a common front that united labour, co-operatives, and community groups in opposition to capital. Across the country, new groups were on the march, with civil servants, provincial employees, and postal workers leading a contingent of public-sector unionists, many of whom were women.

This resistance on the part of labour did not develop spontaneously, of course, but as a result of new types of worker exploitation. Technological change was altering the working environment, as it had for almost a century, but in ways that brought the message of redundancy home to workers who had never expected to meet it face to face. Many crafts had been undermined well before the war, but others did not become obsolete until after 1945. Between 1950 and 1957 the proportion of diesel locomotives used on the railways rose from 25 to 80 per cent, and other improved equipment, as Rosemary Spiers has shown, allowed the CNR to develop the "run through," in which trains no longer stopped at particular terminals for servicing and crew changes. The layoffs resulting from such developments were a prelude to those of the 1980s, when the Liberal government would terminate much of CN's VIA Rail service. Whole communities were decimated in the process, and the number of employees on the Canadian National declined from nearly 128,000 in 1952 to fewer than 80,000 in 1971. On the railways as a whole, the work force dropped 40 per cent in the same period. The railway brotherhoods, something of an aristocracy of labour given to viewing themselves as untouchable by serious challenge, did little to oppose this erosion until, in 1964, the "run through" caused a number of wildcat strikes, prompting a royal commission under Mr. Justice Samuel Freedman of the Supreme Court of Manitoba. In a controversial ruling, he recommended that employers should be required to negotiate on technological change implemented during the life of a union contract.

Other work sectors were also devastated by technical change but got no respite from the courts. The skilled crafts that had hung on to their workplace authority for so long were the most affected, often losing 70 per cent of their numbers. Toronto's powerful Typographical Union, which had made labour history during the nineteenth century and nourished a sense of itself as a power in the newspaper publishing business, was overtaken by computerized typesetting. New methods in the printing trades promised to cut labour costs by almost 30 per cent, but employers relished even more the thought of crushing a union they had been forced to bargain with for almost 150 years. After a 1964 union walkout, precipitated by the computer issue, the organized printers were never allowed back into their workplaces. For six and a half years, stalwart typos walked ragged picket lines outside of Toronto newspaper offices, defeated but still defiant. As the bulk of the strikers retrained, drifted to other work, were secured jobs by the ITU across the continent, or just melted away in dejection, the international union finally decided to cut its losses, now amounting to some $13 million, and call it the end of a rather long, depressing day. Capital, aided by technology, had won a decisive victory and driven effective unionism from its ranks.

Protection from the kind of technological assault suffered by the printers and railway workers, urged by Freedman's 1964 decision, was slow in coming. Not until 1973 was any federal legislation passed that aimed to lend some authority to the Supreme Court of Manitoba's judgement that workers needed to be shielded from the ravages of technical change. For the most part, however, this 1973 enactment proved a dead letter. Wilfred List, labour reporter for the *Globe and Mail*, commented that "Parliament [has] either deliberately or through lack of appreciation of the matters involved clouded the whole area of dealing with technological change under the law so as to make the legislation almost meaningless." Government inaction prompted some unions to demand a technological bill of rights. They did not get far. Robots began to be introduced into workplaces, doing the labour of six humans and more. As Wallace Clement has pointed out, the 1970s saw vast technological changes in INCO's mining methods until workers in the pits became little more than machine tenders. In Grande Cache, Alberta, open-pit miners worked under the supervision of a computer system that monitored them and their automated tools minute by minute. Indeed, the microelectronics revolution, which had its beginnings in the

1970s and would catch fire in the 1980s, threatened the very existence of the human component of work in the office and in industry. The labour movement began to see, by 1975, that it was entering a new age of challenges and displacements.

Employers were able to draw on more than their power at the point of production, as substantial as that was. They also found support from the state. If militaristic intervention in the social relations of production was not as dramatic after World War Two as it had been earlier under Laurier, King, Bennett, and their provincial counterparts, state intervention was still far from inconsequential. Nowhere was this more apparent than in Quebec, where the Dominion Textile interests of Montreal, Valleyfield, Montmorency, and the Eastern Townships were consistently defended by the provincial police forces in the 1940s and 1950s. Pierre Trudeau himself helped to crush the striking Lapalme mail drivers in the 1960s, notwithstanding his siding with labour in the Asbestos strike of the late 1940s. In 1969, in a preface to the October Crisis of 1970, soldiers were sent to Montreal to buttress provincial police as over 5,000 Montreal firemen and police struck work and the *mouvement de libération du taxi* attacked its competitor, the Murray-Hill Bus Lines, exchanging rifle fire that left a policeman dead. Injunctions, increasingly opposed in the 1960s, lent the armed might of the state legalistic cover, while a Task Force on Labour Relations, headed by Dean H.D. Woods of McGill University, was commissioned in 1966 to search out the cause of industrial rebellion. The task force offered some suggestions of how conflict might be "managed," recommending that employer associations should provide material concessions that would placate unions and that government should protect individual union members' rights from violation. In the end, the task force could simply reassert what capital and labour had known for more than a century: workers and employers occupied distinct ground, and within overlapping territory, relations were governed by adversity.

The state made more effective use of the carrot than it did of the stick. Concessions to labour were wrung from the state in the war years, although they were usually hedged in by provisions that employers could exploit. In the aftermath of World War Two the full-blown system of industrial legality was implemented. Paralleling its establishment was the state development of welfare, fundamental to the Canadianized Fordist regime of accumulation. From 1943 on, when Leonard Marsh issued a rejected but influential report on social security and a "comprehensive" scheme to embrace health insurance, family allowances, unemployment insurance, children's allowances, and workers' compensation, the potential of a benevolent Ottawa was ever present. Unemployment insurance was but one of the many consequences of the depression, with the Unemployment Insurance Bill passing the House and the Senate in 1940. Later to arrive on the scene, but equally significant, were hospital insurance acts, pioneered by Tommy Douglas's CCF government in Saskatchewan in 1946 and followed by British Columbia, Ontario, and, eventually, in 1957, the federal government. Universal old age pensions were adopted in 1951 through agreement between provinces, which essentially controlled the domain of welfare, and the federal government, then headed by Mackenzie King's successor, Louis St. Laurent.

In the 1960s these developments were amplified and extended as the federal Liberals launched a nation-wide war on poverty, advocated medicare, and strove to overcome long-standing economic imbalances among the regions. This had been a persistent and vocal complaint for many years, but it had grown more urgent after the provincial opposition to the Rowell-Sirois Report culminated, in 1941, in Hepburn's attack on federal authority and his withdrawal from the Dominion-Provincial Conference with the words that he would "leave these wreckers of Confederation . . . to carry on their nefarious work." Canada's governments spent increasing sums on health and social welfare, approaching 24 per cent of their total outlays: in 1950 the cost was $1 billion; twenty years later it approached $9 billion. Despite this expenditure, however, a 1976 federal study conceded that between 1951 and 1973 the gap between upper- and lower-income groups actually widened.

These expenditures have been interpreted by some as proof of the selfless concern of the state and its agents. In fact, they were "the price Liberalism [was] willing to pay to prevent socialism," as the *Canadian Forum* commented in the 1940s. As Mackenzie King knew well, such social legislation was fundamentally conservative in intent and was passed to dampen discontents that emerged from the rising expectations of wartime prosperity. After the war, when the possibility of recession was great and when entrepreneurial magnates like C.D. Howe virtually controlled the political economy, welfare measures were even more important and necessary, although Howe seemed at times unable to grasp this elementary political reality. He had, according to King, "the employer's mentality."

Americans with whom Howe dealt during World War Two, when he was Minister of Munitions and Supply, noted that he was one of only two Liberal officials "at home with, and consequently able to deal, without a sense of inferiority, with the representatives of money." By the early 1950s, when Howe had passed through various government ministries, *Fortune* correctly noted that Howe had created "a businessman's country." This new "Dominion of Howe" was committed to American defence policy, was unequivocally anti-Communist, and had, over the previous two decades, issued a wholesale invitation to U.S. capital to take over Canadian resources and manufacturing. Foreign-owned industry in Canada rose sharply from $7.5 billion in 1948 to $17.5 billion in 1957. American-controlled capital in manufacturing between 1926 and 1976 rose to 40 per cent in the 1950s and climbed thereafter to a high of 47 per cent in 1970; afterwards it declined modestly. In some sectors – mining, smelting, oil and natural gas – the figures soared to between 55 and 73 per cent.

But this integration of American and Canadian capital did little to decimate the national bougeoisie. Corporate magnates like Howe, E.P. Taylor, and others reaped the profits of resource-development deals and concentrating economic power. Monopoly, established in the early years of the twentieth century, attained new levels of authority and sophistication in the post-World War Two epoch of finance capitalism, in which central industrial and commercial enterprises came to be orchestrated by a few leading financial institutions. On the eve of the 1980s, the top 500 Canadian companies accounted for more than half the sales in the country and two-thirds of the profits and assets. More significantly, the leading twenty-five companies alone produced nearly one-quarter of the sales, profits, and holdings. Of this dominant group, sixteen were Canadian-owned. According to the 1977 Bryce Commission, Canadian capitalism exhibited higher degrees of concentration than other industrial economies, among them the United States, West Germany, Japan, and Sweden. The 1970s saw this trend continue and deepen, with almost 300 mergers taking place in 1974 alone. Profits for the resulting contemporary super-corporations, such as Bell Canada, soared into the hundreds of millions of dollars yearly.

Against such a background, the state's social welfare offerings and program of industrial legality made excellent economic sense. With its institutions, legislation, and public pronouncements expressing an overt concern for the economic well-being of its population, the state nevertheless shored up capital's accumulative appetite as much as it cared for the poor and underprivileged. At the same time as it expanded the welfare state, for instance, it also built the security state. The implementation of universal programs and *social* security coincided with the state's anti-Communist agenda, realized in its escalating concern with counter-subversion in the 1940s. Acting on Igor Gouzenko's 1945 revelations of Russian spies operating in Canada, the government created a special formal branch within the RCMP to be responsible for counter-espionage work. Within a decade, the Special Branch became an independent directorate, called Security and Intelligence, and in 1970 established its autonomy as the Security Service. As youthful rebellion and nationalist agitation exploded in the 1960s and 1970s this wing of the RCMP engaged itself in illegal surveillance and harassment of domestic dissidents, including "left-wing subversives," Québécois nationalists, social democrats, and unionists.

From 1940 to 1975, these and other developments within Canadian society created new challenges for labour. Waves of militancy were pitted against powerful forces of opposition and containment, producing a history of class mobilization that determined the very character of the modern Canadian labour movement.

MILITANCY, LEGITIMATION, AND THE ARRIVAL OF INDUSTRIAL LEGALITY

The voice of class conflict, virtually silent outside the coal fields in the 1920s, became louder in 1933-34, quieted during the lull of 1935-36 and intensified once again in 1937, only to be stifled by the slump of 1938. But with the escalating wartime needs of the early 1940s and the impact of military enlistments and government expenditures (which meant that productivity climbed during a period of relative labour shortage), conflict increased, reaching a peak in 1943. Some 434 class battles were fought in that year, the only annual count to come close to approaching the previous twentieth-century high of 1920. Cruikshank and Kealey identify a 1941-43 strike wave that encompassed some 425,000 strikers and over 1,100 work stoppages. With capital and the state inching toward a regime of industrial legality under the cover of wartime temporary legislation, it is not surprising that more and more strikes were settled by third parties and, interestingly, that employers won clear-cut victories in fairly high percentages of these contests.

This 1941-43 strike wave flattened out regional bumps in previous patterns of conflict. The Maritimes and Quebec contributed more to the national figures than before, Ontario and British Columbia slightly less. Mining and manufacturing dominated, and workers fared best in short, quick walkouts; the longer a strike lasted the worse were the prospects for labour. Recognition struggles declined, compared to the 1930s, and the usual confrontation erupted around issues of wages and conditions.

The increased willingness of workers to resort to the strike was encouraged by substantial gains in production, as well as by wartime legislation. Between 1939 and 1944 economic output increased by approximately two-thirds. Much of this went into war goods and services, but personal consumption also rose dramatically, perhaps as much as 30 per cent. Real capital formation, according to Pentland's 1968 report to the Woods Task Force on Industrial Relations, was from 50 to 70 per cent higher than the immediate pre-war level. With this productive boom and so much on the economic and political line, the state introduced temporary Privy Council orders that sought to contain class struggle. No doubt this worked, but it had the ironic impact, on occasion, of stimulating workers to think of their rights, which, in the economic climate of need and labour shortage, they were then quick to exercise. PC 7440, for instance, limited wage settlements to rates established during the period of "reasonable" (in practice, given the context, depressed) wage increases; workers no doubt saw the injustice of this legislation and appeared not to be cowed by it. Another order, PC 2685, an empty piece of wartime legislation arguing that fair wages and conditions for workers should be encouraged, along with the right to freedom of association, could not help but move workers into conflict with employers.

As employers refused to fulfil the moral obligations set out in this largely rhetorical order and the government assured both labour and capital that PC 2685 was meant to provide guidelines but not designed to be coercive, strikes resulted.

Win or lose, workers' militancy pushed more and more of the working class not only into conflict but into labour organizations. The number of unionists doubled between 1939 and 1945, rising to 725,000. The most organized sectors of the working class were those directly involved in the war effort. Almost one-half of the approximately 800 strikes fought in 1942-43, for instance, occurred in the metal-producing and mining sectors that were central to the prosecution of World War Two. Workers in the clothing, textiles, and wood products areas were also forced into defiance.

In this context of rising output, consumption, and militancy on the economic front, a vital transformation in Canadian labour relations occurred over the years 1939-48. In the present day, Canada is governed by provincial labour codes that cover fully 95 per cent of the work force, the national government retaining power to legislate only with respect to a restricted number of workers who come under federal jurisdiction. However, during the World War Two period, full national regulation of workers was in force, and this had the effect of increasing union activity and lending the working-class mobilization of the era a particularly national colouring. There was even a semblance of unity within the House of Labour, both the TLC and CLC advancing a set of remarkably common demands. This unity would carry on into the post-war years of prosperity as the ranks of unionized workers across the country more than doubled to 1.5 million between 1945 and 1960.

During the 1941-43 strike wave, which threatened political and economic order at a historic moment of pressured tension, the state was far from unified in its understanding of what was at stake and how the developing crisis in industrial relations could be resolved. This, in part, explains the piecemeal and practically contradictory thrust of many of the wartime Privy Council orders. While some sectors of the state apparatus harkened back to a Mackenzie King-like placebo of voluntaristic conciliation, it was apparent that this was not working and, indeed, could not be effective in the changed and charged conditions of the early 1940s.

To the south, President Roosevelt's National Labor Relations Act, also known as the Wagner Act, after its main author, went as far as capital could reasonably countenance in establishing a regime of industrial legality that included designating long-standing employer tactics – company unionism and overt discrimination against trade unions – as unfair labour practices. Employers were impelled to engage in collective bargaining, workers were acknowledged to have the right to determine who would represent their interests in industry, and the state was granted the power to certify bargaining units. For many in the Canadian business community, represented by the Canadian Manufacturers' Association, the Wagner Act was a threatening piece of class legislation. Sectors of the state that took the blunt employers' point of view most readily to heart recoiled in fear from such a solution.

And yet it was apparent that something must be done. Discussions in cabinet proceeded; Privy Council orders proliferated; reports were commissioned and deposited; labour and capital offered their opposing judgements; and strikes continued. Provinces felt constrained to pass collective bargaining acts, and unique experiments in alleviating class conflict, including the creation of a Labour Court in Ontario in 1943-44, were launched. To break the impasse PC 1003 was enacted in February, 1944. Long hailed by commentators as a milestone in the advance of unionism, PC 1003 was in fact an attempt to amalgamate the hegemonic powers of Wagner Act-type legislation with the curbs on labour that a fearful capital demanded. The new order established the right of employees to belong to trade unions, which in turn were empowered to elect or appoint representatives to bargain with bosses as long as those representatives had the support of a majority of workers in their jurisdiction.

But PC 1003 also, as Peter Warrian and Bob Russell have stressed, allowed non-affiliated bargaining representatives to be elected by workers who chose to deal with employers without unions. Thus the new enactment did not necessarily privilege trade unionism; it simply specified that workers had the right to representation. Unfair practices were designated, not only for capital but also for labour, and the requirements for petitioning for a labour board certification vote were set higher than those stipulated in the American Wagner Act, thereby placing explicit barriers in labour's path. Finally, and perhaps most decisively, PC 1003 was premised on the instruction that labour and capital were to bargain in good faith and make every effort to come to a final collective agreement. Its aim, clearly, was to stop the escalation of class conflict evident in the early 1940s, to regulate the class struggle. In Russell's words, PC 1003 was "a strategic but temporary compromise authored by an uncertain political regime." The order was cast in ambivalence, had a limited life span since it would end with the termination of war and the lapsing of the War Measures Act, and excluded whole sectors of the working class not directly involved in wartime production.

Immediately before PC 1003 was instituted, more than one million worker days had been lost to strikes in 1943. In 1944, this figure decreased by more than half to 490,000, an indication that the order-in-council perhaps placed something of a lid on volatile class relations. But in 1945, with war at an end and the short-lived and impermanent provisions of the last few years about to be dismantled, a new moment of urgency faced organized workers. Labour's leaders understandably wanted to avoid a catastrophic repetition of the defeats they suffered in the aftermath of World War One, and they were acutely conscious of the need to retain what they regarded as victories secured in 1943-44. Militancy thus resurfaced with a vengeance in 1945 as almost 1.5 million worker days were accumulated in strikes. Both capital and labour dug in for a fight, and as the Wartime Emergency Powers of the government came to an official end, a new strike wave rolled across the land in 1946-47. Well over 400 conflicts resulted, some of them huge affairs, and massive confrontations shook logging and lumbering, metal, asbestos and coal mining, steel, textiles, transportation, meat packing, and automobile and rubber production. Involving approximately 175,000 workers and millions of worker days lost, these battles resulted, as Bob Russell has recently argued, in the full-scale entry of Fordism into the politics of production.

The site of the codification of this Fordist industrial legality was the symbolically appropriate automobile industry. A 1945 strike at the Windsor Ford plant set the stage for a series of legalistic decisions that would then be partially generalized across the country in an effort to contain the post-war upsurge of Canadian labour.

In spite of the 1937 Oshawa victory at the General Motors plant, unions in the automobile industry were hardly on solid ground. Ford of Canada remained an open shop. The Windsor plant was the foreman's domain, and while treatment of labour during the war years was mediated by Ottawa's enactments and the realization that workers and the production they fostered were needed, it was clear to the men on the line that a return to pre-war conditions would leave them at capital's mercy. Tools were often laid down during the war to secure some gains for the workers, and walkouts were staged yearly from 1942. Organizers failed to crack the open shop, but two weeks after the war ended, 10,000 auto workers walked off the job, demanding union recognition from one of "the most virulent antiunion companies in Canada." To keep maintenance men and police out of the company powerhouse, workers and their supporters surrounded the Ford plant with automobiles and, in a dramatic and ironic blow against the company, locked their cars and went home. One of the most successful pickets in the history of unionism blockaded a factory with its own products; Fordism was being turned against Fordism. A nation-wide sympathetic strike was discussed, and workers in Kitchener and Sarnia protested with walkouts. The Attorney General claimed that "the actions of the Ford Company strikers . . . constituted open insurrection," but workers across the country voiced their support and offered financial assistance. Labour leaders played the hand of state mediation to good effect and pressed the Department of Labour on the need to impose arbitration if final-round negotiations failed.

The result was a historic settlement, crafted by government arbitrator and Supreme Court Justice Ivan Rand. Rand entered the Ford strike convinced that unionism was central to the protection of workers subject to capital's dominant strength and authority. But the unionism endorsed by Rand had to be led by enlightened leaders, attentive to the democratic rights of its members, committed to industrial harmony, and responsible in its exercise of an economic power that was shorn of any political ends. While he would not have described it as such, Rand's world view was eminently Fordist, premised as it was on acknowledging the need for stability within class relations and securing a balanced negotiation of the interests of capital and labour that would, in turn, ensure the production central to the ultimate well-being of workers, employers, and the wider community.

Rand's success lay in a decision to end the Ford strike that codified all of this, incorporating the accommodationist impulses of the trade union hierarchy and exposing a reluctant capital to the gains that could be registered by making the unions administrators of the laws of the workplace. As Russell points out, under what came to be called the Rand formula unions were not granted the closed shop, for this would be to cede organized labour a monopoly over employment. But unions were to be awarded a hitherto unprecedented legitimacy. When endorsed by a majority, unions were to have the right to grieve on behalf of their members, as well as the right to strike. Moreover, union dues were to be checked off by the employer, Rand considering that all workers in a bargaining unit benefited from union efforts with respect to wages and conditions. Whether each worker actually joined the union, however, was a matter to be decided by individual conscience rather than legislated necessity. To benefit from this check-off, however, union leaders had to act responsibly and uphold contracts and the newly evolving "laws" governing workplace behaviour. If wildcat strikes or rank-and-file actions that disrupted production broke out, unions must contain them and reintroduce order on the shopfloor if they wanted to avoid losing union resources and checked-off dues.

Rand's resolution was a Fordist coup that caught both capital and labour off guard by supposedly giving them what they wanted. For labour it was generally perceived to be a magnificent victory. In the words of former Ontario Labour Minister David Croll, it was "a resounding blow for the advancement of labour's rights in our economy . . . a great milestone in the development of labour-management relations as was the initial recognition of collective bargaining." But by tying union legitimacy and its economistic encasing in the dues check-off to the question of industrial discipline and orderly class relations, employers were disarmed in their arguments that unions spelled trouble. Indeed, within a year capital was occasionally willing to concede how content it was with the benefits of industrial legality. One manager reported that, after the initial shock of recognizing unions wore off, it had to be admitted that "(a) the union is not too difficult to get along with (b) the operators in Ontario are exchanging information on common problems." From a Newfoundland boss came the statement that one advantage of drawing up a year's agreement with a union "is that it stabilizes your labour costs and you know where you stand."

Ultimately the Rand formula, resolving one dispute, could not institutionalize a regime of industrial legality, but it did set the tone for the postwar period. Rand's influence was felt in some of the larger industrial establishments and would eventually penetrate the language of collective bargaining agreements. In the immediate post-war years, however, the state moved to quell labour's increasing and tumultuous concern with union security by passing the Industrial Relations and Disputes Investigation Act (IRDIA) in 1948. This legislation picked up the slack created by the lapsing of PC 1003 and allowed for the possibility of collective agreements establishing the closed shop.

By the end of the 1940s, then, a regime of industrial legality that both organized labour and concentrated capital could embrace was in place, shored up by important legislation and judicial interpretation. Critical to the emergence of this systematic attempt to *govern* trade unionism was the full-blown arrival of Fordism, a larger regime of accumulation premised on the stabilizing impact of social security, high wages, placid and predictable class relations, and general corporate/trade union agreement on the parameters of industrial discipline.

On one level, the specific making of this narrower regime of industrial legality has been distorted by a one-sided focus on state intervention and legislation. For as David Matheson has pointed out in an unpublished study of industrial legality in the 1940s, much of what the state-enacted regime proclaimed and sanctioned had already been developing out of the class struggles of the 1940s. In a study of 121 collective agreemeents, Matheson notes a "generational" differentiation between three types of contracts. First-generation contracts, simple documents often signed before 1939, recognized worker collectivity in a *de facto* way or with a crude recognition clause. They were occasionally little more than letters of intent from employers and seldom ran to more than a cursory page or two. Emerging in the transitional years 1940-45, second-generation contracts were longer (approximately ten pages) and began to address questions such as seniority and grievance procedures, reflecting a concern with formalism and legality that was most often spelled out in management rights clauses. The third-generation contract dates from the end of World War Two. Gone was the casual tone of earlier documents and the limited concern of even the transitional contracts of the early to mid-1940s. Instead, contract provisions proliferated. Whereas a typical second-generation collective agreement had some twenty-seven clauses, Matheson found third-generation contracts with seventy provisions and sixty sub-provisions running on for pages and pages. Both Matheson and Warrian note the increasing significance of the management rights clause, usually a final provision in the contract stipulating that anything not covered in the agreement was to be conceded to the managerial prerogative. The vast majority of collective agreements signed before 1945 had no management rights clause or contained no provision delineating unfettered corporate authority. After 1945, however, seven of every ten contracts signed, in Warrian's sample of 176 agreements, included explicit recognition of management rights.

Both state policy and shopfloor negotiations thus structured the new regime of industrial legality in ways that legitimized unionism at the same time that unionism was contained and dressed in the respectable garb of accommodation. Militancy won what unions in Canada struggled for since the early nineteenth century. As Russell notes, the late 1940s were the first time in Canadian history that a case could be made by trade unionism's leadership that it was in the working-class interest to subscribe to the letter of the regulatory law of industrial relations. But to say this is not to say that the new regime of industrial legality was an unmixed blessing for workers or for unionism. The former, after all, were circumscribed under the new regime, not only by capital and the state but also by their own institutions, which took on an increasingly bureaucratic cast and legalistic orientation. As Ian McKay concludes, before the reign of Rand, workers about to strike a boss might ask, "Are we stronger than our employers? How long can we hold out?" After the 1940s, union leaderships were more concerned with other questions: "Does this conflict with the collective agreement? When does this go before the conciliation board? How can we sell this politically?" The check-off saved unions the immensely time-consuming task of collecting dues directly from their members, but it also separated the union and its leadership from regular contact with its members. One astute manager's assessment was that the check-off worked to stifle militancy in the lumber camps. Union delegates sent into the bush to collect dues "kept the men stirred up," he reported, adding that "union agents with a steady income aren't trouble makers." And as contracts grew to unwieldy lengths and descended into the impenetrable discourse of legal jargon, workers simply neglected to pick them up, haul them home, and pour over their contents.

Finally, in an era predating the sanctity of contracts worker strength dictated the course and pace of class conflict, but by the later 1940s collective agreement language and industrial discipline exercised increasing influence. Grievances that once precipitated walkouts were now procedurally resolved. Collective agreements, while freeing workers from so many insecurities, also incarcerated them in notions of what the shopfloor was and was not. In the past, workplaces had often been the site of heated debate and discussion about the direction of class action. Not so in the legalistically governed workplaces of high Fordism, where the shopfloor was the site of uninterrupted production, not a debating society. If there was a grievance it would be handled by the structures and institutions, not by direct action. As much as was gained by the arrival of industrial legality, then, so too was something lost. A part of that loss was the restructuring of industrial unionism away from its mobilizing movement-oriented character of the early 1940s and into its legalistic, business form of the post-war period.

UNIONISM

Unionism made great gains during the war and immediate post-war years, with membership expanding rapidly in both the long-established craft unions of the Trades and Labor Congress and the newly formed industrial unions of the CIO, affiliated with the Canadian Congress of Labour. In the TLC, membership soared from 160,378 in 1938 to almost 360,000 in 1946. During the 1940s the CCL unions almost tripled in number and membership. The original 448 branches expanded to over 1,000 between 1940 and 1946, and membership grew from 100,000 to 315,000 in the same period. It was among workers in the CIO-dominated sectors of resource extraction and mass production that militant action was concentrated, although TLC unions also entered the fray.

The new unions of the CIO were a mixed group. Some, like the International Woodworkers of America, were the direct descendants of a long line of labour militants who traced their lineage back to the IWW and the WUL. A major struggle was waged at Fraser Mills in 1931, but the more substantial organizational breakthrough came in the early 1940s. Led by left-leaning Scandinavian loggers, the IWA organized 90 per cent of the work force on the Queen Charlotte Islands, won significant support among Vancouver Island workers, and launched a drive to unionize the company towns of the Lower Mainland of B.C., where huge employers dominated life in the community as well as the sawmill.

Lumber workers gained their first taste of victory in 1943, an October strike winning them union recognition on the Queen Charlotte Islands and a master contract. In 1946 the loggers led a province-wide strike involving almost 35,000 workers and challenged the government intention of maintaining wartime wage controls. Under the slogan "25-40 Union Security," the woodworkers defied state and employer, demanding a twenty-five-cent-an-hour increase, a forty-hour week, and a range of union provisions, including the dues check-off. Three thousand strikers marched on the capital of Victoria, while in Vancouver "tag days" reminiscent of the relief strikers' tactics of the mid-1930s raised thousands of dollars for the workers in spite of the opposition of the Vancouver City Council. Forced back to work by a government order issued by provincial Labour Minister Humphrey Mitchell, the IWA eventually settled for far less than its original demands. But a contract was secured, as well as partial union security, and organization boomed. Ten thousand workers joined the union during this tumultuous confrontation, raising the membership of the B.C. district to 27,000. By 1946 the IWA was the largest union in the coastal province and one of the four biggest in Canada. In northern Ontario, at the same time, bushworkers in the Lumber and Sawmill Workers Union waged similar struggles, some 5,000 workers in the Thunder Bay area leading the largest walkout in the history of Ontario logging in October, 1946. Employers had to acknowledge total defeat.

Like the IWA, the International Union of Mine, Mill and Smelter Workers was of central importance to the upsurge of CIO unionism and the CCL's opposition to the government's wartime policies. As in logging, workers concentrated in company towns of northern Ontario's mining frontier had a tradition of radicalism, the constitution of Mine-Mill borrowing freely from the advocacy of class struggle associated with the lapsed Western Federation of Miners, active at the turn of the century. But there was also a more immediate structure of subordination to overcome. Union organizer Bob Miner recalled the conditions of the 1920s and early 1930s, when the mine owners kept religious institutions, leisure activities, schools, and housing firmly under their thumbs. "You worked, ate and slept company," Miner noted, and in Dome, near Timmins, children went to bed with prayers of thanks for the livelihood the company town provided: "God bless mommy, God bless daddy, and God bless the Dome." When Miner's father, a Communist who once harboured Tim Buck during one of a series of "Red Scares," was asked by a minister and a mine manager to intervene in a carpenters' strike to secure harmony as well as some material benefit to himself, he "hit the preacher and knocked him into the ditch." Forced to move from the town because of this rash but understandable and honourable act, the Miner family felt the ultimate power of the company. It was made clear that anyone who bought their house would be fired.

The need to overcome this kind of autocracy led miners in northern Ontario to battle for union rights in 1941-42. Local 240 of Mine-Mill demanded recognition in Kirkland Lake, and after two years of listening to CIO officials caution against strike action, the local petitioned the government for a conciliation board. Previous landmark decisions by state-appointed controllers, such as those at the Peck Rolling Mills in Montreal and Hamilton's National Steel Car Company, convinced Canadian unionists that they had little to look forward to from state intervention in labour relations. In both cases, union efforts to secure wage increases or recognition were crushed. In Kirkland Lake the situation would be no different. After stalling for a long time, a conciliation board was finally appointed, and it recommended recognition of the union. Management refused to comply, forcing a confrontation. After more delays, in the form of a government-supervised strike vote, the workers walked out. They were immediately attacked by the press, led by the *Globe and Mail* (owned by gold-mining interests concerned with the battle at Kirkland Lake), and chastised for their anti-patriotic wartime strike. With winter upon them, the miners were "frozen out." Government intervention, in support of the recommendations of the conciliation board, was not forthcoming, although Ontario Premier Mitchell Hepburn did provide the mine owners with constables ordered to protect strikebreakers. A costly defeat, the

Kirkland Lake strike bankrupted the early CCL and decimated Mine-Mill. Company power returned to the mines.

Bob Miner remembered that for the workers who participated in the strike, "it was pretty well disastrous. They lost their jobs, their homes, everything." Although his comment supports some academic interpretations that lay stress on the "suicidal" and "disastrous" character of this struggle, Miner, in fact, would not have agreed with such pessimistic assessment. Like Harold Logan and Laurel Sefton MacDowell, he knew that out of the defeated miners' efforts would come "the march toward PC 1003." Kirkland Lake produced a committed cadre of labour leaders, brought ethnic groups together, united segments of the TLC and CCL, earned labour widespread support, and, in the end, forced the state and employer to accept change and collective bargaining, whatever the ultimate containments of those processes.

Whether or not it had been orchestrated by the employers, and in spite of the vast material cost, Bob Miner viewed the events of the early 1940s as ones of accomplishment. "The Kirkland Lake strike was one of the most advantageous, for the working class as a whole, that ever took place. As a result of what took place there, we obtained labour legislation in Ontario in 1943, which made recognition of unions compulsory once a majority backed the union." However much it is now possible to question this fixation on legislation (which Miner, like so many workers, understandably misread slightly) and its supposed unambiguously positive consequences for labour, it nevertheless remains the case that workers battling for union recognition had little choice but to struggle for an end that capital and the state were reluctant to concede. As it turned out, those two forces proved capable of deflecting what the workers eventually won to their own advantages.

Within the mass production sector, the gains of union mobilizations could be counted in rising CIO union memberships, especially in the electrical and steel industries. The United Electrical, Radio and Machine Workers (UE), for instance, grew out of the development of the electrical industry in the 1920s and the resulting new wave of consumer goods. Predominantly semi-skilled and often female, the work force in this field had few ideological or organizational benchmarks to guide it in its post-1937 history. Led by Communist C.S. Jackson, the UE grew slowly and won support in plants in Brockville and Hamilton. Prior to the 1943-44 legislation favourable to unionism, it enrolled a mere 3,000 members, but its real strength began to emerge in 1946, after battles in Brockville, Montreal, and Hamilton. In the last city, the strike at the Westinghouse works was part of a concerted effort to win union rights at a number of plants, Stelco being the most important. One in five Hamilton workers was on strike, and as one participant in the 1946 upheaval recalled: "In those days the union was evangelical, it was missionary. We had the feeling we were building something for posterity, that we were charged with a mission."

That sense of mission spread across Ontario, where rubber workers and steel workers joined electrical workers in massive 1946 strikes involving almost 30,000 workers and two million working days lost. The president of Stelco's local union, which succeeded in turning back the company's successful early resistance to the Steel Workers Organizing Committee in the 1946 attainment of union recognition, spoke for many workers when he argued, thirty years later, that labour won benefits "which could not be measured in dollars and cents." In the 1946 challenge to managerial prerogatives, workers had, in union leader Reg Gardiner's words, experienced "the feeling of freedom [that came from] breaking the hold that Stelco had on us." By 1951, the United Steelworkers of America claimed a Canadian membership of 55,000, boasting that average earnings in the industry more than doubled over the course of the union's brief life. Electrical workers accomplished similar achievements, and by 1947 were supported by 20,000 dues-paying supporters.

The CCL unions were not alone in making progress during these years. Within the TLC, textile workers at the Dominion and Valleyfield works in Quebec waged a strong battle for the same demands as those of the loggers of the west coast in the form of "25-40 Union Security." Marshalling the full power of the state, Duplessis jailed Valleyfield leaders Kent Rowley and Madeleine Parent, while the companies hired thugs and used provincial police to escort strikebreakers to their jobs. Seamen on the Great Lakes faced similar tactics, as their strike for the eight-hour day was undermined by "scabherding" contingents of Ontario Provincial Police and the RCMP. The federal government intervened to declare the docks public property and denied picketing seamen access to them. A four-year battle was fought by the printers against the Southam newspaper chain in the 1946-49 years, while an industry-wide strike of 125,000 non-operating railway employees in 1950 necessitated a special session of Parliament to deal with a so-called national emergency. In towns like Paris, Ontario, strikes such as the 1949 textile workers' struggle at Penmans Limited challenged corporate paternalism and divided communities.

A catalogue listing of these and many other conflicts would enhance our appreciation of the struggles of these years, of the victories and defeats. But it would tell us very little about the human sacrifice and effort that went into such battles, or of the cultural context that helped to extend unionism politically into a social movement. That remains, for the most part, a hidden history. However, there are signs of the significance of these years, uncovered by oral history projects such as those undertaken some time ago by the McMaster Labour Studies publication series. One of the more revealing documents in this set is entitled *Organizing Westinghouse: Alf Ready's Story*. It details, through focusing on a single but strategically important figure, the virtually unstudied daily routine of union organizing. It was pitted against a gruff political economy of management that saw only profit and loss. "You see, in this electrical industry," claimed one Westinghouse boss, "we have to buy many commodities. . . . To us, labour is just like copper, rubber, steel, paint, and so on. It's a commodity that we need. And we're going to buy it for the lowest price we can." Alf Ready did not agree with that view of human beings: "We were slaves," he recalled, "only they didn't have to keep us." He worked to ensure that this attitude would not survive. His persistent attempts to establish UE at Westinghouse included economic demand and political challenge, as well as creative cultural acts that lent abstract goals a concrete meaning.

Ready began his "art of organizing," for instance, in 1941, with a symbolic destruction of the company union. When the glossy newspaper of this association ran pictures of the company union's leaders, Ready cut them out, mounted their heads on pictures of rats, and pasted them onto a drawing of a cheese, upon which the "rat" union leaders nibbled. He then labelled the creation "The remains of the Company Union" and hung it in the department from which many of the company union's leaders were recruited. Ready had no time for those who tried to curry favour with the employer. "Fellows filed by there by the hour," Ready recalled with glee.

But the real union remained to be built. Ready circulated throughout the plant, armed with a pink requisition slip to make it appear that he was on a company errand, and spoke with workers in all areas about setting up a union. His father, a milkcart pusher in the aircraft shop, collected dues. Union slogans and messages were chalked on stairway risers, written on toilet paper, stuck on the wall. One day, as the janitors went to the washroom, workers flooded the shops with shredded paper (the remains of union leaflets) scrawled with the slogan "United we Stand." As Peter Friedlander has shown in a study of the emergence of a UAW local in Hamtrack, Michigan, such symbolic repudiations of the deferential climate of the workplace are far from minor interludes in the class struggle. They are often the stuff of which resistance is built, the foundation on which more episodic and consequential struggles arise.

From these mundane beginnings, Ready began organizing lunch-hour meetings: "People came from everywhere – it was nothing to see two or three thousand out there on a noon hour." These gatherings in the park brought out an unprecedented boldness. Workers who at first hid behind trees to stay out of sight of their supervisors came out into the open. In 1944, UE won a recognition vote by an overwhelming majority, and by 1946 UE's efforts had branched out beyond Westinghouse to other Hamilton plants, including Stelco and Firestone. Community support sustained the unionists during the confrontations of 1946, and with the recognition of essential human rights, workers at Westinghouse won the respect long denied them.

Alf Ready, like many union pioneers in the mines and on the shopfloors of mass production industries, was not a radical. Radicalism was the farthest thing from some of these workers' minds. In Kingston, for instance, at the Alcan works, a company union evolved into a CIO affiliate and, in the labour upsurge of the mid-1940s, won many of the same kinds of concessions that began to proliferate as collective bargaining and union recognition were legitimized. United Electrical played a role in the first stages of this process. And where UE went, in the 1940s, non-radicals were likely to bump into Communists. Like so many workers who began to organize in the 1930s and 1940s, Alf Ready was motivated by a Communist worker. A Communist steel worker named Bert McLure helped Ready with the UE drive in Hamilton and "introduced [him] to unionism."

For all the successes of industrial unionism in the 1940s, however, there would prove to be no place for the Communists who led or aided so many organizational drives. As much as the arrival of industrial legality, the parallel campaign to contain communism within the labour movement sapped the social movement content of industrial organization and pushed it back into the corner of business unionism. Indeed, without posing any conspiratorial intrigue, it is appropriate to suggest that industrial legality and the suppression of the Communist presence in trade unions were necessary complements to one another, both having as their end the *governance* of labour and the institutionalization and assurance of industrial discipline.

LABOUR'S COLD WAR

Bob Miner remembered that in the struggle to organize the mines of northern Ontario, "it didn't take . . . very long to realize that the people who were doing the work and scrupulously carried out every decision of the union – whether or not they agreed with it – were Communists. That's what influenced me to become a Communist too." Pioneers of industrial unionism and early organizers for the CIO, Communists were a substantial force in the labour upheaval of the 1940s, especially in Mine-Mill, UE, and the IWA. Within the CCL, one-third of the membership was affiliated with unions associated closely with the Communist Party; one-half of the CIO organizers, at least, were reputed to be Communists. At the local level, the Communists often led organizational efforts and undertook the routine but vital tasks of keeping fledgling unions from disbanding. This won them the admiration of militants like Bob Miner and the respect of many rank-and-file workers. However, this layer of activist cadre did not necessarily grasp either the finer points of Marxist theory or adhere rigidly to the line and political direction emanating from Toronto's party headquarters. Their communism was a product of their militancy and their intense activism rather than a measure of doctrinal purity or, even, steady adherence to the party. As Jack Scott, who organized WUL unions and the unemployed in the

1930s and returned from World War Two to play a role in the upheavals of the late 1940s, noted of his own entry into the Communist Party in the early years of the Great Depression, "I didn't know communism from rheumatism."

Nevertheless, if Communist energy and commitment pushed activists into the party, which was often seen as the only radical game in town, and secured the allegiance of many workers, the changeability of official Stalinist Communist Party policy led to a measure of cynicism. Driven underground in 1940-41, the Communist Party was renamed the Labor Progressive Party; by 1944 it was publicly supporting the King Liberals in electoral contests and working against its former "social fascist" associate, the CCF. This social democratic party had recently scored unprecedented political success and was attempting to win the support of the trade union movement in order to gain the strength to form a third-party opposition. The Communist and social democratic rivalries of the 1940s exhibited a vehemence seldom witnessed in Canadian labour. To be sure, at the local level party activists and worker allies from both camps could often get along, and the lines of demarcation were never drawn in practice as strongly and starkly as they were between intransigent leaderships. Still, when the Communist Party abandoned its conciliatory stand toward constituted authority after the war, the confrontation with the CCF escalated, exacerbated by the predictable involvement of the employers and the state. One part of the emerging anti-Soviet Cold War would be fought out in the trade union movement.

This period, then, has been cast in the academic literature as one of "Communist domination" of the labour movement. Appropriating the language of social democracy, academics from Harold Logan to Desmond Morton have argued the case for the CCF and its anti-Communist crusaders: Charles Millard, David Lewis, and many lesser lights, such as Shaky Robertson and Eileen Tallman, who were associated with Millard's Steelworkers. Rarely, if ever, is social democratic domination spoken of, and never with the same degree of vitriol reserved for the Communists of the 1940s, although CCL secretary-treasurer Pat Conroy regarded young CCF members in the unions as "trade union illiterates . . . whose primary motivation was not to build a labour movement but to capture it for the CCF." This political reading of the history of the 1940s is lent authority by the Stalinist policy of the CPC itself, and a scholarship pitting "a heroic democratic socialism" against the "dark forces" of communism points to the CPC's willingness to alternatively encourage and discourage class struggle as evidence of its disregard for the workers' true needs.

The story of the Communist Party in these years is one with many unfortunate chapters, a history with much to atone for. But even this does not justify interpretations depicting tragic rifts within the labour movement as a battle between good and evil, an either/or dichotomy that was resolved in the inevitable victory of those practitioners of "the good fight." Irving Abella's *Nationalism, Communism, and Canadian Labour* remains one of the few substantial studies to document all that was lost with the rash of "commie bashing" that broke out in the 1940s. However, even he argues that in particular cases, the demise of communism was necessarily a positive development in the history of Canadian labour. "In the long run," he contends, "the expulsion of the Communists proved a benefit for SWOC." But the Steel Workers Organizing Committee did not exist in isolation. Its anti-communism spread to other unions and set a particularly problematic tone for the labour politics of the 1940s. The results of this anti-communism were far from beneficial for the workers' movement as a whole.

A case in point was the British Columbia-based International Woodworkers of America. Under orders from national CCF secretary David Lewis, the CCF dedicated itself to ridding "British Columbia of Communist domination." As Jerry Lembcke has shown, this crusade was preceded by CCF factionalism and opposition to Communists in leadership positions in the IWA; one consequence of the divisiveness that emerged from this assault on the B.C. district was a weakening of the organizational drive on the mainland. By 1944, the criticisms directed against Communist president Harold Pritchett and his supporters in the IWA escalated into a disruptive campaign. CCF advocates and outright reactionaries aligned with a White Bloc tied to the conservative American woodworkers of the Pacific Northwest and attempted to break up large IWA locals, rechartering the smaller units under non-Communist leadership. Meetings were attended solely to cause antagonism; the union's "no-strike pledge" was constantly held up to derision; and Communist organizers of proven worth were fired by the international's head officers.

In the post-war climate of anti-communism and the Cold War, the situation deteriorated. Adding to anti-Communist strength was the passage of the American Taft-Hartley Act, which outlawed the closed shop, required union officials to file non-Communist affidavits, and curtailed labour rights established in the 1930s. Communist leaders from the B.C. district were denied admission to the United States and thus blocked from attending conventions and meetings of the international union. Their resignations were demanded. Union books were audited and poor bookkeeping lent credence to the charges of financial mismanagement. The international conducted a vicious program of red-baiting, enhanced by radio broadcasts in which the "reign of terror" in effect in the Soviet Union was imaginatively portrayed. The CCL and the CCF lent such efforts increased potency, sending Steelworker organizer Bill Mahoney to break the back of the Communist labour movement on the west coast. He tackled the Vancouver Labor Council, the British Columbia Federation of Labor, and the IWA. During this time, the Communist leadership of the IWA retained the support of its rank-and-file membership, but they had been so harassed by the autumn of 1948 that they seceded from the international union to form the Woodworkers Industrial Union of Canada. Rumour had it that a leading west coast Communist trade union figure was wandering around with $100,000 in a brown paper bag.

The WIUC split from the IWA was a controversial move, opposed by some woodworker leaders as well as, some say, the Toronto leadership of the CPC. But party figures in B.C. orchestrated the move and lived to regret it. The repressive assault of the CCF, the Canadian Congress of Labour, and the Cold War warriors in the international union and the American state department succeeded in reducing the woodworkers to the status they had held in the early 1930s. Between 1948 and 1950, the WIUC attempted to represent its membership in the west coast logging industry. But employers were hostile, the Canadian labour movement was unsympathetic, the IWA broke its strikes, and provincial police intervened. At the same time, the Labour Relations Board denied the WIUC's legitimacy, often refusing to certify secessionist locals or to sanction the union's strikes. In August, 1950, the dissident woodworkers returned to the ranks of the IWA. The Communists had finally been defeated.

The official organ of the WIUC, *The Union Woodworker*, correctly asserted that the assault on communism in the IWA struck a fatal blow to labour unity. "A year ago," it declared in 1949, "the main bulk of the labour movement was more or less united in a common front. Today, it has been driven asunder, transformed into warring factions, with the remnants of the CIO raiding and wrecking in obedience to [a] policy of 'divide and conquer'. A united CIO movement no longer exists." As Abella shows, the anti-Communist drive "cleansed" the Steelworkers, the United Automobile Workers, the Leather and Fur Workers, and many other unions. The International Union of Mine, Mill and Smelter Workers, a centre of Communist strength and support for the "no-strike pledge" during World War Two, was decimated by an attack from "the steal union."

Even within Mine-Mill, a supposed site of Communist domination, the CCF-CPC rivalry could rear its head in an ugly way. In Trail, British Columbia, the Consolidated Mining and Smelting local of the union was controlled by "right wing CCFers." When a Communist, Jack Scott, was elected to be a delegate to a Mine-Mill convention in San Francisco he attempted to cross into the United States only to be detained by Immigration officials. Refusing Scott entry, the border guards told him that the president of his own union had written to them that a Communist would be attempting to cross into the United States. Upon his return to Trail, Scott was greeted with front-page headlines in the local newspaper detailing his abortive attempt to attend the Mine-Mill convention and condemning him as part of the ubiquitous "Communist conspiracy." Small wonder that Mine-Mill fell on particularly tough times. Only in Sudbury did it remain a union of strength, but even there the CIO was the more potent presence. "What a friend we have in Jesus, since we joined the CIO," International Nickel employees used to sing, adding in more sober tones that they were "not joining anything but the CIO." Within the AFL-TLC, as Rick Salutin's portrait of Kent Rowley reveals, things were little better, and the United Textile Workers was red-baited into retreat in these years.

Unions led by Communists did survive these years, but not without difficulty. The case of the United Electrical, Radio and Machine Workers' Union is instructive. UE was a constant thorn in the side of the CCL leadership, an especially irksome union to the likes of Charles Millard and his allies Aaron Mosher (president of the CCL) and Pat Conroy (secretary-treasurer). As it challenged capital and the state, UE also pilloried the anti-Soviet character of Canada's foreign policy, the Marshall Plan, and the Korean War. Unable to destroy UE from within, the CCL was forced to expel it on a technicality late in 1949 and to charter a rival body staffed by those experienced in searching out Communist sympathizers. In rejecting a UE appeal to be allowed back into the Congress, Conroy charged that the union's leadership and staff were "prisoner[s] and political slave[s] of the Communist party . . . vassal[s] of Uncle Joe Stalin . . . crawling on their bellies to Uncle Joe Stalin to obtain leadership at the expense of the Canadian workers." With the CCL whipped into an anti-Communist frenzy by the onset of McCarthyism in the United States and war in Korea, these words found a warm reception in 1950, and UE was categorically rejected.

And yet UE hung on, retaining most of its membership in the face of CCL raids and attacks from the state. In Quebec, Duplessis virtually outlawed the electrical workers' union. Rank-and-file members, by no means committed to communism, stayed loyal to their leaders, although the Brockville local succumbed to the second raid of the CCL-backed International Union of Electrical, Radio and Machine Workers in 1953. Interviews with UE members conducted by Jim Turk no doubt present a rather rosy picture of the democratic nature of the union, but they do indicate that Communist leaders survived because they established structures that linked workers to their union spokespersons. A steward's system bridged the gap between leaders and led, and executive and membership meetings were convened regularly and were attended by the union's leading figures. More important, at the workplace itself, UE won workers' respect through solid contract settlements, aggressive handling of complaints, and avoidance of unnecessary and unpopular strikes.

Finally, unlike the steel and rubber industries, electrical manufacturing lacked a range of occupations and a hierarchy of historically solidified job classifications. Informal work groups in steel and rubber often developed within the industrial union, functioning autonomously rather than processing grievances through the union. In electrical production plants, however, this was a rare occurrence because of the homogenization of semi-skilled labour involved in the work process, which facilitated the development of a union that seemed closely associated with the rank and file. This meant that the issue of "Communist domination" was irrelevant to many workers. The CCF and the distant CCL, rather than locally rooted Communists, appeared to be the interlopers, partisan and irresponsible agents of disruption.

The United Electrical Workers was thus able to withstand somewhat the climate of anti-communism that prevailed during the Cold War. Other unions were less successful, even when Communists functioned as they did within UE. During the Penmans 1949 strike in Paris, Ontario, textile workers affiliated with the Trades and Labor Congress, most of them female, felt the sting of anti-communism as editorials in *The Financial Post* and Toronto newspapers criticized "a Communist-inspired and conducted strike" that was said to have torn "the heart out of this once peaceful, friendly community of 5,000." A citizens' league dedicated to the defeat of "Communism and other subversive activities, thereby assuring all God-fearing and right-thinking citizens the right to go about their normal affairs," supplemented the efforts of these distant but authoritative sources. As workers and police clashed on picket lines, Paris was said to be "shaping up like another Lachute and Valleyfield or any one of a dozen other violence-ridden strikes called by Communist-run unions since the Soviet Union resumed its prewar line of class struggle." Union organizers such as Madeleine Parent, Kent Rowley, Val Bjarnason, William Stewart, and Helen Muller were stigmatized as Communists. But as research by D.A. Smith suggests, few of the strikers saw these figures in this light. One striker commented that "I couldn't see anything wrong with Bjarnason, Parent and Stewart. To me they were OK . . . I think they were just working for working-class people." In conjunction with the repressive capacity of the state and the municipality, the pervasive power of the company, and the fragmented work force, anti-communism exacted its price from the working class of Paris and helped to seal the union's fate in defeat. As Joy Parr has recently argued, gender figured prominently in this struggle, with womanly militance as unlikely a candidate for conventional endorsement as was a union leadership composed of outsiders easily scapegoated as Communist agitators.

Across Canada the Penmans story of defeat was repeated again and again, the anti-Communist card played with increasing confidence. Among Canadian seamen it would take a particularly tragic turn as a union was crushed by the combined forces of capital and the state, armed with the ideological zeal of the Cold War and gangster tactics of intimidation. Precedents had been established for state intervention in the anti-Communist battles within the labour movement, and as early as 1944 the Canadian government may well have facilitated the granting of landed-immigrant status to a Textile Workers' Union of America organizer, Sam Baron. In conjunction with other red-baiters in the textile industry, Baron drove Kent Rowley and Madeleine Parent from positions of leadership in the AFL-affiliated United Textile Workers of America. But Baron's influence in Canadian trade union circles would be negligible when compared to that of another "import" to the Canadian anti-Communist labour team: Hal Banks would long be remembered, in the words of one judicial authority, as "the stuff of the Capones and Hoffas – a bully, cruel, greedy, dishonest, power hungry, contemptuous of the law." His rise signalled the fall of the Canadian Seamen's Union.

The CSU had its origins in the late 1930s, when a Communist-led contingent broke from the Toronto-based National Seamen's Union, a unique company union led by Captain H.N. McMaster and his daughter. Famous for its strikebreaking, blacklisting, and racketeering practices, the NSU was quickly displaced and the new organization claimed a membership of almost 6,000 by 1939, enrolling over 90 per cent of the seamen working the Great Lakes. Agreements were reached with the bulk of the employers and connections formally established with the AFL and the TLC. Wartime expansion of Canada's ocean-going fleet provided further growth, doubling the CSU membership and establishing it as the dominant union on lake and sea-going ships by 1947. Soon after the Hitler-Stalin Pact was signed, recently recruited Communist Pat Sullivan led a 1940 strike on the Great Lakes that earned the union notoriety for its militant defence of its members and resulted in Sullivan and three of the Seamen's officials being sent to an internment camp. Such confrontation would be rare in the years of Liberal-Labor Progressive Party alliance in 1944-45, but it resurfaced in 1946 with a particularly violent clash that won the CSU sole bargaining rights and turned back an aggressive employer offensive.

By this time, however, the union was increasingly forced to take defensive measures. Shippers and the Liberal state colluded to dismantle the Canadian merchant fleet as owners sold their vessels to international buyers, sailed under non-Canadian "flags of convenience," and hired foreign crews at wage rates far below union scale. The Cold War began to back the Communist-led Seamen into a corner, and the situation worsened as Sullivan (lent to the TLC as secretary-treasurer in 1943) resigned his presidency, denounced the CSU as "communist dominated," and established a rival union. This action combined with the American-based Seafarers' International Union campaign to discredit the Canadian union. After a series of bloody 1948-49 battles that extended from the Great Lakes to Europe and saw employers, the state, and red-baiters in both the Canadian and American labour movements pitted against the CSU, the organization was expelled from the TLC in 1949 and its certification revoked by the Canadian Labour Relations Board in 1950. Being "Communist controlled and directed," the CSU was "no longer within the meaning of the Industrial Relations and Disputes Investigation Act." Industrial legality carried the rider, "no Communists."

Throughout this time, however, the CSU members stood by their union, and rank-and-file workers rebelled at their international officers' attempts to drive the Seamen from the workers' movement. One Toronto delegate at the 1948 TLC convention condemned these actions as "stabbing the seamen in the back . . . stabbing the entire labour movement in the back." The fiercest opposition to the CSU was yet to come, however, in the person of Hal Banks.

A March, 1949, strike of the seamen revealed the unequal character of the opposing forces involved in the struggle against the CSU. As the union protested wage cuts and abolition of the hiring hall, major employers signed "sweetheart contracts" with the Seafarers' International Union. To enforce those contracts and to oversee opposition to the CSU, Banks was brought to Canada, his criminal record and unsavoury past virtually ignored by the Montreal courts that granted him citizenship on the recommendations of leading labour lieutenants. Shortly thereafter, armed thugs were dispatched to Halifax aboard CNR trains and, escorted by RCMP forces, opened fire on seamen picketing a CN-owned steamship. These were but some of the "broad-shouldered boys" that Banks would use to "recruit" for the SIU. As protests mounted, it was clear that the state itself was backing the anti-Communist drive in the seafaring trade. Transport Minister Lionel Chevrier was "not able to say" whether the Halifax strikebreakers were Canadians, Minister of Labour Humphrey Mitchell downplayed the violence and the strike as a "jurisdictional dispute," and C.D. Howe, ever the voice of capital, judged the whole affair just one more indication of how difficult it was for ship's officers to get "a fair day's work out of the crew." Banks, supported by state, employers, and a powerful segment of the labour bureaucracy, soon vanquished the CSU.

A decade later the price of this "victory" over "Communist domination" was revealed: 2,000 seamen had been blacklisted, not by employers but by the union; wage costs in the industry declined; and employers and union officials defied the law to the detriment of workers in the trade. Things deteriorated to the point that, by the early 1960s, a clean-up was necessary. The government appointed a commission of inquiry headed by admiralty judge and justice of the British Columbia Court of Appeal, Thomas G. Norris. The resulting hearings and consequent Norris Report detailed the sordid corruption of Banks's ruinous rule of the SIU, but it also exposed the upper echelons of the Canadian labour movement as foolishly complicit in the whole mess. When criminal charges were laid against Banks he simply returned to the United States, leaving a legacy of collaboration and corruption.

The Canadian labour movement thus entered the 1950s largely purged of Communist influence. In conjunction with the institutionalized regime of Fordist legality, in which the rule of the contract took softened precedence over the bluntness of class struggle, this successful anti-Communist drive sealed the fate of industrial unionism. What had once seemed a mobilization of workers that promised large social change was reduced to a more pragmatic business unionism. Labour's Cold War, effective in most unions, had also led to tactics of intimidation and new forms of domination that far exceeded those of many of the Communist-led unions. While certain Communist practices in the trade union movement no doubt deserved stiff rebuke, and while the CPC's subserviency to Stalinist directives worked to the detriment of the labour movement, Communists had, when all is taken into account, achieved much of significance.

In spite of the highly publicized wartime "no-strike pledges," for instance, it is clear that Communist-led unions rarely imposed such a ruling on their memberships. As the 1943 recognition strike on the Queen Charlotte Islands and the 1941-42 Kirkland Lake Mine-Mill battle revealed, Communists participated in militant job actions even during the period of the popular front. Despite the shifting policy of the Communist International, the Communists won the support of many workers for one simple reason: at the local level they were capable of sensing the mood and needs of their membership. Nor were Communists given to lining their own pockets or to packing the union staff with loyal incompetents. As a disciplined cadre, they were often the first to make material sacrifices and to call to task union staff who failed to do their jobs properly. This is not to deny that some shady dealings were made; it is to suggest that they were not the monopoly of the Communists.

Yet, for all of this, the Communists had to go. Millard won the day, and as a consequence the labour movement in the post-1950 years would operate on the policy that "Loyalty was more important than ability." During the upheavals of the 1960s and 1970s, that orientation, a product of the internecine struggles of the 1940s, would come under attack as the trade unions were besieged by a younger, more militant rank and file that knew little of the ideological turmoil in which the "old guard" had been forged.

COMING TOGETHER

The 1950s marked a point of departure for Canadian labour, as the strains and tensions of the post-war upheaval dissipated in years of relative prosperity and supposed calm. This decade marked the apparent "end of ideology," a condition achieved in part by the crushing of the Communist presence within the trade unions and managerial adoption of "human relations" orientations to the perennial "labour problem." Strikes were less common than they were throughout the 1940s and were more often successful in winning wage, condition, and benefit agreements. Basic survival and recognition of unions were no longer central as they had been in the 1930s and 1940s, guaranteed as they were by the arrival of industrial legality. The organized working class appeared to have reached a new plateau of authority and power, and union membership stabilized. The more than 65 per cent of workers who remained outside of unions were concentrated in smaller industries and businesses or were part of sectors like the emerging white-collar stratum that, historically, had proven difficult to organize.

Labour's relative effectiveness throughout the 1950s and the widening parameters of union demands, which increasingly reflected concern over automation, job security, and company-financed benefits, drew some hostile fire from capital and the state, especially during the closing years of the decade, as the economy dipped into recession. Militancy was perhaps most pronounced on the west coast at this time. British Columbia accounted for 28 per cent of the large strikes in the decade and about 21 per cent of all worker days lost to labour conflict. In 1952 and 1959, when notable strikes occurred, B.C. provided 50 to 60 per cent of national worker days lost and workers involved in strikes. Led by lumber and construction workers, many of these struggles were wildcat strikes, and the regional conflicts of the 1950s prefaced the nation-wide rank-and-file revolt of the 1960s. They drew antagonistic response, most noticeable in the passage of the Labour Relations Act (1954) and the Trade Unions Act (1959). Such B.C. legislation placed new restrictions and penalties on union workers engaging in "illegal" strikes and picketing, and defined worker organizations as legal entities that could be sued for a range of damages in the event of their involvement in activities that violated the law.

For the most part, however, the 1950s were years of consolidation for labour. More large strikes were fought in the manufacturing sector in central Canada and the extractive industries (fishing, lumbering, non-ferrous mining and smelting) that had been at the very centre of the organizing drives of the 1930s and 1940s. Conflicts in the auto industry accounted for more than 16 per cent of the significant battles of the 1950s. Regionally, too, the trade union movement strengthened its foundations, although perhaps at the expense of regional autonomy. Newfoundland's union with Canada in 1949 increased the number of organized workers in the country to over one million. The region had seen a range of organizational activities over the course of the nineteenth and twentieth centuries, and seal skinners, craftsmen in various trades, and miners at the Wabana deposits on Bell Island were all unionists. As Peter Neary has argued in one study of Bell Island and Conception Bay, they had been a unique blend of the traditional and the modern, their culture a hybrid of imposed industrially oriented structures and the ancient ways of the outports of old Newfoundland. But according to William Gillespie, this combination produced a vibrant regional labour movement. At the time of Newfoundland's entry into Canada, Gillespie claims, over 41,000 workers were organized; they immediately joined Canada's "national" labour movement. Nine years later, under the impact of political integration, international unionism, and the rule of Joey Smallwood, Newfoundland's union membership had fallen to 33,000.

The question of who would control these and other dues-paying workers constituted one aspect of the divisions in the House of Labour that remained to be resolved in the aftermath of the post-war workplace and legal gains and the silencing of Communist organizers. The Trades and Labor Congress of Canada, affiliated with the American Federation of Labor, still contended for jurisdictional rights with the Canadian Congress of Labour, which was aligned with the Congress of Industrial Organizations. The purging of Communists in the late 1940s and early 1950s, and the resulting union suspensions, merely exacerbated a difficult situation. Unions were raided by other unions, their members enticed away from TLC and CCL bodies on the grounds that the rival union could provide higher wages and more lucrative benefits. By 1952 it was clear that labour unity was suffering seriously from these activities referred to by one CCL delegate as "the worst attempt at mass raiding in the annals of Canadian labour."

Within the trade union movement two positions were forming, one that supported TLC-CCL unity and one that dismissed the possibility. Those who hoped for unity were led by such people as R.C. McCutchan of the TLC's Retail Clerks International Protective Association, who declared in 1953, "Have you got to wait for the boss to drive you together? . . . Let's control our Canadian policies to the extent of saying: 'Well, if you Yankees can't get together, we in Canada have brains enough to do it'." But this advice was rejected, the majority of TLC delegates aligning themselves with plumbers' leader John Bruce, who refused any compromise with CIO unions. "You can't live with snakes," he claimed, "and I say they are traitors."

Ironically enough, given McCutchan's mildly nationalistic advocacy of unity, the first step was taken in the United States, where new leaders emerged in both the AFL and CIO in 1952. George Meany of the plumbers (AFL) and Walter Reuther of the UAW (CIO) struck a no-raiding pact in April, 1953, and by 1955-56 the unity movement in both Canada and the United States accomplished its aims. The first Canadian convention of the united labour bodies convened on April 23, 1956, and even the remnants of the OBU joined the newly forged national labour organization, the Canadian Labour Congress. A product of compromise and conciliation, the CLC struck a crucial financial arrangement on dues that stood midway between the monthly membership rate of four cents charged by the TLC and the ten cents levied by the CIO.

In the divisive realm of politics, the long-standing divergence between CIO support for the reform-oriented CCF and the TLC advocacy of non-partisanship was overcome to some extent in the agreement to support a political education department that would play a role in the creation of a new party linked to trade unions, co-operatives, farmer organizations, and other progressive blocs. This was possible, of course, because by the 1950s the CCF, as we shall see, seemed to be running out of steam. At the same time, even the "old guard" within the TLC recognized that the Liberal and

Conservative parties offered labour no real voice and even worked directly against trade unions in moments of crisis.

But in 1956 it seemed that such moments of state-directed assault could be overcome by a labour unity that bridged many historic divides. As a young Montrealer, Claude Jodoin, headed up the recently formed CLC, it appeared that Quebec might be enticed to join a workers' movement that was reaching out to draw together all regions of the country and that promised to go beyond past squabbles, although the Catholic *syndicats* remained aloof.

No sooner was this promise raised, however, than a violent jurisdictional dispute reminded labour of the fragility of its new-found unity. In New-foundland the Brotherhood of Carpenters and Joiners and the International Woodworkers of America came to blows over who would prevail among the province's loggers. Two powerful corporate interests – Bowater and Anglo-Newfoundland – refused to deal with the IWA, which the workers in the industry embraced, and the government denied the union certification. Joey Smallwood, once a trade unionist but now a "Father of Confederation," proclaimed his intention of freeing "the loggers of Newfoundland from the tyranny of a foreign union." Architect of Newfoundland's joining Canada, Smallwood could still use the rhetoric of the new province's special nationhood when it served class purpose. It was all rather an old story. IWA left-winger Harvey Ladd added to the conflict by threatening that the establishment of a woodworkers' union would preface a revolution in Newfoundland.

Smallwood wanted nothing of that and he took a swift, arbitrary, and dictatorial course: outlawing the IWA, he set up his own union, the Newfoundland Brotherhood of Wood Workers. Clashes between loggers and police increased, and in one confrontation a policeman was killed; vigilante actions followed. The IWA was routed and the wider labour movement crushed. Under the Labour Relations Amendment Act (1959), secondary boycotts and sympathetic strikes were vetoed and the province was given the right to dissolve any union whose officers were convicted of criminal activities. Between 1958 and 1962, the number of organized workers in Newfoundland declined precipitously to 16,000 while union locals were reduced from 186 to 109. The debacle of organized labour culminated in 1961, when Smallwood handed his union's contracts over to the Carpenters, who refused any CLC interference in their right to represent the Newfoundland loggers. The IWA considered this a high price to pay for the appearances of consolidation.

By the end of the 1950s, then, the workers' movement was in something of a holding pattern. It secured large wins in the late 1940s, but it paid for these victories by trimming its own militant and radical sails. The trade unions were tamed in the process. Now entrenched, they were also more cautious. Between 1955 and 1965 the percentage of unionized workers in

Canada actually dropped, falling from 33.7 to 29.7 per cent. With the Communist presence routed, what direction did labour politics take? Not surprisingly, it followed the general trend: the fortunes of the CCF roughly paralleled those of trade unionism, exploding mercurially in the early to mid-1940s and settling uneasily into the 1950s, a decade that would end with social democratic recognition that something new had to be tried if a reformist third party was ever to register any significant electoral gains.

THE RISE AND FALL OF THE CO-OPERATIVE COMMONWEALTH FEDERATION

The early 1940s were, as David Lewis's memoirs record, the first and most successful period of a labour-social democratic alliance. This was also a time that saw the CCF do daily battle with Communist Party members in the Labor Progressive Party. "All levels of the CCF spent enormous amounts of time and energy fighting off communist pressures to form a united front with them," recalled Lewis. Given what was clearly an obsession on the part of Lewis and other CCF leaders with the need to rid the left of all Communists, it is amazing that the social democrats were also partly successful in courting working-class voters and gaining union support. So much energy was squandered in factional battle. When the state-supported campaigns of repression and smearing aimed at the CCF, employer hostility, and the impoverished coffers of the social democrats are taken into account, the accomplishments of the mid-1940s are quite striking. Much was the product of the tireless efforts and remarkable energy of a dedicated corps of moderate socialists, many of whom received their political training in the CCF Youth Movement of the 1930s.

The CCF received its first union affiliation in August, 1938, when the United Mine Workers of Cape Breton endorsed its reform program. But CCF-labour connections remained informal and often quite weak. While many CIO leaders were CCF advocates, few in the more conservative TLC were linked to the cause of reformism. The war provided the catalyst that thrust the divided labour movement into a concerted campaign for political action. In the West, both Saskatchewan and British Columbia provincial CCF parties grew rapidly, and in the former province the CCF formed the government in 1944; in B.C. it attained the status of official position in 1941. One in four Albertan voters opted for the CCF in the 1944 provincial election, while in Nova Scotia the percentage of the popular vote going CCF almost doubled between 1941 and 1945. Even in Quebec, where social democracy might have been expected to stagnate, the numbers voting CCF increased more than thirteen times between 1939 and 1944. Much of this represented a protest unassociated with working-class constituencies.

Farmers in the West, for instance, were attracted to the CCF because it provided a populist alternative to Liberals and Conservatives and a counter to Social Credit.

In Ontario the labour movement was most supportive of social democracy. There, a 1942 CCF-trade union conference produced a spate of union affiliations. In the 1943 provincial election, the workers of Ontario's industrial cities, mill towns, and mining communities rallied to the CCF banner, electing thirty-four members to the provincial legislature; more than half of them were trade unionists. The Liberals were decimated and the Tories narrowly voted into office: the CCF increased its share of the popular vote by 405 per cent, and the future looked bright indeed.

In fact, though, many of the union affiliations established at this time were allowed to lapse, large employers bankrolled anti-CCF campaigns, and the embittered divisions between Communists and social democrats split labour constituencies. As workers feared the election of anti-labour Conservative politicians and as the Labor Progressive Party forged a Communist-Liberal coalition in the closing years of World War Two, the labour vote slipped through CCF fingers. By 1945 the CCF was in political retreat. In Ontario, the thirty-four seats won in 1943 dwindled to a mere eight in 1945. While the CCF vote remained at the level of the 1943 election, the superior (and lavishly funded) Tory machine of George Drew brought out multitudes of Conservative Party supporters; the victorious Tories increased their share of the popular vote from less than 500,000 in 1943 to almost 800,000 a short two years later. They also used a "special branch" of the Ontario Provincial Police to spy on the CCF and the trade unions. One week after the Tory romp provincially, the 1945 federal election also ended in CCF defeat. Industrial Ontario, casting 260,000 votes for the CCF, failed to elect a socialist candidate, and the party became a regional voice of protest: Saskatchewan's 167,000 CCF voters (barely one-fifth of the entire federal vote) did manage to elect eighteen MPs (almost two-thirds of the total), but the national picture was bleak. Labour had responded weakly to the CCF call, and only in areas of established militancy (Cape Breton, Winnipeg, and British Columbia) did workers vote the socialist ticket. This trend continued in the later 1940s. "All very depressing" was Lewis's candid assessment.

The only possible bright spot for the CCF was that things were worse for the Communists. Driven underground in the early years of the war, they contested only ten ridings in the 1940 election and polled fewer than 15,000 votes. In the 1945 federal election, the Communist Party, under the guise of the LLP, forged a Liberal-Labour coalition that attracted barely 110,000 votes. Only one Communist, Fred Rose, was sent to the House of Commons (and he was an incumbent, elected first in 1943). By far the greatest number of progressive workers voted CCF. And Fred Rose's parliamentary career would soon come to an end, the Gouzenko revelations driving him from office. Tried under the Official Secrets Act in the spring of 1946, Rose was sentenced to six years' imprisonment on charges of Soviet espionage.

These years were not ones of total victory for the Liberals, however. The Saskatchewan 1944 election saw the CCF win an astounding forty-seven of fifty-two seats; the Liberals collapsed in the 1943 Ontario election; and some Liberal defeats in by-elections in August, 1943, saw CCF, Communist, and Québécois nationalist candidates capture the voters' allegiances. Nevertheless, with the election of 1945 the Liberals re-established their firm hold on the reigns of federal political power. Sustained through the early and mid-fifties by "Uncle Louis" St. Laurent, close ties to corporate power, and an astute Ottawa "mandarinate" of senior civil servants, the government party ruled confidently and authoritatively until the electorate grew bored, tired, and eventually outraged enough by the Liberal Party's mishandling of the Trans-Canada Pipeline fiasco to bring Diefenbaker and the Conservatives into office in the election of 1957. Meanwhile, the Cold War and the complacency of the early 1950s nearly eliminated both Communist and social democratic oppositions. The CCF met with irreversible lack of support, and, even when the numbers of elected members rose, success was more a consequence of the shifting boundaries of the electoral system than of increased support. In the 1958 federal election, the CCF secured less than 10 per cent of the popular vote. A change was in order; 1943 seemed a long time ago.

At the 1958 Convention of the Canadian Labour Congress, union leaders called for "a fundamental realignment of political forces in Canada . . . in a broadly based people's political movement which [would embrace] the CCF, the labour movement, farmer organizations, professional people and other liberally minded persons interested in basic social reform and reconstruction through our parliamentary system of government." A joint CCF-CLC National Committee for a New Party was eventually organized, and New Party clubs emerged, primarily among non-working-class strata in Ontario and Quebec. The recession of the late 1950s lent strength to the new movement, and within unions thoroughly alienated from the Liberals and Conservatives, but aware of the futility of endorsing the CCF, the threat of rising unemployment was also an inducement to action. The resistance of the old guard CCFers was slowly diminished: a Peterborough by-election won a federal seat for a New Party candidate in 1960; the Quebec Federation of Labour endorsed the New Party early in 1961; and T.C. Douglas, stalwart social democratic leader in Saskatchewan and provincial Premier, agreed to run as the New Party's federal leader.

Thus, social democracy was revitalized, the fall of the CCF giving way to the rise of what would soon be known as the New Democratic Party. Its founding convention took place at the Ottawa Coliseum, with over 2,000 delegates from unions, the CCF, and the clubs meeting in the summer of 1961. Wary of appearing to be a party dominated by labour, the first convention was nevertheless financed and orchestrated by those skilled in the practice of trade union organization. Moderation was essential to the existence of the New Party, as the interests of the old CCF constituency were to be balanced with those of labour and a new generation of socialists. A relationship of complete equality between the groups was not maintained, however. If labour gave the New Party its first impetus to move into the political arena, the experienced leaders of the CCF maintained their hold on the actual reigns of the New Party's political power, however democratically it was wielded.

Many members active in the New Party clubs, envisioning a movement dramatically different from the old CCF, never became members of the NDP they helped to bring into being. Others, like Saskatchewan CCF MP Hazen Argue, found the New Party tainted and linked with other political forces. Argue made a critique that seemed to affect social democracy's political fortune for a decade and more, prefacing his defection to the Liberals with these words of warning: "It would be most dangerous to the democratic process to have a party gain power, the effective control of which resided in a handful of labour leaders outside the House of Commons." Even in its most innocuous, subdued, and conciliatory formulation, the ability to resolve class distinctions remained the test of social democracy's success. Perhaps St. Laurent had been right when he characterized CCF partisans as nothing more than "Liberals in a hurry."

IMMIGRANTS AND INCOMES

There were substantial material reasons why neither social democracy nor a legitimized labour movement was able to move with much dispatch throughout the 1950s. Slowing the pace of these political and economic mobilizations, however much they were incorporated into the new Fordist regime, was the recomposition of the working class itself.

The rapid economic development of the post-war years, labour shortages in certain sectors resulting from wartime mobilization, and the low fertility rates of the depression era all led to increasing liberalization of immigration regulations. A wave of new immigrants flooded the Canadian labour market after World War Two. Between 1946 and 1961, well over 2 million immigrants arrived in Canada, and during the 1950s immigration played a central role in the growth of the labour force. Two-thirds of the labour force growth of the early 1950s was provided by such new Canadians, while in a less dramatic increase during the more economically depressed later 1950s, immigrants contributed to one-third of the expansion. By 1957, the number of immigrant arrivals (just under 300,000) approached the annual figures for the peak immigration years of 1910-13. In such metropolitan centres as Montreal, Toronto, and Vancouver the foreign-born population soared. Across Canada as a whole there were almost 800,000 more foreign-born residents in 1961 than there had been a decade earlier. As of 1961, foreign-born Canadians comprised 15.6 per cent of the general population, while their numbers increased almost 40 per cent over the 1950s, outpacing the natural increase of the native-born. Taking pre- and post-war immigrants together, one in five Canadian workers was born outside the country.

Two features of this new immigration are notable. First, the relative significance of British immigration declined markedly. English-speaking immigrants from the British Isles remained the single most important group in the post-war period, with approximately 475,000 coming to Canada in the 1950s. But the massive influx of Italian immigrants, commencing in 1951 and cresting in 1956-61 (and that would set the stage for Toronto later to be the largest concentration of Italians in the world outside of Rome), brought 250,000 new immigrants to Canada. In the late 1950s Italian immigrants actually outnumbered those from the British Isles. When these Italians are considered in conjunction with other groups such as the Greeks and the Portuguese, the important place of southern Europeans in the labour market of the 1950s and 1960s becomes clear.

The second notable characteristic of this new immigration was the extent to which it was destined for the workplaces of the country. Earlier waves of immigrants, after all, had at least in part ended up on the land. But farm ownership was even less of a possibility than it had been in previous decades and agricultural employment was shrinking fast in the post-war world. This decline would only accelerate in later decades: between 1951 and 1981 the percentage of the work force employed on farms plummeted from 15.6 to 4 per cent. Almost 90 per cent of the new immigrants of the 1950s were direct wage workers, with over 70 per cent located in the craft, mass production, service, and recreational sectors associated with the mixed economy of high Fordism. This extended far beyond the labour force involvement of native-born Canadians in similar occupations (57.8 per cent), and among labourers, as well, the foreign-born were overrepresented.

The lot of the immigrant was not an attractive one when compared with that of the Canadian-born worker. But for the immigrants themselves the positions secured in Canada usually represented an advance, so limited were the possibilities in the Old World they left behind. Still, in Canada, 48 per cent of the post-war immigrants earned less than $3,000 annually, which was near the poverty line for a family. Moreover, a wage hierarchy divided British immigrants from their less affluent Polish and Italian counterparts. In the former group, incomes of family heads in 1961 averaged $5,341, compared to the much lower $3,992 and $2,918 for the latter two immigrant communities. Only through the pooling of family earnings did non-British immigrants of the post-war period narrow the gap between themselves and the native-born in this realm.

To be foreign-born in Canada on the eve of the 1960s was likely to find oneself on the lowest rung of the wage ladder: in the metropolitan centres such immigrants earned, on the statistical average, at least $500 less per year than their Canadian-born counterparts. In this, they were not all that unlike the oldest Canadian immigrants (or, after aboriginal peoples, the first Canadians), the French Canadians. The average Québécois personal income in 1961 was $1,383, significantly below the national norm of $1,564 (and this far outdistanced the figures from Atlantic Canada, which ranged from Newfoundland's $934 to Nova Scotia's $1,197). For workers caught in such structural inequalities, daily life and identification with class demands or the labour movement's particular perspective would no doubt have been different than they were for the more prosperous native-born, who were also more likely to be unionized.

CLASS AND NATION: QUEBEC

Unionism in Quebec, as we have seen, was marked by the presence of national unions that provided workers with an alternative to the American Federation of Labor. The centre of this distinctively Quebec labour movement was the Confédération des Travailleurs Catholiques du Canada (CTCC), a body originating in religious difference. Most successful in the 1920s and 1930s, the CTCC was led by Pierre Beaule and attracted activists like Alfred Charpentier. A future leader of the CTCC, Charpentier carried the new "gospel" across the province in the early years of organizing. By 1939, the Catholic union centre claimed a membership of almost 50,000, 238 union locals, eighteen study circles, a like number of trade federations, seven regional groups, and twelve city centrals.

In the opening years of the 1940s, as Canadian labour struggled to gain legitimacy, French-Canadian workers became increasingly active in the class contests of the time. By 1943-44, the CTCC was involved in more conciliations and arbitrations with various state agencies (fifty-seven) than it had been in any five years throughout the 1930s: a record-breaking 154 strikes were fought in Quebec in 1942-43, involving 48,000 workers. Much of this activity was conditioned by escalating worker militancy, but corporate autocracy also played a part in the emergence of conflict. Large American-owned firms were not above a practised ethnocentrism, in which they expressed aversion to dealing with French-speaking Catholic clergy. On specific occasions they attempted to destroy all unionism and, failing on that count, encouraged workers to join international unions headed by English-speaking labour leaders.

As labour and capital in Quebec drifted toward an impasse in the 1930s and 1940s, Catholicism itself underwent a mild radicalization. The encyclical "Quadragesimo Anno" issued by Pope Pius XI in 1931 led to this development, establishing workers' rights to share in the profits of industry.

With the rise of Gérard Picard to the presidency of the CTCC in 1945 an older, more conservative generation of leaders was replaced: lay leaders emerged to take the place of priests. A group of aggressive young organizers, among them Jean Marchand, was recruited from Laval University and the traditional tie between Church and state was weakened as the newly reordered CTCC broke decisively from the Duplessis regime. In consequence, membership almost doubled between 1943 and 1948, when over 93,000 Quebec workers were enrolled in 428 *syndicats*, and some of the losses of the 1938-43 years were offset by new advances. By 1955, 100,000 Quebec workers had joined the CTCC unions, and 43 per cent of organized workers in Quebec were controlled by the Catholic unions. For the first time in almost forty years, moreover, these *syndicats*, although Catholic in form, were less closely linked to the Church. Non-Québécois workers diluted the traditional cultural homogeneity of the Catholic unions, weakening the hold of religion and strengthening more secular working-class concerns, while the inclusion of women altered the traditional character of the *syndicats*.

All these factors led to the militancy and confrontation that became a part of the industrial-capitalist transformation of Quebec. Over the course of the 1940s, employment in manufacturing in the province rose by 87 per cent, the value of output jumped 312 per cent, the volume of production climbed 92 per cent, and investment increased 474 per cent. Between 1939 and 1950 employment in manufacturing soared by 200,000, an increase in a mere eleven years as great as the gain in the entire preceding century from 1839 to 1939. Approximately 700 strikes were waged during this same period, or roughly 40 per cent more than were conducted in the two decades leading up to 1936. One of these strikes, the 1949 confrontation in the asbestos mines of the Eastern Townships, was an example of a type of conflict between labour and state-supported capital that revealed the new level of class polarization emerging throughout significant parts of Quebec.

As a fibrous and non-combustible product that could be employed in the making of fireproof fabrics and materials, asbestos gained commercial value throughout the 1930s and 1940s. By 1949, production in the non-Communist world was dominated by six producers in the Eastern Townships and their rivals in the Belgian Congo. The largest Quebec concern was the Canadian Johns-Manville Company, which created the town of Asbestos. Negotiations between the CTCC unions in the mining towns and the employers commenced late in 1948, the first contract in the industry expiring on January 1, 1949. According to the company representatives, the union demanded wage and working condition changes, the elimination of asbestos dust inside' and outside the mills, welfare provisions, recognition of the Rand formula, and the "takeover" of management rights. Capital and labour stood deadlocked well into 1949 and Quebec Department of Labour officials failed to effect a conciliation. With only two possible options – arbitration through legal channels or an illegal strike – the miners walked off the job in mid-February, 1949, blocking production in most mines in the region.

A militant solidarity combined with a festive sense of community to oppose state and employer. Over the course of the next four and a half months the workers battled provincial police and government condemnation as well as employer determination. Strikebreakers were imported, workers were evicted from company houses, and mass demonstrations and silent processions brought Quebec nationalists, intellectuals, and workers together in opening scenes of what would later be recognized as a "Quiet Revolution." Religious leaders spoke of the "dishonour to the province of Quebec" and proclaimed their opposition to the "conspiracy" crushing labour. By early May, community polarization and rising tension culminated in striker pickets and barricades by which the workers secured control of the town of Asbestos. Not until the Riot Act was read was "order" restored, but the resumption of legal authority was secured only through hundreds of arrests, police beatings of strikers, and a violent routing of the unionists that engendered much bitterness and resentment. More than a month and a half later a settlement was reached, but it was to prove an empty one for many of the strikers, significant numbers of whom were not rehired. "Blacklegs" who remained at work were liable to find their cattle slaughtered, barns burned, or windows broken. Perhaps psychologically gratifying, such acts of vengeance did little to win the disgruntled workers material concessions from the companies.

After five months of pitched battle, the workers were left with the bitter aftertaste of defeat. But they also gained significant successes, which would bolster the workers' position in the 1950s. There were signs, however faint, of English-Canadian labour's support for the strike, and the caricature of Catholic workers' conservatism and caution had been erased. Church leadership in the labour movement, and the links that this had forged among the clergy, the state, and the employers, was weakened; in the 1950s, the CTCC would remain a Catholic body, but the chaplain was more a religious figurehead than a union leader. The long-standing bond between the confessional unions and the Duplessis machine was also broken as workers came to recognize that the product of such an alliance was repression. By 1952 the CTCC launched an anti-Duplessis Political Action Committee. Asbestos 1949, for all that it cost the workers of the Eastern Townships, signalled the structural transformation of Catholic unionism.

Led by Picard and Marchand, Catholic unionists in Quebec continued to encourage the secularization and militancy first introduced in the 1920s and so evident by the time of the Asbestos confrontation. In conjunction with the Quebec-based CIO unions of the Canadian Congress of Labour, the CTCC presented the more radical face of Quebec labour. Together, these bodies claimed the allegiance of approximately 135,000 workers, but the craft associations of the Trades and Labor Congress, organized throughout the 1940s and 1950s in the Fédération Provincial du Travail (FPT), still remained numerically dominant with 130,000 members. All three labour organizations had been united in the Asbestos battle of 1949, but in the years after 1952 the FPT tied its fortunes to the Duplessis government and distanced itself from the increasingly radical and politicized wing of Quebec labour. A strike wave swept through the textile industry in 1952, drawing thousands of workers into the streets.

The new vitality of the Catholic workers' movement was apparent in the 1952 strike against the Montreal department store, Dupuis Frères, during which elderly, disabled, and female sales personnel waged a successful struggle for increased wages, the forty-hour week, paid holidays, and union security. As the company attempted to convert to a self-service operation and as Mayor Camillien Houde denounced the strikers as Communists, nationalists in the Quebec labour movement saw that Quebec capital was as oppressive and as exploitative as American or English-Canadian interests. Michel Chartrand, rising union spokesperson, pointed out that the CTCC would have no relations with those who "defended the French language while starving those who used it."

With the merger of the Canadian AFL-CIO forces in 1956, Quebec labour overcame some of the organizational and ideological division that separated leading sectors of the trade union movement in the 1952-55 years. The creation of the Quebec Federation of Labour (QFL) in 1956 was followed by the Murdochville steel workers' stike of 1957, in which combined CLC-CTCC forces were defeated by provincial police, hired thugs, and strikebreakers, and nearly bankrupted by legal costs. One worker died in the battle, and to this day steel workers in Quebec remember the strike as one of the first lessons learned in opposing repression. "Murderville," as they recall, told them much of what to expect in their dealings with employers.

As the regional economy succumbed to recession in the later 1950s, unemployment rose to over 8 per cent, but the decade as a whole saw the wage differential between Quebec and the rest of Canada narrow and the ranks of unionized workers expand modestly: between 1950 and 1960, the Catholic *syndicats* grew in membership from just over 80,000 to approximately 102,000. During this time of stable and moderate expansion, the CTCC opposed the Duplessis regime, reformed and secularized its organization, and worked for a more effective unionism that would enhance the bargaining power of its members. During the 1960s and 1970s, the Quebec working-class experience would reveal different features. Just as the Asbestos strike of 1949 signalled the end of an epoch in the history of Quebec workers' efforts, the conjuncture of the 1960s – where national and class aspirations and grievances fused to reorient workers' demands – transformed the character of class conflict in Quebec. In the process Québécois workers led their Anglophone brothers and sisters into a new epoch of rebellious challenge and political turmoil.

The early years of the 1960s witnessed the beginnings of change. Duplessis and the Union Nationale were displaced as the Liberal Party consolidated its electoral strength. The revival of the economy after the recession of the late 1950s simply accelerated the trend toward industrial-capitalist development and urbanization. Finally, within the labour movement itself, Marchand led the CTCC decisively away from its religious origins. In 1961 the organization was officially renamed the Confederation of National Trade Unions (CNTU). Although this change was motivated largely by secularization, it may also have resulted from Marchand's desire to reassure Pearson's Liberals. By affirming the autonomy of the Quebec unions, he succeeded in checking the drift toward amalgamation with the AFL-CIO unions that had been evident since the 1956 merger and that would have linked the CNTU to the recently established New Democratic Party.

By 1965, then, the long-standing rivalry between national and international unionism within the province resurfaced with a vengeance and consolidated around a growing hostility between the CNTU, now led by Marcel Pepin, and the internationally based QFL, headed by Louis Laberge. The latter secured a rare independence and autonomy within the CLC on the grounds that his own unions in Quebec were constantly threatened by possible raids and that international unionism in the province was engaged in a constant battle with the CNTU. In 1964 alone, the QFL lost 10,000 members to the CNTU, and over the course of the 1960s the Confederation grew rapidly, from 80,000 to 250,000 members.

This tremendous expansion was the product of more than simple raiding tactics. Indeed, it was linked to the weakening of the CNTU's Liberal ties and its advocacy of militancy on the economic front, reform in the social arena, and radical nationalism in political action. Many factors contributed to the abandonment of the Liberal Party, including political corruption, anti-labour action, and the inability of federalists to placate the grievances of Quebec nationalists. As Trudeaumania swept the country in the late 1960s many of the CNTU members recalled the new Liberal leader's words to Montreal's mail-truck Lapalme drivers – "Mangez la merde." Once enrolled in the CNTU, *les gars de Lapalme* resisted poor pay and long hours, forming a co-operative company and winning a mail-delivery contract. But their efforts in the late 1960s collapsed as the post office split their contract among a group of new companies. Trudeau's brusque words of dismissal let these and other protesting workers know that they had little to look forward to from a politician whose career had been, ironically, so closely linked to labour's much-heralded awakening in the Asbestos strike. As radical nationalism flourished in the mid-1960s, concentrated in the Rassemblement pour l'indépendance nationale (RIN) and the post-1963 rise of the Front de Libération du Québec (FLQ), alternatives to bargaining within existing political structures grew more and more attractive to militant workers. Grouped around Michel Chartrand's radical core in the Montreal Central Council of the CNTU, militants supported extra-parliamentary forms of social, cultural, and political action.

Far more democratic than international unions, CNTU locals retained more of their dues at the local level, possessed greater independence of action, and were less bureaucratic and centralized than their AFL-CIO counterparts. They supported a range of demands that extended beyond the workplace, backing the McGill-Français movement, opposing the nuclear arms race, condemning American involvement in Vietnam and imperialist aggression around the world, and demanding the release of imprisoned FLQ leaders Charles Gagnon and Pierre Vallières. With thousands drawn to this eclectic attempt to address class and national questions, Quebec became the syndicalist centre of direct action in North America, and the CNTU the voice of a broad amalgam of unionists, the unorganized, the unemployed, tenants, and consumers. Rejecting the outright endorsement of the social democratic NDP, the CNTU of the late 1960s sought mass mobilization on three fronts: job action and collective bargaining efforts; pressure group activities to address specific consumer grievances; and, finally, political opposition to structures of power, especially those operating at the municipal level. The CNTU also lent its support to cultural attempts to reconceive the social order, stimulating co-operative buying and selling of goods, establishing publishing co-ops that provided books and mass-circulation newspapers to the developing movement, and financing films and literary works of social and political worth.

Nevertheless, the perennial problem of institutional fragmentation remained, and the CNTU and QFL continued as distinctive bodies. The massive repression of the October Crisis in 1970 galvanized working-class unity as much as it stimulated radical resentment. When workers at *La Presse* struck in October, 1971, they were supported by a violent demonstration of 14,000. Chanting "This is only the beginning," the crowd overturned police barricades to vent their rage at the economic and political system seen to be controlled by Montreal Mayor Jean Drapeau, Premier Robert Bourassa, and the Power Corporation. Less than a year later, the prophetic note of that 1971 chant was thrown in the face of authority. A Common Front composed of the CNTU, QFL, and the Quebec Teachers' Corporation embraced nationalist and socialist demands and, on March 9, 1972, rejected government offers of a 4.8 per cent wage increase for all public-sector workers. Two hundred thousand workers responded with a one-day general strike on March 28, 1972, openly defying state directives to remain on the job. On April 10, after days of fruitless negotiation, the Common Front pulled its members from the province's schools, hospitals, government offices, and other public-sector work sites. "Never again will we be divided," declared Laberge.

But this unity was destroyed as the state moved to crush the incipient rebellion. The Common Front was legislated back to work and the three leading figures within the Common Front alliance (Pepin, Laberge, and teachers' leader Yvon Charbonneau) were jailed. Disputes erupted within the workers' movement as some claimed that the actions of March-April, 1972, were the utmost in extremist folly, destined to lead to frustration, demoralization, and defeat. As in 1919, lack of programmatic direction and the immense weight of authority of the state defeated the general strike.

The Common Front revealed the potential of the working class to control the social and economic structures of the entire province of Quebec. At Sept-Isles, St. Jerome, and Montreal, workers seized the reigns of authority in the workplace, liberating themselves from traditional restraints. Equally significant were the Common Front's demonstration of the force of public-sector workers and the volatility of this previously overlooked stratum in the event of confrontation. Indeed, across Canada to varying degrees, the question of public-sector unionism was, by the 1970s, raising perplexing questions for politicians and unionists alike. What was an essential service and what curbs could be placed on working-class rights in these economically and politically crucial areas? What was the working class when it seemed that it now wore white collars as often as it donned workshirts and overalls? And how did the increasing feminization of certain kinds of work associated with government employment and the service and welfare sectors affect the workers' movement?

These and many other questions were raised by the explosion of labour militancy in Quebec in the 1960s and 1970s. In Quebec and across the country, white-collar and public-sector workers, Francophones as well as Anglophones, would add new strength to trade unionism's potency, at the same time that they revealed the limited impact that organization could have in specific job classifications and the power of the state to curb working-class initiatives in particular realms. Quebec's labour upheaval and political turmoil captured national media attention and riveted eyes on the unique and particular oppressions of French-Canadian workers. But in other parts of the country, too, the 1960s and 1970s gave rise to rebellious challenge as a youthful revolt rocked not only the usual pillars of political and economic life, but an increasingly staid business unionism as well.

YOUTH, POPULAR CULTURE, AND ENGLISH-CANADIAN NATIONALISM

The Canadian labour force, like Canadian society in general, grew younger over the 1960s and 1970s. People between the ages of fifteen and twenty-four accounted for little more than 15 per cent of the country's population in 1951, but by the mid- to late 1970s the figure jumped to 19 per cent. In the decade and a half between 1961 and 1975 the numbers of youth participating in wage labour rose dramatically. The percentage of wage earners in the

14-19 and 20-24 age brackets rose from 36 and 69 per cent, respectively, to 51 and 76 per cent. Throughout the 1960s and 1970s the average annual participation rate increases of workers under twenty-five years of age were between 4.4 and 5.3 per cent, outpacing the average annual labour force increase of just over 3 per cent. This lent an increasingly youthful appearance to the Canadian working class: almost one in four of all working Canadians were between the ages of fourteen and twenty-four in 1978.

Some of the youths entering the labour market for the first time in these years continued to live with their parents, sustaining the family's capacity to consume in the face of inflation. For a time this family strategy, so reminiscent of nineteenth-century, pre-World War Two, and immigrant forms of adapation, allowed the family unit a piece of "prosperity," although this was often somewhat illusory. However, job satisfaction was low. A work ethic survey undertaken by the Department of Employment and Immigration found that young workers under the age of twenty were the least satisfied with their jobs, while in the 20-34 age group there was a notable gap between work aspirations and realizations: as more and more young people crowded into a finite number of jobs, the possibilities for "advancement" were constricted.

Within this context of limited potential, youthful grievances found an outlet in cultural developments of the 1960s and 1970s that placed an accent on youth and libertarian anti-authoritarianism. Popular culture, in these decades, fused home and workplace requirements in a populistic assault on the "establishment," an imprecise target that seemed to include the older generation and the bastions of social and economic power, both of which seemed rigidly separate from the experiences of the young.

The anti-establishment wave gained momentum with Elvis Presley, whose "white" version of black musical style galvanized youth across North America. None, perhaps, were so enchanted as Presley's own people, the migrants from the South who, together with black Americans, manned the assembly lines in automobile plants in Ohio and Michigan. Presley's 1950s Canadian tour was followed by other entertainers and in the 1960s British rock groups and American folksingers (all of whom, like Elvis, drew on black jazz and blues artists) followed in his wake. New fashions, scientific advances in birth-control methods, a loosening of the ties of sexual prudery, and drug experimentation paralleled the transformation in music that was at the centre of the emergence of a counter-culture.

Much of this culture was apolitical, extended well beyond class boundaries, and only supported the consumerism of a capitalist order promoted as pluralistic. But at the same time, in its essential questioning of social convention and defiance of established authority, developments within popular culture easily drifted toward a more explicit challenge. One sociological study of sexuality and family planning among low-income urban Québécois married couples revealed how much had changed in the tradition-bound relations of the sexes. Before 1969-70 two-thirds of all pregnancies were unplanned and a mere 25 per cent of women used contraceptives after marriage or the first pregnancy; in the 1970s, however, 86 per cent of these couples were using some method of birth control, and half the women were taking oral contraceptives. Finally, the emergence of the New Left in Canada, with its explicit ties to the American civil rights movement and opposition to the war in Vietnam, was related to the general cultural climate of dissidence, although it attempted to focus previously incoherent or unarticulated strands of opposition into a more direct challenge.

The rise of a popular culture centred on youth and open expression of discontent was often perceived as a product of campus rebellion: the expanding number of university students necessarily attracted attention to those in the classroom rather than the workplace. But even at the height of university enrolments, less than 20 per cent of all Canadians aged eighteen to twenty-four were students, and young workers were caught up in many of the same activities and processes of change that swept so prominently through the ranks of post-secondary school institutions.

Within Canadian unionism, for instance, a rank-and-file membership that came of age after the anti-Communist purges of the 1940s and 1950s was less loyal to its leadership than workers of another generation. Younger workers were simply less likely to identify closely with an entrenched labour bureaucracy whose accomplishments in the recognition struggles of the post-war period or the economic and job condition gains of the 1950s meant less to them than they had to their fathers and mothers. Moreover, with unions expanding in size (by 1970 well over 2 million Canadian unionists paid dues of almost $100 million) and with international offices far removed from Canadian memberships, some youthful dissidents accused the labour movement of being top-heavy and centralized. The results would be felt throughout the 1960s and 1970s.

By the mid-1960s, for instance, illegal wildcat strikes were commonplace: in 1965-66, 369 such struggles were waged in defiance of union leaders. Many of these battles were epic confrontations that won workers considerable concessions from capital. Throughout these tense moments of conflict, workers fought their employers, the state, and their unions, rejecting contracts, fighting police, and defying court injunctions. Typical of the complex levels of developing antagonism were strikes of Hamilton and Sudbury workers and Montreal longshoremen in 1966. Negotiations at Inco were disrupted by a 16,000-member wildcat that union officials subdued only after weeks; nevertheless, it helped to win Sudbury's miners the highest rates in North America. When the contract was eventually approved, however, only 57 per cent of the unionists were in favour of a settlement. To the south, in Hamilton, worker discontent erupted in a violent clash at the Steel Company of Canada, where workers fought police and union leaders, destroyed property, and won themselves a reputation for militancy and the highest steelworking wage in the world. On the Montreal docks, the first illegal strike in years was fought by dockers resisting the stevedoring companies' demands that new cargo-handling machinery be used and gangs reduced in size accordingly. Similar developments on the railways forced Parliament to guarantee 18 per cent wage increases before it ordered strikers back to work, and 12,000 postal workers led one of the largest nation-wide wildcats in the 1965-66 upheaval, partly improving the depressed wage environment in which they earned $3,000 less than policemen and firemen of comparable seniority and $2,000 less than unskilled labourers employed by municipalities such as Vancouver.

Three features stand out in the wildcat wave of 1965-66. An unpublished essay by Joy McBride notes the extent to which this was a revolt of the young, how it was directed against all levels of constraining authority (employer, state, and bureaucratized union), and the resulting tendency of conflict to culminate in violence. The tone of this rank-and-file rebellion was captured nicely in a later statement by a railway wildcatter:

> We've got three enemies, the company, the government, and the union. We can't beat them all now, but we're starting something. It's the young guys that are responsible for this. They started it. If it weren't for them, we wouldn't be here now. They're different. They're fearless. They don't give a damn for the company or the government or the union. It's a new generation. . . . We're our own boss now.

Young workers were directly singled out as the cause of the Stelco and Inco wildcats, and managers at Ford's Oakville plant, the DuPont operation in Kingston, and Montreal's Domtar Packaging all agreed that youthful "hotheads" were responsible for precipitous walkouts and violence. "Always before we could talk reasonably [at the bargaining table]," noted one company official in Winnipeg, "but there are some younger men on the committee and they don't have the experience." Managers threw up their hands in despair as young workers led wildcat strikes at the drop of a hat: adherence to the norms of industrial legality crumbled as workers walked out over demands for free lemonade or milk rations and against muddy walkways or no loitering signs in plant washrooms. Signs of the times, these "reasons" for striking were nothing less than the inconsequential tip of an iceberg of alienation, resentment, and class tension. Plumbers in Midland, Ontario, and labourers in a Saskatchewan potash mine had the temerity actually to tell the truth. According to their union representatives these workers failed to show up on the job simply because they did not feel like working that day.

The situation in Canadian industry in the mid-1960s was thus slipping out of control as work discipline and organized labour's capacity to govern its memberships appeared to collapse. In the absence of the usual regulatory constraints, strikes took on a particularly "wild" character. Typical of contemporary descriptions of these conflicts was a newspaper account of a four-day "quickie" wildcat at Hamilton's Stelco plant:

> Mob rule shut down the sprawling works of the Steel Company of Canada Limited, putting 16,000 persons out of work. Wildcat strikers defied and mobbed their union leaders, shoved police aside and closed off access to the company's plant and offices. . . . The strike appeared to be well organized, but neither the union nor the company could identify those behind it. Some attributed it to young hotheads, others to communists and still others to a group of Canadian autonomists within the union.

Time and time again union leaders, four out of five of whom were between the ages of fifty and seventy, were booed, threatened, cajoled, even manhandled by their young memberships. Trade union hierarchies allied themselves with municipal authorities, the companies, and local media in an effort to cool down their rebellious ranks; during the Stelco walkout, USWA officials urged police to shut down all taverns in the vicinity of the plant to curtail the solidarities emerging in meeting places that bypassed official union structures. A union official involved in the attempt to contain the Inco wildcat confessed how far out of control the situation was: "I saw the molotov cocktails, the guns and the dynamite. The union lost control of the situation. Eventually we took truckloads of arms of one kind or another away from the picket lines."

What emerges from this brief picture of the 1965-66 upheaval (and much more similar evidence presented by McBride) is a sociological profile of working-class rebellion paced by youthful exuberance, the emergence of semi-autonomous structures of working-class self-activity, and a history of grievance and frustration vented not only against the company but also against the union and the extent to which it accepted so fully the penchant for discipline and order at the core of the post-World War Two regime of industrial legality. As militants stoned the house of a boss, setting the surrounding grounds on fire, or drove a union official into the protective custody of the police, it was not surprising to hear labour leaders charge that their members were not "playing their proper role as both workers and union members." That was entirely the point: *proper* roles were being cast off.

In other areas, too, this process was evident. Young workers of the 1960s were also members of the youth-oriented mass culture of these years and, as such, showed open hostility to bureaucratic structures and impersonalized relations. Ironically, much of the imported American dissident culture of the time led Canadians to embrace nationalism as a protest against the American "establishment." Among trade unionists, however, the immediate issues were not the lack of Canadian content in television and radio, the high levels of foreign ownership in the resource and manufacturing sectors, or the number of non-Canadians staffing university faculties. The main issue was that perennial point of contention, international unionism. Within the Canadian labour movement in the 1960s and 1970s the national question was manifested in breakaways, and a new round of internecine warfare splintered the already divided forces of Canadian trade unionism.

Since the 1920s, a strictly Canadian labour movement had been espoused by some in the trade union movement. By the 1950s, two key figures in the drive to organize workers into autonomous Canadian unions were Kent Rowley and Madeleine Parent. Driven from the United Textile Workers of America in a 1952 purge of a dozen Canadian staffers accused of "disastrous and irresponsible leadership" and "Communist" leanings, Rowley and Parent countered by setting up the Canadian Textile Council (CTC), an organization established during the UTWA years when they anticipated their expulsion. The CTC provided a base for the organization of national textile unions independent of the AFL-CIO, with Brantford, Ontario, acting as a centre of recruitment to the fledgling movement. But throughout the 1950s, progress for the nationalists in the labour movement was limited, and Rowley, Parent, and their followers gained little support until the populist and poorly conceived nationalism of the Diefenbaker years (1958-63) and Liberal Finance Minister Walter Gordon's anti-Americanism of the early to mid-1960s helped revive working-class concern with the national question. By the mid-sixties a number of Canadian locals left American unions to found small independent Canadian bodies.

Rowley orchestrated the founding of the Council of Canadian Unions in 1967, later to be known as the Confederation of Canadian Unions (CCU), a central body offering a home to those national unions that broke from the AFL-CIO-connected Canadian Labour Congress. The Canadian Textile Council was expanded to become the Canadian Textile and Chemical Union (CTCU), and in 1971 Rowley and Parent led a strike at the Brantford Texpack plant. The strike drew public attention to their crusade for national unionism and fused a number of dissident strands into a coherent moment of challenge and opposition to American capital and its incursions on Canadian social and economic life.

The Texpack struggle erupted in the aftermath of an American takeover of the Brantford plant in the 1960s. A large American multinational, the American Hospital Supply Corporation, planned to phase out production at the Ontario factory, using the facility as a warehouse for distributing goods produced in U.S. and Asian plants, repackaged, and labelled "Made in Canada." The more than 300 workers, many of them women, thus stood to lose their jobs or be channelled into unskilled, low-paying warehouse work. Picket lines at the Texpack plant were thus aimed at resecuring jobs as well as educating the Canadian working class as to the dangers of the branch-plant economy.

Unionists affiliated with some American internationals, such as the steel workers and the auto workers, supported the Texpack struggle, as did the nascent women's movement and the left wing of the New Democratic Party, the Waffle. Countless young new leftists were also drawn to the daily skirmish outside the Brantford plant, and local police battled picketers with riot gear and paddy wagons that seldom left the scene without arrested strike supporters. Sympathetic academics took their places beside angry workers, while lawyers refought the day's battles in later courtroom confrontations. In the end, the workers at Texpack won a new contract that would preserve their jobs for the remainder of the decade. Labour unity and youthful support won Rowley and the cause of national unionism an important victory.

Less successful, but equally brutal, was the Artistic Woodwork strike of 1973, where an unorganized immigrant shop was won to the CTCU only to have a dictatorial management insist on a contract clause that surrendered any vestige of worker autonomy. As in Brantford, young and old leftists, as well as many in the political centre, united with progressive unionists to back the strikers. The owners of the picture-frame factory eventually capitulated and the strike was won. But in the immediate aftermath, victory was turned to defeat: management hounded unionists, foremen threatened leading activists, and the CNTU Artistic certification vote ended in the crushing of the union and the demoralization of the workers.

Texpack and Artistic involved struggles of workers affiliated with national unions. In both instances, the powerful and established international bodies had shown little interest in organizing these troublesome sectors, where chances of victory were slight and the benefits of drawing such "marginal" workers into the trade union mainstream few. But the nationalist mood of the late 1960s and early 1970s probably saw more influential developments within international unionism itself, where discontent with American labour leadership led to breakaways from Canadian unions. Outside of Quebec the hegemony of international unionism in the Canada of the mid-1960s was unambiguous, with 71 per cent of all organized workers in the country belonging to American-affiliated unions; eight of the ten largest unions in Canada were internationals. One part of the wildcat strike wave of 1965-66 was undoubtedly fuelled by discontent with the distant and bureaucratized leadership of these Washington, Detroit, and Indianapolis-based unions. Matters worsened as wildcat strikers were denied strike pay or clashed with union officials who attempted to force unwanted contracts on them. By 1970, Ed Finn, prominent labour figure, would note that there was a growing "nationalist sentiment among Canadian unionists," and "Unless the internationals heed these incipient rumblings and grant effective self-government to their branches in this country, the next decade could see a titanic – and ultimately successful – struggle for Canadian union emancipation."

At the time Finn wrote, there were a mere 124 independent organizations of workers in English Canada supported by less than 60,000 workers, who represented under 3 per cent of the unionized labour of the country. But over the course of the 1970s the national question refused to go politely away, and breakaway movements and raiding made the issue important to labour, particularly in the West. Members of the International Brotherhood of Pulp, Sulphite, and Paper Mill Workers seceded amicably to form the Pulp and Paper Workers of Canada, while fifteen locals of the Retail, Wholesale, and Department Store Union in Saskatchewan successfully disaffiliated. Between 1970 and 1975, the membership of the CCU more than doubled, and the union joined forces with the Canadian Association of Industrial, Mechanical and Allied Workers (CAIMAW) and the Canadian Association of Smelter and Allied Workers (CASAW). CASAW led one of the largest successful raids on an international union in the early 1970s, winning jurisdiction rights over the 1,800 Alcan workers in Kitimat, B.C., whose previous affiliation had been to the USWA. CAIMAW, formed in 1964, grew slowly and sporadically over the course of the 1960s and into the 1970s, attracting some 6,000 members to its ranks. These largely western breakaway movements were supplemented by eastern developments within Toronto's immigrant construction-worker community in the Bricklayers, Masons, and Plasterers International Union and among chemical and oil workers in Montreal and paper workers in Ontario. By 1978 national unions unaffiliated with the CLC had managed to secure some 665,000 members, or roughly 20 per cent of the organized workers in the country.

Aside from the national question, more and more Canadian unions took on national colouring as public-sector unionism expanded in the 1970s. With the rise of various public employee alliances and unions in the post-1960 years the old American-based internationals, which often treated the entire country north of the 49th parallel as little more than a state federation of labour, were less dominant in the Canadian Labour Congress. The workers' movement, as a consequence, took on new kinds of strengths and weaknesses.

NEW STRENGTHS FOR AN OLD MOVEMENT

Organization in the public sector dates at least from 1889 when railway mail clerks first formed an association. This early effort was followed by various federal government employee attempts to forge a moderate sense of collectivity in 1909; organization began among the letter carriers and postal workers in 1891 and 1911, respectively. The latter groups would initiate a more militant public-sector unionism, eventually breaking from other government employees and the tradition of associations to set up the Letter Carriers Union of Canada and the Canadian Union of Postal Workers.

Together they claimed a membership of 36,000 by the end of the 1960s. That decade, moreover, would see the first wave of conflicts in the public sector, serving as a preface to the even more wide-ranging upheavals of the 1970s.

Civil servants, including British Columbia and Saskatchewan government employees, customs officers, and a wide range of Quebec workers, were adamant in demanding the rights of collective bargaining by the early 1960s. They constantly ran into strong opposition from the state, summarized in the haughty response of political authority that "The Queen does not negotiate." Postal workers, however, took the first steps in letting the Queen's advocates in Ottawa know that this stand had to end. They nurtured a weak recollection of a history of combativity that originated with their support for the Winnipeg General Strike and a 1925 work stoppage broken by some of their own members. In 1965 the postal workers defied the government, the moderate leadership of their own employee associations, and public outrage to extract a wage settlement, launch the Canadian Union of Postal Workers (CUPW), and begin the rise to prominence of Jean-Claude Parrot. As the post office introduced automation and the government sought to turn the workplace into a Crown corporation (a plan not to be realized until the 1980s), workers endorsed more militant leaders and continued to demand humane treatment and economic justice.

All of this pushed the state to respond with a Public Service Staff Relations Act in 1967 and two accompanying bills. They conceded bargaining rights to the postal workers and other civil servants, but the Act defined union jurisdictions in ways that insulated the state from rank-and-file action. The right to strike and even the parameters of negotiations were severely circumscribed, to the point that there was great pressure to avoid explicit conflict and settle disputes through arbitration. What the state had done was offer its increasingly unruly employees bargaining rights and wage concessions, at the same time that it curtailed what the new unionism in the public sector could actually address, actively organize around, and accomplish. What it gave with one hand, it guarded well with another. Still, some 260,000 government workers now had rights they previously lacked.

No doubt the state acted as it did because its arms were being twisted. Aside from the postal worker militancy of 1965 it faced threats from another quarter. Months before the passage of the 1967 legislation, two workers' bodies that resembled company unions renounced their government "staff associations" to create a more aggressive and united organization, the 120,000-strong Public Service Alliance of Canada. By the mid-1970s it would rank, along with another public-sector body, the Canadian Union of Public Employees, among the very largest worker organizations in the country.

As far as combativeness was concerned, however, the posties were still the shock troops of change, the one body of public-sector workers that consistently challenged the state. Given the stressful working conditions experienced by inside postal workers, who were ordered about by military-type supervisors and "would-be postmaster 'generals'," the resentments of CUPW members were understandable. In 1969 they initiated a work-to-rule campaign, and by 1975 postal workers had waged some thirty job actions and strikes directed at issues of technological change, job security, hours, and pay. The introduction of automatic mail-processing, based on the postal code, thrust CUPW into the role of arch-opponent of an economistic dehumanization: sorters working on the automated system were being paid fifty cents an hour less than manual sorters, in spite of an obvious speed-up of their work. Losing the battle against the code, CUPW remained sufficiently strong to stop the mails in 1975 and win some concessions in hours and wages from the state. Amidst charges of "irresponsible elements" within its leadership and condemnation of its supposedly "illegal actions," the union succeeded in increasing its membership.

Other public-sector bodies grew as well, most notably CUPE. Between 1963 and 1973 it doubled its membership, attracting thousands to its ranks every year. In mid-1975, with 210,000 supporters, it became the largest union in Canada. A significant part of this growth can be attributed to its efforts to organize hospital workers in the 1960s, many of whom were denied the right to strike by provincial legislation. These health workers threatened to take to the streets in a 1974 illegal defiance of the Ontario Hospital Labour Disputes Arbitration Act, presenting, like their Quebec counterparts, a common front to various hospital boards. Wage increases were eventually won, often without recourse to strike action, and the 1974 campaign to secure "catch-up" pay increases for hospital workers encouraged nurses to join the rebellion. In New Brunswick, Nova Scotia, B.C., and Manitoba, nurses demanded settlements similar to those won in Ontario. Like Ontario's secondary and elementary school teachers, whose unions totalling 105,000 members struck schools in December, 1973, these workers discovered their place in a class society and expressed their discontent openly. Challenging the legalistic restrictions that had circumscribed their protests in the past, hospital workers and teachers defied the barriers of "professionalism" to demand legitimate status within the Canadian labour movement. They would suffer through denunciations, state opposition, and attempts to sabotage contract negotiations as they joined thousands of federal, provincial, and municipal civil servants struggling to improve their lot in the mid-1970s.

The organizational explosion in the public sector was, of course, paralleled by similar developments in more traditional union strongholds, and militancy was also evident among blue-collar workers, where it often assumed different forms. Moreover, the motivations for the union drives and workplace actions of teachers, health-care workers, and civil servants were not unlike those causing building tradesmen, railway labour, and factory operatives to strike. Double-digit inflation, which was officially 12 to 13.5 per cent by 1974-75, reduced purchasing power and led to rising worker demands. Strikes and walkouts increased greatly and by the mid-1970s were consuming 0.53 per cent of all working time. Demands needed to be great to catch up to runaway inflation. Railway workers struck for a 38 per cent wage increase in 1973, only to be followed by strikes of Ontario hospital workers and public employees seeking settlements that included provisions for 45 to 60 per cent pay increases. White-collar labour, new to the union scene, literally had to follow suit if anything approaching an acceptable living standard was to be maintained.

Many of the workers in the public sector embracing a militant stand for labour in the 1960s and 1970s worked in job settings dominated more by white-collar than by blue-collar employees. Few fit the image of the archetypal proletarian. Yet, as studies by David Coombs and Graham Lowe reveal, the early years of the twentieth century saw the erosion of status and privilege associated with the prim and proper "black-coated" worker, traditionally a male ally and confidant of the employer. As an administrative revolution altered the corporate structure of Canadian capitalism in the early twentieth century, the modern office, staffed by a newly created stratum of clerical workers subordinate to managerial authority, emerged as a central component of the economic order. Between 1901 and 1961, white-collar work rose from a relatively insignificant place among the occupational groups making up the total labour force to a position of dominance, encompassing almost 40 per cent of all Canadian workers. By 1971 the clerical subsection of white-collar workers was the largest occupational grouping in the country, with over 1.3 million working members.

In the workplace experience of these clerks, two developments were of paramount importance. First, the feminization of clerical workers meant that whereas 22 per cent of those employed in this sector were women in 1901, 60 to 70 per cent of all clerical workers in the 1960s and 1970s were female. As a female job ghetto, then, clerical work was particularly subject to the low wage structure that capital found easy to rationalize. Second, office work was itself increasingly fragmented, routinized, and restructured through automation. Before the advent of microtechnology, white-collar workers were in greater demand, and employers often used the possibility of career advancement as a means of encouraging employees to work for lower wages. But by the 1970s this illusion was no longer necessary. As one business school professor remarked: "White collars are where administrators look to save money, for places to hire. It's the law of supply and demand. Once you're in a big supply, you're a bum."

Such developments led to generally deteriorating wage conditions. In 1971, clerical workers in Canada saw their wages relative to those of other workers decline 10 per cent. Their take-home pay was only 70 per cent of that of their counterparts in other work sectors. By the early 1970s the "white-collar blues" became a much-discussed issue, and one CLC officer noted that "most large offices are nothing but quiet factories." Subjected to the same insecurities and tedium as factory operatives, white-collar workers had become part of the working class.

The history of office-worker unionization began in the 1940s when the Steel Workers Organizing Committee lent support to bank clerks' efforts to organize under the auspices of the Office and Professional Workers Organizing Committee. Clerks worked in what CIO-organizer Eileen Tallman described as "Neanderthal" conditions. The patriarchal hold of the banks was so firm that even male bank clerks earned meagre weekly earnings, and their personal lives were monitored to the extent that they were not allowed to marry until their annual salaries rose to approximately $1,500. Bankers apparently felt that this amount would enable the workers to assume family responsibilities and provide for their dependants without "dipping into the till." Rebelling against these restrictions, tellers organized locals in Toronto, Vancouver, and Montreal and struck against two banks in the latter city, where young clerks took home only $8 to $12 weekly. Opposed by managers and priests, this first bank strike was crushed, and the office and professional workers' union behind it disappeared, its essentially male leadership drawn off by wartime armed service recruitment.

By the late 1940s the leading role in organizing white-collar workers passed to the Retail, Wholesale and Department Store Union. After establishing a base in a few dairies, bakeries, and a food chain in 1946, the RWDSU began to organize employees at Eaton's, Canada's third-largest employer and a force that was keeping wages low in the retail field. Dedicated CIO organizers Lynn Williams and Eileen Tallman worked on the Toronto-based Eaton's drive, which turned on the demand of equal pay for equal work. Struggling to overcome a segmented work force, in which employees were distinguished by gender, age, wage, and a multitude of job classifications, the organizers learned that the response to unionism varied from one group to the next. Across the spectrum of departments, Williams and Tallman found that a segmented labour force conditioned a fragmentary cultural context that created barriers to unity. Women in part-time sales, working for "extra" family income, were difficult to organize, as were prestige salesmen in heavy appliances or long-time employees selling fine china goods to an established clientele. Drivers, pressured and structured into persistent overtime, however, were strong union advocates.

Between 1948 and 1952, Eaton's Toronto stores were leafleted, and, as in the industrial union struggles of the 1930s and 1940s, cultural activities were set up to draw workers to the cause. The "Mugwump," a cartoon or *papier mâché* caricature of the worker who could not decide whether or not to join the union, was created to demonstrate the urgency of decisive action and commitment. Banquets, dances, and social affairs were held, all of which proclaimed openly the existence of pro-union forces and broke down long-entrenched relations of subordination. Williams created a forty-four-team league captained by organizers, each of whom had a weekly membership objective. Gains were being registered by the young CCF organizers, but they encountered difficulties as union supporters moved on to other jobs. (Labour turnover at Eaton's approached 35 per cent of the staff yearly.) In addition, the company was gaining support through wage increases, the creation of a pension plan, and opposition to the collectivist orientation of the union. Eaton's stalled union certification proceedings until the Christmas season of 1951, when workers were busiest and thousands of casual labourers were hired for a few weeks. Such developments provided the company with a substantial number of workers who would be apathetic enough to fail to vote for unionization. When the votes were tallied the union lost by a mere 800 ballots, almost 9,000 having been cast. Later efforts came to little and a historic opportunity to win union rights for the workers of a major white-collar employer led to nought.

The defeat of the Eaton's campaign symbolized the constricting potential for white-collar workers that would prevail throughout the 1950s and much of the 1960s. Not until public-sector unionists moved to the forefront of organized labour in the mid-1970s was interest in white-collar organizing revived. The CLC led a well-financed attempt to recruit office workers to the Association of Clerical and Technical Employees. But barriers remained, including what Michael Katzemba has described as the fear of "trouble" that is a significant part of the psychology of the office. ACTE was able to enlist only 7,000 new members. The percentage of unionized offices actually declined from 7 per cent in 1975 to less than 3 per cent in 1976. Since most of the work force in these white-collar sectors was actually female, the history of class and gender once again came together in a conjuncture of central importance to the workers' movement.

WOMEN: AT HOME AND AWAY

The twentieth century has witnessed a shift in attitudes and practices regarding women and wage labour. Once defined as a stage in the life cycle between two phases of dependency (childhood and marriage), and an undesirable interlude at that, female involvement in paid labour has now become commonplace in contemporary Canada, with large numbers of women working in manufacturing, service, and sales occupations. The female participation rate in the labour force climbed from 16.2 per cent in 1911 to almost 40 per cent in 1971, much of the increase (a virtual doubling) coming between 1941 and 1971. Whereas 832,000 Canadian women worked for wages in 1941, over 3 million were pursuing waged work at the beginning of the 1970s. Such figures point to the partial elimination of traditional prejudices and barriers blocking entry to wage labour, but they mask certain critically important social and cultural realities. For women have always worked, if not for wages, providing a force sustaining working-class households and experience for decades, even centuries. Often casually employed or marginalized in outwork, it has proven particularly difficult to place women in the usual occupational classifications. Given to voicing their discontents at the workplace by leaving one job to secure another (often the only option for workers who lacked union protection and legal recourse), women workers' visibility has been clouded historically by the high turnover rates in specific work sectors. To discuss women and the working class, however, is to recognize more than the expanding place of women in the labour force and the problems that intrude on analytical and empirical work in this area. It is also to understand the pivotal role women have played in reproduction – through child-bearing and child-rearing, as well as in unpaid domestic labour – and in the political economy of the family.

Until the 1940s the bulk of women employed in wage labour toiled as laundresses, sweatshop workers in the garment industry, or factory operatives in light manufacturing, producing goods like boots and shoes or textiles. As the clerical work force expanded, women came to dominate the office, and female employment possibilities widened with the expansion of health care that paralleled the rise of the welfare state. Domestic service, the nineteenth century's major female occupation, declined as women were drawn to these more "liberating" jobs. World War One drew many married women into the labour force and, for a brief moment, invalidated long-cherished notions of the distinctions between men's and women's work. A similar process occurred during World War Two, when state and employer welcomed some women into the ranks of a labour force depleted by male recruitment to the armed forces. But even in the war-induced "emergency" situation of the early 1940s, as Ruth Pierson has argued, the confinements of domesticity hung over women's entry into wartime industry. Young single women were recruited first, childless married women next, and finally and reluctantly, mothers. Day-care facilities were established to ease the burdens of this last group. By 1943, more than 250,000 women worked in industrial pursuits of strategic importance to the war effort. Countless others laboured in the service sector and worked in agriculture: teachers and female students over the age of fifteen formed the majority of the almost 13,000-member Farmerette Brigade, whose hard labour at twenty-five cents an hour did much to keep the country and its soldiers fed.

As in the aftermath of the Great War, many of the gains made during the war period were eclipsed with the return to a post-1945 "normalcy." In industrial cities like Hamilton, where women had worked at Stelco, National Steel Car Company, Westinghouse, and Sawyer Massey, work in the primary sector was never completely redefined as a male preserve, but a series of pressures – from the state, the employers, and returning veterans –

constricted opportunities and undermined the sense of women's independence cultivated in the war years.

The family, not the factory, re-emerged as the centre of women's lives and, as Hugh and Pat Armstrong have shown, the 1950s and 1960s saw women segregated in occupations designated unofficially as female. On occasion, as after the defeat of striking Paris, Ontario, women workers at the Penmans mills in 1949, women's movement back into the family was a consequence of a brutal capitalist assault on female working-class militancy. Joy Parr argues that as the 1950s opened Paris's mill families had come to distrust "class-based actions as a way to bring about social change." Instead, they "turned back for meaning in their lives to the gender- and community-based solidarities" that had nurtured them for decades. What they would find there, however, was limited and limiting.

More than half of employed women in the immediate post-1950 years worked in traditional feminine spheres of service: typists, maids, teachers, waitresses, nurses, telephone operators, tailoresses, clerks, and janitors were the dominant women's occupations. As women workers who were thought to be peculiarly adapted to such maternal service-oriented tasks, they earned approximately half the income of their male counterparts and only in rare circumstances did women's wages approach 75 per cent of those of men. Poorly paid, such women workers were conventionally seen as duplicating at work what they were supposedly physically and temperamentally suited to in the home.

More women entered the labour force than men during these years and married women became more likely to seek employment, so that the proportion of single women in the work force declined from 80 per cent of all female workers in 1941 to 34 per cent in 1971. However, throughout most of the post-war period, women's working lives were characterized by subordination and poor pay at the same time that their domestic situations were similarly circumscribed. If unmarried, the woman could support herself and such dependants as she had only through rigorous budgeting and underconsumption. Married women contributed to the family wage but they seldom did so as the equal of men, whose earnings, on average, made their wives' paycheques appear paltry indeed. In spite of increasing numbers of women who gained entrance to the professions, the sociological literature reveals that a gender-based structural inequality still predominated from 1950 to 1970, the years when vast numbers of women entered the labour force.

This material context structured women into dependency on men, a process that must be seen as the material foundation of the underside of family life. Less a haven in a heartless world than a site of all the contradictions of modern capitalist society, the family could be a social unit of survival and adaptation, a place where resources and support networks were shared and developed to cope with the problems of everyday life. But it could also be the embodiment of inequality and violence, as it had been throughout history, with wife-battering, child abuse, and cruelty figuring in its ugly underside. While such domestic violence reaches across class divides, there is no question that in Canada as elsewhere the particular oppressions and exploitative core of working-class life contribute greatly to masculine identities asserting themselves, at times, in aggressive acts of physical intimidation and worse.

Employers could easily claim that they had no responsibility for these problems, but the low wages, alienating jobs, and unemployment that worked in their interests could not help but feed into family violence. Such employers, of which the government was among the largest, successfully secured a pool of inexpensive labour because of wage differentials based on gender. They envisioned that this underpaid and underemployed work force would remain compliant as long as the sanctity of the family remained intact. Thus, there were concrete pressures to stay out of the sphere of the family, thereby reinforcing the notion of the domestic realm as the private refuge of individuals, untainted by public scrutiny and intervention. Capital and the state perpetuated a conception of the family and of women's maternal role within it that was little more than a rationale for low wages and patriarchal authority.

To look at the 1940s and 1950s is nevertheless to see the extent to which these decades mark an important transition in gender, family, and class relations. On the one hand, the continuity of powerful ideologies of the family and appropriate gender roles is evident in this period. But so, too, on the other hand, are there hints of challenges and resistance that would build slowly and intersect with the emergence of a women's movement in the mid-1960s.

In a study of female cotton workers in Quebec between 1910 and 1950, Gail Cuthbert Brandt delineates a movement away from the traditional two-phase life cycle of the 1940s, in which single women worked in the mills until their early twenties and left the work force upon marriage. Women moved between two cycles of dependency: as young workers they handed their wages over to their parents; when married, they were engaged in unpaid domestic labour and child-rearing, and relied on their husbands' earnings. After 1940, however, more workers were practising family limitation, higher wages allowed earlier ages of marriage, and women workers' life cycles took on a more complex structure. Young women worked for a shorter period before marriage and, after a finite period of child-rearing, returned to the work force as married women, supplementing the family income and expanding the consuming potential of the conjugal unit. Between 1941 and 1951, there was thus a decline in the labour-force participation of female cotton workers in the 25-34 age bracket, and a 40 per cent increase in the proportion of workers aged forty-five years and older. A study of the entire Quebec female labour force by Nicolas Zay contains similar findings. Meg Luxton's oral histories of three generations of home workers in the one-industry town of Flin Flon, Manitoba, demonstrate how housewives in the years 1940-59 experienced the modernization of domestic labour, "financing" the purchase of household commodities through babysitting, taking in boarders or laundry, sewing, providing services such as haircuts or Tupperware parties, and carefully budgeting the husband's wage.

These tendencies, in conjunction with the rapid dismantling of employment opportunity and child-care facilities in the aftermath of World War Two, suggest the extent to which women were moved back into the nuclear family. Female cotton workers, Brandt argues, faced technological changes and workplace disciplines that eroded what little autonomy and few skills they possessed in the 1920s and 1930s. As their youthful working lives were shortened through marriage and they could only return to work in middle age when the working-class family finally reached an economic plateau, women conceived of themselves as a transient, family-oriented stratum of the labour force. Their concern with the social aspects of collectivity and working-class solidarity in general, and unionism in particular, was correspondingly diminished. In Luxton's study of Flin Flon, it is not so much a sense of class that emerges from her "second generation" of housewives who established their families during the 1940s and 1950s. Rather, the development of a community of women is most visible. Their ties to each other, consolidated through moments saved by washing machines, improved kitchen technology, and the mechanization of cleaning, were ultimately forged within a family mediated by the realities of working-class life, but clearly affected by changing patterns of consumption that blurred class distinctions. Fordism deepened many distinctions at the same time as it proclaimed the end of one vital difference: class.

In failing to fight adequately the segregation of women in the most menial and ill-paid work sectors, and in perhaps acquiescing to if not adopting much of the familial ideology of the times, the labour movement itself bore some of the responsibility for the general drift toward an insular, family-centred culture of consumption in the 1950s, when the man's wage often provided women with money for housekeeping, while women's wages, when earned, were easily characterized as "pin money." Mass culture, the appearance of a measure of working-class affluence for some, and the economic climate of buoyancy in the late 1940s and early 1950s lent such developments force, but capital, not the working class, would reap the final rewards, as one strike in northern Ontario demonstrated.

The largest industrial dispute in the 1950s was the Inco strike of 1958 in Sudbury, a three-month confrontation that pitted 14,500 workers and their families against the mining company, which lost almost 700,000 worker days to the strikers. Affiliated with the International Mine, Mill and Smelter Workers (a survivor of the anti-Communist purges of the 1940s), the Sudbury workers and their union were crushed in what one workingman later described as "a premeditated smashing of the union." An indecisive union leadership failed to develop a co-ordinated strike strategy and appeared to be alienating the rank and file with its undemocratic and arbitrary stifling of discussion in union meetings. A Women's Strike Committee was formed to pressure the company and the union, formalizing the supportive role that many wives and mothers had been playing since the beginning of the strike. Two months of demoralization and suffering pushed the confrontation in a new direction.

Inco, which had built up large inventories, let the strike run from late September into early December without even making an offer to the union. Then, after saving almost three months in wages, it initiated a new phase of "negotiation." Company spokesmen, the mayor of Sudbury, and officials from surrounding communities orchestrated a huge rally at the Sudbury arena. Two thousand women attended, some ostensibly urged to go by their priests. There they heard appeals to their "protective instincts . . . a basic quality of all women here today." This was to prove a variant of Betty Friedan's "feminine mystique" of particular use to capital.

Whatever the forces behind the arena rally, there can be no doubt that within the community and among the striking miners there was a strong sense of familial pressure to settle and get back to work. One Mine-Mill official described the denouement: "During the strike I am quite sure the company realized there was an opportunity to give the union a real good shaking. They mobilized an awful lot of the community notables, so to speak. They got the wives to speak against the union. They were in a position of strength." Calling for a settlement at pre-strike wages, demanding that civic officials intervene to end the strike, and asking the company to assume its appropriate paternalistic responsibilities by providing relief to alleviate distress in the district, the mobilized wives defied a vacillating and inept union leadership in the interests of the family. "This is a meeting of wives," they proclaimed. "Our men are booed down or forced, physically, out of [the union] hall if they ask questions. How do they propose to shut the women up." Even if some wives remained staunch in support of the strikers, this wifely construction of the Mine-Mill leaders as intimidatingly coercive and the overt public questioning of the masculinity of union leaders who could not silence women in the same physical ways that they shut up their male members were effective ways to undermine a strike obviously gone wrong.

In the days to follow, the media made much of the rebellion of the wives, the state was drawn into the conflict, and tensions mounted within the striker community. One unionist assaulted another for causing his name to be removed from Mine-Mill's welfare list. "He took the bread out of my kids' mouths," he stated in explanation. The miners eventually returned to work for a paltry 6 per cent wage increase over three years, what one union official described as "a few pennies more." Worse, morale among the workers was destroyed and the cause of unionism blackened. Inco had won an unambiguous victory.

As an unpublished study by Bill Pentney notes, miners were defeated partly by the intervention of the wives, whatever the forces manipulating them to act. Of course, there were other factors at work: economic recession, corporate power, and a faction-ridden and indecisive union leadership, among other things, tilted the balance in capital's favour. All of this, set within the family-bound context of the 1950s, may well have resulted in workers and their wives opting for a course that looks, at first glance, to be eminently conservative. But it would be wrong simply to dismiss the Sudbury wives of 1958 as only a force buttressing capital's rule. That, to be sure, was the short-term consequence of the particular ways in which wifely concern was mobilized and manipulated. But the wives' assertiveness represented something of a rebellion against the confines of domesticity and femininity, a restatement of social values that had particular relevance within workers' experience: the right to work; the calling to order of a company that was perceived to be wielding its power in an irresponsible manner. And in riding so thoroughly roughshod over the strikers, Inco perhaps erred in winning too total a victory, when a more magnanimous, benevolent win would have secured them a longer-lasting, and hegemonic, hold over their workers. As one worker opponent of Mine-Mill, affiliated with the rival Steelworkers, remembered, "I think the company, in the long run, lost the strike because people had a great determination, a great hatred for the company." Some of the hatred was no doubt held by wives. Twenty years later, during another strike at Inco, wives would prove a force sustaining militancy and class resolve, reversing the stand that their counterparts had taken in 1958.

Strikes, some of them wildcats, were fought at Inco in 1966, 1969, 1974, 1975, and 1978-79, the latter being the longest conflict in the history of Sudbury miners. Led by local militant Dave Patterson, this last battle turned on issues involving wages, conditions, and grievance procedures, and won the workers union securities and a substantial hourly rate increase. But the costs were also high, including 261 days during which they had drawn no wages. Millions of dollars of support from the United Steelworkers of America sustained them, on one level, but equally important, perhaps, was the militant solidarity of the entire working-class community.

A miner expressed this sense of unity in a letter to the *Globe and Mail* that condemned Inco's anti-labour stand: "They had misread the workers' will to fight for a decent living wage. . . . The whole exercise was designed to lower the pride of the ordinary workers, to teach the pensioners a lesson for daring to picket Inco's Toronto office and to restrict the effectiveness of stewards to obtain redress for aggrieved workers."

An exemplary role was played by the strikers' wives, who formed a support group called Wives Supporting the Strike. Unlike the 1958 Women's Strike Committee, this group won the allegiance of many women who feared the conflict would disrupt family life and wipe out the little security that employment provided. The Wives Supporting the Strike overcame the insularity of the family to develop collective aid, organizing babysitting co-operatives, car pools, mass suppers, and educational groups that provided new knowledge of the issues at stake in the conflict. Women picketed and joined women's demonstrations in Toronto. The actions of these women led to a new awareness of the ways in which cultural and political issues could combine with struggles in the workplace in an attempt to establish a more humane society. One woman expressed the new sense of elation she had discovered:

> I'll never be quite the same again. Now I have a vision of another day. I guess I learned that ordinary women like me can fight a big multinational company like Inco and win – can challenge the government. . . . I learned that there are other ways of organizing our daily lives, ways of living as a community together, ways of being husbands and wives that I never imagined before. . . . Maybe all together, we could make a better world.

The evolution that occurred in Sudbury between 1958 and 1978 can be understood only by examining the development of the women's movement as a whole. During these years the movement was revitalized after half a century in which it had lain somewhat dormant in the aftermath of World War One. In kitchens, offices, universities, and industrial plants, the question of woman's role became, once again, a topic of discussion. A diffuse and eclectic amalgamation of individuals and groups, the women's movement extended beyond class at the same time as it exercised a powerful post-1960s influence within trade union circles.

Women remained less unionized than men in the early 1970s, with 43 per cent of male workers belonging to unions compared to just 27 per cent of female workers. Great provincial variations further complicated this differentiation, with Quebec and British Columbia having the highest degree of unionization among women, Ontario and Nova Scotia the lowest. Yet in spite of the generally poor record in this regard, the rate of unionization among females increased markedly between 1966 and 1976. The number of women unionists more than doubled to over 750,000, while women rose from 17 to 27 per cent of organized labour. In the growing public-sector organizations women became a considerable presence. CUPE's 1976 membership of almost 220,000 was 41 per cent female, while in PSAC, various provincial employees' unions, nurses' associations, retail clerks' unions, and internationally affiliated organizations like the ILGWU, women comprised from 40 to 100 per cent of the membership. Put another way, the number of male unionists increased by 40 per cent between 1966 and 1976, while the ranks of female members soared 160 per cent. Representation of women on union executives in this period, however, was still negligible. Wage gaps were hardly lessened, and women's employment failed to penetrate the high-wage, thoroughly organized construction, manufacturing, and transportation sectors. The record of women and unions in the immediate pre-1975 years is thus one of unmistakable advances and distressing continuities.

Both in their homes and in their workplaces, then, female workers experienced profound changes in the 1960s and early 1970s. Moving away from the insular, family-centred constrictions of the 1950s, they fought their way into the labour movement and redefined the very notion of collectivity. An older woman in Flin Flon (born in 1891) spoke to Meg Luxton of her own experiences and what they told her about historical process:

> Women's politics are like an iceberg. Only the tip shows and it never looks like much. But underneath is a vast mass of women, always moving, usually very slowly.... When I was young, women didn't even have the vote. Well, we thought about that and it didn't seem right so finally lots of women got together and worked for it and now we got the vote. Most people assume women will put up with things the way they are. But that isn't so. When women see a thing needs changing, things change.

This woman was undoubtedly overly sanguine, and history reveals that working-class gains are usually won and preserved only through struggle, constantly renewed and defended. If workers were to implement change in the sixties and seventies, it was apparent that battles at the workplace were insufficient. A politics of change was also required. For that, at the level of mass politics at least, workers had only one readily available option, the New Democratic Party.

THE NDP: A LEGACY OF CLASS AMBIVALENCE

Throughout the 1960s and early 1970s, in its first fifteen years of existence, the NDP operated in ways that recall its predecessor, the Co-operative Commonwealth Federation. The continuities between the two political formations were marked from the very beginning, when the new party's share of the popular vote in 1962, its first federal campaign, was 13.5 per cent, roughly the same as that captured by the CCF in 1949. The NDP did, however, manage to gain six more seats, electing nineteen MPs. But support came from the old radical CCF constituencies in Toronto, northern Ontario, Cape Breton, Winnipeg, and British Columbia. Tommy Douglas's defeat in Regina was a humiliating blow, reminding the NDP that the struggle for power was a much more problematic process than the dream of victory. As

Diefenbaker's confused mishandling of the nuclear arms question alienated his cabinet and Canadians in general, casting the country into another election in 1963, the NDP was forced to fight another costly campaign and lost ground to the Liberals.

In the provinces the picture was even more discouraging, with the NDP failing to preserve CCF seats in Manitoba, falling behind an innovative Conservative, John Robarts, in Ontario, and missing a major opportunity to advance in British Columbia, where the old CCF working-class strongholds of the Lower Mainland seemed unenthusiastic about the arrival of the new party. The worst defeat lay in the loss of CCF forces in Saskatchewan to the Liberals in 1964. Three brief years after its founding, the NDP, like the CCF in 1958, had failed to secure a broad base of support.

In the years that followed the NDP returned to the hard work of organizing in the local constituencies and built the support it mistakenly assumed to exist from the beginning. Gains were registered in 1965-66, and particularly in the industrial cities of Ontario, working-class voters were won to the NDP. Pierre Trudeau's dramatic and popular emergence as leader of the front-running Liberals slowed the NDP federally, but provincial victories attested to the developing strength of the new social democracy and its capacity to govern. The accent was on youth and new leadership (precisely the same constellation that challenged bureaucratic unionism and worked so well for the Trudeau Liberals). Ed Schreyer consolidated Manitoba's ethnic communities around the NDP and opposed old-line traditional parties with a program that included medicare, government-controlled automobile insurance, more public housing, and better roads. It was a mixture of New Deal-type liberalism and Swedish social democracy, but it won Schreyer, then thirty-three years old but a veteran campaigner with a decade of political experience behind him, a narrow victory in 1969. Canada acquired its first New Democratic Party government.

Some party members were opposed to what they regarded as Schreyer's unambiguously socialist campaign, a reflection of how diluted the NDP commitment to and understanding of socialism had become. Others, in what came to be known as the Waffle movement, were advocating a more explicitly radical program that turned on nationalist rejection of things American, including, of course, internationally affiliated unions. Wafflers harangued party leaders, challenged their socialist commitments, demanded new agendas, and treated the labour hierarchy with disdainful contempt. If the Waffle had to choose its class side, it would align with rank-and-file rebels in the unions rather than the upper echelons of the labour bureaucracy. The NDP, of course, had precisely the opposite set of allegiances.

What stands out in both of these developments within the NDP is the ambivalence of class politics within social democracy in the 1960s. To be sure, Schreyer's victory was in good part bankrolled by union contributions, although party coffers would also be filled by small businesses and large corporations, especially through undeclared donations and advertising in the party newspaper. So concentrated was Manitoba's workers' movement in Winnipeg that the provincial NDP necessarily depended electorally as much on Schreyer's "rural touch" as it did on a pro-labour stand. The first provincial NDP government was at least as much a creation of the votes of Ukrainians, Franco-Manitobans, and native peoples as it was of workers.

During this time, Wafflers, with their fixation on the national question, drove stalwart old-line labour leaders, whose histories were forged in the intimate relations of the CIO-CCF in the struggles of the 1940s, into defensive cul-de-sacs in which the only option seemed the outright repression of a faction described by the Steelworkers' Larry Sefton as "pathological." Former Ontario NDP leader Stephen Lewis recalled acrimonious meetings at the Ontario Federation of Labour building called to discuss whether the Waffle should be dissolved and banned or whether some compromise with its presence in the NDP could be tolerated. Sefton told Lewis that "he and others had fought for this party, built it, fought the Communists in the trade union movement, had brought it to this point today," and that the Waffle had to go. Lynn Williams treated Lewis like Inco; "he just wasn't moving an inch," recalled the younger Lewis. The trade union leaderships forged in the loyalty tests of the Cold War and the hard-nosed realism of industrial legality were used to operating in a specific way. In the end the trade union tops got their way: the Waffle was expelled and the majority of its members went on to found the Movement for an Independent Socialist Canada. The Waffle episode, stretching from the late 1960s into 1972, was over.

As Stephen Lewis pleaded for relief from Ontario Wafflers who dogged him at public meetings to question his credentials as a socialist and a nationalist, two successful western provincial campaigns finally silenced the radicals' demands for a more resolute nationalist stand. In Saskatchewan, Allan Blakeney led the NDP to a decisive 1971 victory, reviving faith in the potential of the old CCF farmer-labour alliance. A year later, social worker Dave Barrett resuscitated the flamboyant non-conformism that was once a staple in British Columbia politics and, in the context of unemployment and a sagging resource sector, defeated Social Credit pillar, Premier W.A.C. Bennett.

Provincial victories recast the role of the NDP as something more than a perpetual loser, while the Waffle banishment publicized the pragmatic, non-radical nature of the party. This provided the background to the NDP's 1972 federal election campaign, in which David Lewis effectively assaulted the rich companies, styled as "corporate welfare bums" living on Liberal Party largesse. With public sentiment now moving against Trudeau, the Liberals were nearly defeated. When the votes were counted, Trudeau survived, but only barely: his party won 109 seats, the Conservatives 107, while Social Credit elected fifteen members and David Lewis's NDP held the balance of power with thirty-one members and 18.1 per cent of the popular vote.

Workers benefited from these social democratic victories as western NDP provincial governments introduced legislation that raised minimum wages, protected jobs, and restructured the machinery of labour-capital relations. Labour representatives were hired into government administration and in provinces such as Ontario close links were forged with major unions, including the Steelworkers and the United Automobile Workers. But such NDP electoral wins and the consequent reform legislation and policy were sustained by the relative prosperity of the late 1960s and early 1970s. A new period broke toward the end of these years, signalling a devastating onslaught on the material standards of Canadian working-class life.

By 1974 spiralling inflation that settled into an average annual rate of 13 per cent ate away at worker income. As the Liberal minority government fell in 1974, working-class voters seemed forced to choose between the Liberals, who campaigned against wage-and-price controls, and the Stanfield Tories, who demanded them. Trudeau's posturing brought results: a Liberal majority was secured easily and the NDP suffered a serious setback, its share of the popular vote declining three percentage points and its elected representatives nearly halved, to sixteen. Further provincial defeats in British Columbia (1975) and Manitoba (1977) were not long in coming. So, too, were wage controls. Trudeau, who once characterized controls as "a proven disaster looking for a place to happen," now gave them that very space, establishing an Anti-Inflation Board limiting over four million workers to wage increases of 8 per cent for inflation and 2 per cent for increased productivity. When the three provincial NDP premiers in the West acquiesced to the anti-inflationary controls at the same time as federal leader Ed Broadbent and Ontario's Stephen Lewis opposed them, it seemed the NDP talked tough when in opposition but carried a rather small stick when in power.

FORDISM AND THE CANADIAN WORKING CLASS, 1940-75

The years 1940-75 stand out in the historical experience of Canadian unionists as ones of accomplishment, victory, and prosperity. For the first time ever organized labour managed to force some semblance of security from capital and the state, with the result that many of its ranks could actually settle into lives where stability was not undercut at every turn. To be sure, the main beneficiaries of these years were English-speaking, male unionists in the trades and mass production, many of whom worked in traditional strongholds of regional and industrial privilege. Many workers, from one end of the country to the other, through their lack of union affiliation, inability to maintain a public recognition of their skill and worth, regional location, gender, ethnicity, or race, remained outside of some of the advantages these years bequeathed to sectors of the Canadian working class. And yet there is no denying how different this period was from past contexts. "The post-war settlement worked for us," one immigrant trade union official active in the anti-Communist purges of the 1950s recalled from the vantage point of the early 1980s.

These years of high Fordism have left their imprint on the historical record as working for all kinds of Canadians. To complement the benefits afforded unionized workers by the new regime of industrial legality, the post-World War Two welfare state consolidated a range of other securities: universal family allowances and old age pensions unencumbered by shame were introduced; unemployment assistance was implemented; there were the beginnings of a move toward public health care with the Heagerty Report of 1943; and attempts to establish effective public housing for the needy were taken. All of this continued through the 1950s and gained increasing force and recognition in the climate of the 1960s, when state-sponsored and promoted "wars" on poverty offered considerable aid to the indigent, the handicapped, and youth. What organized labour received with the high wage and collective bargaining rights, those excluded from its ranks appropriated through the widening channels of the state's welfare programs.

In fact, these twinned developments of industrial legality and statist welfare contained and constrained as much as they provided security. The "rights" of organized labour meant little if industrial discipline was not observed and if the contending class parties of the capitalist order were not accommodated to the respectable rules of the new regime. Contractual obligations, union responsibilities and the policing of organized workers, managerial rights, and the patriotic duty to suppress communism as a voice within the workers' movement all loomed rather large in the making and sustaining of industrial legality.

Nor did the recipients of the largesse of the welfare state simply appropriate their slice of the socio-economic pie without cost. Entire regions, known for their capacity to mount irksome campaigns of political protest, were structured into dependency on federal grants and economic power, just as the cushions of allowances and unemployment/health care systems demanded of recipients a certain logic of accommodation to the structures of state authority. For the poor, access to the safety nets of the welfare order came much easier if the fall from respectability did not pitch the unfortunate into a closed corner from which no program could provide an adequate escape.

All of this had been bankrolled by an expansive economic growth that saw rising exports, increasing U.S. investment, and, from 1947 on, Canadian successes in reducing tariffs and lessening quotas on resources entering the lucrative American market. By the early to mid-1960s, U.S. policies – spending on Vietnam and on social programs – stimulated the Canadian economy even more, and the reduction of the value of the Canadian dollar simply enhanced the attractiveness of export potential. Declining U.S. energy reserves and the signing of the Canada-U.S. Auto Pact in 1965 reinforced this trend toward strong surpluses in Canadian merchandise trade.

There were, of course, downturns in this upward spiral of economic advance. Inflationary pressures mounted, first in the late 1950s and again in the early 1970s, signalling the ways in which the post-war economic boom necessarily undermined the state's penchant for stable fiscal and monetary policies. Deficits clearly had to be managed and the marriage between Keynesianism and an economy tilted heavily toward the export of staples contained some problematic contradictions. When the Bank of Canada tried to resolve some of the resulting dilemmas by implementing policies aimed to curb rising inflation it pitched the country into its first post-war recession in the late 1950s, setting the stage for the labour militancy and wage demands of 1965-66. The consuming potential of the working class in the late 1960s, coupled with the North American expenditure on guns and butter (Vietnam and social programs), did put the crisis of social Keynesianism and the Fordist regime of accumulation on hold for a few more years.

By the mid-1970s, however, the socio-economic indicators were clear. Understated official unemployment rates climbed to over 6 per cent in 1971, a figure not registered since the recession of the late 1950s and early 1960s. Inflation, meanwhile, continued apace, driven by external global forces and internal Canadian government policies and domestic developments: the consumer price index was rising at a troubling rate comparable to the boom years 1948 and 1951. This unprecedented conjuncture of high rates of unemployment *and* inflation, which had historically diverged (in 1948 the consumer price index percentage change was a whopping 14.4, but the unemployment rate was a minuscule 1.6; by 1975 the comparable figures were 10.8 and 6.9), spelled the demise of the post-World War Two regime of accumulation, in which high wages, working-class "affluence," and the "benevolence" of welfare and industrial legality secured labour and capital their respective stabilities.

Fordism in crisis necessitated a state response. It was not immediately forthcoming. Troubled by the immediate ravages of unemployment, which have a way of affecting electoral politics far more directly than the incrementally debilitating erosions of inflation, the state initially eased monetary policies and increased the money supply, which rose substantially between 1970 and 1973. Locked into two- and three-year contracts, many unions saw inflation eat away at their wage packages. By 1974 the level of strike activity was rising as workers sought "catch-up" contracts. Between 1973 and 1976 the state addressed the entire social security system with a federal-provincial review of the provisions of Canadian welfare.

All of this coincided with a deteriorating international recessionary context, which saw decreased demand for Canadian exports and a rising deficit that reached a record high in 1975. The state was impaled on the multiple horns of a many-sided fiscal crisis. Programs were cut back, and, as we shall see in the next chapter, challenges were raised against the single most powerful group of Canadians now scapegoated as responsible for pushing inflation to new heights: organized labour. The rhetorics and rationales of the mid-1970s began to take on a new, combative tone; new directions were being charted. Keynesianism was dead; the Fordist regime of accumulation and its attendant class relations had run their course. In the fallout from this process Canadian workers were to see their institutions, their standards of living, and their social place undermined and denigrated in an onslaught of state-directed, employer-endorsed attack.

Chapter 7

HARD TIMES: ECONOMIC DOWNTURN, THE STATE, AND CLASS STRUGGLE 1975-1991

THE SOCIAL FORMATION

For many – organized workers, the trade union hierarchy, and the federal and provincial bureaucrats who concerned themselves with labour relations – the post-war years had been, with some minor interruptions, a long boom of success. The conscious embrace of Keynesianism was never as full and as unambiguous as many economists assumed, and large capital and its highest placed political advocates viewed the welfare state as something less than a mixed blessing, but this reality has been lost in a mythology of the 1950s and 1960s as decades of liberal progress and social advance. It is surely something of an historical irony that, by the early 1980s, most commentators were convinced that the Keynesian revolution fundamentally altered class relations in the advanced capitalist economies of the Western world when, in fact, the only sustained and principled champions of Keynes were the trade unions and their political arm, reformist social democratic parties. These were the very forces that came to power incompletely and sporadically, usually in times of economic belt-tightening. In Canada, as elsewhere, this was a scenario unpropitious for the realization of the Keynesian vision. Similarly, the unspoken logic of Fordism was appreciated most directly by labour and its defenders, for whom full employment, the high wage, "responsible" unionism, and the payoff of working-class consumption were the *sine qua non* of the good life. Yet Fordism's strongest backers were seldom in a position to realize its program of class harmony.

What must be appreciated in any assessment of the Keynesian/Fordist history of the 1940-75 years is the two-sided nature of this period and its class relations. On the one hand, as outlined in the last chapter, the prosperity growing out of monopoly capital's consolidation and its imperialistic conquest of the globe enabled capital and the state to concede much to a working class whose combativity was generally tamed and domesticated. Yet, on the other hand, the price of class harmony was always paid in the controlled currency of *limited* Keynesianism/Fordism, the exchange made by ruling authority with considerable reluctance and always with an open eye to other priorities. At the time, the price exacted from capital and the state seemed, to labour leaders and much of the Canadian working class, an extremely high one, well worth the incremental concessions and structured industrial legality demanded by old class adversaries. As long as the price continued to be paid, in short, the post-war settlement stuck.

Throughout the years stretching from the end of World War Two into the mid-1970s the myth was propagated, until it achieved something of the stature of a natural state, that under the new Keynesian/Fordist regime of accumulation full employment and its attendant security of working-class income would prevail at the top end of the business cycle, interrupted only by short-lived slumps. Keynesianism/Fordism was believed to have produced a steady state of prosperity and economic boom, punctuated by slight downturns of quite limited duration. For two decades this actually approximated economic reality, the distortions of the military-industrial complex and the Cold War's spendthrift on-and-off-again détente only becoming apparent with American capital's defeat in Vietnam. However much Canada was simply along for this essentially American ride, the ultimate consequences always trickled down to a northern continentalist political economy intricately related to the world power to the south.

In terms of class relations the outcome was that the working class and its central organizations, the trade unions, lapsed into a complacent confidence. As Paul Kellogg has suggested, this confidence was expressed in the view that since all workers could find jobs and register income hikes in the era of Keynesianism/Fordism and its dominant material buoyancy, there was no necessity for trade unions to struggle for anything other than the sectional interests of workers in specific jurisdictional areas. The job of the unions was to look after their own rather than to link all workers together. Samuel Gompers's age-old strategy of getting "more, more, and then more" for certain workers was generalized as it never had been in earlier, less secure times. This worked, after a fashion, as long as the slumps were minor and the long boom continued.

By 1975, however, the slumps were anything but minor and it was not economic boom but economic downturn that exhibited the most pronounced tenacity. Canada was no exception. With double-digit inflation running parallel to business slowdown, with official unemployment persistently approaching 10 per cent, with state-declared recession occurring with greater frequency than the more politically profitable periods of good times, and with markets for Canadian products and resources unsure in a precariously unbalanced international order, the years 1975-90 signalled the end of the Keynesian/Fordist era. A state of class harmony gave way to a state of siege: as the economy dipped, the unions found themselves under severe attack. Their confidence in the illusory and limited program of state-embraced Keynesianism/Fordism left them, moreover, relatively defenceless. All that organized labour regarded as normal crumbled in a class war waged from above. The 1980s would be hard times for workers.

These hard times had their origins in the economic unravelling of the long boom and its descent into a spiralling downturn. They were signalled first and most loudly by a mid-1970s state assault on trade union rights and freedoms as established in the immediate aftermath of World War Two, and deepened in the practical alliance of capital and the state throughout the 1980s, a unity premised on the need to contain and ultimately crush working-class resistance. These materially induced hard times drove workers to an economic wall they had not faced since the 1920s and 1930s, and the ideological climate shifted dramatically against labour with the rise of the New Right, which registered gains politically on all levels: provincial, federal, international. Finally, throughout all of this the conventional leadership of the working class seemed capable, both economically and politically, of launching only the most rearguard of actions, with the result that the voice of working-class opposition was muffled and weak.

Even among non-working-class supporters of labour on the left, many began to abandon the working class and champion other, more fashionable, sectors. The pivotal place of the working class as an agent of social change was, in the climate of hard times, increasingly challenged, if not denied – feminists, ecologists, and others took its place. Within the labour movement itself this trend was reproduced among a layer of the trade union hierarchy, where labour-progressive coalitions were promoted in the name of "social" unionism. Seldom, however, did such coalition-building register decisive victories, and more than one alliance of labour and other reform-minded groups ended in acrimony and mutual distrust. Hard times undermined workers economically, fragmented them politically, and assailed them ideologically.

The Keynesian/Fordist climacteric was exposed in the working-class militancy of the mid-1960s. After more than a decade and a half of relative class stability, the aggressive explosion of youthful resistance and the organizational breakthroughs in the public sector culminated in wage gains that many policy-makers considered a serious threat to economic well-being. As the Liberal government's economic advisers assured the state that full employment had been achieved by 1965, inflation was soon regarded as the major development undermining the fiscal order. Kept well in check throughout the 1950s, inflation inched upward over the course of the 1960s: measured in terms of percentage changes in the consumer price index, it stood on the verge of cracking the 5 per cent barrier by 1969, the first time such heights were reached since the post-World War Two/Korean War years of 1948 and 1951. Both unions and corporations seemed intent on pushing the Keynesian/Fordist regime to its limits, convinced that the state would intercede to stifle the ill effects of rising labour and consumer costs. Attempts were made to do just this, but they proved largely ineffective, in good measure because so much of the inflationary surge within the Canadian economy was a product of its reliance on external goods and because the state proved incapable of tackling the twinned evils of inflation *and* unemployment.

This was accentuated when the runaway inflation of 1973-74, induced by crisis in the Middle East and the quadrupling of oil prices, pushed the capitalist economies of the West into a recessionary plunge. In Canada the rate of increase of gross national expenditure dropped from 7.5 per cent in 1973 to just over 1 per cent in 1975. Canada's competitiveness in the manufacturing sector dipped dramatically in this same period as relative unit labour costs rose substantially, peaking in 1976. Early attempts to stem this problematic tide through monetarist practices aimed at curbing rising unemployment only exacerbated the situation by increasing the money supply, lowering interest rates, and strengthening the Canadian dollar relative to U.S. and other currencies. All of this encouraged inflation, and when the 1973-74 recession hit hard and fast the Canadian state was unprepared to deal with the devastating drop in demand for Canadian resources. Between 1970 and 1975 the state found itself mired in a worsening situation of uncontrollable debt: a trade balance surplus of $3 billion at the beginning of the decade turned into a deficit of over $450 million a mere five years later. Meanwhile, corporate spokespersons expressed alarm that more and more of the national income was being diverted from profits, dividends, and interest to wages and salaries.

By 1975 the stage was thus set for the state abandonment of Keynesianism/Fordism. Convinced that profit could be sustained only by tackling inflation head on and, in the process, constraining the wage-hungry unions, the state moved decisively into a program of restraint, in which steady decreases in the growth of the money supply would be complemented by interest and exchange rate policies and supplemented by stringent efforts to control increases in wages and, ostensibly, prices. Wages came under most direct attack in the new climate of anti-Keynesianism. Prime Minister Trudeau, never one to miss an opportunity to up the theatrical content of politics, announced his program of wage and price controls on Thanksgiving Day, 1975. With the Anti-Inflation Board restraining what it was possible for wage earners to win, labour's slice of the economic pie shrunk and income was redistributed from labour to capital. One estimate suggests that wage levels in the years 1975-78 were reduced 7.7 per cent as a direct result of the AIB controls. Prices were not so rigidly policed, but they did fall in the initial years of the Trudeau Liberals' Anti-Inflation Program. Within a few years, however, they were soaring again, outstripping wage gains by considerable margins. Meanwhile, more than a million "official" jobless walked the streets in 1978, and among younger workers recognized rates of unemployment were between 12 and 18.5 per cent; Quebec and Atlantic Canada were the most severely affected regions. In this climate of restraint, wage controls were obviously excessive and unnecessary, and the Anti-Inflation Program was discontinued in 1978.

The labour leadership, entrenched in the Canadian Labour Congress, fought against all of this to some extent, but its opposition was fragmented and fairly inconsequential. The CLC mounted a "Day of Protest" on October 15, 1976, and almost one million Canadian workers left their jobs in what was hailed as a one-day "general strike." But as the Anti-Inflation Board rolled back wage gains won in defiance of controls, the CLC changed its tactics and embraced Liberal Party initiatives to restore some of the close connections between labour and the Liberals that prevailed in earlier epochs. Joe Morris of the CLC led a post-1975 drive toward tripartism: a corporatist, King-like vision of government, business, and labour cooperation. But this bureaucratic pipedream was opposed by militant critiques from the nationalist Confederation of Canadian Unions, Quebec's CNTU, and various CLC affiliate unions. Tripartism gained little substantial support from rank-and-file workers who were mystified by the apparent collusion between their leaders and their proverbial enemies, capital and the state. Even the most accommodated of trade union heads swallowed hard at Trudeau's words of warning to those who would oppose his program of controls: "We'll put a few union leaders in jail for three years and others will get the message."

One of labour's figureheads who got the drift of Trudeau's anti-union tide was Morris's successor, Dennis McDermott, former head of the United Automobile Workers of Canada and, as of 1978, leader of the CLC. When the Sudbury miners, led by the youthful militant Dave Patterson, defied the trend and fought the powerful Inco interests and when postal workers refused to submit to the Liberal state, McDermott issued pious condemnations of these "stupid" confrontations and "ideological ego trips and permanent, perpetual obstruction." This did little to help the most militant sectors of the labour movement. The Canadian Union of Postal Workers, for instance, could hardly abide McDermott's comments when it had been the victim of government coercion, the strikebreaking Postal Services Continuation Act, under which union leader Jean-Claude Parrot was jailed for the crime of not instructing his members to obey the law and break their own strike. McDermott was also unreceptive to those in the labour movement who wanted to fight unemployment with implementation of the four-day work week. Constrained by the state, limited by its leadership, the Canadian workers' movement was drowning in the seas of hard times.

This economics of malaise made for strange political bedfellows. Originating in the federal state's abandonment of Keynesianism/Fordism, the Anti-Inflation Program was proclaimed by Pierre Trudeau and the Liberals. But social democrats in power provincially, such as British Columbia's New Democratic Party Premier, Dave Barrett, behaved little differently. Indeed, Barrett legislated 60,000 provincial woodworkers back to their jobs in the fall of 1975, opting for "responsible" class relations and constrained wage demands. Allan Blakeney, NDP head of the Saskatchewan state, created his own provincial variant of Trudeau's AIB, the Public Sector Price and Compensation Board. A future Trudeau patronage appointee, Manitoba NDP Premier Ed Schreyer was perhaps the most enthusiastic supporter of "controls" among social democrats in power, allying himself with the Prime Minister's view of a "new society."

Whatever the political solidarities of the controls program, they failed as politics and as economics. Politically, the controls marked the end of the first Trudeau reign, as Joe Clark and the Tories finally broke through to federal power in a 1979 election that installed a precarious Conservative minority government in Ottawa. But so wracked was the economy by five years of restraint policy, with its attendant soaring interest rates and foreign debt, disgruntled workers, rising unemployment, and plant closures, that the inept Tories could hardly bend over to pick up the pieces without falling flat on their faces. It did not take long for the Joe Clark jokes to start registering: Trudeau was back in power after a 1980 election precipitated when the Tories lost a non-confidence motion over their first John Crosbie budget. For all the political musical chairs, however, the economy was now characterized by what appeared to be permanently high levels of inflation, which, in terms of changes in the consumer price index, never fell below 7.5 per cent in the late 1970s and early 1980s, and deteriorating levels of productivity and business growth. "Stagflation" was the new, and apt, description of economic life.

Trudeau, finally recognizing that his 1975 controls program had been something less than a political success, entered the 1980s with a fresh approach. The new government tried to bury the economic reality of persistent recession in an avalanche of constitutionalism: it repatriated the Constitution and made much ado about its Charter of Rights and Freedoms. When the smoke cleared to reveal that the economy was still being governed by a scorched-earth policy, Trudeau turned on the tap of economic nationalism to try politically to dampen down and obfuscate the harsh meanings of hard times. But a National Energy Program could do only so much to keep the electorate's mind off of interest rates that lurched to unprecedented highs of over 22 per cent and unemployment that officially stood at close to 13 per cent but was likely more realistically pegged around 20 per cent. In a year and a half in the early 1980s well over 1.2 million jobs were lost in Canada. Much of this catastrophe took place in the previously privileged heartland of Canadian capitalism, south-central Ontario.

As the "have" province took a beating and the "have-not" regions suffered through more of the hard times they had historically known, it was all too apparent that the long boom of the post-World War Two years was definitely over. The Trudeau Liberals, banking on riding out the early 1980s recession by exploiting the politics of economic nationalism, found themselves caught out on an energy resources gamble. The increased revenues and megaprojects they envisioned evaporated and collapsed in an unfolding world-wide recession that set oil prices back to something approximating the pre-1973 standard. It was one thing to leave behind Keynesianism/Fordism; it was another to make something else work.

Pierre Elliott Trudeau reached into his mixed bag of tricks to draw out a solution composed of one part theatre and one part restraint. Both parts were, by now, standard fare for Canadians. Appearing on television in October, 1982, the Liberal leader declared that the new fight against inflation had to be waged voluntarily and that controls, such as those imposed a few years before, would not be forced on Canadians. Instead, Trudeau championed *choice*: "To choose to fight inflation, as a free people acting together – that is the course we choose." Most Canadians, of course, made no such choice, most emphatically not the public-sector workers Trudeau targeted. They were placed, *temporarily*, under the jurisdiction of the Public Sector Compensation Restraint Act, which curtailed the right to strike by extending collective agreements in the public sector and limited/rolled back wage hikes to 6 per cent for the first year of the legislation and 5 per cent for the second. Hardest hit, not surprisingly, were the lowest paid, who were, again not surprisingly, the largely female clerical workers: they saw their employer, the federal government, cut back a negotiated pay increase of 12.25 per cent to the "acceptable" level of 6 per cent. These workers earned an average of $18,000 annually. They could not have felt empowered by the state's program of restraint by choice.

The "six-and-five" controls that applied, technically, only to federal government employees were a signal for all to obey. Private-sector unions fell into line, and the new restraint "choice" had a chilling effect on wages throughout the economy. Provincial governments also wasted no time in following the federal lead, and rare was the government that did not pass legislation controlling its hirelings. In Quebec and British Columbia, in particular, unprecedented attacks on trade union rights and civil liberties led to mass mobilizations of protest. By the mid-1980s the federal government was phasing out its "six-and-five" controls, but as Leo Panitch and Donald Swartz have argued, the last two decades have definitely seen the erosion of the old system of industrial legality. Whether or not the new regime is, as they claim, one of permanent exceptionalism, in which trade union rights as consolidated in the aftermath of World War Two are forever to be sacrificed to the exigencies of the state-defined moment, remains to be seen. But there is no doubt that with the rising wave of back-to-work legislation, which over the course of the 1970s and 1980s increased fivefold and more, one part of the hard times workers face is state opposition to their essential organizations of defence.

It is difficult not to see the balance sheet of class relations in these years of the late 1970s and early to mid-1980s as one in which workers continually lost. Living standards dropped, union memberships declined, unemployment was persistently high, and strike levels fell off. Indeed, employers grew increasingly aggressive as they sensed a labour movement ravaged by economic restructuring and besieged by state assault. As most of the old guard, blue-collar, industrial unions in the steel, construction, forestry, and machinery-electrical sectors lost members between 1982 and 1985, and as the expanding public-sector unions grew under the repressive umbrellas of federal and provincial restraint legislation, union clout weakened. The number of strikes waged over the period 1982-85 declined significantly and was, on annual average, down more than 30 per cent from comparable figures for the 1970s. More and more class battles, moreover, were initiated as employer lockouts, almost one in four conflicts in 1983 being provoked by an increasingly confident capital. Strikers as a percentage of union membership dropped precipitously: over the course of the 1970s this figure rarely dipped below 10 per cent, and in years of intense class battle – 1972, 1974, and 1976 – it registered unprecedented highs of from 20 to 50 per cent; by 1985 it tapered off to a bare 4.4 per cent. Not since the early 1960s had the number of days lost to class conflict been so low.

Emboldened by the many ways in which the downturn tipped the scales of class struggle in their favour, employers pushed concessionary contracts down unionists' throats: in 1984 almost 300,000 workers were bound by 136 agreements that called for a wage freeze or actual pay cut. Writing in the pages of *The Financial Post*, James Bagnall commented in 1986 that "Canadian employers are transforming the face of collective bargaining." Master agreements were being torn up, wage rates were pegged to profitability, two-tiered contracts establishing differential rates for new employees and veteran workers had become the norm in meat-packing and some transportation sectors, and in industries such as construction hourly wage cuts of $4.50 (Newfoundland) were standard and moonlighting unionists took one-third of the jobs at rates well under trade scale (Quebec).

Indeed, the once union-proud building trades workers were taking a particular beating, as an incomplete list of developments in 1986 alone attests. In British Columbia some 40,000 construction workers were locked out, invited back to their jobs for $4 less an hour than their earlier mean hourly wage of $19. Quebec's organized construction workers claimed that 90 per cent of their members were unemployed; they had lived without a negotiated agreement since 1979. Prairie provinces such as Saskatchewan and Alberta turned into virtual open-shop territory seemingly overnight. In the early 1980s upwards of 75 per cent of all construction-related jobs were union-controlled in the prairie West, but by 1986 the comparable figures were 5-15 per cent, and wages plummetted. Three hundred union firms disappeared between 1983 and 1986, and unemployment in the industry stood at a staggering 50 per cent.

"It's absolute chaos out there," declared Raymond Gall, director of the Sheet Metal Workers International Association. To curb the chaos, Gall and others clamped down hard on dissidents in their own midst who were opposed to the increasingly concessionary bargaining of the beleaguered building trades unions. When George Ward of Gall's Sheet Metal Workers called a joint management-union statement on the need for concessions at the bargaining table "the biggest pile of garbage I've ever seen in my life," he was charged by Gall with "malicious and provocative statements" contrary to the union constitution. Oppositionists in Hamilton's International Brotherhood of Electrical Workers and members of the carpenters' and labourers' unions felt the equally heavy hand of bureaucratic repression when they, too, challenged their leadership's capitulation to the contractor bosses. Hard times were getting harder, and harder to take.

To add insult to injury, the simultaneous retreat of liberalism and social democracy as ideologies of reform ensconced in particular Canadian political parties now abandoning the mantle of Keynesianism/Fordism failed to legitimize the new politics of restraint. Indeed, as the facade of reform commitments crumbled under the pressures of hard times, outright reaction seemed to be the major ideological beneficiary. As the Keynesian/Fordist historical moment ran out of time in the 1970s, the global political order was revamped by the rise of the New Right.

Heralding the marketplace as the architect of social values and decrying the influence of big government and big unionism in determining too much and intervening too often, the neo-Conservatives of the New Right championed individualism, familialism, and fundamentalism in education and religion. In place of collective responsibility and welfare programs and policies, they advocated a rough-and-tumble acquisitive egoism, a social Darwinism shored up by the sustaining supports of nuclear families and Godly faith, and freed from the curbs of trade unionism. Where societies have nationalized production to some extent, the New Right promotes privatization. Where capital remains private but constrained by government nonetheless, neo-conservatism calls for deregulation. The rise to power of Margaret Thatcher in Britain and Ronald Reagan in the United States was the most visible political sign of the New Right's lock on the political economy of Western capitalism in the 1980s, and the hegemony of Friedmanite economics in policy circles was the most pronounced statement of neo-conservatism's expanding influence ideologically.

The New Right came to power in Canada slowly, guardedly, and with a sense of the limitations placed on its agenda by historical commitments to social programs (health, education, and welfare) and the principles of universality as expressed in family allowances and old age pensions. Neo-conservatism's most potent presence was always slightly marginalized, exemplified in the peripheralized power of the Bennett and Vander Zalm regimes in British Columbia or among the crudely right-wing backbenchers of Ottawa's reigning Conservatives. Indeed, the Progressive Conservative Party win in the 1979 election was anything but the coming to power of the New Right: Joe Clark, Flora MacDonald, and John Crosbie were old-line Conservatives who had trouble worshipping single-mindedly at the altar of entrepreneurial capital; they always packaged their particular politics in a public commitment to something beyond the cash nexus. As Bothwell, Drummond, and English note, at the close of the 1970s the zealous neo-conservatives of Canada's *Western Report* "contrasted the thin ideological gruel of the Canadian Conservatives with the hearty broth of Reaganism" and found the dish somewhat wanting.

After what seemed to many the shortest run for the roses in Canadian political history, Clark and his Conservatives returned to the status of official opposition in 1980. The knives came out, and most of them were planted deftly in Clark's back. Clark's leadership was contested and, in 1983, the far right within the Conservatives aligned with others to anoint Brian Mulroney, a lawyer turned corporate magnate with his eye on the main chance and his ideological sights set firmly on undoing the wrongs of the Trudeau years. Surging to a stunning 1984 electoral triumph over Trudeau's replacement, John Turner, and the long-suffering leader of the NDP, Ed Broadbent, Mulroney's Conservatives won an amazing 211 seats. The Liberals kept a mere forty, while the NDP hung grimly on with thirty-one.

Even this was no New Right sweep. Mulroney won on the basis of vague promises to reconcile Canadians and head a government with integrity. People expected a businessman to do something about inflation and unemployment, and the populist appeal of "downsizing" government attracted many who never before had voted Conservative but were disgusted by the excesses of patronage under Trudeau and irked by the Philosopher King's fondness for sheltered Crown corporations. Mulroney seemed to be the man for the job.

What he was, was the man for the job, again. Mulroney's huge majority simply whetted his appetite for a second, repeat electoral conquest. No doubt committed to privatization and deregulation, his political eyes of adoration unambiguously focused on Reagan and Thatcher, Mulroney's program of "bodyslimming" the state and the economy nevertheless took a back seat to opportunistically exploiting the possibilities of the hour.

In his quest to keep what he had courted and won, Mulroney was pushed into a problematic corner by one set of forces, drawn back into better light by another. Against him were the scandals, corruption, and flagrant use of patronage that characterized his first term, along with the stumbling threat to universal programs that the New Right Tory penchant for cutbacks exposed and the perils of privatizing what some regarded as national treasures. Working for him was the modest economic recovery of the mid-1980s: as the Canadian dollar skidded downward relative to U.S. currency, bottoming out around seventy cents, cheap goods and resources flowed south, production boomed, and unemployment no longer stared so many Canadians in the face. To cut his losses, Mulroney blustered through the attacks on patronage, backtracked a bit on cuts to social programs, and stalled half-heartedly the privatization process. A few carrots were dangled in front of the noses of the disgruntled, including the trade unions. Union leaders were summoned for a National Economic Conference, and funding for the tripartite Canadian Labour Market and Productivity Centre was maintained. One of the Centre's biggest advocates was Shirley Carr, president of the Canadian Labour Congress. Her predecessor, Dennis McDermott, was adroitly kicked upstairs by Mulroney, posted to Ireland as the Canadian ambassador. It all seemed very cosy.

By 1986 inflation and unemployment were down and prospects for their continued decline seemed good. The number of annual strikes and lockouts stabilized, although 1986 and 1987 saw more workers and much higher percentages of unionized labour involved in conflicts. Most important, from 1985 to 1987, the incidence of wage settlements below the rate of inflation climbed from 49 per cent to 87 per cent, an indication that the softening of hard times was benefiting employers more than workers. While a Vector union report suggested a bright future for Canadian labour, noting that 55 per cent of those polled preferred to work for a union company, Jeff Rose, head of the Canadian Union of Public Employees, caught the real meaning of the moment when he recognized that "Employers are more self confident and more aggressive." As the CLC pleaded for "an economic pick-up, an end to union busting, and more honesty at the bargaining table," salary hikes for executives jumped 22.5 per cent. Those at the top obviously did not beg; they took.

All of this gave Mulroney the latitude he needed: he called and won a second election in November, 1988. It was fought over the age-old issue of freer trade with the United States, and as the Liberals under Turner and the New Democrats under Broadbent lined up to fly the Canadian flag, Mulroney and the Conservatives talked loud and long about investment potential, job creation, and the prosperity of continentalism. They won. Mulroney had his much cherished second electoral wind. It blew strongest from Quebec, where economic ties to the United States worried Francophones far less than a Liberal Party that might refuse the province its historic special status; sixty-three of the seventy-five Quebec seats went to Mulroney, more than one-third of the 169 elected Conservatives.

There were signs well before the 1988 election that the mild economic recovery of the mid-1980s was over. Speculative capital took a beating on meltdown Monday in October, 1987, as the stock market crashed. In a telling indication that Fordism had definitely come to an end, non-union labour was doing better than organized workers in terms of upping take-home pay. With inflation rising on the eve of the Tory election win in 1988, economists coined a new term to describe the decline in economic growth now seen as inevitable for the remainder of the decade and well into the 1990s. "Slugflation" designated an economy of sluggish growth and rising moderate inflation; it might better have been translated as slugging out inflation by cracking down hard on workers. But this could not be done easily and a price was paid. The Canadian Labour Market and Productivity Centre reported that Canada's productivity performance was the worst of seven major industrial nations. All signs, noted the Conference Board of Canada, pointed to a recession. By the summer of 1990 the new downturn was undeniable. Statistics Canada reported that Canadian manufacturing was operating at less than 81 per cent capacity and this measure of productivity had fallen for seven consecutive economic quarters. Hard times, which never really disappeared, were back with a vengeance: tens of thousands of jobs were gone; interest rates were climbing again; and a rising Canadian dollar curbed exports and exacerbated a growing federal deficit.

Mulroney's Conservatives reacted predictably, drawing their rhetoric and rationale from the ideological arsenal of the New Right. They jumped harder on the freer trade bandwagon, tried to cover their deficit-driven backsides with a highly unpopular Goods and Services Tax (GST) that added a 7 per cent surcharge to everything from aerobics classes to zucchini served in your local Yuppie vegetarian restaurant, and plunged the country, à la Trudeau, into yet another whirlwind of constitutional crisis. Nothing seemed to work. Freer trade was not producing jobs and prosperity, the GST was universally reviled, and Meech Lake, while lowering a constitutionalist fog over the economics of recessionary downturn, pitted regions against regions and drove Mulroney's own Francophone lieutenants into self-imposed exile from the federalist project.

The working class could not be blamed for all of this, but Finance Minister Michael Wilson turned the guns on the unions for, in his words, causing inflation by pushing hard for wage increases to offset the perceived costs of the GST. Wilson and the Tories insisted most consumers were really going to benefit and other taxes dropped would actually reduce the price of most items. But as consumers saw a newspaper jump five cents (10 per cent up), the cost of washing a car increase fifty cents (25 per cent up), and entrances to movies push past $8 (12 per cent up), they wondered how all this came about because of a 7 per cent additional tax, let alone how such figures were reflections of price declines.

Meanwhile, the more draconian elements of the New Right pushed more directly into the ideological marketplace. Neo-conservative think tanks such as the Fraser Institute, backed by many of the country's large corporations and financial institutions, churned out publications attacking rent controls, denouncing the monopolistic ill-service of the post office, and bemoaning collectivist approaches to medicare, education, and welfare. "Privatize everything, regulate nothing" was the rallying cry of the hour. Lobby groups such as the National Citizens' Coalition cost unions hundreds of thousands of dollars in legal fees as they sponsored disgruntled union members who fought in the courts to restrict the use of union dues to pure-and-simple business union matters of direct connection to collective bargaining. British Columbia and Saskatchewan governments rewrote labour codes, the better to suppress unionism and encourage capital. As the old-guard Stalinist economies of eastern Europe crumbled, the New Right grew bolder. Brandishing a copy of *Newsweek* with a cover story on "The Decline of the Left," Saskatchewan's Premier Grant Devine assailed NDP "socialism," promised to privatize firms worth $2 billion, and grew effusive in his ecstasy that collectivization and its advocates were dead. "This is their Alamo, this is their Waterloo, this is the end of the line for them," he gushed. Small wonder that by the beginning of 1990 the days lost to strikes had dropped off 66 per cent in one short year.

Throughout all of this the unions were in a mess. Internecine squabbles at the top, raiding, and suppression of dissidents had never been sharper and more debilitating since the days of AFL-CIO rapprochement. In Quebec one CNTU leader described the 1980s as a decade of setbacks for workers and the unemployed.

It was also a period of scapegoating the weak as the state consumed its own. Nowhere throughout the 1975-90 period was the clash between labour and the state more visible than in the public sector, a weak link in the chain of class relations. Once broken, that mangled link could be usefully exposed to all other workers to show them the high price of resistance, just as Reagan used the Professional Air Traffic Controllers Organization (PATCO) as an example in his brutally militaristic crushing of a 1981 strike. There would be no PATCOs in Canada; the limitations of the New Right were different north of the 49th parallel. But there would be plenty of hard blows. Mulroney's idea of labour relations in the public sector was to give the workers "pink slips and running shoes." And if public-sector labour did not get a jump on its adversarial employer it would get cooked in the hot pot of media denunciation, its wounds salted with back-to-work legislation and snide dismissal of its productive utility and social value. CUPE complained in 1982 that "public sector workers have been maligned for alleged featherbedding, earning excessive incomes, engaging in irresponsible strike activities and, in general, being a burden and a parasite on society." Such workers were thus ripe for a cannibalistic picking.

CANNIBALIZING THE CLERKS: PUBLIC-SECTOR WORKERS AND STATE ATTACK

In 1976 more than one-third of Canadian workers were employed by the state or Crown corporations. Unionization rates among these people were extremely high, with some estimates reaching to 90 per cent, and in the late 1970s public-sector unions became the largest worker organizations in the country. The Canadian Union of Public Employees displaced the Steelworkers and Autoworkers as the largest union in Canada by 1977, its membership having soared from 75,000 in 1961 to over 225,000 fifteen years later. Less spectacular was the rise of the Public Service Alliance of Canada, a body that nevertheless boasted a membership of almost 160,000 by 1977. By the mid-1980s, the three largest unions in Canada were the 304,000-member CUPE, the 254,000-strong National Union of Provincial Government Employees, and PSAC, with its 182,000 members. The combined memberships of these three megaunions account for nearly half of the estimated total membership of the organized public sector in Canada.

Indeed, the doubling of Canadian trade union membership between 1960 and 1980 was virtually a product of the expansion of the public-sector unions. This altered the nature of the country's labour movement, displacing the historic dominance of Americanized "international" unions and underscoring the importance of "national" bodies. In 1940, on the eve of the breakthrough in the mass production industries, the public sector accounted for a bare 3 per cent of Canadian unionists. Forty years later, in 1980, that percentage was almost 37. Trade union growth in the public sector was a product of the Keynesian/Fordist age: the expansion of the welfare apparatus in conjuncture with the state-endorsed unionization of its labour force thrust the public-sector unions into the limelight of class relations. This was a long, incremental process, drawn slowly out of the World War Two years, the pace of events quickening throughout the 1950s and 1960s until a 1967-70 explosion of legislation and unionization altered significantly the makeup and meaning of the Canadian workers' movement.

Much is implicitly made of this public-sector breakthrough, especially by nationalistic advocates of the superiority of Canadian trade unionism. In making comparisons with the faltering state of the American workers' movement, commentators often note that the U.S. unions exercise a hold over barely one in seven workers, while in Canada that figure peaked at one in every 2.5 workers in 1983. The percentage of workers organized in Canada has dropped of late, but it remains more than double that of the United States (36 per cent compared to 16 per cent). To be sure, this is an important reality, recently explored sensitively by David Kettler, James Struthers, and Christopher Huxley. Their assessment of unionization and labour regimes in the U.S. and Canada makes it apparent that there is far more to the differential rate of unionism separating the experience of workers in the two nations than the high rates of public-sector organization north of the border. In the complex divergence of Canadian and American political economies – in which regional differentiation with respect to resource/export dependencies, the open shop, and how labour fits into the established political order figure prominently – public-sector unionism is but one of many explanatory factors that demands a nuanced appreciation. Nevertheless, inasmuch as the much-lauded *strengths* of public-sector unionism in Canada are often promoted as exercising both a quantitative and qualitative impact on unionism as a whole, it is worth considering the *limitations* of the public-sector breakthrough in Canada.

The making of public-sector unionism in Canada has an undeniable ambivalence encasing its history and meaning. On the one hand, the organization of the clerks has increased the ranks of organized labour and expanded the boundaries of class struggle. A part of its realization did, of course, as the last chapter emphasized, flow out of the demands of public-sector workers for union recognitions and rights. On the other hand, unlike the industrial unions, much of public-sector organization (unionization in the postal service is something of an exception here) was a product of legislation and amalgamation rather than overt class struggle. Intricately related to the Keynesian/Fordist moment and its class latitudes, the organization of the Canadian public sector in the 1945-75 years was as often a top-down process, imposed by the state and governed from the first by the dictates of a highly bureaucratized set of associational mergers, as it was a mobilization or initiative with critical rank-and-file or militant input. However much one applauds the actual unionization of workers who were previously impaled on the class relations of a weak associationalism and a consultative process that denied collective bargaining and its premises, there is also no underestimating the extent to which federal policies and legislation such as the Public Service Staff Relations Act *created* a public-sector unionism that was, as a consequence, quite different from that which might have been forged in the course of more overt class battle.

CUPE, NUPGE, and PSAC were all, in varying degrees, a product of this historical set of class/state relations. All grew out of the long and slow march of policy concessions of the post-World War Two years and attained their historic place as major players in the Canadian trade union movement through mergers; their certification as unions and their winning of collective bargaining rights were relatively quiet and quick. Extensive membership campaigns were often not necessary and the state conceded somewhat placidly what most employers in the private sector long resisted ardently. For all the exceptions that might confirm the rule – in which the case of municipal workers might be cited repeatedly – the organization of public-sector workers proceeded differently from the unionization of the private sphere. Necessarily accommodated by the state, set in a particular period, the organizational drive in the public sector was understandably more bureaucratized and conciliatory.

Ironically, no sooner was this state-class compromise sealed than it began to come apart. As the Keynesian/Fordist climacteric culminated in seemingly irrepressible federal deficits and a persistent scissor-like crisis of runaway inflation and rising unemployment, the state looked for ways to pump some sustaining savings into the obviously materially depleted body politic. What it gave in a moment of Keynesian/Fordist largesse, it could take away in leaner times of need. Much of the class struggle of the 1975-90 years, as it involved workers in the public sector, would grow out of just this context. As the state sat down to sustain itself in the worsening climate of the late 1970s and 1980s, it cannibalized its own.

The main course, but also the most difficult to digest, would be the postal workers, targeted as the militant vanguard of the public sector. Jean-Claude Parrot led the Canadian Union of Postal Workers in their battles against Trudeau's controls in the 1975-78 years. The hiring of non-union casual labour and the union's demand to be consulted on the implementation of technological changes sparked a confrontation in 1978 that ended with the workers legislated back to their jobs and Parrot in jail. In 1977, after countless studies of the poisoned atmosphere within the post office, the case of A.G. Steele, an Ottawa mail sorter, revealed the workers' plight. Accused of misplacing a package, Steele was questioned by his supervisors, taken to a police station, jailed for eight hours while his apartment was ransacked, and approached by a management informer who attempted to make him confess guilt before a hidden recording device. In the end, the post office admitted that it had been in error and that Steele simply rerouted an improperly sorted package.

Things did not improve much at Canada Post over the course of the 1980s. The Crown corporation still insisted on the right to search worker lunch pails and garment bags; a law professor arbitrator ruled in 1988 that this was not a violation of personal privacy "nor an indignity perpetrated on employees." A 1989 task force concluded that "A lot more than mail needs to be sorted out at Canada Post." Liberal MPs in the Toronto area heard "horror stories reminiscent of 19th century workhouses." Among the charges were that supervisors demanded gifts and bribes from workers, sexually harassed and assaulted employees, and ordered that mail be sent through the system twice to meet volume quotas. Racism was said to be rife in the post office, and gender/family sensitivity at a minimum. Women off work because of miscarriages were interrogated about the cause of their absence; medical notes were demanded of workers attending funerals of immediate family members. CUPW countered with a campaign of resistance to arbitrary authority: workers were urged to carry soiled diapers in bags that inspectors would be searching; identity tags were worn on shoes to make supervision as difficult as possible; and unionists were told to demand overtime to compensate for the time lost to searches conducted at the end of shifts.

By the end of the decade the union and the Crown corporation were deadlocked in a backlog of grievances, 52,000 all told. After ten years of strikes (1978, 1981, 1987, and 1988) and a $2 million union campaign against the Tory push to privatize, stress levels in the post office were at an all-time high. Over the course of 1987-88 the Crown corporation spent $190 million on so-called "extraordinary restructuring costs," most of the expenditure related to fighting two seventeen-day strikes by its largest unions, a sum that averaged out to $4,200 for every man and woman employed at Canada Post. The 1987 strike saw postal pickets assail Tory homes on Thanksgiving, country-wide picket-line violence, and massive, federally orchestrated strikebreaking. As the *Globe and Mail* editorialized that "Canada Post is truly the black hole of labor relations," the Tories pushed their panacea of privatization, whereby 4,000 jobs would be eliminated in contracting out mail service to convenience stores and pharmacies, and Canada Post organized scab armies of single mothers, retired people, immigrants, and part-time workers, some of whom actually got caught crossing picket lines with arms. Nine days into the strike, the government introduced legislation that aimed to force the posties back to work under the threat of five years' exile from any job associated with Canada Post or the union. CUPW itself faced possible daily fines of $100,000. The Liberal Party had the temerity to oppose this kind of legislation, which it had all too willingly turned to when it was in power, with the cute question, "Why the billy-club treatment?" Parrot, who stood his ground in 1978, had a different demeanour in 1987. Claiming that "he was not a candidate for suicide," the CUPW leader made sounds of compliance, pointing out that the Tories would be gone in two years anyway. They would not be; but in 1989 Canada Post did show a profit (almost $100 million) for the first time in thirty years.

This was small solace to London, Ontario, postal worker Peter LeMay. Hurt in a car accident, LeMay had been on sick leave for six months. When he reapplied for his job he was given the cold shoulder by Canada Post officials. He committed suicide shortly after. His 650 co-workers in the London post office refused to work and waged an illegal strike in protest. Parrot attended the funeral and Canada Post launched an inquiry into the LeMay case, as well as disciplinary proceedings against the wildcat strikers.

It is only necessary to ascertain the number of person days lost to strikes in the federal public sector between 1975 and 1981 to understand how loudly the voice of CUPW speaks in the national class struggles of these years. According to figures presented by Jacob Finkelman and Shirley Goldenberg, from the October, 1975, postal workers' walkout to the June, 1981, CUPW strike, 1,858,940 striker days were lost to seventeen federal public-sector work cessations. Approximately 1.5 million days of this lost time were attributed to three CUPW strikes, or fully 80 per cent. Moreover, this does not include another Canada Post struggle, led by the Letter Carriers Union of Canada. Only the 1980 clerical workers' strike against the federal government, involving 45,000 public servants and almost 300,000 days lost, rivals the battles waged by the postal workers.

And yet two related points about the postal workers as public-sector unionists and federal employees need stressing. First, as by far the most militant of government employees, perhaps even the leading edge of militancy within the labour movement as a whole, the postal workers and their leadership stood somewhat removed from other public-sector workers. They were the exception that proved the rule of public-sector workers' vulnerability. For when the postal workers struck they had little of the clout of the older, private-sector industrial unions. Their work stoppages were always depicted as hurting the public more than the employer: as strikes unfolded the media were quick to focus on welfare recipients who needed their monthly cheques and single mothers who depended on the family allowance. The national interest was often equated with the mails moving, and business wailed about losses and international repercussions if the postal service was not in operation. Newspaper editorials, television clips, and a wide array of other multi-media messages got the basic propaganda point across all too effectively: when the state's employees struck, the people suffered.

Not only did the largest public-sector union in the country, the Canadian Union of Public Employees, face this kind of ideological containment; it also was handcuffed by its highly fragmented character. Composed of thousands of small locals, CUPE, unlike CUPW, was incapable of mounting a concerted challenge to state power, indicating another aspect of public-sector weakness. In 1990, for instance, CUPE was scheduled to negotiate 659 collective agreements, covering less than one-quarter of its 370,000 members. The endless bureaucratic demands of simply meeting the obligations of such contractual negotiations assured that the country's largest union would always be on the sidelines of militancy.

Second, for all the national attention federal public-sector strikes received, the strikes fought out in the private sector over the course of the later 1970s were always markedly greater in number than those fought in the entire public sector, which contributed, on average, about 20 per cent of strike activity in the years 1975-81. Of all of this conflict, however, the federal public sector lagged significantly behind other segments of government employees in terms of strike activity. Rarely in the immediate post-1975 years did the federal public sector contribute more than 5 per cent of the total work days lost to strikes in Canada. When all of this is taken into account it suggests the need to appreciate the *limitations* of federal public-sector militancy paced by the postal workers as well as the dimensions of non-federal public-sector strikes.

In the case of the latter process, there can be no doubting that, like CUPW and all federal public-sector unions, organized government employees were severely constrained not only by the ideological assault of the state on all public-sector workers, but also by the ways in which the provinces followed suit and reproduced the repressive legislative atmosphere of the federal Liberals. The 1975-78 Anti-Inflation Program controls and the supposedly voluntary "six-and-five" restraint legislation of 1982 stopped many federal public-sector workers in their tracks.

The provinces, which after all were responsible for hiring the vast bulk of public-sector workers in the vital and burgeoning health and education fields, wasted no time in implementing their own form of controls. By the early 1980s these areas of health and education were absolutely pivotal to both the state and its public-sector workers. One-third of provincial budgets might be allocated to health care, while more than 60 per cent of public-sector strikes took place within the educational and health arenas. When Ontario hospital workers went on a wildcat strike in 1980 and when Alberta nurses walked off their jobs in a legal strike in 1982, they were promptly legislated back to work. Provincial back-to-work legislation, imposed only ten times between 1950 and 1969, was resorted to in fifty-eight instances from 1975 to 1987. The width of the coercive net cast over public-sector workers in this period was truly phenomenal and quite unprecedented. When Ontario aped the federal "six-and-five" legislation with its own Inflation Restraint Act (Bill 179), for instance, it unilaterally curtailed collective agreements, banned strikes for a year, and generally set a wage ceiling of 5 per cent. Bill 179 covered 565,000 provincial, municipal, and regional civil servants, as well as all workers in schools, hospitals, Crown corporations, and companies contracting with the province or funded by it, including day-care centres, nursing homes, and health services.

As the decade wore on it became all too apparent that the public sector was going to be continually eaten away by the state. With the Tories in power federally there were promises of 5,500 job cuts in the federal civil service; but there were nevertheless to be *more* tax collectors, *more* Mounties, and *more* soldiers. International bodies, most prominently the International Labor Organization (ILO), censured British Columbia, Alberta, Ontario, and Newfoundland for their zealous clampdowns on public-sector unionists in 1985-86. In February, 1986, as Quebec imposed a 3.5 per cent lid on public-sector pay raises, Saskatchewan became the first province to invoke Section 33 of the Charter of Rights and Freedoms to exempt its own back-to-work legislation from the guarantee of freedom of association. Premier Grant Devine then ended rotating strikes by 12,000 Saskatchewan public-sector workers, three out of five of them earning less than $24,000 a year. Teachers and municipal workers found themselves at the mercy of unsympathetic local authorities across the country, while the Ontario Public Service Employees Union charged the government with spying on workers through an electronic monitoring process. In Newfoundland, Fraser March led 5,000 public-sector workers into a direct confrontation with Premier Brian Peckford, the second illegal strike among the government employees in less than a year. Arrests and marches on the legislature ended only after a month of bitter combat.

Nurses found themselves on the front lines of a battle in which the odds seemed always against them: 18,000 were ordered back to work in Quebec in June, 1986, but many of them were again on picket lines in 1988, joined by their peers in Saskatchewan, Alberta, Manitoba, and British Columbia. Walkouts, strikes, and slowdowns among nurses were endemic in the late 1980s as the National Federation of Nurses Unions waged a persistent uphill battle for "recognition and respect." Wearied by the endlessness of the fight, many nurses simply opted out and headed for greener pastures: Statistics Canada reported a decline in the numbers of working nurses in 1989, and Ontario alone lost 3,600 such hospital workers. State authorities boasted a large arsenal of repression and drew liberally on strike bans, contempt of court citations, and fines.

Provincial governments such as that of Quebec had their own methods of dealing with the crisis in health care; they obviously did not believe in sparing the rod. Treasury Board president Daniel Johnson announced in the midst of a 1989 walkout of the 43,000-member Quebec Federation of Nurses that "Nurses cannot think they are above the law. . . . It's uncivilized to close hospitals with one week's notice because you don't get your billion dollars." Under Quebec's Bill 160, the Essential Services Act, Johnson noted, illegal nurse walkouts would be subject to individual daily fines of $100 per striker, loss of an extra day's pay for every day off the job, and slash of seniority for each day of the walkout. The union itself was threatened with a $100,000 fine, while key officials were liable to $25,000 penalties. Quebec's anti-scab legislation was overridden as Johnson allowed the hospitals to hire strikebreakers in the face of what he characterized an "intolerable" situation that assailed the "very legitimacy of the democratically elected government." As of September, 1989, Quebec's nurses were at the head of a seething mass of discontented public-sector workers. Most of the 43,000 nurses were in fact back on the job, but 95,000 hospital support staff went out in illegal sympathy strikes, and almost 50,000 health care professionals marched beside them. To add fuel to the fire, 7,000 CEGEP teachers, 85,000 public school teachers, 16,000 school support staff, and 43,000 civil servants were also engaged in one-day rotating strikes against the Quebec state. Approximately 260,000 of the province's 350,000 government employees took job action.

Liberal Premier Robert Bourassa used the strikes to pave the way to another electoral victory, pleading with the public to come to the aid of "old people who have been abandoned and sick children who have been abandoned," and even pro-Parti Québécois journalists deplored the "ritualistic madness" of public health care workers going on strike. When it was all over and done with the Liberals remained in power and the nurses' federation was on the verge of bankruptcy, the Quebec Hospital Association drawing on Bill 160's provision allowing the withholding of union dues in the event of illegal worker walkouts. The nurses had not counted on the hospitals being so quick to deduct ninety-six weeks of dues for the nurses' federation, sixty weeks for the hospital staff unions, and twenty-four weeks for the health care workers' organization, a sum that totalled hundreds of thousands of dollars. Nor had they figured on a judge insisting on immediate payment of a $250,000 fine.

Nurses across the country nevertheless did not allow this kind of draconian reaction to dull their demands. In 1989 British Columbia nurses wanted a 33 per cent wage increase and a 43 per cent hike in benefits. Two years later, in the dead of winter, Manitoba nurses walked picket lines, defied the sneers of hospital administrators, and faced down the usual charges of their callous indifference to suffering patients – most of whom were well looked after by nurses who kept essential services going – in an attempt to get wage parity with their counterparts in other regions. Dragging on for thirty-one days, this Manitoba confrontation pitted almost 11,000 nurses against Premier Gary Filmon's Conservative government, threatening to be the longest nurses' walkout in the history of the country. When the unionized nurses rejected Filmon's first offer with a resounding 94 per cent majority, the provincial government began to make noises about legislating the strikers back to work. But intimidation was wearing a little thin. Manitoba Nurses Union leader Vera Chernecki noted, "I don't know if the nurses would go back to work." Indeed, when Chernecki and other union leaders negotiated a modest agreement and returned the unionists to the hospitals, some 300 strikers refused initially to budge, holding out for a better deal. A bare 60 per cent of the membership voted in favour of the settlement.

Labour militancy in the public sector seemed to be well established by the end of the 1980s. Five of the six major 1989 strikes were in the public sector, four of these related to the upheavals in Quebec alluded to above. But this militancy, tragically, was as useful to capital as it was to a labour movement that remained relatively insulated from a program that could win actual state power for the working class. Much of the public-sector conflict of the late 1980s was actually precipitated by the state, which used the unpaid wage bill of the strike to balance its books and the useful public relations attack on the "greed" of protected state employees to consolidate its hegemony.

Indeed, one could argue that as the public sector increased in importance within the class struggle, the militant capacity of the working class actually to win something from capital and the state lessened. With public-sector strikes leading the pace of class struggle in 1989, the actual number of days lost to work stoppages dropped precipitously and labour victories were few. As early as 1986 word was out that provincial governments, such as Richard Hatfield's in New Brunswick, were willing to force public-sector workers into strikes to save money, balance budgets, and show the electorate they could run a tight ship. In May of that year, Hatfield's Tories entertained contract disputes involving 16,000 teachers, non-academic support staff in the schools, and non-medical hospital workers. There was no lack of militancy on the part of the workers, and there was tough talk of strikes and illegal job actions in defiance of the state. But in the end, the settlements recorded the limits of public-sector militancy and its leadership: contracts stipulating no wage increases in the first year were signed by most unions.

The cannibalistic assault of the state on its own public sector was thus the leading edge of a tough-minded anti-unionism associated with all levels and political colourings of state power in the late 1970s and 1980s. As a CUPE brief to the Macdonald Commission of the early eighties on the future of Canada's economy noted: "The public sector has become the most common scapegoat for the economic problems of Canada." This scapegoating generated considerable acrimony and some militancy, but it also ground down much of the working class. PSAC, losing members over the course of the 1980s, settled a forty-two-month contract in 1989 at an average raise of just over 4 per cent yearly, when inflation was predicted to more than eat away this modest wage hike. Where mass mobilizations of protest did stimulate solidarity and break down the entrenched sectionalism of the workers' movement, moreover, the state did not back easily away from the fight. It usually emerged the victor. As the history of public-sector-led class struggle in British Columbia and Quebec in the early 1980s indicated, the cannibalistic state was a tough opponent, regardless of whether it came to the table dressed in the garb of progressivism or the New Right.

A TALE OF TWO PROVINCES: THE ASSAULT ON THE PUBLIC SECTOR IN QUEBEC AND BRITISH COLUMBIA

There appear to be few similarities between Canada's Pacific coastal province, British Columbia, and its distinctive Francophone society, Quebec.

Their economies, cultures, and politics are as different as night and day. And yet, in 1982-83, the provincial states in these divergent regions set their coercive sights directly on the public sector and attempted to ride out the difficulties of hard times on the backs of government employees. In the process, trade union and civil rights were trampled and popular resistance peaked in massive mobilizations. Yet the state, for the most part, emerged from this self-created cauldron of conflict intact and triumphant, however bruised. Some of the players ended up being displaced, but the nature of state power remained basically unchanged.

No provincial government, it could be argued, did more to consolidate a positive working relationship with its own labour force than the early Parti Québécois (PQ). Quebec's working class was the most combative, militant, and radical in Canada throughout the 1970s. From the Common Front days of 1972 on it was an activist contingent quick to strike and willing to place a wide range of social issues on the bargaining table of class relations. Some of this got translated into the national arena as militant Montreal locals of federal unions stood their ground against the tide of repression or thrust leaders like Jean-Claude Parrot into the national limelight.

When the PQ came to power in 1976, it alone among provincial governments bucked the Trudeau restraint program. Headed by René Lévesque, the PQ was engaged in a higher politics than economic controls, squaring off against the federal Liberals in a sovereignty-association push that was to be tested in a 1980 referendum on Quebec independence. Lévesque and the PQ bought a bit of time and labour support for sovereignty-association in 1979 when they placated a common front of public-sector unionists, but this mortgaging of class relations was torn up as the 1980 call for a "Oui" vote soured and the Quebec economy faltered badly in the early 1980s recession. Cuts in social spending resulted, and the PQ experimented with the privatization and deregulation so championed by the New Right. But it wasn't enough. By 1982 it was apparent that the PQ could no longer pay the price of keeping labour on side. Instead, it desperately needed to shore up its fragile and now gutted economy, structured around the most vulnerable kind of small, consumer-goods manufacturing – textiles, shoes, garments – and to dispel the debilitating view common among Anglophone and American investors that the province was a hotbed of labour radicalism as well as a region of socially progressive government programs with a corresponding tax structure to foot the bills.

With sovereignty-association shelved and the bill for past labour relations largesse now overdue, the PQ moved to counter the economic downturn with the programmatic overkill of the rights of public-sector unionists. It began inauspiciously with the legislating back to work of some Montreal transit workers in January, 1982, but quickly escalated in mid-year. When the Common Front public-sector unions of teachers, CNTU affiliates, and the QFL balked at demands that they forgo salary increases, the Quebec state passed Bill 70. This legislation tabled previously signed contracts and decreed in advance of their impending expiration a 19.5 per cent wage cut for the first three months of 1983. Affecting some 300,000 public-sector workers, Bill 70 effectively banned strikes, extended collective agreements, and lowered salaries.

As if this were not enough, Bill 105 was introduced. It extended the coverage to a few previously excluded sectors of workers, decreed a further extension of all public-sector collective agreements through to December, 1985, and limited wage increases to less than the annual rise in the consumer price index. Job security and working conditions were eroded, as well, with seniority clauses taking a beating and working-class autonomy limited by the centralizing of power and decision-making in the hands of administrative personnel. Some 109 contracts were altered, and public-sector workers' pockets were looted to the tune of over $650 million.

The Common Front unionists quite correctly perceived this as a war waged against them, an aggressive action that commenced with their being stripped of the traditional means of counter-attack, the right to strike. Still, they defied the PQ and its legislative arsenal and walked off the job illegally, some 300,000 in number. This January "general strike" was met with yet another piece of labour legislation, Bill 111, an Act To Ensure the Resumption of Services in the Public Sector, which was passed in February. It provided for fines, imprisonment, and the decertification of bargaining agents, overriding the federal Charter of Rights and Freedoms and the provincial Charter of Human Rights. Those targeted were refused the right of trial and denied the opportunity to present evidence or secure legal protection. To be absent from work was to be guilty. Most union leaders quickly complied with the state's dictatorial demand that they get their members back to work, although the teachers stayed out for a month. Nevertheless, in the face of what was undoubtedly the harshest legislative assault on unionism since 1919, the strike was broken.

For the rest of the decade this guillotine of state attack hung over the collective neck of the Quebec working class. As the 1982-83 legislation lifted in 1985, the PQ simply added on some new bills, amending the provincial labour code and tightening its regulatory control over monetary decisions in the public sector. More and more public-sector workers were designated "essential," and thereby denied the right to strike. Other trade unionists were split off from their brothers and sisters as the state stipulated that collective bargaining was to take place, not in concerted constituencies of solidarity, but within a host of sectoral "sub-tables." This effectively squashed Quebec's historic Common Front.

To be sure, forces beyond the state contributed to this sorry end, among the most significant the rivalries and acrimony within the labour movement and its hierarchy that were encouraged by the repressive divide-and-conquer tactics of the PQ. Nor would the PQ itself ride out the storm. But when it went down to electoral defeat in the mid-1980s, the regrouped Liberal Party was able to pick up where it had left off. The Bourassa Liberals made no move to restore the 20 per cent cut in public-sector wages that PQ Finance Minister Jacques Parizeau secured over the course of his years in office. They simply upped the legislative ante in 1986 with the passage of Bill 160, which, as we have seen in terms of the struggles of Quebec's nurses, provided for the crushing of any unionists who would defy government orders and engage in illegal strike activity. The Quebec Federation of Labour's Louis Laberge called Bill 160 "vicious, illegal, immoral . . . an atomic bomb to sink a canoe."

Laberge's angry rhetoric was, however, matched by a curious nationalistic defence of Quebec labour's own distinctive society relation to the state. In a 1987 interview he remembered with fondness the positive contribution of the PQ, stressed the tripartite climate in Quebec, and was surprisingly generous in his assessment of the new Liberal provincial government:

> I believe the climate in Quebec is a lot better than it's been before. The climate was bad in 1973 when three of us – myself, the president of the CNTU, and the president of the teachers' group, were jailed. The election of the PQ in 1976 helped improve the climate. We did get good pieces of legislation on health and safety and others under the PQ regime. Even today you cannot find anything comparable to what we've had from the PQ government. We cannot forget that. The PQ lost the last election because of internal disputes. They were so divided amongst themselves that nobody could help them, even we couldn't. With this new government we have been pleasantly surprised. The government started off with deregulation, privatization, for instance, the sale of Quebecair. . . . Since then they have been more careful. . . . Management and labour and government have all been working a little closer together for the past 15 years.

Perhaps Laberge's head was clouded by his heavy involvement in the Solidarity Fund, a Quebec trade union exercise in venture capital that by 1989 boasted 72,000 shareholders, assets of $232 million, and a piece of fifty-six small and medium-sized companies. Tax-exempt by agreement with the government, the Solidarity Fund aims, according to its president, former Campeau Corporation VP Claude Blanchet, to create jobs. Laberge sees it as changing the very "mentality" of workers and managers. But just how saving the Quebec Nordiques hockey team with a $3 million investment transforms anything is a little hard to answer. So are dissident unionists' questions about why the Solidarity Fund investments are overwhelmingly in non-union companies. Laberge sees things differently: "Our place of work is there. We have to produce things that can be sold, otherwise the employer who doesn't make any money will probably close down the shop and we would have no job. We're not interested in negotiating with an employer who doesn't make a profit. To us, the word 'profit' has never been a dirty word. I'd rather negotiate with an employer who does make a profit." As one journalist commented, "It's a long way from the infamous 'common front' strikes of the seventies, when Mr. Laberge and two other union leaders went to jail for telling workers to defy back-to-work injunctions."

Thousands of miles away, on the other side of the country, things were also very different in the 1980s than they had been a decade before. In British Columbia, an NDP government was replaced by Social Credit, and under Premiers Bill Bennett and William Vander Zalm the once ostensibly socialist province was turned on its political head. Throughout the 1980s, B.C. would be the most uncompromising site of the politics of the New Right in Canada.

British Columbia's introduction to the downturn came early, with the Barrett NDP government in power, but the recessionary collapse of the 1980s was stayed for a time as the more developed manufacturing economy of central Canada was hit with a pronounced wave of plant closures. When the regional economy finally came to feel the pinch of hard times, however, the pain was perhaps more forceful. Almost entirely dependent on the resources of its forests, British Columbia's export-oriented economy tumbled in the early 1980s. Unemployment, seemingly under control in 1980-81 at roughly 7 per cent, soared to 16 per cent in 1983, well above the national average. Natural resource revenues fell catastrophically. As the new global division of labour lessened reliance on North American products and resources, British Columbia came to the shocked realization that timber could be secured more cheaply from the once obscure corners of the world than it could from the harvests of its own backyard. For the provincial state the economic collapse spelled disaster: the government took in less because the forest industries were selling less, people were cutting back on their buying, sales taxes were reduced, and, finally, personal incomes were cut by unemployment, meaning income tax revenues were reduced. At the same time, state expenditures on welfare and social services necessarily climbed. By mid-1983, a budget deficit of over $1.6 billion was projected.

Obviously concerned with the state of the regional economy and the new international division of labour, the ruling Social Credit Party – a curious right-wing coalition, a segment of which was a natural environment for the most vitriolic neo-conservatism – looked around the province and saw an economic apocalypse looming. There were those willing to tell them what must be done. Consultations were soon arranged with Michael Walker and his colleagues in the B.C.-based New Right "think tank," the Fraser Institute. Premier Bill Bennett took kindly and quickly to the blunt advice he received from Walker and others.

Between February, 1982, and March, 1984, British Columbians were treated to a series of televised chats with Bennett. They were not unlike those mounted nationally by Trudeau, although Bennett had more trouble reading his lines than did the federal Liberal leader. The views of the British Columbia governing party were unequivocal. There was a need for "restraint"; British Columbians could not "picket their way to prosperity"; the province, like it or not, must adapt to "the new economic reality," where victory could only be won by those tough and able enough to compete in world markets. If the west coast could become a high-tech Silicon Valley of the North, or if B.C. could catch some of the rays of a new economic order's "Pacific Sunrise," basking in the light of the prosperity of the Far East, well, so much the better.

On July 7, 1983, Bennett and the Social Credit Party introduced a provincial budget, accompanied by some twenty-six bills. These bills represented a direct attack on trade union rights, human rights, and the autonomy of communities and groups to control or influence spending in the social arena. As a collective assault on organized workers and all oppressed sectors of society, as well as a concerted attempt to centralize power in the hands of the provincial state, the 1983 legislation was as forceful a political move as any Western New Right government had made. It was applauded by none other than ultra-conservative American economist Milton Friedman, who appreciated that Bennett was attempting to do in one fell swoop what Thatcher, Reagan, and others only dared to do over a number of years and campaigns.

Much has been written about the 1983 Bennett budget. Here it is important to stress how central the assault on public-sector workers was to the project. Five of the twenty-six bills attempted to curb the much-maligned powers of civil servants and their trade union organizations. The Public Service Relations Amendment Act, for instance, removed the right of the British Columbia Government Employees Union to negotiate anything but wages. Wage restraint, however, was quickly addressed by the Compensation Stabilization Amendment Act, which extended previously established controls and limited bargaining to a range of minus 5 per cent to plus 5 per cent. More ominous still was the Public Sector Restraint Act, which in its original wording would have given the government the right to fire employees at the expiration of a collective agreement "without cause." Later that wording was removed, but broad termination conditions remained. In one devastating blow, Bennett and the Socreds sought to liberate capital and the state from the fetters of the post-war settlement, striking out at public-sector unionism as the weak link in the chain of trade union defence mechanisms.

Most states intent on cannibalizing the clerks did so slowly, with some consideration given to how to obscure the act. Bennett's innovation was that he refused such obfuscation. (The difference between Bill Davis in Ontario and Bill Bennett in B.C., it was commonly said, was that Davis thought you could catch more flies with honey than with vinegar, while Bennett knew you could get even more with shit.) Before presentation of the budget the government reduced school financing, eliminating 1,000 teaching posts. The day after the twenty-six bills were introduced the state indicated the direction in which it intended to proceed: 400 employees received pink slips, and the state expressed its resolute intention of terminating 1,600 civil servants by October 31, 1983, when the BCGEU contract would lapse. Many of these posts were in the Human Resources ministry, and the 400 firings severely disrupted social services, affecting battered wives, abused children, welfare recipients, and the disabled. The devastating forecasts were that full-time equivalent positions for employees of government ministries would be reduced from about 46,800 to just under 40,000 in 1983, and further slashed in 1984-85 to about 35,400. In the parlance of Social Credit and the New Right this was "downsizing."

Done in the name of economy, these job eliminations also had their convenient ideological and political sides. Bennett made much of civil servant "laziness," lack of productivity, and privileged "job tenure." Fraser Institute head Michael Walker noted that public-sector workers provided "an ideological consistency and a lag in adjustment to new ideas and political directions." In the age of the new reality, "when the government of British Columbia is attempting to make the transition to a new vision of the future, it is appropriate that the continuity of ideas provided by the civil service be broken." Materially and ideologically, then, jobs had to go and with them the people who had been doing the work and thinking the wrong political thoughts.

This sledgehammer attack, coupled with the deep cuts in almost all areas of social spending, mobilized a vibrant mass opposition. From mid-July through mid-November, 1983, B.C. was an intensely politicized province. A *Globe and Mail* correspondent wrote, "Class warfare used to be a joke in this province. . . . [Now] no one is laughing." Trade unions in the public and private sectors banded together in a provincial opposition known as Operation Solidarity. Human rights groups and their supporters came together in a massive province-wide organization known as the Solidarity Coalition. Orchestrating all of this was the British Columbia Federation of Labor president, Art Kube.

An impressive culture of resistance broke somewhat out of Kube's tight organizational control and encouraged thousands to attend nightly meetings, read the movement's newspaper, *Solidarity Times*, and involve themselves in politics and daily discussions in ways never before imagined possible. Demonstrations of 50,000-80,000 were held. As the BCGEU prepared to go out on strike at the end of October there was talk of a general strike and a timetable of strike action that threatened massive public-sector walkouts and private-sector union involvement if the state intervened with a heavy hand to order protesters back to work or to jail their leaders. As

Bennett and the Socreds made a mockery of the traditions of the legislature, using their majority to stifle debate and ram bills through the House, it was obvious to many in the province that parliamentary procedures were a charade. The real opposition was in the streets with the Solidarity mobilization, something that Bennett himself – always keen to poke hard at the NDP – enjoyed acknowledging.

In spite of the intensity of working-class protest, little was won by the anti-Socred stand of literally millions of British Columbia workers and their supporters. BCGEU workers stayed off their jobs for a couple of weeks, teachers struck successfully and illegally, militants called for a general strike, but the state stood firm. And in the face of this firmness the leadership of the Operation Solidarity-Solidarity Coalition, always tightly in the hands of a few trade union leaders, folded. When the going got really tough, a broken Kube retreated to the sidelines. In the end, in what was perhaps one of the sorriest denouements in the history of Canadian class struggle, International Woodworkers of America leader Jack Munro flew on the state's own jet to Premier Bennett's Kelowna home. There, only hours before the B.C. Federation of Labor-led Operation Solidarity promised province-wide labour walkouts to defeat the oppressive restraint legislation, Munro and Bennett shook hands. The tap of class struggle was turned off. No workers were told why or for what. In the weeks to come they would learn: the teachers were victimized; the BCGEU settled for zero per cent in the first year of its new contract and sacrificed workers laid off, part-timers, and job conditions; *Solidarity Times* found its trade union financial support withdrawn; and the "social unionism" promoted by many labour leaders was crudely sacrificed as none of the human rights issues of the massive mobilization were addressed in the Munro settlement that many bluntly called a sell-out.

The fallout from this derailment was immense. Within the workers' movement, acrimony and internal dissent were rife. Munro was reviled by those on the left, defended by those on the right. He was voted out of a B.C. Federation of Labor vice-presidency a short time later. Two years later, Art Kube, mastermind of the Solidarity mobilization, retired from the provincial labour scene to take up a CLC posting in Ottawa: he was the federal body's new "expert" on coalitions. His own coalition, however, was in tatters. Bill Bennett had no Ottawa backers, although his own chief adviser, Norman Spector, was able to land a powerful behind-the-scenes post with the Mulroney Conservative government.

However much the players changed, the British Columbia "reality" was not all that new. As the 1980s wore on Vander Zalm replaced Bennett, the usual skirmishes between the BCGEU and the state took place, the building trades were locked out, and the provincial labour code went through a series of revisions, all of which, not surprisingly, undercut trade union rights and powers. In 1987 the Vander Zalm Socreds implemented legislation that increased state involvement in collective bargaining to an unprecedented level in Canada, allowed employers to restructure their productive relations to avoid unions, and curbed what few powers remained for organized labour, cutting back working-class capacity to resist. The mainstream B.C. Federation of Labor unions called for organized workers to boycott the Labour Relations Board, and tripartite experiments such as the Pacific Institute for Industrial Policy, bankrolled by the federal Labour Market and Productivity Centre, took a nosedive in the estimation of the trade union tops. B.C. Fed head Ken Georgetti described the Institute as "in a very, very deep coma." Bombastic Jack Munro, having now worked his way back into the labour hierarchy after his 1983-84 wrist-slapping, seemed to have been rudely awakened from his class-collaborationist dream. Noticing that Vander Zalm and the employers were cracking down hard on labour, Munro publicly attacked the co-operative tenor of the Institute as nothing less than a sham. "We were duped," he yelled. "We were double-crossed."

This seesaw of seeming militancy, derailment, and co-operation with capital and the state has, in fact, been the trajectory of a 1980s workers' movement constrained by both hard times and a vacillating trade union leadership. As in the case of Quebec's Louis Laberge, B.C.'s labour leadership has often talked tough, done little, and retreated into the pipedream of corporatist collaboration. Whereas Ken Georgetti replaced Art Kube in the aftermath of the latter's Solidarity failure, inching toward opposition and militancy in the later 1980s, he, too, like Quebec's Laberge, now epitomizes the new pragmatism of the trade union bureaucracy. As one newspaper report from 1990 noted:

The B.C. Federation of Labor, once the knee-jerk, extra-parliamentary opposition, now does extensive public-opinion polling every three or four months to tailor its message and moderate its policies. Jack Munro, the long-time sometimes irascible head of the woodworkers, currently sits on at least two provincial councils, alongside employers, to advise the Vander Zalm government on various land-use options. Mr. Georgetti has just been named to the premier's new environmental round table. The Federation and its arch enemy, the Business Council of British Columbia, have just agreed publicly – for probably the first time – on a major new government initiative, the restructuring of the workers' compensation system.

This process underscores the extent to which hard times, and the state's response of cannibalizing the public sector, push labour's leadership into ever more restricted corners of certain defeat. In this context it is worth exploring the nature and meaning of the current labour leadership in more detail.

A TALE OF TWO BUREAUCRACIES: THE GOOD COP/BAD COP MYTHOLOGY OF TRADE UNION LEADERSHIP

The question of labour's leadership is handled in a curiously schizophrenic way by most commentators and historians. On the one hand, much historical comment backs away from a generalized, theoretically informed assessment of the importance of leadership. The justification of this lack of attention usually turns on a dual, perhaps related, analytic and political position. Intellectual trends, which focus on "history from the bottom up," and a deeply entrenched quasi-syndicalist belief that leaders themselves are only a product of what the rank-and-file produces, coincide to shield labour leadership from serious scrutiny. On the other hand, labour leaders themselves have seemed particularly conscious of late of the need to promote themselves. The proliferation of larger-than-life biographies, exemplified by Bob White's *Hard Bargains: My Life on the Line* (1987) and Jack Munro's *Union Jack* (1988), has contributed to the mythologizing of labour leadership. In the place of a serious examination of the phenomenon of trade union leadership, then, we have a duality that is in fact connected: avoidance of the study of leadership allows the leadership issue to be collapsed into personality, usually packaged and promoted with considerable forethought.

But labour leadership in the contemporary Canadian workers' movement is too important a question to be sidestepped or left to hagiography. Indeed, the meaning of leadership is related to precisely the same set of historical forces that have set the stage for much of the current history of Canadian workers. The reigning trade union hierarchy was forged in the cauldron of the very same limited Keynesianism/Fordism that the 1975-90 years have seen deflated, if not defeated. Yet if there is a fundamental discontinuity, there has also been an important continuity in the leadership of the workers' movement and its basic loyalties and orientations.

This essential starting point is often lost on academic and political commentators who are captivated by the personalities of labour leadership. They fail, consequently, to appreciate the extent to which differences in style among the trade union leaders are secondary to the overwhelming consensus prevailing within the labour bureaucracy over the fundamentals of what the political economy of trade unionism should be. Put simply, virtually the entire labour leadership in the Canadian workers' movement of the post-1975 years accepts and lives to perpetuate the premises of the post-World War Two settlement, in spite of the blunt reality that the settlement has been gutted by capital and the state in the recent past.

Virtually created by the post-World War Two reform moment, trade union leaders in Canada are overwhelmingly committed to the principles of reformist politics, a basic tenet of which is the divide that dichotomizes class struggle, relegating the economic battle at the point of production to trade unionism and the parliamentary contest over the direction of the state to the New Democratic Party. This false separation is then reproduced in the intense sectionalism of trade unionism itself. Labour's leaders stand fast, not for the interests of workers as a whole, as a *class*, but for *their* union's rights over particular workers and their dues. This holds, regardless of whether union leaders adopt an archaically steadfast commitment to age-old jurisdictional boundaries or opt, as have some recent colonizers among the labour bureaucracy, for raiding other unions as a means to expand their dues base. The seeming contradiction between union leaders who accept jurisdictional boundaries and those who deny them evaporates when one understands that what is at stake in the United Steel Workers of America organizing warehouse workers, the Retail, Wholesale, and Department Store Union taking taxi drivers under its wing, or the Canadian Automobile Workers marching in to take over already unionized Newfoundland fishermen or gobbling up airline flight attendants has nothing to do with working-class solidarity and everything to do with a conception of the working class as "property" that will be owned by one or another wing of trade union officialdom.

With the coming of industrial legality in the aftermath of World War Two, trade union leaders bought deeply into the notion of workers as property. This was an old process encouraged and furthered by the state, for whom such a class-as-property equation always entailed certain corollaries: those who own property have rights, as did trade union leaders and the institutions they headed, but they also have responsibilities as well, especially the appropriate maintenance of that property. There is no substantial indication that the contemporary Canadian trade union leadership, regardless of minor squabbles over jurisdictions, questions the parameters of this state-embraced understanding of property maintenance. Virtually to a person, Canadian trade union leaders accept the need to control and police their own rank and file, thereby keeping the lid on class struggle and maintaining unionism within the boundaries of respectable organization.

This point can be made with respect to the currently fashionable panacea of "social unionism." Embraced by the progressive wing of the labour bureaucracy, social unionism is supposedly the antithesis of business unionism. It promotes causes and endorses oppositional movements that reach well beyond collective bargaining into the realms, for instance, of world peace and environmental preservation. Social unionism also preaches coalition-building, stressing that labour should unite with other progressive sectors to implement reform and better the lot of the weak and the underprivileged. This is often contrasted with the more narrow unionism of a less progressive old guard within the labour movement. Among this old guard, collective bargaining issues themselves are sacrosanct and little attention is apparently paid to the wider issues of social change. These business unionists want little to do with other potential coalition partners, and instead keep narrowly to trade union circles. The social-versus-business union dichotomy is reinforced by the promotional imagery of labour leadership: the progressive wears tweeds or fashionably tailored suits, keeps him or herself trim with trips to the gymnasium and a carefully monitored diet, and watches language so as not to offend any quarter; the rougher burly macho redneck wing of officialdom dresses in polyester and promotes itself as the tough-talking, straight-shooting defender of the boys (and girls).

This politics of difference and style, these competing masculinities (into which women in the trade union hierarchy also purposively fit themselves), convey a sense of difference that is superficial. There are indeed good and bad cops within the labour hierarchy, but as in the real world of the police this distinction is of far less significance than the ties that bind these factions together. At issue is not which union leader is enlightened and sophisticated but what union leadership does as a structured feature of the workers' movement. And on this final score there does not appear to be all that much difference separating social from business union hierarchies, save for the extent to which social unionism and business unionism appeal to different constituencies and engage in seemingly oppositional public relations.

Social unionism, for instance, might be seen as simply a progressive facade behind which a wing of the labour hierarchy adroitly masks its traditional business unionist refusal to use and extend the class power of the unions to launch a struggle for social change. It actually understates working-class power by accepting the current conventional wisdom that class as the central agent of socio-economic transformation has been undermined, and new social movements of women, ecologists, and peace advocates are more potent than class because they can more easily mobilize masses of supporters. Yet for all of the capacity of these movements and causes to galvanize vocal world-wide protest, they lack the economic teeth to chew into those forces that profit from oppression, ecological devastation, and war-mongering. A real social unionism would indeed link up with these sectors, but it would rightly stress the extent to which only mobilizations led by the working class and backed by the working-class capacity to stop the productive forces of advanced capitalist society in their tracks have the actual power to transform social relations. Yet this is precisely *not* what the much-vaunted current social unionism is about.

Instead, social unionists speak of themselves and those they lead as but one segment among many, all the while using their own powers and considerable financial and bureaucratic clout to control coalitions and steer them in directions the labour hierarchy can tolerate. Unlike the old-guard business unionists who are more arrogantly honest in the refusal of the need to mobilize outside of their own union ranks, the new-wave progressives among the labour heads now have a viable excuse to cover their own commitment to limiting the role the working class can play in transforming society. At the same time they exercise undue bureaucratic and, at times, charismatic control over social movements. This has been evident of late in sectors of the peace movement, in the anti-free trade coalitions, and in the forces opposing the Tory Goods and Services Tax.

Both social unionists and business unionists are thus in fact united in the view that workers are simply one interest group among many within a pluralist social order, that their own particular bargaining with the state can produce only specific, curtailed consequences, largely confined to the wages/job conditions category, and that ultimately a politics of opposition must be channelled into the parliamentary arena, where workers and others should align themselves with the New Democratic Party. The only difference between social unionists and business unionists is that the former camp is willing to commit its rhetoric, and orchestrate its activity and language with more care, to wider projects, while the latter narrow their agenda and appeal more crassly to what they perceive as the parochialism and sectionalism of rank-and-file workers, which they play a role in constructing.

For all the talk of social unionism current among progressive labour leaders, there has been precious little attempt to use union power in ways that step outside of the long-established conventional relations of business unions, employers, and the state. And where social unionism appears to have run a bit ahead of itself, its promise of coalition-building for social change being taken seriously by masses of workers and their allies, the end results have been illuminating. In British Columbia's Solidarity, for instance, the "social" side of unionism's opposition to the Socred state collapsed into a capitulationist business unionism and sectionalism at the eleventh hour. The province's leading "redneck" labour patriarch, Jack Munro, was sent into the fray to stop the struggle that social unionist Art Kube was unwilling to carry on. And when it was all over and done with, social unionists and business unionists stood as one against all of those who wondered how a momentous opposition could be terminated so abruptly. For social and business unionists in B.C. the derailment of Solidarity was rather easily moved into the need to support the NDP in the next provincial electoral contest. To be sure, social and business unionists adopt different stances, even support different prospective leaders, within the NDP. But in the end, the NDP *is* the end.

The good cop/bad cop mythology can be explored by taking on the issue of personality into which the more generalized matter of labour leadership is habitually pressed. Bob White is one of labour's unquestioned progressives; in his recently published autobiography he flies the colours of social unionism with pride, proclaiming that by age seventeen he knew "that the labour movement is a great vehicle for social change, not just inside the plant but in the community as well." Jack Munro, in contrast, is widely perceived as a blustering business unionist, a burly dinosaur who has somehow managed to stave off extinction. For Munro social unionism and coalitions of the working class and other groups are little more than a "grand scheme" destined to "go down the tube." Comparing these labour leaders can be useful.

We live in an age when all seems presentation. The respective dustjacket images of White's and Munro's autobiographies seem to convey strikingly divergent messages. White is packaged skilfully, a cosmopolitan sophisticate at home in the boardrooms of the nation's corporations or walking a picket line. The front cover strikes a serious pose of intense determination, a literal gaze of the leader who can deliver. Dressed in the white shirt, matching suspenders and tie, and business suit of archetypal respectability, White's seemingly manicured hands are placed in a symbolic gesture of pointing to what is to be negotiated while his orderly greying hair conveys the sense of experience all union leaders rely on. A complementary pose adorns the back of the book. There White walks a picket line, his hair more tousled, his dress more casually hip (leather coat, sport jacket, turtleneck), a pursed smile setting off the wrinkled visage of a man who cares. Striking workers, meanwhile, are photogenically faded into the background, placing White himself in an illuminating relief. *Hard Bargains: My Life on the Line*, as a title, constructs White as simultaneously a real worker, drawn out of the hard times of working-class life, and a trade union leader adept at the "crunch" bargaining that gets his members what they need. White's is a life apparently experienced in the production routines of the wage as well as the production of results. As the backcover blurb states, White "is without doubt the single most influential figure in the Canadian labour movement. Respected by workers and business leaders alike, White has become a major voice in national affairs. All his life he has bargained hard, and, more often than not, won."

Jack Munro strikes a different pose. He stares out at the reader from the cover of his book, *Union Jack*, a seeming incongruity. He, too, wears the white collar, tie, and suit, but it jars with the baseball cap atop his head. Unfashionably long sideburns and scraggly neckhairs convey the sense of a man who has no time for "sissified" narcissism, and frame a face that seems to conform to Bill White's comments on contemporary trade union leaders: "When I see the face of a labour leader on the T.V. now it's always fat. All jowls like hogs ready for the knife, it's hard to imagine the sight of any of them striking fear in the capitalists' hearts." Munro's business unionism, however, probably is not meant to strike class fear into anyone, as the comments on the back of the book indicate. The ball cap pegs Munro as one of the boys, tough and straight-shooting, a leader among his rough and tumble woodsworker members, the kind of figure who can draw the praise of populist journalist Jack Webster, Tory politician Pat Carney, and Liberal leader Jean Chrétien. When you are called "a hell of a good guy" by people like these, ordinary workers are meant to sit up and take notice.

That is what one part of business unionism is all about. Another part, unquestioning loyalty to the union as an institution, is conveyed by the title of Munro's biography, a play on appropriate words that link the workers' movement to an empire headed by the monarch.

There appears, then, to be considerable difference between the social unionist, Bob White, and the business union boss, Jack Munro. Yet, symbolically, both appear under their union, White sitting beneath the Canadian Automobile Workers' insignia, Munro's green ball cap sporting the initials of the International Woodworkers of America. Their histories also differ in emphasis and style, but in substance they reflect some remarkable convergences.

Munro commences his own story with a brazen account of how he scuttled, classic business unionist style, the Solidarity mobilization in British Columbia. He revels in his "realism" and "responsible" behaviour: Munro was the man who stopped "the bullshit." Describing the coalition forces of Solidarity as "every goddamn group in the country," including, to Munro's chagrin, "the Rural Lesbians Society" and "the West End Gay Community," Munro recounts how "These people were drunk on their own power." "We trade unionists," he notes, "we were the moderates in all of this." Things were "out of control." So Munro, the bad cop, ended the province-wide agitation, which he nervously saw drifting toward good cop Art Kube's general strike, and thereby saved union treasuries and secured his place and continuity in history. He ends his account of "Derailing the Solidarity Express" with the complacent conclusion: "But the IWA and I have survived. . . . And what about all the hotshots who were going to set the world on fire? Well, they aren't here anymore. But I am."

White would never be so crassly blunt. Whereas Munro's narrative unfolds in a language of expletives and crude stereotyping – his current wife is described as "the little broad . . . the boss" – White, conscious of his image among feminists, is more careful. And a little less believable. The opening chapters of *Hard Bargains* depict a family background that is heroic and honourable: White's parents, working-class immigrants in southwestern Ontario, are loving, religiously devout, temperate, honest, and free from bigotry. White himself was apparently a rather exemplary youth. While a bit of a shirker around the house, he did not like the taste of beer, was polite with adults, could not tell a lie, and picked fights only with "bullies I'd caught pushing another kid around."

Throughout the book, White takes the time to inform us of his personal life, of his pride in his son's non-conformist wearing of an earring along with a tuxedo, and of the busy union leader's willingness to help out a young girl with a drug problem. His exemplary role in the delivery room, in spite of his non-attendance at prenatal classes, is mentioned. Lesson One of the public life of a social unionist has been learned, perhaps a bit too obviously: the personal can be turned to valuable political purpose. When

Munro addresses such personal matters he does it matter of factly; his shortcomings as a husband and father are secondary to his life as a worker and union leader in the making.

All of this is veneer. Many see only this surface of contrasting image, representation, conscious public profile. Scratch the accessible facade, however, and the histories of White and Munro, as well as their practice as trade union leaders, converge. Both White and Munro rose up the union ladder by learning the two ironclad rules of the labour oligarchy's political economy: unswerving loyalty to the union leadership; and the necessity of leading rebellious workers back to their jobs after negotiations fail to get them everything they want. Munro and White were groomed for their positions by incumbent leaders. As they both came to power in the mid-1970s, a time of working-class ferment, their roles were almost exactly the same. The 1973 IWA convention was "a Jack Munro convention," and Munro recalls his message: "I said that the type of infighting that had gone on in the past had to stop. I wanted to restore faith in the leadership and put an end to wildcat strikes that were getting out of hand. I wanted to get rid of the different factions in the IWA." Three years later, in the 1976 Ford strike, UAW leader Dennis McDermott and his hand-picked successor, Bob White, "scrambled to find a compromise that the membership would accept, recognizing that they had to make the best of a bad situation."

The meaning of Munro's and White's histories, for all the difference in rhetoric and representation, is thus quite simple: these men made it to the top because they could be counted on to lead in particular ways. When, in 1960, Jack Munro first aligned with the union, he was a plant chairman, responsible, in his words, for "seeing that the agreement is policed." By 1962 he was a business agent, hired by Jack Moore, the IWA regional head he would later replace. His first duty was "to help the local get a dues increase from the membership in order to hire a permanent third business agent – me."

White's first serious lesson in unionism came in a Woodstock strike when he was a youthful twenty-two. A young militant strike leader, White was told by one of the Canadian UAW honchos: "any dumb sonovabitch can take them out. The test is: Can you put them back?" The union bureaucracy then urged compromise on the strikers and negotiated a settlement with management that the local unionists apparently thought was less than what could have been achieved. White made his choice: he swallowed "a bitter pill" and led his fellow workers back to their jobs. Twenty-five years later, White would have loyalist lieutenants do the same thing. During 1982 negotiations with Chrysler, workers at an Ajax trim plant exploded in anger. "Holy Christ," reported one of White's hired guns, "This is almost a riot. I've never been at a membership meeting like this in my life. They're ready to lynch me. . . . The whole place is yelling *Sell Out!*"

A year later, in the 1983 General Motors-UAW negotiations, White and his bureaucracy's role in suppressing working-class anger appears on film. In a conscious, blatantly self-serving, and amazingly successful move to mythologize his break from the Detroit-based UAW and the founding of the CAW, White allowed the collective bargaining process to be filmed and his conversations with UAW leaders to be clandestinely taped. The result is a highly acclaimed film, *Final Offer*. When 3,000 Oshawa General Motors truck plant workers wildcat in the midst of negotiations, the film, for all of its staging, cannot avoid exposing the vehemence with which White and his loyalists respond to their union base getting out of hand. The account of this episode in *Hard Bargains* is subdued and understated. On film the language and tension of the moment reveal a union bureaucracy seeking desperately a settlement with employers, slamming the lid on working-class self-activity with a harshness that has to be seen to be believed and appreciated. Social unionism fades in the actual battle of class struggle, its layers of protective posturing peeling off to expose a business unionist core.

When Jack Munro and Bob White end their respective books, we should not be surprised with the conclusions. The business unionist speaks of the need for a new generation of experienced leaders to come to the fore. He recognizes that his day will eventually come, and he will have to move over for someone else. But, suggests Munro, "Luckily for me, nobody . . . is saying that just yet about the presidency. I think they still like me." White says almost exactly the same thing: "If the CAW is to remain a dynamic organization, it needs periodic changes in leadership. It needs new, younger people to take over: men and women who have their own style, their own teams, and their own directions. . . . I'll be moving on some day, but where to, I don't know. I honestly don't know." The only difference between the social unionist and the business unionist is that the former has the savvy to promote his own future by coyly implying that his horizons extend beyond trade unionism. Also, it should come as no surprise that social unionist Bob White convinced his supposed opposite, business unionist Jack Munro, to "commit his life to paper." They are truly brothers under the skin. And they need not worry about the next generation of labour leaders.

Like their predecessors, they have done their best to make sure that the leadership layer beneath them remains true to their conception of what union leadership is and remains. Style aside, those who climb their way to the top of the trade union hierarchy are committed to the fundamental premise of a now tottering forty-five-year-old regime of industrial legality: the working class is a "property" that has to be managed so that it can reap its own dividends. The job of union bureaucracies is to do just that, making sure that the workplaces of the land do not rampage out of control. Labour's leaders don't so much live by labour's legalistic, state-imposed codes as they are an integral part of that coding. In the realm of politics, another institution with its own bureaucratic structures plays a similar and complementary role.

SLOW-CIALISMS IN ONE PROVINCE: LABOUR AND
THE NEW DEMOCRATIC PARTY IN HARD TIMES

The close relationship between social democracy and the labour movement in Canada is almost taken as a given in political and academic commentary. The labour leadership, to a person, lines up behind the New Democratic Party, the rare exceptions proving the rule of alignment. But for workers as a class the linkage is more problematic. From its founding in the early 1960s, when it commanded the affiliation of hundreds of union locals representing almost 15 per cent of all Canadian organized workers, the NDP has slowly lost ground. During the post-1975 years of hard times, union affiliations dropped off until, by 1984, just over 7 per cent of all Canadian unionists belonged to labour organizations that hitched their cart to the political horse of social democracy.

Since unionists affiliated with the NDP are more likely to vote New Democrat and more prone to have a working-class leftist self-image than non-affiliated unionists, the inability of the affiliation movement to grow and draw in more unionists is a reflection of the failure of social democracy to deepen its relationship to class in Canada. And of this declining number of locals and percentage of unionists, the regional imbalances are striking. The NDP-labour movement connection was almost entirely an Ontario and British Columbia phenomenon, with the former province providing over 550 of the 730 union-NDP affiliations and over 75 per cent of all unionists in the country affiliated to the NDP. Thus, the NDP is not a labour party in the true sense of the word, and the often-voiced perception that it is controlled by Big Labour is a myth propagated to undercut the New Democrats' electoral chances. To be sure, labour delegates at NDP conventions routinely figure as approximately 25 per cent of all of those present, and the unions contribute substantially to the party coffers, especially in election years (roughly $2.1 million in 1984). But there is no getting around the blunt reality that approximately only one in four unionists votes NDP. This means that unionists are more likely to vote social democrat than non-unionists, but it is hardly cause for celebration in NDP circles.

Indeed, for much of the difficult post-1975 years there was little to cheer about within the NDP. The 1980 federal election saw the party wiped out east of the Ottawa River and there were some in New Democrat circles who embraced the view that whole regions, such as the Maritimes, were "lumpenized" by underdevelopment and would never again be a base for social democracy. Other federal pundits wanted to capitalize on Quebec's historic electoral discontent and try to build a social democratic alliance with the Parti Québécois. This fragile hope shattered as the Bourassa Liberals swept Pierre Marc Johnson's PQ aside and moved to cut their own deals with Mulroney's Ottawa. By the mid-1980s the NDP was clearly flagging, its leader, Ed Broadbent, riding out a rough period by trying to move the party more to the centre, a strategic retreat challenged by many in the ranks and some in the caucus. There was talk of a Liberal-NDP alliance to turn back the Tory tide: polls showed the New Democrats at one of their lowest points ever, a meagre 15 per cent in 1983, and the figure would bottom out at as low as 11-12 per cent; the Conservative Party seemed poised to sweep the next national election; and provincially and regionally the country was ruled by Conservatives, save for Howard Pawley's NDP-led Manitoba, Quebec, hardly a hopeful site for New Democrats, and the Yukon, where Tony Penikett's NDP captured power in the territorial legislature in 1985.

At the 1983 Regina convention of the party, Broadbent and his supporting cast of labour leaders were doubly angered by challenges from Ontario's Left Caucus and the more threatening demands from western figureheads Allan Blakeney (Saskatchewan) and Grant Notley (Alberta). The latter duo proposed that the historic Regina Manifesto of 1933 be updated to promote a "social contract" that would embrace an incomes policy. For the labour bureaucracy and the federal leadership of the NDP this all smacked too much of capitulation to wage controls and they squashed the western initiative, offering an olive branch of provincial rights. A year later the NDP seemed a minor player as the Tories and Mulroney rode their landslide victory into Ottawa. The NDP could take some solace that it had almost held its own since 1980; compared to the Liberals it did quite well.

A comeback seemed in the making. With the Liberals long discredited and as the ruling Progressive Conservative Party plummeted in public opinion, its patronage record making a lie of Mulroney's election promises and its backbenchers caught with their hands in too many tills, Broadbent and the NDP seemed the only credible parliamentary alternative. The social democratic message of humane welfare and unemployment policy, national day care, and an equitable tax system seemed to be finally registering with the voting public. By 1987 Broadbent and the NDP climbed in the polls; apparently 40 per cent of Canadians would vote social democratic. More surprisingly, in Quebec the NDP seemed ready to break through long-standing barriers to emerge as an actual contender for provincial power. A new leader, Michael Agnaieff of the Quebec Teachers' Union, as well as the support of Laberge's QFL, solidified the NDP as a presence in Quebec for the first time. Even in the Far North, the NDP began to register federal victories. In 1987 Audrey McLaughlin won a by-election for the NDP, replacing the powerful retired Tory incumbent, Erik Nielsen, an Ottawa fixture since the late 1950s. Social democracy seemed to be getting its act together. And then it all came apart.

As the 1988 election approached, free trade dominated the electoral agenda. John Turner and the Liberals grabbed the "Canada First" thunder, while Broadbent and his advisers decided to talk to voters about many matters as well as free trade and in the process got lost in the one-issue political shuffle. At the same time, Quebec opted for its own nation and plumped free trade's economic high side, and discontented NDPers defected. The most notable personal instance of this process was the early pre-election passage of Jim Laxer, former radical Waffle leader who had himself been waffling on basic social democratic commitments for some time, to the Liberals. When the votes were counted the NDP increased its number of seats to forty-three and its popular vote to just over 20 per cent. It gained ground in Saskatchewan and British Columbia, but lost footing in Manitoba, the Maritimes, and industrial Ontario.

The trade union bureaucrats backed Broadbent to the full in the 1988 contest. They wanted to beat down free trade. They lost. Angered by this defeat, they saw little to make them all that happy in its aftermath. Bob White distributed a quasi-open letter to the party, assailing the NDP for not making free trade the central issue of the campaign. He also chastised the party for relying on union funds and personnel to mount the electoral charge at the same time as it ignored trade union advice and direction.

When Audrey McLaughlin, having sat in the federal House as an NDPer for only two years, was elected to lead the party in November, 1989, replacing Broadbent, the labour hierarchy hardly called the shot. The trade union tops almost certainly wanted someone else. Coming from the Yukon (which many union heads had never set foot in), identified as weak on economic and labour concerns, and supposedly lacking the charisma and authority that it takes to win votes and maintain party discipline, McLaughlin squared off against British Columbia's Dave Barrett, who secured the reluctant backing of a number of labour leaders. Shirley Carr, president of the CLC, visibly cast her lot with Barrett at the eleventh hour, a rather crude statement on the class/gender divide that many NDPers on the convention floor were kicking around. Bob White, ever the social unionist with an eye on image (and perhaps on the future leadership of the party should Audrey come up short), stood by McLaughlin; Jack Munro was, of course, with Barrett. Peace was predictably made in the end, but union leaders were more than a little miffed that a party they supported so staunchly, with their funds if not necessarily their members' votes, seemed drifting so obviously away from them.

Indeed, throughout the hard times of the 1980s it was fairly apparent that the NDP kept its distance from the overt class struggles of the time. When in opposition, social democrats could do little to stem the tide of provincial neo-Conservative union-bashing. On occasion, as in British Columbia in 1983, social democracy's rather self-serving and complacent insistence that extra-parliamentary oppositions were of far less significance than what was being done and could be done within the halls of provincial legislatures, actually proved counterproductive. Dave Barrett seemed more concerned with the NDP's displacement in the midst of the Solidarity upheaval than he did about the class battle raging around him. Uninvited to a podium at one massive rally, he was asked to comment on the turnout. Describing it all as a "sprint," he suggested the real race was being "run in the legislature." However, the provincial House was itself something of a Socred-orchestrated circus, governed by closure, all-night sittings, and votes at three o'clock in the morning. Barrett himself was eventually forcibly ejected and, this being his second eviction in one sitting, refused re-entry for the remainder of a session. The social democratic opposition was thus leader-less in the midst of the most dramatic class struggle in the province's history. "We are observers, and we observed," Barrett would later comment.

Social democrats, Barrett's characterization aside, were often a little more than observers. In Manitoba, Howard Pawley brought the NDP back to power in 1981, but it was hardly an unambiguous victory for labour. Indeed, it was preceded by acrimonious splits within the ranks of provincial social demo-crats as former cabinet minister and labour lawyer Sid Green defected, biting the hands that fed him, blaming the unions for undue meddling in NDP affairs, and taking a few malcontents with him to form a new party. It failed to elect a single candidate in its first campaign. Under Pawley, who spoke out against union influence in the formation of the NDP twenty years earlier, the Manitoba government faced the recession of the early 1980s and managed to get provincial employees to contribute to a job-creation fund. The race to socialism was hardly being run at a breakneck pace. Pawley waged the fight for the retention of social services, faced reactionary opposition to the NDP's attempts to address the grievances of Manitoba's Francophones in 1983, and won re-election in a 1986 contest that saw the NDP committed to massive provincial hydroelectric development.

No doubt there were many class battles fought out in the social demo-cratic struggles for socialism in one province, but workers and trade union-ists could be excused if, while blinking, they missed the Manitoba NDP's unambiguously pro-labour socialist stance. The social democratic state lost a lot of ground with unionists when, in the summer of 1987, it pushed a "final offer" solution to labour/capital conflict, in which both parties in a dispute would submit their last demand and a "neutral" third party would choose one of the two options. The Manitoba Federation of Labor was in an uproar, and Jeff Rose of CUPE claimed that the NDP government had divided workers as bosses never could. But most of the press ink and a good deal of tension were generated around the language question and the Paw-ley government's upholding of the federal state's abortion law.

As Nelson Wiseman concludes in his history of the CCF-NDP in Mani-toba, social democracy established itself in the mid-1980s as part of the political mainstream. In the midst of hard times, this meant that the NDP was as likely to demand belt-tightening of labour as any other party in power. The difference was that its call for restraint was couched in more authority and could be counted on to generate less grumbling among the union hierarchy and less militancy within the ranks of the workers' move-ment. "Slow-cialism" had its advantages.

This may have had something to do with the most startling provincial political development in the 1980s. Ontario, in comparison with western bastions of social democracy, has always been perceived as an unlikely candidate for an NDP provincial win. Moreover, its NDP strength has more of an unambiguous class colouring than that of other regions, social democracy being strong electorally in the centres of labour power associated with northern resource extraction (Sudbury), southern Ontario industrial might (Windsor, Hamilton, Oshawa), and immigrant radicalism (sections of Toronto). Since the so-called Golden Age of Canadian socialism, when social democracy actually challenged Tory rule in Ontario in the war-torn early 1940s, however, this class-driven protest has never really gelled in provincial politics. For forty-two years Tories ruled Ontario, the modern period under the tutelage of machine-builders Leslie Frost, John Robarts, and Bill Davis.

The long reign of Ontario Conservatives ended in May, 1985. Led by the hard right, Frank Miller having replaced the retiring (in more ways than one) Davis, the provincial Tories were overly confident and seemingly oblivious to the electorate's misgivings about Miller and his proposed dose of neo-conservatism as an answer to the recession-plagued woes of the country's most industrialized region. What should have been a major opportunity for a party of left reform turned into something of a sleeper as Bob Rae attempted to lull voters with a minimalist approach to social change. Electors obviously could not distinguish this from the message of David Peterson's new-look Liberals. As the Tories sputtered and stalled, the Liberals surged forward, capturing the middle ground Rae and his advisers so unardently sought. When the final tally was in, the political map of Ontario had been redrawn. In a final ironic twist Miller and the Conservatives won, with fifty-two seats, but they ended up losing big. Peterson and the Liberals captured more of the popular vote and secured forty-eight seats. The NDP managed to grab twenty-five seats, less than it won in 1975 when it secured the status of official opposition but midway between what it counted in the 1977 (33) and 1981 (21) elections, the latter a particularly bad showing under the leadership of Michael Cassidy. This was thus a classic minority government. But the way the parties negotiated the right to rule was historically unprecedented.

Rae, in a blueprint case of social democracy's negotiation of the parliamentary process, offered both the Conservatives and the Liberals his pledge of support should they agree to a specific agenda of reforms. When the Tories refused, the Liberals snapped up the agreement, which included legislation on human rights, equal pay for work of equal value, changes in severance pay, and restrictions on doctors billing above established Ontario Hospital Insurance Plan (OHIP) rates. Most of this legislation was in fact abstract and either failed to alter fundamentally the special oppressions aimed at, or simply held specific lines in a period of hard times. Nonetheless, "slow-cialists," long perceived as liberals in a hurry, made the Grits run a bit in Ontario in the mid-1980s.

Peterson took it all as an opportunity to train for his own race. He basked in the political sun of holding the greedy doctors in check, talked loudly about commitments to women's equality, and looked every bit the man in charge as the NDP was nudged politely to the sidelines. Waiting out the requisite two years demanded in the NDP-Liberal accord, Peterson called a 1987 election and swamped the already sinking Tories, who could muster only enough support to elect sixteen candidates. Rae and the NDP did little better, winning nineteen seats. The Liberals commanded an astounding ninety-five ridings. Never were Ontario's New Democrats more gloomy; it was hard to realize that you had buried yourself alive.

The NDP did not so much dig itself out of this electoral grave as it was brought back to the living political surface by hard times and the subsequent fallout. In Ottawa, Mulroney and the federal Tories so alienated the Canadian public by the end of the 1980s that whatever the populist appeal of neo-conservatism, provincial Conservatives were very much on the defensive. Unions were insisting that free trade was costing the country hundreds of thousands of jobs, many of them in Ontario where a plant closure movement was upping the body count of unemployed daily. To add to provincial Tory woes, their party was torn apart by its lack of leadership, splits among its varied constituencies, and a catastrophic depletion of party coffers. The Tories, who had ruled Queen's Park for generations, were simply not in the running electorally by the end of the 1980s. Peterson and the Liberals should have coasted to an easy win. The polls said they would, and this prompted Peterson to call an early election, just three years into his 1987 mandate.

As the province prepared to elect a new government in September, 1990, the Peterson Liberals virtually handed victory to the NDP. They proved incapable of subduing a major scandal concerning fund-raising, appeared too eager to wage a costly $40 million election, angered much of their constituency with tax policies that showed no signs of easing up on the high costs of governing in hard times, and were apparently blind to the failures of their own policies. Seldom had the arrogance of power been so blatant. Originally and mistakenly targeting the now toothless Tories as the main contender, Peterson let Bob Rae and the New Democrats score some early campaign points. When Liberal strategists perceived that the NDP, not Michael Harris's Conservatives, now represented the major threat to the continuity of Peterson's rule, the Liberals shifted gears and Peterson began to backtrack on his party's intransigent stand on taxes and to fly the panic-flag of anti-socialism. It simply cost the Liberals credibility and made Peterson look shrill and defensive.

In the highest voter turnout since 1975, 66 per cent of Ontario's eligible voters kicked the Liberals out of office and stunned pundits and politicians of all stripes: the NDP won seventy-four of 130 seats with 38 per cent of the popular vote. "Slow-cialism" had come to another province, and for the first time. Old-timers whose roots reached back to the founding of the CCF cried on election night. There was talk of seeing "the New Jerusalem that Tommy Douglas spoke about." But if NDP diehards finally reaped the fruits of long labours in social democracy's trenches, plenty of newcomers rode high on the tide of victory: a good number of those elected had virtually no political experience and were running in their first campaigns. But there was no doubt that Ontario had spoken, not so much *for* the NDP as against the Grits and Tories. Peterson, who lost in his own London riding, was quick to exit provincial politics, resigning in disgrace as leader. His replacement as MPP, one of twenty-nine women elected, nineteen as New Democrats, formerly ran a shelter for battered women.

Hard times and the prospect of the country's boom province going bust in plant closures, unemployment, and rural collapse set an agenda in Ontario in 1990 that only the NDP could address with credibility. There was little socialism in the campaign, save for Peterson's below-the-belt punches at its inevitably ruinous results. Rae, in the populist parlance of the contemporary NDP, addressed "ordinary people," and his electoral promises of cuts in dependency on nuclear power, rejection of Sunday shopping, environmental sensitivity, increasing the minimum wage, changes in the administration of automobile insurance, pay equity, and refusal of the free trade agreement cut a moderate swath across a spectrum of constituencies, a nice and relatively non-contentious program of "slow-cialism."

The unions and their leadership were behind Rae, of course, but so were many other groups. Native people, fed up with inaction on land claims and enraged by the use of federal troops and provincial police in squashing the Oka, Quebec, uprising in the summer of 1990, saw the NDP as the only alternative. Church groups and unions came together against Sunday shopping. As the Ontario health care system tottered, nurse unionists, Ontario Public Service Employees' Union members in staff positions, thin-skinned doctors who remembered Peterson's mauling of them and their ill-fated mid-1980s strike, and teachers all voiced their discontent with Peterson. Rural regions, long committed to conservatism, had seen enough of the slick, red-tied Liberal leader; concerned with the environment and caught on the horns of rising expenses and declining sales, country folk and residents of Ontario's small cities and towns abandoned the Tories and opted for the New Democrats. Bob Rae, after all, having cleaned up his act, almost looked like a farm boy in a suit. One former cabinet minister and leadership candidate in the Conservative Party suggested that the electorate had "slit its throat."

The new NDP cabinet contained twelve rookies and eleven women. It was also willed a $700 million deficit (which, under scrutiny, ballooned to over $2 billion), a convenient peg on which to retire any notion that the NDP was going to do anything precipitous. The new government moved so slowly many wondered how it was possible for a state to stand so still. There was no socialist transformation, and Rae spent a good deal of his time issuing statements meant to placate Bay Street and Wall Street. Talks with corporations threatening shutdowns proceeded without acrimony; public ownership of what used to be called natural monopolies in the energy sector was backed away from even when it seemed appropriate and necessary. Most of the headlines stressed the same theme, "Rae preaches caution, not revolution." Not a few articles keyed on Rae's unpublished manifesto, "What We Owe Each Other," a speech to the NDP provincial council that attacked Marxism's political failures and economic naiveté, calling instead for a socialism attentive to values and love. It was hard to take seriously the corporate capital howling about what the NDP would do in Ontario when, months after the election, its major concession to the working class was to appoint Bob White to the managerial committee of Skydome in Toronto.

There were, nevertheless, signs that class was a telling feature within the newly empowered Ontario NDP. Barely in office, Rae and his colleagues had to deal with charges that an MPP in their midst was guilty of unfair labour practices. According to the *Globe and Mail*'s Michael Valpy, a battle brewed in Toronto as mayoral ambitions split ascendant social democracy down its class middle. On the one side stood the downtown, radical-chic, fern-bar frequenting, anti-growth, anti-development element: fashionable social democrats who wanted to crack the mayoralty nut, previously avoided by the NDP, by running Jack Layton. On the other side was the more visibly proletarian element from Toronto's West End. They wore blue collars and often worked in construction. Many came from immigrant backgrounds. They weren't fashionable, and they didn't much like a politics of fashion. They wondered what an anti-development NDP campaign, and a possible anti-growth NDP mayor, might mean for working-class Toronto.

"Slow-cialism" being what it is, however, the contentious issue for Rae's ruling social democrats, in 1990, was more complicated than a class-driven labour-versus-capital opposition. As Wayne Roberts perceptively noted, business was going to do what it could to subvert the new government, but it would also work with it, and labour's leadership was going to provide "volunteer traffic cops . . . organizers who see the economy through the eyes of workers who start at 7 a.m., who can talk quietly to business and help put the pieces in place for slow and steady progress." The real problems for a ruling NDP were going to come from two other sources. A fifth column of enemy bureaucrats presented the first hurdle: senior civil servants had for generations cut deals with other bureaucracies and countless capitalists and wanted those arrangements to continue, unchallenged by meddling politicians, whom they have always seen, regardless of party, as merely coming and going with each volatile swing in government-making. And social activists who wanted poverty ended, day care developed, and the environment cleaned up were not likely to accept easily the pace of change dictated by the NDP's gradualism.

"Slow-cialism" in Ontario, sustained by the labour hierarchy, was thus far more a product of a popular alliance of disgruntled social elements than it was a working-class victory. Peterson's Liberals gambled that the "declining middle" would not opt for the NDP and that the recessionary downturn could be rhetorically denied throughout the hoopla of an election campaign. They were wrong. The question that remained to be answered in 1990 was whether or not the NDP could be right. As far as the labour movement was concerned, the first months of social democratic rule in Ontario were nothing if not uneventful: Rae and his colleagues tinkered with the regime of industrial legality, trying to make the arbitration process a little more palpable for unionists, and they addressed gay rights in the public sector, but they rocked the boat of class relations quite gently.

As the province trudged along in the worsening economic climate of recession, it seemed a curious twist of irony that disgruntled workers were going to have to confront a state that they and their leaders would be reluctant to make look bad, let alone topple. Perhaps that was the very point of the NDP victory in Ontario in 1990. Who better to keep the lid on class relations in hard times than New Democrats. Barely four months into its mandate the NDP faced the grim headlines: "Jobless rate at 5-year high as Ontario hit the hardest." In one month alone, the "have" province recorded a leap in the unemployment rates of 26,000. Bob Rae, who in January, 1990, had written that "We owe each other love, and the action that flows from that," sang a different tune in January, 1991. Now in power, Rae's politics of love turned "tough." He spoke of empty coffers, grimaced, and speechified that he had no "interest in being known as Bailout Bob." Some on Bay Street, panicked by the September, 1990, NDP win, no doubt smiled knowingly. It was enough to make conspiracy theory look almost plausible.

MASS CULTURE: SPECTACLE AND HARD TIMES

If this is the fate of social democratic politics in an age of hard times and the collapse of the promise of Fordism, what of the potential politics of mass culture? Interpreting mass culture is now something of an academic industry, with growth areas such as communications theory, film studies, and examination of various media colonizing traditional disciplines and analytic traditions. For all of the output, however, the peculiarly class and Canadian content of mass culture in the late twentieth century remains, at best, a continuing puzzle. Here I embark on a brief comment that should be taken as suggestive and tentative. There can, as yet, be no sure footing on the slippery slope leading to an understanding of mass culture in our time.

One central reason mass culture remains a puzzle, and one difficult to fit together, is that it moves and changes its meaning with the shifting contours of political economy and class struggle. Thus, twentieth-century mass culture, I have suggested, might well have a different impact in the 1920s than in the 1960s. And, correspondingly, in the post-1975 years of hard times and the demobilization of the Fordist project, mass culture takes on new roles and prospects. Put bluntly, those roles and prospects seem to present workers more and more with the allure of a numbing spectacle. As the capacity of the economy to continue to deliver the goods of consumer demand falters and fades, and the traditional defences of social democratic politics and union organization are declawed, mass culture increasingly obscures the hard realities of working-class life in a series of grandiose theatres, the purpose of which seems to be to swamp the oppressed and exploited in wave after wave of exaggerated event and strained carnivalesque gaiety. The elaborately constructed hypernovelty of this mass culture is, of course, a facade that merely marks its fundamental routinization and conformist content. Mass culture in the age of spectacle presents an ironic coupling of oppositions. Individualism and collectivism, isolation and involvement, withdrawal and participation can all coexist because of technologies and promotions that fragment the substance of being at the same time that they deliver the spectacle to ever-widening, but increasingly atomized, audiences. People no longer even have the mundane sociability of waiting in line for a movie as they pick up their video and retire to their VCR-equipped recreation and living rooms.

The French theorist Guy Debord comments on this culture of the spectacle, pointing to its politics of domination and suppression:

> Spectacular domination's first priority was to eradicate historical knowledge in general; beginning with just about all rational information and commentary on the recent past. . . . History's domain was the memorable, the totality of events whose consequences would be lastingly apparent. . . . The precious advantage which the spectacle has acquired through the *outlawing* of history, from having driven the recent past into hiding, and from having made everyone forget the spirit of history within society, is above all the ability to overcome its own tracks – to conceal the very progress of its recent world conquest. Its power already seems familiar, as if it had always been there. All usurpers have shared this aim: to make us forget that *they have only just arrived*.

This is not the kind of grand interpretive sweep that has been common in efforts to understand the particulars of Canadian experience or the nuts and bolts of labour's current situation. And yet it fits well with the unfolding of the 1975-90 years. As this chapter has shown, the spectacle, as Debord conceives it, is not only evident in televised sporting events – and many, especially male, working-class lives are ordered by the absurd calendar of proliferating megacontests, in which January is a month of football bowls, Super and otherwise, Canada Cup hockey is played months before snow flies and the Stanley Cup won in the sweltering arenas of spring, and the boys of summer battle for their so-called World Series rings in the frigid nights of late October – but in the political economy. Are not Bob Rae and Bob White, as well as Wayne Gretzky and Ben Johnson, forged in this culture of the spectacular? To acknowledge this, in some way, is to appreciate Debord's point that, "With the destruction of history, contemporary events themselves retreat into a remote and fabulous realm of unverifiable stories, uncheckable statistics, unlikely explanations and untenable reasoning."

Debord also points to the transiency of a mass culture premised on the spectacle: "When the spectacle stops talking about something for three days, it is as if it did not exist." Even allowing for a certain metaphorical exaggeration, this is an important matter in the shifting meaning of mass culture in our time. Hollywood, from the *film noir* output of the 1940s and before, found it difficult to erase workers. Out of the 1960s ferment of youthful revolt and blue-collar blues and the 1970s trade union offensive, for instance, came flawed Hollywood attempts – *Blue Collar*, *F.I.S.T.*, *Norma Rae* – to address the question of class. There had always been a little of this, as well, in the television sit-com portrayal of the working-class buffoon, from Ralph Kramden to Archie Bunker. My point is not that this representation of labour was at all adequate, only that it was, during the highwater mark of Fordism, difficult to suppress.

With the passing of the Fordist moment, which simultaneously acknowledged working-class difference and attempted to cover it over in a placatory plastic, the agenda of mass culture's spectacle seems in fact to be just this suppression. Maverick filmmaker John Sayles went against this trend with the movie *Matewan*, an historically sensitive, if not unproblematic, reconstruction of early twentieth-century coal-mining wars. But *Matewan* was a decided financial flop and failed to last more than a few days in most of its commercial runs. More telling are the films of David Lynch, especially *Blue Velvet*. As Frederic Jameson has noted, *Blue Velvet* is a nostalgic return to the 1960s, but one can read this 1980s pilgrimage as an anxious avoidance of the cleavages of class, which are lost in the mythological pluralism of a small-town milieu that merges Good and Evil in a nauseatingly repetitive string of obscenities and chilling violence that nevertheless draws both the characters and their audience into a widening series of social transgressions. The 1990 film, *Last Exit to Brooklyn*, seemingly set against the background of overt *class* violence in the post-World War Two years, actually follows a similar trajectory. Individual quests for gratification and identity and brutal assaults on persons leave the class context of this historically situated movie somewhat suppressed. Television, it might be argued, has accomplished the same kind of thing. In a host of popular shows, from *Who's the Boss* to *The Fresh Prince of Bel Air*, what is working-class is what is very often left out or left behind. The spectacle, as in the films of Spike Lee, *Roseanne*, the *Cheers* gang, and *The Golden Girls*, can now talk of race, age, and gender (admittedly in ways that are problematic), but it has for the most part forgotten or trivialized class.

But what of Michael Moore's *Roger and Me*, the amazingly successful depiction of the collapse of Flint, Michigan, and the devastating human costs of rampant unemployment that General Motors executive Roger Smith wants to avoid facing? *Roger and Me* is probably less of an exception to my assessment that the contemporary spectacle of mass culture silences class than it would apparently seem. For what *Roger and Me* does, in an admittedly brilliantly orchestrated play on the spectacle by Moore, is splice the physical suppression of class – the actual collapse of production in Flint – into a parade of spectacles that parody themselves. Bob Eubanks and Miss Michigan, Pat Boone and the country club set, law and order as a black bounty hunter on the eviction circuit or a guest night for the local elite at the jail, the ever-evasive "public" Roger Smith and the bumbling "private" seeker of simple truth and an honest conversation, Michael Moore: these are the spectacles and actual substance of *Roger and Me*. Class in Moore's depiction is actually marginal, the fallout from Fordism's crisis that never really appears, save in the pathetic guise of poor people being evicted or reduced to selling their own blood to eat, breeding and butchering rabbits for meat. And even this human tragedy is, to Moore, often little more than a spectacle to be "shot," regardless of the consequences. I cheered loudly at the end of the film when the public relations promoter for GM was designated as a new casualty of unemployment, but I bowed my head in uncomfortable embarrassment as the rabbit breeder was shut down by the state. As Moore continued his parody, the audience broke into unrestrained laughter at the woman's announcement that she was intending to become a veterinarian. When the tragedy of displaced workers is this kind of parodic appendage to the spectacle itself, then the spectacle has indeed silenced class. *Roger and Me* catapulted Moore from the obscurity of the muckraker into Hollywood prominence precisely because it makes our society laugh when its humane impulse would be to cry; and in the way the laughter is solicited, I would argue, comes the capacity to forget. This has its uses, not only for all the me's in the audience, but also for those who would take their stands with Roger.

This kind of reading of mass culture of course depends on seeing the commercial products of the United States as hegemonic. To accept this as the reality in the 1990s is not, however, to deny that there are a range of other possibilities. There is indeed a spectrum of contemporary cultural output and practice, much of which may well tilt and destabilize the politics of the spectacle. In popular music, for instance, rappers, heavy metal practitioners, and youthful female vocalists all have elements of spectacle in their self-presentation and promotion, but they package themselves differently and carry their messages to the consuming public with a variety of political meanings, particularly with respect to race and gender. Of all musical genres in the mainstream, perhaps country remains truest to some kind of populist sensitivity to class place, but this is both subdued politically and somewhat marginalized commercially, appealing as it does to a rugged individualism that thrives on class difference at the same time as it denies it. Madonna, more than any other pop star, has managed to work something of an oppositional message into her presence, but it speaks with the voice of gender stripped, largely, of class understanding. One wonders how much of Madonna's audience, which is often under the age of ten and relatively innocent sexually, as opposed to a dwindling element of new leftists from the 1960s, actually appreciates her stand. While it would be narrow and close-minded to deny the challenge Madonna raises, there is also no backing away from the mixed message she cultivates, in which there can be no mistaking the "me first" content of "the material girl's" purpose.

On the fringes of mass culture as spectacle lie pockets of more overt political challenge, bands and performers who, like Billy Bragg or Easterhouse, historicize rather than anesthetize, bringing class, as a potential, back into focus. In Canada the soft commercial side of this process has been epitomized by Bruce Cockburn, the harder edge by the 1980s West Coast punk band D.O.A., now defunct. But these are rare currents, easily lost in the swirl of spectacle, hardly pivotal in the swings of the market.

Also easily lost, and lost sight of, are the indigenous local manifestations of a popular, as opposed to truly mass, culture. Embedded in oral traditions and regional political economies, these instances of popular culture defy the spectacular's laboured repression of history and instead sustain, through song and storytelling, a sense of the way lives have been lived among particular groups and within specific regions. Most likely to survive on the margins, these popular cultural forms co-exist comfortably with the regional and ethnic imbalances of Canadian political economy. In Atlantic Canada, immigrant communities, Francophone Quebec, the North, and enclaves of the prairie and coastal west, or, indeed, wherever folk traditions survive and align with a recognition of oppression, popular cultural forms stand as a potential alternative to the relentless incursions of the spectacle. As in the ongoing publication of oral histories and stories in *Cape Breton's Magazine*, they also affirm that specific traditions and ways of life have not been obliterated by economic hardship, but survive and nurture a sturdy defiance.

More conscious efforts to challenge mass culture as dehistoricized and classless spectacle are, of course, constantly being made in the name of workers and the oppressed. Work poets such as Tom Wayman and Phil Hall, small publishers, activists, and oral historians like Rolf Knight and Howard White, folksinger Phil Thomas, playwright of Montreal's

Anglophone workers David Fennario, and artist of the Winnipeg General Strike Robert Kell are but a few of the regionally ensconced cultural workers engaged in efforts to present work and workers in ways that step beyond the spectacular's confinements.

The people and popular cultures that stand outside of mass culture as spectacle – whether indicative of a new and emerging attempt to represent labour in poetry, prose, theatre, and art or instances of residues materially embedded in specific locales and social groups – should not be underestimated. In conjunction with a wide array of locally rooted challenges to mass culture, from various avant garde forms to a range of anti-authority cultural activities, they represent strivings to overcome the domination of the spectacle. But however significant they are, no purpose is served in mythologizing them: they pale in comparison to the market-driven and mass-oriented productions and constructions of the media-prompted and profit-paced cultural industry. That phenomenon, it can be suggested, reproduces in the cultural arena what has also been happening in the spheres of political economy: the suppression and repression of class in Canada; the incorporation and domestication of dissent. To be sure, there remain spaces between the lines of mass culture in the age of spectacle that can be stretched out to reopen the question of class and a politics of opposition. But those spaces are not likely to be tested on the cultural terrain itself. Rather, mass culture and its spectacles will move, and the limited, largely non-commercial work poetry, prose, and art of our time will register with wider constituencies only when forces and agendas beyond the purely cultural reassert labour's potential power.

Mass culture, tempered by hard times and class defeats, is difficult to comprehend outside of the spectacle as an event conditioned by this depressing – socially and economically – context. There remain, of course, pockets of working-class cultural resiliency in the age of the spectacle, with neighbourhood, community, and workplace ties capable of being a reservoir of collectivist values and mutual aid. Still, the structures and underpinnings of this limited realm of semi-autonomy have undergone continuous erosion in the last half-century.

Cultural life is of course increasingly commodified. This has been an ongoing process since World War Two. But we are now in a different cultural marketplace. As the Fordist promise and actualization of an expansive consumerism have soured in the last fifteen years of hard times, mass cultural forms have, more and more, given way to the trappings and hype of the spectacle.

Within this restructured cultural marketplace, much has changed in little less than three decades. Madonna, as an overt opposition, does not quite measure up to the lyrical accomplishments of the early Bob Dylan or the Rolling Stones, circa 1968; eight-year old girls may learn much from "Material Girl" but it will not move them politically the way "Maggie's

Farm" and "Street Fighting Man" did an earlier generation of rebels. Countercultural experimentation with drugs in the 1960s took its toll in many ways, but it at least had two sides, conditioning stands of questioning and defiance, registered not only in campus rebellion but also in rank-and-file union upheavals and wildcats. In the 1990s, with drugs a rare growth sector in the international economy and the meaning of drug use decidedly different, the balance sheet is no longer ambiguous. Corporate moves to implement drug testing in the workplace are but a symbolic demonstration that capital intends to scapegoat the few, the better to terrorize the many. They proclaim the weakness of a workers' movement that can neither offer its ranks alternatives nor curb capital's hypocritical moral assault.

Mass culture as spectacle numbs appreciation of more than the past; it also debases the possibility of grasping the options of the present. Thus universal literacy, a fundamental bedrock of the capacity of culture to be oppositional in the late twentieth-century advanced capitalist economies and generally accepted as a societal accomplishment by the 1960s, can no longer be assumed. In the age of television, video, and the tabloid press, cultural awareness is constructed not through words but in the quick, often visual, fix. Not surprisingly, over half of a sample of workers in British Columbia mills had trouble reading at a Grade 4 level. While this shocking statistic troubled management, which worried that the elementary posted notices of the workplace were not being understood properly, corporate executives took the cues appropriate to the age of spectacle. At MacMillan Bloedel plans were made to reduce the complexity of written instructions, cut the amount of posted directions on the job, and provide voluntary, "non-threatening" adult education programs for employees. They seemed to grasp intuitively what this study of working-class literacy assumed: "It is also not clear that improving reading skills is the answer to enhancing job performance. Certainly no general literacy training will be effective." What is not required to appreciate the spectacle is simply not worth having.

All things considered, this kind of cultural "development" is an ill wind that blows no good for the possibilities of working-class resistance. It requires immense faith in mass culture's ambivalences to regard it as a force capable of being turned to working-class purpose. Certainly this will not be done without much effort and struggle, a project that will necessarily entail moving the cultural in conjunction with a range of socio-economic structures and processes more narrowly political and material.

STABBING BACK/BACK-STABBING

In spite of the odds stacked against labour during the hard times of the 1980s, it was nevertheless true that workers took a stab at fighting back. Public-sector workers were often, as we have seen, at the centre of the fray.

But there were periodic outbursts of class struggle from more traditional quarters, revealing the extent to which the working class could still mount militant challenges against capital and the state. To be sure, in the generalized downturn of material life, upturns in the class struggle were often related to apparent improvements in the economic climate. Thus, over the course of the 1980s the number of striking workers, both absolutely and as a percentage of unionized labour, rose in 1986-87, a direct response to the illusory lifting of the recessionary curtain in the mid-1980s.

This upsurge in combativity affected a wide range of workers and touched many regions. Eighty strikers at a New Brunswick bottling plant walked picket lines for 432 days, battling strikebreakers, organizing a provincial and then a national boycott, facing state injunctions and company intimidation. The B.C. Federation of Labor hierarchy used a one-day general strike to blow off militant working-class steam and allow unionists to vent their frustration at the Social Credit gutting of the provincial labour code. Mills, factories, and schools closed as 250,000 workers walked off their jobs in June of 1987. In spite of the largely symbolic nature of the protest, Attorney-General Brian Smith moved to try to squash the job action, noting that "This strike is an offence against the state and not just the Government." One year later, with the economy moving decisively against Canadian workers, a Kitchener Uniroyal tire plant organized by the United Rubber Workers exploded as the union refused to address the employer's demand for a productivity clause in the contract. A truck loaded with tires was destroyed by a Molotov cocktail, three trailers were also damaged by fire, and 100 police were called in to quiet the situation, which resulted in twenty-seven arrests. As the federal Tories gutted VIA Rail service in September, 1987, with job cuts projected to approach thousands by 1989, a national rail strike was shut down only when Ottawa imposed a back-to-work order on 50,000 unionists. Officials of the union complied with the legislation, but wildcat strikers were a sign of anger in the ranks and several hundred irate workers stormed the Parliament buildings in protest, restrained only by police in riot gear.

The most polarized site of class relations in the late 1980s, however, was Alberta. Lagging behind their brothers and sisters in other sections of the country, Alberta's unionists saw their wages eroded over the course of the decade. Unemployment rates were up, organized labour down. A rash of fierce labour-capital confrontations broke out in the summer of 1986. At Zeidler Forest Industries in the Slave Lake district, at the Suncor Incorporated oil plant in Fort McMurray, and at the Fletcher's meat-packing outlet in Red Deer tough employers demanded concessions from workers, slapped injunctions on defiant unionists, and drew on the police to arrest strikers. Some of these class battles were resolved, but corporations were often successful in staving off union bids for improvements. At Lakeside Packers a United Food and Commercial Workers (UFCW) strike was held at bay for two years while the company planned a $6 million expansion. Members of the IWA Local 1-207 at Zeidler's remained on strike for four years after they walked out in opposition to a two-tiered wage payment system; picket-line violence led to twenty-two dismissals, while in the forests themselves suspicious fires erupted and tree spikings were rumoured to be widespread.

But in Edmonton the Alberta class battles of the mid- to late 1980s raged most dramatically. Peter Pocklington, fresh from his failed attempt to take over the federal Tory leadership with a crass combination of big dollars and blunt New Right ideology, struck a pose of defiant determination. He wanted to drive unionism from Gainers, his Edmonton meat-packing plant. With meat consumption declining in the face of new trends in health and diet, Pocklington demanded that 1,000 workers accept a five-year wage freeze, a two-tiered payment system – with new employees going for the abysmal rate of $6.99 an hour – and other insulting givebacks. To cave in to such corporate tyranny spelled the end of unionism in a province already showing signs of becoming a haven for heartless open-shop bosses. The workers, most of whom earned $7-$12 an hour, demanded one dollar more an hour over two years. Gainers told them to forget it. "We live in a market society," pontificated Pocklington, as if the workers did not already know this. He also played to nationalist and regionalist sentiment with his denunciations of outside agitators and union troublemakers, most of whom he saw as imports from the U.S. and Toronto. It apparently posed no contradictory problem for Pocklington to condemn American unionism at the same time as he opened a non-union meat-packing plant in California. Labour was, and should remain, local; capital was global.

For much of the summer the Gainers UFCW picket line was the focus of national media attention. As strikebreakers were bused in to the plant, violence erupted and local police spent most of their waking hours patrolling the struck work site, protecting the scabs. Eventually police outnumbered strikers by a two-to-one ratio. The entire annual overtime budget of the Edmonton police force was eaten up in a few days. Huge rallies of 10,000 were organized against the provincial labour laws and the actions of the police; one day 3,500 marched on the plant. As the buses were smashed and battered, pelted with rocks and sticks, mass arrests took place. A fifteen-year-old boy and a seventy-five-year-old woman both ended up in jail one week, the arrest figure climbing to 252 for one busy seven-day period. In one sweep 125 picketers were charged. The police superintendent walked through the crowd pointing out individuals and saying, "Take that one and take that one." Some of the pro-strike protesters were arrested 500 metres from the plant gate. One of the first taken into custody was Alberta Federation of Labor president Dave Werlin, a Communist who would later challenge Shirley Carr for president of the CLC. All told some 600 went to jail during the conflict, clogging the courts for weeks. Asked by a reporter if he was a "terrorist," one striker replied, "I never really thought of myself as that. . . . When you see people coming in to take your job, something just snaps." The picket line was eventually subdued, with an injunction limiting the total number of pickets at the plant to forty-two, no more than twelve of whom could congregate together at any one time.

By autumn negotiations were under way. The Alberta Labour Relations Board ruled that Gainers was bargaining in bad faith by denying striking workers their pension rights and trying to terminate the employees' pension fund as a condition of settling the strike. An inquiry into the explosion concluded that Pocklington should pay his workers $1.03 over two years, almost exactly what the union demanded. From across the country came moral and material support, as the Gainers strike symbolized a new combativity within Canadian working-class circles. The CLC asked its 8,000 affiliated union locals to contribute $100 weekly to "adopt a Gainers striker," and organized labour promoted a national boycott of the company's products. The ongoing "Battle of 66th Street" was shaping up as one of the most protracted and militant class struggles of the 1980s.

Even the ruling Conservative Party in Alberta was shocked and embarrassed by Pocklington's provocations. Premier Don Getty eventually put some pressure on the millionaire meat-packer to settle (rumours later circulated of huge interest-free loans), and as Pocklington blinked once the labour tops in the union closed their eyes and prayed for mercy. They didn't get much, but the strike was wound down. Wages were frozen for two years and then workers were to get a 3 per cent pay hike for two more years. Pocklington was allowed to loot the workers' pension fund. For strikers convicted of picket-line charges a deal was worked out whereby they could be granted leaves of absence for up to one year in the event that they had to go to jail. When one union official announced the settlement terms to the strikers he was jeered. Barely 60 per cent of the workers, who were off the job for more than six months, wanted to go back under the poor conditions offered, but the UFCW leadership pushed to end the fight. One senior union source suggested that the labour bosses caved in when they should have hung tough. The strikers had battled for months; both the provincial government and all official inquiries and labour boards exposed Pocklington's intransigence; the boycott was taking a bite out of the company assets; and the scabs were thinning out, leaving the plant wrecked and without a labour force. "We had him where we wanted him," said this disgruntled insider. "Just squeeze – that's all they had to do. And they stroked."

Too many labour battles in the hard times of the 1980s ended like this or worse. The renewed campaign to organize the retail giant, Eaton's, dormant since the 1950s, culminated in a much-publicized Retail, Wholesale, and Department Store Union (RWDSU) organizational drive. Six Eaton's branches in southern Ontario fell to the union, but the newly organized workers found the corporation impossible to move when it came to a first contract. After a six-month strike in 1984 the RWDSU held on to the Eaton's workers but could not protect them or improve their lot. In Brandon, Manitoba, the Eaton's outlet was organized by the UFCW. After the provincial Labour Relations Board imposed a first contract, the store fired half of its employees and demanded humiliating contract concessions from the union. Labour activists dubbed this "corporate terrorism," but there was no question they were losing the difficult battle. By 1987 almost all of what was won in 1983-84 had faded; unionists faced a spate of decertifications. Three years later, when there was a move on the part of Eaton's security guards and another imposed first contract was threatened, the company laid off 100 workers.

Things were little better in the banks. The CLC invested $2 million in an attempt to organize 500 VISA workers, but the outcome, while securing a union foothold, was anti-climactic: unionized workers were no better off in terms of wages than their unorganized counterparts. Canadian Labour Relations Board condemnations of anti-union tactics by financial institutions like the Canadian Imperial Bank of Commerce sounded great and gave advocates of banking unionism a moralistic boost, but they did little to alter the depressing realization that after years of effort so little had been accomplished. Of 175,000 workers in the banking sector, 90 per cent of whom were low-paid women, barely 1 per cent were organized in 1986. Automation – with the proliferation of cash-vending machines – was steadily eroding the numbers employed, making a bad situation worse. Cliff Evans, vice-president of UFCW, looked back over fifteen years of trade union effort in the banking sector and concluded that it had made "absolutely no difference." This may have been a bit overstated, but his description of the main enemy was certainly apt: "The people that control the banking industry are probably the mafia of the industrial relations world, because they don't care what they have to do to get rid of the union."

Similar conditions prevailed at the phone company, which like the banks relied on a large, underpaid female work force. Bell Canada's clerical workers were unionized, but it was clear that their organization generally acquiesced to managerial demand. Late in 1985 some 17,000 Bell clerks fomented open revolt against a contract settlement that downgraded job classifications and instituted a wage freeze; the membership deplored it as a "sell-out."

At least at Eaton's, CIBC VISA, and Bell unions got a foot in the door. Not so in Nova Scotia's Michelin tire plants. The multinational, headquartered in France, was the province's largest manufacturer with a work force of 3,000 in several factories. Late in the 1970s the company made it clear it would leave the province if it had to deal with unions. The provincial government promptly passed legislation – appropriately christened "the Michelin Bill" – stipulating that for a union to win certification it must gain the support of a majority of all workers employed by a company, not just the bulk of the labour force at a particular work site. Since two of the Michelin plants were located in rural areas where support for unionism was weak, this effectively stopped organization of the tire works in its tracks. Repeated efforts to secure union certification of Michelin, involving the Rubber Workers, the CLC, and Bob White's Canadian Automobile Workers, failed, the 40 per cent of the work force that was pro-union stymied by popular fears and misunderstandings as well as a hostile employer and its cute relationship to the provincial state.

In this climate of hard times, two developments marked out the mid- to late 1980s as a specific moment in which things got even tougher for the labour movement. Both exposed the extent to which unionists themselves were conceived as property to be managed by those who owned and controlled them. The first was warfare within the labour hierarchy, the second the ways in which some workers opted for a trade unionism that declawed itself, or, worse, struggled themselves to make the labour movement an even more constrained representative of the working class.

With union certifications harder to come by, and with those in the labour force who were unorganized increasingly difficult to reach with the message of the workers' movement, internecine squabbling within the trade union bureaucracy reached new heights. This took many forms. Often it involved an overt grab at another union's members. Even when this promised to amalgamate workers who should obviously have come together, as in the 1989 merger of Parrot's CUPW and the Bob McGarry-led Letter Carriers Union of Canada, the result was often acrimony and division. When CUPW narrowly won the bargaining rights for all postal workers in a Canadian Labour Relations Board-monitored free vote of the memberships of the unions, it charged the LCUC of using extortion tactics in withholding millions of dollars of assets.

Old antagonisms pitting the defeated LCUC against the victorious CUPW resurfaced later as the International Brotherhood of Electrical Workers launched a raid on the postal workers' union. Among Ontario's teachers a curious legislative regulation segregated men and women in separate union jurisdictions. All teachers had to be members of the umbrella-like Ontario Teachers Federation, but women teaching in the public school system were required to join the Federation of Women Teachers' Association of Ontario (FWTAO), while men were placed in the Ontario Public School Teachers' Federation (OPSTF). In a cumbersome, politically complex, and extraordinarily costly legal contest, these two unions squared off in court over the right of women who wanted to be represented by the male OPSTF to join the labour organization of their choice. Feminist "experts" lined up behind the FWTAO, arguing that women needed separate organizations, extolling the virtues of the women's union and its leadership. It was a sign of the times, and the preoccupation with gender and its seemingly apparent opposition to class, that almost no one advocated one big union of all teachers with a leadership executive apportioned according to the gender balance of the bargaining unit.

The most contentious jurisdictional dispute, however, and one that, as usual, put Bob White at the centre of attention, involved a seemingly incongruous power play linking sectors of the working class that many thought were quite separate. The product of a merger of meatcutters and retail clerks in 1979, the United Food and Commercial Workers (UFCW) was created overnight as one of the largest CLC private-sector affiliates. It was already coming apart by the mid-1980s. In Vancouver, the union was placed under trusteeship when Local 2000 called for Canadian autonomy. According to UFCW local leader Leif Hansen, the takeover "smacked of [the] commando-type tactics that one might expect in a banana republic."

On the other coast, Newfoundland fishermen and fish-plant workers also chafed under the bureaucratized and distanced control of the American-based UFCW. Wracked by a growing union nationalist autonomy sentiment that upped discontent with American bureaucracies, Canadian regionalist attachments, and the purposeful manipulation of specific leaders lusting for the limelight, the UFCW in Newfoundland was ripe for a revolt. It would be led by the charismatic former Liberal MP, Richard Cashin. He and his lieutenants commanded an army of some 20,000 fish workers. After months of battling "international" headquarters, they took their leave of the UFCW in the spring of 1987, forming the Newfoundland Fishermen, Food and Allied Workers Union, the better to hook up with Bob White's CAW. The UFCW, for its part, slapped a trusteeship on the Newfoundland local and screamed about theft of union funds. Cashin and company soon resigned *en masse*, promoting affiliation with White's auto workers.

Millions of dollars would be spent on this union takeover as hundreds of labour board hearings and court proceedings were launched. The UFCW distributed 10,000 cassette tapes to Newfoundlanders, denouncing the raid and slamming defectors. The catchy lyrics hit hard at White, who was chastised as an Upper Canadian colonialist:

Bob White's in Toronto
He's tryin' to save face
But he's given up his principles
And he's raidin' all over the place.

Cashin, for his part, was depicted as an unreliable dreamer with a craving for the good life:

Richard's dreams they're not real
They're just theories he's read
He's got dollar signs in his eyes
And delusions in his head.

Ultimately the UFCW retreated into a classic sectionalism:

I don't wanna be an auto worker
You can't catch your fish with a Chrysler New Yorker
I don't wanna join the car union
When catchin' fish is what I'm really doin'.

A year later the mess was still not resolved, though White and Cashin captured the allegiance of most of the Newfoundland workers. The CLC took a stab at mediating the dispute but then backed off, covering its trail in the smoke of legalism. In 1989 the battle spilled into Prince Edward Island, where the CAW was charged with intimidating Cavendish UFCW workers: vehicles apparently were damaged, cars forced off the highway, and a worker toolbox glued shut with the word "Traitor" scrawled on a note. White's organizers were told to stay away from the plant for six months.

Criticism of CAW action drew Cashin onto the rhetorical soapbox. His call for a revival of old-time labour values understandably fell on many receptive rank-and-file ears, but his dismissal of the bitter denunciation of White's raid as little more than an expression of how "now we're getting legal and bureaucratic in the labour movement," was hardly destined to please others in the labour leadership. Nor were many other union bosses placated by White's answer to the question of why fishermen should join an auto workers' union. "They drive cars, don't they," quipped White. With logic like this nobody's rank-and-file property was safe.

Indeed, the animosity in the upper echelons of the CLC was so thick you could cut it with a knife. At a meeting of Congress "heavies" called to discuss the raiding issue in March, 1987, anti-White feeling ran high. One unidentified male trade union head told reporters, "We all play by one set of rules but the perception now is that Bob thinks he can play by another. . . . You don't respond with cannibalistic fervor when you see another union having internal problems." A woman added, "He looks like he is power hungry." John Freyer of NUPGE suggested that all the media attention had gone to White's head, but Leo Gerard of the Steelworkers said simply and bluntly that it was a straightforward matter of trade union principles being broken.

There was no settling the UFCW-CAW rift, although the workers them-selves voted strongly for Cashin, White, and the CAW. But the tension all of this generated within the CLC was displaced, by 1990, in grumblings about Shirley Carr's tenure as president. In the right place at the right time, Carr was the first woman, the first public-sector unionist, and the first member of an all-Canadian union (CUPE) to head the 2.1 million-member CLC. But after four years at the helm it was far from clear if she was the woman for the job. For years the CLC had been declining in influence until, in 1986, it represented only 58 per cent of Canadian unionists. Many in the labour hierarchy were agitated by Carr's volatility. Her job, they thought, was to smooth things with the federal Tories, to concentrate on research and lobbying. Carr's penchant for corporatist ventures like the Productivity Centre seemed to fit poorly with her bombastic insults of Prime Minister Mulroney as, among other things, a skunk, dead meat, Dracula, or Margaret Thatcher in Jockey shorts. There seemed no predictability to Carr. There was also not a great deal of capacity to manage the increasing financial crisis of the CLC, which was, in the words of James Bagnall of the *Financial Times*, "losing wads of money." Staff cuts were made, and then unmade; dues increases were needed. In the words of one union figurehead, Carr had done "a lousy job." All of this was thrown in Carr's face at a late 1989 Bristol Place Hotel Meeting in Toronto. The knives came out, and Bob White wielded his most menacingly.

As the labour hierarchy battled, the ranks burned. Hard times generated lots of dissidents, but not all of them embraced a course of resistance congruent with what might loosely be recognized as the principles of trade unionism. James McCambly's Canadian Federation of Labor, a building trades-dominated body of more than 200,000 that split from the CLC in the early 1980s, continued to espouse political neutrality at the same time that it cosied up to the Tories. It successfully secured a $15 million federal grant to team up with Wood Gundy in launching the country's first national labour-sponsored venture capital fund. With shares marketed at ten dollars, Working Ventures Canadian Fund, Incorporated, in the words of one right-wing columnist, embraced "investment objectives . . . [with] an appropriately capitalistic ring." In a 1987 interview, McCambly was quick to promote his CFL as a particular kind of organization attuned to "the problems that women face." He stressed that women "are looking for a different style of unionism" and that they did not get turned on "by statements like 'we're going out on strike' or 'we're tough'." In depicting women as "interested in effective negotiations geared to non-confrontation," McCambly rationalized his own CFL's accommodations to capital and the state by cloaking it in a dubiously essentialist understanding of women's ostensible passivity. This was as much a blow struck against feminism as it was an endorsement of it.

Another labour body that took an even more jaundiced view of labour militance and women's activism was Ed Vanderkloet's fundamentalist Christian Labor Association of Canada. Headquartered in Mississauga, this small contingent of 8,500 railed against feminism, socialism, and strikes. Employers liked them because they worked cheap, in some sectors for $4 less an hour than those affiliated with traditional unions.

Matters of principle even seemed to get lost in the rub of hard times against mainstream organized workers. So desperate for dues-paying members were the declining Steelworkers in 1989 that they took to organizing security guards, some 35,000 of them being employed in Ontario alone. The Ontario Labor Relations Board stipulated that such security guards could only belong to unions of guards, a restriction that existed in no other Canadian province. (The USWA grabbed a quick 13,000 security guards in a Quebec organizational coup.) Union efforts to organize the guards were thus challenged by companies employing these "rent-a-cops" as well as by the guards' association at Inco, where the USWA already represented production workers. What the Steelworkers did not seem concerned with was what role security guards play when unionists go on strike. Did the USWA really want to enrol in its ranks the same workers who would be, in so many instances, hired to protect strikebreakers? How did the Steelworkers plan to manage a future strike at Inco if they took in the guards whose job it could well be to escort scabs and thwart striking workers? For the USWA leadership these were merely rhetorical questions: dues were dues.

Some on the left tried to move unionism off of this kind of pure-and-simple business unionist footing, but they found their battles with the bureaucracy draining and usually defeating. By 1985 *The Financial Post* was reporting on the "Broken Dreams of a Union Boss," detailing the rise and fall of Steelworker reformer Dave Patterson. Once the militant young leader of Sudbury's miners, Patterson was elected Ontario district director of the international union in the early 1980s. He campaigned as a new voice of new needs within the labour movement, and was rightly seen as an oppositionist, threatening to the long-entrenched trade union hierarchy of the USWA. It was not long before Patterson was frozen out. When he refused to back Canadian Lynn Williams for the international leadership, his days were numbered. Youth and independence counted for something among the ranks, perhaps, but they cut no favour with the upper chambers of labour's leadership. "In 1981 I thought I could change the world," reported Patterson. "In 1985," he reflected soberly, "I say that if I want to change anything, it's going to take time."

Patterson ended up defeated in his bid for re-election, the press reporting that he was heading back to Sudbury to work at Inco. Had he made it there he would have found it a different place. Between 1958 and 1982, Sudbury was a centre of working-class militancy, and the workers waged six strikes; this class combativity paid dividends as unionized steel workers won high wages and secured considerable job benefits. But from 1982 to 1990 the terms of class trade shifted decidedly to the steel bosses. From the high-water mark of almost 21,000 Inco employees in 1971, the labour force shrank back to 8,000 by 1990; as productivity soared each worker was more "efficient" but also more insecure. No strikes rocked class relations at Sudbury's Inco plant over the years 1982-90.

Other unions also had their reformers. In CUPE Judy Darcy, once associated with the far left, mounted a series of late 1980s challenges to the established union bureaucracy. Her run for the presidency of the Ontario division in 1986 resulted in charges of "red-baiting" and backed Darcy into recantations that she had "matured." Two years later a deal was supposedly cut by which Darcy and another aspiring union leader, Les Kovasci, would share the spoils of office. Darcy was to have a new post created for her. But the expected and perhaps promised votes from the ranks never materialized. There was a refusal to ratify Darcy's new post, and in her stead a relative unknown was elected. By the early 1990s, after a successful stint as secretary-treasurer, Darcy was poised to assume the national leadership of CUPE. Elected to the presidency of the 400,000-member union in October, 1991, Darcy dismissed the relevance of her leftist past, saying, "This union is beyond that." The *Globe and Mail* captured one part of Darcy's rise to power with the headline, "Former radical new CUPE president." As labour journalist Wilfred List reported as early as 1986, the many challenges facing labour in the 1980s often froze out "the ideological left." Reform was a hard row to hoe. Oppositionists either made their peace with the bureaucracy or faced a constant battle.

Nowhere was this truer than in what many considered the cesspool of international unionism, the Teamsters. Headed by a string of notorious, supposedly gangster-connected leaders (from Jimmy Hoffa to Jackie Presser), the Teamsters, by the mid-1980s, were a caricature of the militant trucker unionism that galvanized Minneapolis in the 1930s and helped to kick off the U.S. strike wave of the early depression years. In Canada, Mr. Teamster was Senator Edward Lawson, who, as director of the Canadian Conference, hauled down $300,000+ yearly as a union official and, for attending a mere seventeen days in the Canadian Senate, raked in a further $50,000 and perks. Long-exiled from the CLC, the Teamsters were nevertheless a union with 90,000 members and a lot of power to disrupt business.

A busy man, Lawson was a director of the company that owned the Vancouver Canucks and kept his international travels manageable by flying on his own jet. A made-in-America Canadian union boss, Lawson was in good standing in the upper echelons of the international for many years but could not get much support in his home local of Vancouver, where he failed to rank higher than seventeenth in a delegate election in 1986. Placing first in the Vancouver local election that humiliated Lawson was Diana Kilmury. A trucker for twelve years, she headed up the reform slate of the Canadian division and backed the Teamsters for a Democratic Union (TDU), a U.S.-based opposition caucus. TDU faced a union hierarchy with a history of stopping at absolutely nothing to keep its hold over the massive Teamster resources secure. At the 1981 union convention, Teamster dissidents were hounded and threatened by BLAST, the Brotherhood of Loyal Americans and Strong Teamsters, a goon squad reputedly orchestrated by Presser and company.

As Kilmury and others pushed for Canadian autonomy they found their politics rebuffed and their rights as union members denied. Kilmury claimed that she had been denied union benefits due her after a 1978 truck accident solely because she was a reformer. By the end of the 1980s Lawson was forced to pledge to reform and clean up the Canadian Teamsters, not in response to Kilmury and the reform slate but because of the shakeup of the international union by criminal proceedings in the United States. What with legal action looming over his head as an international officer and a palace coup following Presser's death, Lawson no doubt gained a sense of social conscience. He was rumoured to have struck a deal with those instituting the lawsuit; it wouldn't do to have a Canadian senator convicted in the United States. Lawson ended up losing a jet, but he kept himself in the real driver's seat.

The McCamblys and Vanderkloets on the accommodationist and right-wing edges of the labour movement took pot shots at mainstream trade unionism and siphoned off members. Reform slates and oppositional caucuses were thorns in the side of the entrenched bureaucracies. But these "deviations" were a marginal phenomenon. Even the CFL's considerable membership represented only 6 per cent of the organized workers in the country, roughly comparable to the ranks commanded by Quebec's CNTU.

More menacing was the threat posed by a single union opponent, willing to use the courts to strike a blow against the principle of collectivism and able to draw on the resources of powerful anti-union interests. Led by a retired London, Ontario, millionaire insurance salesman, Colin Brown, the National Citizens' Coalition (NCC) has a history of opposition to medicare, the indexing of pensions, and curbs on election advertising. In 1985 Brown and the NCC teamed up with Merv Lavigne, a disgruntled community college teacher who wanted no part of the Ontario Public Service Employees Union (OPSEU), which was the certified bargaining agent for Lavigne and his counterparts across Ontario. Lavigne, who crossed an OPSEU picket line in 1984, formed a dissident oppositional committee against the job action, publicly condemned the strikers, and launched an NCC-backed legal action resting on the Canadian Charter of Rights and Freedoms. It sought to stop trade unions from spending money on issues and campaigns supposedly removed from the arena of collective bargaining. Specifically, Lavigne objected to OPSEU, the Ontario Federation of Labor, and the CLC spending his dues on donations to political parties, disarmament campaigns, the endorsement of free choice on abortion, opposition to public funds going to build Toronto's domed stadium, help for striking British miners, promotion of international recognition of the Palestine Liberation Organization, and aid to Nicaragua. To curb labour in this way spelled suffocating defeat for trade unionism. As CLC president Dennis MacDermott noted, the Lavigne objections, if recognized in the courts, would "render the labour movement absolutely impotent."

The Lavigne case was disingenuous at best. But in taking it into the courts and publicizing the matter profusely, the NCC struck a blow against the politics of unionism by challenging even the most modest of trade union involvement in issues that reached beyond the bargaining table. Jim Clancy, president of OPSEU, estimated that barely $1.36 of every $1,000 in union dues supported causes objected to by Lavigne. Yet the court battle, which dragged on for years, cost the union over $400,000. The publicity generated out of the case, with its constant questioning of the right of unions to be involved in political matters, was worth even more to the New Right. Eventually the Ontario Court of Appeal ruled that the use of compulsory union dues for political causes was not a violation of the Charter, arguing that the directing of such dues in these ways is an internal union matter. Lavigne's option, in the Court's eyes, was not to fight the minuscule employment of a portion of his dues in causes with which he disagreed through the courts but rather to work within the union to promote his ideas and elect leaders who would act on them. Not forced to join the union, Lavigne could not be identified with its views and practices. When the NCC appealed the case to the Supreme Court, the ruling was again that it was legitimate to spend dues dollars on social and political objectives. Lavigne lost; unionism won.

Still, the Charter of Rights and Freedoms, with its reification of individual rights, proved to be something of a nightmare for trade unionist collectivism. As the 1980s wore on it was apparent that the Charter's ostensible guarantee of freedom of association was a hollow proclamation. In 1987 and 1990, the Supreme Court of Canada ruled (in close, contentious 4-2 and 4-3 decisions) that the Charter's freedom of association did not include the right to strike or to bargain collectively. Just as the regime of industrial legality within which trade unionism had lived for four decades was unravelling, the Charter unleashed a potential flood of anti-union litigation. As a British Columbia prison guard challenged the BCGEU's right to use his dues to fight Social Credit legislation and an editor at the *Winnipeg Free Press* opposed his union contributions going to the NDP, many in the labour movement saw Charter cases, not contracts, as the major challenge to trade unionism in the 1980s. A 1990 compilation of Charter jurisprudence relating to collective bargaining and trade unionism listed 115 separate cases. When the courts rather than the workplace and the political arena become the site of class struggle, the workers' movement is already the loser.

The Canadian working class struggled to make a stab at fighting back throughout the 1980s, then, but the process of resistance was weakened by various kinds of back-stabbing. When internecine warfare raged in the upper echelons of the CLC or erupted in one union's raid on the membership of another, the strength of the workers' movement, already constrained by hard times, was undercut. Unionism's clout was further weakened as a debilitating round of legal challenges, some mounted from within its own ranks, forced it to defend basic rights. Hard times took their obvious toll.

THE GOOD, THE BAD, AND THE UGLY: THE WORKING CLASS IN A TIME OF PERMANENT CRISIS

For Canadian workers the years 1975-90 have been ones of permanent crisis. Barely a year has gone by that has not seen either the overt threat of recession and job loss or the debilitating consequences of spiralling infla-tion. In politics, the rare moments of euphoria associated with massive mobilizations or electoral wins have been tempered by sustained state attacks on what had seemed unassailable labour rights. With the rise of the New Right, the ideological climate has definitely cooled toward the work-ing class, whether organized in unions or dependent on some wing of the welfare state. And, structurally, local technological changes in the labour process and global shifts in the entire nature and meaning of production often undercut working-class strength. This is a bad and ugly period for labouring people and their organizations.

At the beginning of this period of hard times, in the late 1970s, much labour talk focused on the challenges posed by technological change and the dangers to health and safety in various work environments. These remain pressing concerns. Whole realms of work are threatened with virtual extinction because of the microchip revolution and robotics. It is already estimated by major North American car manufacturers that 80-90 per cent of all new plants will soon be controlled by computerized technology. Machinists and draftsmen can easily be replaced by the computerized control of drills and lathes; work that was once highly skilled, some of it a virtual profession, is now reduced to machine-tending or eliminated alto-gether. Simple technology such as the word processor increases productivity in the clerical sector by 50-300 per cent, displacing many workers. Video display terminals are now part of work in airports, shopping malls, librar-ies, gas stations, banks, and countless offices.

This new technology creates new and profoundly disturbing health and safety problems. One-half of VDT operators report routine eye strain, head-aches, anxiety, and depression. More ominous is the threat of low-level radiation, now known to be linked to birth defects. One union organizer has predicted that those operating the new VDTs "are going to be the asbestos workers of the future," a reference to the physical toll lung cancer has taken on asbestos workers over the course of this century. Work, then, is hardly conducive to health. Indeed, it often kills. Miners still died in cave-ins in Quebec and Cape Breton in the 1980s, just as they did a century ago. Over 100 workers per 100,000 employed die annually in forestry. The IWA pushed for a conference on logging deaths in 1988 as sixty-seven fatal injuries occurred, fifty-one in British Columbia alone. Industrial workers exposed to many cancer-producing chemicals find themselves paying the price of their work as they enter their middle years. Estimates are that

10,000 workers in Canada suffer from potentially lethal, cancer-like job-related diseases.

If you don't die on or because of the job, you are likely to be injured. More than a million work-related injuries and illnesses occur in Canada every year. As many as 70 million annual working days are lost to work accidents and diseases, a figure six times greater than the time lost to strikes and lockouts. For all the media attention to crime and its increasing threat to Canadians, the likelihood of being assaulted in the workplace by a machine or accidental mishap is twenty-eight times greater than the chance of being a victim of an assault officially recognized by the Criminal Code. Canada Post, where one in five employees is injured, 67 per cent of these in a disabling way, is more dangerous than the Canadian Penitentiary Service, which has a rate of thirteen injuries per 100 employees. With work accidents and deaths up 10 per cent in Ontario in 1986, the Ontario Federation of Labor called for job fatalities to receive the same attention as police killings. As the 1990s commenced the health and safety of Canadian workers seemed precarious at best: someone was injured at work every seven seconds; there were four fatal job accidents over the course of twenty-four hours of working time; and each minute $7,500 was expended in workers' compensation for deaths and diseases associated with employment.

Technological change and health and safety thus remain concerns of all Canadian workers; union efforts to address these issues have been considerable. Yet as threatening as these issues of technology and injury/death are, there is no denying that they pale in comparison to the recent realization that the entire Canadian, indeed global, economy is in the process of massive restructuring. As the 1990s unfold, Canadian workers and their unions are coming to grips with the understanding that microchip companies such as Atari, Apple, and Wang are moving their assembly operations to low-wage countries such as Mexico, Taiwan, and the Philippines, ensuring that the growth sector of the economy actually generates few jobs in Canada. Death in the forests gets less union press than the absolute decline of forestry products and their traditional markets. This process of displacement surfaced at the 1986 CLC convention as Steelworkers resisted the health and safety demand that asbestos be phased out of all construction work and the industry closed down because of its hazardous health implications. Tragically, but understandably, jobs, not lives, were what the union eventually had to choose.

The trends over the course of the 1980s in Canada were thus clear. Economic sectors dominated by heavy industry and mass production unionism have wilted, as have the highly traditional remnants of the skilled craft-dominated areas of the economy, such as the building trades. Jobs have been disappearing in those very productive spheres where unionism has been an important component of class relations for generations. Where employment growth has taken place, it has been in the service sector.

Between 1981 and 1987 this area rose from 66 to 70 per cent of all jobs in Canada. The implications of this service-paced economy are great. More and more jobs are characterized by low wages. Women, paid less than men and more likely to be locked into occupations of low-status service, are an increasing presence in the labour force. Since 20 per cent of service-sector jobs are part-time, compared to 6 per cent in the goods-producing sector, many jobs are no longer nine-to-five, five-day-a-week occupations.

To be sure, this service sector is often seen as less seasonal, less cyclical, and less volatile than the sphere of commodity production. In the 1981-82 recession employment in goods production dropped 13 per cent, but in service the dip was a bare 1 per cent. But it is also an economy in which authority is more rigidly in the hands of a managerial/professional stratum and in which unionism is weaker and less likely to be a strong factor in the social relations of the workplace. Moreover, in the economic downturn of the late 1980s and early 1990s, even the service sector has been hard hit, job losses in retail, transportation, and fast foods climbing as there is less money to consume, a problem that can only be exacerbated as the Tory GST registers in the shrinking budgets of working-class families.

Even within the long-established centres of production, other developments have tended to accentuate this process whereby unionism has been weakened. One of these trends, much promoted throughout the late 1970s and early 1980s, took its cues from the need of capital to overcome the adversarial tensions of class life. Known as QWL, or Quality of Working Life, this "soft sell" of workplace relations was backed by segments of the state and even supported, for a time, by some unions. QWL programs were implemented in companies such as Canadian General Electric, Domtar, General Foods, General Motors, Inco, Westinghouse, Petrosar, Shell Canada, Macmillan Bloedel, Union Carbide, Esso, Cominco, Canadian Tire, and National Cash Register. The idea was that workers themselves would participate in redefining their jobs, co-operate with management in making decisions about how best to restructure the workplace, and, in the process, become more conscious of the shared interests of labour and capital. For companies the key was productivity; contented workers would be better and more economically profitable workers. It was also obvious in some cases that QWL was brought in to undermine union authority. At one large Canadian chemical plant, the workers threw out their union after being introduced to the QWL system.

QWL began its life in Canada in 1976, at the point that the class combativity of the 1965-75 years was peaking. One of every two unionists in the country walked a picket line in that year. Ontario set up a Quality of Working Life Centre and the federal government backed in principle the idea of QWL. The motivation behind such innovations and attempts to steer class relations in smooth and harmonious directions was thus fairly transparent. Vestiges of QWL remain, but many companies reached for this solution only out of exasperation associated with rising strike levels and increasing odds that they would have to face overt union and working-class resistance.

The best insurance against worker insurgence, most corporate decision-makers agree, is not shopfloor dialogue but audacious corporate control. And nothing solidified this more than the many threats associated with the post-1975 period of hard times. Over the course of the 1980s much of the QWL force, which grew out of the necessity to stem the class combat of earlier times, was thus spent; the attrition rate of specific company plans was quite high, approaching 50 per cent. As studies from Europe and the United States showed that job loss resulted in 68 per cent of the cases where QWL-type work redesign was carried out, it was also apparent to even the most accommodationist of unionists that this system of mediating class tensions was something of a game of Russian roulette for the working class as a whole. By the late 1980s only fragments of the QWL movement remained, but they spoke of their soft sell in ever softer voices. In 1988 the Ontario government closed the doors of its Quality of Working Life Centre.

By this time, the QWL mode of integrating workers into the spirit and practice of the company team had been superseded by a more heavy-handed capitalist paternalism. The case is illustrated well by a specific instance of corporate relocation. When Goodyear, a multinational run out of Akron, Ohio, with sales and production orchestrated around the globe, allowed its unionized Etobicoke tire plant to lapse into technological obsolescence, it rebuilt in Napanee, an eastern Ontario community of 5,000 hungry for jobs. Projected to employ almost 1,000 in what was hailed loudly as the world's most modern tire plant, Goodyear's invasion of Napanee also hinted at many other spin-off jobs as the suggestion spread that industries and services would cluster around the huge operation. Plugging into the local high school, where youth were quickly mobilized to support the coming of the new company and its promise of employment, Goodyear donated its own technology (paid for by government grants) to the school's Industrial Arts program and offered its arrival as an answer to community needs. In a bread-and-circus atmosphere of festive celebration, the company launched its promotional campaign in a ground-breaking ceremony that featured a Canada Day giveaway of 50,000 Goodyear caps, thousands of pounds of cake and watermelon, a lavish fireworks display, and the proverbial Blimp. More than 20,000 crowded into the local fairgrounds for the party, and when the first few hirings were to occur, 1,000 applicants were in line. But virtually anyone with a union past was screened from employment; Goodyear preferred to hire fresh young boys off the farm and just out of school. Everything was done to see that the new factory was non-union.

Paternalism, seemingly banished from the mass production sector with the rise of the CIO unions in the 1930s and 1940s, thus returned with a vengeance in the 1980s and 1990s. At Goodyear, those interviewing for initial jobs were required, contrary to law, to have their spouses interviewed so as to assure managerial elements that the company's demands would not pose family problems that might undermine the stability and corporate commitment of the newly recruited work force.

The Goodyear story was reproduced with a slight twist in the auto sector, as Japanese firms crashed the Big Three's Ontario party to set up plants in Alliston, Cambridge, and Ingersoll. Japanese managerial practices were highly paternalistic and, coupled with the technological sophistication and the small-town, rural roots of the freshly recruited work forces, this made for new challenges to unionism. As capitalism came to the back country in the 1980s, it rode high in the saddle of a frontier-like mentality in which class relations were no longer encumbered by the historically conditioned ground rules of the post-1945 years.

This new-found corporate confidence makes it far more difficult for the workers' movement to address a range of social issues put on the trade union agenda in earlier times. Issues of gender and race, for instance, remain matters demanding trade union attention in the 1990s. But as the women's movement has been forced on the defensive in the 1980s and 1990s, battling to preserve what little was won during the 1960s and 1970s on fundamental issues such as pay equity and freedom of choice on abortion, so, too, has the labour movement's capacity to address the linkage of gender and class stalled somewhat. The percentage of women on union executive boards held constant from 1978 to 1987 at slightly less than 20 per cent. More than 36 per cent of the country's 3.5 million union members, however, were women. Public-sector unions moved to ensure the presence of female union leaders in labour bodies in which the work force was overwhelmingly composed of women, and organizations such as the CLC and the Ontario Federation of Labor guaranteed that a certain number of vice-presidencies would be assigned to women, but the picture in the private-sector, largely American-dominated trade unions is far from ideal. Of 340 union executive board members who were women in 1987, only two came from U.S.-based internationals, where fully 21 per cent of the membership is female. This underrepresentation of women in leadership posts in some unions, along with capital's increasing refusals to countenance any form of social bargaining, has meant that union demands for adequate and affordable day care, paid parental leaves, programs to deal with sexual harassment at the workplace, and affirmative action hiring procedures have either been slipping from sight or been curtly dismissed.

Similar backsliding may well be evident around the labour movement's commitment and capacity to expose and fight racism, both within its midst and as shown by employers. The 1980s opened, for instance, with an innovative and highly effective OFL campaign, "Racism Hurts Everyone." Fact sheets were distributed, a handbook for shop stewards was produced, conferences were organized, instructors were trained, and a major public awareness campaign, including creative use of television advertisement, was launched. The OFL hired Mutale Chanda to co-ordinate the drive, and throughout the 1980s it continued to expose discriminatory practices and call for an end to racism. Within its own ranks workers of colour formed the Ontario Coalition of Black Trade Unionists. Specific unions, such as CUPE's largest Canadian municipal body, Local 79, have linked the struggles against racism and sexism in organizing hundreds of women of colour employed in Toronto's Metro Homes for the Aged. But for all of the positive accomplishments of the 1980s with regard to unionism's record against racism, hard times apparently dictated that Chanda's contract with the OFL not be renewed. Ronnie Leah notes that some trade unionists considered this "a setback" in the struggle against racism and that "many trade unionists are dissatisfied with the slow pace of change."

Many see "national" oppression as a significant factor to address in the workers' movement, as important to overcome as the oppressions of race and gender. Since the mid-1960s, as we have seen in the last chapter, there has been much discontent with the dominance of the Canadian labour movement by U.S.-based "internationals," as well as considerable movement to establish independent, autonomous Canadian unions. On one level, the growth of public-sector unionism, which by definition is Canadian unionism, and the devastating job loss in the old-line AFL-CIO unions have shifted fundamentally the national affiliation of Canadian unions. The breakaway movement of the late 1960s and the early 1970s, by which small unions and individual locals left their American "internationals" to join bodies such as the Confederation of Canadian Unions (CCU), has actually been made more mainstream and respectable with the establishment of the Canadian Automobile Workers in 1985 and the move to independent status of the Canadian section of the IWA one year later. In 1966, barely three in ten organized workers in Canada belonged to Canadian unions. Twenty years later that ratio had reversed, with six in ten unionists belonging to labour bodies that were distinctively Canadian.

To be sure, nationalists and many union dissidents continued to oppose the financial and bureaucratic injustices of a resilient American dominance. The CCU, perhaps relying on some creative bookkeeping, found it relatively easy throughout the 1980s to come up with surveys of international unions that showed a net drain of Canadian working-class dues dollars to the United States. In unions like that of the longshoremen there were many who pushed autonomy as an answer to the stifling lack of democracy imposed on locals by U.S. labour bosses and their Canadian hirelings.

But as hard times structure the possibilities for workers and their leaders it is more and more difficult to see Canadianization as some kind of panacea. Talk of huge amalgamations, such as Bob White's proposed

Canadian Metalworkers Federation, modelled on European trade union practices, has been around for more than a decade but has come to little. White's CAW has had an excellent public relations ride, but many, repulsed by the concession-bargaining of the UAW Solidarity House hierarchy in the extremely tight times of the 1980s, lose sight of the common interests of all auto workers, regardless of nationality, regardless of accommodationist leaderships. In the tense 1982 Chrysler strike, as White appeared to be frozen out by UAW head Doug Fraser, Detroit auto workers – in defiance of their own leaders – crossed the border to walk Windsor picket lines. White repaid them by settling the strike in Canada first, a *nationalist* accomplishment that undercut American workers and gained Canadian labour far less than might have been won by a co-ordinated international strike that would have forced Chrysler's Lee Iacocca to do more than meet face to face with White.

This set the stage for the 1985 White-orchestrated break from the UAW and, again, for contract negotiations to be settled first in Canada, a priority for White, who needed to establish that his Canadian union was an autonomous and legitimate bargaining entity. "Here we are in our first negotiation as a new union," White recalled of 1985, "and we were about to settle a major strike ahead of the Americans and set the pattern for the American agreement. That tasted sweet." Lost in all the nationalist hoopla was *The Financial Post*'s view that Owen Bieber had actually out-negotiated White, getting his 70,000 Detroit auto workers an up-front bonus of $2,100 U.S. to make up partially for past concessions. White got his membership $1,000 in their own devalued currency. To be sure, White's CAW has secured some contractual tidbits for its members of late, but it must also be recognized that it confronted the Big Three within a context far more favourable to workers than that faced by the UAW, the Canadian federal government being committed to the preservation of Ontario's auto industry.

The relative weights of the national question and hard times can perhaps best be assessed by looking at trade unionism in an epoch of permanent crisis in terms of the exacerbating tensions of regional industrial decline. In the mid-1980s the depressed Cape Breton mines were the site of a CCU organizational drive. A narrow majority of the miners stuck with their international affiliated union. Months later it was revealed that 4,000 adults had left industrial Cape Breton in the 1984-86 period. As the Sydney Steel Corporation modernized out of existence 800 jobs, trimming the work force to 700, the region experienced a ravaging depopulation. A federal mobility allowance program subsidized the "move down the road" and provided $3,000 for a family of four to relocate to Ontario if a job for the "breadwinner" could be lined up. Whatever the attractions of a new, national unionism, these were of less import than the acute pressures of economic restructuring and the subsequent disappearance of the wage itself.

As the Canadian working class entered the 1990s, hard times oversha-dowed all else. The recession of 1990 slashed its way through working-class incomes, securities, organizations, and hopes. War in the Persian Gulf may have bumped Mulroney's ratings up and boosted morale in Canada's high-tech arms sector, heavily mortgaged to American militarist interests. But it did little to ease this painful economic context. With energy prices uncer-tain and the Canadian state spending millions daily on an imperialist adventure halfway around the globe, inflation, kept in check by the eco-nomic downturn, began to creep upward again.

Nor were there the mixed blessings of increased employment. Between January, 1990, and January, 1991, official unemployment soared to between 8 and 14 per cent in the country's major industrial cities. Displaced Maritimers, forced into the central Canadian labour market in the mid- to late 1980s, began drifting back home, destitute and dejected. In fishing communities like Lockeport, Nova Scotia, gutted by Tory policies, sixty families depended on the local food bank in 1991; not a single domestic unit had been forced into such dire circumstances five years earlier. Halifax's Metro Food Bank recorded a jump of 40 per cent in the numbers relying on it between late 1989 and early 1991. Clement Gignac of the National Bank of Canada reported that wage and other union demands were on the decline, explaining further that it was all organized workers could do to protect their jobs.

Those who looked for the unions to do much more in 1991 often found themselves disappointed. On issues small and large, there were plenty of indications that the labour movement was at a loss for principled positions and the words and actions to articulate and implement them. What would a nineteenth-century craft union, with its own mechanisms of job control and ways of dealing with workers it judged to be exceeding the standard rate, hogging and rushing their way to the detriment of their fellow union-ists, have made of the 1991 trial of five steel workers for breaking the Employment Standards Act, which limits the amount of overtime allowed? The original complaint that precipitated this issue of overwork into the courts came from the union to which these overzealous workers belonged, Local 1005 of the United Steelworkers of America. Although it had the good grace not to name its own members, the USWA consulted with the Ontario Ministry of Labour and targeted specific Stelco departments, thereby exposing particular employees to charges. Some of these unionists, with Stelco's obvious blessings, were apparently logging ninety-hour work weeks. Unionism clearly lost some of its footing when it depended on the courts to discipline those in its ranks who broke with fundamental commit-ments to collectivism.

More ominous was the quietude of Canadian labour as George Bush and the Pentagon orchestrated Mulroney and his Tory government, effortlessly easing the Canadian state into its role as supplementary firepower for a bellicose militarism. Mainstream Canadian unionism has always aligned itself with patriotism and backed the state in its promotion of specific twentieth-century wars. But seldom has the matter been handled so easily as it was in the Gulf War of early 1991; in the past, many within labour's ranks demanded discussion and debate, and considerable numbers called for strike action to thwart those who would wage war. The best the CLC could offer in 1991, however, was a contradictory rhetorical statement supporting Canadian troops in the Gulf but deploring their use in any offensive activity.

The point is not a simple one, in which the past is judged preferable to the present or the present is automatically assumed to be better than what has preceded it. Workers clearly have benefits and rights in the here and now that would have astounded nineteenth-century labour and surprised, perhaps, their own mothers and fathers. They take for granted much that earlier generations fought for as answers to labour's woes. Yet the consequences of various victories and defeats have spun new and contradictory layers of consequences; the implications of all of this layering have never been clearly foreseen, and while the positive achievements of struggles might be glimpsed the negative outcomes of what often seemed historic steps forward could seldom be perceived in the glare of "progress." And so workers have come to face hazards and stresses and setbacks that could hardly have even been imagined by those who struggled for working-class betterment before them. The present is not only different from the past, it is also almost always more complex.

But however bad and ugly the current hard times are for Canadian workers, the one positive good that it is difficult to erode is that workers appreciate what has historically been struggled over even if it is difficult, at times, to grasp exactly what it is that the struggle will result in. They know, for the most part, that their hope as workers – and the maintenance of their futures and those of their children – lies not in individualism and its acquisitive answers but in collectivity and the claims it makes for all humanity. Whatever the accommodations of unionism, however much it has been integrated into the state apparatus and its leaders structured into compromise and conciliation, workers grasp intuitively that without organization and resistance their lot would be worse. One only has to walk a few picket lines with workers who have been willing to leave their jobs for weeks to squeeze a few more cents an hour out of their parsimonious employers to know this.

As the hard lessons of hard times etch themselves into the material lives of Canadian workers, cutting across the diversities of region, skill, ethnicity, race, and gender with a swath of commonality, this fundamental grasp of the realities of life under capitalism is the good that can turn aside the bad and the ugly of what has of late seemed a permanent crisis of both the institutions and confidence of the working class. Workers themselves, in conjunction with their allies, will build new strategies and new leaderships, restructuring rather than abandoning the one basic defence – the trade union – they have against capital and its increasingly combative allies in the state. They have done this in the past, out of depths of deprivation and defeat that compare only too unfavourably to the present. With this done, the logic of class oppression and exploitation will lead to new, more overtly offensive, political agendas.

For all of the bad and the ugly of the last fifteen years, then, the good has not yet been suffocated and silenced. Workers will build a new and a better Canada through new and better class-based organizations and politics, through a class-struggle leadership and a program that rests on the collectivist class foundations of two centuries of experience. There is a lot to go up against, of course, not the least of labour's problem being the structural and ideological capitulations and collaborations within its own house, which have been so astutely nourished for much of this century by capital and the state, and which now leave many working-class militants and their advocates fighting defeatism and despair. Some may actually succumb to these forces. But for workers as a class this is not really a way out, and this is why every time that the working class is pronounced dead and buried it has managed to rise up and shake its class fist in the face of those who have proclaimed it totally subdued.

This persistent resurrection of class happens not because workers are better human beings than other people, or because they are smarter and more courageous, but, rather, because they, and they alone, have no other options. Whatever their many differences, workers alone in this society produce the goods and services that make our economic, cultural, and political life what it is. They, and no other social grouping, provide the labour that is then turned into profit, which allows the few to direct and control the many. Workers alone can withdraw that labour and in the process pressure the transformation and change of society. Others will, of course, be vital allies, but it will be class that counts, in the end, if the end is to come in ways that improve life for all Canadians.

Women can struggle for their own liberation, but if they ignore the exploitations of class that allow one contingent of owners to live off the labour of workers, they will only ensure that some women are materially better off than others. Environmentalists can fight for Mother Earth, but if they lose sight of who really profits from ecological destruction they will only nudge the corporations to hire better public relations experts and they will only make working-class children feel guilty about the non-recyclable juice boxes in their parentally packed schoolday lunches. Advocates of peace can fight for a world free of war, but unless they address the immense profit of war industries and the immediate need to convert jobs in this sector to productive uses they will be destined to fail, just as they will have done nothing to stop the class war on the domestic front, which has its own kind of routinely dulling carnage. And the battle to stamp out the cancer of racism will be stopped in its tracks if the labour movement is not centrally involved in reconstructing a world untainted by the prejudice of colour. More than 125 years ago Marx suggested that labour in white skins would never be free until labour in black skins was equally free. The tragic reality is that after all of this time not only does this remain as true as it was in Marx's day, but the corollary is also true: peoples of colour, not only at home but also around the world, will never be free until all labour, including white labour, is emancipated.

This is, of course, a two-way street. Workers are not just paid labour, and they are not just that section of exploited humanity that has managed to secure the benefits of unionism. They are wives and the young, they are women as well as men, they are people with sexual identities and political commitments and beliefs, including attachments to environmentalism and peace. The absolute importance of making class matter will only be frustrated if these integral components and values of working-class life are not addressed by organizations and leaderships with explicit class composition and purpose.

I am thus not advocating a rejection of the much-proclaimed need for labour to align itself with other progressive forces in mass coalitions of oppositional protest. But I am adamant on two matters usually passed over in silence by promoters of a social unionism linked to coalition politics. First, it must be understood that such coalitions will go nowhere if they themselves do not recognize and address class exploitation and inequality. They must proceed on the basis of a political understanding of the need to create a society in which inequalities are abolished, an undertaking of transformation that will necessarily rely, first and foremost, on the potential and power of workers. Second, as long as the current leadership – economic and political – of the Canadian working class is unchallenged and allowed to speak for the workers' movement within such coalitions, indeed, allowed to lead them, then protest will only be derailed and defeat ensured. And, it needs to be said, the whole process of building coalitions will be poisoned and the trust that should unite labour and its allies squandered. Those who would argue differently have their heads buried in some quite substantial sand with respect to the contemporary history of the working class. The call for social unionism and the promotion of progressive coalition-building thus demands putting class politics at the centre of such mobilization, confronting, at the same time, the troubling issue of leadership.

All of this may seem utterly utopian. But it has never been more necessary. And if the necessity of social transformation is to be translated into actions that will realize what is needed, it will be workers – in all of their diversity, but also in their final unity – who will make that need come alive, because, quite bluntly, they have no choice and they have the potential power. During the devastating Ontario plant closures of 1981, workers sometimes occupied the factories and reached back into their past to draw on the tactics of the sit-down strike. They demanded their jobs back. It was not the world they sought to change; rather, they wanted merely to turn back a moment of injustice. But the words of one sit-down striker echo the ultimate fate and possible destiny of the working class as a whole: "We had nothing. . . . We really had to take it."

Bibliography

For the nineteenth-century years I have been able to draw upon a literature that confronts the problematic dimensions of plebeian and working-class cultural experience. My own research in original source materials has also been concentrated in this earlier period. Varying assessments of this historiographical context are found in Greg Kealey, "Writing About Labour," in John Schultz, ed., *Writing About Canada* (Scarborough, Ontario: Prentice-Hall, 1990), 145-74; Bryan D. Palmer, "Working-Class Canada: Recent Historical Writing," *Queen's Quarterly*, 86 (1979/ 80), 594-616; David Bercuson, "Through the Looking Glass of Culture: An Essay on the New Labour History and Working-Class Culture in Recent Canadian Historical Writing," *Labour/Le Travailleur*, 7 (1981), 95-112; Gregory S. Kealey, "Labour and Working-Class History in Canada: Prospects in the 1980s," *Labour/Le Travailleur*, 7 (1981), 67-94; and Desmond Morton, "Labour and Industrial Relations History in English-Speaking Canada," and James Thwaites, "History and Industrial Relations in Canada," both in Gérard Hébert, Hem C. Jain, and Noah Meltz, eds., *The State of the Art in Industrial Relations* (Kingston and Toronto: Queen's University Industrial Relations Centre and Centre for Industrial Relations University of Toronto, 1988), 243-79.

In the twentieth-century treatments of labour, however, little attention has been paid to culture. For this reason, my argument is weighted toward the institutions/ political context of working-class life in the years after 1919. But as I attempted to stress in the introduction, a culture does not exist "above" institutions and politics, and in advanced capitalist societies where the institutional/political forces of repression are highly developed the union and labour political action are of vital importance, and are themselves part of cultural experience.

What follows is a partial listing of sources relevant to this study. Particular efforts have been made to include reference to the more obscure unpublished works referred to in the text, but this by no means encompasses all of the pertinent writing in the field. See, for instance, Douglas Vaisey, *The Labour Companion: A Bibliography of Canadian Labour History Based on Materials Printed from 1950 to 1975* (Halifax: Committee on Canadian Labour History, 1980), updated in subsequent issues of *Labour/Le Travail*. The following abbreviations have been employed: *Canadian Historical Review (CHR)*; *Labour/Le Travailleur* – after 1983, *Labour/Le Travail – (L/LT)*; *Histoire Sociale/Social History (HS)*. The countless economic histories and standard texts used in discussions of particular social formations cannot be adequately acknowledged, but I have relied on William L. Marr and Donald G. Paterson, *Canada: An Economic History* (Toronto: Macmillan, 1980) most persistently.

This bibliography is arranged according to the sequence of the text, but is prefaced by a preliminary listing of "essential" texts that cover a wide range of working-class history.

Essential Texts

Early and pioneering attempts to locate the place of workers in nineteenth-century capitalist social formations are found in H. Clare Pentland, *Labour and Capital in Canada, 1650-1860* (Toronto: Lorimer, 1981), and Stanley B. Ryerson, *Unequal Union: Roots of Crisis in the Canadas, 1815-1873* (Toronto: Progress, 1968). Eugene Forsey's *Trade Unionism in Canada, 1812-1902* (Toronto: University of Toronto Press, 1982) provides a detailed listing of trade unions, labour political actions, and strikes in the nineteenth century. A rare and preliminary attempt to catalogue regional strike activity is found in Jean Hamelin, Paul Larocque, and Jacques Rouillard, *Répertoire des grèves dans la province de Québec au XIXe siècle* (Montréal: Presses de l'École des hautes études commerciales, 1971). Useful in this regard are the suggestive overviews produced recently for the *Historical Atlas of Canada*. See, for instance, Bryan D. Palmer, "Labour Protest and Organization in Nineteenth-Century Canada," *L/LT*, 20 (Fall, 1987), 61-84; Douglas Cruikshank and Gregory S. Kealey, "Canadian Strike Statistics, 1891-1950," *L/LT*, 20 (Fall, 1987), 85-145; and Kealey and Cruikshank, "Strikes," in *Historical Atlas of Canada*, III: *Addressing the Twentieth Century* (Toronto: University of Toronto Press, 1990), Plate 39.

Late nineteenth-century community studies include Palmer, *A Culture in Conflict: Skilled Workers and Industrial Capitalism in Hamilton, Ontario, 1860-1914* (Montreal: McGill-Queen's University Press, 1979); and Gregory S. Kealey, *Toronto Workers Respond to Industrial Capitalism, 1867-1892* (Toronto: University of Toronto Press, 1980). Martin Robin's now dated study, *Radical Politics and Canadian Labour, 1880-1930* (Kingston: Industrial Relations Centre, Queen's University, 1968), can be read with profit.

Overviews of the institutional/political history of workers, all of uneven quality, include Harold Logan, *Trade Unions in Canada* (Toronto: Macmillan, 1948); Charles Lipton, *The Trade Union Movement of Canada, 1827-1959* (Montreal: Canadian Social Publications, 1966); Desmond Morton, *Working People: An Illustrated History of Canadian Labour* (Toronto: Summerhill, 1990). Stuart Jamieson's *Times of Trouble: Labour Unrest and Industrial Conflict in Canada, 1900-1966*

(Ottawa: Queen's Printer, 1968) provides an introduction to twentieth-century strike activity, while Pentland, *A Study of the Changing Social, Economic and Political Background of the Canadian System of Industrial Relations* (Ottawa: Task Force on Labour Relations, 1968), serves as a schematic overview of labour-capital relations. Craig Heron, *The Canadian Labour Movement: A Short History* (Toronto: James Lorimer, 1989), is disappointingly conventional and thin, at best, on nineteenth-century material. For a striking visual snapshot, see Kealey and Cruikshank, "Organized Labour," in *Historical Atlas,* III, Plate 38.

Western labour radicalism receives coverage in A. Ross McCormack, *Reformers, Rebels, and Revolutionaries: The Western Canadian Radical Movement, 1899-1919* (Toronto: University of Toronto Press, 1977); David Bercuson, *Confrontation at Winnipeg: Labour, Industrial Relations, and the General Strike* (Montreal: McGill-Queen's University Press, 1974); and Bercuson, *Fools and Wise Men: The Rise and Fall of the One Big Union* (Toronto: McGraw-Hill, 1978). Kenneth McNaught discusses the rise of the early radical social democrat, J.S. Woodsworth, in *A Prophet in Politics: A Biography of J.S. Woodsworth* (Toronto: University of Toronto Press, 1959). Canada's most persistently radical region, British Columbia, is the object of study in Paul Phillips, *No Power Greater: A Century of Labour in B.C.* (Vancouver: B.C. Federation of Labour, 1967).

Documentary collections of value include Michael S. Cross, ed., *The Workingman in the Nineteenth Century* (Toronto: Oxford University Press, 1974); and Irving Abella and David Millar, eds., *The Canadian Worker in the Twentieth Century* (Toronto: Oxford University Press, 1978). Two significant collections of essays highlight different historiographical traditions. Gregory S. Kealey and Peter Warrian, eds., *Essays in Canadian Working-Class History* (Toronto: McClelland and Stewart, 1976), concentrate on local and cultural aspects of workers' experience, while Irving Abella, ed., *On Strike: Six Key Labour Struggles in Canada, 1919-1945* (Toronto: Lewis and Samuel, 1974), probes the episodic struggles of the twentieth century. Michael Earle, ed., *Workers and the State in Twentieth-Century Nova Scotia* (Fredericton, New Brunswick: Acadiensis Press, 1989), addresses the most industrialized province in Atlantic Canada and focuses on the evolution of industrial legality. Bryan D. Palmer, ed., *The Character of Class Struggle: Essays in Canadian Working-Class History, 1850-1985* (Toronto: McClelland and Stewart, 1986), gathers together essays on the various regions and periods of labour's history, as does Gregory S. Kealey and W.J.C. Cherwinski, *Lectures in Canadian Labour and Working-Class History* (St. John's, Newfoundland: Committee on Canadian Labour History, 1985). A focus on the labour process is evident in Craig Heron and Robert Storey, eds., *On the Job: Confronting the Labour Process in Canada* (Kingston and Montreal: McGill-Queen's University Press, 1986). Note, as well, a widely read sociological study, James W. Rinehart, *The Tyranny of Work: Alienation and the Labour Process* (Toronto: Harcourt, Brace, Jovanovitch, 1987).

The best place to begin an examination of Quebec is still with the works of Jacques Rouillard. See, especially, his *Histoire du Syndicalisme Québécois* (Montréal: Boréal Express, 1988). See, as well, Jean Hamelin *et al., Les Travailleurs québécois, 1850-1896* (Montréal: Presses de l'Université du Québec, 1974); Hamelin *et al., Les travailleurs québécois, 1941-1971* (Québec: Institut supérieur de sciences humaines, 1976). The peculiar legal context of unionism in Quebec is addressed in Pierre Verge, "Law and Industrial Relations in Quebec: Object and Context," in Hébert *et al.,* eds., *The State of the Art in Industrial Relations*, 73-105.

Gender and the history of the working class now comprise a vibrant field. For an introduction see Bettina Bradbury, "Women's History and Working-Class History," *L/LT*, 19 (Spring, 1987), 23-44; Linda Briskin and Lynda Yanz, eds., *Union Sisters: Women in the Labour Movement* (Toronto: Women's Press, 1983); Gregory S. Kealey, ed., *Class, Gender, and Region* (St. John's, Newfoundland: Committee on Canadian Labour History, 1988). A useful general recent statement is Elizabeth Fox-Genovese, *Feminism without Illusion: A Critique of Individualism* (Chapel Hill: University of North Carolina Press, 1991).

Of the many popular histories of labour, few have influenced this study. Most are official histories, celebrations of particular events and movements, or explicitly informed by other scholarly studies. One invaluable development, however, emerged out of the McMaster Labour Studies Program. Among the impressive products are Craig Heron *et al., All That Our Hands Have Done: A Pictorial History of the Hamilton Workers* (1981); and a group of pamphlets put together by Wayne Roberts: *Miner's Life: Bob Miner and Union Organizing in Timmins, Kirkland Lake and Sudbury* (1979); *Organizing Westinghouse: Alf Ready's Story* (1979); *Where Angels Fear to Tread: Eileen Tallman and the Labour Movement* (1981); and *Baptism of a Union: Stelco Strike of 1946* (1981). Derek Reimer of Sound Heritage has edited a similar work for British Columbia: *Fighting for Labour: Four Decades of Work in British Columbia, 1910-1950* (Victoria: Provincial Archives, 1978). For Quebec, see *L'Industrialization à Hochelaga-Maisonneuve, 1900-1930* (Montréal: Atelier d'Histoire Hochelaga-Maisonneuve, 1980). Illustrated provincial histories include Bill Gillespie, *A Class Act: An Illustrated History of the Labour Movement in Newfoundland and Labrador* (St. John's: Federation of Labour, 1986); Doug Smith, *Let Us Rise: A History of the Manitoba Labour Movement* (Vancouver: New Star Books, 1985); and Warren Caragatta, *Alberta Labour: A Heritage Untold* (Toronto: James Lorimer, 1979). The best such urban collection of photographs is *Working Lives: Vancouver 1886-1986* (Vancouver: New Star Books, 1985). Unmatched in its sophistication and innovation, however, is Benjamin H.D. Buchloh and Robert Wilkie, eds., *Mining Photographs and other Pictures, 1948-1968: A Selection from the Negative Archives of Shedden Studio, Glace Bay, Cape Breton* (Halifax: Nova Scotia College of Art and Design, 1983).

Partisans of the workers' movement have also written histories. The radical orientation is epitomized by Jack Scott's writings, the most well known being *Sweat and Struggle: Working Class Struggles in Canada* (Vancouver: New Star Books, 1974). More conservative is the CLC-centred Jack Williams, *The Story of Unions in Canada* (Toronto: Dent, 1975); see also Morden Lazarus, *Years of Hard Labour: Trade Unions and the Workingman in Canada* (Toronto: Co-operative Press, 1974). Histories of specific unions that merit particular mention include Ian McKay, *The Craft Transformed: An Essay on the Carpenters of Halifax* (Halifax: Holdfast Press, 1985); and Sally Zerker, *The Rise and Fall of the Toronto Typographical Union, 1832-1972: A Case Study of Foreign Domination* (Toronto: University of Toronto Press, 1982).

I: PRODUCING CLASSES, PATERNALIST AUTHORITY, 1800-1850

On the character of the social formation, note Richard E. Rice, "Ship Building in British America, 1787-1890: An Introductory Study" (Ph.D. thesis, Liverpool, 1977); Gerald Tulchinsky, *The River Barons: Montreal Businessmen and the Growth of Industry and Transportation, 1837-1853* (Toronto: University of Toronto Press, 1977); Jacob Spelt, *Urban Development in South-Central Ontario* (Toronto: McClelland and Stewart, 1972); and the work of Leo A. Johnson, especially *History of the County of Ontario, 1615-1875* (Whitby, Ontario: County of Ontario, 1973); "Land Policy, Population Growth and Social Structure in the Home District, 1793-1851," *Ontario History,* 48 (1971), 41-60. See also Gary Teeple, "Land, Labour, and Capital in Pre-Confederation Canada," in Teeple, ed., *Capitalism and the National Question in Canada* (Toronto: University of Toronto Press, 1981). Graeme Wynn, *Timber Colony: A Historical Geography of early nineteenth century New Brunswick* (Toronto: University of Toronto Press, 1981), is a lucid account of the vital importance of one key staple, while his "'Deplorably Dark and Demoralized Lumberers'? Rhetoric and Reality in Early Nineteenth Century New Brunswick," *Journal of Forest History,* 24 (1980), 168-87, is an interesting discussion of labour. The importance of seafaring labour is addressed in Judith Fingard, *Jack in Port: Sailortowns of Eastern Canada* (Toronto: University of Toronto Press, 1982); Eric W. Sager, *Seafaring Labour: The Merchant Marine of Atlantic Canada, 1820-1914* (Kingston and Montreal: McGill-Queen's University Press, 1989).

Quebec's agricultural crisis is analysed in numerous works by Fernand Ouellet, the most accessible for an English readership being *Economic and Social History of Quebec, 1760-1850* (Toronto: Macmillan, 1980). This interpretation is called into question but not, in my assessment, convincingly refuted by R.M. McInnis, "A Reconsideration of the State of Agriculture in Lower Canada in the First Half of the Nineteenth Century," in D.H. Akenson, ed., *Canadian Papers in Rural History*, III (1982), 9-49. I have been influenced to soften statements in this interpretive realm, however, by Allan Greer, *Peasant, Lord, and Merchant: Rural Society in Three Quebec Parishes, 1740-1840* (Toronto: University of Toronto Press, 1985). See also Greer, "Fur Trade Labour and Lower Canadian Agrarian Structures," *Historical Papers* (1981), 197-214.

Throughout this chapter, I have drawn primarily on my own research notes from the *Upper Canadian Sundries*, the *Montreal Gazette* (1819-50), the *Kingston Whig* and *Kingston Chronicle and Gazette* (1811-40), and assorted other archival holdings and published sources. The Upper Canadian elite and its policies and practices have been scrutinized in a number of recent studies, some of which I use in this chapter, others of which I take exception to. See Peter A. Russell, *Attitudes to Social Structure and Mobility in Upper Canada, 1791-1841* (Kingston and Montreal: McGill-Queen's University Press, 1989); David Keane and Colin Read, eds., *Old Ontario: Essays in Honour of J.M.S. Careless* (Toronto: Dundurn Press, 1990), esp. the articles by Romney (pp. 192-216) and Johnson (pp. 217-33). A useful collection of articles is Victor L. Russell, ed., *Forging a Consensus: Historical Essays on Toronto* (Toronto: University of Toronto Press, 1984). A rare detailed look at an occupation is William N.T. Wylie, "The Blacksmith in Upper Canada, 1784-1850: A Study of Technology, Culture, and Power," in Donald H. Akenson, ed., *Canadian Papers in Rural History*, VII (1990), 17-214.

Pentland's notion of feudal social relations is elaborated in "The Development of a Capitalistic Labour Market in Canada," *Canadian Journal of Economics and Political Science*, 25 (1959), 450-61, although his published book redefines such relations as paternalistic. Critiques of Pentland include the wild and wonderful "H. Clare Pentland, the Irish, and the New Canadian Social History," in Donald H. Akenson, *Being Had: Historians, Evidence, and the Irish in North America* (Port Credit, Ontario: P.D. Meany, 1985), 109-142; and, in Des Morton's words, "For those who enjoy theological disputation," Allan Greer, "Wage Labor and the Transition to Capitalism: A Critique of Pentland," *L/LT,* 15 (Spring, 1985), 7-24. On paternalism, note the discussions in Patrick Joyce, *Work, Society and Politics: The Culture of the Factory in Later Victorian Britain* (New Brunswick, New Jersey: Rutgers University Press, 1980), and Genovese, *Roll, Jordan, Roll: The World the Slaves Made* (New York: Pantheon, 1974). There are pertinent, although differing, discussions in Gerald Sider, "The Ties that Bind: Culture and Agriculture, Property and Propriety in the Newfoundland Village Fishery," *Social History*, 5 (1980), 1-39; David Terence Ruddell, "Colonial Capital and Labour: Principles and Practices in the Quebec District, 1760-1840," paper presented to the McGill Conference on Class and Culture, 1980. On Seaman's Minudie paternalism I benefited from seeing an unpublished study, Danny Samson, "Communal Resources and the Transition to Capitalism in Minudie, Nova Scotia, 1795-1840," seminar paper, Queen's University, 1988. Note, as well, Larry MacDonald, "France and New France: The Internal Contradictions," *CHR*, 52 (June, 1971), 121-43. Christian Norman, "A Company Community: Garden Island, Upper Canada at Mid-Century," in Donald H. Akenson, ed., *Canadian Papers in Rural History*, II (1980), 113-34, is the best recent treatment of Calvin. Invaluable studies include F.L. Barron, "The Genesis of Temperance in Ontario, 1828-1850" (Ph.D. thesis, University of Guelph, 1976); and Graeme H. Patterson, "Studies in Elections and Public Opinion in Upper Canada" (Ph.D. thesis, University of Toronto, 1970).

Material life is probed in Robert Tremblay, "La formation matérielle de la class ouvrière à Montréal entre 1790 et 1830," *Revue d'histoire de l'Amérique français*, 33 (1979), 39-50; Michael Katz, *The People of Hamilton, Canada West: Family and Class in a Mid-Nineteenth Century City* (Cambridge, Mass.: Harvard University Press, 1975). Wage rates are taken from a range of primary materials and from other studies: Robert F. Gourlay, *Statistical Account of Upper Canada* (Toronto: McClelland and Stewart, 1972); Leo Johnson, "Prices and Wages in Canada West, 1840-41," paper presented to the McGill Conference on Class and Culture, 1980; and Russell, *Attitudes to Social Structure and Mobility*. Judith Fingard charts the pattern of poverty in early Canada in "The Winter's Tale: The Seasonal Contours of Pre-Industrial Poverty in British North America, 1815-1860," Canadian Historical Association, *Papers* (1974), 65-94.

The trauma of Scots immigration can be gleaned from James Hunter, *The Making of the Crofting Community* (Edinburgh: John Donald, 1976), while David Gagan, "Mid-Victorian Rural Canada West: 'A Good Poor Man's Country'," paper presented to McGill Conference on Class and Culture, 1980, has some impressionistic data on immigrants that I have used. The nature of population in French Canada can be drawn out of Fernand Ouellet's *Economic and Social History of Quebec, 1760-1840* (Toronto: Gage, 1980), or *Lower Canada, 1791-1840* (Toronto: McClelland and Stewart, 1980). Joanne Burgess, "The Growth of a Craft Labour Force:

Montréal Leather Artisans, 1815-1831," *Historical Papers* (1988), 48-62, is helpful. For material on the Irish, I have relied on Terrence M. Punch, "The Irish in Halifax, 1836-1871: A Study in Ethnic Assimilation" (M.A. thesis, Dalhousie University, 1977), and Donald H. Akenson, "Ontario: Whatever Happened to the Irish?" in Akenson, ed., *Canadian Papers in Rural History*, III (1982), 204-56. Other minor studies, most notably T.W. Acheson, "A Study in the Historical Demography of a Loyalist County," *HS*, 1 (1968), 53-65, have also been consulted. A recent synthesis is Cecil J. Houston and William J. Smyth, *Irish Immigration and Settlement: Patterns, Links, and Letters* (Toronto: University of Toronto Press, 1990).

On apprenticeship, see David Terence Ruddell, "Apprenticeship in early nineteenth-century Quebec, 1793-1815" (M.A. thesis, Laval University, 1969), which appears in published form in Jean-Pierre Hardy and David Thierry Ruddell, *Les apprentis artisans à Québec, 1660-1815* (Montréal: Les presses de l'Université du Québec, 1977); P.H. Audet, "Apprenticeship in Early Nineteenth Century Montreal" (M.A. thesis, Concordia University, 1976); David Sutherland, "The Stanyan Ropeworks of Halifax, Nova Scotia: Glimpses of a Pre-Industrial Manufactory," *L/LT*, 6 (1980), 149-58.

On the respectable, see the important and neglected study by Richard Rice, "A History of Organized Labour in Saint John, New Brunswick, 1813-1890" (M.A. thesis, University of New Brunswick, 1968), as well as Catherine Vance, "Early Trade Unionism in Quebec: The Carpenters and Joiners General Strike of 1833-1834," *Marxist Quarterly*, 3 (1962), 26-42; F.H. Armstrong, "Reformer as Capitalist: William Lyon Mackenzie and the Printers' Strike of 1836," *Ontario History*, 59 (1967), 187-96.

The rough are the subject of important examination in Pentland, "The Lachine Strike of 1843," *CHR*, 29 (1948), 255-77; Ruth Bleasdale, "Class Conflict on the Canals of Upper Canada in the 1840s," *L/LT*, 7 (1981), 9-89; Raymond Boily, *Les Irlandis et Le Canal de Lachine: La Grève de 1843* (Montréal: Leméac, 1980); Michael S. Cross, "The Shiners' War: Social Violence in the Ottawa Valley in the 1830s," *CHR*, 59 (1973), 1-26.

Comment on law, the penitentiary, and crime can be found in Palmer, "Kingston Mechanics and the Rise of the Penitentiary, 1833-1836," *HS*, 13 (1980), 7-82; William R. Teatero, "'A Dead and Alive Way Never Does': The Pre-Political Professional World of John A. Macdonald" (M.A. thesis, Queen's University, 1978); John Beattie, *Attitudes Towards Crime and Punishment in Upper Canada, 1830-1850: A Documentary Study* (Toronto: University of Toronto Centre of Criminology, 1977); and Paul Craven, "The Law of Master and Servant in Mid-Nineteenth-Century Ontario," in David H. Flaherty, ed., *Essays in the History of Canadian Law, I* (Toronto: University of Toronto Press, 1981), 175-211. Kathryn M. Bindon's "Hudson's Bay Company Law: Adam Thom and the Institution of Order in Rupert's Land, 1839-1854," *ibid.*, 43-87, adds appreciation of the Far West. Most useful is Eric Tucker, "'That Indefinite Area of Toleration': Criminal Conspiracy and Trade Unions in Ontario, 1837-1877," *L/LT*, 27 (Spring, 1991), 15-54.

Although I have presented new data in the section on rough justice, my own "Discordant Music: Charivaris and Whitecapping in Nineteenth-Century North America," *L/LT*, 3 (1978), 5-62, is a necessary background study. See, as well, Allan Greer, "From Folklore to Revolution: charivaris and the Lower Canadian rebellion of 1837," *Social History*, 15 (January, 1990), 25-43.

Much remains to be done on the underground history of dissent and insurrection, but note J.B. Walton, "'An End to All Order': A Study of Upper Canadian Conservative Responses to Opposition, 1805-1810" (M.A. thesis, Queen's University, 1977). One of the best treatments of the rebellion remains Edwin C. Guillet's *The Lives and Times of the Patriots* (Toronto: University of Toronto Press, 1968), while previously cited works by Ryerson and Ouellet deserve mention. John Brewer's *Party Ideology and Popular Politics at the Accession of George III* (Cambridge: Cambridge University Press, 1976) should be required reading for those seeking to understand the nature of ritualistic combat in the political realm. Works on reform and rebellion that merit attention include Sean T. Cadigan, "Paternalism in Upper Canada, 1800-1841" (M.A. thesis, Queen's University, 1987); P.A. Buckner and David Frank, eds., *Atlantic Canada Before Confederation: The Acadiensis Reader*, I (Fredericton: Acadiensis Press, 1985), especially articles by Keith Matthews (pp. 212-26) and J.M. Beck (pp. 227-44); and Paul Romney, "On the Eve of Rebellion: Nationality, Religion, and Class in the Toronto Election of 1836," in Keane and Read, eds., *Old Ontario*, 192-216.

On gender and class in the paternal order, see Katherine McKenna, "The Life of Anne Murray Powell, 1755-1849: A Case Study of the Position of Women in Early Upper Canadian Elite Society" (Ph.D. thesis, Queen's University, 1987); Jane Errington, "Pioneers and Suffragists," in Sandra Burt, Lorraine Code, and Lindsay Dorney, eds., *Changing Patterns: Women in Canada* (Toronto: McClelland and Stewart, 1988), 51-79. Peter Ward's *Courtship, Love and Marriage in Nineteenth Century English Canada* (Kingston and Montreal: McGill-Queen's University Press, 1990) supposedly addresses this intersection of class and gender but its selective use of evidence and nostalgically romantic view of the history is hardly believable. I have drawn instead on unpublished research by Annalee Golz, presented in "Family, Economy, and State in Nineteenth-Century Ontario," seminar paper, Queen's University, 1990, and on Cadigan, "Paternalism." On domestic patriarchy, see Allan Kulikoff, *Tobacco and Slaves: The Development of Southern Cultures in the Chesapeake, 1680-1800* (Chapel Hill: University of North Carolina Press, 1986).

Alison Prentice, *The School Promoters: Education and Social Class in Mid-Nineteenth Century Upper Canada* (Toronto: McClelland and Stewart, 1977), points out how class seeped into all aspects of social experience, as does Bruce Curtis, *Building the Educational State: Canada West, 1836-1871* (London, Ontario: Althouse Press, 1988). The beginnings of the labour movement in this period are sketched in Stephen Langdon, *The Emergence of the Canadian Working Class Movement* (Toronto: New Hogtown Press, 1975).

II: CLASS DIFFERENTIATION AND ANTAGONISM, 1850-1880

Gustavus Myers, *A History of Canadian Wealth* (Toronto: Lewis and Samuel, 1972), discusses the first railway boom, while Pentland's review of this reprint of a 1914 muckraking classic, "Were Canadian Capitalists Different? How the West Was Won," *Canadian Forum* (September, 1972), 6-9, contains insight. Valuable analytic advances of early capitalist development and the nature of the workplace can be gleaned from essays by Bruce Laurie and Mark Schmitz in Theodore Hershberg, ed., *Philadelphia: Work, Space, Family, and Group Experience in the 19th Century* (New York: Oxford University Press, 1981). Michael Katz, Michael Doucet, and Mark Stern have carried their work forward from the 1851-61 period covered in Katz, *The People of Hamilton, Canada West*, and I have drawn on their findings in *The Social Organization of Early Industrial Capitalism* (Cambridge, Mass.: Harvard University Press, 1982). An unpublished work, Alan Conter's "The Origins of a Working-Class District: A Portrait of St. Ann's Ward in the 1850s," McGill University, 1976, focuses on the capitalist development in a Montreal working-class district and can be read profitably with John McCallum's *Unequal Beginnings: Agriculture and Economic Development in Quebec and Ontario until 1870* (Toronto: University of Toronto Press, 1980); J.I. Cooper, "The Social Structure of Montreal in the 1850s," Canadian Historical Association, *Annual Report* (1956), 63-73; and Brian Young, *George-Etienne Cartier: Montreal Bourgeois* (Montreal: McGill-Queen's University Press, 1981).

Useful studies that open out into an understanding of the hinterland economies include Kenneth G. Pryke, *Nova Scotia and Confederation* (Toronto: University of Toronto Press, 1979); Ian McKay, "Capital and Labour in the Halifax Baking and Confectionary Industry During the Last Half of the Nineteenth Century," *L/LT* (1978), 63-108; Alan Brookes, "'Out-Migration' from the Maritime Provinces, 1860-1890: Some Preliminary Considerations," in P.A. Buckner and David Frank, eds., *Atlantic Canada After Confederation: The Acadiensis Reader*, II, 34-63; Martin Robin, *The Rush for Spoils: The Company Province, 1871-1933* (Toronto: McClelland and Stewart, 1972); Gerald Friesen, *The Canadian Prairies: A History* (Toronto: University of Toronto Press, 1984); Alan Artibise, *Winnipeg: A Social History of Urban Growth, 1874-1914* (Montreal: McGill-Queen's University Press, 1975).

Labour's place in the social formation of this epoch is given attention in J.V. Barkans, "Labour, Capital and the State: Canadian Railroads and Emergent Social Relations of Production, 1850-1879" (M.A. thesis, McMaster University, 1976); Ian McKay, "The Working Class of Metropolitan Halifax, 1850-1889" (B.A. Honours Essay, Dalhousie University, 1975), part of which appears in a general collection of articles, Rosemary Ommer and Gerald Panting, eds., *Working Men Who Got Wet* (St. John's: Memorial University Maritime History Group, 1980); and Eric Tucker, *Administering Danger in the Workplace: The Law and Politics of Occupational Health and Safety in Ontario, 1850-1914* (Toronto: University of Toronto Press, 1990).

Useful economic histories include O.J. Firestone, *Canada's Economic Development, 1867-1953* (London: Bowes and Bowes, 1958); Firestone, "Development of Canada's Economy, 1850-1900," in *Trends in the American Economy in the Nineteenth Century* (Princeton, N.J.: Princeton University Press, 1960), 217-52; E.J. Chambers and G.W. Bertram, "Urbanization and Manufacturing in Central Canada, 1870-1890," in Ostry and Rymes, eds., *Papers on Regional Statistical Methods* (Toronto: Canadian Political Science Association, 1966), 205-28.

Paul Campbell Appleton, "The Sunshine and the Shade: Labour Activism in Central Canada, 1850-1860" (M.A. thesis, University of Calgary, 1974), provides a yet-to-be-appreciated discussion of mid-nineteenth-century strikes and working-class experience. J.I. Cooper, "The Quebec Ship Labourers Benevolent Society," *CHR*, 30 (1949), 336-43; Margaret Heap, "La grève des charretiers de Montréal,

1864," in Fernand Harvey, ed., *Le Mouvement ouvrier au Québec* (Montréal: Boréal Express, 1980), 49-68; and Gregory S. Kealey, "Artisans Respond to Industrialism: shoe makers, shoe factories and the Knights of St. Crispin in Toronto," Canadian Historical Association, *Papers* (1973), 137-58, are important studies for the 1860s and 1870s. Charles Bruce Ferguson, *The Labour Movement in Nova Scotia Before Confederation* (Halifax: Public Archives of Nova Scotia, 1964), contains much on the immediate pre-Confederation labour movement, as well as a great deal on earlier years. See also Kenneth Pryke, "Labour and Politics: Nova Scotia at Confederation," *HS*, 6 (1970), 33-55. These last two publications contain asides on law and labour that are fleshed out in the previously cited Earle, ed., *Workers and the State in Twentieth-Century Nova Scotia*; Eric Tucker's study of the legal zones of toleration vis-à-vis conspiracy; and Paul Craven, "Workers' Conspiracies in Toronto, 1854-1872," *L/LT*, 14 (Fall, 1984), 49-72. Judith Fingard takes a stab at understanding the underclass that so often found itself in courts and jails in *The Dark Side of Life in Victorian Halifax* (Halifax: Pottersfield Press, 1989).

Associational life is currently drawing more attention. Previously cited studies by Palmer and Kealey contain arguments, as do articles by these authors in Kealey and Warrian, ed., *Essays in Working-Class History*. A significant and sophisticated discussion of the Orange Lodge, at variance in some ways with the interpretation put forward here, is Cecil J. Houston and William J. Smyth, *The Sash Canada Wore: An Historical Geography of the Orange Order in Canada* (Toronto: University of Toronto Press, 1980). The gendered content of associational life is the subject of Mary Ann Clawson, *Constructing Brotherhood: Class, Gender, and Fraternalism* (Princeton, N.J.: Princeton University Press, 1989). I have benefited greatly from discussions with Darryl Newbury, now researching masculine identity, class, and associational life. I draw on some of his unpublished researches here, particularly his M.A. research for "'No Atheist, Eunuch or Woman': Male Associational Culture and Working-Class Identity in Industrializing Ontario, 1840-1880" (Queen's University, 1992).

Work on the family includes Bettina Bradbury, "The Family Economy and Work in an Industrializing City: Montreal in the 1870s," Canadian Historical Association, *Papers* (1979), 71-96; Bradbury, "The Fragmented Family: Family Strategies in the Face of Death, Illness and Poverty, Montreal, 1860-1885," in Joy Parr, ed., *Childhood and Family in Canadian History* (Toronto: McClelland and Stewart, 1982), 109-28; Bradbury, "Pigs, Cows, and Boarders: Non-Wage Forms of Survival among Montreal Families, 1861-1891," *L/LT*, 14 (Fall, 1984), 9-48; John Bullen, "Hidden Workers: Child Labour and the Family Economy in Late Nineteenth Century Urban Ontario," *ibid.*, 18 (Fall, 1986), 163-88; Chad Gaffield, "Seasonal Labour and Family Formation in Mid-Nineteenth Century Canada West," paper presented to the McGill Conference on Class and Culture, 1980; essays in Normand Séguin, ed., *Agriculture et Colonisation au Québec: Aspects Historiques* (Montréal: Boréal Express, 1980); and Michael Katz, "Social Class in North American Urban History," *Journal of Interdisciplinary History*, II (Spring, 1981), 579-606. Joanne Burgess, "l'industrie de la chaussure à Montréal, 1840-1870: Le passage de l'artisanat à la fabrique," *Revue d'histoire de l'Amérique français*, 31 (1977), 187-210, is the foundation upon which a discussion of family inheritance of craft skill in the leather trades is now developing. See also David Gagan, *Hopeful Travellers: Families, Land, and Social Change in Mid-Victorian Peel County, Canada West*

(Toronto: University of Toronto Press, 1981); and Ward, *Courtship, Love and Marriage.* Discerning readers will note that I am critical of the historiographic consensus that has emerged around a rather unproblematic notion of a co-operative "family economy." I have been influenced by the evidence of coercion and gendered power discussed in Golz's unpublished research, cited above, and Kathryn Harvey, "To Love, Honour and Obey: Wife-Battering in Working-Class Montreal, 1869-1879," paper presented to the CHA, Quebec City, June, 1989. I cannot stress too much the significance of Peter DeLottinville's study, "Joe Beef of Montreal: Working Class Culture and the Tavern, 1869-1889," *L/LT*, 8/9 (1981-82), 9-40.

Foster Vernon, "The Development of Adult Education in Ontario, 1790-1900" (Ph.D. thesis, University of Toronto, 1969), provides an introduction to mechanics' institutes, while early responses to poverty are outlined in James Pitsula, "The Relief of Poverty in Toronto, 1880-1930" (Ph.D. thesis, York University, 1979).

Bernard Ostry's "Conservatives, Liberals and Labour in the 1870s," *CHR*, 41 (1960), 93-127, stood as the major account of the nine-hour movement for some years. It should now be read in conjunction with the appropriate chapters in the Palmer and Kealey studies of Hamilton and Toronto, and also beside John Battye, "The Nine Hour Pioneers: The Genesis of the Canadian Labour Movement," *L/LT*, 4 (1979), 25-56. Langdon's *The Emergence of the Canadian Working Class Movement* places the 1872 struggle at the centre of the process of class formation, but more illuminating is his wider unpublished study, "The Political Economy of Capitalist Transformation: Central Canada from the 1840s to the 1870s" (M.A. thesis, Carleton University, 1972). Another unpublished thesis, Robert Storey, "Industrialization in Canada: The Emergence of the Hamilton Working Class, 1850-1870s" (M.A. thesis, Dalhousie University, 1975), contains much of interest.

Studies of relevance in comprehending the nature of class experience in these years include Dorothy Susanne Cross, "The Irish in Montreal, 1867-1896" (M.A. thesis, McGill University, 1969); Desmond Morton, "Taking on the Grand Trunk: The Locomotive Engineers Strike of 1876-1877," *L/LT*, 2 (1977), 5-34; Judith Fingard, "The Decline of the Sailor as a Ship Labourer in 19th Century Timber Ports," *L/LT*, 2 (1977), 35-53; Debi Wells, "'The Hardest Lines of the Sternest School': Working-Class Ottawa and the Depression of the 1870s" (M.A. thesis, Carleton University, 1982); Jin Tan, "In Search of Chinese Labour Militancy: Manifestations of Coolie Protest in British Columbia and the New World, 1850-1855," unpublished manuscript, Ontario Institute for Studies in Education, 1982; and Paul Craven and Tom Traves, "Dimensions of Paternalism: Discipline and Culture in Canadian Railway Operations in the 1850s," in Craig Heron and Robert Storey, eds., *On the Job*, 47-74.

III: THE CONSOLIDATION OF WORKING-CLASS OPPOSITIONS, 1880-1895

A full elaboration of the economic, social, political, and cultural developments in the industrial heartland of Ontario, along with extensive documentation, will be found in Gregory S. Kealey and Bryan D. Palmer, *Dreaming of What Might Be: The Knights of Labor in Ontario* (New York: Cambridge University Press, 1982). T.W. Acheson's "The Changing Social Origins of Canadian Industrialization: A Study in the Structure of Entrepreneurship" (Ph.D. thesis, University of Toronto, 1971) and the major articles drawn from it are invaluable in understanding capitalist consolidation. Michael Bliss, *A Living Profit: Studies in the Social History of Canadian Business, 1883-1911* (Toronto: McClelland and Stewart, 1974), contains some interesting digressions. For the hinterland economies, note the sources cited for Chapter Two above.

For Quebec, see Fernand Harvey's essay on the Knights of Labor in Harvey, ed., *Le mouvement ouvrier au Québec*; Harvey, *Révolution industrielle et travailleurs: Une enquête sur les rapports entre le capital et le travail au Québec à la fin du 19e siècle* (Montréal: Boréal Express, 1978); Jacques Martin, "Les Chevaliers du travail et le syndicalisme international à Montréal" (M.A. thesis, Université de Montréal, 1965); Victor Oscar Chan, "Canadian Knights of Labor with Special Reference to the 1880s" (M.A. thesis, McGill University, 1949); Robert W. Cox, "The Quebec Provincial Election of 1886" (M.A. thesis, McGill University, 1948).

The Provincial Workmen's Association is addressed in Ian McKay's introduction to "C.W. Lunn, *From Trapper Boy to General Manager*," *L/LT*, 4 (1979), 211-22; Sharon Reilly, "The History of the Provincial Workmen's Association, 1879-1898" (M.A. thesis, Dalhousie University, 1979); and McKay, "Workers' Control in Springhill, 1882-1927," paper presented to the Canadian Historical Association, Halifax, 1981. Extremely insightful is McKay, "'By Wisdom, Wile, or War': The Provincial Workmen's Association and the Struggle for Working-Class Independence in Nova Scotia, 1879-97," *L/LT*, 18 (Fall, 1986), 13-62.

Russell Hann, "Brainworkers and the Knights of Labor: E.E. Sheppard, Phillips Thompson, and the *Toronto News*, 1883-1887," in Kealey and Warrian, eds., *Essays in Canadian Working-Class History*, 35-57; Frank W. Watt, "The National Policy, the Workingman, and Proletarian Ideas in Victorian Canada," *CHR*, 40 (1959), 1-26; Phillips Thompson, *The Politics of Labor* (New York: Belford, Clark, 1887); Peter DeLottinville, "The St. Croix Cotton Manufacturing Company and Its Influence on the St. Croix Community, 1880-1892" (M.A. thesis, Dalhousie University, 1979); Gerald Henry Allaby, "New Brunswick Prophets of Radicalism: 1890-1914" (M.A. thesis, University of New Brunswick, 1973); Gene Homel, "'Fading Beams of the Nineteenth Century': Radicalism and Early Socialism in Canada's 1890s," *L/LT*, 5 (1980), 7-32; Ramsay Cook, "Henry George and the Poverty of Canadian Progress," Canadian Historical Association, *Papers* (1977), 142-57; Edward McKenna, "Unorganized Labour Versus Management: The Strike at the Chaudière Mills, 1891," *HS*, 4 (1972), 186-211; Gillian Creese, "Class, Ethnicity, and Conflict: The Case of Chinese and Japanese Immigrants, 1880-1923," in Rennie Warburton and David Coburn, eds., *Workers, Capital, and the State in British Columbia* (Vancouver: University of British Columbia Press, 1988), 55-85; Norman J. Ware, *Labor in Modern Industrial Society* (New York: Russell & Russell, 1935); an unpublished Carleton University seminar paper by Debi Wells, "'Unknown Scribes of Unknown Worth': The Working Class at the Turn of the Century in Canadian Poetry and Novels of Social Criticism," (1979); and Mary Vipond, "Blessed are the Peacemakers: The Labour Question in Canadian Social Gospel Fiction," *Journal of Canadian Studies*, 10 (1975), 32-43, are among the many studies drawn upon here.

For comment on religion and workers in the late nineteenth century, see G. Levine, "In God's Service: The Role of Anglican, Methodist, Presbyterian, and

Roman Catholic Churches in the Cultural Geography of Late Nineteenth Century Kingston" (Ph.D. thesis, Queen's University, 1980); Doris Mary O'Dell, "The Class Character of Church Participation in Late Nineteenth-Century Belleville, Ontario" (Ph.D. thesis, Queen's University, 1990); and unpublished papers by Lynne Marks, "The 'Hallelujah Lasses': Working-Class Women in the Salvation Army in English Canada, 1882-1892," presented to the Berkshire Conference on the History of Women, New Brunswick, New Jersey, 1990; "The Knights of Labor and the Salvation Army: Religion and Working-Class History in Ontario, 1882-1890," presented to the Canadian Historical Association, Victoria, 1990.

On gender, note the unpublished work of Golz, cited earlier, and Karen Dubinsky, "'The Modern Chivalry': Women and the Knights of Labor in Ontario, 1880-1930" (M.A. thesis, Carleton University, 1985); Dubinsky, "'Improper Advances': Sexual Danger and Pleasure in Rural and Northern Ontario, 1880-1929" (Ph.D. thesis, Queen's University, 1991); Fingard, *The Dark Side*, 95-116.

IV: THE REMAKING OF THE WORKING CLASS AND ITS OPPOSITIONS, 1895-1919

Mackenzie King and the "labour problem" are the subject of Paul Craven, *"An Impartial Umpire": Industrial Relations and the Canadian State, 1900-1911* (Toronto: University of Toronto Press, 1980); Bob Russell, *Back to Work? Labour, State, and Industrial Relations in Canada* (Scarborough, Ontario: Nelson, 1990). On the merger movement and other aspects of the late nineteenth- and early twentieth-century economy, see Tom Naylor, *The History of Canadian Business, 1867-1914*, 2 vols. (Toronto: Lorimer, 1975); David Frank, "The Cape Breton Coal Industry and the Rise and Fall of the British Empire Steel Corporation," *Acadiensis*, 7 (1977), 3-34; H.G. Stapells, "The Recent Consolidation Movement in Canadian Industry" (M.A. thesis, University of Toronto, 1922). An invaluable study of the war years is Naylor, "The Canadian State, the Accumulation of Capital, and the Great War," *Journal of Canadian Studies*, 16 (Fall-Winter, 1981), 26-55. The place of American capital in this period can be discerned from Wallace Clement, *Continental Corporate Power: Economic Linkages between Canada and the United States* (Toronto: McClelland and Stewart, 1977); Herbert Marshall, Frank A. Southard, Jr., and Kenneth W. Taylor, *Canadian-American Industry* (New Haven: Yale University Press, 1936). American management techniques are the subject of Daniel Nelson, *Managers and Workers: Origins of the New Factory System in the United States, 1880-1920* (Madison: University of Wisconsin Press, 1975).

The immigrant experience has recently received sustained treatment. Donald Avery's *"Dangerous Foreigners": European Immigrant Workers and Labour Radicalism in Canada, 1896-1932* (Toronto: McClelland and Stewart, 1979) tends to homogenize the ethnic experience and should be read in conjunction with more focused studies of particular group and local histories. See, for instance, Bruno Ramirez and Michael Del Balso, *The Italians of Montreal: From Sojourning to Settlement, 1900-1921* (Montréal: Éditions Du Courant, 1980); Ramirez, *On the Move: French-Canadian and Italian Migrants in the North Atlantic Economy, 1860-1914* (Toronto: McClelland and Stewart, 1991); Robert F. Harney, "Montreal's King of Italian Labour: A Case Study of Padronism," *L/LT*, 4 (1979), 57-84; Allen

Seager, "A Forecast of the Parliament of Man: Aspects of the Alberta Miners' Movement, 1905-1945," paper presented to the McGill Conference on Class and Culture, 1980. An exceptional collection of essays on the Finns, edited by Varpu Lindstrom-Best, is *Polyphony: The Bulletin of the Multicultural History Society of Ontario*, 3 (1981). See, as well, Lindstrom-Best's *The Finnish Immigrant Community of Toronto, 1887-1913* (Toronto: Multicultural History Society of Ontario, 1979).

The material circumstances of Canadian workers are scrutinized in Terry Copp, *The Anatomy of Poverty: The Condition of the Working Class in Montreal, 1897-1929* (Toronto: McClelland and Stewart, 1974); Michael J. Piva, *The Condition of the Working Class in Toronto – 1900-1921* (Ottawa: University of Ottawa Press, 1979); David Millar, "A Study of Real Wages: The Construction, Use, and Accuracy Check of a Constant-Dollar Plotter," unpublished research paper, University of Winnipeg, 1980; Eleanor A. Bartlett, "Real Wages and the Standard of Living in Vancouver, 1901-1929," *B.C. Studies*, 51 (Autumn, 1981), 3-62; Jacques Rouillard, *Les Travailleurs du Coton au Québec, 1900-1915* (Montréal: Les Presses de l'Université du Québec, 1974); and Craig Heron, *Working in Steel: The Early Years in Canada, 1883-1935* (Toronto: McClelland and Stewart, 1988). Ian M. Drummond, *Progress without Planning: The Economic History of Ontario* (Toronto: University of Toronto Press, 1987), attempts to present the counter argument that things were really quite good for workers. Early attempts to probe the nature of inflation and real wages in these years include R.H. Coat's comments in Canada, Department of Labour, Board of Inquiry into the Cost of Living, *Report* (Ottawa: Government Printer, 1915), and H. Michell, "Statistics of Prices," in *Statistical Contributions to Canadian Economic History*, vol. II (Toronto, 1931). J.S. Woodsworth, *Strangers Within Our Gates* (Toronto: University of Toronto Press reprint, 1972), and Edmund Bradwin, *The Bunkhouse Man: A Study of Work and Pay in the Camps of Canada, 1903-1914* (Toronto: University of Toronto Press reprint, 1972), are early works addressing living and working conditions of immigrant workers.

Robert Babcock, *Gompers in Canada: A Study of American Continentalism Before the First World War* (Toronto: University of Toronto Press, 1975), provides an invaluable account of early international unionism's development, though the interpretation diverges from that presented above. For treatment of one union, see James Douglas Thwaites, "The International Association of Machinists in Canada to 1919" (M.A. thesis, Carleton University, 1966). Desmond Morton, "Aid to the Civil Power: The Canadian Militia in Support of Social Order, 1867-1914," *CHR*, 51 (1970), 407-25, examines the use of state force to suppress strikes, while detailed examinations of conflict in the pre-World War One period are found in Ian McKay, "Strikes in the Maritimes, 1901-1914," in Buckner and Frank, eds., *Atlantic Canada Since Confederation*, 216-59; Craig Heron and Bryan D. Palmer, "Through the Prism of the Strike: Industrial Conflict in Southern Ontario, 1901-1914," *CHR*, 58 (1977), 423-58. Henry C. Klassen, "'The Bond of Brotherhood' and Calgary Workingmen," in A.W. Rasporich and H.C. Klassen, eds., *Frontier Calgary: Town, City, and Region* (Calgary: University of Calgary, 1975), 267-71, offers some comments on a western city other than Winnipeg or Vancouver. On Alberta miners I have relied on Allen Seager, "A Proletariat in Wild Rose Country: The Alberta Miners, 1905-1945" (Ph.D. thesis, York University, 1982), while other work sectors are treated in Warren Cargata, *Alberta Labour: A Heritage Untold* (Toronto:

Lorimer, 1979). Cape Breton miners and steel workers are the subject of Paul MacEwan's *Miners and Steelworkers: Labour in Cape Breton* (Toronto: Samuel, Stevens Hakkert and Company, 1976), but I have relied more explicitly on David Alexander Frank, "The Cape Breton Coal Miners, 1917-1926" (Ph.D. thesis, Dalhousie University, 1979), and the many papers and articles drawn from this important study. Frank's arguments are challenged in Ralph Wayne Ripley, "Industrialization and the Attraction of Immigrants to Cape Breton County, 1893-1914" (M.A. thesis, Queen's University, 1980). The Lethbridge 1906 coal strike forms the pivotal event in William Baker, "The Miners and the Mediator: The 1906 Lethbridge Strike and Mackenzie King," *L/LT*, (Spring, 1983), 89-118, while the 1916 Hamilton munitions strike receives sustained examination in Myer Siemiatycki, "Munitions and Labour Militancy: the 1916 Hamilton Machinists' Strike," *L/LT*, 3 (1978), 130-52. The unskilled receive a rare word in Craig Heron's discussion of "Hamilton Steelworkers and the Rise of Mass Production," *Historical Papers* (1982), 103-32.

My discussion of politics draws heavily on work cited in the "essential texts" section of the bibliography as well as studies listed in later sections. There is some material, as well, in Ian Angus, *Canadian Bolsheviks: The Early Years of the Communist Party of Canada* (Montreal: Vanguard, 1981), while Gene Howard Homel, "James Simpson and the Origins of Canadian Social Democracy (Socialism in Toronto, 1890-1914)" (Ph.D. thesis, University of Toronto, 1978), ranges well beyond the apparent limitations of the title. Also important are the articles drawn from Wayne Roberts, "Labour and Reform in Toronto, 1896-1914" (Ph.D. thesis, University of Toronto, 1978). Socialist activity on the east coast is discussed in David Frank and Nolan Reilly, "The Emergence of the Socialist Movement in the Maritimes, 1899-1916," *L/LT*, 4 (1978), 85-114. Labourist thought and its evolution in Winnipeg can be charted in Allen Mills, "Single Tax, Socialism, and the Independent Labour Party of Manitoba: The Political Ideas of F.J. Dixon and S.J. Farmer," *L/LT*, 5 (1980), 33-56. The most useful statements on labourism are Craig Heron, "Labourism and the Canadian Working Class," *L/LT*, 13 (Spring, 1984), 45-76; Suzanne Morton, "Labourism and Economic Action: The Halifax Shipyards Strike of 1920," *ibid.*, 22 (Fall, 1988), 67-98. For labour politics in urban B.C., see Allen Seager, "Workers, Class, and Industrial Conflict in New Westminster, 1900-1930," in Warburton and Coburn, eds., *Workers, Capital, and the State*, 117-40. Views of the Socialist Party of Canada may well shift with a reading of J. Peter Campbell, "'Stalwarts of the Struggle': Canadian Marxists of the Third Way, 1879-1939" (Ph.D. thesis, Queen's University, 1991).

Work on the General Strike and the class conflicts of 1919 makes up an important component of the historiography within the field of working-class studies. A central recent statement is Gregory S. Kealey, "1919: The Canadian Labour Revolt," *L/LT*, 13 (Spring, 1984), 11-44. Aside from studies that I have mentioned earlier, see D.C. Masters, *The Winnipeg General Strike* (Toronto: University of Toronto Press, 1950); Norman Penner, ed., *Winnipeg 1919: The Strikers' Own History of the Winnipeg General Strike* (Toronto: James Lewis and Samuel, 1973); Nolan J. Reilly, "The General Strike in Amherst, Nova Scotia, 1919," *Acadiensis*, 9 (Spring, 1980), 56-77; Fred Thompson, "A Rebel Voice: Fred Thompson Remembers Halifax, 1919-1920," *This Magazine* (12 May 1979), 22a-22b; H.C. Pentland, "Fifty Years After," *Canadian Dimension*, 6 (1969), 14-17; and A.B. Woywitka,

"Drumheller Strike of 1919," *Alberta History*, 21 (1973), 1-7. Important recent statements include Glenn Makahonuk, "Class Conflict in a Prairie City: The Saskatoon Working-Class Response to Prairie Capitalism," *L/LT*, 19 (Spring, 1987), 89-124; the conceptually informed James R. Conley, "Frontier Labourers, Crafts in Crisis, and the Western Labour Revolt: The Case of Vancouver, 1900-1919," *ibid.*, 23 (Spring, 1989), 9-38; and the popularly pitched Allen Seager, "Nineteen Nineteen: Year of Revolt," *Journal of the West*, 23 (October, 1984), 40-48. Background to western labour radicalism, aside from McCormack's previously cited study, can be obtained from Joseph Harry Sutcliffe, "The Economic Background of the Winnipeg Strike: Wages and Working Conditions" (M.A. thesis, University of Manitoba, 1972); Allan Donald Orr, "The Western Federation of Miners and the Royal Commission on Industrial Disputes in 1903 with Special Reference to the Vancouver Island Coal Miners' Strike" (M.A. thesis, University of British Columbia, 1976); Alan F.J. Artibise, *Winnipeg: A Social History of Urban Growth, 1874-1914* (Montreal: McGill-Queen's University Press, 1975). The One Big Union is a much-discussed moment in the history of Canadian labour but one of the more significant studies remains unpublished: Peter Warrian, "The Challenge of the One Big Union Movement in Canada, 1919-1921" (M.A. thesis, University of Waterloo, 1971). An interpretation at odds with the one presented here is found in David Bercuson, "Labour Radicalism and the Western Industrial Frontier, 1897-1919," *CHR*, 58 (1977), 154-75. The experience of the IWW is probed in A. Ross McCormack, "The Industrial Workers of the World in Western Canada: 1905-1914," Canadian Historical Association, *Papers* (1975), 167-90; and more recently, in Mark Leier, *Where the Fraser River Flows: The Industrial Workers of the World in British Columbia* (Vancouver: New Star Books, 1990).

On women workers, see Wayne Roberts, *Honest Womanhood: Feminism, Femininity, and Class Consciousness among Toronto Working Women, 1893-1914* (Toronto: New Hogtown Press, 1976); Joan Sangster, "The 1907 Bell Telephone Strike: Organizing Women Workers," *L/LT*, 3 (1978), 109-29; Star Rosenthal, "Union Maids: Organizing Women Workers in Vancouver, 1900-1915," *B.C. Studies*, 41 (1979), 36-55; Marie Campbell, "Sexism in British Columbia Trade Unions, 1900-1920," and Susan Wade, "Helena Gutteridge: Votes for Women and Trade Unions," in Barbara Latham and Cathy Kess, eds., *In Her Own Right: Selected Essays on Women's History in B.C.* (Victoria: Camosun College, 1980), 167-204; Deborah Gorham, "Flora MacDonald Denison: Canadian Feminist," in Linda Kealey, ed., *A Not Unreasonable Claim: Women and Reform in Canada, 1880s-1920s* (Toronto: Women's Press, 1979), 47-70; Linda Kealey, "Canadian Socialism and the Woman Question, 1900-1914," *L/LT*, 13 (Spring, 1984), 77-100; and the very important article by Jacques Ferland, "'In Search of Unbound Prometheia': A Comparative View of Women's Activism in Two Quebec Industries, 1869-1908," *L/LT*, 24 (Fall, 1989), 11-44. Craig Heron has made an initial effort to address the meaning of children's education and the family in "The High School and the Family Economy in a Factory City: Hamilton, 1890-1940," paper presented to the Canadian Historical Association, Victoria, 1990. See, as well, David Frank, "The Miner's Financier: Women in the Cape Breton Coal Towns, 1917," *Atlantis*, 8 (Spring, 1983), 137-43; Jane Synge, "The Transition from School to Work: Growing Up Working Class in Early Twentieth-Century Hamilton," in K. Johwaran, ed., *Childhood and Adolescence in Canada* (Toronto, 1979), 249-69. For early public-sector organizing, see Anthony Thompson, "'The Large and Generous View': The Debate on Labour Affiliation in the Canadian Civil Service, 1918-1928," *L/LT*, 2 (1977), 108-36.

The emergence of Catholic unionism is discussed in Jacques Rouillard, *Les Syndicats Nationaux au Québec de 1900 à 1930* (Québec: Les Presses de l'Université Laval, 1979); Brian Hogan, "Church and Union: The Case of Hull, 1912-1921. An introduction to R.P. Joseph Bonhomme OMI, 'Notes historiques sur l'association ouvriere de Hull'," *L/LT*, 7 (1981), 131-49; Allan B. Latham, *The Catholic and National Labour Unions of Canada* (Toronto: MacMillan, 1930).

V: DISSOLUTION AND RECONSTITUTION, 1920-39

The starting place for an understanding of this period is John Herd Thompson and Allen Seager, *Canada, 1922-1939: Decades of Discord* (Toronto: McClelland and Stewart, 1985). Important state activities are addressed by Russell, *Back to Work?*, and Barbara Roberts, *Whence They Came: Deportation from Canada, 1900-1935* (Ottawa: University of Ottawa Press, 1988). On industrial legality, see, for Nova Scotia particulars, Earle, ed., *Workers and the State*; McKay, *The Craft Transformed*.

For discussions of the merger movement and the Americanization of Canadian capitalism, note the studies cited earlier. An important study is Tom Traves, *The State and Enterprise: Canadian Manufacturers and the Federal Government, 1917-1931* (Toronto: University of Toronto Press, 1979). The nature of the depression and the imbalance in the economy of the 1920s are the subject of wide-ranging comment. Among the more accessible works are Michiel Horn, *The Dirty Thirties: Canadians in the Great Depression* (Toronto: Copp Clark, 1972); Linda Grayson and Michael Bliss, eds., *The Wretched of Canada* (Toronto: Doubleday, 1973). Important discussions of workplace relations are Bruce Scott, "A Place in the Sun: The Industrial Council at Massey Harris, 1919-1929," *L/LT*, 1 (1976), 158-92; Margaret McCallum, "Separate Spheres: the Organization of Work in a Confectionary Factory – Ganong Bros., St. Stephen, New Brunswick," *L/LT*, 24 (Fall, 1989), 69-90. On welfare capitalism, see Heron, *Working in Steel*, and Joy Parr, *The Gender of Breadwinners: Women, Men, and Change in Two Industrial Towns, 1880-1950* (Toronto: University of Toronto Press, 1990).

On the defeat of labour and the rise of the Communists, see Angus, *Canadian Bolsheviks*; William Rodney, *Soldiers of the International: A History of the Communist Party of Canada, 1919-1929* (Toronto: University of Toronto Press, 1968). Labour's decline in the West is outlined in Kathleen O'Gorman Wormsbecker, "The Rise and Fall of the Labour Political Movement in Manitoba, 1919-1927" (M.A. thesis, Queen's University, 1977); and W.J.C. Cherwinski, "Organized Labour in Saskatchewan: The T.L.C. Years, 1905-1945" (Ph.D. thesis, University of Alberta, 1972). The demise of the craft worker is explored in Craig Heron, "The Crisis of the Craftsman: Hamilton's Metal Workers in the Early Twentieth Century," *L/LT*, 6 (1980), 7-48.

For material life in the 1920s, see the previously cited studies by Bartlett, Copp, Millar, and others, as well as Leonard Marsh's studies in the McGill Social Research Series, which are an invaluable source, as is M.C. Urquhart and K. Buckley, eds.,

Historical Statistics of Canada (Toronto: MacMillan, 1965). My speculative assertions on the Americanization of mass culture in the 1920s draw on lecture notes graciously made available to me by Professor John Herd Thompson of McGill University. An exceptional source is E.R. Forbes and A.A. MacKenzie, eds. (Clifford Rose), *Four Years with the Demon Rum* (Fredericton, N.B.: Acadiensis Press, 1980).

Veronica Strong-Boag, "The Girl of the New Day: Canadian Working Women in the 1920s," *L/LT*, 4 (1979), 131-64, is a pioneering breakthrough in delineating the structural contours of women's working experience in the 1920s. This work is expanded in Strong-Boag, *The New Day Recalled: Lives of Girls and Women in English Canada, 1919-1939* (Markham, Ont.: Penguin, 1988). Mary Vipond, "The Image of Women in Mass Circulation Magazines in the 1920s," *Modernist Studies*, 1 (1974-75), 5-13, is noteworthy, as is the Quebec study, Marie Lavigne and Jennifer Stoddart, "Ouvrières et travailleuses Montréalaises, 1900-1940," in Marie Lavigne and Yolande Pinard, eds., *Les Femmes dans la Société Québécois* (Montréal: Boréal Express, 1977), 125-44. See, as well, Catherine Macleod, "Women in Production: The Toronto Dressmakers' Strike of 1931," in Janice Acton, Penny Goldsmith, and Bonnie Sheppard, eds., *Women at Work: Ontario, 1850-1930* (Toronto: Women's Press, 1974), 309-30. An extremely important discussion of gender in the 1920s, with insights into its relation to mass culture, is Suzanne Morton, "Men and Women in a Halifax Working-class Neighbourhood in the 1920s" (Ph.D. dissertation, Dalhousie University, 1990). Legislation crucial to women is discussed in Margaret E. McCallum, "Keeping Women in Their Place: The Minimum Wage in Canada, 1910-1925," *L/LT*, 17 (Spring, 1986), 29-58. See, as well, Linda Kealey and Joan Sangster, *Beyond the Vote: Canadian Women and Politics* (Toronto: University of Toronto Press, 1989); Elaine Bernard, *The Long Distance Feeling: A History of the Telecommunications Workers Union* (Vancouver: New Star Books, 1982); and an innovative discussion of gender identities, Mark Rosenfeld, "'It was a Hard Life': Class and Gender in the Work and Family Rhythms of a Railway Town, 1920-1950," *Historical Papers* (1988), 237-79. The central text on women and radical politics is Joan Sangster, *Dreams of Equality: Women on the Canadian Left, 1920-1950* (Toronto: McClelland & Stewart, 1989).

On coal miners and communism, I have relied most on the studies of Seager, Frank, and Angus, mentioned above. See, as well, A.B. Woywitka, "A Pioneer Woman in the Labour Movement," *Alberta History*, 26 (1978), 10-16. There are now a number of "oral biographies" of individuals who were active in the Communist movement. Among them are: Bryan D. Palmer, ed., *A Communist Life: Jack Scott and the Canadian Workers Movement, 1927-1985* (St. John's: CCLH, 1988); David Frank and Donald MacGillivrary, eds., *George MacEachern: An Autobiography* (Sydney, N.S.: University College of Cape Breton, 1987); Howard White, ed., *A Hard Man to Beat: The Story of Bill White, Labour Leader, Historian, Shipyard Worker, Raconteur – An Oral History* (Vancouver: Pulp Press, 1983); Doug Smith, *Joe Zuken: Citizen and Socialist* (Toronto: Lorimer, 1990); Peter Hunter, *Which Side Are You On Boys: Canadian Life on the Left* (Toronto: Lugus, 1988). The official party history is *Canada's Party of Socialism: The History of the Communist Party of Canada, 1921-1976* (Toronto: Progress, 1982).

June MacPherson, "'Brother can you spare a dime?' The Administration of Unemployment Relief in the City of Montreal, 1931-1941" (M.A. thesis, Concordia

University, 1975), and Bettina Bradbury, "The Road to Receivership: Unemployment Relief in Burnaby, North Vancouver district, and West Vancouver" (M.A. thesis, Simon Fraser University, 1976), provide some local detail on processes outlined in national studies. Kingston data are from an undergraduate essay, Gudron Leys, "The Impact of the Great Depression on Kingston and the Response of the Propertied Class" (Queen's University, 1979), while the comments on Newfoundland rely on material in S.J.R. Noel, *Politics in Newfoundland* (Toronto: University of Toronto Press, 1971). But note, as a recent rejoinder, Jim Overton, "Economic Crisis and the End of Democracy: Politics in Newfoundland During the Great Depression," and Sean Cadigan, "Battle Harbour in Transition: Merchants, Fishermen, and the State in the Struggle for Relief in a Labrador Community in the 1930s," *L/LT*, 26 (Fall, 1990), 85-150. Ronald Liversedge, *Recollections of the Onto-Ottawa Trek* (Toronto: McClelland and Stewart, 1973); Lorne A. Brown, "Unemployment Relief Camps in Saskatchewan, 1933-1936," *Saskatchewan History*, 23 (1970), 81-104; Richard McCandless, "Vancouver's Red Menace of 1935: The Waterfront Situation," *B.C. Studies*, 22 (1974), 56-71; James D. Leach, "The Workers Unity League and the Stratford Furniture Workers: The Anatomy of a Strike," *Ontario History*, 60 (June, 1968), 39-48, are indispensable. On relief activities, see Pierre Berton, "Bloody Sunday in Vancouver," in *My Country: The Remarkable Past* (Toronto: McClelland and Stewart, 1976), 177-96; Patricia V. Schulz, *The East York Workers' Association: A Response to the Great Depression* (Toronto: New Hogtown Press, 1975); and sections of Fern Sayles, ed., *Welland Workers Make History* (Welland, 1963). The standard treatment of many of these themes is now James Struthers, *No Fault of Their Own: Unemployment and the Canadian Welfare State, 1914-1941* (Toronto: University of Toronto Press, 1983). For the gendered construction of state policy, see Ruth Roach Pierson, "Gender and Unemployment Insurance Debates in Canada, 1934-1940," *L/LT*, 25 (Spring, 1990), 77-104.

The social democratic experience is analysed in Norman Penner, *The Canadian Left: A Critical Analysis* (Toronto: Prentice-Hall, 1977), and Penner, "Social Democracy in Canada," paper presented to the Commonwealth Labour History Conference, Warwick University, 1981. Understanding of this milieu requires knowledge of the social gospel, explored in Richard Allen, *The Social Passion: Religion and Social Reform in Canada, 1914-1928* (Toronto: University of Toronto Press reprint, 1975), and Michiel Horn, *The League for Social Reconstruction: Intellectual Origins of the Democratic Left in Canada, 1930-1942* (Toronto: University of Toronto Press, 1980). David Lewis offered his comments on the CCF experience in *The Good Fight: Political Memoirs, 1909-1958* (Toronto: Macmillan, 1981).

The traditional account of the CIO in Canada is Irving Abella, *Nationalism, Communism and Canadian Labour: The CIO, The Communist Party of Canada and the Canadian Congress of Labour, 1935-1956* (Toronto: University of Toronto Press, 1973). It can now be compared to specific industry studies, where interpretation often differs from that in Abella. See, for instance, John Manley, "Communists and Autoworkers: The Struggle for Industrial Unionism in the Canadian Automobile Industry, 1925-1936," *L/LT*, 17 (Spring, 1986), 105-34; Jerry Lembcke and William M. Tattam, *One Union in Wood: A Political History of the International Woodworkers of America* (New York: International, 1984); Michael Earle, "The Coalminers and Their 'Red' Union: The Amalgamated Mine Workers of Nova

Scotia, 1932-1936," *L/LT*, 22 (Fall, 1988), 99-137; Laurel Sefton MacDowell, *'Remember Kirkland Lake': The Gold Miners' Strike of 1941-42* (Toronto: University of Toronto Press, 1983); and, more generally, Heron, *The Canadian Labour Movement*, 65-93. The important history of northern Ontario loggers has recently been addressed in Ian Radforth, *Bush Workers and Bosses: Logging in Northern Ontario, 1900-1980* (Toronto: University of Toronto Press, 1987); and Bruce Magnusson, *The Untold Story of Ontario's Bushworkers: A Political Memoir* (Toronto: Progress, 1990). See also Duart Snow, "The Holmes Foundry Strike of March, 1937: 'We'll give their jobs to white men'," *Ontario History*, 69 (1977); and, for Quebec, Evelyn Dumas, *The Bitter Thirties in Quebec* (Montreal: Black Rose, 1975); Conrad Black, *Duplessis* (Toronto: McClelland and Stewart, 1977). An exemplary study, yet to be equalled in Canada, is Peter Friedlander, *The Emergence of a UAW Local, 1936-1939: A Study in Class and Culture* (Pittsburgh: University of Pittsburgh Press, 1975).

Agitational propaganda and cultural activity is the subject of Frank Watt, "Literature of Protest," in Carl F. Klinck, ed., *Literary History of Canada*, 1 (Toronto: University of Toronto Press, 1965), 473-92; Richard Wright and Robin Endres, eds., *Eight Men Speak and Other Plays from the Canadian Workers' Theatre* (Toronto: New Hogtown Press, 1976); Dawn Fraser, *Echoes from Labor's War: Industrial Cape Breton in the 1920s* (Toronto: New Hogtown Press, 1978); Bettina Bradbury and Yolanda Kingsmill, "Poverty, Politics and the Press: A Cartoon History of the Depression Years in British Columbia," unpublished manuscript, Vancouver, 1977; John Bentley Mays, "A Visual Trip to the Depression," *Globe and Mail*, 14 November 1981; and Donna Phillips, ed., *Voices of Discord: Canadian Short Stories from the 1930s* (Toronto: New Hogtown Press, 1979). I have also drawn on an undergraduate essay, Anne MacLennan, "Food for Thought: The Changing Mood of the Depression as Indicated by Selected Urban Literary Works" (McGill University, 1980).

An overview of Catholic unionism is found in the introduction to *Quebec Labour* (Montreal: Black Rose, 1972), while the Antigonish movement is explored in Robert James Sacouman, "Social Origins of Antigonish Movement Cooperative Associations in Eastern Nova Scotia" (Ph.D. thesis, University of Toronto, 1976), and a number of published articles based on this dissertation. Racial fragmentation in British Columbia is the subject of W. Peter Ward, "Class and Race in the Social Structure of British Columbia, 1870-1939," *B.C. Studies*, 45 (1980), 17-36. Many of the articles in Warburton and Coburn, ed., *Workers, Capital, and the State* take a different view.

VI: CLASS, CULTURE, AND MOVEMENT, 1940-1975

There is still no adequate contemporary history of Canada, although Robert Bothwell, Ian Drummond, and John English, *Canada Since 1945: Power, Politics, and Provincialism* (Toronto: University of Toronto Press, 1989), can be used to obtain some insights and empirical data. But it requires great patience to separate the relevant from the ridiculous. On the most successful political leader of the period, see Richard Gywn, *The Northern Magus: Pierre Trudeau and the Canadians* (Toronto: McClelland and Stewart, 1980). Robert Bothwell and William Kilbourne, *C.D. Howe, A Biography* (Toronto: McClelland and Stewart, 1979), tells us something of a strategically placed political-economic figure, while an understanding of the Liberal Party emerges from a reading of Reginald Whitaker, *The Government Party: Organizing and Financing the Liberal Party of Canada, 1930-1958* (Toronto: University of Toronto Press, 1978).

The nature of concentrated economic power is addressed in a voluminous literature that now includes John Porter, *The Vertical Mosaic* (Toronto: University of Toronto Press, 1965); Wallace Clement, *The Canadian Corporate Elite: An Analysis of Economic Power* (Toronto: McClelland and Stewart, 1975); Clement, *Continental Corporate Power: Economic Linkages Between Canada and the United States* (Toronto: McClelland and Stewart, 1977); Jorge Niosi, *The Economy of Canada: Who Controls It?* (Montreal: Black Rose, 1978); Robert Sweeney, "The Evolution of Financial Groups in Canada and the Capital Market since the Second World War" (M.A. thesis, Université de Québec à Montréal, 1980).

The role of the state in restructuring social and productive relations in this period is addressed in Russell, *Back to Work?*; Earle, ed., *Workers and the State*; Dennis Guest, *The Emergence of Social Security in Canada* (Vancouver: University of British Columbia Press, 1980); McKay, *The Craft Transformed*; most of the essays in Michael S. Cross and Gregory S. Kealey, eds., *Modern Canada, 1930-1980* (Toronto: McClelland and Stewart, 1984); Jeremy Webber, "The Malaise of Compulsory Conciliation: Strike Prevention in Canada During World War II," in Palmer, ed., *Character of Class Struggle*, 135-59; David W.T. Matheson, "The Canadian Working Class and Industrial Legality, 1939-49" (M.A. thesis, Queen's University, 1989); Peter Warrian, "Labour is Not a Commodity: A Study of the Rights of Labour in the Canadian Postwar Economy, 1944-1948" (Ph.D. thesis, University of Waterloo, 1986); Judy Fudge, "Voluntarism and Compulsion: The Canadian Federal Government's Intervention in Collective Bargaining from 1900-1946" (Ph.D. thesis, Oxford University, 1987).

Railway labourers in the period are the subject of a useful study, Rosemary Ellen Speirs, "Technological Change and the Railway Unions, 1945-1972" (Ph.D. thesis, University of Toronto, 1974), while Inco's miners and their experience are the centre of Wallace Clement's study, *Hardrock Mining: Industrial Relations and Technological Changes at Inco* (Toronto: McClelland and Stewart, 1981). An important assessment of labour in the World War Two years is Laurel Sefton MacDowell, "The Formation of the Canadian Industrial Relations System during World War Two," *L/LT*, 3 (1978), 175-96; a wider-ranging study is H.C. Pentland, "The Canadian Industrial Relations System: Some Formative Factors," *L/LT*, 4 (1979), 9-24. On the IWA I have drawn most heavily from Jerry Lembcke, "The International Woodworkers of America in British Columbia, 1942-1951," *L/LT*, 6 (1980), 113-48, which should be read against Abella's *Nationalism, Communism, and Canadian Labour*. A useful local study is David Brian Akers, "Capital Organizes Labour: Company Paternalism, Industrial Unionism, and Alcan Workers in Kingston, Ontario, 1941-45" (M.A. thesis, Queen's University, 1987).

Differing assessments of industrial unionism and the anti-Communist drive in the labour movement can be gleaned from Terry Copp, *The I.U.E. in Canada* (Elora, Ontario: Cumnock Press, 1980); Copp, ed., *Industrial Unionism in Kitchener, 1937-1947* (Elora, Ontario: Cumnock Press, 1976); and James Turk, "Labour During the Cold War: Oral History in the Study of the Survival of the United

Electrical Workers in Canada," paper presented to the Canadian Oral History Association, Montreal, 1980. The development of the 1946 steel strike in Hamilton, which I have neglected here because of the existence of other accessible sources, is explored in an unpublished paper by Robert Storey, "Unions, Workers and Steel: The Blurring of the Picket Lines," University of Toronto, 1979. I have benefited from seeing a lengthy unpublished research paper on the Penmans Ltd. Paris, Ontario, strike of 1949 that was forwarded to me by D.A. Smith. Note the treatment in Parr, *Gender of Breadwinners*. The sordid history of the CSU is examined in John Stanton, *Life and Death of a Union: The History of the Canadian Seamen's Union, 1936-1949* (Toronto: Steel Rail, 1978); and more recently in the diametrically opposed William Kaplan, *Everything that Floats: Pat Sullivan, Hal Banks, and the Seamen's Unions of Canada* (Toronto: University of Toronto Press, 1987), and Jim Green, *Against the Tide: The Story of the Canadian Seamen's Union* (Toronto: Progress, 1986). On Newfoundland, see Peter Neary, "'Traditional' and 'Modern' Elements in the social and economic history of Bell Island and Conception Bay," Canadian Historical Association, *Papers* (1973), 105-36; Peter Neary, "Canada and the Newfoundland Labour Market, 1939-1949," *CHR*, 62 (1981), 470-95. Ernest Bugya Akyeampong, "Labour Laws and the Development of the Labour Movement in Newfoundland, 1900-1960" (M.A. thesis, Memorial University, 1980), is countered by William E. Gillespie, "A History of the Newfoundland Federation of Labour, 1936-1963" (M.A. thesis, Memorial University, 1980), which challenges Akyeampong's argument that the regional labour movement thrived in the aftermath of Confederation.

Quebec is the subject of much study, most of it focusing on the institutional and ideological evolution of labour. See Alexander Fraser Isbester, "A History of the National Catholic Unions in Canada, 1901-1965" (Ph.D. thesis, Cornell University, 1965); Samuel Henry Barnes, "The Ideologies and Policies of Canadian Labor Organizations" (Ph.D. thesis, Duke University, 1957); Pierre Elliott Trudeau, ed., *The Asbestos Strike* (Toronto: James Lewis and Samuel, 1974); and Daniel Drache, ed., *Quebec – Only the Beginning: The Manifestoes of the Common Front* (Toronto: New Press, 1972).

White-collar unionism occupies a prominent place in Robert Laxer, *Canada's Unions* (Toronto: Lorimer, 1976), while its historical origins are the subject of recent historical and sociological inquiry in studies such as Graham Lowe, *Women in the Administrative Revolution* (Toronto: University of Toronto Press, 1987); David Coombs, "The Emergence of a White Collar work force in Toronto, 1895-1911" (Ph.D. thesis, York University, 1978). White-collar inhibition concerning unionism is the subject of Janet J. Mayer, "Hegemony and Class Imagery: A Study of Monopoly-Sector White-Collar Labour," paper presented to the Canadian Political Science Association, Montreal, 1980, and is also an issue in Michael Katzemba, "Working in an Office," in Walter Johnson, ed., *Working in Canada* (Montreal: Black Rose, 1975), 122-30. An extremely useful collection of articles on public-sector unionism is Mark Thompson and Gene Swimmer, eds., *Conflict or Compromise: The Future of Public Sector Industrial Relations* (Montreal: Institute for Research on Public Policy, 1984).

On women workers, see Ruth Roach Pierson, "Women's Emancipation and the Recruitment of Women into the Labour Force in World War II," in Susan Mann Trofimenkoff and Alison Prentice, eds., *The Neglected Majority: Essays in Cana-*

dian Women's History (Toronto: McClelland and Stewart, 1977), 125-45; Veronica Strong-Boag, "Working Women and the State: the case of Canada, 1899-1945," *Atlantis*, 6 (Spring, 1981), 1-9; Hugh and Pat Armstrong, "The Segregated Participation of Women in the Canadian Labour Force, 1941-1971," *Canadian Review of Sociology and Anthropology*, 12 (November, 1975), 370-84; Martin Meisser *et al.*, "No Exit for Wives: sexual division of labour and the culmination of household demands," *Canadian Review of Sociology and Anthropology*, 12 (November, 1975), 424-39. On the role of wives in the Sudbury strikes, I have used Bill Pentney, "Mine-Mill versus Inco, Sudbury 1958: A Study in Class, Culture, and Conflict," undergraduate essay, Queen's University, 1979, and Meg Luxton, *More than a Labour of Love: Three Generations of Women's Work in the Home* (Toronto: Women's Press, 1980), a study I have drawn upon for other material as well. Note, too, Gail Cuthbert Brandt, "'Weaving it Together': Life Cycle and the Industrial Experience of Female Cotton Workers in Quebec, 1910-1950," *L/LT*, 7 (1981), 113-26; Nicolas Zay, "Analyse statistique du travail de la femme mariée dans la province de Québec," in Michèle Jean, ed., *Québécoises du 20e siècle* (Montréal: Éditions du Jour, 1974), 124-40. On women, work, and unionization, see Julie White, *Women and Unions* (Ottawa: Canadian Advisory Council on the Status of Women, 1980); Paul Phillips and Erin Phillips, *Women and Work: Inequality in the Labour Market* (Toronto: Lorimer, 1983); Pat Armstrong and Hugh Armstrong, *A Working Majority: What Women Must Do For Pay* (Ottawa: Canadian Advisory Council on the Status of Women, 1983); Peta Tancred-Sheriff, ed., *Feminist Research: Prospect and Retrospect* (Kingston and Montreal: McGill-Queen's University Press, 1988). An important theoretical statement is Lynne Segal, *Slow Motion: Changing Masculinities/Changing Men* (London: Virago, 1990).

Nationalism and the breakaway movement are addressed in R.B. Morris, "The reverter clause and breakaways in Canada," in Teeple, ed., *Capitalism and the National Question in Canada*, 89-100; Philip Resnick, "The Breakaway Movement in Trail," and Paul Knox, "Breakaway Unionism in Kitimat," in Resnick and Knox, eds., *Essays in B.C. Political Economy* (Vancouver: New Star, 1974); Rick Salutin, *Kent Rowley: The Organizer; a Canadian Union Life* (Toronto: Lorimer, 1980). I draw on Joy McBride, "The Wildcat Wave: Rank and File Rebellion in the Canadian Labour Movement, 1965-1966," seminar paper, Queen's University, 1986. Wayne Roberts, *Cracking the Canadian Formula: The Making of the Energy and Chemical Workers Union* (Toronto: Between the Lines, 1990), is a stimulating recent study.

Politics and labour's involvement in the CCF-NDP have drawn extensive comment, starting with Gad Horowitz, *Canadian Labour in Politics* (Toronto: University of Toronto Press, 1968). David Lewis, *The Good Fight*, is essential reading and an institutional overview of social democracy's experience can be developed from G.L. Caplan, *The Dilemma of Canadian Socialism: The CCF in Ontario* (Toronto: McClelland and Stewart, 1973); Leo Zakuta, *A Protest Movement Becalmed: A Study of Change in the CCF* (Toronto: University of Toronto Press, 1964); Walter Young, *Anatomy of a Party: the National CCF, 1932-1961* (Toronto: University of Toronto Press, 1969); Desmond Morton, *NDP: The Dream of Power* (Toronto: Hakkert, 1974); Morton, *Social Democracy in Canada* (Toronto: Samuel Stevens, 1977); Keith Archer, *Political Choices and Electoral Consequences: A Study of Organized Labour and the New Democratic Party* (Kingston and Montreal:

McGill-Queen's University Press, 1990); Nelson Wiseman, *Social Democracy in Manitoba: A History of the CCF/NDP* (Winnipeg: University of Manitoba Press, 1983); James A. McAllister, *The Government of Edward Schreyer: Democratic Socialism in Manitoba* (Kingston and Montreal: McGill-Queen's University Press, 1984). The Communist experience is less well served, but see Ivan Avakumovic, *The Communist Party of Canada: A History* (Toronto: McClelland and Stewart, 1975); Palmer, ed., *A Communist Life*; Norman Penner, *Canadian Communists: The Stalin Years and Beyond* (Toronto: Methuen, 1988).

I have drawn much of the more current material from my own files from Vancouver, Toronto, and Montreal newspapers and from W.D. Wood and Pradeep Kumar, eds., *The Current Industrial Relations Scene in Canada* (Kingston: Queen's University Industrial Relations Centre, 1979). See also Jenny R. Podoluk, *Incomes of Canadians* (Ottawa: Dominion Bureau of Statistics, 1968); Warren E. Kalbach, *The Impact of Immigration on Canada's Population* (Ottawa: Dominion Bureau of Statistics, 1970).

VII: HARD TIMES: ECONOMIC DOWNTURN, THE STATE, AND CLASS STRUGGLE, 1975-1991

This chapter is developed out of my own particular perspective on times I have actually lived through. I draw on my own newspaper clippings, but I am especially indebted to the Industrial Relations Centre at Queen's University, which provided me with access to its own clippings file for the later 1980s. Also extremely useful for raw data is the yearly publication of the Centre, *The Current Industrial Relations Scene in Canada*. See, as well, *The Report of the Royal Commission on the Economic Union and Development Prospects for Canada (Macdonald Report)*, (Ottawa: Government Publishing, 1985), a three-volume assembly of information on the labour market, unemployment, and strikes and lockouts. There is not all that much to draw upon for insight into the political history of this period so I have turned occasionally to Bothwell, Drummond, and English, *Canada Since 1945*, and to David Bercuson, J.L. Granatstein, and W.R. Young, *Sacred Trust? Brian Mulroney and the Conservative Party in Power* (Toronto: Doubleday, 1986). The essays in Kealey and Cross, eds., *Modern Canada*, cited earlier, are helpful, as are Daniel Drache and Duncan Cameron, eds., *The Other Macdonald Report: The Consensus on Canada's Future That the Macdonald Commission Left Out* (Toronto: Lorimer, 1985); and Robert Argue, Charlene Gannage, and D.W. Livingstone, eds., *Working People and Hard Times* (Toronto: Garamond, 1987). On the end of Keynesianism, see Cy Gonick, *The Great Economic Debate: Failed Economics and a Future for Canada* (Toronto: Lorimer, 1987). Perhaps the most influential short text dealing with the matters addressed in this chapter is Leo Panitch and Donald Swartz, *The Assault on Trade Union Freedoms* (Toronto: Garamond, 1988), but see as well Paul Kellogg, *Downturn: The Origins of the Employers' Offensive and the Tasks for Socialists* (Toronto: International Socialists, 1988). On the ravages of unemployment, see Patrick Burman, *Killing Time, Losing Ground: Experiences of Unemployment* (Toronto: Wall and Thompson, 1988). For a brief statement of themes central to the period, see Bryan D. Palmer, *Work and Unions in Canada* (Ottawa: Department of the Secretary of State, 1988). Note, as well, Alfred A. Hunter, *Class*

Tells: On Social Inequality in Canada (Toronto: Butterworths, 1986); Harvey J. Krahn and Graham S. Lowe, *Work, Industry and Canadian Society* (Toronto: Nelson, 1988).

There is almost no Canadian writing on Fordism, but Bob Russell's *Back to Work?* is a beginning. For a perspective from which Canadian analysis can learn, see Mike Davis, *Prisoners of the American Dream: Politics and the Economy in the History of the U.S. Working Class* (London: Verso, 1986). There is little on the New Right as well, but for introductory statements see Warren Magnusson *et al.*, eds., *The New Reality: The Politics of Restraint in British Columbia* (Vancouver: New Star Books, 1984); James Pitsula and Ken Rasmussen, *Privatizing a Province: The New Right in Saskatchewan* (Vancouver: New Star Books, 1990); Stan Persky, *Fantasy Government: Bill Vander Zalm and the Future of Social Credit* (Vancouver: New Star Books, 1989). For those who want a taste of the real item, consult Douglas K. Adie, *The Mail Monopoly: Analysing Canadian Postal Service* (Vancouver: The Fraser Institute, 1990); Sandra Christensen, *Unions and the Public Interest: Collective Bargaining in the Public Sector* (Vancouver: The Fraser Institute, 1980).

Public-sector unionism is dealt with in Thompson and Swimmer, eds., *Conflict or Compromise*; and in its federal spheres in Jacob Finkelman and Shirley B. Goldenberg, *Collective Bargaining in the Public Service: The Federal Experience in Canada*, 2 vols. (Montreal: Institute for Research on Public Policy, 1983). The trials and tribulations of public-sector unions are presented in James Clancy, Wayne Roberts, David Spencer, and John Ward, *All for One: arguments from the labour trial of the century on the real meaning of unionism* (Toronto: OPSEU, 1985); Cynthia Ryan, *Collective Bargaining Laws Under the Charter: A Digest of Case Law* (Kingston: Queen's Industrial Relations Centre, 1990); *Labour Law Under the Charter: Proceedings of a Conference Sponsored by Industrial Relations Centre/School of Industrial Relations and Faculty of Law, Queen's University* (Kingston: Queen's Law Journal and Industrial Relations Centre, 1988). "Notice of Expert Evidence on Behalf of the Federation of Women Teachers' Associations of Ontario in the Matter of a Board of Inquiry pursuant to the Human Rights Code" (with respect to complaints of Margaret Tomen/Linda Logan-Smith) is illuminating on the question of teachers' unionism, sex segregation, and "expert" testimony.

A rare worker-produced history of a contemporary struggle is Raymond Leger, *423 Days on the Picket Line* (Fredericton, N.B.: RWDSU Local 1065, 1988). On international unionism and Canadian/American comparisons, see David Kettler, James Struthers, and Christopher Huxley, "Unionization and Labour Regimes in Canada and the United States: Considerations for Comparative Research," *L/LT*, 25 (Spring, 1990), 143-60. For a conservative, but usefully sceptical, view of the argument that Canadian and American unionisms are fundamentally different, see Leo Troy, "Convergence in International Unionism Et Cetera: The Case of Canada and the United States," working paper, Queen's Industrial Relations Centre, Kingston, March, 1991.

On union leadership, see Pradeep Kumar and Dennis Ryan, *Canadian Union Movement in the 1980s: Perspectives from Union Leaders* (Kingston: Queen's Industrial Relations Centre, 1988); Bob White, *Hard Bargains: My Life on the Line* (Toronto: McClelland and Stewart, 1987); Jack Munro and Jane O'Hara, *Union Jack: Labour Leader Jack Munro* (Vancouver: Douglas and MacIntyre, 1988); Will

Offley, "The Munro Doctrine," *New Directions* (January/February, 1990), 33-37; "George North: the last angry words of a principled trade unionist," *ibid.*, (May/ June, 1990), 31-34. The CAW/UFCW confrontation has received surprisingly little in the way of analysis, but background on the industry context can be gleaned from Bryant Fairley, Colin Leys, and James Sacouman, eds., *Restructuring and Resistance: Perspectives from Atlantic Canada* (Toronto: Garamond Press, 1990); Wallace Clement, *The Struggle to Organize: Resistance in Canada's Fishery* (Toronto: McClelland and Stewart, 1986). On Shirley Carr, see James Bagnall, "The State of the Unions," *Financial Times of Canada*, 15 January 1990. My own account of the Solidarity uprising in British Columbia is Bryan D. Palmer, *Solidarity: The Rise and Fall of an Opposition in British Columbia* (Vancouver: New Star Books, 1987).

On the NDP, sources other than those cited earlier include: Wayne Roberts, "NDP Future Shock," *Socialist Studies Bulletin*, 21 (July-September, 1990), 11-17; Desmond Morton, *The New Democrats, 1961-1986: The Politics of Change* (Toronto: Copp Clark Pitman, 1986); Jonathan Pierce, "Social Democracy on the Frontier: The Case of the Yukon," in Mike Davis *et al.*, eds., *Fire in the Hearth: The Radical Politics of Place in America* (London: Verso, 1990), 317-30. Keith Archer, in *Political Choices*, addresses the question of NDP/union affiliation. An illuminating statement is Bob Rae, "What We Owe Each Other," New Democrats News Release, January, 1990, Legislative Library of Ontario.

Issues of importance are addressed in Jesse Vorst *et al.*, eds., *Race, Class, Gender: Bonds and Barriers* (Toronto: Between the Lines, 1988), especially the article by Ronnie Leah, pp. 166-95; Donald V. Nightingale, *Workplace Democracy: An Inquiry into Employee Participation in Canadian Work Organizations* (Toronto: University of Toronto Press, 1982); Donald M. Wells, *Empty Promises: Quality of Working Life Programs and the Labor Movement* (New York: Monthly Review, 1987). The service sector is addressed in Ester Reiter, "Life in a Fast-Food Factory," in Heron and Storey, eds., *On the Job*, 309-26. On mass culture consider the arguments in Guy Debord, *Comments on the Society of the Spectacle* (London: Verso, 1990); Fredric Jameson, *Postmodernism: or, the Cultural Logic of Late Capitalism* (Durham, North Carolina: Duke University Press, 1990).

Index